MW00770850

GUAM

THE BATTLE FOR AN AMERICAN ISLAND IN WORLD WAR II

JAMES H. HALLAS

STACKPOLE
BOOKS

Essex, Connecticut
Blue Ridge Summit, Pennsylvania

STACKPOLE BOOKS

An imprint of The Globe Pequot Publishing Group, Inc.
64 South Main Street
Essex, CT 06426
www.globepequot.com

Distributed by NATIONAL BOOK NETWORK

British Library Cataloguing in Publication Information available

Library of Congress Cataloging-in-Publication Data available

Names: Hallas, James H., author.
Title: Guam : the battle for an American island in World War II / James H. Hallas.
Other titles: Battle for an American island in World War II
Description: Essex, Connecticut : Stackpole Books, [2025] | Includes bibliographical references and index.
Identifiers: LCCN 2024034221 (print) | LCCN 2024034222 (ebook) | ISBN 9780811776899 (cloth) | ISBN 9780811776905 (epub)
Subjects: LCSH: World War, 1939-1945—Campaigns—Guam. | Operation Forager, 1944. | World War, 1939-1945—Casualties—Guam. | World War, 1939-1945—Campaigns—Mariana Islands. | Guam—History—Japanese occupation, 1941-1944. | United States—Armed Forces—History—World War, 1939-1945.
Classification: LCC D767.99.G8 H36 2025 (print) | LCC D767.99.G8 (ebook) | DDC 940.54/2667—dc23/eng/20240923
LC record available at https://lccn.loc.gov/2024034221
LC ebook record available at https://lccn.loc.gov/2024034222

♾️™ The paper used in this publication meets the minimum requirements of American National Standard for Information Sciences—Permanence of Paper for Printed Library Materials, ANSI/NISO Z39.48-1992.

CONTENTS

CONTENTS

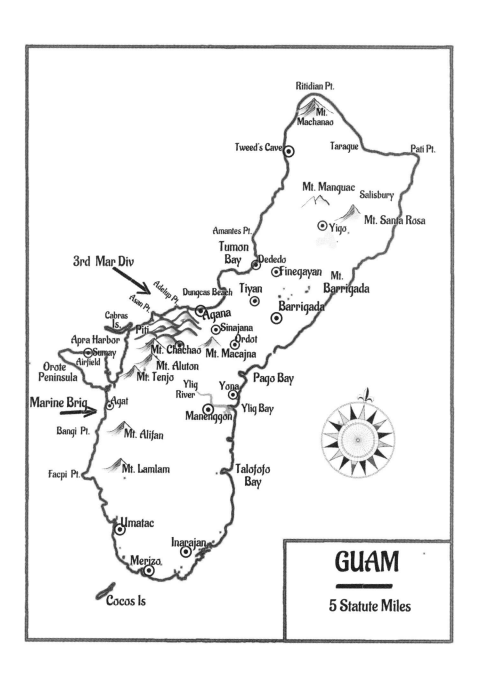

GUAM

5 Statute Miles

INTRODUCTION

OILY BLACK SMOKE WAS STILL BILLOWING SKYWARD OVER THE WRECKAGE OF THE U.S. Pacific Fleet at Pearl Harbor when Japanese planes appeared in the skies over Guam on the morning of December 8, 1941. An American territory since the end of the Spanish-American War over forty years before, the picturesque island in the Marianas chain—3,340 miles from Honolulu and twenty hours ahead by time zone—had been an irritant to Japan since the end of World War I.

That was about to change.

After two days of air attacks, fifty-five hundred Japanese troops waded ashore in the early morning hours of December 10, 1941 (Guam time), easily overwhelmed the token U.S. garrison, and announced that the twenty-three thousand native Chamorros were now part of a new world order that would bring prosperity to all. The forced change of ownership gave Guam the dubious distinction of being the first American soil formally surrendered to an enemy in World War II—and the only one with a significant U.S. civilian population.[1]

Historians typically refer to the seizure of the island in 1941 as "the first battle of Guam" and the return of U.S. forces in 1944 as the "second battle." There was argu-ably a third "battle," that being the struggle of Guam's Chamorros under Japanese rule between the bookends of loss and liberation. As Guam's captured U.S. military personnel left for POW camps in Japan in January 1942, the island's civilian popula-tion embarked upon what would turn out to be two and a half years of Japanese rule. It was an occupation that gradually progressed from tolerable discomfort to a waking nightmare of beheadings, rapes, and mass murder as the war turned against Japan.

The story of the perseverance of Guam's civilians through those years of enemy rule, and their loyalty to an America that had declined to grant them the privileges of full citizenship and did not always treat them equitably, is one of the more inspiring—and perhaps one of the more neglected—of the war. The islanders may have been taken for granted by Washington, but they never took America for granted; nor did they doubt that America would return while they fought their "battle" as best they could alone.

And eventually America did return as U.S. forces made the long slog across the Pacific toward Tokyo. They came to the Marianas in June 1944 to obtain island bases for the airfields that would allow the newly introduced B-29 Superfortress bombers to devastate Japan. They would also come as the liberators of Guam's Chamorro population, though that happy event was incidental to the military goals. While not ignoring the civilian issue—preinvasion orders included reminders to the troops that the Chamorros were Americans—there was no emotional preinvasion rhetoric comparable to General Douglas MacArthur's widely advertised "I shall return" promise to the Filipinos.

The U.S. return to Guam, which began with landings by the 3rd Marine Division and 1st Provisional Marine Brigade on July 21, 1944, saw bitter fighting for a beachhead over the first four days. Resistance was fierce as the Marines fought to seize the high ground dominating the landing beaches. On the night of July 25–26, the Japanese commander launched one of the largest enemy counterattacks of the Pacific war on the center of the 3rd Marine Division's line, overrunning elements of the 21st Marines and penetrating in some spots to the rear areas, including the division hospital. The attack was broken by noon the next day and proved to be the de facto end of the battle as it left Japanese forces too disorganized to mount an effective defense after withdrawing to the northern part of the island. III Amphibious Corps (IIIAC) commander Major General Roy S. Geiger declared victory on August 10, though thousands of Japanese remained at large in Guam's jungles—the last known straggler not emerging until 1970.

The loss and subsequent liberation of Guam has attracted relatively little attention from military historians or the general public over the years. Speaking of the loss of the original garrison in the opening days of the war, historian Roger Mansell, who devoted himself to recording the stories of Guam's American POWs, observed, "The guys on Guam, they were a footnote. After Pearl Harbor, Guam just disappeared off the radar."[2] In fact, unlike the heroic but equally doomed battle put up by the defenders of Wake Island, the Guam garrison surrendered after only token resistance. The reasons for that decision were sound—circumstances on Guam were much different from those on Wake—but left nothing much to celebrate as a feat of martial arms.

The return to Guam in 1944 and the bitter fighting for the beachhead have been overlooked for other reasons, overshadowed early on by the bloody battle for Saipan that preceded it and by the command controversy that arose during that campaign. The subsequent highly publicized fighting at Iwo Jima and Okinawa only cemented that obscurity. Perhaps the following pages will help in some small measure to correct that historical oversight. The men who liberated Guam demonstrated the same courage and tenacity shown by their comrades who fought in better-known battles, and they deserve to be remembered.

A couple of technical issues—or decisions—may be best addressed here as well. Many place-names on Guam have been changed or altered since World War II: the capital Agana, for instance, is now known as Hagåtña. In another possible area of confusion, the American reference to "Chonito Cliff" in the fighting for the Asan beachhead was actually a corruption of "Chorito Cliff." I have elected in all cases to retain place-names as used by the American military at the time—and as generally referenced in later writings—in hopes of avoiding unnecessary confusion.

Another decision involves the use of the term "Chamorros" to refer to the civilian population during the war years. This too was the commonly used term at that time. After the war, widespread anger with Saipanese Chamorros who aided the Japanese occupying forces on Guam led to a preference for the term "Guamanian" to differentiate the island's people from those hated collaborators. Today, while that hostility lingers, there has been a movement back toward acceptance of "Chamorro." My own feeling is that either title should be a source of pride, and that conviction has persuaded me to use the terms interchangeably.

Finally, a word on war. Many of the incidents and events described in the following pages are disturbing, even given the distance of time and the insulation offered by the printed word. If there is one thing that characterizes combat, from the earliest confrontation, when one man bashed another to death with a rock, to the more sophisticated lethalities of the present day, it is ugliness. War is ugly, and it is cruel. Guam was no exception, and I have sought in the following pages to convey that reality without blinking.

PROLOGUE

AGANA, GUAM, DECEMBER 8, 1941

Dawn was still a half an hour away when an urgent message arrived at Guam's expansive Government Palace, rousing naval governor Captain George J. McMillin from what was probably an already uneasy night. As the early hour suggested, the radio message from Hawaii contained bad news. The U.S. Fleet at Pearl Harbor, thirty-four hundred miles away and twenty hours behind Guam on the clock due to the International Date Line, had come under Japanese attack at 0755 Hawaiian time.

As McMillin hurriedly phoned staff members, Navy radiomen at the island's communications center tuned in to stateside news broadcasts to learn more about the attack. A follow-up military radio dispatch soon arrived to dispel any lingering hopes that there had been some sort of terrible mistake:

From: SECRETARY OF THE NAVY
To: ALL U.S. SHIPS AND STATIONS
EXECUTE WLS AGAINST JAPAN

The meaning was simple: all naval forces were authorized to proceed against Japan as if a formal declaration of war were in place.[1]

McMillin, a 1911 Naval Academy graduate described by a subordinate as "a wonderful and gifted commanding officer,"[2] hastily assembled key personnel at his offices in the Government Palace. Also known, somewhat less grandly, as "Government House," the imposing edifice located on one side of the palm-lined Plaza de Espana in the heart of Guam's capital served as the island's seat of government as well as the naval governor's official residence.[3]

A heavy-set six-footer, the fifty-two-year-old McMillin had spent two years on the staff of the Navy War College, followed by a year as executive officer aboard the battleship *Idaho* from 1938 to 1939, before arriving on Guam with his family in

April 1940 as the island's thirty-eighth naval governor. In addition to his administrative duties as governor, he served as commandant of Guam's Naval Station and the island's small Marine garrison.

Guam had long been considered a comfortable posting, but recent months had brought nothing but worry to McMillin as relations with Japan deteriorated and open hostilities became more and more likely. Now, with the attack on Pearl Harbor, those fears had come to pass to a degree none could have imagined, observed McMillin's vice governor, Navy commander Donald T. Giles, a forty-three-year-old native of snowy Syracuse, New York. "Although we had known that war was imminent, we were stunned, both because the target of the Japanese attack [Pearl Harbor] had not been foreseen with any accuracy and because of the manner in which the attack had occurred," he admitted.[4]

Giles had arrived on Guam the previous May, delighted to find himself in a veritable tropical paradise. Now it appeared that paradise could become his grave. No one attending Governor McMillin's early-morning conference entertained any doubts that their newly declared enemy would soon be on their doorstep. An isolated outpost surrounded by Japanese possessions, Guam had been an irritant to Japan for some twenty years. Japanese-held Rota, fifty-four statute miles to the north, was visible on a clear day from Guam's high northern plateau. Saipan, the center of Japanese government in the region with its modern airfield and military facilities, was only another seventy-three miles north of Rota.

There was little the Guam garrison could do to resist. McMillin could call on 153 Marines and less than three hundred sailors to defend the island, along with about eighty Insular Force Guard volunteers, consisting of poorly armed, half-trained native Chamorros. Another 160 Chamorros were enrolled in the unarmed naval militia. The available forces were much too few, the Japanese were much too close, and everybody knew it. There would be no heroic but futile last stand at Guam. "Our war plans were specific," recalled Giles. "We would burn all classified material, destroy all equipment and supplies that could be of any possible use to the enemy, disperse the natives and surrender."[5]

At the Pan American Airways facility on Apra Harbor—the only regular air link with the outside world—word went out to the Guam-bound China Clipper, which departed Wake Island on its weekly run at 0600, that conditions were "unsuitable" and the big, lumbering seaplane should cancel the flight. The warning was gratuitous by a matter of just a few minutes. Clipper captain John H. Hamilton had been alerted by radio of the Pearl Harbor attack soon after takeoff. He immediately turned back for Wake's airfield, where he had to dump six thousand pounds of gasoline in order to bring the ship down for a landing.[6]

As alerts began to go out to military units and civilian leaders on Guam, McMillin ordered the arrest of the handful of Japanese nationals on the island. Prominent among them was Takekuna ("Samuel") Shinohara, owner of a restaurant popular with naval and Marine officers who was reported to have brazenly—and perhaps presciently—hoisted a Japanese flag outside his Agana residence that same morning. Shinohara and about two dozen other potential fifth columnists—most of them suspects only because of their nationality—were hastily rounded up and confined in the concrete jail near the post office at Plaza de Espana.[7]

With no idea as to how much time he had left before the Japanese military arrived, Giles instructed his communications officer to burn any remaining classified documents and destroy all coding machines. At 0730 most phone lines mysteriously went dead, forcing the use of messengers by automobile and on foot. An hour later, the officers heard the drone of approaching planes. As they were all too well aware, Guam had no airfield. The nearest air base was Aslito Field on Japanese-held Saipan.

"There they are!" announced McMillin somewhat unnecessarily.[8]

War had arrived in paradise.

CHAPTER 1

DOLLARS CANNOT BUY YESTERDAY

SHAPED SOMEWHAT LIKE A DISCARDED SOCK AND ENCOMPASSING A TOTAL AREA OF 228 square miles, Guam is the southernmost and largest of the nearly two dozen islands and islets comprising the Marianas chain. The island is roughly thirty-four miles long and varies in width from about five miles at the narrowest to nine miles at the widest. The southern half of the island in 1941 consisted of hilly ridges covered with *neti*, or sword grass. The northern half rose into a broad three-hundred to six-hundred-foot-high limestone plateau covered by thick jungle. With a tropical rain forest climate comparable to that found in the Amazon Basin, the temperature seldom exceeds an average of eighty-seven degrees Fahrenheit. Humidity averages about 90 percent. The island is soaked by almost daily rains from July to December.

A barrier reef up to seven hundred yards wide in places surrounds the greater part of the island. There are few potential landing beaches and many miles of high coastal cliffs. The best access lies along the southwest coast, which is also the location of Apra Harbor, the best deepwater port in the Marianas. However, any hostile landing would have to contend with a rugged line of hills running just inland along the coast. The highest peak, near the southern end, is 1,334-foot Mount Lamlam. Extending north are 869-foot Mount Alifan, 1,022-foot Mount Tenjo, 1,046-foot Mount Chachao, and 1,082-foot Mount Alutom.

Total population at the outbreak of the war was about twenty-three thousand native Chamorros and approximately six hundred U.S. military personnel. Most civilians resided in the south, which was also the center of agricultural production and location of Agana, the island capital. As many as ten thousand Guamanians resided in Agana. About five thousand others lived in a half dozen main villages, including Agat, Umatac, Merizo, Inarajan, Yona, and Sinajana. Second only to Agana was Sumay, with a population of about two thousand, on the northeast shore of Orote Peninsula, which forms the lower side of Apra Harbor. In addition to the Marine Barracks and rifle range, Sumay was home to the headquarters of the Pacific Cable Company as well as the site of Pan Am facilities for the Hawaii-to-Manila "China Clipper," the latter including a wood-frame, twenty-room hotel for overnight passengers. Piti, the site of the naval station and port of entry for Apra Harbor, was located about five miles southwest of Agana.

Life was slow paced for both the native population and military personnel. "The weather was always warm and balmy, even during the rainy season when the mild tropical rains gently dampened the island," reminisced Marine corporal Martin Boyle, a six-year veteran from Kansas. "During the typhoon season the high winds would almost blow the island away, but the people were always braced for them, and after a couple of exciting days the winds would move on, soon to be forgotten, and the people would resume the lazy ways of the tropics."[1]

Many Chamorros maintained small truck farms—which they called "ranches"— outside the villages. They alternated between their villages on weekends and the ranches during the week, tending to small vegetable plots and raising a few chickens, goats, pigs, and cattle. Corn was the chief food staple. The only export of any significance was copra—the dried meat of the ripe coconut. Produce was transported to market in ubiquitous two-wheeled carts pulled by plodding carabaos, but subsistence farming was the rule. A military study published in 1939, noted that 81 percent of the native population was engaged in or depended upon agriculture. "However, the industry only keeps pace with the needs of the inhabitants and little effort is made to provide for more than the immediate needs," observed the author.[2]

Archeological studies indicate that Guam was settled as early as 1500 BC by people from Southeast Asia. The first known contact with Europeans took place on March 6, 1521, when explorer Ferdinand Magellan's round-the-world expedition made a brief stop before continuing on to the Philippines. The visit did not end happily as Chamorros who paddled out to see the visitors blithely helped themselves to assorted booty, even including a ship's skiff. There was a confrontation, and at least one Chamorro was killed. Magellan then sent out a raiding party that killed seven more Chamorros and burned forty or fifty homes to the ground.

Forty-four years after this inauspicious encounter, on January 26, 1565, Miguel Lopez de Legazpi arrived with a four-ship "fleet" and formally annexed the island and the rest of what would become known as the Mariana Islands in the name of Spain's King Philip II. The Spanish subsequently posted a small garrison on Guam, which became a way station for galleons on their way to and from the Philippines, but made no particular effort to develop the island. Relations with the native

Chamorros were relatively amiable until 1668, when a contingent of proselytizing Jesuits arrived. The newcomers christened the islands the "Marianas" in honor of the Spanish queen and set about introducing the "heathen" population to the blessings of Christianity, by force if necessary.

Violent clashes broke out as the Chamorros resisted the Jesuit assault on their social structure, which included a belief in spirits. The clashes escalated into an armed rebellion in 1670. The Spanish brought in military forces from the Philippines to crush the rebels, but resistance was not completely quelled until 1693. By then, the number of Chamorro inhabitants—estimated at about fifty thousand throughout the Marianas when the Spanish first arrived—had been reduced by war and disease to as few as four thousand or five thousand. A census taken in 1710 indicated that the native population of the Marianas—all of whom had by then been forced to relocate on Guam—had been reduced to a mere 3,539.[3] Numbers crept upward over the next two hundred years—to over eighty-five hundred by the 1890s—but by then intermarriage and relationships between Spanish, Chamorros, Filipinos, and others had largely transformed the original Chamorro bloodline into a population of mixed ethnicities that was now, thanks to Spanish perseverance, also staunchly Catholic.

In succeeding years, the island remained a remote way-stop, manned by a small Spanish garrison that was often out of contact with the outside world for months on end. They were so out of touch that when Captain Henry Glass of the USS *Charleston* came along in June 1898 and fired twelve shells into the old—and, as it turned out, abandoned—Fort Santa Cruz in Apra Harbor, Spanish governor Juan Marina mistook the barrage as some sort of honorary salute. He sent out a welcoming party, only to learn to his chagrin that the United States and Spain had been at war since April. Fifty-four Spanish soldiers and a gaggle of Guamanian auxiliaries were disarmed without incident, the American flag was hoisted aloft, and over three centuries of Spanish dominance ended with a scarcely a whimper.

When the war concluded two months later, the United States took possession of the Philippines and Guam for $20 million. Ironically, the acquisition of Guam was almost an afterthought, brought to the table by naval officers who argued that the island would provide a good base for the Pacific cable and be useful as a coaling station. The William McKinley administration went along but expressed no interest in the rest of Spain's possessions in the Mariana, Caroline, and Marshall Islands, which were subsequently purchased from Spain by Germany for a bargain $4.2 million.

A navy yard was established at Piti on Apra Harbor in 1899. The first Marine garrison arrived on Guam that same year. The Marine Barracks was constructed in 1901 outside the village of Sumay overlooking the harbor. A relay station for the trans-Pacific cable was established in 1903 at Sumay. As Guam would be serving primarily as a U.S. Navy coaling station, it seemed expedient to place the island and its inhabitants under naval administration. Governance over the next four decades was left to a succession of naval officers who ran the island like a ship and varied widely in competence regarding their approach to and interest in the welfare of the civilian population.

The results were generally beneficial. The population increased by 128 percent between 1901 and 1940. Schools, courts, police, and other governmental services were established. The inhabitants adopted American culture far more readily than they had Spanish—though their commitment to Catholicism remained unshaken. Villages sponsored baseball teams; there was a local Boy Scout chapter, a chamber of commerce, a Rotary and an Elks Club, and a Masonic Temple—even a Coca-Cola bottling franchise, the first to operate outside the continental United States.

American rule, while not oppressive, was characterized by a combination of benign but superior paternalism and unabashed racism. In 1937 a naval governor complained it was impossible to get efficient work done on the island unless an American was in charge. "It is seldom that we can get a native able to exercise executive responsibility of any sort," he wrote, adding, "Education and evolution may correct this."[4] Various edicts through the years reflected the darker side of U.S. rule. One sought to ban intermarriage between any white person and "any person whole or part of Chamorro or Filipino extraction."[5] Schools were segregated. Chamorros were allowed to join the U.S. Navy, but only as mess attendants. Periodic efforts were made to discourage use of the Chamorro language to the point that in 1922 Chamorro-English dictionaries were collected and burned. In other areas, the exercise of authority could be petty to the point of absurdity. One naval commandant issued an edict that forbade "whistling in the streets because whistling was an unnecessary and irritating noise."[6] In an effort to bring the rat population under control, another governor levied a twenty-five-cent tax on all male Chamorros who failed to deliver a monthly quota of five rat heads.

Some governors were more forbearing than others. Most notable perhaps was Governor Willis Winter Bradley, a World War I Medal of Honor recipient, who arrived in 1929. Bradley implemented numerous reforms and programs to improve the schools and roads and establish a library. Most significantly, he issued a proclamation granting Guamanians the same rights as were guaranteed in the U.S. Constitution's Bill of Rights and authorized formation of an advisory-only Guamanian Congress. The gesture did not change the reality that Guamanians did not enjoy the privileges of full U.S. citizenship, could not vote, and "had no effective guarantee against deprivation of life, liberty and property, except that provided by local naval law," but Bradley was trying.[7] The islanders expressed their appreciation with a parade in the governor's honor. His Navy superiors were less enthralled, and in 1931 Bradley was recalled. Guamanians were considered U.S. nationals, but citizenship and any true powers of self-determination would be a long time coming. In the interim, they might be most accurately described as colonial subjects, albeit largely complacent ones.

Despite Guam's supposed military value, the island remained a backwater on the way to the Philippines during subsequent years, a transformation hastened as the U.S. Navy moved from coal to oil to power its ships. Various plans to fortify the island were broached, but little came of them beyond a lot of empty talk. A half dozen coastal guns were installed, and in 1921 a Marine Corps seaplane squadron was stationed at Apra Harbor, but that was about all.

Bitten by the empire-building bug, the Japanese were more opportunistic. Upon the outbreak of World War I in 1914, a Japanese naval force rushed to seize German possessions in Micronesia—including Saipan and Rota in the Marianas as well as the Caroline and Marshall Islands. That brash landgrab left Guam as the only American territory in what now promised to be a Japanese-dominated lake. Except for the British-occupied Gilbert Islands and Guam, Japan had gained control of all of Micronesia in one fell swoop. The islands were placed under Japanese mandate, and when peace finally arrived four years later, the war-weary victors lacked the stomach to challenge the new owners.

Funding concerns and pacifist sentiments subsequently gave birth in 1922 to a feel-good arrangement in the form of Article XIX of the Washington Naval Disarmament Treaty, which called for the nonfortification of the Pacific Islands. The agreement primarily benefited the Japanese, who did not want to see a well-defended American bastion in their new backyard, insisting "there was a feeling that every gun of Guam would be pointed at the heart of Japan and threaten her freedom of action in that part of the Pacific."[8] The agreement extended to 1936; by 1930 the six coast artillery guns previously emplaced at Guam had been removed, leaving the island essentially defenseless. The island's Marine seaplane squadron was withdrawn in 1931. In a show of good faith—or, depending on one's perspective, naïveté—the Japanese governor of Saipan was invited to drop by and inspect the disarmament efforts for himself.

Those gestures notwithstanding, the Japanese continued to carp about Guam, referring to the island as "an important American naval base" and a "cancer disturbing the peace of the South Sea Islands."[9] This paranoia extended even to improvements to Apra Harbor to facilitate the Pan American Airways weekly San Francisco–Manila–Hong Kong clipper service implemented in October 1935. Those improvements were of no great military significance: the company leased shoreside facilities and the former Marine Corps seaplane ramp on the Orote Peninsula and built a small hotel to accommodate passengers staying overnight on stopovers by the massive thirty-two-passenger Martin M-130 flying boat.

Meanwhile, the Japanese were making major improvements to their own holdings, including an airfield and a seaplane base on Saipan and facilities that were clearly more military than civilian in nature. U.S. suspicions deepened when Japan, which had been operating its possessions under a League of Nations mandate, walked out of the League in 1935 and closed the islands off to Westerners. Efforts to collect intelligence on Japanese activities in the region began early on with a trickle of information from the few travelers to the northern Marianas as well as from agents posing as crewmen on trading ships. Perhaps the most notorious effort involved Marine lieutenant colonel Pete Ellis. Posing as a "copra trader," Ellis ventured into the Japanese mandates, only to die under "mysterious" circumstances—probably the effects of advanced alcoholism rather than any foul play, though no one would ever be sure—in the Palaus in May 1923.

Guam itself began to figure more heavily in the intelligence-gathering effort when the Office of Naval Intelligence began intercepting Japanese radio traffic from a facility located at Libugon Hill on the heights behind Agana. Two six-hundred-foot towers had been erected in 1920, and by 1929 a specially trained cryptological team was regularly pulling Japanese radio transmissions from the ether. By 1935, considerable progress was being made in breaking the Japanese diplomatic "Purple Code" and military "Red Code." As Guam gained importance in the eyes of war planners, Congress in 1938 authorized the secretary of the Navy to appoint a board of naval officers to examine U.S. defenses in the Pacific. Chaired by Rear Admiral Arthur Hepburn, former commander in chief of the Pacific Fleet, the board had much to say about the potential benefits of a fortified Guam.

Previous U.S. strategy for war in the Pacific, as codified in various renditions of the so-called ORANGE plans, recognized that the Philippines could not be held against a serious enemy attack, though planners hoped it would be possible to retain control of Manila Bay. Under that scenario, the U.S. Pacific Fleet would steam from Hawaii's Pearl Harbor and fight its way through the Japanese mandates to Manila Bay. There the Navy would be in a position to cut Japanese trade routes and put an early end to the conflict. Revisions to the plan in 1927 and 1928 addressed the fate of Guam, conceding that the island would likely be lost in the early days or weeks should war break out with Japan.

Ironically, only two years before, a fictional account of a war between Japan and the United States set in the year 1931–1932 had attracted considerable attention in both countries. Authored by British naval writer Hector C. Bywater, the imaginary future conflict featured numerous scenarios that would be eerily echoed over a decade later with the Japanese attack on Pearl Harbor. In the book, titled *The Great Pacific War*, Bywater devoted an entire chapter to the American defense of Guam, which in his scenario fell to the Japanese only after two thousand well-armed Marines with artillery and aircraft exacted a bloody toll on the invaders.

The actual state of affairs seven years after Bywater's imaginary clash was much less encouraging. Presented in December 1938, the Hepburn Report observed that Guam was "at present practically defenseless against determined attack by any first-class power based in the Pacific." The report urged that the island be developed into a major advanced fleet base. Hepburn argued that a well-fortified Guam would serve as a counter to Japanese-held islands such as Saipan, provide a stepping-stone for any U.S. advance, and make "hostile operations against the Philippines a precarious undertaking."[10]

Congress demurred. Some members fretted that fortifying Guam would only provoke the Japanese. In a speech to the House of Representatives, Congressman J. M. Robinson of Kentucky dismissed military concerns, airily pointing out that Japan, Italy, and Germany had all offered assurances that they had "no designs whatsoever against the United States."[11] Isolationists such as former president Herbert Hoover argued that the vast Pacific Ocean provided a natural "moat" protecting the United States against Japanese attack. Opposing expenditures for the fortification of Guam, Republican senator William E. Borah jeered that apprehensions about Japan were mere "jitterism" and declared there was no pressing need "to decorate that sand dune on the other side of the Pacific."[12]

The appropriation failed. However, two and a half years later, as relations with Japan continued to sour, the nonchalance exemplified by Representative Robinson and Senator Borah began to wane. Proposals to fortify Guam were renewed, and $4.7 million was appropriated for improvements to Apra Harbor and construction of a seaplane base. Nearly seventy American contractors from the San Francisco–based J. H. Pomeroy Company arrived with heavy equipment to begin work. Surveys were conducted for an airfield on Orote Peninsula west of the Marine Barracks at Sumay.

But by then, many feared—rightly as it turned out—that the situation was beyond repair. In August 1941, the Navy's chief of operations, Admiral Harold Stark, advised Admiral Husband Kimmel, commanding the U.S. Pacific Fleet at Pearl Harbor, "I fear . . . that it is pretty late to start on Guam anything more than we already have in hand. We will make all the progress we can, remembering that 'dollars cannot buy yesterday.'"[13]

In a letter dated October 6, 1941, Vice Admiral Richmond Kelly Turner, head of the Navy's War Plans Division, opined, "Guam is not really defendable no matter how many troops and fortifications you put there."[14] Turner's view was shared by many others in the Navy, including Admiral Harry Hill, who later observed, "I don't believe any reasonable expenditure of men and armament would have made it possible to make Guam impregnable. It was cut off. It was 1,500 miles inside the Marshalls, and 1,000 miles from the Philippines, and 2,500 miles from any base of ours."[15] It would be foolish to pour time and treasure into Guam for facilities that would only end up benefiting an invader.

RAINBOW war plans, the latest strategy for U.S. operations in the Pacific, reflected this skepticism, rating Guam as a Category F, the lowest priority. Should war come with Japan, as seemed more and more likely as the weeks passed, Guam would be conceded to the enemy.

While penurious politicians may have dismissed Guam as a remote sand dune, American military personnel considered the island a Pacific paradise—the stereotypical "white man's tropics," as one writer put it.[16] The weather was balmy, the beaches were pristine, the natives were friendly, and military responsibilities were far from onerous with duty hours from early morning to only about noon in many cases. "Guam was like most Asiatic duty," recalled Navy radioman Joseph R. Young. "Lots of drinking and not too much work."[17] Captain (later General) Merwin H. Silverthorn arrived in April 1930 aboard the transport USS *Henderson*. The voyage from San Francisco took twenty-two days, which included a three-day layover in Honolulu. He found that his official duties concluded by 1300, which allowed plenty of time to enjoy the nine-hole golf course out beyond the Marine Barracks at Sumay. It was twelve miles by road to Agana, which had movie theaters that showed Hollywood films for a dime, a bowling alley, and ample watering holes. Naval officers and men, often accompanied by their families, enjoyed spacious homes and were tended to by native cooks and maids who did laundry, made beds, and ran errands. Even enlisted men lived like minor potentates, hiring civilian houseboys for a pittance to shine their shoes, make their bunks, and keep the barracks clean and neat.

Edward ("Ed") E. Hale, a twenty-seven-year-old electrician's mate second class, arrived on Guam in early September 1941. Assigned to the USS *Penguin*, a World War I minesweeper converted to patrol gunboat based at Piti Navy Yard, Hale—fresh off an overcrowded cruiser—could scarcely believe his good fortune. "It was the South Seas I had read of and dreamed of but thought too good to be true," he recalled. "The coral beaches, littered with colorful shells; turquoise waters of perfect swimming temperature, teeming with fish of every color and shape; forests of coconuts and bananas, papayas and pineapple . . . the carabao carts, loaded with fruit and vegetables of all seasons. Beautiful dusky maidens with black hair and brown eyes watched from the often pane-less windows of grass-covered huts." Patrol duty was so relaxed that sailors often trailed fishing lines from *Penguin* in hopes of catching marlin, sharks, dorado, or yellowfin tuna.[18]

Another member of *Penguin*'s fifty-four-man crew, a twenty-year-old former Indiana farm boy named Eddie Howard, echoed Hale's enthusiasm in letters home. The dock at Piti, he wrote, was only a seventy-cent taxi ride and three miles from Agana, which offered "pool halls, a theater and a dance about once a week." Added Howard, "Regulations—none. Go ashore in civilian clothes or in swimming trunks. Eat like an officer. Plenty of golden colored butter, etc. . . . Can get natives to do our laundry for $4.00 a month. We [on board ship] have a native to do all our work for us. He shines bridgework, cleans floor plates and dries bilges for a dollar apiece each pay [day]. Around $14 a month. Some life, eh?"[19]

Navy radioman Clarence G. Rhodes and his family spent three years on Guam from 1936 to 1939 and liked it so much he requested two extensions. "We found the native people to be most considerate of other people, kindhearted and as innocent as children," he remembered. "It was one place in the world where an American dollar had not spoiled the people. If they liked you, money was of no concern. If they liked you, they would work for you for nothing. If they did not like you, you didn't have enough money to pay them to work for you. A lot of Navy people made the fatal mistake of talking to them like they were slaves. The next morning they would just simply not show up. The lady of the house would never know why."[20]

Marine corporal Boyle was especially taken with Guam's maidens—he and his buddies consorting with the bar girls at watering holes in Sumay and Agana. "The graceful, high-cheeked native girls were always gay, always laughing and always willing," he observed. Local prostitutes were given Navy medical exams every Monday, a schedule that earned them the nickname "Monday ladies."[21] As far as Boyle was concerned, he'd landed in high clover. "With a can of beer going for a dime and the best stateside bourbon selling for a buck and a half a bottle, there wasn't anything more that a young-hot-blooded Marine could ask for," he enthused.[22]

— ∙ —

The question as 1941 wore on was just how long Corporal Boyle and his fellow leathernecks would remain peacetime Marines chasing after bar girls. As early as June 8, Governor George J. McMillin, concerned by the deteriorating diplomatic situation with Japan, recommended to the chief of naval operations that all U.S. military dependents on Guam be evacuated immediately due to the infrequent availability of transport and "the international situation in the area."[23]

The Navy was in agreement, and McMillin subsequently oversaw the evacuation of all U.S. civilian women and children from Guam, including his own wife, Annabel, and teenage son and daughter. The last of the 104 military dependents left on October 17 on what was to be the final trip of the USS *Henderson*. The lone exception was a Mrs. John Hellmers. The wife of a Navy chief petty officer, she was eight months pregnant and per her doctor's orders was allowed to stay until she gave birth to her baby. A photo of the ship and passengers in the monthly *Guam Recorder* newspaper bore a cheery "Aloha" headline, in a sort of "whistle in the graveyard" dismissal of the somber reason for the departure.

By now all the signs pointed toward war, with some of the intelligence information generated by the top-secret radio intercept station in the heights above Agana. Station B, part of a U.S. network set up to collect and record Japanese navy coded message traffic for analysis and decryption, reported on October 19 that thirteen new naval auxiliary ships were now present in the Japanese mandates.[24] Presumably in response, the *Penguin* was ordered to switch from daytime to nighttime offshore patrols to watch for hostile vessels.

Another indication of potential trouble came on November 5 when Japanese special envoy Saburō Kurusu stopped over via the China Clipper on his way to Washington to participate in diplomatic talks aimed at easing tensions between the two countries. Clipper passengers were typically treated to dinner at the Government Palace, but special envoy Kurusu declined the invitation, the first time in memory that anyone had done so. Suspicious that the Japanese visitors were gathering intelligence on Guam's defenses, Governor McMillin ordered that Kurusu and his entourage be restricted to the Pan Am hotel when the diplomat's departure was delayed by threat of a typhoon. McMillin's suspicions were not unwarranted: landing in Apra Harbor, the diplomats were provided a sweeping view of coastal facilities, information that embassy personnel subsequently passed along to the navy vice minister.

Unbeknownst to the Americans, the Japanese had established a lookout station on nearby Rota to keep an eye on ship movements and any potential effort to reinforce the Guam garrison. Other intelligence-gathering efforts were less subtle. By the middle of October, Japanese reconnaissance flights, conducted by seaplanes from the 18th Naval Air Unit based at Saipan, had noticeably increased in number. It appeared the Japanese were unimpressed with President Franklin D. Roosevelt's Executive Order No. 8683, issued in January, which designated the airspaces over Guam "as Naval Airspaces Reservations for the purpose of national defense."[25] Once putting in an appearance every week or two, Mitsubishi F1M2 "Pete" observation floatplanes based at Flores Point on Saipan now appeared overhead nearly every day, flying with impunity over the island, which had no aircraft of its own to contest the intrusions. Heralded by the distinctive throb of their unsynchronized engines, the Petes droned nonchalantly over Orote Peninsula, just out of rifle range, before heading off to inspect potential coastal defenses. The U.S. State Department protested to Tokyo with no result. After a while, spotters didn't even bother to report the intrusions as "there was nothing anyone could do but stare at 'em," remarked a Marine sergeant.[26]

A report from Japanese air surveillance at the end of November noted the presence of "1 tanker, 1 ship that looks like a gunboat and 2 small vessels"; there appeared to be no airfield or aircraft on the island; the barracks, cable station and fuel tanks on Orote Peninsula, as well as the Naval Repair Station, wireless station and other prominent targets were spotted; no enemy surface or air movements in the area were detected, but "judging from the accelerated road construction, etc. it appears that preparation of lookout posts and gun positions may be considerable."[27]

Over drinks in the officers' club, a newspaper correspondent heading home from the Orient on the China Clipper predicted that Japan would be at war with the United States within two weeks. The next day, Captain William T. Lineberry, commanding officer of the U.S. Naval Hospital on Guam, ordered personnel to paint red crosses on the rooftops of the hospital buildings so they would be identifiable from the air as nonmilitary facilities. Reports from higher command confirmed the news correspondent's suggestion that the diplomatic situation was rapidly deteriorating. On November 24 the acting chief of U.S. Naval Operations advised all commands, "Chances of favorable outcome of negotiations with Japan very doubtful. This situation coupled with statements of Japanese Government and movements of their naval and military forces indicate in our opinion that a surprise aggressive movement in any direction, including attack on Philippines or Guam is a possibility."[28]

Ten days later, on December 4, Governor McMillin received a coded message to "destroy all secret and confidential classified matter" and to retain only what cryptographic channels were necessary for essential communications. A Japanese attack was expected sometime after Christmas.[29] On December 7, Guam's station ship, USS *Goldstar*, then in the Philippines on a supply mission—which included acquisition of fifteen hundred cases of San Miguel beer and one thousand tons of rice—was ordered to delay its return "on account of the serious international situation."[30] Navy radioman Harold ("Hal") E. Joslin and the seven other sailors manning the intercept station at Libugon realized something was up from the amount of Japanese radio traffic crowding the airwaves. "We knew the Japanese fleet was out of area, but we didn't know what they were up to," he recalled.[31]

No one entertained any illusions about the outcome of a Japanese invasion. "If the Japs ever decide to hit this rock, I'd be the second guy to ever walk on water," one Marine joked darkly.[32] The island's government departments and naval station at Piti were manned by 274 regular Navy personnel. The naval component included the USS *Penguin* crewed by four officers and fifty men; the USS *Robert L. Barnes*—fondly known as the "Barney Maru"—an immobilized tanker permanently moored in Apra Harbor and now used for fuel storage and to train Guamanian mess attendants for service with the fleet; and two small naval patrol craft, YP-16 and YP-17. The obsolete *Penguin* mounted the only practical antiaircraft armament at Guam—this consisting of a 3-inch antiaircraft gun and two .50-caliber machine guns. As for ground forces, the Insular Force Guard, a sort of Guamanian militia first formed during World War I and reinstated only a few months earlier, could not be expected to stand against trained troops.

The main professional infantry presence on Guam in November 1941 consisted of 153 Marines at the Marine Barracks at Sumay, commanded by Lieutenant Colonel William K. MacNulty. The forty-nine-year-old Pennsylvania native had enlisted in 1915 and served in France with the Marine Brigade during World War I, where he was wounded and received the Silver Star for bravery. Subsequently commissioned from the ranks, he added a Navy Cross to his decorations during the second Nicaragua campaign in 1928 for saving a trapped platoon from a bandit ambush. Despite his military record, the colonel does not appear to have inspired great respect on Guam, where he had expected to quietly conclude his career before heading off into retirement in January. Pan Am employees derisively referred to him as "Clipper MacNulty" due to his enthusiasm for entertaining civilians—notably ladies—arriving aboard the weekly flights.[33] Unfortunately, the now middle-aged warrior would prove one of a number of leadership disappointments in the trials to come.

Marine sergeant Earl B. ("Benny") Ercanbrack, a twenty-nine-year-old Texan with twelve years of service in the Corps, including three years in China, was ready to fight, but he also knew a doomed cause when he saw one. "Months before the Japs attacked, even before war was declared, we knew that we would either be captured or killed," he recalled. "We never talked about it but we all knew it. We didn't have much of anything with which to fight but we had made up our minds that we would fight."[34]

At Sumay, twenty-year-old PFC Carroll D. ("Barney") Barnett and another Marine were ordered to bury all records, plus any money in possession of the paymaster's office. The men had already been told that with war likely to break out at any time, there would be no payday. The Marines emptied the arsenal and divided up all the ammunition. "Thereafter, we kept our old obsolete Springfield rifles from World War I and the small amount of ammunition on our bunks," recalled Barnett. "The worst part was that there were not enough rifles to go around."[35]

⌐⌐

Admiral Harold Stark's observation to Admiral Kimmel on August 19 that "it is pretty late to start on Guam" was more prescient than he may have realized. Only five days prior to that remark, Imperial Japanese Navy planners had advised their army counterparts that a schedule of preparations for war against the United States and Great Britain must be completed by October 15. Among the list of targets in the Japanese crosshairs was Guam.[36]

Contingency plans for the seizure of Guam dated back to at least 1924 or 1925, when the Japanese General Staff established a Committee for the Research of Military Preparations against the United States. A revision of the Imperial Defense Policy in 1936 again called for the seizure of Guam. So long as the island remained in American hands, it would present a threat to Japanese naval activity in the region, disrupting sea lanes and possibly even serving as a springboard for raids against Japanese bases.

On January 6, 1941, the Japanese army and navy high commands agreed to seize Guam upon the outbreak of hostilities with the United States "to ward off threats by the enemy to insular areas in the South Pacific." Following air attacks to destroy enemy vessels and defense facilities, the navy would escort army forces to Guam and assist in landing operations. The army would occupy Apra Harbor, capture Agana, and "then mop up any remnants of the enemy on the island." The plan was titled "G Operation."[37]

Ten months later, with diplomatic talks with the United States at an impasse—
and amid mounting concerns over the impact of a U.S. oil embargo imposed in
July—the Japanese military began to move forward with war plans. On November
5, commander in chief of the Combined Fleet Admiral Isoroku Yamamoto issued
Combined Fleet Top Secret Operation Order No. 1. The 151-page document out-
lined the planned attack on Pearl Harbor as well as near simultaneous movements
against Malaya, the Philippines, Guam, Wake, Hong Kong, Java, and the Bismarcks.
On the night of November 16, the six carriers and accompanying ships of the Pearl
Harbor Carrier Striking Force began to steam east from Japan's Inland Sea. "Attack
on Guam will commence immediately after our first air attack against America is
confirmed to have been carried out," read the order.[38]

Three days after Yamamoto issued Operation Order No. 1, Imperial Headquarters summoned fifty-one-year-old Major General Tomitarō Horii, a plainspoken
veteran of the China campaigns known for his stubbornness and determination, and
directed him to prepare to seize Guam. The assault would be carried out by Horii's
South Seas Detached Force (*Nankai Shitai*), a brigade-sized unit built around the
144th Infantry Regiment. Supporting elements were drawn from the 55th Infantry Division, including various signals and medical units, an engineers company, a
mountain artillery battalion, and even a company of cavalry. Assembled in Korea
before sailing for Japan, the roughly fifty-five-hundred-man South Seas Detached
Force would be joined by four hundred Special Naval Landing Force (SNLF) troops
from the 54th Keibitai (Naval Guard Force) based on Saipan.

General Horii subsequently met with Vice Admiral Shigeyoshi Inouye, commander of the Fourth Fleet, which had overall responsibility for naval operations in
the Central Pacific area, to hammer out the details of naval support. The invasion
task force, commanded by Rear Admiral Aritomo Gotō, would consist of the heavy
cruisers *Aoba*, *Kako*, *Furutaka*, and *Kinugasa*, light cruisers *Tatsuta* and *Tenryu*,
destroyers *Kikuzuki*, *Yuzuki*, *Uzuki*, and *Oboro*, and nine transports, submarines, a
minelayer, and four gunboats. Once ashore, the South Seas Detached Force would
neutralize enemy military facilities on Orote Peninsula, seize Agana, and secure Apra
Harbor. Landing areas were selected with the caveat that the final decision on where
to go ashore would be made by 1000 hours the day before the actual assault.

General Horii summoned key officers to his headquarters at Marugame on
November 17 to review the operational plans. Three days later he sent sealed orders—
to be opened only after the troops departed from Japanese harbors—to each unit in
his detachment. The South Seas Detachment boarded transports that same day and
proceeded to Chichi Jima in the Bonin Islands some 830 nautical miles north of Guam

where they practiced boarding motor barges. "The bay is filled with large ships," wrote Private Sagaei Matsuura. "It seems as though there are about seven or eight men-of-war here too." Another member of the detachment observed to his diary,

> *29 November: America has disguised herself till now. We are going to meet the enemy at Guam Island with ever-increasing spirit."*
>
> *4 December: Worshipped the Imperial Palace at 0830. Gave 3 Banzais! There was a speech. Japan–America, War! It looks as though the hardships we have borne until now will be rewarded! We have received life for Showa's reign. Men have no greater love than this. Convoy to sail! 0900! Now, prosper, fatherland! . . . The South Seas Detachment will cooperate with Fourth Fleet to capture Guam. If there is no separate order, the landing will take place on 10 December.*[39]

A recent graduate of the Imperial Japanese Military Academy, Second Lieutenant Yutaka Yanagiba commanded a company in the 144th Infantry Regiment's 2nd Battalion. "[On the way to Chichi-Jima] I was given a map of Guam Island said to have been drawn up from air photos," he observed. "All place names were then turned to the Japanese language and I was ordered to remember the geography."[40]

The plan called for a main landing by the bulk of the fifty-five-hundred-man South Seas Detachment in the south at Merizo. This force would proceed up the coast and capture Agat, where General Horii would establish his headquarters before seizing Orote Peninsula and securing Apra Harbor. Secondary landings would be conducted by the army's Tsukamoto Battalion, followed by the Hayashi Detachment—naval troops led by Commander Hiroshi Hayashi—at Tumon Bay less than four miles north of Agana. This force would move south to seize the capital. Another battalion-sized force would go ashore at Talofofo Bay on the eastern coast and move inland to occupy Mount Tenjo. The nine transports of the invasion fleet would arrive at the embarkation point three nautical miles offshore by midnight. The first wave would board motorized barges at 0200.

The Guam defenders later charged that a "fifth column" of Japanese civilians on the island had provided key intelligence to the invasion planners and even sabotaged Guam's phone lines—Japanese-born Takekuna ("Samuel") Shinohara, owner of an Agana restaurant popular with Navy and Marine officers, was cited among the most prominent suspects. The accusations were strongly denied by those civilians after the war. In retrospect, there is no evidence to believe that any of the thirty-nine adult resident Japanese nationals at the outbreak of the war were conducting organized spying, though Shinohara was to become a key collaborator during the occupation and would subsequently be charged with treason.

In fact, Japanese intelligence on the island's defenses suffered from serious gaps that nearly any resident could have easily corrected. One of the more amusing misconceptions was encountered by Japanese businessman Kanichi Ogawa, who was familiar with Guam through his family's shipping business. Sometime in 1941 he was summoned to an audience with the Japanese Naval Staff. A navy commander asked him about the number of tanks on Guam.

"I have never seen them," said Ogawa.

"A Japanese submarine has seen them," replied the commander.

Ogawa later discovered that what the submarine crew described as tanks were actually "bulldozers and dump trucks nonexistent in Japan at that time." In fact, there were no American tanks on Guam.[41]

A more serious intelligence failure involved a drastic overestimation of the number of enemy troops on Guam. An examination of the operation by U.S. intelligence after the war revealed that the Japanese believed there were three hundred to five hundred Marines on Guam, backed up by about fifteen hundred "native soldiers." The Japanese misconception of U.S. strength prompted planners to assemble an unnecessarily large invasion force, which essentially amounted to swatting a fly with a brick—and a fly without wings at that. Japanese intelligence also observed, "It seems that artillery positions are being constructed at several points along the coast and inland on the island." In fact, the garrison had no artillery whatsoever. Finally, the decision to land forces at Merizo and then march north along the coast failed to recognize that there was no roadway over the six miles between Umatac and Agat.[42]

But those revelations lay a few more days into the future. On December 2, General Horii was informed by Imperial General Headquarters that the invasion was to take place on schedule. That same day, the general directed the South Seas Detachment, "Commence landings on 10 December and invade Guam island." The convoy left the Bonins on December 4 and reached Rota before dawn on December 8. There it rendezvoused with the auxiliaries carrying the SNLF troops from Saipan and towing the landing barges to be used in the assault. From there, the ships would continue in scattered groups to their respective anchorages off Guam in time to launch the landings on the morning of December 10. "Guam Island will be attacked and occupied," observed an unidentified soldier in his diary. "During the voyage all necessary preparation of arms, such as 150 rounds of ammunition, were in readiness. With these we can kill. It is heavy, but I feel like taking more."[43]

CHAPTER 2

WAR COMES TO PARADISE

War came to Agana during Mass.

December 8 was a special day on Guam: the annual celebration of the Feast of Immaculate Conception, a holy day of obligation honoring the Blessed Mother. Celebrants had been streaming into the capital for days in anticipation of the festivities. Dressed in their Sunday best—blissfully unaware of the disaster unfolding at Pearl Harbor or the urgent discussions in Governor George McMillin's office just across the Plaza de Espana—they packed Agana's spacious old Dulce Nombre de Maria Cathedral for the 8 a.m. High Mass conducted by Bishop Miguel Ángel Urteaga Olano. Following Mass, a procession would carry the cathedral's treasured statue of Guam's patron saint, Our Lady of Camarin, through the streets of the capital in joyful celebration.

Among the celebrants was six-year-old Carmen Artero and her seven-year-old sister, Maria. They were two of a host of white-gowned child "angels" who were to scatter flower petals during the procession while singing praises, "It is a fragrant gift we give to you, our Blessed Mother." But Carmen and her sister would never get the chance to offer their fragrant tribute that Monday morning. "Right during Mass we heard drones of airplanes coming," recalled Carmen, "and I got so excited because I thought, 'Oh my gosh, Pan Am is coming!'" Assuming the noise signaled the approach of the weekly Pan Am Clipper, she nudged the girl next to her, exclaiming, "Pan Am is coming! Pan Am is coming!" Her sister warned her to hush up, but as the sound of aircraft grew louder, Carmen grew even more excited. "Not one Pan Am, I think, so many Pan Ams coming. . . . I hear many many," she exclaimed.

At the front of the church, Bishop Olano paused from the service to confer with a messenger. The two spoke quietly for a moment as a babble of worried voices began to rise from the crowded pews. The bishop returned to the podium and called for

17

quiet. "And he told us the Japanese have started the war on Guam and they were not going to continue the Mass," said Carmen. The people should leave the cathedral and run home. "And so, everybody starts shrieking, crying, screaming—all the grownups because we kids didn't know what was going on," observed Carmen.[1]

It was just past 0830, recalled Chief Radioman Hugh Myers, when the planes came into view at the Libugon Hill intercept station. "Those are planes from one of our cruisers," remarked one of the radiomen. Then they saw the red disc "fried egg" insignia of Imperial Japan on the wings.[2]

Eighteen seaplane bombers from the Saipan-based 18th Air Unit swept over Agana before breaking into two groups. Half proceeded toward Piti Navy Yard and the radio intercept station at Libugon Hill behind the capital. The others raced toward the Pan Am facility and Marine Barracks at Sumay. The bombs tumbling down on the Pan Am facilities below Sumay drew first blood. One hit near the flagpole; another blew apart the hotel kitchen, killing two Guamanian kitchen workers—Larry Lujan Pangelinan and Teddy Flores Cruz—who became the first fatalities of the war on Guam. A third bomb set the installation's big Standard Oil fuel tank on fire, black smoke billowing skyward as the flames took hold; a fourth landed in the water near the main office. Fleeing the building, forty-year-old maintenance man Juan Wesley was struck by a bomb fragment that sliced open his abdomen. As his intestines started to spill out, he pulled off his T-shirt and used it to plug the gaping wound. Clasping the shirt tightly to his abdomen, he made his way home and eventually to the naval hospital in Agana, where doctors were able to save him.

Private First Class Frank Nichols was on a detail painting the Marine Barracks on the height overlooking Sumay when the bombs started to fall. "I was surprised as hell," he remembered. "I was on the upper level of the painting scaffold and in the rush to get off of there, I knocked over a gallon of paint, dropping it right on the head of the Marine just below me. We all ran and scattered into the jungle surrounding the camp. The Jap planes bombed everything, the first attack hitting the radio shed and the barracks. I remember seeing the basketball backboard tumbling over and over after a bomb blew it over. Even at the time, it seemed as if it were happening in slow motion."[3]

Twenty-three-year-old Corporal Harry E. Anderson of New Lenox, Illinois, was fatally wounded when shrapnel tore through the radio shed. Another blast tore off a Marine's leg. Oblivious to the chaos, a tractor operator—his ears stuffed with cotton to protect against engine noise—continued mowing the adjacent golf course fairways. Belatedly recognizing his peril, he raced the tractor toward a wooded area until it collided with a tree. He then jumped down and disappeared into the undergrowth.

The bombing created mass panic at Sumay village. "We thought it was the end of the world," observed Jesus C. Lizama.[4] Carmen Babauta, who was tending to a new baby, remembered, "People were crying running." Her husband yelled for her to grab the baby and run to the church. "We all tried to find some place to hide. . . . Everyone was crying and scared. We got together on the back side of the church and hid there."[5]

Moored at a buoy in Apra Harbor after returning from her nightly patrol, the USS *Penguin* had already sent a number of crewmen ashore to prepare for a long-anticipated ship's beach party. In addition to her leaky boiler, the tired old vessel's radio was on the fritz so there had been no contact with shore. *Penguin*'s skipper, thirty-seven-year-old Lieutenant James Haviland, had no idea hostilities had broken out until a boat from the navy yard motored out to deliver a written message marked "Confidential." Tearing open the envelope, Haviland perused the contents and turned to his exec, Ensign Edwin A. Wood. "War has been declared," he announced.[6]

There was little time to absorb the news. Minutes later, they heard the crump of bombs in the distance, then the sound of airplane engines as three aircraft, sun glinting on their wings, headed directly at them. "General quarters!" shouted Haviland. "All hands prepare to get underway immediately!"[7] The crew jumped into action as the klaxon blared. Sailors manned the ship's 3-inch gun and two .50-caliber machine guns. Mooring lines were cast off, the engine room brought up steam, and the 188-foot-long former minesweeper started through the channel toward the open sea. Then the Japanese were on them. Machine guns hammered, tearing up the deck and riddling the lifeboats. Bombs sent up cascades of water around the ship. The gun crews fired back but were handicapped by lack of a range finder. As they were forced to guess the distance to targets, their fire had no noticeable effect.

In the boiler room below deck, Watertender Ed Howard had little idea what was going on outside except that the *Penguin*'s guns were all firing. "Every time they'd fire, the ship would shake, you know," he recalled. "It really wasn't made for that. The ship would shake and the insulation would fall down and there we were. . . . [W]e were hitting these rough swells, and we're going full speed."[8]

Up on deck, Ensign Robert G. White was directing return fire from the 3-inch gun when a bullet glanced off the gun mount and tore into his chest. The twenty-one-year-old Kentuckian, who had only joined the crew in March after finishing midshipman's school, collapsed into the arms of Seaman First Class Edwin J.

("Knobby") Settles. Blood spurted all over. Settles could see White's heart in the open wound. "He had just a little—like a horseshoe right over his heart. And when his heart would beat, the little piece of meat would raise up and the blood would jump out," he recalled. The young ensign looked up at Settles and asked, "Would you contact my parents?" As Settles nodded, White died in his arms.[9]

The planes swung around for another pass. This time their bombs hit close amidships, opening holes in *Penguin*'s side. As water poured into the ship, the attacking aircraft finally turned back toward Agana. Ensign White was the only fatality, but nine other men had been wounded. The most seriously injured were Seaman First Class Earl M. Ratzman and Coxswain Rex E. Wilson, both of whom suffered abdominal wounds—Ratzman was actually holding his own guts in place; Wilson had a puncture in the pubic region. Lieutenant Haviland had been wounded in the left forearm by a bomb fragment but continued in command.

Realizing the ship was doomed, Haviland ordered her scuttled to keep her out of Japanese hands. The seacocks and portholes were opened. The ship's thirty-foot boat had been riddled and was useless. As *Penguin* began to settle at the stern, the crew stripped to their skivvies, donned life jackets, and took to the water. Ensign White's body and the most seriously wounded were placed aboard the two undamaged life rafts, and the crew struck out for Orote Peninsula. Despite fears of sharks, they all made it ashore, as did the ship's two canine mascots. Two hours later, standing on the rocky peninsula, they watched the Stars and Stripes, still flying from *Penguin*'s stern, finally sink beneath the waves.

At the Station B naval intercept station up on Libugon Hill, twenty-five-year-old Harold Joslin, who had joined the Navy four years before to escape the family dairy farm in tiny Sequim, Washington, initially thought the approaching aircraft were friendly. He was quickly disabused of that notion as the planes began strafing and bombing, coming in so low the sailors could see the pilots in the cockpits. Hiding in the tall sword grass outside the station, some of the radiomen popped away at the planes with their .45-caliber pistols in an exercise of defiance and futility. Despite the pathetic show of resistance, the bombers managed to miss the radio facility and its array of towering V-shaped antennas designed specifically for the long-range interception of Japanese naval communications.

"In between raids we continued the very difficult task of destroying everything at the station," observed Joslin. "The traffic files were tightly bound and had to be torn apart and the sheets separated. We placed everything in a huge pile in the center of the operating spaces, including equipment which we had smashed with a sledge-hammer, poured gasoline on the pile and soon had a blazing fire which we hoped would destroy all evidence of a tell-tale nature." They removed the keys from their special Japanese typewriters and pitched them into a nearby bog. All realized that if the enemy discovered typewriter keys with kanji ideograms, they would immediately recognize that Libugon was something other than an ordinary radio station, with predictably unpleasant repercussions for the seven intercept specialists involved.[10]

The planes departed at about 1100, but the respite was brief. Two hours later the attack resumed. Land-based bombers went after the radio towers on the hills behind Agana, then spent the next couple of hours buzzing around strafing roads and villages. One pilot strafed the naval hospital, the machine-gun fire punching through the roof with its newly painted red crosses, some of the bullets lodging in the wardroom floor. Frustrated Marines at Sumay fired at the planes with their rifles. "Don't do that or you'll draw their fire!" someone shouted. "They have machine guns!"[11] Finally, the enemy bombers reassembled over Agana and flew off to the north toward Rota and Saipan.

As the day ended, the worst damage had been inflicted on the harbor area. The *Penguin* had been sunk; a bomb had hit patrol boat YP-16 at the navy yard dock, setting the boat on fire with flames spreading to sister boat YP-17, damaging her as well; machine shops and warehouses at Piti Navy Yard had been gutted. While not hit directly, the USS *Barnes* had taken some near misses at her permanent mooring and was leaking oil. "At Sumay, the gas tanks of the Pan American Company were on fire," observed Ed Hale; "the village was deserted, the Marine Corps base almost deserted."[12]

Aboard the *Barnes*, Filipe Cruz and his fellow mess attendants training for service with the U.S. fleet had gone to general quarters during the air attack on nearby Orote Peninsula, though just what they were supposed to do next was a mystery to Cruz. The *Barnes* had no armament beyond two machine guns safely stowed away in one of the lower holds. After three bombs exploded close to the stationary vessel, the bosun's mate told the men to swim to the reef and await orders. Cruz pulled off his shoes and took to the water.

On shore later in the day, the ship's executive officer told the assembled Guamanian sailors that the island was surrounded. "His last order to us was to return to our home, burn our uniforms and disguise ourselves as civilians," said Cruz. "A final warning was issued to us to the effect that, in the event of capture by the enemy, we were not to disclose information of any military value whatsoever." They dispersed, and Cruz began the long walk back to his home in Merizo at the southern end of the island.[13]

In Agana, eleven-year-old Justo Leon Guerrero's family was packing clothes and other essentials when a truck drove by their house, klaxon horn blaring. A voice from the truck was shouting, "Get out of town! Get ready to get out of town! A truck will take you all out of town! Japan has bombed Standard Oil! Get ready, the truck will be here soon!"

Another truck soon came along as promised, and the family began to climb aboard. Noticing that Justo was carrying his puppy, the driver told him to leave the dog. "Then I'm not coming too!" retorted Justo. The driver relented and told him to climb aboard. Justo asked where they were going. "Machananao," his mother told him, referring to an area near Yigo miles to the north.[14]

Also among the throngs fleeing Agana, was Ben Blaz's family—mother, father, and eight children ranging in age from toddler to midteens. As they trudged up the road toward their family farm, five miles inland, thirteen-year-old Ben caught up to his father in the lead. "Papa," he asked, "why are we doing this?"

"We are at war," said his father, without looking at him.

"Papa," insisted Ben, "what is war?"

His father, who worked for the government as an immigration officer, did not answer. He just squeezed the boy's hand, and Ben saw that he was crying. Except at funerals, he had never seen his father cry before.[15]

Agana, which that morning had been preparing for celebratory fiestas, was a virtual ghost town by evening. Residents had hastily gathered what possessions they could and fled into the surrounding hills. The two-hundred-foot smokestack at the power plant, the city's tallest landmark, stood idle—the plant's furnace having been used earlier that morning to incinerate stacks of confidential documents shuttled over by bicycle and pickup truck from government offices. The Gaiety Theater, which the night before had enjoyed a packed house for the movie *Flight Command*, starring Robert Taylor as a naval aviator, was closed. Even the city's dogs seemed strangely muted, as if perplexed by the suddenly deserted streets. By nightfall, besides the bewildered dogs and a few stray civilians, only government officials and military personnel remained in the capital.

Street patrols were conducted by sailors from the *Penguin*, now resting on the sea bottom off Orote Point. After swimming ashore that morning, the near-naked survivors had been helped up the peninsula's sharp volcanic cliffs by Marines from the nearby barracks. Ratzman and Wilson were loaded into a taxi and rushed off to the naval hospital in Agana. The others piled into a Marine quartermaster's truck, which dropped them off at the Plaza de Espana. Though most of them were still without shoes or clothing beyond their skivvies, the officious individual in charge of the Navy storeroom refused to issue them replacement clothing without proper authorization. "You fellows will have to do the best you can for yourselves," he told them.[16] Nothing if not resilient—be it under enemy air attack or in the face of bureaucratic idiocy—the sailors scrounged up a grab bag of civilian garb, Navy dungarees, and even some Marine clothing from the post supply. After gulping down a bit of stew and bread from an emergency kitchen set up in the home of one of their officers, they reported to the armory by the Plaza de Espana where they were organized into night patrols to police the capital.

Governor McMillin kept naval headquarters on Hawaii informed of events with a series of succinct radiograms. The initial attack had been conducted by twelve light and six medium bombers, he reported. The *Penguin* had been sunk. The Standard Oil bulk storage facility was on fire, but other damage was not extensive. "Civilians machine gunned in street. Two native wards hospital and hospital compound machine-gunned." An attack by six twin-pontoon single-engine bombers had damaged buildings at Piti Navy Yard. Civilian casualties were estimated at about fifty. Two Pan Am employees had been killed. Military casualties included Ensign Robert G. White, killed and three Marines in serious condition.[17]

Though Commander Donald Giles expected a Japanese invasion at any moment, the only real excitement that evening was a message that arrived after sunset reporting that some men in a dugout canoe had landed at Ritidian Point on the northernmost end of the island. A search party rounded up three of the intruders and hauled them back to Agana, where they identified themselves as Chamorros from Saipan.[18] They said they were among ten Chamorros enlisted by the Japanese to act as "interpreters" during the seizure and occupation of the island. They had been dropped off in two groups of five that morning by a Japanese patrol boat, one group on the northern end of the island, the other on the southern end. Their immediate mission was to advise the Chamorro-speaking Guamanians not to offer resistance to the Japanese "or they [would] be punished severely."[19] Civilians were to evacuate Agana, stay away from the shoreline, and not interfere in the landings. In addition to warning civilians of the impending attack, the infiltrators had been directed to cut American communication lines and identify shoreline fortifications. The prisoners volunteered that the landings were to take place the next morning about three miles up the coast from Agana.

Fearing the infiltrators could be Japanese plants intended to mislead him, McMillin was skeptical about their revelation regarding the landing site. "I was not inclined to accept the story at the time since I thought it might be a trick to have the Marines moved from Sumay to the beach during the night, in order that they might make a landing in the Apra Harbor area without opposition," he observed.[20] The "interpreters" were unceremoniously crammed into the Agana jail with the other internees, and no effort was made to mount a defense in the area they had identified. As it turned out, they were telling the truth about the location of the landing, though they were wrong about the timing.

Japanese planes returned the following day, again attacking the Pan Am facility and Sumay barracks and strafing villages and roadways. Responding with small arms fire, the defenders managed to hit the fuel tank of one plane—the pilot made it safely back to Saipan—but otherwise the air attack continued unimpeded. One bomb narrowly missed the jail where the Japanese civilians were confined. The explosion blew out the front of the adjoining building, rocking the jail, shattering a window, and throwing the captives into a panic. A Navy nurse at the island hospital coldly confided to her journal that the bomb "missed a splendid chance for a good deed. . . . A better aim would have wiped out most of Guam's Fifth Column!"[21]

Despite the air attacks, some Americans remained optimistic, failing to recognize the devastation the Japanese had wreaked on the fleet at Pearl Harbor and the ramifications for the garrison at Guam. "We expected our navy to come and rescue us within a day or two or something like that," remembered Pharmacist's Mate Third Class Alfred ("Al") Mosher of the Japanese air attacks. "We kind of laughed it off and thought it would be a temporary thing."[22]

Mosher's commanding officer, Captain William Lineberry, who had previously ordered red crosses painted on the hospital roof, promptly punctured that delusion. "He didn't mince words," recalled hospital corpsman Peter B. Marshall, a Missouri farm boy who had enlisted in the Navy in 1939 to see the world. "He said by this time tomorrow we would all be prisoners of war or killed. I don't think I slept a wink that night."[23]

About two hours after sunset, Governor McMillin summoned Commander Giles and other ranking officers to his quarters for a damage assessment. The prognosis was grim. "The Japanese had destroyed our radio communications with the outside world, and many of the island's telephone lines were dead," observed Giles. The *Penguin* had been scuttled. "Japanese aircraft had laid waste to Sumay and destroyed the [ammunition] magazine there. We had no aircraft or antiaircraft guns to protect us, and enemy aircraft were bombing and strafing indiscriminately." Invasion was clearly imminent.[24]

Civilian leader Pedro Martinez asked whether he should destroy his ice plant to keep it out of Japanese hands. McMillin gently advised him that the ice plant had no strategic value. Pedro had a large family, he remarked; his main concern now should be their survival. "I am finished as far as this war is concerned, but we will defeat the Japanese," he added. "The Americans will come. My advice to you, Pedro, is to let the Americans fight the Japanese."[25]

McMillin had already concluded that surrender was inevitable. The small garrison would not be able to resist a landing in force, and there was obviously no hope now that the U.S. Fleet would come steaming to the rescue. All too aware of Japanese atrocities in China, he also feared that offering serious—but ultimately futile—resistance could result in the wholesale massacre of military personnel and civilians. At least one officer spoke up against McMillin's decision. "When the governor mentioned surrendering after a token resistance, Lieutenant Colonel [William] MacNulty remarked that that was contrary to the traditions of the Marine Corps. . . . They were ready to fight to the last," observed Giles.[26]

But MacNulty was overruled. McMillin then took steps that—while his subsequent report does not admit it—would simplify the mass surrender of military personnel. There would be no attempt to defend Guam's beaches, though patrols would conduct periodic checks. The Marine garrison—except for those assigned to Insular Patrol police duties—would remain in the Sumay barracks area. The eighty men of the Insular Force Guard would take up positions around government buildings at the plaza in Agana along with twelve Marines from the Insular Patrol, a few stray Marines from Sumay, a handful of clerks from the Navy's administrative offices, and the surviving crew members from the USS *Penguin*.

The *Penguin* contingent was based with most of the Insular Force in the armory near the Government Palace. At about 2130 a report came in that a light had been seen offshore. Ed Hale and another sailor on watch took a truck out for a look but detected no activity. Their watch ended at midnight without any further excitement, but at 0130 they were roused once again after signal rockets were reportedly seen offshore.

This time the two sailors drove about two miles north to Dungcas Beach, where they found a lot of tracks in the sand but no Japanese. As they started back in their truck, a sedan with six of their *Penguin* shipmates rolled up from Agana. "Each had an automatic and a couple of rifles," recalled Hale. "When we said we were returning to Agana, they said they would go on to Recreation Beach [Dungcas Beach] and look around."[27] Though Hale did not know it, his decision not to linger probably saved his life.

—◆—

The Japanese invasion force picked out the silhouette of the island against a moonlit horizon as they approached just after midnight. "Using a spy glass, they saw the landing shore and the line of breakwater at the base of the island, but no light was to be seen," noted a Japanese report. The sea was relatively calm despite a stiff northwest wind. "The moonlight shining on their faces, the soldiers became ever more persuaded of certain victory," observed the report.[28] The vessels reached their anchorages at about midnight, and the transports began lowering landing barges. All seemed to be going according to plan. "It was reported that the Orote Peninsula area was covered with thick black smoke and that the enemy minesweeper *Penguin* was sunk outside the harbor," noted a Japanese summary of the situation.[29] Final reports from the 18th Naval Air Unit indicted that no enemy gun positions had been detected and that there appeared to be no mines in the harbors or bays.

The Tsukamoto Battalion began landing operations off Tumon Bay at about 0215 in six motorized barges and four small landing boats. In the moonlight, the boats were visible at a distance of three hundred meters; the beach "appeared as a belt forested with palm trees."[30] While there was no opposition, the boats were unable to find a passage through the coral reef. The barges finally motored further up the coast toward Amantes Point, where the troops were able to wade ashore. By then it was 0310. Heading inland, they captured two American sailors who had chosen that inopportune time to go visit their girlfriends in Tumon.

Aboard a separate transport, four hundred Special Naval Landing Force (SNLF) troops from the Hayashi Detachment were supposed to follow the Tsukamoto Battalion, but "finding the coast of that bay unsuitable," according to Japanese records, they turned south and landed instead at Dungcas Beach just north of Agana.[31] They lighted the way to shore with flares that were visible from the capital, inadvertently alerting McMillin that a landing operation was probably underway.

According to Commander Giles, the landing barges were spotted by a handful of patrolling Insular Force guardsmen, one of whom took a shot in their direction before he and his comrades fled to spread the word. Japanese records indicate that "some resistance was encountered in the area of the Tsukamoto Battalion."[32] Whether this was a reference to the shot fired at the naval troops or possibly to activity by the six sailors Ed Hale had encountered on his way back from Dungcas Beach is unclear.

Twelve miles down the coast, the fifty-five-hundred-man South Seas Detachment landed at Bile Bay near the village of Merizo on the south end of the island. The first boats came ashore at 0425 without incident. "There were neither American soldiers nor residents around the landing beach," noted a Japanese report.[33] Merizo school principal Manuel T. Charfauros was cooking an early breakfast in his outdoor kitchen when he was accosted by a Japanese soldier. "You got wife?" the soldier inquired hopefully.

"No," answered Charfauros. "She's not here."

Prodding Charfauros with his bayonet-tipped rifle, the soldier escorted him down the street to the village schoolhouse, where a Japanese officer continued the interrogation. "Where are the Americans?" he demanded.

"They are in Sumay," said Charfauros.

"Are there any Americans here?"

"No. Only the priest."

"Where is the priest?"

"I don't know—out somewhere."

"Are there any mines in the ground?"

"I don't know."[34]

As the hours passed with no one to fight, an officer assembled village residents and read a prepared statement. "The Japanese Army is here to protect you, by the grace of the Emperor," he declared. "Your people and ours are all of one color."[35]

To the officer's possible chagrin, his solemn promise lost much of its intended effect as the Japanese belatedly discovered that the coastal road did not extend to Merizo. They would not be able to march north to Agat to seize Orote Peninsula as originally anticipated. Their plan in shambles, the newly arrived protectors of the people reembarked on their boats and motored up around Facpi Point to land at Agat, leaving the residents of Merizo to their own devices for the time being. By the time they arrived at Agat, the battle for Guam would be over.

A third force, the Horie Battalion, coming ashore in the area of Talofofo on the east coast, also ran into trouble as it encountered rough seas. The original plan had been to land at Ylig Bay. Thwarted by high waves, they were forced to come in at Talofofo. Four of the large landing boats and one of the smaller craft were damaged; they made it to the beach but soon sank. Fortunately, there was no sign of the enemy. The battalion struck out on a rudimentary road that soon degenerated into a trail that forced the sweating infantrymen to proceed in single file in the direction of Mount Tenjo. They too were destined to miss the pending battle.

～～

Back at the Plaza de Espana, the mixed bag of defenders remained on edge following a report that a shot had been heard from the direction of Dungcas Beach just up the coast. Chief Bosun's Mate (CBM) Robert B. Lane, a thirty-nine-year-old Navy careerist in charge of training the Insular Force Guard, dismissed the report as the product of jittery nerves. "The Japs won't come here," he assured the men. "They've got more than they can handle to save Tokyo!" But a few minutes later they distinctly heard more shots, including the rattle of machine-gun fire. This time there was no denying it. "We knew there were no Americans down there with machine guns," observed Ed Hale.[36]

The contingent of Insular Force guardsmen, sailors, and Marines hastily deployed around the 2.5-acre plaza. The indigenous guard, formed a mere six months before, had only rudimentary training. "Those fellas hadn't even shot a rifle before," recalled Marine Ray Church, part of the Marine detachment assigned to the Government Palace. "The poor little militia guys. But they were brave. They were right there."[37]

Many of the guardsmen were armed with older-model Springfield rifles marked on the stocks "Do Not Shoot. For Training Purposes Only." Only that day they had also been issued three World War I–era Lewis machine guns. These featured round, top-mounted pan magazines containing forty-seven rounds of 30.06-caliber ammunition and had an effective range of about 880 yards. None of the Insular Force guardsmen had ever fired one before. Weapons were in short supply among other defenders as well. *Penguin* crewman CBM Robert W. O'Brien recalled, "I shared a .45 with seven other men. If I got it [killed], number two took the gun; if he got it, number three took the gun and so on."[38]

Insular Force guardsman Pedang ("Pete") Cruz was issued one of the three obsolete Lewis guns that would form the core of the defense. He positioned the gun at the northeastern corner of the plaza covering a road leading directly into the government building complex. Another machine-gun crew set up by the bandstand in the plaza but was driven out by an infestation of ants. They finally took up position at an embankment on the western side of the plaza. For his part, Pete Cruz was feeling less than heroic. "I was so scared that, given the chance, I would have fled from the spot," he admitted. "I couldn't flee, of course, because Chief Lane kept checking on us every few minutes. The only thought in my mind was: If I must die, I hope to God I kill some Japanese first."[39] Unbuckling his .45-caliber pistol, he handed it to his unarmed ammunition carrier, Vicente ("Ben") Chargualaf, telling him to use it only to protect them whenever he had to stop firing in order to reload the machine gun.

The *Penguin* contingent took up their own positions, recalled Hale. "[Electrician's Mate First Class Ralph H.] Gwinnup took group of men along a hedge. [Machinist's Mate First Class Verne N.] Bairey gathered another group by the bandstand. I took several native boys to the hedge and followed it to the northwest corner. There we turned over three concrete benches for a bulwark and prepared."[40]

The defenders were divided into two contingents, with Chief Lane in charge of one and Chief Robert O'Brien from the *Penguin* leading the other. O'Brien observed, "By now we were as ready as we could be and were deployed in the grass, behind bushes. . . . A bush couldn't stop a beer can, but we had nothing else. I guess the shock of war starting without any forewarning had really fouled up what little organization there might have been."[41]

The Japanese SNLF troops were already headed south along the two-lane macadam road to Agana, well ahead of their army comrades thanks to the unplanned detour to Dungcas Beach. At the village of Apurguan about a mile from the capital, they encountered a makeshift jitney—a converted sedan—crammed with seventeen civilians trying to make their way north to Yigo about fifteen miles away. The Japanese opened fire, riddling the vehicle, then closed in to bayonet anyone showing signs of life. Thirteen civilians were killed, including four members of one family. One passenger survived by jumping off the jitney as the shooting began and fleeing into the brush. Three others were later found seriously wounded but alive in the tangle of corpses.

Nurses at the naval hospital complex heard shots from time to time, but their first casualty didn't arrive until 0400 when Bill Hughes, the civilian Public Works labor foreman, reported for treatment. "Hughes had been driving his wife and sister-in-law in from their ranch when Jap soldiers leaped on the running board," reported a nurse. "The soldiers used their bayonets and Hughes stepped on the gas, knocking their assailants off the car. Both women were bayonetted, the sister-in-law fatally. Hughes himself was badly bayonetted about the arm."[42]

Out on the plaza, one of Ed Hale's shipmates emerged from the darkness beyond the perimeter. "They are coming," the sailor advised. "Lots of them. They've got machine guns and bombs, and they're pulling carts of some kind."[43] Marine sergeant George J. Shane confessed, "On a scale of one to ten, our pucker factor at that instant was fifteen."[44] At about 0430, Pete Cruz heard the clink of metal on metal and spotted shadowy figures moving toward him in the bright moonlight. He opened fire.

The Japanese replied with a hail of bullets. Lying next to the gun, Roman Camacho, a young civilian who had insisted on joining Cruz, suddenly exclaimed, "I've been hit, Pete."[45] Struck by a bullet that traversed his chest, he fell silent. Cruz's ammunition carrier, Ben Chargualaf, was next, hit by a burst that almost tore off his left arm. Cruz kept firing until the machine gun jammed. As word came to pull back, he grabbed the gun and ran toward the armory. Two guardsmen found Chargualaf crawling along the plaza crying for help, his arm hanging by a ribbon of torn flesh. He begged to be taken to the hospital. The guardsmen helped him as far as the government building guardhouse, where he succumbed to his wounds. Japanese overrunning Cruz's abandoned gun position paused to bayonet the prostrate Camacho, who was probably already dead, before continuing into the plaza area.

Armed with a .45-caliber pistol and twenty-two rounds of ammunition, Ed Hale waited as the sound of gunfire drew nearer. He entertained no illusions about his chances. "Most of the native boys with me had bayonets on their rifles," he recalled. "I felt indescribable pity for them and their mothers and sisters." Suddenly word passed down, "Go to San Ramon Hill! The Japs are coming down San Ramon Hill!"[46]

Jumping up, Hale and the others ran through some trees on the plaza, climbed a fence, and made their way along the road to the rising ground behind town. "A third of the way up the hill we scattered in the brush—behind logs or stumps where we could watch the road," Hale remembered. The moonlight made everything seem weird and confusing. Down below, he saw figures filtering across a clearing behind the Government Palace. "They were everywhere," he recalled. He raised his pistol and emptied the full magazine. There was no return fire. "Suddenly everything seemed quiet nearby, but the firing and blood-curdling yells were coming from the plaza now," he observed.[47]

His moment of solitude ended abruptly as a grenade exploded just a few feet away, showering him with dirt and sand. A second grenade plunked down just beyond his feet, but he managed to flop down behind a mound of dirt as it exploded, and the blast passed over him. Apparently assuming he was dead, his assailants moved on, leaving him to take stock of his situation. His group of guardsmen was nowhere in sight. Down in the plaza, things seemed to have quieted down for the moment. Day was just breaking. The defenders had mostly retreated into the armory building, taking cover behind the thick concrete walls. That shelter was about to become more tenuous as Hale could see the Japanese dragging up field guns.

From his position in the plaza, Commander Giles, incongruously clad in the white linen suit he typically wore when conducting civilian affairs—his only nod to his military rank being the naval cap on his head and a .45-caliber pistol—realized that "the jig was up," as he put it.[48] Contacting Governor McMillin at his command post in the Government Palace, he said they were about to be wiped out. McMillin told him it was time to surrender.

As Marine Ray Church recalled it, "The governor's aide [Giles] came running down the stairway. He had a sheet tied on a broom handle. He was waving this sheet back and forth and running down to where the Japanese were. We thought we'd never see him again."[49] Giles's first stop was his Chevrolet automobile parked near the offices. Reaching inside, he gave three long blasts on the car horn. He assumed anyone in the military—the American military, at least—would recognize this sequence as the signal to "secure." The plaza defenders ceased fire immediately. Japanese fire also tapered off. From across the plaza, Giles heard a voice shout, "Come!" It was 0545.[50]

Accompanied by Chief Lane, Giles started across the plaza. Despite the possibility that he might be embarking on his last walk on earth, he prudently turned his heavy gold Naval Academy ring around to face his palm to make it less conspicuous in hopes that it might not end up as a souvenir in some Japanese soldier's pocket. Enemy soldiers with bayoneted rifles took them into custody without incident. Giles noted that they had foliage in their helmets and attached to body nets and seemed very businesslike. After a brief exchange with a Japanese officer who couldn't speak a word of English, the two Americans were ushered into the presence of navy commander Hiroshi Hayashi, whose command of the English language was little better. Resorting at times to pantomime, Giles managed to convey that the American "number one man" was back at the Government Palace. With some shoving and a prominent display of bayonets, he and Lane were escorted back to the plaza, where they found all of the defenders stripped to their underwear and lined up under the watchful eyes of a couple of Japanese machine-gun crews.

"We didn't know what to expect," observed Ray Church, after the defenders were ordered to come out with their hands up. "I was laying behind this hedge there. This Jap came up and knocked my helmet off with his bayonet and I was taken prisoner."[51] One of the Marines—nineteen-year-old PFC John Kauffman of Arlington, Virginia—had already been murdered, bayoneted to death as the prisoners exited the armory and were shoved, punched, and beaten into line on a grassy area to the left front of the Government Palace. "I thought they were going to kill us all," recalled PFC Harris Chuck. "They corralled us into three ranks, shoving and pushing and poking bayonets at everyone."[52]

Kauffman, who had a reputation as "a hothead," apparently lost his temper at being shoved around by one of the Japanese and angrily blurted, "Fuck you!"[53] Whether or not the Japanese understood the language, he recognized Kauffman's defiance and promptly gutted him with his bayonet. "He was in the rank right in front of me," said Chuck. "He dropped to the ground—dead. Much later, when we were marched away, they let him lie there with his insides hanging out."[54] Two other Marines—PFCs William W. Bomar Jr. and William H. Burt, both members of the

Insular Patrol—were also killed that morning at or near the plaza. According to various accounts from survivors, Bomar—and possibly Burt—was beheaded, but the circumstances are unclear.

Governor McMillin had been captured in the reception room of his quarters about twenty minutes after Giles's cease-fire signal. "The leader of the squad of Japanese who entered my quarters required me to remove my coat and trousers before marching me into the plaza, where officers and men were being assembled, covered by machine guns," he reported.[55]

Upon Giles's return with Commander Hayashi, they retired to the Government Palace to formalize the surrender. With the linguistic assistance of one of the previously detained Japanese civilians, the terms were soon hammered out, though McMillin stubbornly rejected the first draft when it failed to ensure fair treatment of the Guamanian civilians.[56] The agreement was amended, and McMillin signed. He then called Lieutenant Colonel MacNulty at Sumay to advise him of the surrender. He directed MacNulty to disarm his Marines and await the arrival of the Japanese.

Up on the hill, "scared, weak and cold," Ed Hale considered disappearing into the jungle but eventually decided to join his shipmates down on the plaza and share their fate, whatever it might be. Burying his pistol, he walked down the hill, passing a small group of Japanese carrying a machine gun. They wore dark green uniforms with wrap leggings and helmets with nets for affixing camouflage. They paid him little attention. "They seemed calm, as if going out for a walk," he recalled. Arriving at the plaza, he was accosted by a Japanese soldier who searched him and made him strip to his underwear before he was allowed to sit down with the other prisoners.[57]

CHAPTER 3

THE SURRENDER

FORTUNATELY FOR SERGEANT EARL ERCANBRACK, WORD OF THE SURRENDER reached Sumay before the Japanese arrived. "I had a patrol of sixty-three Marines the third day that had been ordered to make a suicide mission to stop the Japs at a crossroad near Sumay," recalled Ercanbrack. "We had nothing but small arms with which to fight. Just before the Japs arrived at my sector word came that the governor had surrendered the island and that we should give up the fight."[1]

Ercanbrack marched his men back to the barracks. The Marine detachment—some men with tears in their eyes—stood at attention as the flag was lowered and a white flag, improvised from an old mattress cover, took its place as a token of surrender. The Stars and Stripes was buried to keep it out of Japanese hands. In a last-minute gesture of defiance, a demolitions team blew up the detachment's ammunition magazine, a private first class climbing a couple of telephone poles to connect the wires to trigger the blast. The quartermaster stores warehouse and the Navy's twenty-five-thousand-barrel fuel oil tank had been set on fire by a civilian employee of the Public Works Department, but four thousand barrels of Pan Am aviation fuel fell into Japanese hands when would-be arsonists were kept at bay by the burning Standard Oil tank farm. The power plant, cold storage plant, commissary store, and all the island's bridges remained intact. "We disassembled our rifles and threw the bolts into the jungle," recalled PFC Frank Nichols. "We gathered at what was left of the barracks in Sumay and awaited the Japs."[2]

Japanese troops soon arrived, forced the Marines to strip, shoved them around some, and finally loaded them into trucks and brought them to Agana to join the other prisoners. "From the first attack on, the Marines at Sumay didn't do a damn thing," recalled PFC Carroll D. ("Barney") Barnett. "Our weapons were useless relics, many of us were unarmed and Colonel [William] MacNulty was absolutely useless.

No one had much respect for him. He was simply sent to Guam to finish out his years until he could retire."[3] While Governor George McMillin's decision to forego serious resistance certainly saved some of their lives, most of the leathernecks presumably would have agreed with PFC Barnett that it was not the Marine Corps' finest hour.

———

Eleven men were killed in the fight for the Plaza de Espana: one Navy ensign, three Insular Force Guard guardsmen, and a civilian volunteer (Roman Camacho); two Navy enlisted men; three Marines; and a civilian employed by Navy Public Works. Eight men were wounded. The ensign, twenty-nine-year-old Graham Paul Bright, a Naval Academy swim team standout from Pittsburgh, Pennsylvania, died in a misguided attempt to reach the plaza in his car. He was intercepted by Japanese soldiers who riddled the car with machine-gun fire, then pulled the young officer out of the vehicle and bayonetted him, leaving his body in the roadway.

Four Americans had taken refuge in an office in the Government Palace. They included thirty-nine-year-old Chief Motorist's Mate Malvern Smoot, Navy yeomen Joe Blaha and Lyle W. Eads, and a Navy civilian employee, thirty-six-year-old John V. ("Jack") Kluegel. Peering through a window, Smoot thought the men surrendering on the plaza were being lined up to be shot. He and the others ran out the back door toward the Government Palace horse stables, hoping to escape up the steep slope to the rear.

It was a vain hope. A machine gun ripped as they were spotted by Japanese soldiers. Smoot shot back with his .45, but was hit in the head and killed instantly, slumping down against the horse corral fence. Following on Smoot's heels, Kluegel was also killed. Blaha went down as a bullet shattered the bone near his hip and another hit him in the back. Eads escaped being shot when he tripped over a flowerpot and went sprawling. Blaha called out to him, "Stay down, Eads and hide yourself."

A Japanese soldier came up and bayoneted Smoot and Kluegel, who were already dead. Seeing that Blaha was still alive and conscious, he strolled over and drove his bayonet into Blaha's chest. Blaha felt air bubble from the hole in his chest as he struggled to breathe through a punctured lung. The homicidal Japanese failed to notice Eads. As the sun rose, Blaha saw flies gathering on Smoot and Kluegel. All he could think was, "I am still alive." Eventually another group of Japanese soldiers happened along. Spotting Blaha, they were about to finish him off when an officer intervened. Eads took that opportunity to get to his feet and surrender. Both men survived, though Blaha's wounds crippled him for life.[4]

In addition to the eleven men killed at the plaza, the morning's toll included the six sailors from *Penguin* who had gone up the coastal road to reconnoiter the Tumon Bay beaches earlier in the morning: Signalmen 3rd Class Robert W. Ernst and Seba G. Hurd, Boatswain's Mates First Class Rollin G. Fraser and Frank J. O'Neill, Coxswain Leo J. Pineault, and Gunner's Mate First Class John Schweighardt. In his last letter home on November 27, Fraser had written, "We expect to be blown out of the ocean at any time."[5] Captured by the landing force after a brief shootout—which the Japanese subsequently described as "a small engagement on the northwestern beach"—the sailors were stripped, wired together, and bayonetted to death.[6] At least twenty-two civilians—and possibly as many as thirty or more—were also killed before the surrender. Governor McMillin subsequently reported total losses between the initial air attacks on December 8 and the final surrender on December 10 as thirteen officers and men of the U.S. Navy and Marine Corps, four members of Guamanian military units, one American civilian, and an estimated forty to fifty Guamanian civilians. Wounded included thirty-seven sailors and Marines, eight members of the Guam military, and an unknown number of Guam civilians.[7]

Rear Admiral Atsushi Kasuga, commanding Japanese naval personnel, came ashore with his staff at 1000 and established his headquarters in Sumay as the island was to come under navy jurisdiction. At 1400 he reported by telegram on the success of the landing. "So far, our side has incurred no loss," he reported. "The enemy seems to have lost its fighting spirit due to our fierce aerial attacks in the past few days."[8] General Tomitarō Horii entered Agana that evening and took up residence in Government Palace.

According to Operational Order A No. 21, "The detachment met with complete success its combat goals, obtaining in battle, results better than expected, though some enemy soldiers still remain at large."[9] Contrary to expectations, there were no land batteries; "rather only a few machine guns had been placed [at] strategic sites." The wireless telegraph station, cable station, port facilities, machines, and equipment had been wrecked. "As for the warehouses, they had buckets filled with oil at every nook and corner as to be ready to be set on fire. So probably there had been no time to destroy them by the time of the Japanese landings."[10]

Efforts to notify Tokyo of their success went somewhat less smoothly than the invasion itself. Seaman Koji Takayanagi, a radioman with the 5th Special Base Force, observed, "The army was scheduled to send the occupation declaration to Japan via Saipan. They tried to send the declaration to Saipan for as long as two hours, but there was no response from Saipan. So, the army came to the navy with a cipher telegram saying, 'Navy-san, please send this.' The navy sent the telegram to Saipan by the TM-type short-mobile radio telegraphic apparatus."[11]

It was later claimed in some quarters that Japanese losses were as high as two hundred men—an impossible number in light of the weak resistance. The Japanese admitted to losses of only one killed and six wounded. Even if a low count intended for home consumption, that number is likely closer to reality. "The conquest of Guam was very easy," remarked Lieutenant Yutaka Yanagiba, "and it was like a [vacation] journey overseas. The Japanese military suffered only the death of a navy man."[12] The lieutenant would have received little argument from the conquered. "We didn't put up much of a fight," admitted civil engineer, now prisoner of war, Lieutenant Junior Grade Jack Schwartz.

Though distasteful, Governor McMillin's decision to quickly capitulate may well have averted a wholesale massacre. Two months later, the 144th Infantry troops that helped capture Guam were responsible for one of the Pacific War's more notorious atrocities, murdering about 160 Australian prisoners of war at Rabaul. The prisoners were taken into the jungle at Tol Plantation in small groups and systematically bayoneted or shot. The few survivors told of grinning Japanese soldiers emerging from the bush with bloody bayonets to round up their next batch of victims.

Though shoved around by their captors, the men held at the Plaza de Espana managed to avoid a similar fate. Finally allowed to retrieve their clothes, 450 captives were initially crammed into the adjacent Insular Force Guard building, which had a capacity of about 80. The Americans were soon separated from the others and moved into the cathedral and nearby St. Vincent de Paul Society building. The move to the cathedral wasn't much of an improvement. "Under appallingly crowded conditions, prisoners slept on the pews or wherever else they could find an open space," said Commander Donald Giles. "The cathedral had only one toilet, and there were insufficient bathing facilities. There was little water, either for washing or for drinking, and what was available flowed at such low pressure that it came as a mere dribble."[13]

Giles, Governor McMillin, and members of their administrative staff were confined at the naval hospital along with medical personnel, including five Navy nurses. Among the latter, Chief Navy Nurse Marion Olds had watched from her window the morning of the surrender as Japanese soldiers poured through the gates and onto the hospital grounds. "They scrambled for the shade of trees, dropping their packs and guns as they flopped to the ground," she recalled. "And then they did an amazing thing. They produced bamboo fans and started fanning themselves. It was almost laughable."[14]

So far, Olds had witnessed no acts of brutality. The nurses had not been molested, though their armed guards showed no regard for the women's privacy, frequently rifling through their rooms and helping themselves to whatever struck their fancy. Olds's worst brush with her captors resulted from failing to properly bow to her guards. "You are not bowing to the sentry or to me," an officer admonished her. "You are bowing to the emperor; you are now a conquered people." Another nurse was slapped by a soldier when she failed to understand his instructions, but otherwise they were not physically abused.[15]

The most terrifying moment for hospital corpsman Peter Marshall occurred when the staff was called out to the center of the compound and lined up in in front of a couple of machine guns. "I had never been so scared in all my life," he admitted. "My heart was pounding. I could feel sweat running down my body." Instead of being shot, the captives were treated to a lengthy propaganda speech on the virtues of Japanese rule and then sent back to their duties.[16]

Assuming the Japanese would kill any prisoners, PFC Barney Barnett and a few of his buddies hadn't waited at Sumay for the enemy to arrive and take their surrender. As the others began to assemble, Barnett ducked into the bushes. Later in the morning, he and four companions piled into a truck and drove away from camp, intending to hide out until the American fleet arrived—a salvation they expected within a few weeks. Instead, they drove right into a Japanese unit. "As we headed uphill, from both sides of the road about fifty Jap soldiers suddenly stood up and aimed their rifles at us," recalled Barnett. The five Marines raised their hands.

Taken back to the now deserted barracks area, they were stripped of clothes, watches, wallets, rings, and other items of value or interest to their captors. Naked as jaybirds, they sat on the lawn while the Japanese looted the barracks. As day waned, they were given some clothes and spent the night in the empty pool room, but morning brought more uncertainty. Rousted out at sunrise, they were escorted outside and stood up against a fence facing two machine guns and what appeared to be a firing squad.

As an officer shouted orders, the soldiers noisily worked their rifle bolts, but instead of firing on command, they charged at the prisoners, screaming at the top of their lungs. "Just as they came within a few feet, they turned their rifles sideways and struck each of us," said Barnett. "We were sent sprawling against the fence and onto the ground." This sadistic little game was repeated three times before the soldiers pointedly loaded their weapons. "Now we knew the end was coming," said Barnett. As the Marines prepared for death, a messenger ran up and spoke to the officer. Twenty minutes later, the Marines were escorted away. Just how close they had actually come to death or whether the Japanese were just having some cruel fun, they would never know.[17]

Also taking to the bush, *Penguin* crewmen Edwin Settles and Walter ("Maggie") Magelsenn found refuge with a Chamorro family in an outlying valley. Their benefactor agreed to feed the two sailors, but insisted that they stay hidden in heavy brush up on the mountainside. "And the very next day when they [Japanese patrols] started combing . . . we were in this underbrush, and they would miss us. I mean, they was within a few yards of us," recalled Settles.

Over the next two or three days, the Chamorro brought them food late at night, but the pressure was mounting. Finally one night he blurted, "I wish you boys would leave." He was worried about his wife and two children, he confessed. "I don't want them killed. But I love Uncle Sam and if you insist, I will take care of you as long as I can." No, Settles told him; they would go.

At daylight, he and Magelsenn started down the paved road toward Agana to turn themselves in. An occasional truck full of Japanese soldiers ground past them. "[As] each truck would go by, we would raise our hands up and keep walking and look at them and smile, and they would look at us and smile," remembered Settles. Finally arriving at Agana, they walked in on a startled Japanese officer who "jumped up and screamed and sounded like Donald Duck," recalled Settles. Regaining his composure, the Japanese gave them some cheese and Chesterfield cigarettes. Settles saw a squad of soldiers assembling outside and was sure they were about to be taken out and shot. He turned and shook hands with Magelsenn. Good-bye, he said. This was it. Instead, they were taken to a headquarters building, where they were confronted by a lieutenant wearing a sword so long it dragged on the floor. The lieutenant stood them at attention. He was going to interrogate them, he advised, and if they lied, he would cut their heads off. "What's your general quarters?" he asked Settles.

Settles, who had manned one of the machine guns on the *Penguin* and was pretty sure he had hit one of the Japanese planes that attacked the ship, said he had no general quarters: he just scrubbed the deck and washed paint. This went on for a while with Settles moving himself ever lower in the chain of command until the lieutenant lost his temper. Screaming in an apparent rage, he pulled out his sword and leaped forward, swinging the weapons with both hands, so close that the blade passed under Settles's chin. "I thought he [had] cut my head off and it was so sharp, I didn't feel it," recalled Settles. "They had Magelsenn sitting in a chair, and he jumped up and screamed when the thing went in under my chin that way. He thought they cut my head off, too."[18]

Apparently appeased, the lieutenant put away his sword and had the two sailors escorted to the cathedral where they joined the rest of the prisoners.

—◦—

Guam's civilians were making their own adjustments. Fourteen-year-old Maria Santos Martinez's family had sought refuge in the jungle. "Our family hid there and it was so dark and we couldn't find each other," she remembered. In the morning her father left to cut *tuba*—source of a popular alcoholic drink—and when he climbed down from the coconut tree, he saw a Japanese unit coming from the direction of the Tumon Bay beaches. "They stopped at the house of my aunt and found a young woman by the name of Maria Camacho whom they dragged out and raped," said Martinez. "They held onto her father and while a bayonet was pointed at him, the battalion took turns on the young woman. My father ran back to us in the jungle and told us about what he saw."[19]

Thirteen-year-old Justo Guerrero was playing around at the family ranch when he noticed three Japanese soldiers approaching. "This was the first time I ever saw a Japanese soldier," he said. "One of them just stopped and glared at me. The other two went into the chicken ranch and took a hen and her eggs and then they all left. They never said a word. We had five or six baskets for chickens to lay eggs—they took the only hen that was laying eggs."[20]

Over the next couple of days, the Saipanese Chamorro interpreters circulated around, ordering civilians to report to the plaza to register and receive identity tags. Walking into town to register, young Rosita ("Rosie") Guitierrez and her family passed the body of Ensign Bright still lying in the road by his bullet-riddled car. They knew the ensign well. He and two other young officers had rented her aunt's home next door, and he had often taken the time to speak to Rosie in a friendly fashion.

Over the next few days, Chamorros were registered, issued cloth identity tags, and released. All private motor vehicles were confiscated to be used by the occupying forces or handed out as rewards to Japanese civilians. A dusk-to-dawn curfew was imposed. An edict went out that all radios and cameras were to be turned in. Anyone found with an illegal radio would be subject to execution. On Orote Peninsula, the two thousand residents of Sumay village were evicted from their homes, a process that reportedly included a half a dozen rapes. The vacated buildings and the former

Marine Barracks were taken over by Japanese troops. The Chamorro Insular Force Guard veterans were eventually "released" to work as stevedores unloading cargo; many would subsequently be forced to dig manganese out of an open pit mine near the radio towers at Libugon.

Japanese soldiers wandered the streets of Agana. "There was the smell of pickled radish [*daikon*], dried seaweed, fish, sea-slugs and sea-cumbers and the odor of soybean soup [*misu*] . . . from every corner of the city where hungry troops were preparing their meals on open fires," observed Pedro C. Sanchez.[21] "Foreigners are luxurious," company commander Lieutenant Yutaka Yanagiba confided to his diary a day after the surrender. "There are swimming pools, a golf course and automatic record-changing phonographs." The civilian population seemed friendly enough. A Chamorro child presented one of his enlisted men with a chicken—at least Yanagiba thought it had been a gift. "If he had robbed the chicken from villagers, I intended to make him take responsibility," remarked the lieutenant, "but as a Chamorro child followed immediately after him, I felt relieved to think that the soldier was given the chicken. Then we took a picture together and sang a song."[22]

Relations with the Japanese were less idyllic for Bishop Olano, the island's ranking cleric. Attempting to enter his residence, he was barred by the crossed bayonets of two Japanese guards. "This is my house," he remonstrated with them.

"Emperor, emperor," they replied stubbornly.

Finally gaining permission from higher authority to retrieve some clothing, the bishop found his house had been ransacked. Trunks had been emptied and clothes strewn on the floor where they apparently served as makeshift bedding. Most of his personal possessions had vanished. "Bread, pieces of ham, lard, sugar covered the floor," he recalled. Soldiers had hung their clothes out to dry on lines strung along the veranda. Olano noticed one of the Japanese was wearing his bishop's shoes. "I was about to call his attention [to this] when upon second thought I decided to refrain from doing so," he remarked.[23]

The new masters of Guam issued a proclamation to the Chamorros, advising, "Our Japanese Army has occupied this island of Guam by order of the Great Emperor of Japan. It is for the purpose of restoring liberty and rescuing the whole Asiatic people and creating the permanent peace in Asia. Thus our intention is to establish the new Order of the World."[24] Guam's civilians were assured they need not worry "as we guarantee your lives" and would not plunder private property. However, warned the occupiers, "those who conduct any defiance and who act spy [*sic*] against our enterprise shall be court-martialed and the Army shall take strict care to execute said criminals by shooting!"[25]

Six days after the disaster at Pearl Harbor, the U.S. Navy admitted it was unable to communicate with Guam by either radio or cable. The last reports from the island indicated that Japanese troops had landed at several points. "The capture of the island is probable," stated an official Navy communique.[26]

This somber news was followed on December 16 by a Japanese radio announcement that "Japanese forces landed at the port of Apra on western Guam at dawn on December 10, attacking a number of strategic points." Japanese forces were in possession of the capital Agana; they had captured over 380 prisoners, "including George McMillin, the governor, the commandant of the naval station, the vice governor and many officers," and had been in complete control of the island since December 12, noted the report.[27]

The news, at least in military and high political circles, was not unexpected, but the public was dismayed. Newspaper reporters and columnists pointed out that Congress had repeatedly denied funds to fortify Guam. Columnists Drew Pearson and Robert S. Allen observed, "For years the Navy tried to get funds to fortify this vital little insular possession and congress repeatedly blocked the plans." The column then quoted "a few of the gems" uttered in the House when Congress debated and voted down an appropriation for Guam on February 23, 1939. The cast of villains included Representative John M. Robinson of Kentucky, who had previously declared, "The real danger to our country does not come from Japan. Japan, more than 7,000 miles from our shores, and with a navy only two thirds as large as ours, could make no successful attack on the Hawaiian islands or continental United States if we mind our own business and stay neutral."[28]

Speaking out against what he considered a smear campaign against the records of certain congressmen, Senator David Walsh (D-Massachusetts), chairman of the Senate Naval Affairs Committee, "noted for the record that the Navy never did ask congress for authority to fortify Guam but proposed only that it be authorized to dredge and otherwise improve the harbor." The proposal was defeated by the House of Representatives and never came to a vote in the Senate, he declared, "because the Navy did not insist upon it."[29] Once again, defeat found itself an orphan.

For the American prisoners on Guam, recriminations as to who or what was to blame for their fate had become a moot point. By Christmas Eve, the reality of their situation was beginning to sink in. Packed into the cathedral, the mixed bag of Marines, sailors, civilian contractors, and Pan Am employees were now under the watch of Japanese army troops who were more strident and less tolerant than their naval predecessors. "Prisoners were punished severely for the slightest infraction or assumed infraction," recalled Commander Giles. "Punishment was delivered on the spot. . . . Normally it took the form of beatings, bamboo canes being the favorite delivery instruments. . . . [T]his was followed by a smashing fist to the face." The bayonet was also "used with alacrity."[30]

The men who had operated the highly classified radio intercept station at Libugon were especially nervous. It had been anticipated there would be time to evacuate these key personnel before hostilities broke out, but the speed and magnitude of the Japanese assault across the Pacific dictated otherwise. After destroying the incriminating material at the station, the detachment, led by thirty-year-old Chief Radioman Donald ("Don") W. Barnum, headed into the hills where they intended to set up emergency radio equipment to maintain communications with the Philippines. As it turned out, they lacked some crucial parts and were never able to get on the air.

On the third day they saw Japanese soldiers sweeping the surrounding hills. Radioman First Class Markle T. Smith tied a skivvy shirt onto a stick, and the radiomen followed him out toward the approaching enemy. "We were soon captured, placed in a circle, and forced to strip to our skivvies," said Harold Joslin, who also brought his pet dog with him. "We were all loaded on a truck, including the dog, and were taken to Agana, where everyone else had assembled. That was the last I saw of the dog."

They hoped they had adequately covered their trail. "We all wore radioman insignia on our uniforms, and could claim we worked at the naval radio station as long as the Japanese did not find any incriminating evidence to the contrary," observed Joslin. While they hoped for the best, it seemed inevitable that the Japanese would eventually identify them. "We were sure they knew we were intercept operators," said Joslin. "So every time somebody came around, some of the Japanese officers, we were sure they were looking for us in particular."[31]

Ironically, the Japanese fastened instead on Chief Radioman Hugh Myers, who spent three weeks hiding in the jungle before finally emerging to surrender on January 3. Myers's duties had consisted primarily of radio upkeep and repair at the main station in Agana, but he was generally aware of the secret intercept activities at Libugon. Over the next week, he was repeatedly interrogated and threatened with execution by the Japanese, who were convinced that a hidden radio station was broadcasting intelligence reports from the island. Myers was filled with dread when his interrogators brought him up to the secret intelligence center at Libugon. To his relief, the fire set by the detachment had done its work well. "The heat had been so intense that the panes in one of the windows had partially melted and had cooled in a sagging position," he said. "Even the characters on the keyboards of the typewriters—which I suppose had been Japanese—had been burned until they were ashen and unreadable." His captors asked him the purpose of the facility. The inventive Myers replied that while the main station was located at Agana, radio reception was clearer up on the height, and a small detachment had been assigned to copy weather and press bulletins.[32]

Myers kept Barnum and the radio intelligence unit members apprised of the questioning, and they memorized what he had told the Japanese so their stories would agree should they be interrogated. To the team's good fortune, the Japanese never realized the intelligence prize that was right at their fingertips. They eventually gave up on Myers, and the radiomen were never unmasked.

As the days passed, thoughts among the POWs turned more and more to food. Though Chamorro civilians risked abuse to bring foodstuffs to friends and boyfriends, there was not enough to eat, and what was available from the Japanese consisted mostly of weak vegetable stew and boiled potatoes. "Most of the sailors and Marines and some of the civilians were held in the cathedral," recalled a Navy nurse. "These latter had the worst time. Their rations were one potato and a thin slice of bologna, twice daily."[33] Ironically, this meager fare was often served on Minton china looted from a doctor's quarters. Allowed one religious service on Christmas Eve, the prisoners were "melancholy," observed Ed Hale. "Many of the fellows received gifts of food from native friends or relatives, but for most of us Christmas meant only a very thin breakfast, no lunch, and a light supper."[34]

Adding to the growing discontent, a breakdown in leadership allowed self-interest to erode what should have been a cooperative effort among the prisoners. One POW vividly recalled a fellow captive who hogged several quilts and a hammock, while the prisoner next to him was forced to sleep on the bare concrete floor. Some of the nearly seventy civilian contractors insisted they deserved preferential treatment since they weren't part of the armed forces. Among the military ranks, some petty officers insisted on maintaining their peacetime prerequisites and privileges over lower ranks rather than conceding that all were in the same boat, as it were. It was a cancer that would persist to one degree or another throughout their captivity.

Twelve days after that first miserable Christmas, the captives were told to get ready to move to a permanent POW camp. They were not told where that camp would be. Many continued to labor under the illusion that they would be freed as part of a prisoner exchange. Others thought they would remain confined somewhere on Guam. Both were wrong.

At 0430 on January 10, the prisoners were roused, fed what Giles described as "an unusually hearty breakfast consisting of a piece of luncheon meat, a boiled potato, and a bit of coffee," and told to get ready to depart.[35] Two hours later, the 483 U.S. POWs and nationals were lined up on the plaza for a seemingly interminable head count. At 0730, led by Captain McMillin, Colonel MacNulty, and other ranking officers, they began the four-mile hike to Piti Navy Yard. From what their guards let slip, they were to be sent to Japan.

Approaching the navy yard, they were paraded past a crowd of Chamorros, apparently assembled as a parting humiliation for the captives. "But whenever they felt safe from the eyes of the Japanese guards, they smiled and waved at the Americans," observed Ed Hale, trudging along with the rest.[36] Giles saw only sympathy in their faces. "Some cried openly, and in a few instances, those who were more courageous reached out and grabbed our hands as we passed. Also, when the guards were not looking or were too far away, small packages of food and clothing were thrust into our hands."[37]

The miserable column was counted yet again upon arrival at the dock and then once more before the captives were loaded onto barges and boated out through the vessels crowding the harbor. Much to their surprise, their destination was the former luxury liner *Argentina* Maru, most recently in service as a troop transport during the seizure of Wake Island. As they milled around on deck, Captain McMillin, still wearing civilian clothes, attempted to address his fellow prisoners with a few words of reassurance. Before he could continue, a Japanese officer rushed up and slapped him, then shoved him aside. "You were in charge, but not anymore!" the officer shouted in English. "You and your men are all cowards for surrendering and we will treat you accordingly. We will inflict upon you all the punishment that the human body can endure!"[38]

Filing down into the bowels of the ship, the military prisoners were crammed into two unventilated steerage holds lined with tiers of sleeping shelves. About two feet apart, each tier was six shelves high. Eight men were assigned to each shelf with about twenty inches of room per man. "There was little space between one's face and the shelf above, and there was no room to move," noted Giles.[39] As afternoon waned, *Argentina* Maru weighed anchor, and the prisoners felt the ship get underway.

Despite their predicament, there remained a general feeling that the war would not last long. One prisoner put together a calendar and asked his fellow captives to predict when they would be freed. The most pessimistic estimate was three months.[40]

CHAPTER 4

THE GREATEST GIFT OF ALL

The industrious Japanese wasted no time laying the groundwork for the long-term administration of their new conquest. The original invasion force departed in mid-January to prepare for the invasion of Australian-held Rabaul, leaving about 250 men of the 54th Keibitai to garrison the island and deal with military affairs under overall command of the Fifth Base Force on Saipan. Oversight of the civilian population would be handled separately by the Guam Minseibu (Civil Administration Department), which was also answerable to the navy's Fifth Base Force and was headed by Commander Hiroshi Hayashi of the 54th Keibitai.

Aiding in the pacification effort were the Chamorro "translators" from Saipan and Rota, ten of whom had infiltrated ashore just prior to the Japanese invasion. Another two dozen arrived in January; their number would eventually expand to about seventy-five men and three women, many of whom acted as police, among other roles. Japanese spokesmen assured their new subjects that in the Greater East Asia Co-Prosperity Sphere, participating peoples would work together for the mutual benefit of all. Under Japan's benevolent hand, nations throughout Asia and the Pacific would comprise an empire that would become the richest and most prosperous in the world. All would coexist in harmony.

Guamanians soon learned that this utopian vision did not embrace a continuation of the easygoing American days. As one of the newly arrived civil administrators observed, "The order we received was to see that the people of Guam change their attitude, that is away from the American influence and to obey the rules, orders and regulations of the Japanese, and also to see that they place themselves like Japanese."[1] This transformation included recognizing that their land, houses, cattle, chickens, and so on were all the property of the emperor and were available to them only through his forbearance and the permission of his representatives.

One of the first dictates was to turn the clock back one hour to Japanese time. This was followed by an announcement that Guam would henceforth be known as "Omiyajima," widely translated as "Great Shrine Island." Agana became "Akashi," or "the Red City."[2] The cross was removed from the cathedral in what would prove to be a futile effort to counter the Western influence of Catholicism and encourage the Japanization of the Chamorros. The cathedral itself was subsequently converted into a propaganda and entertainment center. As a Spanish national, Bishop Olano had been sent off with the prisoners aboard the *Argentine* Maru. The remaining Chamorro clergymen were ordered to start every service by requiring all worshippers to bow to the emperor. They were to speak only in Chamorro; no English was allowed. They were to meet with the Japanese governor every month and brief him on their religious activities "and to cooperate by telling the people that the Japanese were winning the war," observed Baptist pastor Joaquin Flores Sablan.[3]

An immediate—and, as far as most Chamorros were concerned, insulting—demand was that all civilians show respect and subservience to their new masters by bowing. "Bowing to a friend required only a slight nod of the head," observed Tony Palomo. "Bowing to an officer or to an institution, like a police station, required the bending of the head and body at a forty-five degree angle. The supreme bow was reserved only to the Japanese emperor and members of his family. This required a person to face north and then bend his entire body forward and down to a ninety degree angle. And in doing so, the person must bow slowly and solemnly."[4]

Civilians walking by a Japanese municipal office were required to demonstrate their obedience to the imperial government by pausing to bow in the direction of the door. Signs posted on office walls, police stations, and sentry boxes ordered, "You must stop here and bow to us."[5] Bows were required wherever the signs were posted, even if the building or sentry box was unoccupied. Those caught failing to comply—or whose respect seemed perfunctory—were typically beaten, sometimes severely. "A poorly done bow to one soldier might earn nothing more than a well-placed boot or a few slaps, while another might resort to stomping or hitting you time and again until your face was swollen," recalled Ben Blaz.[6]

Blaz, who was big for his age, recalled one particularly humiliating incident where a Japanese soldier ordered him to go get a box so that the shorter soldier could stand on it to slap him around the head. The slaps were more severe than they might seem, he added, because the soldiers would hit hard with the open hand and then again in a return motion with the back of the hand. "Rarely, if ever, was this done only once."[7] One Chamorro who failed to bow low enough while passing a police station was beaten so badly his spinal cord was damaged. Paralyzed, he subsequently died.

In masked defiance, some Chamorros turned the bows into insults. Bending stiffly at the waist, they would cheerily declare in Chamorro, "Good morning, asshole!" or "Now that I'm bending over, kiss my ass!" always taking care that none of the Saipanese translators were around to overhear.[8]

Satisfying as those small triumphs may have been, no one could have any illusions about the penalties for disobedience or overt resistance to Japanese authority. Less than a month after the invasion, a number of civilians were escorted out to Agana's Pigo cemetery to witness the execution of two Chamorro men, Alfred Flores and Francisco Borja Won Pat. Flores, who had worked for the Pomeroy Company, a defense contractor, before the invasion, had been caught trying to pass a note to the captured Americans asking what he was supposed to do with a batch of dynamite stored in the harbor area. Won Pat was accused of trying to take items from a Pomeroy Company warehouse, the contents of which were now the property of the emperor.

The two doomed men, blindfolded and with hands tied behind their backs, stood by two open graves facing a five-man firing squad. A Japanese officer read the offenses. A prayer was offered by a priest, and as Flores's mother futilely cried out to God, a volley sent the two victims sprawling. The corpses were dumped into the open holes as shocked witnesses departed. Recording the event in his diary, Fumitoshi Yasuoka, a soldier with the South Seas Detachment, observed matter-of-factly, "Saw two spies whom we caught yesterday being shot."[9] It would turn out to be a portent of things to come.

As the *Argentina* Maru carried its involuntary guests to what would turn out for most of them to be years of imprisonment, Navy radiomen George Ray Tweed and Alfred J. ("Al") Tyson were dodging Japanese patrols in Guam's interior. Soon to be declared missing and presumed dead by the Navy, they had decided to take to the bush rather than surrender.

Tweed, at age thirty-nine, was a sixteen-year Navy veteran. A radio maintenance man, he had arrived on Guam in August 1939. His wife and son, along with other American women and children, had been evacuated in October 1941. His marriage had been on the rocks in any case. He and Tyson, a career Navy man from Rhode Island, were working at the Navy Communications Office in Agana when the Japanese invaded. As the unit broke up their radio equipment with sledgehammers, it was obvious how things were going to end, at least in the short term, but Tweed and Tyson remained optimistic. They figured it wouldn't be long before the U.S. Fleet showed up to liberate the island. "Six weeks, we agreed, was a conservative estimate," observed Tweed. "If the Americans would be here by then, what was the use of surrendering. We could surely hold out that long."[10]

If Tweed had a gift beyond knowing his way around the inner workings of a radio, it was the ability to look out for George Ray Tweed. Following the abandonment of the radio intercept station at Libugon on December 8, he had been called out to help the intercept crew get on line with the relocated emergency transmission station. Tweed drove up from Agana with some of the needed parts, but as soon as the Japanese planes returned, he jumped back into his car and left. "He told no one he was going and made no effort to carry out his assigned duties," remembered Radioman Joseph R. Young.[11] The Libugon team never saw him again and never did manage to get their radio setup operational. Adding to their frustrations, Tweed took their walkie-talkie, which was their sole means of communication with Captain George McMillin. The Japanese reportedly discovered the radio lying alongside the road after the invasion.

Gathering up a stock of canned goods, Tweed and Tyson climbed into Tweed's old REO sedan and headed inland, eventually abandoning the car near Yona on the east coast and continuing into the bush on foot. Assisted by friendly Chamorros, they hid out for weeks, battling swarms of mosquitoes and dodging enemy patrols. As far as they knew, they were the only two Americans still on the loose, but they eventually learned that four other Navy men were hiding out at Manenggon about three miles further inland. A Chamorro led them to the other fugitives, who were camped out in a rude shelter hardly large enough for their sleeping mats. They turned out to be Yeoman First Class Adolphe Yablonsky and Chief Aerographer Luther W. Jones from the Navy Communications Office and two crewmen off the USS *Penguin*, Chief Machinist's Mate Michael L. Krump and Motor Machinist First Class Clarence B. Johnston.

"I knew them all," said Tweed. "Yablonsky, or Ski as we called him, had come to Guam and started to work in the Communications Office a couple of months ago. He had a sharp, active mind and held his own on almost any subject in the office bull sessions. Everyone knew 'Weatherman Jones,' the lanky aerographer. He had come in for plenty of kidding every day at the office when he posted his forecast." Chief Krump was clearly in charge of the group. "He was the leader and looked the part," observed Tweed. "Tall and broad, he was physically the most rugged of the four."[12]

It took the Japanese a few weeks to learn that the six sailors were still at large, but word eventually leaked out. Kanichi Ogawa, who headed the Minseibu's newly installed General Affairs subsection and spoke Chamorro thanks to business contacts before the war, recalled, "Every Chamorro knew this but the Naval Guard Unit didn't because it couldn't understand their language." But eventually the rumors reached Guard Force commander Hiroshi Hayashi. Summoning Ogawa, Commander Hayashi asked, "Is the rumor true that six American stragglers are in hiding?"

"Every Chamorro person is saying so," admitted Ogawa.[13]

The revelation put Hayashi in a difficult position as he had already reported that the island was secure and all prisoners had been sent to Japan. The Japanese became still more alarmed when they learned there were radiomen among the fugitives, suspecting the sailors could be in possession of a transmitter. Search parties were organized. An official report assured the powers that be that the authorities were "making all possible efforts to capture escapees by mobilizing the police officers and village chiefs to cooperate with the navy."[14]

Chamorros forced to assist in sector searches under Japanese oversight often tipped the fugitives off before dutifully beating the bushes, but the pressure mounted. During one close call, a searcher almost stepped on Tweed as he lay concealed in the underbrush. The six Americans soon decided they would have a better chance of avoiding capture if they broke up into two-man teams. Tweed and Tyson struck off on their own. A day or two later, they were nearly caught when a large search swept the area. "We heard them near the spot we had just left, yelling *Whooo-ooo! Whooo-ooo!* like farmers calling hogs," Tweed recalled.[15]

In conversation with a Chamorro friend, the two sailors admitted they were thinking about turning themselves in. A somber look came over the Chamorro's face. "You're too late," he said.[16] The grace period was over. A Japanese officer had told him that since all the other prisoners had been removed to Japan, any American caught in the bush now would be killed.

Back in the United States, information regarding the fate of the Guam captives trickled in slowly. Early reports listed the numbers of prisoners taken but did not identify them individually.

In mid-January, Japan's Domei news agency reported an interview with Captain McMillin at Zentsuji prison camp on Shikoku island, describing him as seeming "well and chipper." McMillin said his treatment had been satisfactory. "I want you to tell President Roosevelt we of the American forces fought valiantly and defended our posts until the last," he added in a considerable exaggeration of fact.[17]

General news accounts quoting a Japanese report that the prisoners on Guam included five nurses encouraged nine-year-old William Robert Jackson to believe his mother, Navy nurse Lieutenant Junior Grade Leona C. Jackson, would eventually return home to the tiny village of Union in northern Illinois. "I know I'll see my mother again, some day," declared Robert, who lived with his grandparents and entertained ambitions of becoming an airplane pilot or a professional baseball player. "I just got a feeling that my mom's all right, and I know I'll see her again."[18]

Other families learned their loved ones were alive in early February as the Japanese began broadcasting statements from prisoners. One of the first was from Commander Donald Giles, who assured his wife, "I am well and safe in the war prisoners camp in southern Japan. . . . Re-address and save all magazines for me. Anticipate exchange of prisoners and return when conditions permit."[19]

Subsequent broadcasts featured messages from various other ranks. Some messages were from the captive personally; others were read on the air by Japanese broadcasters. Twenty-year-old Field Musician Alfonso J. Moreno's message to his mother in Los Angeles was typical: "Dear mother, I am safe and in good health. We are being treated swell. We hope the war is over soon so we can come home. Give everyone my regards and don't worry."[20]

Reprieved from almost certain death in the aborted defense of Sumay, Sergeant Earl Ercanbrack assured his wife in Norfolk, Virginia, in a message read by a Japanese broadcaster, "Safe and well. Not a scratch. Hope you are well. Am in a Japanese prison camp. Excellent treatment. Advise folks. I am very sorry for the way the war must have surprised you. Never fear for my safety. Nothing can harm me as long as I am held by your sacred love."[21]

Not all the news passed on by the War Department came as a relief. As more information arrived from the International Red Cross in May, Mr. and Mrs. Harry E. Anderson of New Lenox, Illinois, learned that their son, Marine corporal Harry Anderson—previously presumed to be a prisoner, according to the Navy Department—was dead. "An amateur radio operator, young Anderson enlisted with the Marines three years ago and had been at Guam since last August," observed the *Chicago Tribune*. "He was wounded, presumably December 7, and later was reported a Japanese prisoner of war. His parents had received no letters from him since the Japanese assault."[22] He was the Andersons' only child.

At about the same time, Jean Kluegel, a schoolteacher in Honolulu, learned that her husband, thirty-seven-year-old Jack V. Kluegel, previously reported as a prisoner, was also among the dead. A graduate of the U.S. Naval Academy and Stanford University Law School, Kluegel was the sixth generation of his family to live in Hawaii; his ancestors had come to the islands with the first company of missionaries aboard the brig *Thaddeus* in 1820. In addition to his wife, he left a three-year-old daughter.

By June, listings of prisoners had been provided through the International Red Cross, and the wheels were turning to repatriate noncombatants. In August, the Swedish liner MS *Gripsholm* docked at Jersey City, New Jersey, with over fifteen hundred repatriated civilians, diplomats, and other qualified internees and noncombatants. Among them was William Robert Jackson's mother, Leona, and the other four Navy nurses from Guam. Not among the repatriates were the civilian contractors captured on Guam or Governor McMillin, who had hoped to be treated as a diplomat or government official rather than as a naval officer. He, Commander Giles, and the civilian contractors would remain prisoners for the next three years.

The Japanese effort to assimilate their new subjects into the Greater East Asia Co-Prosperity Sphere got underway in earnest after the new year, with language training at the island's former elementary schools. The first classes were supervised by instructors from the 54th Naval Guard Unit and the Minseibu staff, but regular teachers arrived from Saipan and the Palaus in September. A school for Chamorro children in Agana held classes to teach simple Japanese vocabulary, reading and writing of katakana characters, arithmetic, children's plays and songs, flag raising, moral discourse, and etiquette. A curriculum geared toward young adults consisted of language and patriotic songs.

School days began with solemn bows in the general direction of Japan. Students would then recite, in Japanese, the fealty oath to the emperor and sing the Japanese anthem, recalled fifteen-year-old Jose M. Torres. The teacher would then typically launch into a tirade against the "hedonistic and morally corrupt Americans," claiming that the Japanese would soon win the war and dictate surrender terms to the Americans in the White House, observed Torres. Failure to pay attention provoked slaps and cuffs from the teacher, which inspired fear and resentment but did little to advance the learning process.[23]

"One day, we were all standing facing the east. I didn't even know what we were doing," recalled Juan U. Baza. "But we were supposed to bow to the east, to the Emperor, the god of Japan, and the world, supposedly. I didn't bow quickly enough. I'll never forget. Nakase Sensei [teacher] kicked me, slapped me first and then kicked me. Kicked my feet and I fell down. Needless to say, I was kind of afraid to go to school."[24]

On the second day of school, Justo Guerrero's teacher criticized the boys for having "American-style haircuts" and told them to get shaved-head Japanese haircuts like his. The next day, ten of the students showed up at school without the required haircuts. "He cursed at us and took the scissors from his desk and grabbed my hair and cut it," recalled Justo. "He did the same to the other boys." That evening, Justo's mother shaved off what remained of his hair.[25]

Such petty tyrannies did nothing to seduce the civilian population as assimilation efforts continued to bump up against forty years of Americanization. One frustrated teacher observed that even the "half-Japanese" students, who received special attention, showed little interest in their new studies. "I talked about the lifestyle in Japan, half in English and half in Japanese, but the second-generation people became pure Chamorros and had no consciousness of their Japanese ancestry," he complained with some annoyance.[26]

Japanese schoolteacher Kiyoshi Nakahashi, who had been brought in to help instruct the Chamorros in the proper attitude, attributed their lack of enthusiasm to "unfavorable education and cultural influence during the American colonial administration." A military report observed, almost with bemusement, that the Chamorros seemed to lack social awareness, "did not have their own characteristic culture and were deficient in the concept of truthfulness, although they were obedient."[27] Their new subjects seemed wholly disinterested in adopting Japanese virtues of discipline, hard work, and sacrifice for the greater good. "Almost all natives on this island don't work but play," observed Lieutenant Yutaka Yanagiba only days after the invasion.[28]

The lieutenant was far from alone in his disapproval of what Japanese tended to view as moral frivolity. "Young girls are seen spending every day idly painting their nails red and doing make-up. They smoke in front of people in an unconcerned manner," a Japanese teacher wrote home.[29] Ueno Fukuo, an agricultural geographer who visited Guam between August and September 1942, observed, "The women wear attractive American dresses and some of them are coquettish. . . . The Chamorros want brilliantine [scented hair oil] and tobacco rather than food. . . . Even the low prestige people in Agana adopted American lifestyles and have household effects which only Japanese upper classes have in Japan."[30]

For their part, Guam's civilians continued to be alternately amused and terrified by their new masters. Jose Torres recalled one "asinine edict" wherein the authorities ordered every family to submit a list of livestock and poultry in their possession, stipulating that none were to be consumed without express permission. The Chamorros simply submitted phony lists and continued to eat as they pleased. "And then came the edict to end all edicts," observed Torres: "The Japanese authorities determined that houseflies had become a problem and must be eradicated. These flies were to be swatted, put in empty matchboxes and turned in to the authorities. This edict produced another guffaw from all of us—matchboxes laden with dead houseflies, indeed."[31]

But if the Japanese could be buffoons, they were still dangerous and unpredictable buffoons. Jose Santos Torres's ten-year-old brother was beaten by a teacher for whistling the American national anthem on his way to school. "I remember my brother when he was getting beaten up by the Japanese with a stick, you know, like a heavy cane," recalled Torres. "He was getting beat up on the head, and the following day he died—brain hemorrhage."[32]

The upheaval in Chamorro life intensified as the Japanese began to implement plans to transform Guam into a major food-producing center. The island had no significant rice production at the outbreak of the war, but in early 1942 the Japanese established rice farms at Asan, Piti, Sumay, Inarajan, Agat, Umatac, and Merizo. Chamorros ages eleven and older were organized into labor battalions to clear land and prepare rice paddies for the ambitious program.

Jose M. Torres was only fifteen years old. "My labor battalion was Labor Battalion Number Six and had approximately thirty men and boys whose initial work was tilling and cultivating by hand soil for rice planting," he recalled. "Members of the work battalions cultivated taro, rice, tapioca, corn and other crops without compensation because their harvests were turned over to the Japanese."[33]

The Minseibu system distributed this communally grown food first to the military, then to Japanese civilians, and lastly to the Chamorros who produced it. How much, if any, the Chamorros received depended on the number of Japanese civilians and military personnel on the island. "The residents must discard the liberalistic attitudes of the U.S. and achieve complete self-sufficiency on the island," the chief of the local section for political affairs lectured Chamorro leaders. "The new world's maxim is 'those who don't work cannot eat.'"[34]

"The Japs made us work even if we had sore eyes, a bellyache or were sick," recalled Thomas Tajalle. "The only time they let us alone was when we had a fever. They would put a hand on our foreheads and if we felt feverish, they would let us off work for the day."[35]

Resentful Chamorros took to singing a defiant little ditty reflecting where their loyalties lay. Forbidden by the Japanese, they sang it nevertheless, even at social gatherings. Typical of an almost endless variety of verses was the plea

Eight of December 1941
People went crazy right
Here in Guam.
Oh, Mr. Sam, Sam
My dear Uncle Sam,
Won't you please come
Back to Guam?[36]

Adding to the frustrations of the Japanese in their attempt to transform their new subjects into compliant members of the empire were centuries of Spanish colonial rule with its fervent Catholicism. Conquered or not, the devout Chamorros were not about to trade Jesus for a Japanese emperor. Their intransigence was encouraged by Guam's ranking Catholic priest, thirty-one-year-old Father Jesus Baza Duenas. The slender, bespectacled Duenas had been ordained in 1938, only the second Chamorro to be named to the priesthood up to that time. When the Japanese expelled all foreign religious leaders with the other POWs in 1942, Duenas and the newly ordained Father Oscar L. Calvo were allowed to remain since both were Chamorros. They agreed to share responsibilities for the island, with Father Duenas tending to the spiritual needs of parishioners in the south and Father Calvo to those in the north.

Unlike the younger Calvo, who made an effort to get along with the Japanese, Father Duenas quickly became an irritant to the invaders with his stubborn defiance of the occupation. Secure in the righteousness of his God, he made little attempt to conceal his disdain for Japanese hypocrisy and his lack of respect for their authority. He defiantly hummed American songs, leafed through forbidden American magazines in public, and vociferously protested Japanese mistreatment of his parishioners. Complicit in helping to shield Tweed and the other fugitives, he was also among those who covertly listened to broadcasts on the few contraband radios that had been hidden from the occupiers.

Exasperated by Duenas's stubbornness and his influence with the civilian population, the occupiers brought two Japanese priests to Guam in November 1942 in a rather heavy-handed ploy to undermine his stature and garner support from the highly religious Chamorros. Undeterred, Father Duenas boldly criticized the two newcomers for propagandizing from the pulpit, adding in a letter, "We consider you Japanese priests as spies."[37] He ignored Father Calvo's cautions, and when one of the Japanese priests warned him about his defiant attitude and advised him to limit his activities to religious affairs, the Jesuit retorted, "I answer only to God and the Japanese are not God."[38] As it turned out, these would be his first bold steps down the path to eventual martyrdom.

Among the new arrivals on Guam following the invasion was a contingent of so-called comfort girls, a disingenuous name for the sex slaves compelled to service Japanese military personnel. Forty-five of these women—mostly Koreans—were shipped to Guam from Japan. They were joined by a number of Chamorro women who were recruited or coerced to staff the brothels. Some of the latter included former "Monday ladies," but other so-called volunteers found themselves with little choice in the matter.

At least five brothels were established, three in Agana, one in Anigua, and one in Susa near Piti. Customers were allowed fifteen minutes or less with a woman, each of whom was expected to service from ten to fifteen men per day. "Soldiers of less than the noncommissioned officer class were Chamorro women's customers," observed Petty Officer Hirose Hisashi of the 54th Naval Guard Unit. "On holidays, called a *hangen joriku* [port and starboard liberty], soldiers stood in line in front of the comfort station and were told, 'Five minutes per person.'"

Hisashi described one of the Agana brothels. "There were about five small cabins, each with four rooms. In each cabin, there were four to five Japanese, Okinawans, Korean, Chamorro and Chamorro-Spanish mixed blood women," he recalled. "The Japanese were professionals aged 25–30. The Chamorro women were divided into dark-skinned ones and Chamorro-Spanish mixed blood ones. For soldiers, dark-skinned women were popular because their services were good. They weren't professionals. All the women regularly received venereal disease checkups at a hospital."[39]

A subsequent U.S. intelligence report on the occupation noted, "There seems to have been comparatively little outright rape, except in the very early days."[40] The operative phrase in the report was "outright rape." Petty Officer Hisashi observed, "All officers had Chamorro girlfriends."[41] Many of those relationships were apparently voluntary. Others were not. Women hoping to avoid being forced into prostitution by agreeing to serve as maids for Japanese administrators often found they had simply contracted for another form of sexual exploitation. Koshimuta Yoriko, the wife of a South Seas Guam office employee, recalled that one of her maids confessed to her, "I have become a maid because I don't want to be a comfort woman." Nevertheless, Yoriko could not help but notice the frequent turnover of maids in some households. "My husband said that it was because masters are taking advantage of them," she observed.[42]

Prominent in the trafficking was Samuel Shinohara, the flag-flying Japanese store owner, who had been gifted one of the confiscated cars in recognition of his enthusiastic collaboration with the invaders. Shinohara also saw to the needs of select Japanese officers. A few weeks after the execution of Flores and Won Pat, Shinohara, accompanied by a Japanese police official, drove up to Jose Flores's ranch in Inarajan in southeastern Guam, asking for Jose's seventeen-year-old daughter Alfonsina.

Shinohara told Alfonsina's mother, Rafaela, that he wanted to take the girl back to Agana to serve as a police administrator's housekeeper. Recognizing Shinohara's true purpose, Rafaela objected. The girl was only seventeen and had never been away from home, she protested. "Yes," replied Shinohara, unmoved, "but you must obey it and if you don't, all of you will be killed." He added that the police official had specified that he wanted a seventeen-year-old girl.

Alfonsina's father Jose also objected, but Shinohara insisted. "This is what this officer wants," he replied. "This is wartime and we must obey the officials." He repeated that failure to comply could result in death. Jose recalled, "Right at that moment, I knew that whether I wanted to give up my daughter or not, they would take her just the same."

Rafaela spoke with Alfonsina, who was crying, and told her she must go or she would be killed. "No," protested the girl, "I don't want to go."

But in the end, she had no choice.

Back at the officer's house in Agana, her fears were quickly realized. "Shinohara told me to go into a certain room and told me to stay there with [the officer]. So I started crying and [at] that time I was only thinking of my parents and never expected that I would be turned over to a man. Then Shinohara said that I must listen and obey or else I will be beheaded. . . . Shinohara said that I must obey because if I didn't it would mean my life and the lives of the people in my family."

That evening the police official forced himself on her for the first time. For the next six months, until the officer left the island, she would be forced to accommodate his sexual demands. Prior to that first night, she had never slept with a man.[43]

The search for the six fugitive American sailors on Guam continued unabated during the spring and summer of 1942. Aside from the embarrassment of failing to capture the evaders, the military continued to believe they had possession of a radio transmitter and were sending intelligence information about Japanese forces. A member of the 54th Naval Guard Unit noted later that the communications section even studied how to trace the transmissions back to the source but without success.[44] In fact, there were no transmissions to trace as the Americans had no transmitter.

The Saipanese police, brought in because they spoke Chamorro, were the most obsessed with finding the fugitives. Police detained Chamorros for interrogation based on gossip, rumor, and sometimes just whim. In August, Joaquin A. Limtiaco, a farmer from Barrigada in northern Guam, was taken to the civil jail in Agana under suspicion of aiding the Americans. It was true, but Limtiaco professed ignorance. "I was asked whether I had some Americans in hiding and I replied in the negative," he testified later. "They started beating me up."[45]

Chamorros would come to refer to these beatings as "being punished," which was a gross understatement of a brutality that sometimes led to the victim's death. Jose Villagomez, one of the Saipanese "investigators," observed of police interrogation procedures: "They held them [suspects] by the collar and tripped them; whipped them, clubbed them, made them take the kneeling position with a board or club across [the backs of their knees] and then they will start kicking the thigh, or drown them. Sometimes they took a hose and put it in a person's mouth; they soaked a towel with water and put it over the face and at the same time talk to the person and keep on pouring water. Kick you on the leg or tie them in the hands and hang them up [from an overhead beam]."[46]

"They seemed to believe if they beat you long enough and hard enough, you would tell them what they wanted to hear," observed Ben Blaz, whose father was called in to the police station and whipped to a bloody pulp from his neck to his waist. The elder Blaz was a former immigration employee, and the Japanese demanded that he reveal the location of any explosives or weapons hidden in the harbor. How he would have such information was a mystery. "There was no telling who they would call, who they would accuse or why," noted Blaz. "They might as well have held a lottery with the names of everybody in a revolving barrel for all the sense it made."[47]

Held in custody for weeks, Joaquin Limtiaco was repeatedly beaten by three to four men at a time. "I was beaten every two or three days and sometimes I was beaten twice in one day for a period of about two and one half hours to three hours each time," he recalled. It started with lashes from a whip—composed of a tendon about three-quarters of an inch in diameter and about three and a half feet long, fastened to a wooden handle about twelve inches in length. "When one man got tired, he would pass the whip to another for him to take it over," said Limtiaco. Other beatings were administered with a wooden club. "Sometimes they made me take the position of having the tips of my toes and my hands touching the floor; sometimes they tied my hands and tied them to a beam," said Limtiaco. Forcing him into a "position of crawling with the tips of my toes and the palms of my hands touching the floor" seemed particularly popular with his tormentors. "From the start of my punishment I took that position and every time I fell to the side, they [would] kick me to resume the same position."

The beatings progressed to water torture. "After they got through beating me up, they took me over to the bathroom, wet a towel over my face, took off my pants, and started pouring water over my nose," he related. While experiencing all the effects of drowning, he was advised that his only chance for relief was to tell what he knew about the Americans. In fact, he had been helping the fugitives avoid capture, but even after weeks of torture, he never gave up any useful information. Finally, the

Japanese naval officer in charge ordered him released on the condition that he "go out and search for all Americans in hiding." He was to report every three days.[48]

In September, Japanese brutality finally brought results. On the morning of September 12, two Chamorros who had reportedly been threatened and extensively tortured led the Japanese to where Krump, Jones, and Yablonsky were hiding in the bush at Yona about four miles southeast of Agana as the crow flies. Accompanying the patrol—which consisted of about fifteen Japanese soldiers along with some Saipanese police—was Officer Adolfo Sgambelluri, a Chamorro who had been playing a dangerous game. While working as a policeman, he had also been passing information to those protecting the Americans. This time, however, he would be unable to help. "We had walked very slowly for about 50 yards or more when I heard a pistol shot," he recalled. "So I hollered, 'Hands up!' as I was ordered to do. The Americans were found sleeping and were awakened by the yelling of the Japs."[49]

The three evaders denied knowing where the other Americans were hiding. Asked where the cooked rice and food at the campsite came from, they said it had been given to them by a native, but they didn't know his name. "Krump, the biggest of the three Americans, was made to stand up and four Japs took turns hitting him in the stomach with their fists, but failed to move him," said Sgambelluri. They then moved on to Yablonsky, the smallest of the three, kicking him in the testicles and choking him.

Finally, the Americans were given shovels and picks and told to start digging. "I thought the Japanese treated their prisoners better than this," remarked Krump, still defiant. Sgambelluri passed the statement on to the translator, who relayed it to the Japanese officer in charge. The officer just laughed. "President Roosevelt is responsible for this," he replied through the translator.

After digging a grave measuring about four by eight feet, the three men were given a notebook to write last letters to their families. All were pretty much the same, observed Sgambelluri, saying they had been captured and were about to be shot and asking family members to "take good care of the kids." Sitting down in the hole surrounded by Japanese soldiers, the three sailors looked around at each other with resigned smiles. "So long boys," said one. They were ordered to sit with their hands around their knees and their heads bowed forward.

"Then the officer took out his sword and swung down on Krump's neck," recalled Sgambelluri. "Krump raised his right hand, the pointed finger out as if to say 'once more' after the first swing." Then the other Japanese lunged forward with their fixed bayonets, taking turns stabbing the three men. The native guides were ordered to shovel dirt over the victims. "And because one of them was moaning, the Japs thrust their bayonets into the grave where I believe Yablonsky was," said Sgambelluri.[50]

Six weeks later, on October 22, the Japanese caught up with Al Tyson and Clarence Johnson hiding in a chicken coop on a ranch in north-central Guam. Loose talk among the civilians apparently led them to the ranch, where they threatened to kill owner Tommy Torres and his family unless he revealed the whereabouts of the Americans. Japanese soldiers surrounded the chicken coop. Tyson, who had separated from Tweed earlier and joined up with Johnston, was standing watch by the fire. Johnston was asleep inside the shelter.

Startled by shouts from the Japanese, Tyson jumped up and ran into the bushes. Johnston, .45-caliber pistol in hand, emerged from the shelter and started shooting, but crumpled under a barrage of bullets that hit him in the face and chest. Tyson, seeing there was no escape, raised his hands and stepped out of the bushes. A Japanese promptly shot him through the forehead at close range, blowing the back of his skull off.[51]

Now, of the six evaders, only Tweed remained.

George Tweed's continued survival would have come as a shock to his family. In May, five months after the fall of Guam, the War Department had informed his wife in Santa Paula, California, that he had been killed in action in December. In truth, he would not have lasted any time at all were it not for the assistance of dozens of Chamorros, many of whom would pay a steep price for their loyalty.

Only a day before Tyson and Johnston were killed, Tweed, who had previously parted company with Tyson, apparently due to personality conflicts, fled to the northern part of the island. There he sought help from rancher Antonio Artero, the thirty-seven-year-old son of one of Guam's largest landowners. Like so many of his fellow Chamorros, Artero—a devout Catholic—could not bring himself to turn his back on the skinny, dirty wretch standing before him. He led Tweed to a rocky crevice in a three-hundred-foot cliff overlooking the ocean in a remote corner of the ranch property. This would become Tweed's home for the next twenty-one months while the Japanese turned Guam upside down looking for him. "Since I was only four miles from the northern tip of the island, I could see most of the west coast for twenty miles," recalled Tweed.[52] On a clear day, even Rota was visible, forty-seven nautical miles to the north.

Artero visited about once a week to bring food and odds and ends to make Tweed more comfortable—including at one point a fancy pair of pajamas. Tweed, who slept in his clothes for fear he would have to flee for his life at short notice, expressed his thanks, then carefully folded up the pajamas and stored them away with the idea of one day returning them to his benefactor. A few sheets of corrugated metal were more useful, serving as a roof for his rock crevice shelter. Tweed built himself a raised floor using bamboo from a nearby grove, a table and chair, and other amenities. He made a lamp from an empty sardine can, using coconut oil as fuel, and fashioned bamboo piping to sluice water off the metal roof of his shelter into a barrel that supplied his drinking water. When Artero gave him a Big Ben clock, he adapted it into a warning system, stringing a long cord he made from *pago* tree bark as a trip wire from the alarm button down to the approach to his shelter. Anyone climbing up would disturb the cord and set off the clock's alarm. Fortunately, the one time the alarm sounded, scaring Tweed half to death, the culprit turned out to be a crow that had landed on the trip line.

In an effort to fill the long, empty hours spent in solitude, Tweed took up the study of algebra, assiduously working out problems from a textbook provided by Artero. He read and reread a small stockpile of old magazines until they literally disintegrated—by which time he had memorized everything from articles to advertisements. When Artero mentioned that his family's shoes had worn out and there were none to be had, Tweed made a pair using wood for soles and deer hide for the uppers. They were so successful that he began spending hours turning out shoes for Artero's eight children, his wife, and his relatives.

Each month, Tweed wrote a letter to his mother, describing his condition and state of mind. Not wanting them to fall into the hands of the Japanese should he be caught or killed, he hid the letters in the hollow of a tree, only telling Artero where to find them. Artero promised that if something happened to Tweed, he would see that the letters were mailed after the war. The prospect of liberation seemed to grow dimmer by the day, which made Tweed feel "pretty low" at times, he admitted. At first he kept setting dates for the Americans to return to Guam, but as each date came and went, he grew more and more depressed. Finally, he stopped setting dates as it became clear that it might be years before Americans returned to Guam. "I felt it was only a matter of time until I would be caught, but I was determined to postpone that day as long as possible," he observed. "I lived from day to day."[53]

Tweed's pessimism was well-founded. Encouraged by their successful hunt for Tweed's shipmates, naval and police personnel continued to threaten and brutalize Chamorros in an effort to learn his whereabouts. It might have worked, except that Artero, well aware that loose talk had led to the discovery of Tweed's fellow sailors, guarded his secret carefully. Virtually no one knew that Tweed was hiding on his ranch. Nevertheless, as the search turned to northern Guam, the danger to Tweed and to the Artero family intensified. "The woods were so full of Japs that Antonio was afraid of stumbling upon one when he brought my food and suggested that he cut down his visits to twice a month," recalled Tweed. Lonely and short on food, Tweed passed long hours playing solitaire. "I went so long without anyone to talk to that I almost lost my voice," he recalled.[54]

Though Tweed, whom many Chamorros found to be self-centered and demanding, may not have fully appreciated it, the Artero family, in addition to taking great risks, was making great sacrifices on his behalf. "We didn't have much food to eat," remembered Carmen Artero, who had been among the stranded child angels at the Dulce Nombre de Maria Cathedral the day the war began. "We ran out of rice and flour and everything else." They relied on breadfruit, taro, and bananas and ate lots of eggs, she recalled. Much of the remaining livestock, cattle and pigs, had to be provided to the Japanese. "Some of the Japanese [would] come by our house and push us off the table and sit down and eat our food and a lot of times that was the only meal we were going to have for the day," said Carmen.

As it neared Christmas, Carmen and her siblings grew more and more excited, knowing their mother had been hoarding ingredients for a pie. "My mom always made the best lemon pie. . . . And so we were all so excited we were going to have lemon pie, we hardly ever had good food to eat since the war started but now we were going to have lemon pie!" she recalled. But when the pie was finished, her mother put it in the gunny sack with the provisions for Tweed.

Carmen was appalled. "You are going to give the pie away?! Isn't that for us?!"

Her mother told her to be quiet, and Carmen accompanied her father out into the bush to deliver the food to Tweed. "I felt real bad," she said; "we took the pie and lots of other food."

After they came home, Carmen's mother said the Christmas novena and the family sat by the door looking at the moon as they had no electricity, just candles. "And we were singing," recalled Carmen.

"And then after that my dad said to me, 'See, that pie, we gave it to somebody who has no one. It is a person who is all alone, but your mama and I we have each other and we have you and you have us and we are so lucky and we're so fortunate, God loving us and blessing us and we have each other. Isn't that the greatest gift of all?'"

"Yes, papa," she said.

"Well, let's pray for the person who has nobody, just his pie," said her father.

And so the Artero family observed Christmas. "Even though the smell of the pie [was] still lingering in the house, we had the smell of the pie and each other," observed seven-year-old Carmen.[55]

CHAPTER 5

UNDER THE HEEL

MERE DAYS AFTER THE JAPANESE ARRIVED ON GUAM, A RUMOR CIRCULATED among the civilian population that the United States would return on December 25, 1941, and expel the invaders as a "Christmas gift" to the Chamorros. When Christmas passed uneventfully, the rumored return date was moved up to New Year's Day, and then to July 4. As each holiday passed without the anticipated appearance of the U.S. military, the rumor mill eventually subsided, though the belief that the United States would one day return to Guam was never in doubt.[1]

On December 10, 1942, the Japanese held a parade to celebrate the first anniversary of Guam's liberation from American colonialism. The procession included a parade float bearing a youngster dressed as a Japanese soldier holding an oversized rifle and standing on an American flag as he pantomimed bayonetting another youngster clad in a U.S. Navy uniform. Writing home to his wife in Hokkaido, twenty-nine-year-old Nakahashi Kiyoshi, who had been assigned to Guam as a civilian schoolteacher, noted that he had arisen early in the morning to mark the first anniversary of the war. "I worshipped the distant Tokyo sky, shouted *banzai* three times and pledged without uttering a word to work for the emperor as his disciple in the second year of the war," he wrote.[2]

Despite Kiyoshi's patriotic fervor, 1943 would not be a particularly good year for the Japanese empire. In defiance of the Japanese edict banning radios, a number of contraband sets remained concealed around the island, providing an audio window on the outside world—and that window offered glimmers of encouragement to hopeful Chamorros. One close-knit group of Chamorros kept a cached Silvertone radio operating through almost the entire thirty-two months of occupation. They first plugged the radio into an outlet at the former Navy aerological shack at Fort Apugan, using a long extension cord and hiding themselves in the bushes. They tuned in regularly to news broadcasts from the Fairmont Hotel Studio in San Francisco. Over the next two and a half years, they operated out of various hideaways, including one where they plugged their extension cord in the wiring atop a utility pole. Using a map torn from a *Pacific Island Yearbook*, they were able to track the progress of the war. Among the news they heard was the launching of the cruiser USS *Guam*, which was christened by Governor George McMillin's wife in November 1943. The "radio gang," as they became known, had their share of close calls—including one occasion when they avoided detection by a search party by suspending the radio on a wire above a cesspool—but they were never caught.[3]

News of events beyond Guam circulated by word of mouth as the radio gang and a handful of other civilians risked their lives to tune in to the outside world. George Tweed, who had access to a radio for a while, actually produced—somewhat rashly, it would seem—a periodic typewritten sheet, *The Guam Eagle*, with abbreviated news accounts on the progress of the war. The sheets were passed from hand to hand among the Chamorros before intensified Japanese pressure forced Tweed to abandon his publishing career and focus more on preserving his own neck.

The news was nearly all bad at first as the Japanese juggernaut swept across the Pacific. But as the months passed, the reports began to improve. The Japanese were stunned in April when U.S. Army bombers, taking off from the carrier *Hornet*, raided targets in the home islands. A Japanese invasion force was turned back from Port Moresby at the Battle of the Coral Sea, easing the threat to Australia, followed by the crushing Japanese naval defeat at Midway in June 1942. The U.S. 1st Marine Division landed on Guadalcanal in August, kicking off a bitter battle of attrition. In the Southwest Pacific, U.S. and Australian forces blocked a Japanese land assault in New Guinea. Among their victims was Guam's erstwhile conqueror Lieutenant General Tomitarō Horii. The general's South Seas Detachment was destroyed in fighting with the Australians in November 1942. Horii himself drowned during the retreat when his canoe was swept out to sea and capsized. The struggle for Guadalcanal finally ended in an American victory and would soon be followed by an advance up the northern Solomons. Japanese forces had taken horrific losses at Guadalcanal and were suffering similarly in the fighting on New Guinea.

Painfully aware of their declining fortunes as the war moved deeper into its second year, Japanese military planners—with the emperor's consent—reluctantly opted for a change in strategy. Instead of expanding offensive operations in an attempt to secure an outright victory, a new plan, settled upon in late September 1943, was to regroup and build up an "Absolute National Defense Sphere." Guam and Saipan, previously regarded as "patrol or relay bases," would form a crucial element of that defense "sphere," part of a natural barrier "defending Japan proper as well as the South Seas regions," as a Japanese military study subsequently observed.[4]

Reorganizing behind a bulwark of fortified islands, the armed forces would await the American advance. Rabaul and the Marshall Islands would screen the main line. Behind this sacrificial outer shell, a second, inviolable inner defense line would extend from the Marianas to the Palaus to western New Guinea. Located only 1,250 to 2,000 miles from Tokyo, this line was to be held all costs. Possession of the Marianas was especially vital as their loss would put the Japanese home islands within reach of the new American long-range B-29 bombers.

Airfields in the defense line would be a key element of what Japanese planners expected to be a decisive fleet engagement. The U.S. fleet would be drawn into a massive trap. Whittled down by air forces flying from unsinkable island bases, the remainder of the enemy fleet would be finished off by Japanese carriers. Defeated and demoralized, the Americans would then agree to a negotiated peace that would leave Japan with the bulk of its wartime conquests. "The fundamental purpose of the Army operations is to secure strategic areas, especially air bases, in the Central Pacific [so] that our air forces will be afforded an opportunity to annihilate the advancing enemy units at sea," observed a Japanese report; "or failing in that, they will be able to prevent the enemy from landing on the beaches and establishing his air bases on the islands."[5]

Early plans to implement the new Japanese strategy called for the 13th Division, which had seen extensive combat in China since 1937, to be transferred to the Marianas. An advance detachment of about three hundred men left for Guam from China in October 1943. By the time they arrived, the transformation of the island from outpost to key air base was already underway with construction of an airfield on Orote Peninsula. Korean and Chamorro labor drafts began work on the field in mid-1943 at the former Sumay golf course—the same site U.S. planners had surveyed before the war but never had a chance to develop.

On November 10, 1943, the 4th Naval Civil Engineer Department arrived with the 217th and 218th Setsueitai (naval construction battalions), each consisting of about eight hundred Korean laborers and one hundred Navy and civilian engineers. U.S. civilian contractors had destroyed most of their heavy equipment before the surrender. Lacking similar equipment, the newly arrived labor units were forced to do the bulk of the airfield work by hand. "Heavy machines were two bulldozers, a crane vehicle and two large-size dump trucks left by America," observed Satomi Yamamoto, a civilian employee of the 218th Setsueitai. "There were only five to seven Japanese-made ordinary trucks. Japanese had a moving vehicle, but it always broke down."[6]

The naval construction battalions were supplemented by Chamorro labor drafts, which took men away from food production—which was already faltering—just as more military mouths arrived. "Every morning two trucks were sent to transport about sixty villagers from each village a day," noted Yamamoto. Workers toiled from 8 a.m. to 5 p.m. and were compensated with two or three cans of rice about five centimeters high. "With only shovels and pickaxes, the work was actually tough," said Yamamoto. "The Chamorros accounted for 60 percent of the total workers, but they did only what was told and were reluctant to immediately comply with orders."[7]

Adding to the growing misery of Guam's civilian population was the continuing search for fugitive sailor George Tweed. By the end of 1943, police were routinely detaining and torturing anyone suspected of having knowledge of Tweed's whereabouts.

They came for Baltazar J. Bordallo at his house in Agana one morning at about 1 a.m. As he entered the interrogation room at the former Bank of Guam, a police investigator hit him in the jaw. Another Japanese began working him over with a whip. They demanded to know where Tweed was hiding. Bordallo replied truthfully that he did not know. His interrogators insisted he was lying. The beatings and questions about Tweed continued over the next five days. "Sometimes they beat me up standing, and sometimes the two Japanese would tell me to get down on my fours and hit me on my back," Bordallo testified later. "I remember the last beating I received and that was to tie both my limbs and hang me up to a beam and I received as far as I can recall at least forty lashes on my back."

Desperate to put an end to the torture, Bordallo promised to search for Tweed, adding that if he did not find him within twenty days, he would forfeit his life. "With a wife and fifteen children—the youngest only an infant—I had to find a way to survive," he explained. "I never knew where Tweed was, nor did I ever meet him. But I was willing to try. It was either his life or mine."[8]

Joaquin A. Limtiaco was also hauled back in front of a police investigator to face questions about Tweed. "I told him I did not know anything about the Americans so he told me to open my mouth and he took his revolver and pointed it to my mouth and then he started pulling the trigger," recalled Limtiaco. When Limtiaco failed to respond, interrogators beat him until he collapsed on the floor. "He was crying and groggy [and] bleeding out of his mouth," observed another detainee who witnessed the assault. Police finally turned Limtiaco loose without having gotten any closer to Tweed.[9]

Twenty-eight-year-old Lourdes Merfalen Payne probably became a suspect as she was married to an American sailor. Police came to her home at Dededo and demanded to know the whereabouts of "the American" Tweed, recalled Lourdes's younger brother, Manny. "The police said the family would be executed if she didn't tell the truth." Lourdes replied she didn't know anything about any fugitive American. Her denials were ignored.

"Each time they're not satisfied with the answer, it was followed with a blow in the face, not with the palm open, but with the fist closed, to my sister's face every time she gave a negative answer," recalled Manny. "This went on for almost an hour, and they finally decided to leave, leaving my sister with a puffy face, bleeding through the mouth and nose."

The situation worsened the following day when Lourdes was ordered to report to the Agana police station. Manny accompanied her. The interpreter and police ordered him to leave, but he didn't go far. He stood just outside the building where he could see his sister through a window and hear what was going on inside. "They were tying up her hands in front of her, and there was a chair just before her and she was told to get on the chair," he recalled. "So they strung up my sister to the beam of that building and I watched her dangling on that rope."

Once again the questions started, with Lourdes denying she knew anything about the American. "Every time she gave an answer, it was followed with a whip, about a yard-long whip, instead of a beating with the hand," recalled Manny. "I can see through the window flashes of blood. Her dress is soaked with blood. She wasn't crying, but I can see tears dripping through her face."

When Lourdes finally lost consciousness, the interpreter, who was doing the whipping, told another man to bring him a container of what Manny assumed was water. As he watched, the interpreter poured the liquid over his sister's head. He realized from the smell that it wasn't water—it was gasoline. As Lourdes started screaming, Manny, crying, ran away, but "from 100 feet away, I can still hear my sister yelling."

The next day, the police dropped Lourdes off at her home. "She cannot eat. She won't eat," said Manny. "She won't talk for weeks." She never knew anything about Tweed or the military. "Her husband never told her anything about the Navy anyway, to begin with," observed Manny.[10]

The campaign of terror could not help but have an effect. "What I could not understand was while many of our people were being brutalized on account of him, Tweed was moving from place to place, attending parties and generally enjoying himself," Bordallo said later. If Tweed were really a hero, he added, he would have come out of hiding and given himself up to put a stop to the systematic torture of civilians.[11] Toward the end of 1943, one of the two Japanese priests assigned to the island wrote an open letter to Tweed urging him to surrender. He said he had been assured by the authorities, "as a special respect to me, a Catholic priest," that Tweed would be treated as a prisoner of war. "The Japanese government will not kill you. After necessary examinations, you will be sent to Japan and placed with the other American prisoners." Copies of the letter were distributed around the island.[12]

Among the dozens of Chamorros who had helped Tweed—who went by the underground name "Joaquin Cruz" during his many months on the run—was Agueda Johnston, the wife of a retired Marine who had been sent to Japan with the other prisoners in January 1942. Former principal of Guam's George Washington High School, she was quietly active in resistance to Japanese rule. Her activities included keeping Chamorros apprised of the progress of the war —ingeniously passing along updates obtained over illicit radios by hiding messages inside the wrappers of bars of soap made by her family. She also provided food, clothing, and reading material for Tweed. When Tweed suggested around the middle of 1942 that he was thinking about giving himself up, she had urged him not to. His continued freedom was an inspiration to the Chamorros and reinforced their faith that the Americans would return, she said. However, as the Japanese increasingly turned to torturing civilians in an effort to discover Tweed's whereabouts, Johnston had a change of heart and told him he should surrender to put a stop to the brutality.

It is unlikely that Tweed was "generally enjoying himself," but he was no longer prepared—if he ever had been—to give himself up. In a letter to Johnston, he chastised Chamorros for gossiping about his possible whereabouts and warned her to keep her own mouth shut. Collaborators would pay a heavy price someday, he added. "I can name at least three men who will face a firing squad when [the American military] arrive," he wrote. "Do you want to place yourself alongside them?" He added, "The Japs would not even know I am in Guam if the people had not talked so much."[13]

Asked years later about her interactions with Tweed, Johnston, who came to be viewed as one of the heroines of the occupation for her resistance to the Japanese, remarked without particular rancor that if Tweed "were any kind of a hero, he would have turned himself in." She herself was interrogated and beaten by the Japanese police but never said a word. "The Japanese could have killed me three or four times, I would not have given them the satisfaction of giving them information about Tweed," she declared.[14]

Tweed's decision to remain in hiding almost certainly saved his life, but it would affect his standing among the Chamorros long after the war ended. Still, he was not betrayed. Johnston observed later that those who protected Tweed did not necessarily even like him. "The people who shielded or helped Tweed did not do this because of him personally, but because he was an American and because of the flag he represented," she wrote in a personal letter after the war.[15] They would continue to pay an outsized price for their patriotism.

⟶ ⬥ ⟵

Thousands of miles to the east of Tweed's island hideout, discussions were underway that would shape the future of Guam's Chamorros in ways they could not possibly have imagined. The Mariana Islands had long been a focus of U.S. war planning for any conflict with Japan. Both the prewar ORANGE and RAINBOW contingency plans had contemplated using the islands as a stepping-stone on a return to the Philippines, but this strategy was now in some doubt.

Among the loudest voices in favor of invading the Mariana Islands was Admiral Ernest J. King, the prickly sixty-five-year-old chief of naval operations. King argued that seizure of the Marianas would sever enemy lines of communication between Japan and bases to the south, provide bases for continued Allied advances toward China and the Philippines, and cut the Japanese home islands off from vital raw materials in the Southwest Pacific. As early as the Casablanca Conference between Allied war leaders on January 14, 1943, King proposed an advance through the Marshall Islands to Truk to the Marianas and then to the Philippines. He continued his lobbying at the Trident Conference in May and at the Quebec Conference in July. Along the way, he found an ally in Army Air Force chief Hap Arnold, who saw the Marianas—with their proximity to Japan—as an ideal base for America's new long-range B-29 bomber. It was anticipated that Guam alone could accommodate a minimum of six long-range bomber strips, eleven medium bomber runways, and six fighter and four emergency airfields. Guam could also be useful as a submarine refueling base station, while Apra Harbor would provide an anchorage for an advanced naval base.

But not all U.S. planners thought invading the islands made strategic sense. One powerful opponent emerged in Southwest Pacific commander General Douglas MacArthur. The egotistical MacArthur saw King's proposal as a threat to his theater of operations—and, presumably, to his personal and professional stature in the war against Japan. Rather than proceeding through the Central Pacific, he advocated a drive from Australia through New Guinea to Mindanao. In a letter to Secretary of War Henry L. Stimson, he promised, "Give me central direction of the war in the Pacific and I will be in the Philippines in ten months."[16]

At the Cairo Conference in November, the Combined Chiefs of Staff tried to placate both sides by endorsing a two-pronged assault. MacArthur would continue his advance along the New Guinea–Mindanao axis in the Southwest Pacific, while Admiral Chester W. Nimitz pressed forward with his island-hopping campaign through the Central Pacific. The Combined Chiefs tentatively called for the recapture of Guam and seizure of the Marianas in October 1944, not quite a year in the future.

On November 1, 1943, the 3rd Marine Division landed on Japanese-held Bougainville in the northern Solomons. Less than three weeks later, American forces seized Makin and Tarawa in the Gilbert Islands chain. The 2nd Marine Division's assault on Betio Island in the Tarawa atoll was particularly bloody. Intelligence failed to reckon with a neap tide that left unusually shallow water over Betio's reef. Lacking sufficient amphibious tractors and with other landing craft unable to clear the reef, Marines were forced to wade hundreds of yards to shore under heavy fire. Over the course of the next seventy-six hours, 978 Marines were killed, and 2,188 others were wounded. Virtually the entire Japanese garrison of 4,690 men—including 1,200 Korean laborers—was killed.

Despite the heavy cost and its implications for the future, the seizure of the Gilberts opened the way to the Marshall Islands, which formed the outer screen to the newly designated Japanese Absolute National Defense Sphere. U.S. plans, as they eventually evolved, called for the seizure of Kwajalein and Roi Namur to take place on January 31, 1944. A plan put forth by Admiral Nimitz, acting as commander in chief, Pacific Fleet and Pacific Ocean Areas, anticipated landings in the Marianas in mid-November 1944. An amended version issued on January 13, 1944, called for the seizure of Saipan and Tinian on November 1. This first phase would be followed by the liberation of Guam on December 15.

Nimitz's decision to bypass outlying islands and strike into the heart of the Marshalls at Kwajalein, Roi Namur, and Majuro in late January and early February 1944 took the Japanese by surprise. All objectives fell quickly. Casualties were light. Emboldened, Nimitz pushed on to seize Japanese-held Eniwetok on February 18. The main island of Engebi was captured at a cost of 85 men killed or missing and 166 wounded. The Japanese lost 1,276 killed and 16 captured.

Thanks to Nimitz's master stroke, the U.S. advance through the Central Pacific was now only 1,025 nautical miles from Guam. The implications were impossible to ignore, even for the average Japanese. "In addition to honorable deaths on Kiska and

Attu islands, I have heard about such deaths on Makin and Tarawa islands," wrote Guam teacher Nakahashi Kiyoshi on Guam a month after the loss of the Gilbert Islands. "I am feeling tense."[17]

—◦—

Only five days after the fall of Eniwetok, teacher Kiyoshi received a firsthand indication that the tide of war had changed as twelve U.S. Hellcat fighters roared in to strafe planes parked along the runway at the newly completed Orote Airfield. The fighters were from USS *Bunker Hill* and arrived over Guam largely by accident.

Part of Task Force 58, *Bunker Hill* stopped by the Marianas following a multi-carrier raid on the Japanese base at Truk. The stopover raid, the first U.S. air attack of the war on the Marianas, was intended not only to show the flag but to obtain much-needed intelligence on Saipan and Tinian. So little was known about Saipan—the first target on the Marianas invasion agenda—that analysts were even unsure of the location of the island's Aslito Airfield, built in 1934. Taking off from *Bunker Hill* at 0810 for a fighter sweep over Tinian, twelve Hellcats from Fighting Squadron 18 encountered a thick overcast. After orbiting for a while, the fighters headed south, where the cloud cover seemed to be thinning, in hopes of finding a target or landmark. En route, one pilot thought he saw land—it was probably Rota—but his radio was out of order, and he was unable to alert the others. A few minutes further south, another island appeared through the broken cloud cover. It was Guam.

The pilots spotted the newly constructed airfield at Orote Point—which had only become operational in January—and rolled in for a strafing attack. The first run caught two Zero fighters that were just landing—both were set afire as they rolled down the runway. In the same run, pilots strafed three twin-engine navy transport planes, another Zero, and two Betty medium bombers parked alongside the runway. After a second run, all aircraft visible on the runway were burning. As the flight came around for a third strafing run from the southwest, two Betty bombers were observed approaching the field. Lieutenant Commander Sam L. Silber led his six-plane division in an attack on the first Betty. After inconclusive runs by Silber and Lieutenant Junior Grade C. T. Beall, Ensign W. S. Stevenson put a burst into the wing tanks and set the Betty aflame. The second Betty was attacked by Ensign T. S. Harris, who lost track of the bomber as it pulled up into the sun. Lieutenant Junior Grade D. E. Runyon cut in, hitting the plane in the engines and sending it into the water in flames.

In addition to discovering the heretofore unknown airfield, Silber's pilots noted a tower of some sort at Manell Point by Merizo and a possible radio station and building at Agfayan Point, both at the southern end of the island. Referring some-what generously to the accidental overflight as "a visual reconnaissance" of Guam, the Task Force 58.3 war diary added, "The airfield on Orote Peninsula was the only one observed by the flight and the probability of another field on the island having escaped their observation is believed negligible."[18]

Actually construction had already begun on a second airfield located at Tiyan, east of Agana. The runway was being carved out of thick jungle—again, mostly by hand—with much of the work done by Chamorro labor drafts. "I remember joining four or five other men in lashing ropes to large rocks and then around our waists and dragging them off like we were cattle," recalled Ben Blaz, who was assigned to one of the Chamorro work parties.[19] The Tiyan field—yet to be discovered by U.S. intelligence—would become operational by May. Clearing for a third airfield near Dededo, three miles northeast of Tiyan, would begin in April, and plans were under-way for still another field to be located near Barrigada to the north as the Japanese rushed to make up for lost time.

The U.S. strike into the heart of the Marshalls and the seizure of Eniwetok stunned the Japanese high command, though they failed to recognize an imminent threat to the Marianas, anticipating that the next blow would fall on the Palaus in the western Carolines. But while the American carrier raid on Saipan, Tinian, and Guam did not alert them to their error, it did make clear that the Marianas could no longer be considered a safe rear area. Efforts soon got underway to evacuate Japanese civilians—mostly women and children—from the Marianas to Japan. Unlike Saipan, where Japanese nationals numbered in the thousands after the island's years as a mandate, there were relatively few Japanese civilians on Guam. Prior to the war, Japanese residents numbered less than forty, many of whom had "mixed-blood sons and daughters totaling 207 persons, through marriage with natives," according to Japanese figures.[20] Those numbers expanded after the occupation, most of the newcomers being Minseibu and South Seas Development Company employees and their dependents. A census document subsequently captured by U.S. forces indicated there were 270 male and 185 female Japanese civilians on Guam as of January 10, 1944.[21]

Word went out in February that Japanese women, children under age eighteen, and civilians age sixty or older would be evacuated from the island. Yoriko Koshi-muta, wife of Takeshi Koshimuta, head of the Omiyato Office of the South Seas Development Company, recalled that a meeting was held at the company's club to discuss the procedure. Though the decision to remove civilians from the island could not be considered a good omen of things to come, she did not indicate that there was any sense of panic. About 180 civilians were subsequently evacuated on March 22 aboard the *Tamahoko* Maru. All those leaving had arrived on Guam as part of the occupation; there were no evacuees among Japanese residents from the prewar days. The ship docked safely at Yokohama on April 1. Forbidden by the military to send a telegram to her husband on Guam to inform him that she had arrived safely home, Yoriko wrote simply, "Send money," allowing him to read between the lines. As it turned out, she would never see her husband again.[22]

❧

Meanwhile, plans to bring in the 13th Division from China had fallen through. Though an advance detachment had already arrived at Guam, the remainder of the veteran division was held back to participate in a massive spring offensive in South China. Replacing the 13th Division, the Japanese 29th ("Thunder") Division, then in Manchuria training for possible combat with the Soviets, was ordered to the Marianas in February. Though it lacked the combat experience of the 13th Division, a postwar study praised the 29th as "the most efficient division of the Kwantung Army," where it had been held in strategic reserve.[23] Commanded by Lieutenant General Takeshi Takashina, the division had been formed in 1941 with personnel drawn from Honshu island's Nagoya district, home to the Mitsubishi Aircraft Company, manufacturer of the famed Zero.

The men were well trained for the large-scale offensive maneuvers expected in China—a training and organization that were less well suited for the defensive tactics that would be required should the Americans invade Guam. Upon being selected for defense of the Marianas, the division's three infantry regiments—the 18th, 38th, and 50th—were reorganized into regimental combat teams with the addition of attached artillery and engineers. Each infantry regiment numbered approximately twenty-nine hundred men with total divisional strength somewhat north of eleven thousand men, according to U.S. order-of-battle estimates.

The fifty-three-year-old Takashina was a former military school instructor who had commanded a brigade in Manchuria before being promoted to lieutenant general and named to lead the 29th Division in October 1943. Period photos show a stocky, full-faced individual, peering calmly if somewhat owlishly at the camera from behind black round-rimmed spectacles. Whatever his appearance, he and his division would prove to be a nightmare for the Chamorro population on Guam.

Upon receipt of a movement order on February 18, the division left its station area on the pretext of embarking on a long-term maneuver. Transported by train to Pusan, Korea, the troops were issued summer-weight clothing before boarding ships for Ujina, Japan, where they received special equipment "for use in South Seas battlefields."[24] The division would form part of the 31st Army organized under the command of General Hideyoshi Obata on February 28 to defend the Central Pacific Area.

Prior to their departure for Guam, General Takashina's staff officer for operations was advised of the crucial importance of his new posting. "The Mariana Islands are Japan's final defense line," he was bluntly informed by the chief of the Imperial Army General Staff. "Loss of the islands signifies Japan's surrender."[25] Lest there be any lack of appreciation among the troops regarding the seriousness of their mission, General Obata issued an order that the South Marianas Area, which included Guam, would "be defended to the death."[26]

The troop transports, escorted by three destroyers, got underway for the Marianas on February 26, with thousands of troops packed into the stifling holds. "The heat, humidity, foul breath and odor which filled the ship was more than enough to make everyone on board sick," remembered Corporal Shoichi Yokoi.[27] None of the soldiers had been told their destination, but they knew they were going into battle, recalled Lieutenant Yasuhiro Yamashita, who sailed with the 18th Regiment aboard the *Sakito* Maru. They were sure they were going to die, he observed calmly.

Many were closer to death than they knew. The convoy was just forty-eight hours sailing distance from Saipan when it was attacked by the submarine USS *Trout*. Two torpedoes slammed into the *Sakito* Maru. Another struck the *Aki* Maru, carrying the 38th Regiment, in the bow. Aboard the *Aki* Maru, twenty-nine-year-old Corporal Yokoi witnessed the aftermath of the torpedo hit on the troop compartment housing elements of the 38th Regiment. "There were about a dozen victims," he said. "Some of them had an arm or leg or both blown off; fragments of flesh were scattered everywhere. It was a terrible sight which I could hardly see." One of the petty officers offered instructions on what to do if the ship sank: "Throw away your rifle and bayonet, take a bar of green bamboo and jump into the sea with it. Once in the sea, swim away as fast and as far as you can from the ship, otherwise you will be swallowed up into a whirlpool created by the sinking ship." Fortunately, for Yokoi, when the *Ong! Ong! Ong!* blare of the ship's alarm was finally turned off, the *Aki* Maru was still afloat.[28]

The *Aki* Maru was able to continue at reduced speed, but the *Sakito* Maru was doomed. A voice on the loudspeaker called for calm as panicked soldiers poured from the hatches. As black smoke billowed from the hold, the captain turned to the colonel in charge of the military contingent and advised, "It is regrettable, but it is time to abandon ship."

Lieutenant Yamashita joined dozens of men clinging to a raft in the frigid water. The raft rocked precariously as panicked swimmers tried to climb aboard. A lieutenant in charge of the regiment's flag flailed at them with his sword, screaming, "If you don't let go of the boat, I'll behead you! Just hang on to the life preservers!" As night fell, men began to slip off and drown one by one. Yamashita could hear voices in the distance singing military songs. The voices seemed thin and uncertain, and after a while the singing stopped. At daybreak he found himself surrounded by floating dead bodies.[29]

Later in the day, Yamashita and about 120 others in his group were picked up by two destroyers. They were the lucky ones. About fourteen hundred soldiers, including the regimental commander, perished in the sinking.[30] Eight tanks and most of the 18th Regiment's artillery and heavy equipment also went to the bottom. However, the U.S. victory came at a cost. *Trout* never returned from that patrol—her eleventh of the war—and was believed to have been cornered and sunk by the destroyer *Asashimo* immediately following the convoy attack, with the loss of all eighty-one hands.

The survivors of *Trout*'s attack arrived at Saipan's Tanapag Harbor on March 3. The next day, the 38th Regiment, numbering 2,894 men commanded by Colonel Tsunetaro Suenaga, continued to Guam along with 203 men from division head-quarters. The 50th Infantry was sent to Tinian. The 1st Battalion of the 18th Infantry remained on Saipan, while the 2nd and 3rd Battalions of the 18th Infantry, along with regimental headquarters and most of the 9th Tank Regiment, went to Guam. Now commanded by Colonel Hiko-Shiro Ohashi, the two reorganized infantry battalions numbered about thirteen hundred men.

The next largest army reinforcement to arrive on Guam was the 6th Expeditionary Force, which sailed from Pusan, Korea, and arrived on March 20. The forty-seven-hundred-man unit was formed from elements of the 1st (Tokyo District) and 11th (Shikoku Island) Divisions of the Kwangtung Army and included six infantry battalions, two artillery battalions, and two engineer companies. After arriving on Guam, the unit was reorganized into the twenty-eight-hundred-man 48th Independent Mixed Brigade commanded by Major General Kiyoshi Shigematsu and the nineteen-hundred-man 10th Independent Mixed Regiment commanded by Colonel Ichiro Kataoka. The three-hundred-man advance detachment from the 13th Division that had arrived earlier was folded into the 29th Division. Other units available to General Takashina, who was responsible for the defense of Rota as well as Guam, included two and a half companies from the 9th Tank Regiment as well as the 24th Tank Company—a total armored strength of about thirty-eight light and medium tanks. There were also a number of antiaircraft units and an engineer regiment.

Japanese naval units on Guam, which as of February 1944 had expanded to about 450 men, were also being augmented with additional coastal defense and antiaircraft units. By July, the 54th Keibitai had expanded to about twenty-three hundred men under the command of Captain Yutka Sugimoto. Other personnel included eighteen hundred men of the two naval construction battalions brought in for airfield work the previous November. Naval air units sent in to man the airfields numbered probably another two thousand men.[31] These forces also fell under General Takashina's overall command. By summer, total Japanese troop strength on Guam was at least 18,500 men, well above initial U.S. intelligence estimates.

Their orders from 31st Army headquarters in March were unambiguous. Defenses must be strengthened "and general preparations for the annihilation of the enemy landing on the beaches must be completed, including the protection of our air bases. . . . Even if we fail to check the landing of a part of the enemy forces, our air bases will be firmly secured and we will be able by persistent opposition to deny him the use of these airfields."[32]

Gratefully debarking from the *Aki* Maru at Apra Harbor, Corporal Shoichi Yokoi thought Guam "appeared to be a fantastically beautiful island." The soldiers were especially fascinated by the coconuts but had no idea how to open them. Shown how to split the coconut open with a machete, Yokoi sampled the milk inside. "It tasted like soda pop which had gone flat," he decided.[33]

Another new arrival, Corporal Masashi Ito, a light machine gunner with the 29th Division, also found Guam a considerable improvement over the bleak wind-swept plains of Manchuria. He and his friends spent their limited free time swimming in the river near their bivouac and catching an eel-like fish that could be as much as four or five feet long and five inches or more in diameter. "A dish of eels broiled in oil was a tasty addition to wartime rations," he observed. Had there not been a war on, "it could have been called a peaceful, pleasant existence."[34]

Stationed at Sinajana in the hills southeast of Agana, Corporal Yokoi's company moved into houses seized from Chamorro families. "We climbed up a ladder onto the wooden floor of a house on high pillars," he said. "There was only a single room under a thatched roof and it was furnished with a number of wooden beds. Unlike the Japanese, the natives here kept their shoes on inside the house so that the floor was filthy. There was no electricity, gas or water."[35]

One group of Japanese officers took up quarters above Chamorro Pedro Peredo's residence in a two-story building in Agana Heights. One evening the officers invited

Peredo and his roommates upstairs to join a party. "Some of the Japanese looked very young," remembered Peredo. "They were drinking and dancing. They wanted to dance the old Guamanian dances. So we joined in and taught them. The more they drank the more they talked and pranced around." The Japanese seemed to forget any distinctions between them and their guests, treating them more like friends, remarked Peredo. "We kept pouring them whiskey." One young Japanese officer said they expected to be sent somewhere else from Guam. But he didn't know where. No one ever told them where they were going, but chances were, it would be "a one-way ticket," he laughed. Peredo was struck by their seeming vulnerability. "They drank and danced and laughed and wept and I felt a little bit sorry for them," he admitted. "They were just boys."[36]

Such instances of camaraderie—even alcohol-fueled examples—would prove to be the exception. The previous oversight by token Japanese naval forces had been bearable, if not always benign. This was about to change for the worse as administration of Guam's civilians now became an army responsibility. Lieutenant General Takashina assumed command of all of the island's forces and imposed harsh security measures enforced by the army's Kempeitai military police. Schools and churches were closed down and a halt imposed on all civic activities. There was no longer any interest in coaxing Chamorros toward Japanese ways and voluntary integration. Guam was a potential combat area under authoritarian army rule. "The military insulted the islanders and confiscated their assets," noted Arahara Yasuke, an administrator with the Minseibu's General Affairs section.[37] Other than their value as a source of forced labor, civilians were considered a liability.

Minseibu administration of the island was dissolved on March 1. The former Minseibu policemen and teachers were absorbed into the Fifth Navy Construction and Service Department and assigned to serve as "vigilant watchers" of the Chamorros.[38] This ominous new role included overseeing the supply of civilian labor to the army and the navy for work on fortifications and airfields. Men and boys between sixteen and sixty—and often younger—were drafted into labor battalions. Equipped only with wheelbarrows, picks, shovels, and other hand tools, they were put to work digging hundreds of air raid shelters and cave positions in cliffs and hillsides, building pillboxes and gun emplacements, and constructing underwater obstacles along likely landing areas. Toiling under the unrelenting sun with their inadequate tools, the work details were "encouraged" by their Japanese masters with kicks, slaps, punches, and clubbings.

Ben Blaz was put to work constructing log crib obstacles barring access to potential landing areas on the island's southwestern coast. Logs were cut and dragged to the site, where they were sharpened at one end and anchored in place to pierce the bottoms of approaching landing craft. Coral had to be chopped out to fill log cribs on the reef. It was grueling work. "We had to carry the logs, rocks and barbed wire across slimy jagged coral, more slippery than ice covered by water," said Blaz. "The logs were unwieldy and required two or three men to maneuver them. If one slipped, all three could expect to go down and the sharp coral could lacerate the skin as easily as carving knives." Everything had to be accomplished at low tide under the eye of impatient Japanese supervisors. "Everyone working in the bays felt he was being screamed at constantly—by the Japanese, by the rising waters, by his own body craving rest," said Blaz.[39]

Arousing the displeasure of their overseers, Joe Crisostomo Aguon's labor group was ordered to form up in two lines facing each other. Once in line, each was further instructed to slap the man or boy standing across from him. Aguon found himself lined up across from an elderly man. When he refused to slap the man, a Japanese guard whacked him with a stick by way of encouragement. Standing across from the reluctant Aguon, the old man whispered, "Go ahead and slap me, I will understand." Their lesson in Japanese work ethics concluded, the men were ordered back to their labors.[40]

The diversion of so many Chamorro men to construct military defenses meant still fewer workers available to grow crops. Women, children, and elderly men were put to work in the fields under the supervision of the newly arrived 170-man Kaikontai (Crop Cultivation Unit), a quasi-military unit specializing in agriculture. Its mission—which seems ludicrous in retrospect—was to use Chamorro labor to accelerate agricultural production so that it was capable of feeding as many as thirty thousand troops, making the island self-sustaining. Kaikontai headquarters was established at a large agricultural plantation operated by Chamorro forced labor at Tai, a sparsely inhabited area about five miles southeast of Agana.

Despite their rather innocuous title, the Kaikontai proved even more demanding and exploitive of the Chamorros than their Minseibu predecessors. "Japan's *Kaikuntai* [*sic*] was ruthless," observed a postwar historical study. "All able-bodied women (and some men deemed too frail for heavier work) and all female children over 12-years-old labored from 8 a.m. daily until sundown in food production. Rice plantings at Piti, Asan, Agat, Inarajan and Merizo were extended. New fields inland were cleared of tangantangan; sweet potatoes, corn, taro, tapioca and other foods were planted. Family quotas of chickens, pigs and eggs were increased. Work days were marred by physical punishment of women and children thought to be not working hard enough. Slapping was an ordinary punishment."[41]

Compounding agricultural woes, the spring of 1944 was one of the driest in years, drastically affecting production. Civilians tried to supplement their scanty rice rations with fruits, taro, and other naturally found foods, but the opportunity to forage was limited due to the time they were forced to spend laboring on military defenses and food production for the Japanese themselves. The Japanese showed no sympathy, dismissing their charges as lazy and "idle in common with other natives in the South Seas islands."[42]

"Babies and young children suffered especially severely at this time," noted a subsequent U.S. intelligence report. "With milk requisitioned for Japanese aviators, mothers were forced to resort to coconut milk and unripe breadfruit for infant feeding. By the time our troops landed on the island many infants had reached a pitiful state of malnutrition and presented the picture of extreme marasmus. . . . The vast majority of infants showed obvious malnutrition, with signs of protein and vitamin deficiency. Many were so weak they could not turn their heads."[43]

CHAPTER 6

THE MARIANAS

Encouraged by the successful leap into the Marshalls and convinced by the February carrier raids that the Japanese bastion at Truk no longer posed a significant military threat, American planners decided to advance the timetable for the Marianas operation, code-named "Forager." Detailed planning for the seizure of Saipan, Tinian, and Guam began in March.

Admiral Chester Nimitz had originally projected landings on Saipan and Tinian for November 1, followed by Guam—code-named "Stevedore"—on December 15. A joint staff study on Forager issued on March 20 moved the date for the Saipan operation up to June 15. Saipan was considered the most important of the three objectives due to its status as the seat of government in the Marianas, its development as a Japanese base and command center, and its airfield. Seizing Saipan first would also prevent enemy air reinforcements from shuttling south through the chain to contest the subsequent invasion of Guam. Anticipating that the situation on Saipan would be well in hand within three days, the Guam assault date—designated W-Day (William-Day) to avoid confusion with Saipan's D-Day (Dog-Day)—was scheduled for June 18. Tinian, only three miles southwest of Saipan, would be seized as soon as practicable.

As originally conceived, the Marianas operation would involve over 127,571 assault troops assigned to capture the three islands: 71,034 were designated for the seizure of Saipan and Tinian, and 56,537 were assigned to Guam.[1] Hundreds of combatant ships and auxiliaries ranging from aircraft carriers to transports to patrol craft would be required. The Northern Attack Force, built around the V Amphibious Corps (VAC)—the main ground units being the 2nd and 4th Marine Divisions—would be responsible for the seizure of Saipan and Tinian. The Southern Attack Force, built around the III Amphibious Corps—the main ground units being the 3rd

Marine Division and 1st Provisional Marine Brigade—would seize Guam. The 27th Infantry Division would serve as Expeditionary Force Reserve, available to either the Northern or Southern Attack Force as needed. The Army's 77th Infantry Division, soon to arrive in Hawaii, would serve as long-term area reserve but would not be available until twenty days after the Saipan landings. That was not considered particularly worrisome. Planners anticipated that the original units would be sufficient.

Overall command of Forager would be under Admiral Raymond Spruance, commander of the Fifth Fleet. Vice Admiral Richmond Kelly Turner would command the Joint Expeditionary Forces as well as the Northern Attack Force. Marine lieutenant general Holland M. ("Howlin' Mad") Smith would be in overall command of all Forager ground forces. Wearing two hats, Smith would also directly command the Northern Troops and Landing Force (NTLF) troops conducting the seizure of Saipan on June 15. The Southern Attack Force, assigned to seize Guam, would be commanded by Rear Admiral Richard ("Dick") L. Conolly. The ground forces committed to Guam—the Southern Troops and Landing Force—would be led by Marine major general Roy Geiger under the purview of General Smith.

While Holland Smith and Kelly Turner were notorious throughout the services for their difficult personalities, the leaders of the Southern Attack Force that would assault Guam were cut from different cloth. Fifty-two-years old, Conolly was recognized as one of the Navy's most capable amphibious commanders, having earned the nickname "Close-in Conolly" for an incident in the Marshall Islands operation when he ordered the USS *Maryland* to "move really close in" to provide support for the Marine landings. Described as "genial, thorough and methodical," he was a team player.[2] "He was a splendid, strong able man who would listen," said Colonel Robert Hogaboom, a member of Holland Smith's staff. "He would send for Marines and listen to them talk about amphibious operations. He would send for me and sit at a table and talk with me by the hour, questioning me, and then he would put on his field boots and go ashore and follow the Marines all through the operations. He studied and mastered the Marines' problems as well as the naval problems."[3]

A similar spirit of efficiency and cooperation characterized General Roy Geiger. A heavy-set fifty-nine-year-old with a penchant for cigars, Geiger had been a teacher and lawyer before enlisting in Marines in 1907 and finding a home. As one of the first Marines to go into aviation, he had spent most of his career flying and commanding flyers. Most recently, he had served at Guadalcanal as chief of aviation during some of the campaign's darkest hours, returning to the United States as director of Marine aviation before being elevated to corps command.

A land command for an officer reputedly "weaned on aviation fuel" may have seemed an anomaly, but Geiger would more than live up to expectations.[4] "If you had a son or a daughter going into battle, you would hope they had a commander like Geiger," remarked a fellow officer.[5] A matter-of-fact man who disliked small talk, he was better educated than most of his peers, a quick learner who demanded excellence and functioned well under pressure. "He did not try to nitpick or micro manage the staff work, but told them what he wanted and let them find the best way to do it," remarked one staff officer. "Before long they knew better than to go to him for a decision without having very thoroughly gathered, analyzed, and presented all of the information needed to make a decision."[6]

Geiger and Conolly would develop a warm relationship in the coming months—a relationship that was mirrored by their staffs. "The team of Geiger and Conolly was unbeatable," observed Lieutenant Colonel William F. Coleman, the IIIAC intelligence officer.[7] Commenting later on the staff dynamic, Admiral Conolly observed, "That's the best relationship I ever had anywhere, anytime, during the war with any other service. It was partly due to the fact that Geiger and I got along very well together, and due to his personality. He was forceful and at the same time very cooperative and human, a wonderful man—very knightly character. . . . He was just a marvelous man."[8]

A dispatch regarding the Marianas operation was received by Geiger's staff on March 27. "Hurrah! We have a job," Geiger's aide, Captain Roy Owsley, noted in his diary.[9] Geiger and key members of the IIIAC staff flew to Pearl Harbor on March 29 and spent the next nine days conferring with the planners for other elements of Forager. A tentative operation plan for the Guam assault was prepared by IIIAC staff and approved by General Smith on April 3 and by Admiral Turner on April 4. The plan was subsequently honed by Marine and Navy staffs during a profitable series of meetings over a period of days at IIIAC headquarters on Guadalcanal.

The defense and capture of Guam had been the focus of a student exercise at the Marine Corps Schools for field officers as far back as 1936—"a favorite operation in those imaginary conflicts which are fought across sheets of paper at the Marine Corps Schools," as one analyst later put it.[10] The accepted school solution over the years was to avoid an amphibious assault across the wide fringing reef along Guam's western coast. Any student who dared depart from the accepted mantra could expect to be rewarded with a failing grade. But advances in technology had made the conventional school solution less imperative by 1944. Newly developed amphibious tractors (LVTs) and trucks (DUKWs) were now able to negotiate reefs that would have been impassable only a few years earlier. These developments gave Geiger's planners far more flexibility than would have been possible previously.

Still, Guam's topography continued to impose limitations. The eastern shore was considered unsuitable for a landing, being to the windward and subject to rough seas. Over time, those pounding seas had created a lip on the reef that made it virtually impassable. Even had that not been the case, an attack from the east would require the landing force to negotiate miles of jungle to reach the key objectives, those being Apra Harbor and the airfield on Orote Peninsula. Elsewhere, steep cliffs barred access along most of the coastline, including Orote Peninsula with its valuable airfield. This left about fifteen miles of potential beach access, all on the west coast extending to the north and south of Apra Harbor—and even here the reef ranged up to several hundred yards wide.

The most attractive landing site was at Tumon Bay, which offered a two-mile stretch of wide sandy beach where the Japanese had come ashore in 1941. The reef was not too wide, and the coastal area sloped gradually up to the high ground further inland. The problem with Tumon was that it was too obvious. Planners assumed—correctly as they later discovered—that these beaches would be heavily defended. The distance from Apra Harbor was also problematical, and the way toward the harbor was barred by highly defensible terrain.

In the end, IIIAC planners settled on simultaneous landings by the 3rd Marine Division and the 1st Provisional Marine Brigade at two separate points on Guam's western shore. The 3rd Marine Division would land on a twenty-five-hundred-yard front between Adelup and Asan Points just up the coast from Apra Harbor. The 1st Provisional Marine Brigade would come ashore about five miles further south on a mile-long front between Agat Village and Bangi Point on the other side of Orote Peninsula. The two would establish separate beachheads and eventually link up, isolating the two key objectives—Apra Harbor, needed as a supply port, and Orote Peninsula with its airfield. The wide separation between the two forces ran counter to conventional doctrine, but planners accepted the risk in light of their limited options. To better coordinate the landings at two separate points—what a Marine officer later described as "creating the situation of two almost separate military operations by the same landing force"—Admiral Conolly divided the Guam forces into a Northern Attack Group (Asan beaches) commanded by himself and a Southern Attack Group (Agat beaches) to be led by Rear Admiral Lawrence F. Reifsnider.[11]

Two alternate plans were developed, should the preferred beaches prove to be too heavily defended or unsuitable for landing. Operation Plan No. 3-44 issued on May 30 provided for landing the entire invasion force in echelon on the beaches between Agat and Facpi Point. A follow-up, Operation Plan No. 4-44 issued on June 9, envisioned a landing by the 3rd Division between Adelup and Asan Points as proposed in the original plan, with the Marine Brigade landing on beaches between Bangi Point and Facpi Point, immediately to the south of the brigade's previously designated landing area.

———

Considering that Guam had been an American possession for over forty years, U.S. intelligence was surprisingly deficient in a number of areas, particularly in the specifics of the island's terrain features. General Holland Smith later observed caustically that "our knowledge of our former possession was almost less than we knew of the most secret Japanese islands."[12] During Guam's long tenure under U.S. Navy rule, it appeared there had been virtually no study of military terrain features.

The Office of Naval Intelligence (ONI) compiled a 345-page study of the island (ONI-99) for distribution in February, but it was based entirely on information predating the Japanese occupation. Other input was gleaned from officers who had served on Guam over the years and from Chamorros now serving in the Navy, but the value was mixed. "An officer who had served in [the Marine Barracks] and was presumed knowledgeable on such matters, provided information on the reefs; he proved to be all wrong," remembered Major Louis Metzger, who would command an armored amphibian battalion during the operation.[13]

Battalion commander Major Henry Aplington recalled, "The land forms shown on the maps were very general and did not show vegetation. . . . ONI 99 had been put together from the best information available but it tended to rely on pre-war reminiscences of officers stationed there, the input from Guamanian mess-boys and anyone else who had knowledge of the island. Its photographs were pretty much personal snapshots of family outings and the wife and children posing on the reef at low tide. Some showed a bit of background terrain."[14]

Hydrographic charts representing Apra Harbor and various bays proved useful, though the remaining coastline, including the anticipated landing beaches, was only generally examined. The charts also failed to indicate the true nature of the fringing reef or the depth of water there. Geiger's headquarters sought permission to land reconnaissance patrols on the island "for the purpose of contacting natives and getting such information as could be obtained in an effort to see behind the curtain," but their request was turned down.[15]

Mapmakers relied on an earlier Marine Corps Schools draft to develop an air and gunnery target map with a scale of 1:20,000, which was distributed for tactical planning. Another, smaller scale map at 1:62,500 was produced for corps use. Neither was ideal, but the 1:20,000 scale map—which was published before adequate aerial photos became available—turned out to be particularly unsatisfactory. "Vast areas of the ground actually covered by dense vegetation appeared as bare terrain," observed a subsequent Marine Corps study. "In many cases, broken ground contour lines indicated the interior had not been thoroughly surveyed. Finally, as troop commanders would soon discover, the map location of roads and trails in northern Guam often turned out to be inaccurate by hundreds of yards."[16] Colonel Ray A. Robinson, 3rd Division chief of staff, later observed, "The map we had showed three ridges between where we landed and Agana. And there were five. Well, those ridges took casualties."[17]

A number of rubber relief maps made up to brief the troops also proved to be "inherently inaccurate," noted III Amphibious Corps planners, though they provided a general picture and had the advantage of being easily portable. Many units later took the rolled-up maps ashore with them—one officer reporting that they also "served a most useful purpose when used as rubber mattresses on the ground."[18] More useful from an instructional standpoint was a plaster relief map prepared by Navy commander Richard F. Armknecht, one of four Civil Engineer Corps officers assigned to the Naval Station on Guam. Armknecht had been attending a conference in Hawaii on December 7, which allowed him to escape capture. His 1:5,000 plaster copies with a 2:1 exaggeration of the immediate beach area were credited with "giving the assault troops the only real visual aid in what they were to encounter in the war of terrain."[19]

Despite that contribution to the war effort, Armknecht apparently failed to endear himself to the 3rd Marine Division's leadership. The engineer, whose duties on Guam "had consisted of taking care of the sewerage system in the town of Agana and advising the Guamanians in regard to the construction of privies," as a division officer acidly remarked, seems to have overestimated his own stature during a briefing that included division commander Major General Allen H. ("Hal") Turnage. Instead of limiting himself to information on Guam's terrain, the Navy commander launched into a harsh critique of the plan to land the 3rd Marine Division at Asan where the beaches were overlooked by rugged heights. "This, he declared, was utterly wrong, it was stupid, and it would end in failure," recalled Lieutenant Colonel John S.

Letcher of the incident, "adding that he would wash his hands of any responsibility for the success of the operation."

His tirade was interrupted by Turnage, a normally imperturbable man, who stood up "eyes flashing" and coldly asked Armknecht who had given him the idea that he was in any way responsible for the outcome of the attack. The engineer admitted that no one had.

"Then," said Turnage, "bear that in mind and hereafter confine yourself to the matters which you were brought here to discuss, namely the topography, climate, and other physical characteristics of the island. When we want your opinions on other matters, we will ask for them."[20]

⌐━◄

At 0921, three hours after sunrise on April 5, USS *Greenling* extended her periscope above the surface off Guam's Talofofo Bay and began snapping photographs of the coast. Skippered by Lieutenant Commander James D. Grant, the Gato-class submarine, built by Electric Boat in Groton, Connecticut, and launched in September 1941, already had eight war patrols to her credit, including at least two that involved special operations. On her seventh war patrol, she had been tasked with landing a party of Marine Raiders in the Treasury Islands and also conducted a reconnaissance of Tarawa. On her eighth patrol, she had managed to sink a freighter, while also reconnoitering Wake Island.

U.S. submarines conducted periodic patrols in the waters off Guam as early as February 4, 1942, when USS *Thresher* attacked a small Japanese freighter only seven miles off Agana. The number of patrols in the Marianas went from only four in 1942 to a total of fifteen between January and November 1943—an indication of the improving war situation. Ship traffic in and out of Guam was not heavy, but now and again the sub skippers would pick off a vessel. In late May, USS *Whale* sank the *Shoei* Maru, a 3,590-ton gunboat carrying naval troops of the Japanese Fifth Base Force returning to Saipan from Guam. The ship went down in about four minutes, apparently with no survivors. On August 27, USS *Snapper*, maneuvering under the nose of a patrol boat puttering around only thirty-five hundred yards astern, sank the freighter *Tokai* Maru, which was moored in Apra Harbor. The stricken freighter came to rest on the harbor bottom beside the German auxiliary cruiser *Cormoran*, which had been scuttled by her crew on April 7, 1917, to keep her out of American hands following the declaration of war on Germany.

Grant, a square-jawed Class of 1931 Naval Academy graduate from Cleveland, Ohio, had been directed not to engage the enemy on *Greenling's* current mission—

all of the shooting was to be done with cameras as he photographed the coasts of Saipan, Guam, and Tinian to assist in the planning for Forager. While Grant might have preferred to be blowing Japanese ships out of the water, *Greenling's* reconnaissance mission was considered so important that USS *Seahorse* had been sent to rampage around the southern Marianas in an effort to draw enemy antisubmarine assets away from Grant's patrol area.

Greenling's mission was already hazardous enough, as it required the sub to approach close to the coast in daylight, often in shallow water, and demanded meticulous attention to detail. Experimentation with various cameras had determined that the 120mm single lens reflex Primarflex was best suited for periscope photography. Unfortunately, the Primarflex was manufactured by a German company, which was unlikely to fill an order now that Germany and the United States were in a state of war. However, by placing want ads in photography magazines, the U.S. Navy Bureau of Aeronautics had been able to acquire ten used Primarflex cameras, which were reserved strictly for subs engaged in photographic reconnaissance missions.

The specialized use required modifications and special handling to compensate for the lower light when shooting photos through a periscope, as well as to deal with vibration from machinery and wave action that could blur the photos. Great care also had to be taken as to location and coverage. With an eight-degree photographic field, the periscope had to be rotated approximately four degrees for each successive shot so the photos would overlap. The sub's location was carefully plotted on a chart with reference to coastal landmarks. A full roll of twelve photos was shot at each stop as the sub moved slowly along the coast. Each roll of film was then numbered, with the same number inscribed on the chart with a vector to indicate the orientation of the camera. Photos were developed aboard the sub and checked for clarity. They were then mounted in a mosaic to verify complete coverage.

Greenling left Pearl Harbor on March 20 and arrived at Saipan on April 2, where she immediately experienced shutter problems with her two cameras. A close call with a Japanese patrol boat on the morning of April 4 persuaded Grant to head south and take a look at Guam. In the meantime, the engineering officer deduced that the camera problems were probably caused by high humidity inside the sub. He put together a makeshift oven, disassembled the cameras, dried everything out, cleaned the parts, and put them back together, which resolved the problems. To prevent a reoccurrence, the cameras were kept in the oven when not in use.

Starting off Talofofo Bay the morning of April 5, *Greenling* slowly worked south over the next two days shooting photos and recording information on tides and depth soundings. Though Japanese air activity was noted during the day, the sub was not detected. One close encounter occurred the night of April 6 when *Greenling* surfaced to recharge her batteries under cover of darkness. Lookouts spotted a Kawanishi H8K four-engine flying boat—code-named "Emily" by Allied intelligence—patrolling only one thousand yards off the port side. Grant hastily took the sub down without being sighted.

On the morning of April 8, the monotony was broken once again when lookouts sighted a burning ship to the east of Talofofo Bay. A Japanese escort stood alongside the stricken ship, and a few hours later a Japanese destroyer also arrived on the scene. Though Grant did not know it at the time, the burning vessel was the *Aratama* Maru, which had run afoul of USS *Seahorse* only about an hour before. *Seahorse* had been stalking a convoy of three lumbering freighters escorted by two destroyers since the previous afternoon, finally getting into firing position at 0221. The sub fired six torpedoes—a spread of three at each of the two freighters. The patrol report observed, "Saw first target hit with a tremendous explosion just under the bridge. A brilliant mass of flames shot high into the air, and the water on both sides of the ship, for a distance of several hundred yards, was sprayed with debris. Took quick look around for destroyers and when the periscope was trained back on the target bearing, the ship was gone, leaving a pall of smoke. The second target was on fire amidships, but on an even keel and not low in the water. Sound reported the destroyers coming in, and we went deep."[21]

The 6,783-ton ammunition ship *Aratama* Maru had been hit amidships and in the bow, killing four men and setting her cargo of gasoline on fire. The crew managed to control the flooding, but the burning hulk eventually drifted aground off Talofofo Bay, where she would remain for the rest of the war. Japanese soldiers slapped around curious Chamorros who came to gawk at the wreck, telling them the ship was American, but the large rising sun insignia painted on the side argued otherwise. The second ship, the *Kizugawa* Maru, was badly damaged with thirty-seven sailors killed, but she remained afloat. The freighter was taken under tow and brought into Guam.

Grant decided to vacate the area and spent the next couple of days photographing Tinian before returning to Guam on April 11—which happened to be his thirty-sixth birthday—to wrap up photo coverage there. The mission was completed on the afternoon of April 15, without incident beyond a brush with a bothersome Japanese patrol boat.

While *Greenling* lurked beneath the sea, efforts were also underway to reconnoiter Guam from the skies above. On April 24, Navy PB4Y-1s from Air Photographic

Squadron 3 (VD-3), accompanied by B-24s from the 392nd Bombardment Squadron based on Eniwetok, made the one-thousand-mile flight to conduct a photo sweep of the island. The Navy version of the Army's B-24 four-engine heavy bomber, the PB4Y-1 Liberator had a range of twenty-one hundred miles and was extensively used as a patrol bomber and by long-range photographic reconnaissance squadrons over the vast Pacific expanses. The B-24s went along to provide protection should Japanese fighters attempt to interfere with the mission.

While results were disappointing due to cloud cover and mechanical problems that forced two of the seven PB4Y-1s to break off, the crews did get a good look at Orote Airfield, which appeared to be "a large and well-developed air base with a large number of planes on it." The photo mission also discovered the new airfield at Tiyan and what appeared to be the beginnings of a third field "just north of Amantes Point." Though the flight had been detected by enemy radar while still 120 miles from the target, the Japanese took no discernible defensive action. Fighters failed to intercept, and crews noticed only one flash from the ground that might have been antiaircraft fire.[22]

Hoping for better results, a second reconnaissance was scheduled for May 7. The photographic element consisted of six PB4Y-1s—four from VD-3 and two from Air Photographic Squadron 4—accompanied by twelve B-24s, ten from the 26th Bombardment Squadron and two from the 431st Bombardment Squadron. As a secondary mission, the PB4Y-1s each carried a one-hundred-pound bomb and the B-24s each carried three one-hundred-pound bombs to drop on targets of opportunity. Preferred targets included the airfield and other military installations on Orote Peninsula and the power plant and telephone exchange in Agana.

The mission took off from Eniwetok at 0620 for the long flight to Guam. Two of the B-24 escorts turned back due to mechanical difficulties, but the remainder of the flight arrived at Guam at about 1100 hours, and the planes made their first runs on a parallel course from the northern end of the island south to Orote Peninsula. They then turned east and made a second parallel run over the southern part of the island.

As the planes made their first run, about twenty-five enemy fighters were seen taking off from Orote Airfield. The fighters gained altitude and began piecemeal attacks just as the formation was completing the second run. "Attacks were made on every section and continued until the formation had gone about 80 miles from the target," noted the aircraft action report. "Most of the attacks were individual and were not coordinated." The majority of the fighters—identified as Zeros—were painted a dark blue, though a few were tan colored and at least one was silver, according to crew reports.

Most of the Japanese pilots attacked from below and behind, which allowed them to stay out of the tail gunner's line of fire but exposed them to the belly turret guns. American gunners subsequently claimed at least seven kills, which seems highly unlikely, though Japanese tactics were clearly ineffectual. The PB4Y-1 piloted by Lieutenant Commander Neil C. Porter claimed three Zeros. One was hit by the belly turret gunner as it attempted an attack from below. "Flames started coming from its engine and it fell out of control through clouds below," noted the aircraft action report. The top turret gunner shot the port aileron and part of the port wing off another Zeke attempting an overhead attack. "The plane and the pieces that were shot off of it were seen to pass close under our plane and fall to the water below." The starboard waist gunner claimed a third victory, hitting a Zero that burst into flames and fell toward the water out of control.

The ball turret gunner in another PB4Y-1 raked a Zero attempting an attack from below. "When hit, the plane turned over and went straight down, burning," noted the after-action report. Still another was claimed by the ball turret gunner in a third PB4Y-1, who reported that the enemy aircraft "fell off on its back, burst into flames and went down in a steep spiral to the water below." The port gunner in the same PB4Y-1 fired on a fighter as it broke off its run. "He saw tracers going into the fuselage near the engine and the plane was last seen in a steep dive but because of the necessity of keeping an alert for more fighters nobody was able to see whether it ultimately crashed or not." The escorting B-24s claimed two fighters shot down and two probables.

Moderate antiaircraft fire from the airfield at Orote and near Agana was reported by at least two of the crews. The bursts were at the correct altitude but lacked the proper lead, as most of the shells exploded behind the planes. Some pilots also attacked the American formation with phosphorus bombs. "In most cases the fighters making these attacks approached on opposite course several thousand feet above our planes and then made a regular dive bombing approach dropping the bombs just as they pulled out of the dive. Some crew members reported that these bombs appeared to be lobbed from the fighters. . . . There were no hits on our planes by phosphorus bombs but several exploded at the correct altitude and some were very close," noted the subsequent action report. Despite the repeated fighter attacks, only one plane, an Army B-24, was hit. A 20mm shell wounded the tail gunner in the arm and leg. The fighters finally broke off their attack, and the formation proceeded as planned to Mokareng Airfield on Los Negros in the Admiralty Islands, where it landed without further incident.

A preliminary examination of the photos revealed forty-two planes on Orote Airfield, including twenty-nine single-engine planes, eight Betty bombers, and five aircraft that appeared to be twin-engine fighters. A smaller number of planes was observed on the new Tiyan Field near Agana. Seven or eight medium to large cargo ships (AKs) were visible in Apra Harbor. More ominously as far as the Marines were concerned, there were indications that the enemy was constructing obstacles on the reef in Agat Bay.[23]

On Guadalcanal, the 3rd Marine Division was recovering from its first campaign, an amphibious assault at Cape Torokina on Bougainville in the northern Solomons. Activated in September 1943, the division consisted of three infantry regiments—the 3rd, 9th, and 21st Marines—along with an artillery regiment (the 12th Marines), a tank battalion, and engineer and support troops, totaling 20,328 men. Their shoulder patch proclaimed their readiness and versatility. The patch consisted of a red shield depicting a caltrop, a three-pronged device designed to always land point up and used in battle against men and horses since Roman times.

Commanded by Major General Hal Turnage, the division lost about four hundred killed and fourteen hundred wounded carving out a beachhead at Bougainville during two months of fighting from November 1 to late December. Literally bogged down in one of the most inhospitable environments in the world, the Marines contended with flooded foxholes, near-impenetrable jungle, cold rations, and ceaseless rain that rotted the clothes off their backs—they even suffered casualties from falling trees. "Everything that God didn't want He put on Bougainville," observed a disgusted veteran of the campaign.[24] Finally relieved by Army troops in late December, the division began trickling back to Guadalcanal to refit even as Bougainville shuddered with a series of earthquakes by way of farewell.

"Following our trying experiences of life on Bougainville, returning to Guadalcanal was liking coming home to an island paradise," recalled radioman Jack Kerins. There were tents, mattress pads, mosquito nets for cots, a large screened-in mess with a concrete floor and wooden tables and benches, and even makeshift showers constructed from fifty-five-gallon oil drums. For the next couple of weeks, guard and work details were kept to a minimum, and time was set aside for rest and recreation as the men recovered their strength.[25]

But as routines were gradually reestablished, it became evident that the 3rd Marine Division would be heading into combat again in the very near future. The much-despised Reising submachine guns in Kerins's outfit—stamped sheet-metal affairs that tended to jam at the most inopportune moment—were withdrawn and replaced with new M-1 carbines. "Our radio section received the new and very efficient SCR-300 radios to replace our antiquated TBYs that were next to being worthless," he recalled. "Drills and training sessions were stepped up in every squad, company and battalion."[26]

In a departure from the past, when the identity of objectives remained a closely held secret, the Marines were told they would be assaulting Kavieng, a major enemy base on New Ireland. The landing was scheduled for April 1. Seizure of the provincial capital on Balgai Bay would tighten the noose around the Japanese bastion on Rabaul. It was not expected to be easy. "Except for one small pier, the waterfront was an open beach with a grass-covered ridge close behind it rising to a height of 30 or 40 feet," recalled Lieutenant Colonel John Letcher, executive officer of the division's artillery regiment. Swamps on either side would force a frontal assault on the ridge, which the Japanese had presumably transformed into a fortress.

"The more we studied the situation the worse it looked and it was universally, though of course very quietly, said that taking the place was going to be a bloody business and a foolish thing to do just to obtain the airfields, because the same result could be accomplished without any fighting by occupying [unoccupied] Emirau Island [about one hundred miles northeast of Kavieng]," observed Letcher. Following a briefing of Jack Kerins's artillery battery in the mess tent, one of the cannon cockers murmured worriedly, "Jeez, if any of us come out of this friggin' mess alive, we'll be damn lucky S.O.B.s."[27]

Thirty-six hours before departure, while combat loading of ships was already underway, the division was advised that the Kavieng operation had been cancelled. Already keyed to a high pitch, the men weren't sure whether to be grateful or disappointed. "By now we were becoming restless. It wasn't that we were looking forward to going into a battle again, especially this one, it was just that this waiting was no good," observed Kerins.[28]

—⌒—

As the 3rd Division stood down, the unit that would form the other component of the Guam invasion force, the 1st Provisional Marine Brigade, was still undergoing birthing pains. Built around two regiments—the 4th Marines and the 22nd Marines—the brigade had been formed on March 22, at least in name. The 4th Marines were sent to occupy Emirau following cancellation of the Kavieng operation, while the 22nd Marines were in the Marshalls. They would not arrive on Guadalcanal until late April. Brigadier General Lemuel ("Lem") C. Shepherd Jr. assumed command of the brigade on April 16 with a mere two months' grace to pull it all together before the Guam operation was scheduled to take place.

Once fully constituted, the brigade would number 9,886 men. Both regiments were well seasoned with combat veterans. The original 4th Marines had been lost in the Philippines at the beginning of the war. The newly reconstituted regiment had been put together with personnel from the former Marine Raider battalions, which had been disbanded in January. Raiders had seen combat during the legendary Makin Raid as well as on Guadalcanal and Bougainville but were phased out when the Marine Corps decided the specialized elite units were no longer needed and were actually a divisive element in an organization that proudly viewed all Marines as elite.

The 22nd Marines had been stationed on Samoa early in the war. More recently, the regiment had participated in the seizure of the Marshall Islands in February, fighting on Engebi, Parry, and Eniwetok. Marine casualties during the entire operation were listed as 254 killed and 555 wounded. The regiment was praised for its "repeated landing operations," with the observation that the "loss in combat efficiency due to fatigue and casualties was compensated for by the outstanding fighting spirit of all hands."[29]

Both the 3rd Marine Division and the 1st Provisional Marine Brigade were in good hands with Generals Turnage and Shepherd. Entering the Marine Corps as a lieutenant in 1913 after attending the University of North Carolina, Turnage had served in Haiti, commanded a machine-gun battalion in France during World War I, and headed Marine forces in North China. Soft-spoken, gentlemanly, and largely unflappable, he was well liked. Some of his superiors had reservations about a supposed lack of forcefulness before promoting him from assistant division commander to 3rd Division commander in September 1943, but the fifty-three-year-old had turned in a solid performance at Bougainville in November. His assistant division commander, Brigadier General Alfred Noble, observed with pardonable pride that the division had become a well-oiled machine under Turnage. "From the planning to the fighting end of it to its administration and everything else, it was very smooth operating because we had spent a lot of time on standard operating procedures," he said.[30]

For his part, forty-eight-year-old Lem Shepherd was considered one of the fair-haired officers of the Marine Corps. A graduate of Virginia Military Institute, he had been wounded three times fighting with the Marine Brigade in France during World War I, where he earned a Navy Cross. Despite that sanguinary record, the cerebral Virginian was known as a "schools man." He had commanded the Marine Corps Schools, where he enhanced his reputation as a teacher of tactics. More recently, he had served as the assistant commander of the 1st Marine Division during the 1943 landing on Cape Gloucester. He detested the Japanese. "Killing a Jap was like killing a rattlesnake," he remarked years later.[31] At the same time, he was considerate of his officers and men, which earned him their respect and loyalty. One of his lieutenants, who later described Shepherd as "one of the greatest Marines of all time," vividly remembered the general's admonition as to an officer's responsibilities: "Rank not only has its privileges but it also has its responsibilities. You are an officer. When you are in the field, you don't eat until your men have eaten and at night you don't get into your hole until your men are in theirs."[32]

"We knew he was as good a man as you could find . . . the kind of general who knows what he's doing and isn't in a big hurry to lose lives needlessly," recalled an enlisted member of the 22nd Marines. "You like to feel the guy making the big decisions is also thinking of the men under him. We believed Shepherd fit the bill in this department."[33]

Time was growing short. Turnage's staff received the operation plan for "Stevedore," as the Guam operation was code-named, on May 11. The Marine Brigade received the plan two days later, leaving Shepherd to organize his newly arrived brigade and conduct planning at the same time. Short on help and knowing the 3rd Division was top-heavy with officers, he asked Turnage, who was a good friend, to give him a few lieutenants. To Shepherd's pique, Turnage refused. "Hal, all I'm asking for is about three or four of your officers to come to the brigade for my headquarters staff and important jobs in my headquarters company," pleaded Shepherd, but Turnage was adamant. Shepherd would subsequently extract a small measure of revenge on Guam, but for the moment he had to make do with what he had.[34]

According to Operation Plan No. 1-44, the Southern Landing Force (IIIAC) slated for the assault on Guam was also to be prepared to assist in the seizure of Saipan should the landing by the 2nd and 4th Marine Divisions on June 15 run into trouble. Otherwise, the Guam landing was to take place on June 18—a mere three days after D-Day at Saipan. At least one officer felt that the June 18 timetable for Guam was too optimistic. Colonel Robert E. Hogaboom, Admiral Kelly Turner's assistant chief of staff for operations, proposed that W-Day on Guam be pushed back at least five to seven days after the Saipan landings. He observed there was a strong probability the Saipan operation would draw out the Japanese fleet. Pushing back the date of the Guam landings would allow any naval confrontation to play out, while also providing time to monitor developments in the land action and the extent to which reserves might be required. Hogaboom's concerns were dismissed, but vindication would not be long in coming.[35]

Dress rehearsals for Stevedore were conducted between May 23 and 27. The 3rd Division held two days of rehearsals beginning May 23 at Cape Esperance on Guadalcanal's northwest coast. Geiger's aide noted in his diary that 747 ships—from carriers and battleships to the versatile LSTs (Landing Ship, Tank) and a multitude of specialized landing craft—were designated for Stevedore. All assault troops and equipment were landed in accordance with the ship-to-shore movement plan, accompanied by actual naval air and gunfire bombardment. The 1st Provisional Marine Brigade was put through its paces in same area on May 25 to 27. "Transport areas, fire support areas, target areas, boat lanes, etc. were laid out near Cape Esperance to simulate as near as possible the exact conditions likely to be encountered at Guam," reported IIIAC. "Ships were assigned to and fired by the shore fire control parties in the same manner as scheduled for the actual operation. The results of these rehearsals were highly gratifying, especially the call fire phase where shore fire control parties called for and spotted fire from all ships present, in many cases overhead fire."[36] If there was a drawback, it was that the rehearsal area had no reef comparable to what would be encountered at Guam. Planners compensated by establishing an imaginary reef offshore where troops had to transfer from Higgins boats to amphibian tractors, but it would prove to be no substitute.

Unlike with the scrubbed Kavieng operation, this time there were no general troop briefings as to the objective. The rank and file remained in the dark. "None of us knew certainly what our next destination would be," observed Sergeant Alvin Josephy, who would accompany the 3rd Marine Division as a combat correspondent. "There were lots of rumors and many arguments."[37]

CHAPTER 7

A FORCED CHANGE OF PLANS

TETERE, GUADALCANAL, JUNE 2, 1944

The 3rd Marine Division was on the move. A bugle roused the men at 0300 in their tent city among the endless ranks of coconut trees at the former Lever Brothers plantation. After a hasty breakfast they slogged or rode several miles down the muddy road to the beach, where loading of men and equipment had already been underway for the past three days. The beach area was jammed with units waiting for LCVP landing craft to carry them out to the troop transports. Large placards listed the names of ships waiting offshore. An old-time regular Marine platoon sergeant who would be coming in with supplies after the initial landing amused himself by tormenting the waiting men with dire warnings. "It is going to be murder for you poor fellows," he jibed. "You know they are counting on sixty percent casualties. I will be there in time to bury a lot of you."[1]

They took the gaffing in stride. They were young. The average age of an enlisted Marine was twenty-one or younger, and their lieutenants and captains were typically not much older. An analysis of men from the 3rd Marines subsequently killed at Guam indicates they ranged from seventeen to thirty-six years of age. The bulk of the dead were nineteen to twenty-one years old. Speaking of the prospect of his first combat, Private Aaron S. Fox observed wryly with the benefit of hindsight, "Strangely enough, when you're seventeen, not that you don't have any fear at that moment, [but] you think that nothing can happen to you or your mother will raise hell."[2]

"I wonder who's going to get this place after the war," one Marine mused, referring to their soon to be former home on Guadalcanal.

"Give it to the Japs," replied a corporal. "As part of their punishment."[3]

The armada offshore was already loaded with hundreds of thousands of tons of everything from lubricating oil and gasoline to hand grenades, rations, and screening

95

to keep flies out of latrines. The *President Jackson* alone carried 89 vehicles, 102 tons of naval ammunition, 190 tons of ammunition for ground forces, 46 tons of rations, 606 drums of gasoline, 77 drums of kerosene, 25 drums of oil, 140 drums of water, and 166 drums of diesel among other supplies. LST 221, just one of dozens of LSTs assigned to the operation, was loaded with 8 tons of 37mm ammunition, 21 tons of 60mm mortar ammunition, 17 tons of 81mm mortar ammunition, 3 tons of 57mm ammunition, 10 tons of hand grenades, 1 ton of rocket grenades, 3 tons of rockets, and 57 tons of 75mm artillery shells, in addition to fuel and extras.

Aboard the USS *Zeilin* it was discovered that the alcohol and brandy brought on board on May 28 for Marine medical units had already been pilfered. Medical officers hastily obtained a replacement supply before departure. Of less interest to thirsty Marines, but of more potential value in the future, a total of 43 million units of penicillin had been procured prior to sailing from Guadalcanal. Most of the life-saving drug had been distributed among the troopships, which would act as hospital facilities during the first days of the campaign. Somewhere, too, in the great masses of equipment and materiél, were stacks of white-painted wooden grave markers, all ready except for the names.

Heavily laden with troops and equipment, the LSTs departed first, leaving on June 1, followed by the faster transport and support groups on June 4. III Amphibious Corps headquarters embarked on the *Appalachian* on June 3 and sailed the next day with the fast transport group. All would assemble at Kwajalein atoll, where they would join the Saipan-bound Northern Attack Force carrying the 2nd and 4th Marine Divisions from Hawaii. Aboard USS *Crescent City*, there was animated speculation among the troops as to their final destination. The general consensus was Japanese-held Truk, but a particularly astute pharmacist's mate observed that an awful lot of Guamanian sailors seemed to have been brought in from all over the fleet. A chief yeoman confided that scuttlebutt had identified the objective as Wake.

As the ships lumbered along toward their rendezvous at Kwajalein, the public address system came to life aboard Lieutenant Paul C. Smith's transport, the USS *Wharton*. "Now hear this, now hear this," announced a disembodied voice. "We have just received word that a successful landing has been made by American and British forces on the beaches of Normandy on the continent of Europe."[4] There was a brief moment of complete silence, recalled Smith. Then hundreds of Marines crowding the deck in the moonlight rose to their feet and cheered.

The reaction was similar on Sergeant Alvin Josephy's transport, the *Crescent City*. "The men went out on deck and whooped and cheered and clapped each other on the back" before gradually returning to card games and bull sessions. Their enthusiasm sprang at least in part from self-interest, admitted Josephy. The general feeling was that once Germany was defeated, the troops in Europe would be sent over to help finish the job in the Pacific, and then everyone could go home. "Perhaps this was a selfish way to look at it," he observed, "but it was realistic."[5]

They were well out to sea when an official announcement put an end to the speculation about their own destination: the target was Guam.

The Japanese continued to anticipate that the next American push would be into the Palaus. They were about to be rudely disabused of that expectation as Admiral Raymond Spruance moved to secure air superiority over the Marianas. With only four days to go before the Saipan assault, Task Force 58 approached to within 192 miles of Guam and at 1300 hours began launching fighters and torpedo bombers to pound Saipan, Rota, Tinian, and Guam. Planes from *Hornet*, *Belleau Wood*, and *Yorktown* were assigned to hit the airfields on Guam. A May 27 intelligence evaluation estimated there were seventy-eight planes at Guam, mostly fighters along with a handful of bombers.[6]

Arriving over Guam, Fighting Squadron 24 leader Lieutenant Commander E. M. Link Jr. saw no enemy aircraft in the air as he led two divisions of *Belleau Wood* Hellcats through holes in the clouds to strafe Tiyan Airfield, referred to in American documents as "Agana Airfield." The attack caught at least eight twin-engine bombers and one fighter parked on the field. "Anti-aircraft fire, medium and heavy, was intense and often accurate," reported Link. Four Zeros suddenly appeared as Link pulled up from a second run at the field. One of them got onto Link's tail but spewed smoke, fell off, and spun into the water as it was promptly riddled by a trailing Hellcat. Another enemy fighter was shot down near an unfinished airfield north of Tiyan, crashing into the trees without burning.

The third division of *Belleau Wood* Hellcats, led by Lieutenant R. F. Ross, went after Orote Airfield, strafing the runway and shooting up at least one fighter and an unidentified twin-engine plane on the ground. Joining up with seven other Hellcats, they took out after five Zeros passing overhead at about twelve thousand feet. The Zeros disappeared into cloud cover, then reemerged to dive on the Hellcats. Ross fired two bursts at one of the Zeros from dead astern. The Zero smoked, burst into flames, and spun into the sea.[7]

A bigger melee was developing over Tiyan Field where sixteen Hellcats from *Hornet*'s Fighting Squadron 2 (VF-2) ran into an estimated twenty-five Japanese fighters, all colored "reddish brown with red sun [insignia]," pilots reported. Squadron commander William A. ("Bill") Dean and his "Rippers" claimed twenty-three kills, including four credited to Dean himself, but lost Lieutenant Junior Grade Howard B. Duff Jr., whose Hellcat was hit by antiaircraft fire over the airfield. Duff brought the damaged plane down in the water north of Orote. "He made a beautiful water landing," reported Lieutenant Junior Grade Daniel A. Carmichael Jr., who watched from above as Duff clambered out of the sinking plane and inflated his life jacket. Flying protective cover for his downed mate, Carmichael suddenly saw a Zero coming at him. "I pulled up in a chandelle as he leveled off and he rolled across in front of me," he reported. "I shot at him from an altitude of 1500 feet, full deflection, at 9 o'clock. He burned when he hit the water."

As Carmichael and Lieutenant Arthur Van Haren Jr. continued to circle Duff, more Zeros materialized. The two Rippers knocked down three of them. Lieutenant L. E. Doner knocked down two more, including a Zero that nearly bagged him first with an overhead run. "He came in from 3,000 feet. . . . I whipped to the left and the tail of my plane was shot up. I had a large hole in my right aileron and something came through the cockpit enclosure. He came in underneath and I nosed in under him and followed him in a climbing turn. Only three guns on the left side were firing. I ran out of ammunition just as he burned and went in," reported Doner of his narrow escape.

In the process of fighting off the Zeros, they lost track of Duff down in the water. Carmichael searched for ten minutes and even returned after the postattack rendezvous to make one more check, but there was no sign of the twenty-six-year-old Pennsylvanian. Duff was listed as missing in action and eventually, in 1946, as killed in action.

Hornet's Rippers saw more action over Guam later in the day when Lieutenant Commander L. E. Harris led another strike on the Tiyan and Orote airfields. Eight interceptors swooped down on them from eleven thousand feet. One made the mistake of pulling up over Harris after making a pass at another Hellcat. Harris got on his tail, "gave him a squirt and he blew up." Lieutenant Junior Grade Franklin T. Gabriel had opened up on one Zero when another made a high-side run on him, pulling him off target. When Gabriel turned into the newcomer, the pilot veered away and attempted a wingover, but to no avail. Gabriel shot him down. He then proceeded to knock down the first plane, following with a run on yet a third Zero from the three o'clock position. "It started to smoke and headed straight toward the water," he reported. "I don't know what became of it as there were two more circling me at the time."

Lieutenant Richard J. Griffin claimed two kills. The first was a Zero flying only six hundred feet off the deck. "It was in a turn at the time. I shot and nosed out as flames gutted from its starboard wing," he reported. "It went into a cloud, came out burning and then went into the water from 400 feet." Griffin followed up on a fighter that appeared to be running from another aerial scrap. "I made a full power run from 6 o'clock firing from 800 feet and closed to 70 feet. He smoked, and, as I rolled over his tail, popped his canopy and bailed out," said Griffin.

In another low-level encounter, Ensign Ross F. Robinson latched onto the tail of a Zero only eight hundred feet off the water and stayed on him for fifteen to twenty seconds—an eternity in dogfighting. "I started him smoking from 6 o'clock. As I got to him, I saw he was burning. I got within 40 feet and then overshot, and as I pulled alongside, I saw the pilot was dead in the cockpit," reported Robinson. "He burst into flames and burned as he went in."

Hornet's Rippers claimed ten kills in the melee, including what they identified as a Nakajima JIN twin-engine Irving but may have actually been a G4M Betty medium bomber. Painted brown with prominent red rising-sun devices, the enemy aircraft was fitted with a radar assembly that looked like wing floats. The Irving/Betty appeared about to make a run on the rescue submarine USS *Stingray* stationed just offshore to pick up downed pilots but broke off when Lieutenant Junior Grade John L. Banks intervened. Closing to within seven hundred feet after a forty-mile chase, Banks gave it a burst that drew flames from the starboard engine. The pilot flew on, making gradual turns in an effort to give the rear gunner a chance to catch the pursuing Hellcat with his 20mm cannon. Banks dropped down below the tail and shot out the port engine, whereupon the plane went into a slow wingover from fifty feet and crashed into the water.[8]

The Navy pilots were not impressed with their opponents, none of whom demonstrated any teamwork or effective defensive or offensive tactics. "Most of them engaged in acrobatics, many times low over the water. At least one was seen to do a split-S at such low altitude that he dove into the sea," observed a pilot summary. Filling out the aircraft action report section marked "Apparent Enemy Mission(s)," one self-assured wag from *Belleau Wood* responded, "Self-preservation."[9]

USS *Stingray* spent June 12 on "lifeguard" duty off Guam's west coast, charged with rescuing any pilots forced to parachute or make offshore water landings. Skippered by thirty-two-year-old Lieutenant Commander Sam C. Loomis Jr., *Stingray* was on her eleventh patrol—her second under Loomis, who had taken command of the Salmon-class submarine the previous November. Loomis had finished at the bottom of his class at the Naval Academy but proved to be a very capable submariner during his previous tour as executive officer on USS *Snook*. "There are some people who are smart who just can't achieve academically," observed a close friend. "You run into these people. Loomis was one of them."[10]

During *Stingray*'s previous patrol, also to the Marianas, she had sunk a Japanese cargo ship and later had a narrow escape of her own when she was apparently targeted by another sub that fired two torpedoes. One passed one hundred feet in front and the other ran down *Stingray*'s starboard side without making contact. Loomis evaded and never did identify the source of the attack. After a hiatus at Pearl Harbor, *Stingray* went back to sea on May 26. Despite experiencing problems with the engines and periscope, Loomis arrived off Guam on June 11 and took up station as the rescue sub.

The crew didn't have long to wait. The next morning they picked up Lieutenant John M. Searcy, a Hellcat pilot with *Hornet*'s VF-2. Half drowned and suffering from shock and cuts about the head, the twenty-six-year-old Texan was unable to hang on to the line thrown over to him. Lieutenant E. G. Weed finally jumped into the water and hauled the bedraggled pilot back to the sub. When Searcy became more conversational, it turned out he had been one of the pilots who chased off the Irving/Betty that had gone after *Stingray* the day before.

Loomis spent the rest of the morning on the surface keeping a wary eye on what appeared to be Japanese Betty bombers flying in over the northern end of the island, occasionally taking the sub down when one got too close. But at 1300, *Stingray* was on the move again as a report came in that a Helldiver had made a water landing inside Apra Harbor. At 1353 the starboard lookout sighted an object on the water about two miles away. Heading toward it at full speed, they found two men in a yellow rubber raft. "Both men were waving their sail, shining a mirror, and, in general, doing all they could to attract our attention," observed Loomis. The two castaways were dive-bomber pilot Lieutenant Richard E. James and Aviation Radioman Second Class David Hamblin Smith from *Yorktown*'s Bombing Squadron 1 (VB-1). Shot down in the harbor, they had climbed into their raft and somehow managed to sail out to the open sea without attracting the attention of the Japanese.

A third rescue call at 1652 ended less happily. *Stingray* was alerted that a pilot had parachuted into a cove just south of Orote Peninsula. Records indicate the pilot was twenty-four-year-old Lieutenant Junior Grade Isaac J. Snowden of Jonesboro, Arkansas, a Hellcat jockey flying off *Belleau Wood*. Struck by antiaircraft fire during an attack on Orote Field, Snowden's fighter caught fire, and he bailed out over the water just south of the peninsula. He appeared to survive the bailout but failed to deploy his life raft, which may have been lost or damaged. Three fighters circling over his location eventually lost sight of him.

As *Stingray* arrived on the scene, she came under fire from Japanese shore batteries on Orote. The first rounds fell short, but another salvo straddled the sub, and Loomis took her under. Coming up to forty-one feet, he used the sub's VHF radio to contact his "chickens"—friendly air cover—who told him they could see dye from the marker all aircrews carried in their life vests but were unable to make out the pilot. Loomis brought the sub closer in but realized the dye marker was so near to shore that he wouldn't be able to turn around even if he could reach it. "We were 1.4 miles SW of Orote Point, the sun had set, our 'chickens' were leaving and neither of them had seen [the] pilot in water. . . . [A]fter careful inspection, we decided to get out of here," he reported. Snowden was never found.

Loomis surfaced after dark. No other pilots were reported down in the water, but *Stingray* spent the night patrolling off the west coast, firing rockets at various intervals just in case. There were no responses. By sunrise at 0554, carrier attacks on Guam's airfields and military facilities had already resumed. At 0946 Loomis was alerted that a Hellcat pilot had parachuted into the water about five hundred yards off Agana after his plane was hit by antiaircraft fire.

The downed pilot was Ensign Donald C. ("Red") Brandt, a twenty-year-old Ohioan from *Hornet*'s VF-2. Brandt had been flying at thirteen thousand feet when a shell exploded alongside his Hellcat, riddling the aircraft and tossing it fifty feet through the air. Brandt coaxed the damaged fighter out over Agana Bay and bailed out at about ten thousand feet just before the plane exploded. His parachute opened but had apparently been sloppily packed. "They had the straps on wrong and I came down sideways and broke all my ribs," he recalled. Upon hitting the water, he was able to cut his way out of the harness, but the wind took his chute along with his life raft, leaving him bobbing in the water with just his Mae West life vest. In addition to broken ribs, he had a deep slash across his left palm and was dangerously close to the Japanese-occupied shore. He spent a lonely two hours bobbing around in his life jacket before an American Helldiver pilot spotted him and dropped him a life raft.

A covering plane radioed *Stingray* that he was circling the downed pilot despite intense antiaircraft fire. Loomis asked if the pilot had drifted any further from shore. The reply came that he was still only about five hundred yards from the beach and not making much headway. Another pilot, apparently not realizing he was talking on an open channel, piped up, "Don't tell them that; they'll never go in." Immediately afterward, a skeptical Loomis received assurances that the downed pilot was at least a mile off the beach and drifting nicely toward the open sea.

Still on the surface, *Stingray* arrived off Agana at 1227. Greeted by a shell that splashed down about four hundred yards off the sub's starboard beam, Loomis promptly took her down, watching through the periscope as two more shells splashed down about two hundred yards ahead of the sub. A radio message indicated the downed pilot had managed to retrieve a raft and climb aboard. A few minutes later Loomis spotted him dead ahead.

Watching from shore, the Japanese could also see the raft, as well as the periscope of the approaching sub. A burst of what was probably small arms fire kicked up little sprays of water near the pilot. Peering through the scope, Loomis could see Brandt ducking down in the raft, not that the thin rubber sides would provide much protection against a bullet.

Brandt sighted the periscope and started waving. Unable to surface and expose the sub to the enemy shore batteries, Loomis approached with about ten feet of the No. 1 periscope and three feet of the No. 2 scope protruding above the surface. Brandt and his fellow *Hornet* pilots had been briefed just the day before on this type of situation: if the sub was unable to surface, it would approach with its periscopes up. The downed pilot was instructed to loop a line from his raft around the scope. The sub would then tow him away from danger.

Loomis made his first pass, but Brandt showed no signs of having a line ready as the sub went by. As Loomis turned for a second attempt, three shells splashed off *Stingray*'s port quarter. Twenty minutes later another shell exploded close aboard, followed almost immediately by another. It was now 1352. "Almost on top of pilot," reported the sub's log. "Now he's paddling away from scope. Missed."

As shells continued to fall around the sub, Loomis came around and tried again at 1453. The frustrated skipper noted in the log, "Pilot missed the boat again. On this try, he showed the first signs of attempting to reach periscope. Maybe shell fire made him think that a ride on a periscope might be all right after all. I am getting damned disgusted, plus a stiff neck and a blind eye." Word came that two Japanese swimmers had apparently gone into the water in an effort to get to Brandt before the sub could pick him up.

On the fourth try at 1516, Loomis practically ran the pilot down, and Brandt finally got a line onto the periscope. For the next hour *Stringray* towed him out to sea while Brandt "frantically signaled for us to let him up," observed Loomis. "His hand was badly cut and it must have been hard for him to hang on with one hand while bumping along in the whitecaps at 2 knots. However, at this stage of the game, I wasn't feeling one bit sorry for him."

Finally, safely out of range of shore batteries, Loomis surfaced and brought the young Texan aboard. Brandt said that during the first and third approaches he had been afraid the periscope was going to run him down so he tried to get out of the way and catch hold from behind, but he couldn't keep up. Loomis grudgingly conceded that the shock of getting blown out of the sky and then falling upside down in a parachute from ten thousand feet would be enough to addle anyone. "We're on speaking terms now, but after the 3rd approach on him, I was ready to make him captain of the head," he confided to the sub's log.[11]

Miles to the east, the invasion armada was gathering as the faster transports joined the LST group at the Kwajalein atoll staging area on June 8. Hundreds of ships crowded the huge lagoon. "When I saw all those ships anchored there, I didn't see how Japan could win the war," recalled tank crewman Harold R. Graham. "I never saw so many ships in all my life."[12] Four days later, while *Stingray* chased around after Ensign Brandt off the coast of Guam, the armada exited the lagoon in a seemingly endless procession and steamed westward toward an assembly area off Saipan.

The morning of June 15 all the planning came to its inevitable moment of truth as the 2nd and 4th Marine Divisions of the Northern Landing Force choked down an early breakfast, boarded their amphibious tractors, and churned toward Saipan's hostile shore. Just over one hundred miles to the east, Admiral Conolly's Southern Landing Force, scheduled to assault Guam three days later, waited for developments. It was "another beautiful day," recalled Major Henry Aplington aboard LST 449. "We had been provided with the maps and frequencies in the event of being committed and on the conn of [LST] 449 my communicators had the radios up so we could follow the action ashore. Fighting came through as heavy and the progress slow but by later afternoon it was evident that 'the good guys' were winning."[13]

Admiral Spruance was confident enough by that afternoon to confirm W-Day for June 18. But as the Guam attack force began to head south for its own rendezvous with destiny, the situation ashore and at sea began to clarify—and the outlook darkened. Reports from Saipan indicated that Japanese resistance was much greater than expected. Heavy fighting was throwing Holland Smith's optimistic timetable into disarray and would soon force him to commit the 27th Infantry Division, the designated Expeditionary Troops Reserve.

Adding to Spruance's concerns, reports arrived that evening from U.S. submarines that the First Mobile Fleet under the command of Vice Admiral Jisaburo Ozawa was steaming from the Philippines toward Saipan. The Japanese had decided to confront the Fifth Fleet in what they hoped would be a decisive naval battle. Spruance estimated the Japanese carriers could be within striking distance as early as June 17. At 1100 hours on June 16, he sent a dispatch to Admiral Conolly postponing the Guam landing with a new date to be set as developments warranted. Conolly's task force, already steaming toward the objective, turned back and reassembled east of Saipan. Vindicated by events, Colonel (later General) Robert E. Hogaboom, who had warned of just such an eventuality, said later, "I think this could have been foreseen. I had predicted that we needed at least seven days."[14]

Meanwhile, the preinvasion bombardment at Guam had already gotten underway. Battleships *Pennsylvania* and *Idaho*, along with cruisers *Honolulu*, *San Francisco*, and *New Orleans*, accompanied by seven destroyers, began shelling coastal defense guns shortly after 0800. There was no return fire.

Aboard *Honolulu*, known to her crew as "the Blue Goose," a Chamorro mess boy who had been gazing anxiously shoreward toward his former home on Facpi Point, approached Lieutenant Commander Samuel Eliot Morison, a former Harvard professor tasked with recording and writing a history of wartime naval operations. The mess boy suggested that Morison, who obviously had important connections, might persuade the Bombardment Unit commander to allow the two of them to take a rubber boat ashore to inform his friends that the Americans were coming. Morison, viewing a visit ashore as "somewhat premature," politely demurred.[15]

In fact, it was even more premature than Morison imagined. The cruiser had just directed a salvo on a camouflaged 5-inch gun emplacement when the order came from the Bombardment Unit commander to cease fire, followed by a further order to "cease present operations" and return to Saipan.[16] Also breaking off was Underwater Demolition Team 3 (UDT-3), which had been preparing to conduct a reconnaissance of the landing beaches.

Waiting anxiously with the 38th Regiment by Guam's Agat beaches, Second Lieutenant Rai Imanishi made note of the shelling in his diary, observing that the enemy ships closed to within ten thousand meters and shelled the shore steadily for two hours. "Our positions were hit fourteen times," he wrote. "Fortunately, none was injured.... We think that at last the enemy will land tonight, and so we will observe strict alert all night. We were issued hand grenades and are waiting for the enemy to come." Instead, the seas the next morning remained empty, apparently much to the combative lieutenant's disappointment. "If the enemy is coming, let him come," he observed to his diary. "The spirit to fight to the death is high. We are anxiously waiting but nothing unusual has happened so far as dawn breaks."[17]

Lieutenant Imanishi would have to wait a bit longer for his personal fight to the death. During the forenoon, Spruance met with Admiral Turner and General Holland Smith aboard Turner's flagship *Rocky Mount* to hash out the change of plans forced by the approach of the Japanese fleet. Though the Guam landings were now on hold, the Southern Attack Force was to remain at sea 150 to 300 miles east of Saipan. This positioning should keep the ships safely removed from the forthcoming sea battle but leave the Guam troops available, should they be needed to reinforce the three divisions already committed to Saipan.

Thanks to the recovery of the Japanese Z Plan—an outline of enemy naval planning for a decisive battle—from a crashed plane in the Philippines the preceding April, Spruance had a reasonably good idea of what to expect from Admiral Ozawa. The Z Plan had been tweaked a bit in subsequent months and was now known as "A Go," but the basics remained the same. The Japanese intended to first hammer the U.S. fleet with land-based aircraft from their island airfields. Ozawa would then launch his carrier planes, which had greater range than the U.S. planes, from a distance that would keep his carriers beyond Spruance's reach. The carrier planes would attack the U.S. flattops, then proceed to airfields on Guam, Tinian, and Rota, where they would refuel, rearm, and resume the attack. What Ozawa did not know was that Spruance's fighter sweeps over Guam, Tinian, Saipan, and Rota had decimated Japanese land-based airpower. That pounding would continue over the next few days in an effort to destroy what was left of Japanese air forces and knock out the island airfields before the confrontation at sea.

An hour before sunset on June 17, as the Southern Attack Force's Tractor Group Three cruised two hundred miles east of Guam, the radar operator aboard the destroyer USS *Stembel* saw his scope suddenly light up. Unidentified aircraft—flying fast and very low—were approaching the formation from eleven miles out.

Stembel sounded general quarters and radioed the alarm to the rest of the group, at the same time racing at flank speed to interpose the ship between the bogies and the group's sixteen troop-carrying LSTs, nine LCIs (Landing Craft Infantry), and accompanying vessels. Skies were partly cloudy, but the intruders—identified as four fast-moving Nakajima B5N (Kate) torpedo bombers—were already in sight. While

U.S. reports indicate the planes were Kates—and one ship's crew said "consensus of opinion was one Val and two Kates"—Japanese sources indicate the raid, launched from Truk four hundred miles away, consisted of five later-model B6N (Jill) torpedo planes and one J1N (Irving) night fighter.[18] From a practical standpoint, it didn't matter much. Both Kates and Jills were crewed by a pilot, navigator/bombardier, and radioman/gunner and carried a 17.29-foot-long, 1,870-pound Type 91 torpedo slung underneath the fuselage.

Racing in toward the massed ships, the Japanese pilots must have thought they'd hit the jackpot. The lead plane peeled off and headed for *Stembel*, but as the destroyer opened up with her guns, the Japanese pilot either became confused or lost his nerve. Dropping his torpedo from four thousand yards out, he veered off to port. The destroyer swung parallel to the anticipated track, and the torpedo missed along the port side.

The remaining torpedo planes headed for the *Agenor*, a 328-foot-long landing craft repair ship, crewed by 22 officers and 231 men. Steaming along about eight hundred yards from *Agenor*, the crew of LCI(G) 468, an LCI fitted out as a gunboat, commenced firing with the vessel's 40mm and 20mm mounts. One Jill launched a torpedo apparently aimed at *Agenor*, then turned away, smoking heavily before crashing into the sea. A second Jill appeared along the same track. LCI(G) 468 took it under fire. "At this time tracers were observed coming very near the ship and a few seconds later the ship was hit by fire either from another ship in the formation or from the machine guns of the attacking plane," noted the ship's after-action report.[19] Three men were wounded, including the skipper, twenty-seven-year-old Lieutenant Junior Grade George D. Mayo, on the bridge. Gun crews aboard LCI(G) 468 and nearby LCI(L) 471 continued to fire at the torpedo plane, "knocking pieces of his fuselage off."[20] Flames broke out along the fuselage, but the plane kept coming. Boring in only fifty feet or less off the water, the Jill released its torpedo at a range of about 150 yards.

Aboard LST 449, Major Aplington watched events unfold. "When the general alarm went [off], I bolted down the passageway and out into the starboard deck to see all AA firing and low in the water, a Japanese releasing his torpedo, seemingly headed directly for 449," he remembered. "At that moment LCI(G) 468, a bone in her teeth, guns firing, and signal flags streaming, surged between us and the torpedo." Apparently intended for *Agenor*, the torpedo instead smashed into LCI(G) 468's starboard side. The 518-pound high-explosive warhead erased fifty feet of the LCI's bow along with the gun crews, knocking out all guns with the exception of the aft 20mm. "There was a flash and 468 was dead in the water, nothing forward of her superstructure, the flags burned remnants, and dead sailors hanging over the gun tubs," recalled Aplington.[21] Lieutenant Paul C. Smith witnessed the massive explosion from his vantage point aboard LST 220. "The whole forward part of the craft blew skyward, and I saw the forward gun crew flung into the air like limp dolls, with arms and legs askew," he said.[22] Debris showered down on nearby LSTs, fatally wounding a nineteen-year-old Marine private first class aboard LST 207 six hundred yards away from the explosion.

LCI(L) 471 continued firing as the Jill turned away spewing smoke. The crew lost sight of the plane as they turned their attention to yet another Jill boring in on them. "This one came in on our starboard bow and we fired on him with all starboard guns," noted the ship's after-action report.

> He was coming in low, 50 or 60 feet off the water, speed about 150 knots and just off our starboard bow. He launched an 18-inch torpedo about 100 feet out from us and slightly forward of bow, missing us by about twenty-five feet. Evidently this was aimed at Agenor also, but it cleared her. Just as the Jap launched his torpedo, our guns blew out a large section of his fuselage; we kept firing into him and as he crossed our bow a great ball of flame issued from beneath his fuselage, accompanied by a shower of debris. He banked off and tried to gain altitude, but was very wobbly. He continued across the bow of the Agenor badly afire, but crashed and exploded in the sea about 3,000 yards to port of the formation.[23]

It was all over in six minutes, from 1759 to 1805. Three Japanese torpedo bombers had been shot down, though who shot what in those few chaotic minutes was unclear. "I remember the results that came from different ships and if you added them all up there were thirty-nine planes shot down," recalled Lieutenant Jim Gallo, a Marine platoon commander.[24] LCI(G) 468 remained afloat, but casualties were severe: one officer and one man were known dead; one officer and twelve men were missing and presumed dead; and four men had been wounded. Most of the casualties had been manning gun stations on the forecastle when the torpedo struck. Among the dead and missing were two seventeen-year-old sailors: Seaman Second Class Dewey Andrew Hayhurst of Portales, New Mexico, and Seaman Second Class Lynn Shields Long Jr. of Jasper, Alabama, both of whom had joined the Navy only six months before. Lynn Long's parents were informed on July 11 that their son had "died from wounds received in action." Dewey Hayhurst's family would have to wait another year before receiving formal confirmation that their son, first declared missing, was dead.[25]

At least one Japanese air crew survived to report that the attack had succeeded in sinking "thirteen transports and left one destroyer listing heavily."[26] In fact, the only casualty was LCI(G) 468. The ship was taken in tow by the USS *Holly* and salvage work began, but it soon became apparent that the damage was too extensive to be repaired with the facilities at hand. On the afternoon of June 18, LCI(G) 468 was cast off and sunk by gunfire from USS *Stembel*.

＿＿＿＿＿

Heavy ground fighting continued on Saipan on June 19 as Admiral Spruance braced for the arrival of Admiral Ozawa's First Mobile Fleet. On Guam, both Japanese airfields were a beehive of activity during the morning. Despite U.S. hopes, days of attacks on the fields had failed to knock them completely out of action. "The bombings became so routine that the Japanese had us sleep at the airfield," recalled Ben Blaz, who had been conscripted to work on the field. "Once the planes departed, they had us out filling in the bomb craters the Americans had left behind. The field was all dirt and crushed coral, so that was simple."[27]

Atsuo Takeda's Fourth Weather Unit rushed to complete a large shelter about one hundred meters from their barracks. Soldiers and islanders mixed cement and carried sandbags all day in the extreme heat. Supervisors berated anyone who slowed down, often slapping them in the face by way of encouragement. Tiyan Airfield was a cloud of dust under the constant attacks. Black smoke billowed from burning oil tanks at the navy yard. "As a plane fell on fire, we were pleased until we found out it was a Zero fighter," said Takeda. "There were only thirty planes on Guam, but almost all of them were destroyed by that time."[28] A Japanese infantry lieutenant expressed his frustration to his diary, writing, "It is especially pitiful that we cannot control the air. We can only clench our fists in anger and watch."[29]

As their situation deteriorated, the Japanese began to see spies everywhere. Twenty-eight-year-old Magdalena San Nicolas was working as a forced laborer clearing fields when the workers were summoned with the call *Itsumari*, the Japanese order to assemble. They gathered near a mango tree where three Chamorros, hands tied behind their backs, waited beside a large, freshly dug hole under the watchful eye of Japanese soldiers with fixed bayonets. "We were warned that whomever whines, cries, or calls out, we'd all be killed," said Magdalena. Eleven-year-old Juan Baza was also present. "Everything was dark, black. I felt so hot," he recalled. "All I could see was these three men. I was so scared."[30]

Permitted to say a few words, one of the Chamorro prisoners indicated that he and his two comrades had been accused of spying. "If I must die, let it be," he added resignedly, "but God knows I am not guilty of any crime."[31] One of the captives began to recite the Lord's Prayer in Chamorro as they were forced to their knees with their heads extended.

"The *taicho* [leader] then splashed some water on his sword, wiped the water off and then slashed it against the neck of one of the men," remembered Doris Untlan, watching with the other workers. "He immediately moved to the second man and then to the third. The third victim's neck was not completely severed, but several Japanese moved in and pushed the bodies into the grave."[32]

Once casting themselves as friends and mentors, the Japanese were beginning to careen out of control.

CHAPTER 8

TURKEY SHOOT

Out at sea the morning of June 19—on what would have been W+1 according to the original Guam invasion schedule—Admirals Raymond Spruance and Jisaburo Ozawa were moving toward what the Japanese hoped would be the decisive battle of the war. Spruance had yet to locate the approaching Japanese fleet, but there was little question that a confrontation was imminent.

At 0540, still fifteen minutes before sunrise, Task Force 58 radars picked up an increase in air activity over Guam, ninety miles away. Four F6F Hellcats from *Belleau Wood* were dispatched to have a look. Arriving over Orote at 0600, the fighters, led by Lieutenant Collin I. Oveland, found the airfield buzzing with activity. As anti-aircraft fire blossomed toward him, Oveland spotted four Zeros maneuvering to hit the Hellcats from above and behind. "Skunks!" he exclaimed over the radio, yanking his F6F into a tight turn.

Racing at the Zeros head-on, Oveland singled out one of the fighters and squeezed his gun button. The enemy pilot snapped into an aileron roll that ended when the plane smashed into the water below. Lieutenant Junior Grade Rodney C. Tabler nailed another fighter that went straight in, but a fresh swarm of Zekes appeared as the Hellcats regrouped. Oveland evaded one by diving away at four hundred knots and radioed the task force for help.[1] It was his good luck that fighters from USS *Cabot*'s Fighting Squadron 31 (VF-31) were only ten miles northwest of his position. Eight Hellcats responded and proceeded to knock down six Zekes, led by division leader Lieutenant Charles H. Turner. The twenty-six-year-old Floridian started by setting a Zeke on fire, prompting the pilot to bail out. He then sent two others into the ocean trailing smoke.

After a brief hiatus, things heated up again as more enemy aircraft were detected approaching Guam shortly after 0800. Fifteen *Hornet* and *Yorktown* fighters were already on the scene with more soon on the way. Eight Hellcats from *Belleau Wood*'s Fighting Squadron 24 (VF-24) were bounced by about fifteen Zeros near Orote forty-five minutes later, but the Japanese got the worst of it, losing seven planes in the melee. Lieutenant Junior Grade Robert H. Thelen of VF-24 knocked down three, burning the first in a head-on run. Another fell victim to Lieutenant Junior Grade L. R. Graham, who gave him a burst from dead astern. The pilot catapulted out as the plane exploded and somehow managed to pull his rip cord and drift down just offshore.[2]

Twelve *Bunker Hill* Hellcats arrived over Orote Field at 0920 to find Japanese planes taking off. Lieutenant Junior Grade Lloyd P. Heinzen and three of his mates rolled in from sixteen thousand feet, strafing the runways from five thousand feet to as low as five hundred feet before pulling up. Caught in a burst of fire while taking off, one Zeke went into a ground loop and crashed in a cloud of smoke and dust. As the Hellcats pulled out, Heinzen spotted what he identified (possibly erroneously) as a Mitsubishi L4M1 navy twin-engine transport plane and a lone Zeke approaching from the southwest end of the field. He made a run on the Zeke but overshot. His wingman, twenty-one-year-old Lieutenant Junior Grade Edward J. Dooner of Narberth, Pennsylvania, compensated with a burst that sent the Zeke plummeting into a cluster of parked aircraft on the field below. Pulling up, Heinzen atoned with a long burst into the transport, sending it crashing into the runway. He reported,

> We soon found ourselves at this low altitude with Zekes and Hamps[3] all around us; many of them were carrying belly tanks. I got on the tail of a Hamp and started fires in both its wing roots. It did a split-S and I lost track of it as I soon learned that a Zeke was on my tail. I made a sharp left turn and saw tracers going past my port wing. I immediately reversed the turn only to have two Hamps make a run on me from 1 o'clock above. Only by turning into these two planes and scissoring with Dooner did we manage to drive them away. I then made a 60 degree run on a Zeke which was carrying a belly tank. The Zeke did a split-S with flaps down at 1,000 feet. I pulled up into a wing-over and got into a position astern of the Zeke and managed to explode it with a short burst.

Dooner radioed that he had taken hits in the oil line and gas tank. He and Heinzen started back toward the carrier, but Dooner couldn't make it. He headed down for a water landing. "His Hellcat either exploded or broke up when he landed and he did not get out," reported Heinzen. Heinzen circled the spot for several minutes but saw no sign of Dooner, who was subsequently listed as killed in action.

The presence of belly tanks as noted by Heinzen indicates that many of the arriving planes were staging through to Guam from airfields on Iwo Jima, Yap, and

Truk to participate in the fleet confrontation. Flying with Lieutenant Commander Elbert ("Go Get 'Em") McCuskey's division, Lieutenant Junior Grade Harry Brownscombe ducked into a cloud after an attack by two Zekes damaged the outboard gun on his port wing. While he was preoccupied, the other three pilots in his division knocked down four Hamps, including one that flew into the side of a hill and exploded.

Attempting to rejoin the others, Brownscombe found his way blocked. There seemed to be Zekes everywhere. "As he was ducking in and out of clouds, he noticed a Zeke below him and started a high-side run," reported McCuskey. "As he was about to shoot, another Zeke, which was scissoring with the first one, presented [him] with a head-on shot. This enemy VF was hit in the engine and in the wing roots. It rolled over on its back and the pilot bailed out." Brownscombe ducked back into the clouds and spotted another Zeke. Closing in, he opened fire from astern. The Zeke rolled over on its back, caught fire, and dived into the ocean.[4]

By 1010, the massacre was largely over. *Lexington* fighters arrived over Orote as the air battle ended and had to content themselves with strafing planes parked along the edges of the runway. Descending through the ever-present antiaircraft fire, they shot up several, but none would burn, possibly because they had been degassed.

Contrary to the wishes of his more aggressive carrier officers, Admiral Spruance had elected to take a defensive posture as the First Mobile Fleet drew near. Viewing the protection of the Saipan beachhead as his primary responsibility and unsure of the exact position of the Japanese fleet, he waited for Ozawa to make the first move. He did not have to wait long.

At 0730 a Japanese reconnaissance plane spotted American carriers 380 miles from the approaching First Mobile Fleet. At 0825, the Japanese carriers began launching planes. At 0957, a radar operator aboard the battleship *Alabama* picked up bogies approaching from 140 miles out. At 1005 Admiral Marc Mitscher recalled his fighters from the aerial brawl over Guam and elsewhere, radioing "Hey Rube!" the age-old circus call to assemble. Dive-bombers and torpedo planes were launched and sent to the east where they would be out of the way, leaving the defense to the fighters.

Lieutenant Junior Grade Arthur Hawkins, a fighter pilot with USS *Cabot's* VF-31, joined the swarm of Hellcats scrambled to intercept the Japanese. "The first wave were mostly fighters; they came in ahead with the big fighter-bombers coming in later," he said. "It must have been a good flight of forty or fifty, some Judys, some bombers but not very many. Our division was vectored out to hit on that first wave. We were in perfect position about 3,000–4,000 feet above them. As they came in, we dove into them from above. My division accounted for thirteen airplanes on that particular hop. I got three. Everybody got three except one guy . . . who got four."[5]

The Japanese pilots seemed to have no formulated defense tactics. The bombers merely scattered, while the fighters made no particular effort to cover them. Forty-two out of sixty-nine Japanese planes in "Raid I," as the Americans came to call the first attack, failed to return to their carriers. Only three or four bombers managed to leak through the U.S. fighter screen. At 1049 a bomber scored a hit on the battleship *South Dakota*, killing twenty-seven men and wounding twenty-three but failing to knock the big ship out of action. It proved to be the only notable Japanese success of the day.

Ozawa followed the first aerial wave with three more. Raid II, made up of fifty-three Judy bombers, twenty-seven Jill torpedo bombers, and forty-eight Zeros, was launched beginning at 0856. They were picked up by U.S. radars at 1107 at a distance of about 115 miles. Hellcats tore into them: of the 128 planes launched, 97 never returned to Ozawa's carriers. Raid III, launched between 1000 and 1015 and consisting of forty-seven aircraft, was more fortunate. The bulk of the formation was directed to the wrong contact point; finding nothing, forty of them returned to their carriers. Seven others had the misfortune to run into a swarm of Hellcats from *Hornet*, *Yorktown*, and other carriers and were splashed.

Ozawa launched his last planes in Raid IV at 1030. Thirty Zeros, ten Zero fighter bombers, nine Judys, six Jills, and twenty-seven Vals lumbered off the flight decks and headed east. Guiding on a misreported contact, they failed to find the American flattops. Some headed back for their carriers and a few proceeded to Rota, but the majority—twenty Zekes, twenty-seven Vals, and two Jills—made for Guam. Nearing the island, they jettisoned their bombs and prepared to land. If they thought they had reached sanctuary, they were in for a rude awakening.

While the clash between the carriers unfolded in the skies over the Philippine Sea, the threat posed by Guam as an unsinkable "aircraft carrier" and potential refuge was not neglected by U.S. tacticians. Concerted efforts got underway to bomb the island's airfields out of commission as thirty-two *Hornet* and *Yorktown* dive-bombers were dispatched to attack the Orote and Tiyan airfields just before noon.

"AA fire at Agana [Tiyan] was medium, mostly 40mm from west of airfield," reported pilots. "Orote Field, however, was well defended with heavy and automatic fire especially from batteries at the east end of the field. A few destroyed planes were observed on both runways; no air opposition was encountered."[6]

The antiaircraft fire was bad enough. Lieutenant Stuart W. Roberts's Helldiver crashed while strafing Orote. Neither Roberts nor his gunner, Aviation Radioman First Class Walter O. Warmouth Jr., had a chance to get out. Lieutenant Junior Grade Oscar W. Diem's dive-bomber was riddled so badly that his wounded radioman had to crawl into the aft fuselage to manually lower the tail hook. They made it back to *Yorktown*, but the plane was a total wreck. Deck crews pushed it over the side.[7]

As this action was developing, Lieutenant Commander Ralph Weymouth of *Lexington*'s dive-bomber squadron, VB-16, tired of burning gas while cutting useless circles in the sky beyond the action, decided to let his pilots get rid of their bombs over Orote Field only sixty or so miles away. Shortly before 1300 he took his dive-bombers, along with about a dozen SBD Douglas dive-bombers and nine Avengers from *Enterprise* and an escort of ten Hellcats, toward Guam. "After about two or three hours [circling during the morning], we received a message to go on in and drop our bombs on the fields on Guam, the Orote Peninsula," recalled Jim Ramage, leader of *Enterprise*'s Bombing Squadron 10 (VB-10). "We were to get down there and see if we couldn't keep the field at least temporarily knocked out in case some of the Japs got through and tried to land."[8] Weymouth's dive-bombers were carrying one-thousand-pound armor-piercing bombs intended for sinking ships. The effect on the runways was disappointing but certainly more productive than dropping the ordnance in the ocean. The five-hundred-pound general-purpose bombs with four-to-five-second delay fuses carried by the Avengers had better effect, deeply cratering the coral-surfaced runways.

Toward midafternoon the cruiser *Montpelier* received word to launch its two SOC Seagull seaplanes to rescue the crew of a downed dive-bomber off Orote Point. Though typically used for naval gunfire spotting and observation, the small two-seater biplanes, fitted with a central float that allowed them to land and take off on the water, were also ideal for pilot rescue. *Montpelier* catapulted her SOCs at 1500. Escorted by a pair of Hellcats from *Enterprise*, the two unarmed floatplanes spotted Lieutenant G. L. Marsh and his rear gunner, Aviation Radioman Second Class W. L. Lindsey, floating in a raft about two miles north of Orote Point. Their SBD had been hit in the engine by antiaircraft fire while bombing Orote Field, but Marsh managed to coax it out to sea before ditching.

Facing rough seas with six- to eight-foot swells and winds of sixteen to seventeen knots, the SOCs—call signs "Ace" and "King"—would likely not be able to take off again once they set down, but the two pilots decided to try it. They got down without mishap and picked up Marsh and Lindsey but, as feared, were unable to get back up off the water. Ace finally started taxiing back to the ships some twenty miles out to sea, while King continued futile attempts to get airborne. Soon the two Seagulls were five miles apart.

The two Hellcats flying cover split up as the SOCs separated. Lieutenant Henry C. Clem, executive officer of *Lexington*'s Fighting Squadron 10, stayed with Ace, while Lieutenant Commander R. E. Harmer watched over King. At this point, things went from bad to worse as a Japanese Zero suddenly swept down on Ace, machine guns chattering. The first strafing run missed the plane by about ten feet as the SOC pilot put out a desperate call for help.

Watching over King, Harmer heard Ace's plea for help and saw the enemy pilot completing his strafing run. As the Zero banked for another try, four Hellcats dove on it, but the agile enemy fighter pulled up in a steep climb. One of the F6F pilots made the mistake of trying to match the climb. It was Clem, who should have known better. As Harmer watched, the Hellcat stalled out. The Zero pilot executed a quick wingover, made a head-on run on the Hellcat, and sent it plummeting into the water. Ace broke in on the radio, "They got one of our boys."

Harmer tried to catch up as the Zero pulled out and ran for Guam. He managed to get in one burst from extreme range. The Zero smoked, but Harmer couldn't close and finally turned back to the SOCs. There was an oil slick where Clem went in, but no sign of the exec. There were, however, plenty of Zeros in the area, a number of which continued to express an inordinate interest in the two water-bound SOCs. Eight miles away, Ensign Wendell Twelves, a Hellcat pilot with Fighting Squadron 15 (VF-15) on USS *Essex*, heard one of the SOCs calling for help. "They were being strafed by two Zeros," recalled Twelves—known to his shipmates as "Doz," as in dozen. "He wanted immediate help from any fighters in the area," said Twelves. "The man was scared. I could hear the desperation in his voice."

Twelves gunned his Hellcat toward the SOCs. "Things had become very busy," he recalled. "The sky was a turmoil of battle. I could see a dozen or more planes turning and twisting in combat. Several were trailing smoke. The combat frequency was full of chatter." As he drew closer, he saw the Seagulls riding high on their single pontoons as they tried to escape out to sea. "I picked up a Zero on my next scan. It was ahead of and below me. Its dark wings glinted in the sun," he said. The Zero was lining up for a run on one of the SOCs.

Twelves had a sinking feeling as he realized he could not get there in time to stop it. The pilot of the Seagull gunned his engine and turned in a wide circle in an effort to throw off the enemy's aim as the Zero swept down. Twelves saw the water around the Seagull turn white under machine-gun fire. He arrived just as the Zero broke off. The Japanese pilot spotted him at four hundred yards, but it was too late; Twelves was already squeezing the trigger. His tracers curved into the other aircraft. Passing overhead, Twelves rolled to the left to set up for another run, but the Zero, only two hundred feet off the water, had already begun to burn. The nose dropped, and the enemy fighter hit the water at a shallow angle. "It skipped and cartwheeled endlessly, leaving a brilliant trail of fire on the water," remembered Twelves.

Turning back to check on the SOC, Twelves saw a second Zero maneuvering for a run on the desperately taxiing planes. He raced in and executed a wingover, which gave him a high-side deflection shot from above and behind the enemy pilot. "I fired several short bursts while sliding through to a stern position. I could see debris coming off the Zero as my bullets struck home." Heavy black smoke poured from the plane. Suddenly it rolled to the right and spiraled into the sea. "It hit the water hard," observed Twelves. "Then it was gone."

Before Twelves could congratulate himself, he found he had become a target himself as tracers streaked past his canopy. A Zero had jumped him from behind and was ranging in with its machine gun before pounding the Hellcat with the more lethal 20mm cannon. Too low to dive away, Twelves threw his fighter to the right and left with all his strength in an effort to throw off the Japanese pilot's aim. The tracers abruptly stopped, and Twelves twisted his head around to find that another Hellcat had taken the Zero under fire. The Zero was smoking and heading down. "A breath of air that I didn't know I was holding escaped my lungs," he admitted. He checked his gauges and looked the plane over for damage. There were numerous holes in the wings, but everything seemed to be in working order.[9] Down below, the two Seagulls were now motoring out to sea, unmolested. Hours later, the airmen were picked up by destroyers *Blaine* and *Anthony*, but the little biplanes, battered by the rough seas, could not be salvaged, and the destroyers did what the Japanese had failed to do and sank them with gunfire.

⌒

The aerial battles over Guam continued into late afternoon as surviving carrier aircraft from the Japanese Mobile Fleet and aerial reinforcements from as far away as Truk streamed in, most of them now low on fuel and looking for refuge. What they got was a massacre as waiting Hellcats tore them apart.

An after-action report summarizing feedback from USS *Cabot*'s fighter squadron observed, "The quality of enemy pilots engaging in this action seemed to vary from very good to very bad. Some Zeke pilots combined daring and good judgement with proficient flying technique, while others seemed confused and frightened."[10] Jim Ramage, flying with *Enterprise*'s VB-10, offered a less formal assessment. "Our F6Fs were right down at treetop level chasing these poor guys up and down the landscape," he observed. "I don't know if any Jap ever landed. I think there were some enemy pilots that either force landed or actually were so scared they just landed right in the water. It was a real massacre."[11]

Leading Fighting Squadron 25 fighters from USS *Cowpens*, Commander Gaylord B. Brown arrived to find a gaggle of Vals coming in with a few Zeros providing cover only twenty-five hundred feet above the torpedo bombers. "Forty enemy planes circling Orote field at Angels 3, some with wheels down," he radioed.[12]

At about this same time, Ensign Wilbur B. ("Spider") Webb of *Hornet*'s V-2 "Rippers" noticed a line of aircraft flying along Guam's mountainous spine, apparently headed toward Orote Field. The procession stretched as far as he could see. Like Brown, he estimated there were at least thirty or forty planes and maybe more. They were low, and many of them had their landing gear down. "What in the dickens are our planes doing that low over the island with their landing gear down?" he wondered to himself.

His confusion cleared as the formation drew closer. The mystery aircraft were Japanese Val dive-bombers, identifiable by their fixed landing gear, flying in divisions of three with Zeros overhead. As they began to bank away and assemble in a landing pattern for Orote Field, Webb could see the big red meatballs painted on the fuselages. The twenty-four-year-old Oklahoman, who had enlisted in the Navy in 1938, talked his way into pilot training, and been commissioned from the ranks, could hardly believe his eyes. It was a fighter pilot's dream. "I just thought, 'Boy, this is it. Make it good and get as many as you can before they know you're here,'" he recalled. As the Japanese seemed oblivious to their peril, he decided to just slide in with the traffic pattern like a wolf in a herd of sheep. As he started in, he flipped on his camera and gun switches, hit the gun chargers for the six .50-caliber Browning machine guns, and keyed his radio for a general broadcast that would forever enshrine him in Navy legend: "Any American fighter, I have forty Jap planes surrounded at Orote Airfield. I need some help!"

Seconds later, positioning himself less than twenty yards behind the first group of Vals, he dropped his landing gear and flaps to avoid overrunning the slow-moving dive-bombers, focused on the Val to the left, and squeezed his gun trigger. The dive-bomber promptly exploded. The two-man crew—pilot and backseat gunner—probably died without ever realizing their danger. Webb shifted to the center plane and fired again. "The top of the Val's vertical stabilizer disintegrated, and several bullets hit the rear seat gunner in the chest," he recalled. "Then the starboard wing of the aircraft came off and the plane exploded."

Webb slid in behind the third Val. By now his speed had started to build up again, and he was in danger of overrunning his intended victim. More alert than Webb's previous victims, the Japanese rear seat gunner opened up on the pursuing Hellcat with his machine gun. Webb held down the trigger on his .50s, but the Val flew stubbornly on. "Burn you bastard, burn you bastard," he chanted as his guns tore into the Japanese. Finally, the dive-bomber exploded, so close that the debris knocked several holes in Webb's Hellcat.

Webb pulled around and slipped in behind another trio of dive-bombers, again starting with the Val on the left. The backseat gunner was firing from less than thirty yards away—so close that Webb could make out the color of his flight suit, helmet, and skin. Suddenly, the enemy gunner seemed to just give up or perhaps he saw death coming for him. He put his hands up in front of his face an instant before several of Webb's .50-caliber slugs tore into him. The Val caught fire, and the pilot bailed out. They were only two hundred feet off the ground; Webb doubted the man's parachute had time to open. The middle Val in the group eluded him, but Webb went after the plane on the right and started him smoking. "Then his tail disintegrated and he just fell," he recalled.

Tracers floated past his Hellcat as ground gunners around the airfield sought revenge. Though Webb did not realize it, he had been taking hits. But by now a swarm of American fighters had descended on Orote. It seemed that everywhere he looked, there was a parachute or a burning plane falling from the sky. "By this time the Vals were gaining altitude and the Zekes came in above them," reported Webb. "I made a head-on run on one from below at 1,500 feet. I fired and saw pieces fly from the plane. It returned fire. A few seconds later a parachute was in the air and the plane crashed." As he came around, he saw another Val coming in twenty feet off the water. "I got on it from above at 7 o'clock. I fired at it and it started to smoke." As he pulled up, the Val plunged into the water.

Circling out to check his guns, Webb saw two more Vals making passes at the field. A Hellcat sent one slamming into Orote's runway. The second fled out over the harbor. "I went back and killed the rear seat man. The plane was smoking when I left and I pulled up quickly to clear the hill and didn't see it again."[13]

All in all, forty-one U.S. fighters participated in the debacle, claiming sixty kills and racking up at least thirty. Another nineteen enemy aircraft were damaged so badly by gunfire or rough landings on the cratered field as to be unserviceable. One Hellcat pilot from *Hornet* knocked down four Vals; then, out of ammunition, he made several dry runs on a low-flying torpedo bomber, intimidating the pilot into making a water landing. As he flew past the floating Val, he saw the pilot and gunner shaking their fists at him. Heading back to USS *Essex*, having downed seven enemy planes during the day, Commander Dave Campbell counted no less than seventeen oil slicks or fires within a one-mile radius of Apra Harbor where planes had gone in.

Unfortunately, the day ended on a dark note for *Essex*'s VF-15. On a sweep over Orote at 1825, squadron commander Charles W. Brewer and his wingman, Ensign Thomas Tarr, went low after some enemy planes descending toward the field. Brewer knocked one down for his fifth kill of the day, but it cost him his life. Zeros pounced on the pair from higher altitude and shot down both Hellcats. Also lost was twenty-three-year-old Ensign Thomas E. Hallowell from the *San Jacinto*, gunned down by two high-flying Zekes near Agana.

Spider Webb called it a day when his guns finally quit for good. Only then did he notice that his canopy was shot up, there were holes in his wings, his radio was out, and the cowling and windshield were covered with oil. Over one hundred holes were later counted in his Hellcat. Back at the carrier, Webb's gun camera film confirmed four victories. The camera had jammed after number four. The Navy gave him credit for six kills and two probables. His Grumman was so badly shot up, deck crews shoved it over the side.

As U.S. carrier pilots celebrated aboard ship that evening, the mood on Guam was understandably grim. A Japanese soldier wrote in in his diary, "The enemy, circling overhead, combed our airfield the whole day long. When evening came, our carrier bombers returned, but the airfield had just been destroyed by the enemy and they could not land. Having neither fuel nor ammunition the fifteen or sixteen planes were unable to land and had to crash. . . . It was certainly a shame. I was unable to watch dry-eyed. The tragedy of war was never so real."[14]

The clash of the carriers continued the next day as Spruance's pilots went after the First Mobile Fleet, but the decisive battle sought by the Japanese had effectively been fought on June 19. Admiral Ozawa lost two carriers to U.S. submarine attacks on

June 19 and a third to Spruance's dive-bombers and torpedo planes on June 20, but the greatest damage was done to Japanese naval aviation.

Japanese losses over the two days totaled approximately 426 planes and 445 aviators. An estimated 160 of those aircraft were knocked down over and around Guam. As Admiral Ozawa withdrew in defeat on the evening of June 20, Japanese naval air power had been thoroughly eviscerated and would never recover. Carriers without planes were little better than floating docks, or as the Japanese Combined Fleet chief of staff observed darkly, "The task force without planes was, as it were, a living corpse."[15] The one-sided debacle would go down in the history books as the Battle of the Philippine Sea, but to American naval aviators it would be forever known as "the Great Marianas Turkey Shoot."

CHAPTER 9

HURRY UP AND WAIT

Off to the east of Saipan, the Guam invasion force continued to wait. "The Pacific weather was perfect, day after beautiful day passed without event," recalled Major Henry Aplington. "The formation [was] seemingly motionless on the calm sea."[1] At night all ships were blacked out, with no lights permitted and no smoking allowed on deck, which was tough for cigarette addicts. "But it did make the tropical heavens clear and sparkling with the stars shining like diamonds," recalled machine gunner Joseph ("Joe") L. Frank, whose machine-gun squad was camped out on LST 125.[2]

Crowded into the transports and LSTs, the troops had little to do but lounge on deck, clean their weapons, engage in endless card games, or gaze out at the ocean and the surrounding ships. "I've been bored with life other times, but never that bad," admitted Corporal Stephen Marusky. "It was just wait, wait, all the time. We didn't know a damn thing. It was enough to drive a guy nuts."[3]

Early-morning calisthenics provided some exercise, with jumping jacks, deep knee bends, and running in place in an effort to keep the men in shape. For his part, Aplington occupied himself by reading and rereading Field Manual 7-20, titled *Rifle Battalion*, "refreshing its guidance in my mind"—a guidance, he observed, that "was no longer an academic exercise."[4] Commissioned in the Marines shortly after graduating from Princeton in 1940, the twenty-seven-year-old had served in regimental operations before being named to lead the 1st Battalion, 3rd Marines five months earlier. At Guam, his battalion was assigned to seize a key thumb of protruding high ground just inland from Red Beach 2, and he intended to be ready.

Just when that critical day would actually arrive remained uncertain. With the Japanese naval threat to Forager now eradicated, Admiral Chester Nimitz was anxious to get the Guam landings underway, but the continued tough ground fighting and heavy losses on Saipan argued for caution. It was abundantly clear that the original timetable calling for the invasion of Guam a mere three days after the Saipan landings had been optimistic in the extreme. A key concern now was the lack of immediately available reserves. The 27th Infantry Division, the designated floating reserve for the Saipan and Guam operations, had already been committed in its entirety at Saipan. The long-term area reserve, the 77th Infantry Division, was still in Hawaii. The Southern Attack Force was afloat within striking distance of Guam but had no available reserves and might itself be called upon should still more troops be needed to secure Saipan.

As the waiting continued, conditions aboard ship gradually deteriorated. The cargo-laden LSTs had not been intended as troop ships. "They were a curious and ungainly, slab-sided, craft, 316 feet long with a 50-foot beam, shallow draft for beaching, and two clamshell bow doors and a ramp," recalled a Marine officer.[5] Whereas a destroyer could crank out thirty-eight knots, the LSTs lumbered along at about nine or ten knots, leading to their nickname, "Large Slow Target." Built to accommodate 125 troops, most were now crowded with twice that many Marines on decks and in holds, packed in among equipment ranging from Jeeps, amphibious tractors, trucks, and trailers to stacked ammunition and fifty-five-gallon drums of high-octane gasoline. Topside, the ships looked like seagoing hobo camps, the decks festooned with tarps and shelter halves stretched overhead to provide the exposed passengers with some relief from the blazing sun and passing rain squalls. Cots and bedding lay strewn about wherever men could find a nook or flat place to lie down. "My bed was on top of two or three 50-gallon oil drums," said Sergeant Neil Stiles. "They were standing on end and that's where my bunk was. Guys were on the deck and anywhere you could find. . . . They had some tarps rigged to keep the sun off and the rain. But, for the most part, it was pretty miserable living."[6]

The sweltering troop compartments in the actual transports were as bad or worse. "The only words that can accurately describe the troop compartment of an attack transport, are 'sweat and stink,'" observed Corporal Dan Marsh.[7] Troops slept in canvas bunks stacked one over the other four or five high and about eighteen inches apart, so close that a man's nose practically brushed the bottom of the bunk above. "And it was hot in those places" recalled Private First Class James L. Swain. "The ventilation wasn't too good. Smelly. There was a lot of gambling going on: cribbage, black jack, hearts. Some reading, if you were able to get ahold of a book."[8]

Over-the-rail toilets had been set up to accommodate the troops on Marine Richard Zenger's LST. "They consisted of a water trough built of several halves of oil drums (halved lengthwise and welded together) with sea water running through under wooden seats spanning the drum halves," he remembered. Personal hygiene became problematic. "Bathing was to grab a bit of soap when it rained and try to get cleaned up in the tropical downpour," recalled Major Louis Metzger. "Invariably the rain stopped when one was all soaped up, which required the wash-down to be from a bucket of salt water. We had rashes and were sticky from salt water all the time."[9]

Assuming they were going immediately into combat, the men had brought little extra clothing, and their utilities began to show the wear and tear of dirt, sweat, and lack of laundry facilities. "Our laundry was tying our rather ragged uniforms to a line and towing them alongside the ship for a time, which at least got the smell of sweat out of them," said Metzger.[10] The officious captain of First Lieutenant Cord Meyer's LST issued a directive forbidding this practice on the unlikely grounds that the clothing could tear loose and form a trail leading Japanese submarines to the vessel. When Marines ignored the directive, the ship's captain ordered two of his sailors to take fire axes and cut the lines securing the laundry. "They had cut no more than two when the outraged Marines seized both sailors and threw them overboard," recalled Meyer. A destroyer picked them up, the captain retired to his cabin, and there was no more argument about Marine Corps laundering practices.[11]

Despite that unhappy incident, in most cases the Navy did what it could to keep the Marines as comfortable as circumstances allowed. One Marine officer recalled that when ice-cream mix ran low in his transport division, the Navy directed that the ice cream be served to Marines only. Nevertheless, there were lines for everything from the heads to meals. "Up to two hours could be spent running all of us through the [chow] line," recalled PFC Joseph Frank. The mob waiting to use the head was "as bad as being raised with a couple of sisters by a widow mother and a maiden aunt," he joked.[12]

The tedium aboard Joseph Frank's LST was briefly interrupted when a Marine accidently set off a smoke grenade he had been playing around with. Under the assumption that there was a fire in the hold, bedlam reigned until the grenade finally expended itself. The careless Marine earned himself fifteen days on bread and water with a full ration every third day. A more deeply mourned casualty of military authority was a store of raisin jack some enterprising Marines were brewing, having hidden the contraband inside the ballast tanks of one of the amphibian tractors. The stash was discovered when an officer conducting a routine inspection was nearly overcome by the fumes emanating from the alcoholic brew. He ordered the contents dumped over the side, though a few Marines armed with tin cups managed to savor a few drops before their precious cache disappeared into the sea.

Finally, five days after the Marianas Turkey Shoot, the ground action on Saipan had improved to the point that III Amphibious Corps could be released from floating reserve. However, the Guam landing continued to remain on hold. On June 25, the ships carrying the 3rd Marine Division headed instead for Eniwetok. They were followed five days later by the 1st Provisional Marine Brigade. Arriving aboard his LST on June 30, Marine corporal Byron G. Sneva found the twenty-mile-wide lagoon crowded with ships. "That evening we got showers, with hot and cold water, our first fresh water showers since the last week in May," he said.[13]

That same day, Admiral Richard Conolly flew to Saipan to confer with Admiral Kelly Turner and General Holland M. Smith, who up until then had been fully occupied with the Saipan operation. As a result of this conference, it was decided to attach the 77th Infantry Division to IIIAC for the Guam operation. W-Day was rescheduled for July 25 to allow time for the Army division to arrive from Hawaii.

The decision was not without debate. Concerned about the approach of typhoon season and not wanting to give the Japanese more time to strengthen Guam's defenses, Admiral Nimitz had hoped to set W-Day for July 15, when at least one regimental combat team from the Army division should be available. U.S. chief of operations Admiral Ernest J. King also expressed reservations about the delay. Seeing the dispatch regarding the decision, he scrawled "too late" just above the proposed July 25 assault date.[14] However, Nimitz ultimately acquiesced to the amended timetable.

The decision to delay was encouraged by information that Japanese troop strength on Guam had been steadily increasing over the past two months. On May 27 the number of Japanese military personnel was estimated at 10,000 to 11,000, revised upward from the May 11 estimate of 8,900 to 9,300. POW interrogations and intelligence captured on Saipan indicated that those estimates were still woefully low. The latest estimate of enemy troop strength as of July 18 was 18,657 (plus aviation ground troops). That estimate was accompanied by a detailed breakdown of individual enemy units compiled from records seized on Saipan—a breakdown that, with a very few exceptions, would prove to be pretty close to the mark. That listing identified the 29th Division and the 6th Expeditionary Force as the main units present on the island.[15] Documents that fell into U.S. hands with the capture of 31st Army headquarters on Saipan—including a defense plan for Guam dated March 25—also provided information on Japanese troop dispositions and indicated that General Takeshi Takashina anticipated landings along the Tumon Bay–Agana Bay–Piti stretch of coastline as well as over the Agat Bay beaches.[16]

This new intelligence gave rise to fears that seizure of the island could be even more difficult than that of Saipan, which was only a third the size of Guam. With that in mind, it was agreed that one regimental combat team of the 77th Division must be available for W-Day, and the remainder of the division was to be available no later than W+2. Admiral Raymond Spruance agreed to the delay "with reluctance," realizing that it would require the Marines to spend even more time baking in the sun on their crowded transports. Nevertheless, he saw little choice. "The character of enemy resistance being encountered in Saipan and the increase over the original estimates of enemy strength in Guam" made it advisable to wait "until the entire 77th Division was available as a reserve," he observed.[17]

Conolly, who along with Major General Roy S. Geiger, had hoped to get the Guam operation underway without delay, obtained one important concession: a greatly prolonged naval bombardment to soften up enemy defenses. Admiral Spruance, concerned about civilian casualties, agreed on one condition: that the bombardment be conducted as systematically and carefully as possible. When Admiral Kelly Turner told Conolly to find someone to oversee that process, Conolly excused himself from the conference cabin on *Rocky Mount*. He returned almost immediately to announce, "I have the fellow, Kelly. It's Conolly!" He would personally direct the preinvasion bombardment.[18]

This was welcome news for the Marines. Recalled General Lemuel Shepherd, "In discussing naval gunfire support, Conolly said, 'Well, I'll give you support. By golly, I'll run my flagship on the beaches if necessary.' And Admiral Conolly would have done it if it had been necessary."[19]

— ◆ —

The troubling intelligence on the Japanese defense did not alter the original landing plan, which called for a double envelopment of the Orote Peninsula and Apra Harbor. Details were provided to the commanders of all major units at a conference aboard Admiral Conolly's command vessel, USS *Appalachian*, on July 10. As previously decided, the assault force would attack over two separate landing areas five miles apart on the western shore: Asan to the north of Orote Peninsula and Agat located to the south.

It was all a lot more complicated than a layman might assume, observed a company commander in the 3rd Marine Division in a letter home:

> *There is a great deal of very intricate planning and timing involved in making a landing party. . . . [T]hings to be considered are the boat assignments of your units, what men will be put in every boat; where they will find that boat to get into it; where they will debark from the ship . . . also at what time they will debark and in which wave each boat will hit the beach. . . . [E]ach boat will proceed to a rendezvous area and join other boats of its*

wave where they will circle for possibly an hour or two before proceeding to a control point and then to the line of departure from which you head for the beach. . . . [T]here is much room for mistakes—boats getting in the wrong wave, men in the wrong boats, hitting the beach too soon, losing direction or missing a control boat, etc.[20]

Key to the plan were the amphibious tractors—LVTs, or "amtracs" as they were familiarly called—that would transport the Marines over the reefs and onto the beaches. The reefs, ranging up to five hundred yards or more in width, were impassable to boats and would become killing grounds should the Marines be forced to wade in under enemy fire—a lesson learned at great cost at Tarawa the preceding November. The 3rd Amphibian Tractor Battalion, with 180 LVTs, would bring the 3rd Marine Division ashore; the 4th Amphibian Tractor Battalion, with 178 LVTs, would take care of Shepherd's Marine Brigade. In addition, one hundred amphibious trucks (DUKWs) would carry in artillery pieces and radio Jeeps. Sixty DUKWs were assigned to the 3rd Marine Division and forty to the Marine Brigade.

The troop-carrying amtracs would be preceded by LVT(A)-1 "amtanks" of the 1st Armored Amphibian Tractor Battalion. The LVT(A)s were armored amtracs fitted with an M-3 light tank gun turret. The 1st Armored Battalion version carried a 37mm gun (later versions would be fitted with a more effective 75mm howitzer) and four machine guns, two of which were located in scarf mounts on the rear deck, with another in the turret and one in the bow. Measuring twenty-six feet long, just under eleven feet wide, and ten feet high to the top of the turret, the LVT(A)-1 had an inch of steel armor on the sides of the cab and open-top turret and a quarter inch elsewhere. The vehicle weighed about sixteen tons and was capable of 20 to 25 miles per hour ashore and 5 to 7.5 miles per hour afloat. "The primary mission of the LVT(A)s was beach assault," noted the battalion history. "They were to lead the first infantry wave across the reef, firing at enemy targets until the infantry hit the beach. Since in that phase of the landing, naval and air bombardment had been lifted, the LVT(A)s provided the last firepower against hostile beaches before the troops were actually ashore."[21]

The 3rd Marine Division would come ashore north of Apra Harbor on a twenty-five-hundred-yard stretch of beach between a set of "devil's horns"—Adelup Point on the left and Asan Point on the right. The village of Asan—home to about five hundred residents—extended for about a mile along both sides of the coastal road at the northern end of the landing beaches. The assault would cross the gravel coastal road and advance over a wide swath of dry rice paddies to seize the rugged ridges overlooking the beaches. The division's landing zone was divided into four beaches coded (from north to south) Red 1, Red 2, Green, and Blue.

The 3rd Marines, commanded by forty-six-year-old Colonel W. Carvel Hall, had what would be the toughest job. Coming in over Red 1 and Red 2, Hall's men were to secure the division's left flank by seizing Chonito Cliff and the commanding terrain to the right of the cliff.[22] The cliff—actually a steep ridge nose overlooking Red 1, pierced by a cut to accommodate the Apra Harbor–Agana coastal road—ran to the water's edge, essentially placing Hall's regiment in a sort of topographical cul-de-sac. Hall, who took pride in ancestors who had served as officers in the American Revolution and for the Confederacy during the Civil War, was new to regimental command, having been in charge of division supply during the Bougainville campaign. He seems to have been a bit of a martinet. One of his battalion commanders recalled him, with thinly veiled disdain, as being of "medium height, spare, rugged hawk-like face, and idiosyncratic, the latter characteristic emphasized by a slight lisp."[23]

The 21st Marines, led by forty-one-year-old Colonel Arthur H. Butler, would come ashore at Green Beach to assault the slightly less precipitous, but still daunting, heights facing the division center. Butler was the lone Naval Academy graduate among the division's three infantry regiment commanders; his service ranged from chasing insurgents in Nicaragua to a stint as an instructor at the Marine Corps Schools. As the regiment's executive officer during some of the fiercest fighting on Bougainville, he had earned the Legion of Merit with Combat "V."

Colonel Edward A. Craig's 9th Marines would land at Blue Beach in the shadow of Asan Point on the division's right. Forty-seven years old, the self-effacing Craig—a man with a sense of humor—was a veteran of the Banana Wars and staff service. He had led the 9th Marines through the Bougainville campaign, earning a Bronze Star for his performance.

The 1st Provisional Marine Brigade would land south of Orote Peninsula on the roughly mile-long stretch between Agat Village and Bangi Point. Located in the shadow of 869-foot Mount Alifan, the landing zone was divided into four color-coded beaches from north to south: Yellow 1, Yellow 2, White 1, and White 2. Protruding from the center of the landing area between Yellow 2 and White 1 was stubby Gaan Point. Yellow 1, on the far left, was only two thousand yards from the Orote Peninsula's steep shoreline cliffs. Potential trouble was also posed by two rocky islets: tiny Neye, located just to the north of the brigade's landing area, and Yona, just to the south.

The 4th Marines, commanded by Lieutenant Colonel Alan Shapley, would land on the brigade right over White 1 and White 2. A crucial early objective for Shapley's Marines was Hill 40 just inland from Bangi Point. A star quarterback at the Naval Academy in the 1920s, Shapley had narrowly escaped death as a member of the Marine detachment aboard the USS *Arizona* during the Japanese attack on Pearl Harbor. Blown into the harbor when the battleship exploded, he managed to swim ashore, while also saving another man from drowning. He subsequently commanded the 2nd Marine Raider Battalion, though he never really bought into the Raider credo, feeling that a well-trained conventional Marine battalion could do pretty much anything a Raider battalion could do. When the Raiders were broken up, Shapley was charged with bringing this assortment of freethinkers back into the conventional fold, which he did, though they would always view themselves first and foremost as Raiders. He also seemed to have a predilection for fellow gridiron veterans—nearly a dozen former All-Americans populated his regiment's ranks.

The 22nd Marines, commanded by Colonel Merlin F. Schneider, would come in over Yellow 1 and Yellow 2, secure Agat Village just to the north, and then move up the coast to cut off Orote Peninsula from the mainland. Sporting a bushy moustache, the forty-three-year-old Oregon native graduated in 1923 from the Naval Academy and had served in China and as commanding officer of the Marine detachment aboard the battleship *New Mexico* before the war. More recently, he had been moved up to command of the 22nd Marines after serving as the regiment's executive officer during the seizure of Eniwetok. He was particularly respected by the regiment's enlisted men "because his empathy leaned more toward we in the ranks, in contrast to his relationship with those junior officers surrounding him," observed one of his PFCs.[24]

The high ground dominating the 3rd Division's landing area remained on the mind of General Allen Turnage as the invasion drew near. In the end, everything hinged on securing those ridges. As one regimental commander advised his officers, "The theory is simple, gentlemen. It's the old school solution—seize the high ground and hold it."[25] Despite his annoyance with Commander Richard Armknecht's lack of tact at the earlier briefing about terrain, Turnage was not oblivious to the threat posed by the heights behind his division's landing area. The division faced possible entrapment in what amounted to a twelve-hundred-yard-deep semicircular bowl, should it be unable to secure the high ground just inland.

Before the division sailed in June, the general assembled his officers for an informal talk, personally shaking each man's hand as they entered the ship's wardroom. "When we were all inside, he made a short speech, the import of which was that no matter what happened on the beaches the troops must push inland and secure the crests of the hills which surrounded the beach and when these had been taken, they must be held at all costs and under no circumstances be given up," recalled Lieutenant Colonel John S. Letcher. "He then expressed his confidence that every one of us would do his duty and wished us all good luck."[26]

＊＊

Though American intelligence was not aware of it, the Guam garrison now included 31st Army commander Lieutenant General Hideyoshi Obata—an accidental honor the fifty-four-year-old veteran of the Burma campaign presumably would have preferred to forego. Described by a navy counterpart as "extremely intelligent and, for an army officer, of extremely broad vision," he had been away from his Saipan headquarters on an inspection tour in the Palaus when the U.S. invasion force arrived.[27] Accompanied by two senior officers, he boarded a plane to hasten back but made it only as far as Guam before air and sea access to Saipan was slammed shut.

Despite Obata's superior rank, he ceded the hands-on defense of Guam to 29th Division commander General Takashina. According to a Japanese staff officer who survived the campaign, their relations were "exact and correct," and though the two shared the same command post, Takashina "had a free hand in preparing for and conducting combat operations. He in turn was scrupulous in keeping the army commander informed, and in accepting his advice and guidance." Division operations officer Lieutenant Colonel Hideyuki Takeda observed that Obata had been an instructor at the Army General Staff College when Takashina was a student there, "so the relationship between the two generals was very amicable."[28]

With invasion clearly imminent, the Japanese intensified construction of defense works. The shift to a defensive mentality among troops that had most recently been training to assault Soviet pillboxes brought its challenges. "Our officers became agitated and tense," recalled Corporal Masashi Ito. "And the fear became reflected in our Orders for the Day, which grew increasingly severe; preparations doubled to the point of frenzy; and for us, waiting, the strain grew unbearable."[29]

The main Japanese defense line extended from just north of Tumon Bay, south to Facpi Point on the western coast. Artillery pieces dragged up into the heights overlooking potential landing beaches were supplemented with dummies fashioned from black-painted coconut logs. At the southern end of the island, gangs of Chamorro laborers were ordered to lay coconut tree trunks across the coastal road in hopes of blocking American tanks. At Asan, workers constructed tank obstacles, digging ditches and implanting tree trunk posts in mazelike patterns.

A comparison of U.S. aerial reconnaissance photos taken between June 6 and July 4 indicated an increase of 141 machine guns or light antiaircraft positions, 51 artillery emplacements, and 36 medium antiaircraft positions. A subsequent Marine Corps study of the Guam operation observed, "Better photographs may have accounted for the discovery of some of the additional finds; still, the buildup was remarkable considering the short period involved."[30]

Unlike Saipan, where the Marine landing had caught the Japanese with numerous large coastal guns still waiting to be installed, the Guam garrison profited from the thirty-three-day postponement of W-Day. The delay gave Takashina extra time to identify likely landing areas, position units, and emplace virtually all of his big guns. These included eighteen 200mm antiboat guns, six 6-inch coastal defense guns, three 140mm coastal defense guns, five 120mm coastal defense guns, twenty-eight 120mm dual purpose guns, and fourteen 75mm antiaircraft guns—this in addition to the artillery organic to his ground units. A document captured on Saipan and dated June 1, 1944, additionally listed a variety of artillery ranging from fourteen 105mm howitzers to forty 75mm pack howitzers; nearly a hundred antitank guns ranging from 57mm to 37mm; 349 7.7mm light machine guns; and 540 50mm grenade dischargers, the latter being familiarly, if not fondly, known to American Marines as "knee mortars"[31]

Military common sense and the brief U.S. naval bombardment that had been hastily called off on June 16 allowed General Takashina to develop a reasonably accurate prediction of likely U.S. landing beaches. Rear Admiral W. L. Ainsworth, commanding the Southern Fire Support Group, later described the interrupted bombardment as the equivalent of "an engraved diagram" showing the enemy "that our probable intentions were to land just about where we did."[32] However, Takashina greatly overestimated the size of the forces he would face, anticipating the enemy would employ four or five divisions in simultaneous landings on two fronts. He wrongly suspected a supplementary landing could be made behind his forces "from the Pago Bay front" on the east coast and considered it possible that the amphibious landings might be supplemented by an airborne assault.[33] He also continued to view the Tumon Bay beaches as particularly vulnerable and devoted considerable time and effort to defense works there.

In early July, Takashina moved the bulk of his forces—which had been scattered around the island to cover multiple potential landing areas—to defend the western beaches between Agat and Tumon Bay. His 29th Division headquarters and most of his service troops were located at Fonte on the plateau overlooking the Asan beaches where the 3rd Marine Division planned to land. Headquarters of the 48th Independent Mixed Brigade, commanded by Major General Kiyoshi Shigematsu, was also located at Fonte. Shigematsu's brigade was responsible for defense of the Agana sector extending from Tumon Bay in the north to Piti in the south.

To the south, defense of the Agat sector was entrusted to Colonel Tsunetaro Suenaga's 38th Infantry Regiment, headquartered on the lower reaches of Mount Alifan. The 1st Battalion was assigned to the Agat area beaches, the 3rd Battalion was assigned to the left flank, and the 2nd Battalion defended the base of Orote Peninsula. In addition to the 2nd Battalion, 38th Infantry Regiment, the Orote Peninsula was defended by the bulk of the 54th Naval Guard Force and two batteries of the 52nd Antiaircraft Artillery Battalion. The latter, charged with defense of Orote Airfield, had 75mm antiaircraft guns that could be depressed for use as ground weapons. With no planes left to service or fly, the Southeast Area Air Depot and 263rd, 521st. and 755th Air Groups were converted into infantry units. Remaining troops, mostly service, engineer, and construction units of dubious combat value, were scattered throughout the island. Armor was positioned in reserve to strike at enemy beachheads: the 24th Tank Company with nine light tanks at Ordot; the 9th Tank Regiment's 2nd Company with twelve to fourteen tanks, mostly mediums, assigned to the 48th Independent Mixed Brigade; and the 1st Company with twelve to fifteen light tanks assigned to the 38th Regiment at Agat.

The general's plan was to stop the invaders at the shoreline and throw them back into the sea, as called for by Imperial Headquarters doctrine. This was the same defense mantra that had repeatedly failed in the past, most recently at Saipan. General Takashina's operations officer, Lieutenant Colonel Hideyuki Takeda, later claimed he had argued against this tactic as it "was not favorable for the Japanese forces." The newly arrived 29th Division did not have sufficient time or materials to prepare proper shoreline fortifications and "thus would be annihilated on the narrow beach by enemy airplanes and naval guns," he said. Better to exploit Guam's rugged interior for a defense in depth to negate the American advantage in firepower.[34]

Colonel Takeda's arguments were overruled in favor of a conventional beach defense. Training for the ranks was to include "calm and accurate fire from as close range as possible from the shore"; "close-in attack against tanks at the beach"; "essentials of night attack, particularly infiltrating attack"; and the ability "to acquire skill in firing at floating targets" and "to hit the target with the first shot and to economize ammunition."[35]

In a nod to the destructive power of naval shore bombardment, General Takashina warned units to avoid revealing their positions prematurely, lest they be destroyed before the landings even began. "Against [the] enemy's attack, efforts shall be made

[to] refrain from accepting the challenge and to conceal our positions during the initial air-raids and naval bombardment," noted a staff officer. "The time and units for commencing firing shall be notified by definite orders."[36] Dummy positions were constructed, including one behind the Agat beaches featuring poles painted to simulate antiaircraft guns, surrounded by dummy crews. Dressed in Japanese uniforms, the dummies were posed in regular firing positions, including loaders stooping to pick up shells and even an officer seeming to scan the sky for planes.

A Chamorro woman employed at 29th Division headquarters later stated that a Japanese staff officer told her that any attempted U.S. landing would be like Tarawa, where the defenders "killed 5,000 Marines" as they struggled ashore. "While the enemy is advancing from the line of coral reefs to the shore," noted a Japanese order, "the combined infantry and artillery firepower will be developed. In particular, when they reach the water obstacles, oblique and flanking fire will be employed to establish a dense fire net and thus annihilate them on water. Every company will make a sudden attack with its firepower."[37] Any troops that made it ashore were to be counterattacked and destroyed.

As W-Day approached, U.S. intelligence assessments of enemy defense preparations were not encouraging. "It would appear that the Japanese believe the most dangerous areas to them are: The Tumon Bay area, the Agana-Piti-area, and the Agat area," noted IIIAC. "These areas are heavily defended, and the approaches to the beaches are barred by obstacles on the reef." IIIAC could expect to run into more hostile artillery than previously encountered "and will probably find it better employed," observed IIIAC chief of staff Colonel Merwin H. Silverthorn in a discussion of enemy capabilities. "Recent experience shows that strong tank attacks may be expected either day or night." Surprise was considered unlikely. Documents captured on Saipan indicated that Japanese defenses were concentrated along the west coast, with inland positions along the high ground. "From a study of facts gathered from all available sources it seems evident that both we and the Japanese have been thinking along the same lines, that is, the beaches we find best for landings are those the Japs find most dangerous to them and have fortified the most," observed IIIAC.[38]

Roughly eight thousand miles from General Takashina's headquarters on Guam, a notice arrived at about this same time at the Pineault family's rented walk-up in coastal Fall River, Massachusetts. The notice was from the local draft board, and it directed Alfred Pineault's son, Leo, to report for his preinduction examination.

Family members informed the board that Leo was not available. He had been killed on Guam three days after the Japanese attack on Pearl Harbor. Draft board officials, presumably red faced, apologetically explained they had been notified by the Navy merely that Leo had been "detached from the service," which they erroneously interpreted to mean he was available for the draft.[39]

Back at Eniwetok, the Marines who would avenge Leo Pineault continued to wait. They had already spent weeks aboard ship, and the novelty had long since worn thin, though Eniwetok was an improvement over cutting circles in the open sea. The food got better, there was an opportunity for quick freshwater showers, and some ships even screened topside movies in the evenings. Schedules were set up to bring groups ashore to stretch their land legs. Combined with regular calisthenics aboard ship, the program was intended to keep the assault troops in reasonably good physical condition, but the effects of nearly two months of shipboard inactivity would not be quickly remedied.

Corporal Fred Addison's LST opened its clamshell doors and lowered the bow ramp so the men could swim in the warm tropical lagoon. "Some of us were diving and doing 'cannon balls' from the side of the bow," recalled Addison. "So far as I can remember, we never for any of these swims had a lifeguard posted nor anyone with a rifle on lookout for sharks. It was a welcome diversion and a lot of fun."[40] Each transport was assigned an islet to use for rest and recreation. "We played touch football practically nude," recalled Sergeant Neil Stiles. "We didn't have any swimming trunks. Some of the guys didn't even have skivvy drawers. We never wore them. We threw them away or wore them out and never got any more because we couldn't keep them clean. We just wore our dungarees."[41] Edward Schubel's buddies amused themselves racing little crabs. "We'd make a big circle and bet on 'em to see whose went out first," he remarked.[42] Refreshments consisted of two cans of warm beer per man. "The two cans always boiled down to one net," observed Lieutenant Paul C. Smith, "because the beer was so warm that as soon as a can was punctured half of it spurted into the air in a gaseous geyser."[43]

PFC Ray Gillespie's outfit disembarked for its recreational interlude on July 3. Gillespie was glad to get ashore, but he did have one complaint: dead Japanese who had been hastily buried after the battle for the island earlier in the year. There were mass graves everywhere. Some of the corpses had been dug up and propped up as if sitting against coconut trees in what was apparently someone's idea of humor. One of these now mostly skeletal residents lounged nearby one evening as Gillespie and some buddies built a campfire and sat back to enjoy their two cans of beer. "The guys began to sing known ballads," recalled Gillespie, who admitted he was virtually tone deaf. "So I joined in, but for only a few seconds, when Squeaky said, 'Shut up, Gillespie! This goddamn dead Jap sings better than you.'"[44]

By now, the assault troops had been briefed on their target until "Guam was coming out of their ears," observed a battalion commander.[45] "With it all, it was surprising how seemingly well acquainted we were with an island we'd never seen," recalled an officer scheduled to go in at Agat. "We could visualize the rice paddies just beyond the Jap beaches. We pictured the town of Agat. We knew how many houses were in the town. We knew it was 1,500 yards from the beach to the sharply rising hills and Mount Alifan; the Harmon Road approach to Mount Alifan was as widely discussed as any Main Street."[46]

The prospect of combat was beginning to look like a relief. "If you spent two months on an LST you'd be willing to storm the gates of Hell just to get off the damn thing," observed Platoon Sergeant Hank Bauer, waiting with the 1st Provisional Marine Brigade. One of the Marines on Bauer's LST was Bud Herrick, who was married to Kathleen Winsor, author of the steamy (for those days) novel *Forever Amber*. Herrick had several copies of the book, and it seemed to Bauer that just about every Marine aboard eventually read it. "Jeez, were they horny!" he recalled. The books were just about worn out after a while. "I think even the chaplain read it,"[47] said Bauer.

Though it might have seemed they'd been consigned to limbo, the wheels determining their future continued to turn. Boarding a hastily assembled transport division, the 77th Division's 305th Regimental Combat Team sailed from Honolulu on July 1 with an advance division headquarters. On July 6, three days before Saipan was officially deemed secure, Admiral Spruance was advised that the 77th Division would arrive at Eniwetok by July 18, four days earlier than originally anticipated. He responded by moving W-Day on Guam up to July 21. It would not be long before some of the thousands of bored Marines would be looking back on their long weeks aboard ship with something close to nostalgia.

U.S. Marine Insular patrolman poses with schoolchildren on Guam in 1914.
NATIONAL ARCHIVES

The Governor's Palace on Agana's Plaza de Espana was the site of token resistance
during the Japanese landings on December 10, 1941. NATIONAL ARCHIVES .

A contemporary illustration by painter Kohei Ezak depicts the landing by the Japanese South Seas Detachment on Guam. NATIONAL PARK SERVICE

Naval gunfire pounds enemy positions on Guam. The lengthy bombardment was widely praised following the operation but still fell short of hopes. US NAVY

Makeshift shelters and tarpaulins festoon the deck of this LST crammed with men, equipment, and supplies. Thousands of Marines spent weeks aboard similar vessels awaiting the green light for the Guam landings. NATIONAL ARCHIVES

Assault troops join in prayer aboard ship on the eve of the W-Day landings on Guam.
NATIONAL ARCHIVES

Crammed with Marines, a landing craft heads toward the Asan beaches on W-Day. The crucial high ground just inland is plainly visible. USMC

Landing craft carrying the first waves of the Marine Brigade head toward the Agat beaches. Orote Peninsula looms at the top of the photo. US NAVY

Marines pile out of their amphibious tractor and take cover as the assault waves hit the beach on W-Day. NATIONAL ARCHIVES

Hit by an enemy shell, a Marine amtrac explodes before it can reach shore. USMC

A Marine rifleman moves past dead comrades sprawled by the amtrac to his left as the Marine Brigade comes ashore at Agat beaches on W-Day. USMC

Troops and amphibious tractors crowd the narrow Agat beaches soon after the Marine Brigade landing. Maanot Ridge looms off to the north.
NATIONAL ARCHIVES

Two Marines struggle under the weight of a badly wounded buddy on one of the invasion beaches. USMC

Scene on Asan Beach an hour and a half after the initial landing the morning of July 21. Asan Point, one of the two "devil's horns" looms in the background. NATIONAL ARCHIVES

Dead Marines lie in a heap next to a knocked-out amtrac on the Agat beaches. The Marine Brigade took numerous casualties from a concealed enemy field piece during the landing on Yellow Beach 2. USMC

A bloody tangle of dead Marines, weapons, and equipment lie strewn in the sand after their position was hit by a mortar or artillery shell on the beach. USMC

Knocked out by the preinvasion bombardment, this 6-inch naval gun capable of hurling a one-hundred-pound shell ten thousand yards was one of three located on the high ground overlooking the 3rd Marine Division beaches at Chonito Cliff. USMC

Still wearing his helmet, a wounded Marine is hoisted aboard an assault transport offshore for further medical attention.
NATIONAL ARCHIVES

A cable system rigged by engineers facilitated the evacuation of wounded down the cliffs in the 3rd Marine Division beachhead. USMC

A flamethrower operator burns out a Japanese emplacement. USMC

Marines look for intelligence information and souvenirs in the wreckage of a Japanese cave position. NATIONAL ARCHIVES

A dead Japanese soldier lies next to a communication wire along a Guam road. USMC

Japanese dead litter the ground following the abortive counterattack to push the Marines back into the sea. USMC

The high ground overlooking the Asan beaches gave Japanese defenders an expansive view of the Marine beachhead. USMC

Two Marine riflemen advance warily on
an enemy emplacement. USMC

Supported by
a Sherman
tank, Marines
advance into a
grove of shat-
tered coconut
trees. USMC

A weary rifleman tries to
catch some rest in the dubious
comfort of his foxhole. USMC

With only a poncho as his shroud, a fallen Marine is lowered into his grave. USMC

Marine dead await burial at Agat. The 1st Provisional Marine Brigade suffered heavy casualties the night of W-Day and on Orote Peninsula. USMC

Riflemen from the Marine Brigade pass two destroyed Japanese tanks in the advance along the Orote Peninsula. USMC

Having first provided the man with a cigarette, Marines coax a survivor of a Japanese naval unit out of his hiding place. Most Japanese military personnel chose death over surrender. USMC

Marines cautiously work their way through what is left of Guam's capital, Agana. USMC

Two U.S. tanks burn after being ambushed during the 77th Division's advance on Yigo in northern Guam. U.S. ARMY

Long columns of troops slog north in pursuit of disorganized Japanese forces following the failed enemy counterattack. USMC

A Marine lugs a machine gun tripod up one of Guam's steep hills, followed by another crew member carrying the gun itself. USMC

Safely within U.S. lines, liberated Chamorro refugees line up for water. NATIONAL ARCHIVES

Marines watch as a demolition team blows up an enemy bunker. USMC

Ignoring the sprawled body of a dead Japanese soldier, Marines gather water and supplies brought in by amphibious tractors. USMC

Hands bound behind his back, a Chamorro man lies with other civilians executed by the Japanese in a murderous frenzy as defeat loomed. NATIONAL ARCHIVES

Marines examine a downed Japanese plane following the capture of Orote Airfield. USMC

A Navy corpsman tends to a wounded boy who came into U.S. lines with other civilians. USMC

A Marine gives his wounded buddy a drink of water as he awaits evacuation to a field hospital or ship. USMC

A Japanese prisoner uses a loudspeaker in an attempt to coax stragglers out of hiding. USMC

CHAPTER 10

RESCUE

WHILE DISTANT MARINES COMMUNED WITH JAPANESE CORPSES, DELVED INTO racy novels, or just stared out over the endless sea, twenty-two-year-old Lieutenant Junior Grade William Rufus Mooney was losing track of time. During a strafing run over Guam's Tiyan Airfield on the afternoon of June 16, the *San Jacinto* pilot's Hellcat had taken a fatal hit from a Japanese antiaircraft gun. "On my second run I got one plane on the ground, but on my third run my engine was hit by anti-aircraft fire as I was coming out of a dive," recalled the St. Joseph, Missouri, native.[1] The Hellcat stayed airborne long enough for Mooney to make a rough water landing about fourteen miles offshore, but he nearly drowned when his parachute snagged on something in the cockpit and started to drag him down with the plane. "I released the chute and bobbed straight to the surface," he recalled. "Then I got out my little one-man raft which was hooked to my life jacket. I looked at my watch as I crawled into the inflated raft. It was 5 p.m."

Mooney noticed blood pooling in the bottom of the raft and only then realized he had gashed open his forehead during the water landing. His section leader, Lieutenant Junior Grade D. G. Steward of Birmingham, Alabama, was circling overhead. Though Mooney could not know it, Steward was calling for help on all emergency channels but with no success. "He stayed over me for two hours and then began to run out of gas and had to leave," remarked Mooney. "I'll never know how he managed to stay that long. But when he went away, I was all alone."

The Guam shoreline was visible off in the distance. Mooney started paddling away from the island, thinking his best chance lay in remaining well offshore. Inventorying his supplies, he found he had a half-inch square of hard candy, a handful of malted milk tablets, and five twelve-ounce cans of water. As darkness fell, he settled down and went to sleep. Morning found him even closer to the east coast of Guam, drawn in by a swift current. He paddled all day against the current hoping to be picked up by a destroyer or spotted by friendly planes, but there was no sign of either. He finally gave in to the inexorable current, hoping he could negotiate the heavy surf now plainly visible along the coastline. "The beach was rugged as all hell," he said. "The whole island from this point looked like it was made of lava with a lot of caves in the steep black cliffs."

As he had feared, his raft capsized in the pounding surf. He lost his wristwatch but managed to save the raft. Mulling his options, he decided his best chance was to spend his nights hiding on the island where he could sleep and forage for food. At daylight, he would paddle out to sea where he was more likely to be spotted by friendly aircraft. Realizing that there was less aerial activity on the east coast, he also decided to gradually paddle around the northern end of the island to the west coast where he would have a better chance of being picked up.

Over the next few days Mooney paddled doggedly up the coast by day and rested ashore at night. He saw no Japanese or natives. Though he searched, there was little food to be found. A few coconuts had drifted ashore but proved to be inedible. He tried eating various leaves and small crabs but was unable to keep them down. His diet consisted primarily of three malted milk tablets a day. "After the first few days I wasn't so hungry," he said, "but my thirst was bad." A heavy rainstorm finally provided relief thanks to the rain cape in his raft. "I just drew up my knees and the rain filled that poncho and I took all the air out of my life jacket and a mouthful at a time, I filled that life jacket," he explained "The water in there kept me alive . . . because it did not rain again."

He saw "all kinds of Japanese planes every day" but no American aircraft. He lost count of the days, but he thought it may have been on the tenth or eleventh day of his ordeal that a couple of Japanese torpedo bombers passed low overhead—so close Mooney could see the pilots. If they saw him, they gave no indication of it. "At first I was afraid some Jap plane would spot me—then I got so I didn't give a damn, for I figured they would at least feed me before they disposed of me," he admitted.[2]

He was paddling along about two hundred yards offshore on the afternoon of July 2, trying to ignore some snipers on the beach who were taking pot shots at his raft, when a flight of Hellcats roared overhead. Mooney flung a dye marker overboard. To his indescribable relief, as the water around the raft turned a bright green, one of the fighters waggled his wings to indicate they had seen him. Ten miles west of Orote Peninsula, Lieutenant R. W. Kiser, senior naval aviator aboard the USS *Washington*, was on rescue station with two Kingfisher floatplanes when the fighter escort came up on the radio. A pilot had been sighted in the water about one hundred yards off the beach on the northeast corner of island, he advised Kiser.

Escorted by the fighters, the Kingfishers headed north. The water was rough with four-foot waves, but Kiser had no trouble locating the raft and managed to set down safely. "After much maneuvering in rough water, I came in close aboard the downed pilot, tied the mooring line around the gun mount band in the rear seat and threw the other end of the line to him," said Kiser. Mooney found out how weak he had become when he could hardly pull himself up into the Kingfisher, but he finally managed to clamber into the back seat, and Kiser lifted off and delivered him back to the USS *Washington*.[3]

"Then they gave me the biggest steak I had ever seen," said the happy pilot, who found he had lost seventeen pounds during his ordeal. "It took me an hour to eat it—I was full long before the hour was up but I thought to myself, 'You never can tell what will happen,' so I just ate and ate."[4]

Mooney was a very lucky man. No airman unfortunate enough to fall into Japanese hands on Guam survived to tell of the experience. Fugitive George Tweed, who presumably heard the story from his Chamorro protectors, later told U.S. intelligence personnel about a pilot who brought his disabled plane down in a water landing just offshore. "The pilot managed to climb out of the ship and began swimming toward shore," related Tweed. "When he was about fifty feet from shore a bunch of Japs lined up and opened fire on him and he was killed before he was able to reach shore."[5]

The unnamed pilot may have been lucky in one respect: at least he came to a quick end. Another airman was not so fortunate. Francisco Castro was toiling with a Chamorro labor party one afternoon when they heard a plane approaching low over the trees. It was a Hellcat and was obviously in trouble. Losing altitude, the fighter roared just overhead before plowing through the brush and jungle vegetation and skidding to a stop not far away. The workers dropped their tools and ran to the crash site. Thirty-eight-year-old Jose L. G. Cruz climbed up onto the wing with the help of another Chamorro and pulled the dazed pilot out of the cockpit. "I could see from a distance that there was blood on his face and around his ear and eye. His head was scraped and you [could] see part of his skull," recalled Leonilla Herrero.[6]

"What are all of these children doing here?" asked the pilot as he began to recover his senses and saw the Chamorro women and children from the work party standing around.

"We are working cleaning the fields for the Japanese," someone replied.

Moments later, a Japanese patrol arrived. Some of the Chamorro women and children were crying as they looked at the injured American. "The poor man was in bad shape," recalled Justo Guerrero. The soldiers pushed the people away. "All of you go back to work," one ordered. They tied the pilot's hands and led him away, half holding him up. "He seemed stunned," observed Guerrero.[7] According to police interpreter Henry Pangelinan, the pilot was summarily disposed of. "The Japanese cut off his cock and made him chew it like a cigar," he said. "Then they killed him."[8] Still on the run, George Tweed heard that the pilot had been tortured for four days, then brought to the island cemetery, where "his head was cut off."[9]

Jose Cruz's impulse to help the injured American proved to be a fatal mistake. The Japanese soon took him into custody. Cruz had kept the pilot's gloves, which his interrogators found suspicious for some unfathomable reason. Cruz was repeatedly tortured and accused of being an American spy. His denials had no effect. "The Japanese made him dig his own grave, then they asked him what he wanted," said Pangelinan. Cruz took a ring off his finger and asked that it be delivered to his wife. "Then one of the Japanese took out his sword and cut off his head."[10]

Civilians were warned they would not live to welcome any American return to the island. "When the Americans take Guam, they will find nothing but flies," the Japanese told them.[11]

＊＊＊

As W-Day drew near, a last-minute suggestion aimed at possibly expediting the attack in the 3rd Marine Division's sector came from an unexpected source: the commander of the 77th Infantry Division, forty-nine-year-old Major General Andrew D. Bruce.

The son of a Saint Louis attorney, Bruce had graduated in 1916 from Texas Agricultural and Mechanical College. He served as a lieutenant in a machine-gun battalion in France during World War I, was wounded in action, and received the Distinguished Service Cross, earning the temporary rank of lieutenant colonel by war's end. Between the wars, he participated in historical work at the U.S. Army War College, served on the General Staff of the War Department revising textbooks on military doctrine, and attended the U.S. Army Infantry School, the U.S. Army Field Artillery School, the U.S. Army Command and General Staff School, the U.S. Army War College, and the Naval War College. Clearly on a command track, when war broke out, he was promoted to brigadier general and assigned to organize a new tank destroyer center. He was promoted to major general in September 1942 and assumed command of the 77th Infantry Division in May 1943.

Under Bruce's command, the 77th Division would earn a reputation as one of the outstanding U.S. Army divisions in the Pacific Theater. Though not combat tested when it set sail from Hawaii in July for the rendezvous with the Guam invasion force, it came to III Amphibious Corps as one of the most thoroughly trained divisions in the Pacific, having undergone rigorous instruction in desert warfare, winter mountain warfare, and amphibious operations. Still, the sudden call to battle was not without problems. In a subsequent critique, the division would admit, "Great difficulty was experienced when the Division was suddenly ordered into the [Marianas] operation and attempts were made to fit the Division into the plans as originally published. The concept for the operations was unknown to the Division until arrival at an Advance CP at Eniwetok. In addition, the Division was not included in the distribution lists of plans published by the units with which the Division later operated."[12]

Despite time constraints and the rush to get equipment and men aboard ship, by July 15 General Bruce had compiled three plans (one preferred and two alternate) for his division's commitment to the Guam operation. The preferred plan detailed the division's role as already delineated by IIIAC—landing the troops in support of the 1st Provisional Marine Brigade. The first alternate plan laid out the division's course of action should it be committed instead to support the 3rd Marine Division at Asan.

The second alternate plan envisioned support of the 3rd Marine Division, but in a less conventional role. Bruce proposed taking the enemy by surprise by landing two of his regiments between Uruno and Ritidian Points on the northwestern coast. From there, they would move southwest to seize the Tumon Bay area, the Tiyan Airfield, and the northern road network from the rear, ultimately cutting the island in two "on the line from Agana (exclusive) to Pago Bay."[13] The landing, to be conducted at around dawn, would take place about four days after the main assaults to the south. The GIs would go ashore without heavy equipment but could easily be supplied and reinforced once the Tumon Bay beaches had been seized.

Bruce argued that the secondary landing would complement and ease the 3rd Marine Division's assault at Asan. It positioned the 77th Division "to become a hammer striking forwards and eventually on the anvil, i.e., the Force Beach Line [3rd Marine Division FBL]," he explained. "Should the enemy divert sufficient forces to halt this division for any appreciable length of time it should be possible for the 77th Division to become the anvil and the forces occupying the FBL to become the hammer."[14]

Arriving at Eniwetok on July 11 in advance of his division, Bruce enthusi-astically approached the Marine commanders there with his alternate plan. The reception was cool. General Allen Turnage, whose division arguably had the most to gain should the scheme work, advised Bruce to drop the idea. One of the biggest sticking points—and it was big indeed—was the fear that the units Bruce proposed to commit to a backdoor assault might be needed at the main beachhead. After the experience at Saipan, no one wanted to be caught without sufficient reserves.

Other drawbacks—pointed out in an analysis compiled by Colonel Walter A. Wachtler, operations officer for General Roy Geiger's Southern Troops and Land-ing Force—was the difficulty of landing on that part of the coast due to cliffs and the rugged jungle terrain any force would encounter as it attempted to move south toward Tumon Bay. Similar cautions appeared in a 1939 Marine Corps Schools study, as well as in a subsequent Japanese study, which noted, "North coast of island generally forms a series of steep cliffs of 100–200m, but landing of small troops is possible. At that time [1944], there were several paths leading from the shore to the cliff, but a foot soldier could barely traverse these paths."[15]

While observing that "the concept is excellent," Colonel Wachtler questioned the feasibility of supplying and supporting the force, the diversion of critical landing craft from the main effort, and General Bruce's assumption that the Japanese lacked a substantial organized reserve. "I am inclined to [the] belief that he does [have reserves]," countered Wachtler.

As for General Bruce's presumptions that the Japanese considered a landing in that area to be too difficult and would be slow to react, Wachtler noted, a touch caustically, "This appears to be based on an assumption of Jap intentions rather than an estimate of his capabilities." In a memorandum to General Geiger, the colonel concluded, "It is believed that the disadvantages outweigh the advantages of the proposed course of action for employment of the 77th Division and it is, therefore, recommended that the original decision to hold it in Corp Reserve, to be landed in order, be adhered to."[16]

General Bruce had forwarded a copy of his proposal to Geiger around July 14, by which time the general had already left for the Marianas with Admiral Richard Conolly aboard the command ship *Appalachian*. Colonel Wachtler's analysis was dated July 18, just seventy-two hours before W-Day. If Geiger had ever entertained any thoughts of giving Bruce's proposal the green light—which is unlikely given the timing—Wachtler's analysis put them to rest. Geiger rejected the idea, observing that it was too major a change to implement at that late date.[17] However, when it appeared that Holland Smith, already embroiled in a heated interservice feud over his relief of Army general Ralph Smith on Saipan, might be considering targeting General Bruce for aggressively pushing his alternate plan, Geiger demurred. "I consider that General Bruce has a perfect right to submit for my consideration any plans which he deems appropriate in furtherance of operations," he wrote Smith on July 23. "I request that no issue be made of this matter. My relations with the 77th Division so far have been entirely satisfactory and I anticipate and desire that they continue so throughout the campaign."[18]

Holland Smith did not pursue the matter further.

Late in the afternoon of July 10, the destroyers USS *McCall* and USS *Gridley* were working their way north along Guam's western shoreline when someone on a cliff just below Uruno Point began flashing a mirror at *McCall*'s bridge. A ship's signalman was summoned and saw that the mystery signaler was now standing in the open, waving a pair of crudely fashioned semaphore flags.

"Please answer by searchlight," signaled the stranger. "I cannot read semaphore but I am proficient in the reception of Morse code by lights."

McCall unlimbered a searchlight and winked out "K," code for "Go ahead."

High up on the cliff, George Tweed was almost overcome with a rush of excitement and apprehension. For the past two weeks he had watched U.S. ships steam past his clifftop hideout, but all efforts to attract their attention with his homemade semaphore flags had gone unnoticed. Now, with the aid of a simple pocket mirror, he had finally been seen. He was unsure of the complete semaphore alphabet, but figured the ship's crew would be able to fill in the blanks.

"I have information for you," he signaled.

The ship's light blinked, "K."

Tweed began waving his flags, but in his excitement wasn't sure he was actually making sense. Calming himself, he began again, more deliberately this time. "The Japs have a battery of coast guns mounted at Adelup Point." He paused. "The Japs kill every American who falls into their hands." The destroyers circled just offshore for about a half an hour as Tweed continued to send bits and pieces of information. Finally, exhausted, he put down his flags. The ships seemed to be getting up speed. Frantic, he raised the flags again and slowly and methodically spelled out, "Can you take me aboard?"

McCall's skipper, Lieutenant Commander John B. Carroll, contacted the patrol leader aboard *Gridley* and asked permission to risk sending in a boat. Permission was granted. Armed with Thompson submachine guns, sixteen volunteers led by

Lieutenant Junior Grade Robert H. Shaw clambered into *McCall*'s whaleboat and headed toward shore. Tweed had just about given up hope when he saw the boat. Practically "delirious with joy," he hoisted his flags for a final message: "Please wait for me. It will take me half an hour to get down to the water." He turned and raced back to his cave where he dashed off a quick note to Antonio Artero explaining his departure. Scooping up a few personal possessions, he half slid, half fell down the steep precipice to the water.

Aboard the whaleboat, the heavily armed rescue party was on edge as they approached shore in the growing darkness. "We were plain scared that the Japs would open up with rifle and machine gun fire when we got in close enough—but they didn't," recalled twenty-year-old Gunner's Mate Second Class Donald F. Conlin, who had been a high school student in Lancaster, Pennsylvania, when Tweed first fled into Guam's jungle.[19] They saw a light flashing on shore and steered toward it, cautiously pulling up about two hundred yards out. "Here I am!" Tweed shouted. "Come on in! There's plenty of water here!"

"No, you swim out," shouted someone in the whaleboat. Tweed began to argue, but the sailors were insistent. Tweed said he couldn't leave his things. "You swim out," came the reply. "If *you're* all right, then we'll come in and get your things."

"Oh, it's *me* you're afraid of," observed Tweed. Someone in the boat piped up, "You ain't just a-lyin'."

Tweed stripped off his clothes and started swimming. "When they saw I was really white, two dozen arms reached out for me," he recalled. "They pulled me over the side and I fell sprawling into the boat. . . . They were the best-looking bunch of men I ever saw in my life." Less than an hour later he was sitting at a table with white linen, china, and silver in *McCall*'s officers' mess. The menu featured baked ham.[20]

Despite Admiral Raymond Spruance's previously expressed concerns about civilians, Agana, Piti, Agat, and other towns were systematically obliterated by both air and naval bombardment as W-Day drew closer. As early as July 6, twelve aircraft from USS *Bataan* bombarded Agana with depth charges fitted with instantaneous fuses. USS *Wasp* reported destroying "about 90% of the buildings in Piti town" as well as part of the causeway leading from the town to Cabras Island by Apra Harbor. Buildings and antiaircraft positions at and around Agana were also targeted, with *Wasp* reporting the destruction of the hospital, Government Palace, and church. "The first was employed by the enemy as barracks; the second as Army headquarters and the third as Navy Headquarters," according to *Wasp*.[21]

Bombs and shells inevitably fell on civilians and enemy alike. "The continuous pounding nearly drove us insane," recalled Chamorro Ricardo J. Bordallo. "There was no escaping the noise. During a barrage, we couldn't speak, couldn't think. We could do nothing but wait for a lull and blessed silence. The lulls were painfully brief. As soon as our ears stopped ringing, the bombardment would begin anew. We would dive back into the shelter, muffle our ears as best we could, and cower in fear again."[22]

Among the unintended victims of the ongoing naval bombardment was thirteen-year-old Irene Ploke and her family in Agana. Irene was the daughter of Chief Pharmacist's Mate John Francis Ploke, now a prisoner in Japan. Married to a Chamorro, her father had taken refuge in the jungle after the Japanese invasion in 1941, but his freedom was short-lived. Two Japanese soldiers showed up a couple of days later and told Irene's mother that if her husband did not surrender, they would start killing people. No one doubted they meant it. At her mother's direction, Irene went out into the jungle to talk to her father. "I said, 'Daddy, there's army soldiers out there, and you have to surrender.' So he said, 'Okay,'" she recalled. Ploke removed his shirt and tied it to a branch. Holding the makeshift flag in one hand and little Irene's hand in the other, he walked out of the jungle and gave himself up.

Now, two and a half years later, with Agana under American bombardment, most residents had fled to the hinterlands, but Irene's grandfather stubbornly refused to leave. The rest of the family took shelter under a bridge, leaving the grandfather and a cousin behind to watch their house. Hours later, they saw two blackened figures approaching. As the two apparitions drew near, the family realized it was the grandfather and Irene's cousin, now black with caked dirt and soot. Hiding in a shelter by the house, they had narrowly escaped death from a bomb or shell explosion. "My cousin was all [covered with] shrapnel," she recalled. "They were buried alive, and somehow my cousin saw a little, little hole with light, and he dug himself out. After he dug himself out, he dug a bigger hole and dug my grandfather out while his eye was hanging [from] his socket. . . . The whole thing was hanging. We started to cry because it [was] really them, you know. So we just held their hands and we started to walk."

As they passed the former naval hospital, a Japanese medic stopped them. Irene feared he intended to kill them. Instead the medic carefully bandaged her grandfather's eye before urging them to run and hide. "To us, he's an angel," she said.[23]

⌒

Angels were about to become even scarcer than usual on Guam. With a U.S. landing clearly imminent, the Japanese military now moved to deal with what they had come to view as the civilian "problem." It was clear to the authorities that two and a half years of "Japanization" had had little effect on the Chamorros. Their loyalty could not be relied on in the coming battle. Corporal Shoichi Yokoi heard rumors that "some locals were making contact with enemy submarines at night by way of torchlight and signals. In one incident, I was told, some locals sang the U.S. anthem and waved handkerchiefs to a submarine."[24]

Recognizing that "the trend cannot be reversed," the Marianas District Group Headquarters decided on July 4 to forcibly relocate all civilians to camps under the supervision of the military police and Kaikontai. Chamorros in forced labor units working on defenses or the airfields would continue in that capacity, but all others would be relocated.[25] Six days later, General Takeshi Takashina issued orders putting the edict into effect. Japanese soldiers and civil authorities combed the countryside, ordering the Chamorros to assemble and prepare to move to what were essentially outdoor concentration camps. The largest of these was located well to the east at Manenggon, a valley area along the Ylig River near Yona village where eighteen thousand people would eventually be confined.

"We were told to leave because if we stayed at the ranch and they found us, they would either hurt us or kill us," said Jesus Mariano Borja. At Agana Heights, Juan Lujan Pangelinan was ordered to escort the people to an assembly area before midnight. "Those found in their residence after midnight will die," he was told.

"The Japanese were going all over the place and chasing everyone from their homes," recalled Vicenta Borja Rosario. "All the people—carry what you can carry—the rest they left behind. They left it all behind. Everyone was walking. Everyone. Everyone. It was very scary. It was nighttime, it was dark. The people were all crying. Everyone was—it was like you didn't know where to go."[26]

Japanese teacher Nakahashi Kiyoshi recorded the evacuation of civilians in his village. "The order was issued at 7 PM, and the movements started at 2 AM. It was not a spring drizzle, it was raining. It was an ominous day. There were constant naval bombardments, and carrier-based planes made the rounds of the sky. . . . We made up a huge line of 2,000 people who were leading horses, and pulling carts and vehicles. They moved forward while flare bombs exploded. . . . There were also sick people carried on stretchers."[27]

Thousands of Chamorros, from infants to the elderly, crowded the muddy trails, carrying what they could. Some rode carabao carts, but most slogged along on foot under the watchful eye of bayonet- and club-wielding Japanese soldiers continually shouting, "*Hiyake! Hiyake!*" (Hurry! Hurry!).[28] The elderly, the sick, and small children were all driven relentlessly on. "We could not help anyone who fell behind or fell down," recalled Edward Aguon. "Even if that person was your grandmother, a sick relative or a dying friend, you had to move on and leave them there, lying on the road covered with mud. I didn't know what lay ahead. . . . Whether we were going to live or be slaughtered."[29]

"We have to carry whatever we can and when we marched the rain came down, and all of us were wet, but we can't stop walking," recalled Juan Martinez Unpingco. "I can hear babies and children crying and some old people moaning due to the hunger and tiresome march." It was hardest on the elderly. "We found some who died and were left behind by their families," remembered nine-year-old Magdalena Lujan Calvo. "Some were still very sick, they were moaning." Jose Rosario Mesa, still a few days short of his tenth birthday, carried his baby brother piggyback. The baby got sick. "It was like he didn't move himself, but I figure out he's sleeping," recalled Mesa. After walking for hours, he was finally allowed to rest, and his mother came to take the baby. The child was dead. "I didn't know he [had] died," said Mesa.[30]

Nearly insane with thirst, twenty-eight-year-old Rosalia Duenas Flores stopped at a water-filled hole in the road. "I was extremely thirsty," she said. "We had no more water, no more coffee, nothing anymore. Everything we brought with us was all gone on the road." Unable to bear it anymore, she dropped down on the road and went to drink from a puddle. "Don't for Pete's sake, drink that," exclaimed her husband. "You might get poisoned." Rosalia shrugged him off. "It's up to God," she replied. "He knows that I am suffering. I'm very thirsty." She cupped her hands and drank.[31]

With daylight, the Japanese grew noticeably fearful of U.S. air observation. "Every time they [heard] an airplane they chased us into the jungle so they won't see us, the Americans," recalled Juana Lujan Calvo DeOro. One soldier turned his attention to Hannah Chance Torres—apparently noticing her Caucasian appearance—as the young mother shepherded her children along the roadway. "And he was screaming something that sounded like 'Americano! Americano!'" said a witness to the confrontation. The soldier began beating Hannah with his sword as she clutched her infant daughter to her chest. Hannah didn't cry out, even as she was repeatedly knocked down. None of the other Chamorros dared intervene for fear they would become the object of the soldier's rage.

Finally Hannah thrust the baby and her two little girls toward her sister-in-law, Mariquita Torres. "Tita, take these children for your children," she pleaded before falling to the ground. This time she did not get up. Mariquita took the children, reluctantly leaving Hannah. Behind them, another woman exclaimed, "Go on, go, go, go on. Don't stop, do not stop. Do not." They had to continue walking, explained Hannah's daughter. "Because they knew if they didn't that they would be killed too."[32]

At last, the long lines of refugees began to stream into Manenggon to find the "camp" was nothing but an empty expanse of grass and scattered rocks along the slow-moving Ylig River. "When we got to the camp there was nothing there," said Isabel Bamba Montague. "Nothing." Told to fend for themselves, the new arrivals cut coconut fronds and constructed rude shelters. As they labored, some Chamorros straggled in carrying Hannah Torres. "It was several hours later before they were able to locate where my father was," said Hannah's daughter. "And my father came.... He kept telling my mother, 'you're going to feel better, just hang in there. The Americans are coming.'" But Hannah Torres never got to meet their liberators. Some hours after arriving, she succumbed to her injuries. Her family wrapped her in a blanket and a bamboo mat and buried her by a coconut tree next to the river.[33]

———

Even some Japanese were stunned by the unraveling taking place among their countrymen as the invasion drew near. "The Kaikontai came down from the plateau looking for woman laborers," teacher Nakahashi Kiyoshi wrote home to his wife. "From their laughing over [the] prospect about what comes next, and their crazy words and deeds, I came to doubt whether they have Japanese character.... [B]oth officers and soldiers acted as if they became savage animals themselves by departing from lofty purposes." Their attitude toward the Chamorros "bordered upon madness," he wrote.[34]

Joaquin V. E. Manibusani was assigned to a work party at the agricultural center at Tai, which was rapidly becoming a preferred site for summary executions. He could plainly see what was coming. "I recall being there at the camp and my men being ordered to catch about ten dogs," he said. "The dogs were tied up and hung upside down from a tree; the Japanese then would practice swinging their swords by killing the dogs. The *taicho* [Japanese leader] would demonstrate to us what he believed to be an art—the skill of slaying a dog. Of course, he was showing off the power of his sharp blade of the sword."[35]

As Manibusani inferred, the killing of helpless dogs soon progressed to the murder of helpless civilians. Among the victims was Guam's popular and outspoken priest, Father Jesus Baza Duenas. The Japanese had long suspected that Father Duenas was complicit in concealing Tweed—and, in fact, the Jesuit knew more about Tweed and his supporters than he let on. His status among the deeply religious Chamorros had protected him thus far, but on July 8, as a U.S. invasion loomed and moral constraints collapsed, the Japanese arrested the priest at his residence outside Inarajan. The young priest's nephew, former island attorney Eduardo ("Eddie") Duenas, was also taken into custody. Confined to a house close to where Father Duenas was being detained, Francisco Lujan and a few other village leaders could hear the priest being beaten throughout the night. His interrogators repeatedly asked about Radioman George Tweed. "Every time the priest denied that he knew the where-abouts of Tweed, he was hit with a club," said Lujan. "We could hear everything from the house where we were. We could hear it when he was hit with a club. We heard when he fell to the floor. We heard the priest keep denying that he knew anything about Tweed. This shouting and torture went on almost all night until about 3 a.m."[36]

At about noon the next day, village leader Ping Cruz and a few other Chamorro leaders were summoned to police headquarters where they found the two Duenas men hog-tied and lying on the ground outside. Their faces were swollen and their clothes spattered with blood. The Japanese took turns kicking the two men. Specta-tors were summoned from a nearby rice field to watch the abuse. Police warned them not to cry out or express sympathy for the pair, but one woman could not restrain herself, crying out, "Ay Yu'us Tata logue. Na para" (Oh, God, the Father please stop). A soldier clubbed her into silence before she could finish her plea.[37]

There was worse to come. The Japanese tied Father Duenas to a wooden plank, propping it up so that his feet were higher than his head. Three of his captors then took turns pouring water over the priest's mouth and nose, forcing him to swallow or drown. "And when his stomach bulged with water, two Japanese took a bamboo pole and pressed it against the priest's stomach," remembered Cruz. "This lasted for about three hours. . . . While they were torturing Father Duenas, they kept asking him where the Americans were. Father never said a word."[38]

Late in the day police finally ordered Francisco Lujan to untie the priest. "When I untied him, he asked me to help him to stand and to hold him under his armpits as he was all sore. He could not stand. He asked me to look for his glasses but I could not see them around." Lujan went to fill a can of water because the priest, despite the hours of water torture, was very thirsty. "I had to help him drink since his hands were tied. He asked for more water, but the police said no."

That evening the two captives were taken by truck to Kempeitai headquarters, located at a house in the hills overlooking Agana. Forty-six-year-old Joaquin Lim-tiaco, who had been impressed into service as a messenger by the Japanese, saw the prisoners in the yard there. The priest had been tied to the post of a chicken coop. Eddie was bound to a nearby tree. "Father Duenas was wearing a yellowish polo shirt and black trousers," recalled Limtiaco. "Eddie also had on a white polo shirt and khaki trousers. There was a nasty cut on his head and I could see blood clots about the wound." In the early morning hours, after the Japanese guards had retired,

Limtiaco and a fellow Chamorro received permission from a Saipanese interpreter to bring some coffee to the prisoners. As the priest thanked him, Limtiaco whispered that he was prepared to untie the men so they could escape into the jungle. "You know that the American bombardment has begun and it won't be long now before the invasion starts," he said.

Father Duenas declined. "I and my nephew were promised by the Japanese that we would be untied tomorrow because they have not found any information from us," he said. He also said he feared for the families of anyone involved in helping them to escape. "I'm positive the Japanese will retaliate against them. Go and look after your families. God will look after me. I have done no wrong," he assured his would-be rescuer. When Limtiaco approached Eddie, he too demurred. "I'm here with Father and I'll do whatever he wants to do," he replied. "If he says we'll escape. I'm for it. If he says no then we won't. I'm with him all the way. It's up to him."[39]

It was a fatal decision. The two men were subsequently brought to Kaikontai headquarters at Tai. There, on July 12, they were summarily beheaded. Two other Chamorros—Vincent Baza and Juan Pangelinan—who had helped Tweed during his years in hiding, were also killed. The four men died not knowing that Tweed had escaped only two days before.

The Japanese net was also closing on Antonio Artero, whose family had taken refuge in a cave to escape the naval bombardment. American planes were constantly overhead. "We were so scared because they were shooting at our house," recalled daughter Carmen. "They're bombing us from the ship, they're shooting us from the air."[40] Juan Pangelinan and his family had joined the Arteros, but one day two messengers—a Saipanese and a Chamorro—arrived to summon Pangelinan. They said the Japanese wanted to pay him for the livestock and produce taken from his farm.

"I warned him that it was a trap," recalled Antonio. "I said the Japanese had taken a lot of livestock and farm produce from me and that I had never heard that they compensated anyone."[41] Pangelinan, who had originally brought Tweed to Artero, replied, "Oh, I want to protect my wife and my kids. I'm going."[42] He left and was subsequently beheaded alongside Father Duenas on July 12. That same day, Antonio went to check on Tweed and found he was gone from his cliffside aerie. A note to Antonio, dated July 10 and scrawled on a sheet of green onionskin paper, advised, "A destroyer is sending in a boat to take me aboard. God bless you, my friend and if we both live until the war is over, you will surely hear from me."[43]

Two days later, messengers Joaquin Limtiaco and Juan Flores arrived with another summons from the Japanese, this time for Antonio. They told the same concocted story used to reassure Juan Pangelinan: the Japanese wanted to compensate Antonio for produce and livestock. "I can't believe you," retorted Antonio. "You're lying." As the two men insisted, Carmen ran up with a gun her father had hidden away. "My Dad took the gun away from me and pointed it at them and said, 'Tell me the truth or I'll shoot you. So help me God I'll kill the two of you right here."

Limtiaco and Flores confessed that they had been told to bring him in, even hog-tying him if they had to. If they couldn't find Antonio, they had been instructed to bring in his family. They'd been told they would be killed if they failed to bring Antonio back. Finally, they revealed that the Japanese had already tortured and killed Juan Pangelinan and Father Duenas.

"You get out of here before I kill you," Antonio told them.

The two men left. They subsequently told the Japanese they had been unable to locate Antonio or any members of his family. For his part, Antonio immediately packed up his family and moved them into Tweed's former hideout. Carmen was assigned to follow along in the rear, erasing their tracks and any signs of passage. "And I could hear Japanese voices in the far distance," she remembered.[44]

As thousands of her fellow Chamorros hid or trudged toward confinement camps, fourteen-year-old Beatrice Flores was searching for her uncle, Baldumero T. Peredo. The uncle had run afoul of the Japanese bureaucracy when he failed to obey the evacuation order to leave Agana. Finding that he was not at the family farm at Tai, Japanese "census officials" threatened to execute Beatrice's entire family if they failed to produce him. Beatrice was appointed to return to Agana and bring him back.

She found Baldumero hiding near the family home in Agana. He was filthy and nursing a badly infected injury to his leg. She was pleading with him to return with her to Tai when they were discovered by a Japanese patrol. Unimpressed by Beatrice's official pass, they escorted the two to a tunnel in the heights behind town, cramming them in with seven Chamorro men, who had also been detained. Three young women, weeping with fear, were soon pushed into the tunnel as well. Two of them, Diana and Josephine Guerrero, were sisters. The third girl was sixteen-year-old Antonia ("Toni") Fernandez. For two days they were held without food or water as they underwent interrogation through a Saipanese translator. "Did they love Americans?" he asked. Beatrice replied, "No, we love the Japanese." But nothing they said made any difference. "The more you tell them, the more they slap you because you're lying," she recalled.

Just before dawn on July 18, the prisoners were dragged down to a swamp outside Agana. The women were detained by the edge of a bomb crater, while the men, including Beatrice's uncle, were herded off into the jungle. "It was still dark, but when we heard the noise like someone cutting down a tree—*swish, swish*—and men screaming we knew the Japanese were killing them," she said. She went numb with fear as the cries stopped and the soldiers came back out of the woods, their uniforms spattered with blood. "Their rifles and everything are all [covered in] blood," she said.

A Japanese soldier tore off Diana Guerrero's dress and hacked at her breast with a bayonet. As the young woman screamed in terror, her sister rushed forward to intervene. "All the time she was shrieking and sobbing because the Japanese were stabbing her, too," recalled Beatrice. "Diane kept on screaming." When the two women finally stopped moving, the Japanese took them by the legs and threw them in the bomb crater. Turning on Toni, the Japanese slashed her arm and cut open her stomach before shoving her into the pit with the other two.

"When it comes to me, when they took me out, I was walking in air," Beatrice recalled of her terror. Someone pushed her head down, and she was jolted by a heavy blow. "I could feel my warm blood pouring out of me and it was as if my heart could not pound fast enough," she recalled. She was vaguely aware of dirt being thrown over her. She could not breathe from the pain in her neck and the dirt that was beginning to choke her, but she forced herself to remain still until the Japanese finally left. She had no idea how deeply she was buried, but was able to use her left hand to push the dirt away from her face.

As she struggled to free herself, she heard moaning. It was Toni Fernandez. "She was asking for water," recalled Beatrice. "I felt about and found what seemed to be moist mud. I took some of that mud and she and I sucked the moisture out of it. Little did I know that the moisture I picked up was that created by the blood of those executed and buried with us. I lay still for a while. When I again checked Toni . . . she didn't move. . . . [T]here were no sounds from her. . . . [S]he was stiff and dead."

Beatrice finally managed to dig herself out of the makeshift grave. In agony from a four-inch gash in her neck, she stumbled away. "I don't know where I'm going. I don't know what happened to me. I don't know nothing," she said later. "I just keep going."[45]

CHAPTER 11

FROGMEN AND TETRYTOL

THE TEDIUM ABOARD THE TRANSPORT AND TRACTOR GROUPS WAITING AT ENIWE-tok came to a close on July 15 as the LSTs finally left the anchorage bound for Guam. The faster transports got underway two days later, just a few hours after the arrival of ships carrying the first elements of the 77th Infantry Division arrived at the lagoon. Over 56,000 troops would be involved in the invasion, including 37,292 Marines and 19,425 Army.

"Everyone was in good spirits, feeling eager, ready for anything," remarked Corporal Fred Addison, who would go in with the 1st Armored Amphibian Tractor Battalion. "Bob Pierce from my crew cut my hair with scissors from a 35-cent sewing kit. I daubed green paint on my knife sheath, pack, canteen cover, etc., as camouflage. I cleaned my A-10 machine gun, the tripod, and my carbine again. I washed socks and a towel. Card games occurred every day and night, and some ran continuously. Pretty soon the players were narrowed down to five or six, and then to just a couple. One man in the 22nd Marines aboard had over $1,700 in winnings, and in 1944 that was one hell of a lot of money."[1]

Major Henry Aplington's LST was already underway and headed for the lagoon entrance when a landing craft came alongside with his regimental commander, Colonel W. Carvel Hall, carrying an assortment of the latest aerial photos showing the 3rd Marines' landing area. Hall spread the photos out on the wardroom table and allowed Aplington a quick look before gathering them up and hurrying on to the next battalion. "Actually, they were, except to give an impression, almost useless," recalled Aplington of the photographs. The critical hill mass inland showed only as a "gray splotch" marked "cloud." Still, he wished he could have had access to the photos during the long wait at Eniwetok instead of receiving a mere last-minute glance.[2]

George Tweed might have been able to provide some insight to assist ground operations, but he was no longer available. "Tweed was interrogated by [Admiral] Kelly Turner's staff and immediately rushed back to the States," remarked IIIAC intelligence officer Lieutenant Colonel William F. Coleman. "Requests for permission for III Amphibious Corps intelligence officers to question Tweed were denied and to the best of my knowledge, the corps never received any of the information obtained from Tweed."[3]

There were the usual final briefings and gear checks. Passwords and countersigns were established for the first five days. The response to a challenge was to be any month of the year, such as "July." The challenger would then reply with another month, such as "April," as the countersign. After five days, the password/countersign would change to any U.S. city and five days after that to any U.S. state. Troops were reminded, "Guam is American territory and the people are American nationals. We will be welcomed as liberators, not as enemies. This is the first operation on American soil in the Pacific exclusive of Attu in the Aleutians." An annex to Operation Plan No. 1-44 cautioned, "The Citizens of Stevedore will be treated with every consideration due American Citizens. All personnel will be cautioned that the molesting of women and the looting of property will be swiftly and severely dealt with." The annex listed thirty-eight Guamanians ranging from administrators and businessmen to civic leaders and clergy—including Mrs. Agueda Johnston—"who are believed to be reliable and will welcome our return" and would be useful in reestablishing civilian structure. Also among the thirty-eight was Father Jesus Baza Duenas, whose decapitated remains, unknown to U.S. intelligence, now lay in an unmarked grave at Tai.

Another annex referred to collaborators, specifically singling out one F. R. Ishizaki, "nicknamed 'Ben Cook,'" and "Mrs. Sawada," widow of a prominent Japanese national, as known fifth columnists. "The above two persons should be apprehended as soon as possible and escorted to Corps CP, when established ashore, without delay," noted the directive.[4] Ironically, the list of fifth columnists did not include Samuel Shinohara, who would later be charged with treason.

As for Japanese military personnel, veterans scarcely needed to be reminded that no quarter was to be expected or given. Lieutenant Cord Meyer, who had first fought the Japanese at Eniwetok, had been "astonished by the behavior of the Japanese, although we had been amply warned." Rather than surrender, "they chose to fight to the last man and to take as many of us with them as they could before they died," he said. "With their last bullet, they would commit suicide rather than allow themselves to be captured. If they were wounded, they would hide a grenade so that those of us who attempted to help would be blown up with them. Only those most seriously wounded or those stunned into unconsciousness by a shell burst could be taken prisoner." Meyer admitted to "a grudging respect for their suicidal bravery,"[5] but that same respect brought a very cold admonition from PFC Charles LePant's battalion commander. "Don't be taken prisoner," he told his Marines. "And I don't want any prisoners."[6]

⸻

As W-Day approached, General Roy Geiger relaxed as best he could with a mystery novel featuring the legendary Fu Man Chu. In the waters off Guam, the underwater demolition teams (UDTs) were already in action.

UDT-3 arrived aboard USS *Dickerson* on July 14, followed three days later by UDT-4 aboard USS *Kane* and UDT-6 aboard USS *Clemson*. They came with thousands of pounds of high-explosive tetrytol to blow beach obstacles and open channels in the reef. *Dickerson* alone carried forty-two tons of tetrytol stored in the upper troop compartment, "which hindered eating facilities and decreased ship's stability," ship's officers complained.[7] The UDT teams also packed a somewhat less warlike accoutrement: hundreds of condoms. The condoms had raised some eyebrows when first requisitioned, but it wasn't as it seemed. "They were not for sexual purposes but used to waterproof our firing caps, which were underwater much of the time," observed Radioman Second Class Robert M. ("Woody") Wood of UDT-4.[8]

A study of aerial photos indicated that the reef obstacles at Guam consisted primarily of coral-filled log cribs. During the initial planning stages, a high-ranking naval officer had suggested the crews of the LVT(A)s could "throw harpoon type devices into the obstacles" and simply drag them out of the way, but that hairbrained idea was speedily dismissed in favor of good old American tetrytol.[9] During their wait at Eniwetok, UDT-4 constructed six-by-four-foot coconut log cribs filled with coral to study the best way to destroy the barriers. Experimentation showed that twenty pounds of tetrytol placed along the seaward side of the crib was sufficient to get the job done.

The UDT plan called for three days and nights of reconnaissance of the reef and obstacles along the designated landing beaches at Agat and Asan. The teams would then begin to systematically destroy the obstructions. In an effort to confuse the Japanese, the teams would also conduct diversionary swims at Tumon Bay, Agana Beach, Dadi Beach, and the beach between Bangi Point and Facpi Point, south of the designated landing area at Agat.

UDT-3's first night recon at Asan on July 14 got off to a shaky start. Clad in jungle-green fatigues, kneepads, rubber-soled sneakers, and work gloves, forty-eight swimmers went in—twelve to each of the four designated landing beaches. The reef was almost dry at low tide as the "swimmers" crawled along the rough coral. "Considerable enemy activity on beach," noted Lieutenant Thomas C. ("Tom") Crist, the thirty-year-old Texan commanding UDT-3. "Men could be heard talking, trucks running, a cement mixer, and many small lights were observed." At 2300, three bursts of enemy machine-gun fire were heard, and when the swimmers reassembled an hour later, three men failed to show up. The rest of the team reluctantly retired. A boat was left to retrieve the missing men if they showed up later, but by morning there was still no sign of them.[10]

Finally, at 0615, lookouts aboard the destroyer *MacDonough* spotted the missing swimmers—Ensign W. J. Dezelle, Ensign Martin Jacobson and Gunner's Mate Third Class J. E. Bagnall—twenty-five hundred yards offshore. "I don't know how they saw us . . . these little heads bobbing up and down in the water," remarked Jacobson gratefully. Pulled from the water, the weary men said they had been trapped on the reef, unable to move with enemy personnel only a few feet away, when it came time to reassemble. "After a while, we thought the enemy had seen us so we started swimming out to sea, to see if we could find the boat," said Jacobson. They had been swimming and treading water since about midnight.[11]

The following day, UDT-3 suffered its first fatality during a daylight reconnaissance of Agat Beach where the 1st Provisional Marine Brigade was slated to come ashore on W-Day. Thirty-one-year-old Chief Warrant Officer Ralph A. Blowers was killed when his landing craft got hung up on a coral head and came under fire from shore. A bullet hit the chief in the neck and severed his spinal cord, killing him instantly. Crewmen aboard LCI(G) 469, providing cover for the swimmers, also came under fire, and five men were wounded by shell fragments. Chief Blowers was brought back to the *Dickerson* and buried at sea that same evening.

Reconnaissance of the 3rd Marine Division beaches revealed that crib-type obstacles had been placed in an almost continuous line along the reef. "These obstacles were piles of coral rock within a wire frame made of heavy wire net, similar to 'Cyclone' wire fencing," noted the UDT-3 report. "The obstacles were three to five feet in diameter, three to four feet high and five to eight feet apart."[12] Over on the Marine Brigade beaches, UDT-4, commanded by thirty-five-year-old William G. Carberry, a lawyer and former Campbell's Soup Company employee, found coral-filled log cribs arranged in an irregular line about 100 to 150 yards offshore and extending over the entire one-mile length of the landing zone. Gaps were blocked by wire cables running from crib to crib. The obstacles were augmented by a two- to three-strand barbed wire fence on a single line of wooden posts along the low-water line about twenty yards offshore. Posts fashioned from tree trunks had been planted on the beach to block vehicles.

Swimmers found no evidence of mines on either landing zone. However, the Japanese continued last-minute work on reef obstacles even with the invasion force gathering offshore, as one UDT ensign discovered when he went to reprimand some of his men for talking too loudly. Hurrying toward the offenders through ankle-deep water, the ensign came up short and hastily retreated when he discovered the chatter came from a Japanese work party busy piling rocks into the wire cribs.[13]

The teams began blowing obstacles four days before W-Day. The procedure employed by UDT-3 was typical. The swimmers embarked after dark from the *Dickerson* in an LCPR (Landing Craft Personnel, Ramped), which towed two rubber boats loaded with thirty packs totaling 630 pounds of tetrytol. As they approached the reef, four LCI(G) gunboats stood five hundred to one thousand yards offshore maintaining continuous fire with their 40mm and 20mm guns on the beach area to discourage Japanese interference. Once the teams reached the reef, the gunboats ceased firing but remained on watch, ready to act if needed.

Paddling or dragging the rubber boats as close to the obstacles as possible, the demolition teams set to work. In some instances obstacles were less than fifty yards from shore, and the reef was completely dry, leaving the teams with no concealment as they lugged the charges toward the cribs. A Primacord trunk line connected the cribs to be blown. One twenty-pound pack of tetrytol was tucked in alongside each obstacle and tied into the trunk line. Once everything was in place, the men were picked up by their boat; the firing signal was given, and a four-minute fuse was pulled as the boat left the area.

The work was not always routine. One night a UDT-4 boat became stuck on the reef at Agat after the fuse on the demolition charges had been pulled. As time ran out, the men ducked flat in the boat as a long line of obstacles blew sky high along the reef. Wood and coral fragments splashed around and onto the stranded boat, but fortunately no one was injured.[14]

Late in the day on W–4, UDT-3's efforts to clear the 3rd Marine Division beaches ran into an even more serious snag when one of the covering gunboats, LCI(G) 348, ran aground on the reef edge four hundred to five hundred yards off Red Beach 2. Efforts pull the gunboat off failed when the lines parted. As the Japanese opened up on the stranded ship with mortar fire, the task unit commander ordered the gunboat abandoned. The crew was taken off in small boats. The enemy fire failed to hit the gunboat, but destroyers *Sigsbee* and *Schroeder* stood by through the night in case the Japanese attempted to board the abandoned vessel. Meanwhile, when UDT-3 went to blow the obstacles, a misfire left many of the cribs intact. The following day, the frogmen revisited the reef in their first daylight mission and relaid the charges—totaling three thousand pounds of tetrytol—masked by a smoke screen put down by planes, smoke shells from destroyers, and smoke rockets from the LCI(G)s. This time the charges fired, taking out 150 coral-filled cribs. Later in the afternoon, a tug managed to pull LCI(G) 348 off the reef under intermittent machine-gun fire.

Over a period of four days, UDT-4 removed about three hundred obstacles from the Agat beaches and blasted coral pinnacles blocking the entrance to a natural channel through the reef at White 1. Just to the north, UDT-3 removed 640 obstacles from the 3rd Marine Division beaches, using ten tons of tetrytol in total. The four LCI(G)s supporting the team with covering fire each expended about ten thousand rounds of 40mm and from twenty thousand to thirty thousand rounds of 20mm, along with two hundred barrage and smoke rockets during the process.

Despite the danger, Chief Blowers was the only UDT fatality during the reef clearing operation. The lack of casualties may have been due in part to Japanese fire discipline. Superior Private Teruo Kurokawa, a member of a 47mm antitank gun crew on Asan Point, later told interrogators that "his piece could have wiped out our UDT teams a number of times but orders were not to fire until a landing attempt was underway."[15] Ironically, Private Kurokawa's obedience to orders came to naught: his gun was subsequently destroyed in the preinvasion bombardment.

For his part, Admiral Richard Conolly was making good on his promise to methodically destroy the island's defenses from the sea. "My aim is to get the troops ashore standing up," Conolly told Geiger. "You tell me what you want done to accomplish this and we'll do it."[16]

The naval effort got underway in earnest on July 8—the start of the most extensive preinvasion bombardment of the Pacific war. The postponement of W-Day from June 18 to July 21 had its drawbacks, but by extending the softening up process, it undoubtedly saved Marine lives on the invasion beaches. For the next thirteen days (exclusive of W-Day), six battleships, nine cruisers, and a host of destroyers poured shells into the island while carrier planes bombed and strafed. The expenditure of shells totaled 836 rounds of 16-inch; 5,422 of 14-inch; 3,862 of 8-inch; 2,430 of 6-inch; and 16,214 of 5-inch. From July 11 onward, at least one battleship division was always present to lend the weight of their 16-inch guns—capable of hurling a twenty-seven-hundred-pound shell up to twenty-four miles—to the preinvasion bombardment.

Progress was monitored by a panel of officers called the "target information board," consisting of representatives from naval, air, gunnery, and intelligence staff sections, as well as from the landing force. "A list of all known Japanese installations was compiled and as firing ships damaged or destroyed one of these installations a notation was made on the list," noted IIIAC. "The list was kept current with addition of new installations as they were discovered by photography or other means."[17]

Carrier aircraft also continued to pound island targets. On July 18, carrier aircraft flew 662 bombing sorties and 311 strafing attacks; on July 19, the numbers were 874 and 392; on the day before the landings, they were 1,430 and 614. A total of 1,121 tons of bombs, depth charges, and rockets were expended in the effort to neutralize enemy positions.

The process was not without cost. Thirty-five aircraft were lost to antiaircraft fire over Guam during June. Sixteen more were lost in the three weeks leading up to W-Day. Between July 6 and 17 alone, combat losses were nine planes, all from antiaircraft fire. A similar number were lost operationally. *Yorktown* lost a dive-bomber and crew in a particularly horrendous "operational" accident on July 16. Returning with a damaged aileron from a strike on Rota, twenty-five-year-old Lieutenant Paul Mullen of Saint Paul, Minnesota, and his backseat gunner, Aviation Radioman Second Class Nicholas J. Boutos, were forced to bail out near two destroyers about five miles off Orote Point. Boutos was fished unconscious from the water by USS *Sigsbee*, but efforts to resuscitate the New York native were unsuccessful. Mullen had survived the jump in better shape and was seen swimming in his life jacket but was inadvertently run down by the USS *Schroeder* as the destroyer rushed to retrieve him. A subsequent search of the area recovered only his life jacket and a small body part identified as a piece of a lung.

For the Japanese, the incessant shelling and aerial bombardment made movement by daylight virtually impossible. A shaken Japanese private wrote, "On this island no matter where one goes the shells follow."[18] Antiaircraft units exacted a toll on American pilots, but their ammunition was running low. "On 17 July there were only eight rounds left for each antiaircraft gun, these were reserved for later use against tanks," noted a Japanese report.[19]

"Most of the beach defenses were destroyed," observed a subsequent Japan Self Defense Force report. "All the palm trees along the seashore were mowed down. . . . Radio stations were fired upon in less than a minute after they started sending signals. . . . In the Agana area, every structure but the church was completely demolished. At Pago, Inarajan and Merizo, all road bridges were destroyed and the movement of motor vehicles and artillery became impossible."[20] The shelling was so intense "we feared that the whole island might sink into the ocean," said Corporal Shoichi Yokoi.[21]

Lieutenant Rai Imanishi recorded his frustration in his diary. "Our positions [at Agat] have been almost completed but they have not been done as we had hoped. . . . [G]reat effort was put into the construction but we still have been unable to complete the cover. We are in a terrible fix."[22] Special "marine squads" were organized to fire torpedoes from large landing barges. Other torpedoes were buried on expected landing beaches as makeshift antitank, antivehicle mines. Bottles were filled with gasoline and equipped with wicks for use against tanks.

The constant shelling was also beginning to take a psychological toll on the Japanese troops. News of the fall of Saipan over a week earlier had stiffened Japanese morale, making the troops angry and more "vigorous" in their determination to preserve Guam as a base for counterattacks by the Japanese navy and air forces.[23] Nevertheless, Lieutenant Colonel Hideyuki Takeda later admitted that the unrelenting bombardment preceding the landings led to "scattered outbreaks of serious loss of spirit." The shelling and bombing were "near the limit bearable by humans," he confessed. As the attacks intensified, some of the men were so affected they "could not perform their duties in a positive manner."[24]

Among the casualties was Corporal Masashi Ito's best friend, Aihara Fumiya. Fumiya was struck by a bomb splinter during an American air attack—"a wicked, jagged piece of metal which entered the rear part of his body and cleaved a path right through him practically to his spine," remembered Ito. "It was a miracle he wasn't killed outright." It might have been better for Fumiya if he had died immediately. He lingered for days in a hospital ward "that looked more like one of our cave shelters" before finally succumbing to his wound, observed Ito.[25]

Corporal Ito's friend was particularly unlucky. Despite the intensity of the shelling, personnel casualties from the preinvasion bombardment were not especially high—roughly one hundred killed—and the survival rate among guns and hardened positions was better than U.S. gunnery analysis suggested. Of the naval guns emplaced in caves, about half remained operational. Positions built with a type of hard coral called *cascajo* and reinforced with concrete had proven able to survive any but a direct hit. Positions built with concrete over one meter thick remained unaffected by naval shelling. Power generators had been tucked away in caves and suffered no damage. Guns and mortars on the reverse slopes overlooking potential invasion beaches remained untouched. Communications also remained unaffected. The Japanese had taken care to lay wire lines in two and sometimes even three separate routes through defiladed areas and protected gullies and ravines. That precaution paid big dividends.

Colonel Takeda could not cite a single instance where military phone lines were cut by naval gunfire. Wire and wireless communications with island units remained intact. General Takeshi Takashina also enjoyed uninterrupted communications with the garrison on Rota and with Imperial General Headquarters in Tokyo.

Major General Kiyoshi Shigematsu reassured his 48th Independent Mixed Brigade that despite the awesome display of firepower, the Americans could be beaten. "The enemy, overconfident because of his successful landing on Saipan, is planning a reckless and insufficiently prepared landing on Guam. We have an excellent opportunity to annihilate him on the beaches," he declared.[26]

Stationed with his transport company near Agat, Corporal Shoichi Yokio found himself looking to the future with a strange inner calm. "I do not know how to explain this," he wrote later. "But I was beginning to be settled into some sort of determination. Not only myself, but also all of us shared the same frame of mind. We quietly hid ourselves in a shelter and calmly waited for the invasion."[27]

The *Indianapolis* with Fifth Fleet commander Admiral Ray Spruance on board arrived on July 20 to join the fire support vessels. By the afternoon of W–1, all forces connected with the impending assault were in position or, in the case of the troop-carrying ships, nearly so. The four major components of the landing force numbered 54,891 men: 3rd Marine Division (20,328), 1st Provisional Marine Brigade (9,886), 77th Infantry Division (17,958), and IIIAC troops (6,719).

Naval forces included fifteen carriers of Task Force 58 along with five escort carriers, six battleships, nine cruisers, and fifty-seven destroyers. Four battleships, three cruisers, and four destroyers had been assigned close-in support missions off Asan, and two battleships, three cruisers, and three destroyers would provide support to the Agat beaches. Their big guns would be supplemented by the rocket-firing LCI(G)s and a multitude of other smaller vessels supporting the landing.

Everything seemed to be on track, though Admiral Conolly had an anxious moment on W–1 when Admiral Spruance messaged to ask if he had made contingency plans to postpone W-Day due to an impending typhoon. Conolly's hurricane specialist assured him that while a typhoon was building, the track would take it several hundred miles to the west of Guam. Any effect on the surf along the western beaches would not be felt for six or seven days.

In a dispatch to the task force, Conolly reported that the weather forecast for July 21 was "excellent" with conditions "most favorable for a successful landing."[28] All known major defensive installations covering the landing beaches had been silenced.

"The extended period for bombardment, plus a system for keeping target damage reports, accounted for practically every known Japanese gun that could seriously endanger our landings," observed General Geiger's naval gunfire officer. "When the morning of W-Day arrived it was known that the assault troops would meet little immediate resistance." Admiral Conolly's staff concurred, optimistically opining, "Not one fixed gun was left in commission on the west coast that was of greater size than a machine gun."[29] They should have known better, but optimism was running high.

W-Day was confirmed with H-Hour set for 0830.

Aboard LST 479 a thirty-two-year-old former parish priest, Lieutenant Anthony ("Tony") K. Conway, now chaplain to the 1st Battalion, 22nd Marines, penned a last letter home to his parents in Lost Creek, Pennsylvania. "We go into Guam tomorrow," he wrote. "I am not so much afraid now. But tomorrow morning I, no doubt, will be plenty scared. But I love the adventure. And then the good I am doing makes fear take a back seat. If the worst should happen to me know that it is God's will, and I gave my life for the church and the God who rules it."[30]

As U.S. commanders focused on last-minute plans and adjustments, the killing spree on Guam was spiraling out of control. On July 15, even as the American invasion force left Eniwetok, several hundred residents of Merizo on southern Guam were rounded up and marched under guard toward a concentration camp at Atate in the Geus River valley. Some of them would never get there.

Toward evening, the crowd was called to order by a Japanese officer accompanied by an interpreter. Falling in with the rest, former Navy messman Filipe Cruz watched as the officer extracted a list from his pocket. Following the attack on the USS *Robert L. Barnes*, Cruz had returned home to Merizo but was soon swept up in a Japanese dragnet seeking Insular Force personnel. His attempts to plead ignorance came to naught when interrogators spotted his military-issue shoes. He and his shipmates spent the next two and a half years toiling on various enemy work details ranging from unloading cargo ships to digging manganese out of open pit mines. Most recently he had been forced to dig trenches and transport ammunition as the Japanese prepared for the coming battle.

Consulting his list, the officer began reading off names for a supposed work detail. There were twenty-eight in all, including schoolteachers, the village commissioner, parents of sons in the U.S. military, former members of Guam's Insular Force Guard, a mother who refused to bow to the Japanese, the woman's two daughters, and other recalcitrant or potentially troublesome Chamorros. Cruz heard his own name, along with those of his father and several shipmates, called out. Separated from the rest, they were escorted through the jungle to a cave that had originally been dug to store ammunition. It was now dark. Cruz could see sporadic flashes like heat lightning off in the distance as the U.S. invasion fleet bombarded shore installations. Their Japanese guards appeared to be drunk. They were engaging in "much merrymaking," noted Cruz. "Particularly amusing to them was our reaction to their sword teasing" as they pantomimed attacks on their captives.[31]

As the Chamorros were ordered into the cave, forty-seven-year-old Manuel Charfauros, a member of the prewar Guam Congress and former Merizo school principal, lagged behind the others just outside the entrance. Suspicious of the Japanese and their so-called work party, he was considering making a run for it, when a grenade exploded. Startled, Charfauros looked down to see another grenade by his feet. He leapt away as it exploded, tearing a chunk of flesh from his left leg.

Crammed into the cave with the others, Filipe Cruz first gleaned what was about to happen when a single rifle shot struck his father. More gunfire tore into Chamorros crowded at the entrance. A moment later a hand grenade landed inside and exploded with a deafening roar. A second grenade followed, then a third, which bounced off Cruz's chest. He grabbed it and tried to heave it outside, but it hit something and bounced back and exploded, driving metal fragments into his right side. Terrified, Cruz made a break for the entrance. "I ran up to the guard at the door, who had another hand grenade in his hand ready to toss in my direction," he recalled. He pushed past the surprised guard and crashed off into the underbrush, followed by a scattering of rifle shots. It was dark and raining, and no one attempted to follow him.[32]

Unable to run due to his torn leg, Manuel Charfauros lay motionless in the rain, feigning death. He could hear labored breathing from inside the cave. Someone else was making a bubbly sound. Several Japanese had lined up by the cave entrance. Charfauros heard footsteps as their leader approached holding a sword. "Suddenly there was a hiss followed by silence," he recalled. "And then another hiss and the bubbling stopped." As Charfauros silently prayed for mercy, the officer approached him and struck him with the sword across the right shoulder, then a second time across his back and yet again at the base of his skull. Somehow Charfauros managed to remain still. The Japanese turned back to the cave and threw hand grenades among the people crowded inside. The multiple explosions were punctuated by cries and groans. Someone staggered to the entrance begging for mercy. Charfauros heard the officer say, "Maila" (Come).

"Please, have mercy and excuse . . . ," said the terrified Chamorro.

"Maila," repeated the officer, followed by a thud as he beheaded the man.

Another captive was more fortunate. Told to come out as he begged for mercy, he recoiled as the sword descended and was struck in the shoulder instead of the neck. Like Charfauros, he lay still, feigning death. Satisfied with their handiwork, the soldiers entered the cave to bayonet anyone still showing signs of life. Lying motionless among the corpses, a few terrified survivors heard Maria Lukban Mesa, a former school principal, pleading for her life just before a Japanese officer plunged his sword into her chest. "It was raining heavily by the time the soldiers came out of the cave," recalled Charfauros. "They collected their equipment and filed down the slope, disappearing into the dark."[33]

Miraculously, twelve people in addition to Charfauros and Cruz survived the butchery, most by pulling the dead and dying over themselves in the cramped confines of the cave and feigning death. A few of them were already staggering out of the cave. Charfauros cried out to one of the survivors for help. Presumably preoccupied with his own troubles, the man retorted, "Aw—you can crawl," and went crashing down into the ravine. Charfauros finally dragged himself to a clump of banana trees a few yards away and propped himself up against a tree trunk. He sat there, shivering violently, until he finally fell asleep.[34]

The killing continued three days later at Fena, near Agat, where over thirty Chamorro teenagers had been drafted to transport ammunition. It appeared that their liberation was at hand. "American planes were already flying over Guam and everybody felt that the invasion was going to take place soon," remarked eighteen-year-old Jose Oficido Cruz.

As the U.S. bombardment intensified on July 19, the soldiers rounded up the teens and ordered them into caves near Fena Lake. Several of the girls were pulled from the group and taken to a separate cave, where they were repeatedly raped throughout the night. The men were given some rice and *daigo*, a pickled radish dish. "After we ate, they told us to go into the cave to rest and sleep because they would be releasing us soon," recalled Cruz. "I thought maybe they were releasing us because of the American invasion."

But once everyone was inside, the horror began as the Japanese threw grenades into the crowded cave and opened fire with machine guns. "Those who did not die from the hand grenades started screaming and calling out to God as they started to push each other towards the back of the cave," recalled Cruz. "I was already at the back and I crawled into a small crevice at the bottom back wall. Others tried to follow me but the back of the cave was small and it just seemed as if the people were trying to crush each other into the back wall to get away from the machine gun fire."

Eventually the shooting stopped, and Japanese soldiers entered the cave to bayonet anyone still showing signs of life. Some of them were armed with bamboo lances that had been sharpened at one end. Huddled in his crevice behind a pile of corpses, Cruz could see their shadows as they went about their gruesome task by the light of what he believed to be oil lanterns. Finally they left, presumably to join in the nightlong rape of the girls who had been taken earlier.

"I stayed in the cave that night and didn't move even my fingers because I was afraid the Japanese were still there and would hear me," said Cruz. "But after a long time, I wanted to get out because it was getting difficult to breathe. I started pushing away the bodies that were around me. I wanted to get some air because the smell of gunpowder and the blood and guts was so strong." He emerged into bright sunlight. It appeared to be around noontime. There were no Japanese soldiers in sight, but when he tried to stand up, he felt a terrible pain in his leg and collapsed. "When I looked down at my leg and pants I could see that it was covered with blood but I couldn't tell whether it was mine or others," he said.

He looked back into the cave at the pile of bodies he had just crawled over. "Some of the bodies were badly dismembered and some had their insides coming out," he remembered. He recognized his brother Pedro. "His body was very bloody and I could tell he was dead." Two other men were lying outside the cave, and he thought they were moaning, though neither was moving. "There was dried blood all over their bodies and they were just staring with their mouths open but I thought that I heard them moaning."

He took off his shirt "because [he] couldn't stand the smell and it became very stiff because of the dried blood." Casting it aside, he hobbled off in the direction of Manenggon.[35]

— ~~ —

Herded into a detention camp at Atate, the Merizo refugees soon learned from the few survivors what had befallen the twenty-eight villagers separated from the rest on July 15. Their fears grew about the fate of another thirty young men who had been taken away the next day, ostensibly to help carry ammunition and supplies. Days passed, and none returned. Their families would later find that the men had been murdered on July 16 at nearby Faha, and this time there were no survivors. But now, some Chamorros decided to fight back.

Five days after the Faha Massacre, eighteen-year-old Juan M. Torres was ordered to accompany a work detail to fetch rice from a depot about a mile away from the camp at Atate. He and his companion were taking a break on their return to camp when a band of Chamorros armed with rifles and swords came down the trail from the direction of the rice depot. Torres asked what was happening.

"The Americans have landed at Cocos Island," replied one of the men. "We are going to kill the Japanese at Atate."

Leading the group was twenty-four-year-old Jose ("Tonko") Reyes. He and three other Chamorros had already killed four Japanese at the rice depot where Reyes got things started by knocking one of the three guards down with his fist. Overpowering two others, the Chamorros dragged them all down to the river and beat them to death with stones. A fourth Japanese was shot dead with one of the captured rifles when he chose that inopportune moment to show up at the depot. Now numbering over a dozen men, the insurgents were on their way to eliminate the seven guards at the Atate camp.

Reyes planned to take the Japanese there by surprise. Two of the men, Juan Cruz Borja and Juan Meno Garrido, would carry a bag of rice to the guard tent entrance and call to the Japanese. Everyone else would stay out of sight. When a guard came to the entrance, Garrido would knock him down, and the rest of the Chamorros would rush the tent before the Japanese could get to their weapons.

Arriving at the tent, Borja and Garrido called out to the guards inside, but when one of them emerged, Garrido hesitated. Unaware of his peril, the guard saw the rest of the Chamorros standing idly around. "You, and you and you, where are your rice bags!" he yelled angrily. Alarmed, Reyes shouted to Garrido, "Hit him or I'll shoot you instead!"

Garrido knocked the guard down, and the Chamorros rushed the tent. From somewhere a woman shrieked, "*Ai*, why are you doing this? Now they will kill all of us!"

The first guard, clad only in a red *fundoshi* ("loincloth"), tried to crab away, then went into a fetal position, crying out in protest as the Chamorros descended on him. A woman in the gathering crowd urged them on, shouting, "Hit him in the balls, hit him in the balls." That proved unnecessary, recalled Torres, as the guard was already quite dead "with parts of his brain splattered all over the surrounding vegetation."

The guard detachment leader escaped into the jungle, but the rest were beaten or strangled to death. The Chamorros dragged the bodies from the collapsed tent and lined them up on the ground before a now somber crowd of detainees. Their guards were dead, but no one had any illusions as to what would happen if the Japanese returned in force. As they hurried to flee the camp, it was agreed that six of the men—including Torres and Garrido—would attempt to contact the Americans. The six volunteers decided their best chance would be to head to the coast and take a canoe out to sea in hopes of being picked up by a U.S. warship.[36]

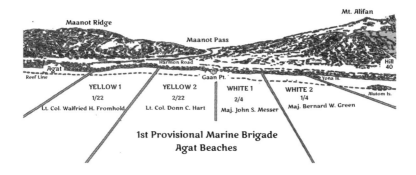

Maanot Ridge

Mt. Alifan

Maanot Pass

Harmon Road

Agat

Reef Line

Gaan Pt.

Yona Is.

Hill 40

Alutom Is.

YELLOW 1	YELLOW 2	WHITE 1	WHITE 2
1/22	2/22	2/4	1/4
Lt. Col. Walfried H. Fromhold	Lt. Col. Donn C. Hart	Maj. John S. Messer	Maj. Bernard W. Green

**1st Provisional Marine Brigade
Agat Beaches**

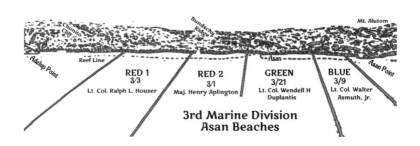

Chonito Cliff

Bundschu Ridge

Mt. Alutom

Adelup Point

Reef Line

Asan

Asan Point

RED 1	RED 2	GREEN	BLUE
3/3	3/1	3/21	3/9
Lt. Col. Ralph L. Houser	Maj. Henry Aplington	Lt. Col. Wendell H Duplantis	Lt. Col. Walter Asmuth, Jr.

**3rd Marine Division
Asan Beaches**

CHAPTER 12

ACROSS THE REEF

IN THE WATERS OFF GUAM, THE COMPLICATED DANCE OF AMPHIBIOUS ASSAULT WAS finally beginning to unfold. The process, mused a Marine officer, involved perhaps "the fastest regression of mankind from civilization to barbarity." One morning a man was enjoying breakfast in the wardroom of his ship, and "three and a half hours and a short boat ride [later] . . . he could be rolling in a ditch with another human being trying to kill him with a knife."[1]

As the LSTs and transports rounded Guam's northern coast in the darkness, the flicker of naval gunfire was visible on the horizon like distant heat lightning. The 3rd Division would debark from sixteen LSTs and twelve transports and the Marine Brigade from sixteen LSTs and eight transports. "Throughout the night gun flashes and star shells were observed in the vicinity of Guam," noted the war diary of USS *Rixey*, approaching the island at about 0130.[2] Some men watched quietly; others tended to last-minute details. No one could predict the future. Chaplain Father Paul J. Redmond passed the time playing bridge with three young officers from the 4th Marines. Within the next few days, he would preside over the burials of all three.

Corporal Fred Addison recalled little overt excitement with the landing now only hours away. "I imagine civilians picture the day as a lot of commotion, with everybody sharpening their knives, reading Bibles, and talking of home in a hysterical way," he observed. "But it was just like most other days except for maybe an hour when we went over the plans." He spent most of the day playing double solitaire. "At 1500 they turned on the showers. I had a good long one, and that felt good. . . . I attended church services as did most men. We could see flashes from naval gunfire on the horizon after dark."[3]

A corporal in First Lieutenant Robert A. Fish's amtank platoon came to him with an unusual dilemma. "He was carrying a sack full of money—$2,000 to

$2,500—that he had won at poker or dice," recalled Fish. "He wanted to know what to do with the money. We went to the ship's exec and checked it into the ship's safe. I have often wondered whatever happened to that money. [The corporal] was killed in the landing when a shot hit the turret of his tank."[4]

Aboard LST 477, half a dozen stowaways who had gone AWOL from Marine air units stationed on Eniwetok had belatedly emerged from hiding. They included a laundry machine operator and an airfield firetruck crewman. Anxious that the "real war" was passing them by and eager for combat, they had stowed away on an LST carrying the 1st Battalion, 4th Marines when the convoy sailed. They could now look forward to a reduction in rank, attachment of pay, and every shit detail their parent unit could provide when they finally returned—if they returned. But for now, they had their wish.

The Marines on Alvin Josephy's transport spent the night sitting around in the crowded hold, singing, talking, and giving weapons a probably unnecessary final cleaning. They weren't allowed topside, and it was hot in the hold. A "tall thin boy" on one of the stacked canvas racks was talking about his wife and two children at home in Chicago. He said he hoped this would be his last campaign. As it turned out, it was, though not in the way he hoped, recalled Josephy. He was destined to be killed in the fighting.[5]

Artilleryman Jack Kerins, assigned to land with the unit's reconnaissance party in the early waves at Asan, spent the night before W-Day in the ship's mess hall trying to write last-minute letters to his parents and his "dream girl" back in Terre Haute, Indiana. Failing, he finally consigned his wadded-up attempts to a GI can and went topside. He stood at the rail conversing with a couple of buddies about nothing in particular as they studied the wash from the bow of the ship bringing them closer and closer to the unknown. "The three of us spent the rest of the night lying on the hatch cover. It seemed we had just fallen asleep when the squawk box blared," he recalled.[6]

Reveille in the sweltering hold of Josephy's transport came via loudspeaker at 0230: *Reveille, Reveille! All up! All up!* Reveille and chow times varied on the LSTs from as early as 0200 to as late as 0400. "Most of us had been wide awake long before daylight because we had been too nervous and excited to sleep, so we kept busy by checking and double checking our weapons, ammunition and hand grenades as we smoked one cigarette after another," confessed PFC George R. Aspley aboard LST 122.[7]

Lieutenant James ("Tom") Brock, a former star football center for Notre Dame's Fighting Irish, insisted he actually slept "quite well," though he admitted he "couldn't help thinking what the next morning would be like." He was slated to land at Asan with the 3rd Battalion, 21st Marines. "We rolled out at about 4 AM and the Navy gave us a treat of two fresh eggs per man, as it was our last meal aboard. I went out on the deck before morning chow while it was still pitch dark and off in the black night I could see huge flashes across the sky, and a few minutes later heard reports from the big guns,"[8] he remembered.

The sailors were already at general quarters, standing gun watches. "The 'head' was crowded with Marines, many of whom had been there all night, smoking and talking about the landing," observed Josephy. "The little red lights around the toilets had been the only illumination in our hold and the 'head' was the natural gathering place. The room was filled with smoke and the heavy odor of sweat."[9]

Jack Kerins found himself standing in a long line that wound down the passageway leading to the troops' mess hall. "There was little conversation. Many of the Marines were still half asleep. The rest of us were deeply engaged in our own personal thoughts," he observed. Breakfast was steak and eggs, biscuits, fruit juice, and coffee.[10] Aboard PFC Joseph ("Joe") Friedman's LST, the morning fare was also steak and eggs. "I declined it," he recalled. "With my stomach doing flip-flops, the last thing I wanted was food."[11]

The day dawned clear and humid. At 0530 the support vessels moved into position and began the prearranged bombardment schedules. Navy fighters and bombers were already taking off from the flattops. The concussive boom of the big guns rolled across the water as battleships, cruisers, and destroyers sent shells hurtling toward the shore. LSTs were jockeying into assigned positions, while the LCI(G) gunboats maneuvered toward the reef.

Aboard the USS *Aquarius* off Asan, First Lieutenant William Putney, assigned as a veterinarian to the 2nd and 3rd War Dog Platoons, toyed with his bacon and eggs in the ship's wardroom. He knew he should eat something but found he had little appetite. Finally, he retrieved his pack and carbine and joined the gathering of men on deck. The naval barrage seemed to be well underway. "Shells from the 16-inch guns of the battleships pounded the hill behind the beach, causing explosions that sent fire and smoke hundreds of feet into the air," remembered Putney. "Small fires burned all along the beach. To my left destroyers were throwing shells onto the beach from close range. They roved back and forth, one firing a series of volleys followed by another firing into the same area."[12] Corporal Stephen Marusky was also watching the show. "First could be seen the yellow-orange belching flame, and then the heavy thunderous report," he recalled.[13]

"Ships everywhere . . . just *boom boom boom boom*," observed corpsman Leo A. Remaklus. "And you think, there can't be nothing alive in there."[14] Marusky wasn't so sure. Off in the distance, Guam loomed like a huge mountain shrouded in the early morning mist. The air was heavy with the acrid smell of explosives. A Marine infantryman remarked, "All I want to do is make it ashore. Once there I'll feel safe." There was a general air of apprehension. "Everybody's nerves were high-strung and tense," said Marusky. "I know mine were and, believe me, I was scared even aboard ship."[15]

PFC Marvin Corff had been playing bridge earlier in the morning with a member of his war dog platoon. Now, as they waited, a fellow card player remarked solicitously, "Corff, I don't want you to get killed 'cause you owe me two dollars."

"Okay, I'll try to remember that," replied Corff.

"I'll be honest, I was very scared," recalled PFC Thurman Clark, another member of the war dog platoon. "I think most of us were the same way. If you weren't, something was wrong."[16]

Slated to go in on Red Beach 1, Lieutenant Paul C. Smith, commanding 2nd Platoon of C Company, 1st Battalion, 3rd Marines, found himself strangely devoid of feeling. The redheaded lieutenant was something of a curiosity in his regiment. A former editor of the *San Francisco Chronicle*, at thirty-five years old he may have been the oldest platoon leader in the division, having used his political connections to wrangle his way into the Marines as an enlisted man. He was certainly the only second lieutenant on a first name basis with admirals and government bigwigs. While undergoing officer training at Quantico, he had been invited out to lunch by Secretary of the Navy Frank Knox, and he had been receiving similar courtesies since joining the 3rd Division after Bougainville. His connections gave him a very special status—sometimes to his personal discomfiture—but none of that mattered now. Going ashore, he would be no more bulletproof than the lowliest private. As he waited with his platoon, divided into three groups that would embark on three different amtracs, his men were pale, tense, and silent. PFC Lawson G. Knotts, a gangling twenty-year-old from South Carolina, finally admitted, "Gee, I'm scared."

"Sure," said Smith. "Everybody is."

"Are you scared, Lieutenant?" asked Knotts.

"Hell no," replied Smith. "It's against the rules for lieutenants."

Knotts chuckled. Smith went to light a cigarette to see if his hand trembled. It did.[17]

Waiting on a multitude of decks, Marines and sailors paused as the disembodied voice of General Roy Geiger came over transport loudspeakers: "Men, this is General Geiger. The eyes of a nation watch you as you go into battle to liberate this former American bastion from the enemy. Make no mistake, it will be a tough bitter fight against a wily, stubborn foe who will doggedly defend Guam against this invasion. May the glorious traditions of the Marine *esprit de corps* spur you to victory. You have been honored."

As the general concluded, the rousing strains of "The Marines Hymn" blared out over the speakers.[18]

At 0630 word came to "land the landing force."

Debarkation of the tractors through the LST bow doors and down the ramp was set for 0730. For many men, finally having something to do came as a relief. As tank company commander Captain Bertram A. Yaffe put it, "Sooner better than later, get it the hell over with."[19] Yaffe noticed that most of his men had left their shoes untied, well aware that some crews on previous operations had drowned when their Sherman tanks swamped. As the first men headed topside from USS *DuPage*, Marines scheduled to come in on later waves offered encouragement: "Go get 'em, gang!" "Give 'em hell, fellows." "Good luck, men." "Save some souvenirs for the rest of us."[20]

Not one to miss an opportunity, PFC Eugene Peterson was distracted by the call for ship's crew's breakfast. "I bolted for the galley and ran to the front of the long chow line," he recalled. "They were serving meatloaf. I grabbed a couple of slices of bread and asked the sailor passing out the meatloaf for a slice. He said 'Beat it, Marine. We already fed you.'" Before Peterson could react, the chief cook stepped forward and pushed the recalcitrant server aside. "Wise up, punk," he reprimanded the man. "This Marine is facing a day of bad news—he don't need any of your mouth." The chief grabbed a towel, wrapped up half a meatloaf, and handed it to Peterson. "Thanks, Marine," he said. "Stay alive."[21]

Miles away, on the receiving end of the unrelenting naval gunfire, Corporal Masashi Ito's infantry unit had been given the order to move. "We began threading our way through the dense jungle covering the hills toward the south," he recalled. The cacophony of exploding shells from the naval bombardment was overwhelming. "The din robbed us totally of all sense of hearing," he said. "It wasn't the same as a boom or a roar that splits the ears; it was more like being imprisoned inside a huge metal drum that was incessantly and insufferably being beaten with a thousand iron hammers. Fortunately for us, we were moving away from the main target area—so although the noise was unbearable, not all that many shells burst close to us."[22]

The first seven assault waves would ride amtracs directly from the LSTs to the beach. Subsequent waves would climb down cargo nets hung over the sides of their transports to Higgins boats bobbing in the water below. Lacking tracks, the Higgins boats would bring them as far as the reef line, where the Marines would transfer into returning amtracs for the last leg to the beach. Burdened down with weapons and forty-pound packs, men had been taught to cling to the vertical strands of the cargo nets to avoid having their hands trampled by the man following from above. Marines in the boats below would hold the nets away from the sides, dodging the occasional falling helmet that some descending Marine had neglected to fasten.

Nineteen-year-old Sergeant John R. Silvestrini of the 3rd Medical Battalion was more than a little apprehensive about the procedure. "The scaredest I've ever been is going over the side of the ship over the cargo net and the Higgins boats were down there waiting and the ocean was rough, the boats were going up. I seen a lot of guys get caught between the Higgins boat. . . . [T]hey got crushed. I was scared going down there. If they got that cargo net today, they got my fingerprints on it yet," he remarked.[23]

Jack Kerins's first sergeant passed down the line of men waiting to start down the cargo net into the boats, handing out salt tablets about the size of a nickel and twice as thick. "Take this now," he ordered. "Let it dissolve in your mouth. It will replace the body salt you'll be sweating today."

"The idiot that came up with that friggin' idea should be shot," muttered a skeptical Marine.[24]

On the tank decks in the bowels of the LSTs, the amtrac crews had started the engines on their LVTs. The huge clamshell doors at the bow remained closed, and the noise was deafening, recalled Major Henry Aplington, accompanying his battalion below. "Motors were roaring and the exhaust fans whining—it was claustrophobic."[25]

Aboard LST 221, Sergeant Buck Daley observed that the amtracs—sometimes referred to as "alligators"—were parked atop what was essentially a floating bomb. The LST's hold had been loaded first with at least six feet of artillery shells and other ammunition, which was then topped with wooden planks. "Then there was a layer of oil drums with fuel, then more planks were added, and then the amphibious tractors were stowed on top of all that. . . . The access to the hold where the alligators were waiting was through a round hatch barely large enough for a man with pack and rifle to climb down the ladder into the dimly-lit hold. There a runner met us with a flashlight and led us to our assigned alligator."[26]

Assigned to the first wave at Agat, George Aspley's platoon descended into the cavernous hold to the waiting LVTs. "Because of all the smog from the running engines, we thought that we were all going to be dead from the exhaust fumes before we ever got out of the well deck," he observed. "Soon, the LST came to a stop, the huge bow doors opening and the ramp lowered. Fresh air rushed in and somehow we all knew that we would at least have a chance to live a few minutes longer before hitting the beach."[27]

In the bowels of LST 219, PFC Hendon H. Edwards was facing his first combat operation. His drill instructor at boot camp had assured the recruits that they had no idea what they were getting into, and now it seemed clear to Edwards that the man knew what he had been talking about. "I was frightened," he admitted. "I knew it was a life and death situation. But I was twenty years old then and I had enough brashness and bravo about me to feel that I could take care of myself. I had played two years on the varsity football team in high school. I had confidence in my fellow Marines, in our training and our weapons, so I felt that with a little luck I'd come out all right."[28]

A Japanese lieutenant was less sanguine. Looking out over the gathered armada from Guam's shoreline, the stunned officer thought that the sea seemed to be "paved" with ships. "This is the day I will die," he confided to his diary.[29]

Out at sea, the LSTs began to disgorge their landing craft. Crowded with more than a dozen other Marines in the tank deck of LST 125, PFC Joseph Frank waited for the three or four tractors ahead of him to lurch down the extended ramp into the sea. It occurred to Frank that kindergarten science teaches that eleven tons of iron won't float. "Not able to leave, I proceeded to my next best scenario," he recalled. "I unbuckled my helmet and pack straps, then proceeded to arrange my gear for jettison." Moments later his LVT clattered down the ramp and lurched into the water—a process that reminded Lieutenant Tom Brock of the times he had watched turtles fall off logs back home. "I could see that the other gators ahead of us had not sunk," observed Frank with some relief, though they were riding awfully low in the water. "You could just barely see them as they slowly moved to a staging area where we would circle."[30]

PFC Marvin Corff was pensive as his landing craft bobbed around off the Asan beaches. "We got aboard and circled for a while," he recalled. "And you know, your senses are so different when you're about ready to invade. The sun is never brighter, the sky is never bluer, the jungle is never greener and the blood is never redder. All of your senses are just tingling. We could see the shells landing in the water next to us."[31]

The assaults at both Asan and Agat would be spearheaded by the LVT(A)s—the armored "amtanks"—of the 1st Armored Amphibian Tank Battalion. The battalion's tanks had been split between the 3rd Division and the Marine Brigade: Companies A and B (thirty-seven tanks) would lead the brigade assault at Agat; Companies C and D (thirty-six tanks) would spearhead the 3rd Marine Division assault. They would be followed by forty-eight troop-carrying LVTs—twelve for each color-coded beach—with the next five waves arriving at three-minute intervals.

Close supporting fire would continue to pound an area from the water's edge to about three hundred yards inland and still deeper—about one thousand yards on each flank—during the approach. Large-caliber guns were to shift fire away when the leading waves were twelve hundred yards from shore. Close-range 5-inch shelling and supporting fire from the LCI(G) gunboats was to continue until the leading assault wave closed to within three hundred yards of the beach. Between 0715 and 0815, eighty-five fighters, sixty-five bombers, and fifty-three torpedo bombers would strafe and bomb along the landing beaches from Agana south to Bangi Point, a distance of about fourteen miles. Naval gunfire trajectories were calculated so shells went no higher than twelve hundred feet, allowing pilots to safely pull out of their runs at fifteen hundred feet.

One last punch remained before the amtracs hit the beach. Prior to leaving Guadalcanal, eighteen LCI(G)s had been fitted with CIT Type 8 rocket launchers. With forty-two launchers per gunboat, each LCI(G) was capable of firing 504 rockets—for a grand total of 9,072—smothering the beaches immediately before the troops arrived ashore. Nine gunboats were assigned to Asan and nine to Agat. They would lead the first wave, fire their rocket salvos, then break off to the flanks.

Waiting to go in, amtank radiomen came on the air to check in with their platoon commanders. "We were a mile or so offshore at this point," said Corporal Fred Addison. "The skies were clear and seas calm."[32] Behind them, the LSTs continued to disgorge infantry-laden amtracs. Small guide boats bustled around, shepherding the landing craft toward assembly points. Landing boats carrying equipment or supplies flew colored flags indicating their cargo: a white flag for water, yellow for gasoline and oil, green for tracked vehicles, red for ammunition.

Watching from the hills overlooking the Marine Brigade's assigned beaches, Second Lieutenant Yasuhiro Yamashita was entranced by the sight unfolding out to sea. "The traces of crafts' wakes were really beautiful, like floating threads of a loom," he recalled. "Then I realized the enemy would soon be invading the beach."[33]

The LCI(G) gunboats led the way, 250 yards in front of the first wave of amtanks as they crossed the line of departure at 0759. Smoke from the bombardment wafted toward them on a slight offshore breeze. At 0815, covering the left flank of the Agat landing, LCI(G) 365 opened fire on Yellow Beach 1 with her 40mm guns from two thousand yards out. Six minutes later, as the gunboat loosed its first salvo of rockets in a ripple of explosions along the shore, she was caught in the cross fire of a 75mm gun on Bangi Point and another on or behind Pelagi Rock southeast of Apaca Point—an early indication that naval gunfire had not been as thorough as promised.

The gunboat took ten hits in quick succession. Down by the bow and listing badly to starboard, with fires in the bosun's locker and in the No. 2 troop compartment, she managed to get off a second salvo of rockets before ceasing fire as the assault waves closed to within 250 yards of the shore. As the ship swung to starboard to turn away, a heavy burst of machine-gun fire tore into the pilothouse and conn from astern. The helmsman was mortally wounded, and the gunboat yawed wildly toward the reef. A seaman seized the wheel and brought the ship around. By now the forward well deck was awash to a depth of six inches. Crewmen threw the rocket projectors overboard along with other loose gear in an effort to lighten the ship and keep her afloat. The LCI(G) limped out to the USS *Fayette*, where twenty-four casualties, including the ship's captain, were taken aboard. Three were dead when received in the collecting station; three more died within a few minutes and another the next day.

Serving as the communications center off the Agat beaches, USS *Ringgold* chronicled the unfolding assault:

> *0715 Aircraft bombing and strafing commenced.*
> *0753: First assault wave on line of departure; other waves approaching line of departure.*
> *0759: Executed "one" flag; first assault wave dispatched to beach.*
> *0802: Second wave dispatched.*
> *0805: Third wave dispatched.*
> *0809 LCI gunboats commenced intensive rocket fire.*
> *0810: Fourth wave dispatched.*
> *0815: Fifth wave dispatched.*
> *0820: Sixth wave dispatched*
> *0825 Wave Six "Able" dispatched.*[34]

Looking out from the open hatch of his amtank as he followed along behind the gunboats, Corporal Stephen Marusky could see perhaps a mile of amphibious tanks to his left and right, saltwater foaming whitely in their wakes as they churned toward the Agat beaches at a speed of about 150 yards per minute, or five miles per hour. Marusky's Company B was heading for the White Beaches on the right, spearheading the 4th Marines. Company A had the Yellow Beaches on the left where the 22nd Marines were to land. Scattered among the surging amtanks, the camouflage-painted LCI(G)s blasted away at the beach. Huge gray hulks of battleships and cruisers continued to lay down fire from thousands of yards offshore, the barrage now seeming to morph into one huge roll of thunder. The noise was overwhelming, remembered PFC Charles Lepant. "*Boom-boom-boom-boom-boom-boom-boom-boom-boom.* There's so much noise. It's *boom-boom-boom*—"[35] Somewhat incongruously, a rainbow arched majestically skyward in the distance, the remnant of early-morning showers.

Up ahead, Guam's green hills and a shore lined with shattered coconut palms were slowly coming into closer view. An air observer reported that many of the rockets intended to soften up the beach area seemed to be falling short.[36] Geysers of water erupted around the tanks as the Japanese opened up with mortars. "Button up," ordered Marusky's tank commander over the intercom. Despite the order, Marusky left his front deck hatch slightly open so he could see more clearly. They were still about five hundred yards out. Above and behind him the two machine gunners and 37mm gunner fired steadily at the beach. Every time the 37mm went off, Marusky's hatch bounced up, allowing smoke and powder to blow through and sting his face. "This and the clattering of the machine guns in the rear added to the confusion," he remembered. At long last, tracks grated on coral about two hundred yards from the beach. Commanding Company A, Captain Owen P. ("Pat") Lillie radioed all hands, "There they are men. Let's go get 'em."[37]

The Japanese were patiently waiting. Despite optimistic evaluations of the damage inflicted on enemy shore defenses, a skillfully concealed fortified gun position burrowed into rocky Gaan Point between the Yellow and White Beaches had gone unnoticed and untouched through day after day of shore bombardment. Jutting out about fifteen yards, the point had served planners as a convenient center point dividing the Yellow and White Beaches. It had not been recognized as a significant threat, explained Captain Ralph J. Parker, operations officer for the 4th Amphibian Tractor Battalion. As Parker recalled it, "All our maps reported this piece of land to be not over sea level in height." In fact, the point was nearer ten yards high and had been honeycombed with defensive positions, including a 75mm mountain gun, one 37mm gun, and emplacements for machine guns and riflemen.[38]

The two main guns "were in a double cave, one above the other. The mouth of the cave could not be seen from the sea, and trees and shrubbery prevented them from showing in aerial pictures," observed brigade staff officer Colonel Edwin C. Ferguson.[39] The gun chambers were protected by four feet of concrete in front and overhead. Above the gun chambers were three square observation posts about three feet high with concrete walls six inches thick. Communication with the guns below was by voice tubes fashioned from two-inch-diameter pipes. Another 75mm gun was located in a pillbox just to the north of the point, along with two concrete 40mm emplacements dug into an embankment roughly five feet above the high-water mark. Though some large shell or bomb craters were subsequently found within fifteen yards of the guns, they had not impacted the positions.

Fred Addison's amtank hit the reef about one hundred yards to the left of the point. Machine-gun bullets whipped the surface of the water, accompanied by the larger splash of exploding mortar shells. Then the guns on Gaan Point came to life. On Addison's right, amtank A-11 listed abruptly to port as a 75mm shell tore a gaping hole amidships, killing both scarf machine gunners. The badly wounded lieutenant commanding the tank dragged himself away from the burning turret toward the driver and radio operator at the bow. Both were dazed by concussion, and the driver had been hit in the back by shell fragments, but they managed to apply a tourniquet to the lieutenant's wounds before they all took to the water. The ammunition passer and the gunner, the latter dragging a mangled foot that would later have to be amputated, also got out, just before a blowtorch of flame shot up from the turret as the vehicle's fuel and ammunition ignited.

As Captain Lillie's command tank (A-18) moved up to fill the gap, a shell hit the muzzle of its 37mm gun. The force of the blast angled downward, killing the radio operator. Lillie, manning the waist machine-gun position, was badly wounded. Watching from his amtank, Addison saw a bandage fluttering whitely in the breeze as a crewman tried to help the stricken captain. Both the gunner and ammo passer had also been hit. The driver, with the radio operator lying dead across his lap, continued to steer the tank, its main gun now useless, toward the shore.

The massacre of A Company continued as amtank A-2 was hit by a round just below the starboard waist gun. The blast killed the starboard machine gunner instantly and wounded the port machine gunner, ammunition passer, and 37mm gunner. All guns except the port machine gun were knocked out. The wounded port gunner continued to fire as the amtank wallowed on.

A hundred yards from the beach, amtank A-7 was bracketed and then hit in the turret. The tank caught fire. Tank commander Sergeant Irwin G. Saville and his 37mm gunner climbed out to find the starboard machine gunner lying dead on the deck. The radio operator had been wounded and burned. They managed to put out the fire with their hands, but when the driver tried to restart the stalled vehicle, the engine refused to turn over. Saville ordered the crew to abandon the tank. The ammunition passer strapped the wounded radio operator into a life belt and swam him back out past the reef, where they were eventually picked up. Saville told the others to follow him to the beach. In waist-deep water he turned to say something and disappeared in a fountain of spray as he took a direct hit from the same enemy 75mm gun that had knocked out the amtank. His companions paused in shock, then continued wading toward the beach. The body of the twenty-one-year-old sergeant from Orchard Park, New York—or what remained of it—was never recovered.

LVT(A) A-5 was hit twice as it made its way over the rough coral reef, but miraculously no one was hurt. Despite a few holes in the pontoons, the tank continued on toward the beach. A-14 was less fortunate. As the tank crawled across the reef in low gear, a direct hit tore away the side of the turret, killing the tank commander and gunner. As the driver pressed on, the tank received three more hits in rapid succession. One machine gunner's arm was severed; the other machine gunner and the ammunition passer were also wounded. The tank lurched forward over the coral as the ammunition passer tied a tourniquet around the machine gunner's arm and administered morphine.

Tank A-12, headed toward the center of Yellow Beach 2, was about two hundred yards offshore when it was hit on the forward starboard pontoon. The blast severed the starboard track, causing the tank to swerve to the right. Almost immediately another shell struck in almost the same spot as the first but a few inches higher. The first shell had killed the radio operator; the second killed the driver. The ammunition passer was badly wounded. The tank commander gave the word to bail out. It proved to be a timely order: they had no sooner scrambled away than another shell penetrated the ammunition compartment, and the tank exploded.

Lieutenant Robert A. Fish's amtank crew benefitted from an error when the driver brought them in to the right of Gaan Point. The mistake may have saved their lives as it kept them out of the killing ground established by the guns chewing up the rest of A Company. On the way over the reef, they passed a five-by-two-foot plywood sign left by Underwater Demolition Team 4. Carefully lettered in black paint, the sign boldly proclaimed, "Welcome U.S. Marines/Agat USO One Thousand Yards." Their tank came in twenty to fifty yards to the right of Gaan Point. "I could see the Japs staring at us as we came ashore," recalled Fish. "Also we were peering into the barrel of a Jap artillery piece that had evidently been disabled by the naval bombardment."[40]

Surviving the run to shore with B Company, Stephen Marusky considered himself blessed. "Three other tanks had hit land mines along the beach while others had never reached the beach," he observed. "A hidden Jap [75mm gun] in a pillbox accounted for about three tanks and six to eight tractors, a few of the tractors blown to hell by direct hits. Mortar fire had knocked out other tanks."[41]

The first waves lurched up on shore at 0832. Aboard the command ship USS *Ringgold*, the log entry noted, "First landing craft reached the beach line. Firing by enemy appeared to be light and ineffective."[42]

Lieutenant Shigenori Yoshida, a surgeon with the 38th Infantry Regiment, was resting on some crates in a cave in the hills behind the Agat beaches when another officer burst in shouting that the enemy was landing in front of the 1st Battalion. It appeared the battalion would be completely annihilated, he said.

Yoshida left the cave and climbed onto the high ground to look, groaning as he saw landing craft stretching from the beach far out to sea. He turned gloomily away. "Well, then, we'll cook our rice and eat plenty of food tonight," he said fatalistically. "We'll eat a good meal and let the rest of life take care of itself."[43]

◆━◆

Six miles up the coast, the 3rd Marine Division's landing at Asan was also underway as the division ventured into the 1.5-mile open maw between Adelup and Asan Points. Led by nine rocket-equipped LCI(G)s and thirty-six amtanks, the initial ship-to-shore movement was spared the heavy resistance encountered by General Lem Shepherd's brigade at Agat, though General Allen Turnage's Marines would soon be introduced to their own piece of hell in the heights beyond the long, curving invasion beach.

Upon exiting their tractors, the 3rd Division Marines would have to cross fifteen to thirty feet of white sand into a shell-torn fringe of coconut trees and brush, before emerging onto the coastal road that ran parallel to the beach. Beyond the road lay an open expanse of dry rice paddies terminating at the foot of the heights manned by the 320th Independent Infantry Battalion, who enjoyed a bird's-eye view of the ground below. "It was the perfect defensive position," observed Alvin Josephy. "Enemy machine gunners and riflemen were dug into the ridge crests; the gullies were filled with mortars. The Japs could see us coming in across the reef; they could see us run to the foot of the hills and try to get up the hills. They could fire straight down on us. It was imperative that we wrest the high ground from them as quickly as possible."[44]

The 3rd Marines faced the toughest challenge at Red Beaches 1 and 2 on the left flank where the hills rose steeply from behind the beaches. The 3rd Battalion on the extreme left was to seize the precipitous Chonito Cliff flanking Red 1, while the 1st Battalion on Red 2 was tasked with securing a steep topographical nose that extended toward the landing area from the ridges beyond. Adding to their peril, both beach approaches were dominated by enemy guns on the devil's horn of Adelup Point, a coral rock finger extending about four hundred yards seaward just to the north. Rising fifty to seventy feet from the water, the point had been fortified with at least seven pillboxes and a battery of coastal defense guns, along with 37mm and 47mm guns and 70mm howitzers, some of which had survived the preinvasion bombardment. One emplacement had been dug into the foundation of the Kroll House at the top of the point. Once the residence of the owner of a San Francisco–based copra export company, the hacienda, now reduced to rubble by naval gunfire, had most recently housed Japanese staff officers. Fortunately for the landing force, a battery of 6-inch guns atop Chonito Cliff had been spotted and knocked out prior to the landing. To the right, the division's other two regiments faced difficult but marginally easier ground, with the 21st Marines landing on Green Beach in the center and the 9th Marines on Blue Beach on the right, just inside the other devil's horn of Asan Point.

Air strikes along the beaches began at 0815. At 0819, the assault waves were reported to be twelve hundred yards from shore, confirmed by parachute flares dropped by the air coordinator to indicate their position. At 0820 the air observer noted that the LCI(G)s were firing their rocket barrages: *The rockets are landing and giving them hell. Good effect on the beach. Landing craft seem to be about 1,000 yards from beach.*[45]

Due to land on Blue Beach at H+5, Captain Calvin W. Kunz's tractor, still a mile out to sea, was unable to locate its boundaries due to the dense smoke and dust. "We were literally moving into an enormous cloud of dust and not a beach," he recalled.[46] Heading toward Red 2 in Lieutenant Paul Smith's amtrac, one of the Marines abruptly lost his breakfast. Smith saw that the culprit was PFC Knotts, the youngster who had asked earlier if he was scared.

Positioned in the hills overlooking Piti, Second Lieutenant Yasuhiro Yamashita of the 18th Regiment was on the receiving end as the naval barrage shifted further inland. "All over, bodies were being blown up as the cannon shells fell," he recalled. "The earth and sand buried the soldiers."[47] Standing offshore, patrol craft USS PC-555 echoed air observer reports: "No return fire was encountered and no Jap movements of troops noticed."[48]

That was about to change as the barrage passed over and Japanese troops emerged from holes and caves on the reverse slopes overlooking the invasion beaches—including one cave on the reverse slopes of Chonito Ridge capable of sheltering two hundred men. The bombardment may have shaken them up, but they were far from broken.

Following the amtanks, PFC Joseph Frank's troop tractor lumbered toward Blue Beach, bordered on the right by Asan Point. "The Japs on and in that ridge were looking right down our cleavage," recalled Frank. Like Adelup Point to the north, the promontory had been fortified with 120mm, 37mm, and 47mm guns, as well as machine guns and three 200mm antiboat guns partially sheltered by concrete walls. Some, but not all, of the guns had been destroyed in the preinvasion bombardment. The LVT to Frank's right suddenly exploded "in a shower of water, bodies and what-have-yous." As the stricken vehicle lurched to a halt on the reef, the survivors took to the water and began slogging toward shore.[49]

Manning an LVT machine gun on the way in toward Blue Beach, PFC Wayne Barham watched the line of tractors churning toward shore like participants in some sort of giant race. Huddled below the gunnels, most of the Marines had a less expansive view of their surroundings. "Some guys were on the bottom of the boat on their hands and knees throwing up; and then there are other guys cracking jokes," said twenty-three-year-old First Lieutenant Jack Eddy.[50] Heading in with the 21st Marines, PFC Frank Chuisano found that his mouth seemed extraordinarily dry. There was little talking. "I got up once to look, but someone yelled, 'Get your ass down!' I didn't say that much. I guess we were scared. I know I was scared." As the tractor jolted over the reef, Chuisano turned to his buddy, PFC Jimmy Barrett, and croaked optimistically, "I'll see you when it's all over."[51]

About four hundred yards from the beach, Lieutenant Tom Brock could see his battalion's objective looming high above the shattered coconut trees. "It looked like a tough hill to climb and surely was when we reached it," he said. "As our boats moved on towards the beach, we could see machine gun fire coming from the hills and mortars and artillery shells bursting along the beach. From a distance, it looked like rain drops falling in a pool of water. . . . A shell landed in a fuel or ammunition dump which caused a huge explosion, and flames shot hundreds of feet into the air."[52] PFC John W. Foley's platoon leader sounded like a broken record as he repeatedly admonished curious Marines in their tractor, "Keep your head down! Keep your head down!" A voice piped up, "There ain't enough room!" Then a shell hit close by. "Why, you looked around and you couldn't see a head sticking up," said Foley.[53]

The din of the big guns was overwhelming, recalled PFC George Bessette; "they're pounding like crazy." As his amtrac neared shore, they began to take small arms fire. The youngster manning the tractor's .30-caliber machine gun near Bessette was immobilized with fright. "He froze to the gun," said Bessette. The lieutenant yelled out, "Hey, Bessette! Get up there and get that gun going!" Bessette climbed up by the gunner. "I was scared and I grabbed the kid's hand and I whispered in his ear, 'You think you're scared, pal? Join the club.' And I pulled the trigger and he was okay. Once he started firing that broke the ice."[54]

Corporal Jack Kerins's recon party from the 12th Marines was supposed to come ashore at Green Beach. As their amtrac clambered up onto the reef, someone opened up a case of hand grenades and started passing them out. Kerins hung two of them from his web gear on each side of his chest and chambered a round in his carbine. "Keep your heads down from here on in," shouted the amtrac machine gunner. Kerins glanced over at Private Harold Boicourt. Still a week short of his twenty-first birthday, the tall Indiana Hoosier had turned a deathly white, and he jerked away reflexively when Kerins reached over to touch his arm. Kerins tried to reassure him with some small talk, but Boicourt just stared back, glassy-eyed. As the tractor finally climbed up onto the beach, a violent explosion rocked the vehicle. Kerins looked up to see the machine gunner draped over his weapon, dead. "Everybody out!" yelled the driver. "It's the end of the line." Forgetting about Boicourt, Kerins rolled over the side and ran across the narrow beach toward a tangle of blasted coconut trees.[55]

Radioman John McClure had a narrow escape when his amtrac got hung up on a coral head on the way in. A farm boy from Bonham, Texas, McClure had enlisted at age seventeen. After a brother in the Army wrote to say he wouldn't advise joining the Army, and another brother, this one in the Navy, wrote to say he wouldn't recommend joining the Navy, McClure enlisted in the Marines. Now, stuck in an immobile tractor on the fire-swept reef, it appeared he had made a very poor decision indeed.

"Our vehicle got one track stuck," he recalled. "And it was stuck good. So the driver was frantically trying to go forward and backward to get out of there. And it wouldn't budge." An artillery shell exploded about one hundred yards behind them. The next round cut the distance by half as the enemy gunners made corrections. As the tracks spun uselessly, the third round exploded about six feet behind the tractor. Seawater cascaded down on the men inside. "Well, that round was so close and such a big explosion that it sort of addled all of us; we were about half out of it, including the driver," remembered McClure. Somewhat miraculously, the blast also bounced the amtrac off the coral snag. The driver gunned the engine and raced for shore. "We went in there and we piled out and ran like rabbits," said McClure, who wouldn't find out until much later that the explosion that probably saved his life had also punctured one of his eardrums.[56]

As demolitionist Hendon Edwards's tractor neared the beach, his lieutenant's voice rose over the roar of the vehicle's seven-cylinder aircraft engine, shouting, "Lock and load!" Their model tractor had no exit ramp, said Edwards. "You had to go over the side and it was about a seven- or eight-foot drop." Edwards had a pole charge—a pole about five feet long with four or five pounds of TNT strapped to the end of it, designed to blow up pillboxes. "When I went over the side—we were loaded down with everything under the sun that we could carry—I dug that pole charge into the sand and tore it all to pieces. Half pound blocks of TNT was all around."

He scrambled in the sand trying to gather up the pieces as small arms and some mortar fire descended on the beach. Other men were frantically digging in the sand or looking for cover. "Well, we had a squad leader by the name of Sgt. [John J.] Creamer, he came to us from the 1st Raider Battalion which had taken Guadalcanal and Tulagi and he was something else," recalled Edwards. "He was going along there kicking us and bootin' us and cussin' at us: *Get up! Move out! Move out! Move out! Let's get up on that high ground. You're gonna be killed if you stay down here!* And sure enough, the mortar fire was coming forward and we were running as hard as we could and just about as it was going to catch up with us it stopped."[57]

As Lieutenant Tom Brock's tractor clambered up onto Green Beach, the left tread went deep into a ditch. Tilted at about a forty-five-degree angle, the vehicle stalled. The Marines bailed out as machine-gun fire snapped overhead and off the sides of the tractor. "Just as we climbed out of our boat another one was pulling up behind us," remembered Brock. "I turned and looked at it, and just as I did, I saw it receive a direct mortar hit and things went sky high." Knowing he had to get his men off the beach, Brock led them inland through the dust and smoke to the shelter of an abandoned Japanese trench. Considering the pounding the beach area had taken, he was surprised to come under fire from a couple of stay-behind snipers, one in a coconut tree and the other in the ruins of a house. "One of my boys spotted the one in the tree, but it took a long time to find him and pick him off," he recalled. "We found the other sniper when we started to move off the beach towards the hills, and he stuck his rifle out from those ruins and shot the heel off one of my boy's shoes. We disposed of him by tossing a hand grenade down into his lap."[58]

Starting to move inland with the 3rd Marines, PFC Robert Dent had a scare that would seem comical only in hindsight. "Just about the time we got out of the amtrac there was a native hut there and all of a sudden we heard a big racket and Lord we didn't know what was going on and it happened that two big hogs ran out from under the hut," recalled Dent. "That was a relief."[59]

The tractor carrying Sergeant Ed Jewsbury and his buddy, Sergeant Jack Watkins, also ground ashore on Green Beach. Jewsbury, a tall twenty-two-year-old from Blackwell, Oklahoma, bailed out on one side, while Watkins went over the other. A mortar shell exploded on Watkins's side of the amtrac. Jewsbury ran around to check on his friend and found him lying in the sand. "I've been hit in the hand," he told Jewsbury. Jewsbury picked Watkins's hand out of the sand and saw two of his fingers had been severed. As he pulled him to his feet to get him back into the amtrac, he noticed blood leaking out from under Watkins's helmet. Watkins said his head didn't hurt, but when Jewsbury lifted the helmet he saw his friend's hair was a mass of blood. He got Watkins back into the amtrac, and it lumbered out to sea. "That was the last time I saw Jack until I ran into him at the Marine Corps Base at San Diego the day I arrived back in the States," observed Jewsbury. "He had just been released from the Naval Hospital that morning. He had a silver plate in his head."[60]

Corporal George Papalias's amtank bogged down in a shell hole on the Red Beaches, and the crew bailed out. Papalias crawled into a shell hole feeling decidedly underarmed with just his .45-caliber pistol. A couple of Marine infantrymen from the following wave slid in behind him. As one of them peered over the edge of the shell hole, a bullet snapped by, creasing the strap on his combat pack. The intended victim seemed to take this as a personal affront. "I'll get that son of a bitch," he exclaimed and took off over the edge of the crater. More infantry piled into the hole. An explosion—Papalias thought it might have been a loose grenade—shredded one man's leg. His thigh "looked like hamburger with lots of blood," recalled Papalias.[61]

Off on the division's right flank, the amtrac carrying PFC Billy W. Sherrill ground to a halt in front of a steep embankment on Blue Beach. Twenty-two-year-old Second Lieutenant Joseph E. Shelly of Fall River, Massachusetts, a forward observer with the 12th Marines, jumped off the front of the tractor and disappeared in a massive explosion. Sherrill thought the lieutenant had set off a mine, but it may have been an exploding shell. "It blew him to smithereens and caved in the front of the tractor and that killed both the driver and the assistant driver," he recalled.[62]

Also on Blue Beach, PFC Wayne Barham jumped out of his LVT into about a foot of water, losing his helmet in the shallows. By the time he finally scooped it up and got it securely back on his head, he found he was alone. The others had scrambled up an eight-foot embankment in front of the tractor and were gone. Climbing to the top, he saw his platoon running across the open flats toward the hills. He started after them. "Smoke filled the air," he recalled. "The acrid smell of gunpowder choked me." Shattered palm trees jutted up like broken femurs, their tops sheared off by the naval bombardment. The twisted steel and shattered concrete of a knocked-out pillbox loomed nearby. Casting a quick look over his shoulder, he saw the next wave was already coming in.[63]

Landing with the same battalion, PFC Joe Frank ran inland and jumped into a shell hole alongside a rifleman from his platoon. Frank asked what was going on. "Hell, I don't know," blurted the Marine. An instant later he jumped up and charged forward. Frank followed, crouching down behind the stump of a shell-blasted coconut tree. "I was on one knee behind that stump, peeking around it when in front of my face I saw pieces of wood flying out of that stump," he remembered. "For a few seconds it didn't sink in, then it happened again and I realized that those were bullets coming through that tree stump." Scuttling away, he slid into another shell hole. A Marine sat at the bottom, serenely spooning the contents of a C ration can into his mouth. When Frank informed him he was a nut case, the man just smiled and kept eating.[64]

"We lost quite a few boys," said Corporal John B. Davis. "I lost W.A. Smith, William A. Smith. We called him 'W.A.' He and I were carrying a coil of wire and we were advancing and he was shot in the head. And then Pete Petosky came up to take his roll of wire so we could carry it up to the individuals up forward and he was shot in the stomach."[65]

The first LVTs made landfall on the Blue and Green Beaches at 0828, followed one minute later by the 3rd Marines on the Red Beaches. PFC Joseph R. Anderson was among the few men who actually laid eyes on a Japanese as he moved inland. There was an explosion as he crossed a dry rice paddy beyond Blue Beach, and he saw an enemy soldier thrown about ten feet into the air. "His torso went one way and his head went another."[66]

PFC Dick Gormley was also trying to get across the paddies, hampered by a load that included a thirty-eight-pound SCR 300 radio, his pack, a musette bag over his shoulder with extra batteries for the radio, his carbine, and ammunition. He was so loaded down with gear, he'd been forced to stand up in the amtrac on the way into the beach. Now, as he lumbered inland, a lieutenant about twenty feet in front of him took a full burst in the chest from an unseen Nambu machine gun. Gormley kept moving.[67]

Out beyond the reef, aboard an LCM (Landing Craft Mechanized) designed to bring vehicles ashore, Alvin Josephy and other Marines crowded around a radioman monitoring the airwaves. The radioman pressed his headphones tighter against his ears and yelled, "First wave ashore!" He listened a moment or two to the traffic between the beach and ships offshore, then glanced up with a smile. "Casualties light."[68]

While it was a simple matter to get killed on any of the 3rd Marine Division beaches that Friday morning, the hottest spot by far was on the division left. Sheltered in caves, dugouts, and wooded folds in the steep slopes overlooking Red Beaches 1 and 2, the Japanese had survived the preliminary bombardment and emerged to man guns and mortars commanding the approaches to the heights.

Corporal Lawrence Radel landed on Red 1 in the shadow of Chonito Cliff, the steep, three hundred-foot-high red clay ridge rising from behind a seawall about four hundred yards to the right and slightly inland from Adelup Point. "One of my duties when we went in, I had to be the last guy on to get the guys to make sure they got off," he recalled. "And I had to push one guy over because he was so scared. I had to push him over. Because all hell was breaking loose. . . . The beach was big and long and wide. They had us zeroed in. I mean zeroed in."[69] At 0912, Lieutenant Colonel Ralph L. Houser, whose 3rd Battalion was tasked with seizing Chonito Cliff, reported "mortar fire and snipers very heavy . . . many casualties."[70]

A Marine Corps study later attempted to put the 3rd Battalion's objective into perspective. "The danger posed by the Japanese in their caves on Chonito Cliff led to some exaggerated news reports of its size," noted the study. "The cliff itself was only the seaward edge of the steep ridge which overlooked the whole length of the Red Beaches; it lay northeast of Red Beach 1."[71]

The coastal highway crossed a concrete bridge over a dry stream bed in the four-hundred-yard gap between Adelup Point and the left edge of the height where the Japanese had constructed an ingenious tunnel system allowing them to fire on both the road and the beach. A draw led inland on the southern edge of the height. Ironically, Houser, who had gone into the Marine Corps in 1935 after graduating from the University of Iowa, had driven along that very same coastal road and through the defile during a stopover on Guam several years before. "If I had known that I would have to assault that cliff I would have looked at it more closely," he admitted to a fellow officer.[72]

The terrain did give the Marines landing on Red 1 one break. While the men were exposed to direct fire from Adelup Point on the way into the beach, once they were ashore, those guns were unable to take Red 1 itself under fire as they were blocked by the tip of a spur extending down to the water from the high ground on the northern edge of the beach. Unfortunately, the benefit was limited as this same spur had been heavily fortified by the Japanese.

Houser's battalion landed with two companies abreast: I Company on the right and K Company on the left. "The idea was to hit the beach in a rush and dash to the initial objective before the Nips could recover from the pre-invasion bombardments," observed battalion executive officer Major Royal R. Bastian, a sharp-looking Louisianan who had majored in chemical engineering at Tulane before the war.[73] I Company planned to push up into the draw to the south of Chonito Cliff but was stopped by enemy fire. Among the early casualties was the company's executive officer, twenty-five-year-old Lieutenant Redge F. Henn of California, who was shot in the left wrist and thigh during the attempt. As he was evacuated to the beach, he told Bastian that the Japanese had recovered before the company could make it to the objective.

K Company crossed the stream bed and started up the south side of the cliff, but immediately came under fire from enemy positions on the height behind them. The support platoon tried to force its way through the cut to wipe out the strongpoint, only to be cut up by machine-gun fire, accompanied by grenades rolled down on them from the heights above. The advance stalled.

The situation was as bad or worse on Red Beach 2 just to the south, where twenty-four-year-old Second Lieutenant Jim Gallo, leading the 1st Platoon in Captain Geary R. Bundschu's A Company, came ashore at 0829. Gallo rolled out of his LVT and landed on his back on a shattered coconut log, knocking the wind out of himself. Mortar fire was falling on the beach, and the sound of naval gunfire was deafening. Catching his breath, Gallo gathered his platoon and started through the dry rice paddies toward their intermediate line objective: a steep ridge nose that extended down toward Asan Village parallel to the direction of the attack.

Referred to in unit documents as "O-A" and by A Company as "Our Ridge," the objective lay immediately south of Chonito Cliff near the junction of Red Beaches 1 and 2 and led up to still higher ground and the division's main "D-1" objective. A Marine Corps officer later described it as "a rock pile 400 feet high and 200 yards square thatched with jungle vegetation. . . . It was so situated that even a handful of well-hidden men, using mortars and machine guns, could repel a much larger force moving up from below."[74] On the morning of July 21, this potential killing ground— soon to be dubbed Bundschu Ridge—was one of the most critical objectives on the 3rd Marine Division beachhead due to its dominating location.

Bundschu, the twenty-five-year-old scion of two prominent California families, including a grandfather who had served as a U.S. congressman—had volunteered to seize the key terrain feature during the first operational briefing by battalion commander Major Henry Aplington weeks earlier. Despite his impressive ancestry, the intent-looking gray-eyed six-footer was no prima donna. An avid outdoorsman who had worked summers digging ditches for $4.68 a day to help pay his tuition at the

University of California, Berkeley, he had enlisted in the Marines after graduation and been commissioned just a month before Pearl Harbor. He was well regarded in the battalion—so conscientious that he wrote periodic letters to the mothers of his men to reassure them their sons were doing well. Jim Gallo considered him "an excellent leader in all respects . . . confident, decisive and matter-of-fact about what he wanted to accomplish."[75] During briefings, the lanky captain assured his men, "If things get confused during landing, just follow me."[76]

Speed was of the essence if A Company hoped to scale the ridge before the Japanese recovered from their initial shock, but Bundschu had already lost that race as they headed inland across the paddies. The company lost two of its three rifle platoon leaders almost immediately upon landing. Leading the 2nd Platoon, Second Lieutenant William Shellhorn, who had hoped to become a Lutheran minister after the war, was killed soon after leaving his tractor. The leader of 3rd Platoon, twenty-nine-year-old First Lieutenant John Wike of Philadelphia, was also killed, leaving Jim Gallo as the sole surviving platoon leader. Sergeants took over the other two platoons, urging the men inland toward the higher ground beyond as mortar shells whispered down on the beachhead.

Gallo had been a standout four-sport athlete in high school in Haverstraw, New York, and a multisport competitor at Colgate College, but Guam's suffocating humidity and weeks of inactivity aboard ship were already taking their toll. He found himself gasping for breath as he and his men trotted across one hundred yards of open rice paddy toward the ridge. Negotiating a low escarpment, they finally pushed into the brush-choked jumble of steep rock faces and deep crevices that formed the forward slope of higher ground. As Gallo picked his way up, he heard something in the undergrowth ahead and called out cautiously, thinking it might be one of his own men. A Japanese soldier shouted back, "Hey, Marine!" and took a shot at him. The bullet cut through the dungaree cloth on Gallo's shoulder without so much as breaking the skin. The loudmouth Japanese didn't get a second chance as twenty-one-year-old PFC Hershel S. Canup of Social Circle, Georgia, emptied an eight-round clip from his M-1 into him.[77]

Off to Gallo's left, Captain Bundschu and the 2nd Platoon had also started up the steep slope with the 3rd Platoon in support when a Japanese light machine gun opened up from a forward position above them. Two Marines and a corpsman were shot down before the machine gunner disappeared back up the ridge to the main line of entrenchments along the crest. "Captain Bundschu called us machine guns up to him, and jumped into the vacated Jap's foxhole," recalled eighteen-year-old PFC Boyd C. Troup. Seconds later, they came under fire from some Marines who mistook them for Japanese in the confusion. Scrambling out of the hole, Bund-schu stood in full view and shouted at them, "Don't shoot! Those are Marines!" The Japanese up on the ridge immediately zeroed in on him. "I was about twelve to fourteen feet below him and I could hardly see him for all the dirt and dust kicked up," said Troup, "but I did see him slump down and thought he was dead."[78] Bundschu had been hit in the flurry, but he was far from dead. Climbing back out of the hole, he made his way down the slope and allowed a corpsman to bandage a gunshot wound in his shoulder before heading back up the ridge where the sit-uation continued to deteriorate. Raked by two machine guns positioned to deliver enfilade fire on the slope, Company A had advanced only about two hundred yards by 0850 and was not even close to securing its objective.

Bundschu had known the ridge would be a tough nut, but the terrain was far worse than anyone had anticipated. In some spots his men were confronted with a sixty-degree incline, forcing them to sling rifles so they could use both hands to grab clumps of sword grass and pull themselves up. Occupying trenches at the top of the ridge, defenders from Captain Yoshihiso Nakamura's 320th Independent Infantry Battalion rolled hand grenades down on them. A Marine slid down the hill clasping a bandage over a stomach wound. Another descended holding a hand to a bloody head injury. Among the casualties was PFC Troup, who "got blasted by a Jap hand grenade" as his machine-gun team attempted to support the push to the crest.[79] Sergeant Robert A. DesForges of Ware, Massachusetts, a former Raider, went down with multiple fragmentation wounds from an exploding shell. All seven corpsmen assigned to A Company became casualties within the first hour.

Creeping forward with Lieutenant Gallo's platoon, PFC Bob Costen saw four or five Marines go down in a cloud of dust as a machine gun opened fire on them. While aboard ship, someone had made off with Costen's clean set of spare dungarees. He found out later that the culprit was one of the men he had just seen cut down. The thief lay dead, face down in the dirt, wearing a purloined jacket with Costen's name neatly stenciled across the back.

Attempting to advance his platoon on the right, Gallo found they were cut off from the rest of the company by a deep gully. He had been issued a relatively new piece of communications equipment that might have helped—a lightweight RPZ Emerson radio receiver that was supposed to let him receive radio messages—but the device did not seem to be working. Carried in a canvas bag, the receiver featured a wire that attached to the wearer's helmet, which was supposed to serve as the antenna. In the scramble up the slope, the wire broke off. Gallo jury-rigged it to a rifle bolt and got some intermittent reception, but it soon crapped out again. He finally tore the thing off in disgust and threw it away.

Landing on Red 2 in the fifth wave behind Bundschu's company, Lieutenant Paul Smith organized his C Company platoon and started inland, narrowly escaping death when a machine-gun bullet tore at his collar but failed to draw blood. As mortars dropped behind them, the platoon corpsman ran up and flopped down beside him. "I have to report Knotts dead, sir," he yelled over the surrounding bedlam. The Arkansas Marine who'd asked Smith if he was afraid had been one of the first in the platoon to be killed. Off to their left, Smith's platoon sergeant and a couple of riflemen were moving against a pillbox concealed among the uprooted trees. The corpsman beside Smith suddenly went down, shot by a second supporting machine gun. "It seemed to me that the lad's dying look was one of amazement that I should have let such a thing happen to him," recalled Smith.

Leaving the corpsman, Smith and his runner, twenty-year-old Corporal Bill Brunelle of Revere, Massachusetts, took advantage of a slight defile and worked close to the machine gun. "Finally, I was right alongside the single forward port of the pillbox," said Smith. "I tossed in a white phosphorus grenade. With all the racket we could hear piercing screams as the phosphorus sizzled into the flesh of the crew inside." Brunelle followed with a fragmentation grenade, and the screaming stopped.[80]

Major Aplington had come ashore just before 0900 and established battalion headquarters behind a wrecked house in Asan Village near a shot-up sheet metal building still bearing a sign reading, "US Navy Pumping Station #1." A single birdhouse set on a pole remained incongruously intact amid the wreckage of the village. At 0920 Bundschu reported to Aplington that he was commanding the attack from a position about 150 yards from the top of the ridge. His lead platoon was pinned down in a depression on the right, and he had committed his reserve platoon to the left side of the ridge but had yet to get to the top.

During the planning stages, Aplington had felt confident that his battalion could fulfill its mission and secure the ridge. Now he found his men in a hornets' nest of Japanese who had all the advantages of terrain. "With their interlocking bands of fire and pre-planned mortar and artillery concentrations, they knew what they were about and died hard," he observed. "We did not know at the time that the 3rd Marines were knocking on the front door of the command post of the commanding general of the 29th Infantry Division in the hill mass ahead of us. The terrain was horrendous with its impenetrable brush and cliff-like outcropping of rocks. The battalion had extreme difficulty making forward progress, as well as the most difficult job of maintaining contact with units on the left and right."[81] Though he didn't know it, things were only going to get worse.

⌐∾⌐

Mortar fire, directed from the high ground, began to intensify on the 3rd Marine Division beaches within fifteen minutes of the landing. Among the victims was one of Lieutenant Paul Smith's best sergeants. A mortar shell landed at the noncom's feet as he helped organize the platoon for the push through the rice paddies. "He fell on his back, hard, as though he had tried a tumbler's flip but got only halfway through it," said Smith. "I went over to him. His whole pelvis and abdominal area was shot away. Little thin stringlike sinews kept unwinding and springing like rubber bands from the hole where his stomach should have been. He never knew what hit him."[82]

PFC Frank Chuisano was trying to dig in when there was a great explosion—or maybe it was a series of explosions—from artillery or mortar fire. "It caught everybody at once," he said. Several men went down, including his gunnery sergeant, a prewar Marine from North Dakota farm country who was killed outright. "God, he was a big son of a bitch, but he was a terrific man," said Chuisano. Chuisano's buddy, PFC Jimmy Barrett, was severely wounded in the legs. When the chaplain went to tend to him, Barrett waved him off. "I'm okay, Father. Take care of the other boys first," he said. Despite his brave words, the nineteen-year-old from Brooklyn, New York, died of his wounds that same day.[83]

"Our wave of men left fifteen or twenty minutes after the first wave," recalled Corporal Henry Karbin. "When we hit the beach, we jumped over the sides into about thirty inches of water. The Japs were dropping mortars all over us. . . . [T]he shoreline was full of men that had been hit from the previous waves. They were all yelling for medical corpsmen. We felt guilty because we couldn't stop and help. We had our own destination to go to and that came first. We moved off the beach off to the right toward Asan Point."[84]

As Pharmacist's Mate Second Class Clyde T. Clark approached the Red Beaches in the fifth wave, a nearby LVT was hit by a shell or mortar round. Black smoke poured from the stricken craft. There was no sign of survivors. Clark, who had joined the 3rd Division as a replacement in January, crouched lower as a shell landed a few dozen feet away, wounding the driver in the face. Another shell slammed into the rear of the amtrac, and one of the Marines was struck in the back of the head. Clark started to go to his aid, but Pharmacist's Mate First Class Graham I. Craig, an older veteran who had served in the Bougainville campaign, waved him off. An instant later a second shell punched through the side of the tractor and exploded, blowing off Craig's jaw, left hand, and fingers from his right hand. Dying in a welter of blood, he tried to speak, but could only manage an unintelligible gurgle.[85]

Amtanks from the 1st Armored Amphibian Tractor Battalion stood on the open reef firing their 37mm guns at Japanese artillery dug into Adelup Point. It was a valiant effort, but they were hopelessly outgunned. At 0915, a sharpshooting gun on the point knocked out three of the tanks, killing five men and wounding seven. One of the drivers, nineteen-year-old Corporal John F. Kelly of Detroit, Michigan, was wounded but managed to escape his tank. He was picked up and taken out to the destroyer USS *McKee*, where his injuries were treated. "I then went topside to talk to the skipper at his request," he recalled. "He wanted to know if I was one of the people who had come from that tank." Kelly said he was, pointing out his abandoned LVT(A) sitting on the reef with a broken track. "He took a pair of binoculars and saw the emplacement for the gun that had struck our tank. He promptly fired his guns on the emplacement and destroyed the gun." Kelly's amtank burned all day with the bodies of three dead crewmen inside.[86]

Before heading for shore shortly after 0900, hospital corpsman Leo A. Remaklus heard that the first wave had met no opposition. That was clearly not the case now. Mortar and machine-gun fire sprayed water all over the men huddled in his landing craft as it churned toward Green Beach. "We got in there and here these Marines were laying on this really nice beach. . . . And a little corporal got up and he called them guys every name he could think of and says. 'We're movin'! We're movin'!' And very soon they started up them hills and the next thing you know they was rolling right back down," remembered Remaklus.[87]

Also on Green Beach, PFC Joseph Friedman steered clear of a tank trap where a cluster of Marines had sought shelter, choosing instead to hunker down behind a sheared-off palm tree. A moment later a mortar shell landed in the tank trap. "The screams from the wounded men in the tank trap were absolutely frightful," he recalled. Starting inland, he found Lieutenant Ferris Wharton and a few other men from his Weapons Company platoon dug in only about thirty feet away. The popular lieutenant, a former physical education teacher in Baltimore, Maryland, had devised a novel way to keep up morale as shells continued to fall. "Hey, Friedman!" he called. "C'mon over and pick up some candy bars!" Friedman scrambled over to take a candy bar from Wharton's outstretched hand before ducking back to cover. Seconds later, a mortar shell whispered in and leveled the lieutenant. As a corpsman bent over the stricken officer, Friedman asked how badly Wharton was hit. The corpsman replied that the lieutenant had suffered a massive wound in the spinal area and probably wouldn't live five minutes.

"Let's get him to the beach area and out to a hospital ship," begged Friedman.

The corpsman replied it was no use. As Friedman knelt by his side, Wharton drew a last breath and died.[88]

———

Circling offshore in a Higgins boat, Colonel Edward Craig watched a hail of artillery, mortar, and small arms fire descend on his 3rd Battalion as it came within range of Blue Beach. A pall of smoke and dust hung over the landing area as naval gunfire continued to pass overhead. Forty-seven years old, Craig had been commissioned as a Marine second lieutenant in 1917, much to the disgust of his career Army officer father, who considered the Marines "a terrible bunch of drunks and bums."[89] He missed out on combat in World War I and spent the interim years in a variety of infantry and staff roles before taking command of the 9th Marines in July 1943.

Anxious to take personal command as his regiment started inland, Craig ordered his boat commander to bring him up to the reef where he could transfer to an amtrac and go ashore. "My boat officer, a brand new ensign, refused to carry out my orders and insisted that he stay in a landing wave," recalled Craig. The colonel threatened to throw him over the side. One of his sergeants offered to do the honors. No doubt convinced that Marines of all ranks were simply crazy, the ensign grudgingly ordered the boat to the reef, where Craig and his command group boarded an amtrac for the run to the beach.[90] To the left and front, other amtracs were churning forward, while others headed back for another load of troops. "Suddenly off to our port an amtrac took a direct hit and exploded violently and virtually disappeared," recalled Major George W. Carr, the regimental communications officer.[91]

Already ashore on Blue Beach, PFC Joseph Frank's machine-gun squad laid down fire as the riflemen advanced toward the hills. "Both to our front and right the ground was full of pillboxes, but the ridge also had some big caves in its sides," he observed. "We had two flamethrowers in the company and they were working those caves, burning them out." A Marine burdened down with a radio ran past Frank, then dropped with a grunt as a bullet hit him in the gut.[92] Leading L Company, Captain Harry B. Barker, a six-foot-three-inch former Grinnell College athlete and veteran of Bougainville, was also hit, wounded in the right arm by a Japanese sniper's bullet. Arm bandaged, he returned to lead his company in an attack against a low hill and was wounded again, this time more seriously as a grenade or shell fragment tore into his neck.

Taking cover by the coastal road, PFC Joseph Kight, an artillery forward observer, spotted Sergeant Dick Manley, a 3rd Battalion mortarman from Pleasanton, South Carolina. Manley was cursing. "What's the matter, Dick?" asked Kight.

Manley replied, "Look up yonder. Look."

Kight looked and saw a column of men walking along the crest. "Boy," he said, "we got up there fast, didn't we?"

"Hell!" retorted Manley. "They're Japs and the damn lieutenant won't let me shoot."[93]

The gunner on Sergeant Jim Milliff's machine-gun crew was killed as they came under fire from the higher ground. A Marine called out to Milliff, "There's a Jap in there!" pointing to a cave entrance up on the hill. Another Marine came along with a flamethrower, and Milliff pointed out the cave. The Marine turned his flamethrower on the entrance. "Seven Japs ran out and we shot them," said Milliff.[94]

The battalion pressed forward. On the left, K Company crossed the rice paddies and seized the ridge beyond with what the operational monograph subsequently termed "astonishing rapidity."[95] Arriving ashore, Colonel Craig's command group was also on the move, though he had already lost his executive officer, wounded by a mortar blast on the beach. Accompanied by his personnel officer, Captain Charles C. Henderson, who was bleeding from cuts to his face and neck from a bullet that had smashed into his carbine, Craig went looking for 3rd Battalion commander Lieutenant Colonel Walter Asmuth Jr. Small arms fire forced them to the shelter of a low mound. "I was looking through my glasses at the ridge ahead when [Henderson] suddenly toppled over across my knees, shot through the throat," said Craig. "I lay him down behind the mound and yelled for a corpsman." Finally locating Asmuth, Craig found the colonel had suffered a gunshot wound to the arm and was about to be evacuated. As Craig returned to his command post in a large bomb crater, some stretcher bearers came through carrying Harry Barker, "one of my best company commanders," recalled Craig. The captain was dead, having succumbed to the wound to his neck.[96]

CHAPTER 13

THE FIGHT FOR THE BEACHHEADS

At Agat, the slaughter of amphibious vehicles heading into the Yellow Beaches south of Orote Peninsula continued unabated as the troop-carrying tractors came within range of the Japanese guns. "First wave of LVTs is about 100 yards from beach and are receiving gunfire on LVTs just on flank on Yellow 1 and White 2," reported the air liaison observer.[1]

"Can you locate source of fire?" came the reply.[2]

"We were in slow-moving amphibious tractors, the kind you had to jump over the side to get out," recalled twenty-one-year-old PFC Thomas ("Tom") E. Backman, part of a brigade signals unit. "As we turned toward the beach, I could see little spurts of water coming up from the ocean and I realized those spurts were probably mortar shells the Japanese were dropping on us." A great cloud of reddish dust hung over the landing beaches as Navy pilots made their last strafing runs. "We grew more tense the closer we got to the beach. But finally the amtrac lumbered out of the water and came to a stop a few yards from the water's edge. We all immediately vaulted over the side and crouched next to the amtrac wondering what to do next."[3]

The first wave—or what was left of it—reached the beach line at 0832. At 0840 the air observer reported, "6 LVT(A)s and 3 LVTs have been hit. Men are wading ashore. . . . 1st wave of LVTs are leaving beach to return. . . . Troops are advancing inland." Three minutes later, at 0843, he added, "I count 6 LVTs stopped in the water. Having good fight on Yellow 2."[4] Out on the reef, the survivors of a burning amtank waved down a trio of LVTs that had delivered their troops ashore and were returning seaward for the later waves. All three stopped, only to be hit in rapid succession by a Japanese shore gun. Two were able to pull out, but the third joined the burning amtank on the reef.

Heading in toward Yellow 2 with the 2nd Battalion, 22nd Marines, platoon leader Second Lieutenant Richard ("Heavy") Pfuhl was still three hundred yards out when mortar rounds began sending up showers of seawater around his tractor. "Two hundred yards out, our LVT bangs the reef and is half swimming, half crawling," he recalled. "It's an amusement park ride with Marines bouncing from gunnel to gunnel and up and down."

Only thirty yards from shore, there was a grinding explosion on the right gunnel, and the amtrac listed to port. "Get your butts outa here!" someone yelled, and the occupants bailed out into about two feet of water. "Fifty yards to my right, a Nip field piece fires north along the breaches," observed Pfuhl. "We are sitting ducks, amtracs dead in the water everywhere. One smoking amtrac, no sign of life, crawls slowly onto the beach and stops." Dazed, Pfuhl somehow made his way to shore, but his company was already taking losses, including one of his veteran sergeants, twenty-seven-year-old Joseph W. Tucker of Dublin, Texas, an eight-year veteran, who was decapitated.[5]

Also killed on the way into the Yellow Beaches was the commanding officer of the 1st Battalion's Headquarters Company, Major Hudson Bridge. The twenty-six-year-old scion of a prominent Saint Louis manufacturing dynasty, Bridge had won a Silver Star during the Marshall Islands campaign for directing the destruction of two enemy emplacements firing on the landing force. "He was a big beast of a guy," recalled Pfuhl. "While we were landing, the gunner on his amtrac got knocked off and the major went forward and began plugging away with the machine gun. . . . He was blown to pieces, apparently by a direct hit."[6] Killed in the same tractor, along with about eight others besides Bridge, was battalion chaplain Lieutenant Anthony Conway, who had been entrusted with just about everybody's gambling money, "the Marines never for a minute considering that he was just as mortal as they," remarked combat correspondent Cyril J. O'Brien.[7] The young priest's precautionary final letter to his parents would arrive home following news of his death.

PFC George Weber, a former farm boy from Schaghticoke, New York, was among a handful of survivors from an amtrac blown out of the water fifty yards off Yellow Beach 2. Weber could be forgiven if he thought he was being persecuted by the fates. Six months before, his landing craft had been hit going ashore at Eniwetok. Now, with blood streaming down his face from a head wound, he made his way to shore and crawled over the sand, taking shelter behind a boulder on the edge of a shell hole near Gaan Point.

About thirty yards away, a Japanese field piece was shooting at amtracs lumbering across the reef. Weber lobbed a grenade at the position, then another, and another. After the fourth, the gun went silent, but a machine gun on top of the emplacement continued to rake the beach. Weber worked in closer and knocked it out with another grenade, then picked up a rifle from the sand and joined a squad heading inland. Having fired poorly during boot camp at Parris Island, he was not optimistic about his contribution to overrunning the Japanese infantry. "I don't know if I killed any," said the one-man demolitions team. "You gotta remember, I never was much of a rifleman."[8]

Twenty-five-year-old Platoon Sergeant Thomas R. O'Neill of Kansas City, Missouri, transferred from a Higgins boat to an amtrac at the reef line. "Overhead a squadron of Navy dive-bombers were making a run on the Orote Peninsula," he recalled. The Japanese suddenly let loose with a barrage of antiaircraft fire. "The lead plane took a direct hit, blowing it to bits." O'Neill chanced a quick look over the side and counted six amtracs burning in the water. His own tractor was about to join them. "We had just reached the reef when we took a hit," he recalled. "There was a sudden explosion. I lost all count of time although I couldn't have been out more than a second. The heat and acid smell of powder was still in the air." The shell had struck the port bow, blowing the port track off. The tractor took on a list, and the driver's compartment was on fire. Either the driver or the assistant driver—O'Neill wasn't sure which—stumbled out of the forward compartment. "He looked as if he'd been hit bad," said O'Neill. "[PFC Jennings H.] Walkup grabbed him, inflated his life belt and pushed him over the side. I never did see the other crew member." O'Neill ordered everybody over the side before the Japanese gunners could follow up with another shell. "We had to wade 500 yards to the beach," he noted. Everything was "all bedlam and confusion. . . . The beaches were under fire. All hands were digging in or seeking cover of some sort."[9]

A line of trenches roughly two feet wide and three and a half feet deep paralleled the shore about fifty feet inland. The main trench was connected to occasional communication trenches leading to rifle or machine-gun pits about eight feet forward of the trench line. Other subsidiary trenches led to shelters in the rear. Earth-covered pillboxes projecting only three feet from ground level, each with two twelve-by-fourteen-inch firing ports, were positioned to fire along the beaches. Japanese crossfire from Gaan Point and tiny Yona Island just off Bangi Point also raked Yellow Beach 2. Among the casualties was a first aid station party, struck down by a shell from a 75mm field gun as they were debarking from their amtrac. The bodies of seventy-five Marines were later counted on the three-hundred-yard strip of sand. "One I still remember was a buck sergeant lying face down with a .45 pistol clutched in his hand," recalled PFC Tom Backman.[10]

PFC James Bradshaw, his section leader, and their platoon leader, First Lieutenant John F. Ford of Framingham, Massachusetts, scrambled into a bomb crater on Yellow 1 and tried to sort out just where they were. They were poring over their map when Ford suddenly collapsed. "We rolled him over and we found a hole in his side," recalled Bradshaw. A mortar shell fragment had torn through his abdomen. "And you were taught not to delay, go on with your business. So we slapped a dressing on this hole. And [we used] his dressing. That was another rule. You always used the man's individual dressing rather than your own. You saved yours for yourself. . . . We slapped a dressing on him and we went looking for our platoon. When we caught up with the rest of the platoon, the assistant platoon commander wanted some maps that the commander had and he went back to get them." When he returned, he said the lieutenant had died.[11]

Still gathering his senses on Yellow 2, Heavy Pfuhl pitched three grenades at a Nambu machine gun that was yards out of range. Off to his right, the field pieces dug into Gaan Point continued to fire. Corralling a bazooka team, Pfuhl directed their fire onto one of the gunports. They appeared to get three hits. "The gun, which commanded the entire cove, was silenced for a few minutes, but it started up again," he recalled. Leaving it to someone else, Pfuhl headed inland.[12]

Burdened down with a seventy-pound flamethrower, eighteen-year-old PFC Ralph M. Contreras, a stocky Mexican-American kid from Dixon, Illinois, came in on Yellow Beach 1 on the Marine Brigade's left. Contreras, who had joined the 22nd Marines after Eniwetok, was a mortar man by training, but on the way to Guam his squad leader had called him over for a chat. "And there on the deck of the ship—I was onboard ship—[was] a flamethrower," he recalled wryly. "He said, 'we're going to show you how to operate this and you're going to carry this in when we go into Guam.' I had never seen a flamethrower before. . . . Didn't know the first thing about it."

Slogging inland with the first waves, it seemed to Contreras—experiencing his first combat—that nothing much was happening at the moment, but this early first impression didn't last long. "We made about 500 yards and all hell broke loose," he recalled. A machine gun located in a pillbox opened up on them, and the call went out for a flamethrower. Contreras crawled forward accompanied by another Marine who was supposed to open the valves at the top of the tank at the critical moment since Contreras wouldn't be able to reach them himself. He recalled,

This kid, this buddy of mine, he was supposed to be my assistant, and we got up there, we were pinned down, because they couldn't get the machine gun and there was all kinds of

fire. . . . I couldn't hit the deck. I had to kind of lean back on them tanks you know. If they ever hit them tanks, they wouldn't find me at all. So I kind of leaned back and I could just hear the bullets going by my ears. . . . And the assistant who was supposed to turn on all these valves for me, he was right in front of me behind a coconut palm that had got busted. And he turned around to say something and then he went down. . . . And when I got up to him, he'd got a slug right through his head, never knew what hit him. . . . I don't know if it was a stray or a sniper or what, but he gets it there and I'm right behind him in the open and I'm not hit and he gets killed. That's the way it was.

Contreras turned his attention back to the pillbox. "So anyway, we got another guy who had to turn on the valves, and we're trying to get up to the pillbox. He says okay and I aimed the thing and squeezed it. Nothing happened. Not a damn thing happened." Disgusted, Contreras threw the flamethrower on the ground and picked up a Browning Automatic Rifle (BAR) from a downed Marine.[13]

Plans for the Agat landing called for the amtanks and LVTs in the first waves to dash inland for several hundred yards before stopping to unload. "By so doing, they would be behind the beach defenses and could attack them from the rear," theorized General Lemuel Shepherd. "I figured that the Japs would believe the amphibs were tanks and take cover, thereby permitting the vehicles to pass over them without injury to the thin-skinned vehicles."[14] This same maneuver—intended to take advantage of the initial shock to quickly establish a deeper beachhead—had been tried and failed on Saipan the previous month, and it fared no better at Agat. It was a lot to expect from the armored amphibs even if all went well—and things were not going well on the Marine Brigade beaches as the Japanese guns continued to take a toll on the tracked vehicles. "The theory was excellent, but the Japs did not cooperate," an amtrac officer remarked wryly of the failed blitzkrieg.[15]

Captain Owen Lillie's A Company command tank made it ashore, though its 37mm main gun was now useless as a result of the hit it took on the way in. The driver managed to get about one hundred yards inland before the tank got hung up on a tree stump and stalled. Gunnery Sergeant Daniel H. Maynard climbed out and saw his ammo passer giving first aid to Captain Lillie. The popular twenty-four-year-old officer, a graduate of the University of Michigan, where he had majored in "letters and law," had been hit in the chest. Maynard stuck the captain with a morphine syrette, but Lillie died a few minutes later. Their radio operator was already dead, killed instantly by the same shell that had knocked out their 37mm gun.[16]

First Lieutenant Robert A. Fish's amtank survived the run into shore and lumbered about fifty yards inland, where it bogged down in a bomb crater. "We could not see anything directly to our front, but off to the right and behind us, Gaan Point was lighting up like a Christmas tree," he said. "The Japs were putting up tremendous resistance from this strongpoint. We could see some of the Japs standing on top of Gaan Point, firing their weapons at the oncoming amtracs."[17] Only three tanks from Company A and eight from Company B managed to make their way inland across the coastal road and into the expanse of dry rice paddies leading to the foothills of Mount Alifan.

The Company B amtanks fared somewhat better on the White Beaches. Spared the deadly fire of the Gaan Point guns decimating Company A just to the north, eight tanks pushed at least some distance inland. PFC Earl M. Hill's amtank had just entered a row of shattered coconut trees beyond the beach when someone in the main turret shouted, "McCrory's hit!" Nineteen-year-old PFC Ralph N. McCrory had been manning one of the .30-caliber machine guns located behind the main turret, a position that left the gunner exposed from the waist up. A treetop sniper had waited until the amtank lumbered by and then fired down on the lanky blonde Texan.

Hill crawled back into the cargo bay and found McCrory lying face down on the stacked 37mm ammunition. He removed the first aid kit from McCrory's web belt and began to look for wounds, but all he could find was a small circular hole in the top of McCrory's steel helmet. He unfastened the helmet and pulled it off. With the helmet came a large part of the young Texan's skull and brain. Hill put the first aid kit aside and covered the dead youngster with a poncho.[18]

The 1st Battalion, 4th Marines, commanded by Major Bernard W. Green, came ashore behind the amtanks on White Beach 2 with two companies—A and B—in the assault. Only thirty yards inland, a machine gun in a pillbox cut down five B Company men, killing two and wounding three. B Company's mortar platoon leader, First Lieutenant Roger E. Smith, was fatally wounded when he attacked a pillbox with only his rifle in an effort to save one of the wounded Marines.

Leading A Company's 3rd Platoon, Lieutenant Max Belko, a former All-American and star tackle for the University of Southern California Trojans football team, had ended up in the water when his amtrac was disabled by a shell on the way into the beach. No one was injured, but as the amtrac began to settle, they all piled out and waded ashore. "We had just secured the beachhead and had contacted the flank units," recalled company commander First Lieutenant Frank Kemp of the push inland. "Lieutenant Belko passed behind me checking his 3rd Platoon. I trained my eyes on an opening in the tall grass ahead of our lines. Twice the enemy had risen above the grass and I sprayed the area with a BAR on full auto. The area had a lot of vegetation growing . . . a lot of cover for the enemy. Only when they fired could we locate their position."

Moments later, Belko went down. "We were standing on a hill well above the beach, when a sniper fired up the hill and hit Lieutenant Belko," recalled Platoon Sergeant Jack R. Christenson. As others ducked for cover, Corporal Bill Dae, an Apache Indian and veteran of the 1st Raider Battalion, remained standing, firing his M-1 rifle at two Japanese, one of whom had just shot the lieutenant. Dae killed them both, but Belko was in bad shape. Platoon Sergeant Ken Champlin went to help the lieutenant and found he had been shot in the stomach. Champlin stuck him with a morphine syrette, but there wasn't much else he could do. Belko lifted a hand, and Champlin grasped it. "That's all she wrote, Champ," murmured Belko. And then he died.[19]

Twenty-three-year-old PFC Roger C. Spaulding headed inland carrying a World War I vintage BAR he had "won" by drawing the low card—the deuce of spades—which entitled him to last choice of the available automatic rifles, this being a Cosmoline-caked relic still wrapped in a 1918-dated newspaper. "By the time I landed, it was getting hot on the ground, and the Jap defenses were making things hotter," he recalled. "I had to go over coconut trees, rush to the next, take cover behind it, then go over again—all the while lugging my BAR, bipod and ammunition."

Charging over a low ridge with his assistant gunner, Spaulding saw a Japanese soldier just down the slope pointing a pistol at him. Flustered, he groped for a grenade, then remembered the BAR. He leveled the rifle at the man and pulled the trigger. One round went off, and the gun jammed. When he looked up again, the Japanese had holstered his pistol and was coming at him with the longest sword he had ever seen. Spaulding grabbed the BAR by the barrel, intending to club his attacker or at least parry the sword, but before they could come to grips, his assistant gunner cut loose with his M-1, and the enemy soldier's head seemed to explode. As the nearly headless corpse collapsed, the sword glanced off Spaulding's BAR. Spaulding and his savior paused to examine the dead swordsman. An officer or noncom, the man was clad in clean khaki shorts and shirt and wore two wristwatches—"the fancy kind with a tiny leather cover over the face for protection," recalled Spaulding. What remained of his helmeted head had been practically severed from his body. Spaulding's assistant gunner grinned and gestured toward his victim with his M-1. "See that, Rog? See that?" he said proudly. "All six of them, right between his eyes!"[20]

Breaking through the crust of resistance at the beach, PFC George Aspley thought many of the Japanese he encountered seemed dazed and disorganized. "We were easily able to shoot or bayonet them as they cowered in their foxholes with their arms covering their heads, or pick them off as they attempted to crawl out of their holes in order to man their machine gun or mortar positions," he observed. He gave no particular thought to the killing. "As for the Japanese, it never occurred to me that they were human beings as they crawled in and out of their bunkers and shell holes," he admitted. "I viewed them more as rats in a city dump crawling around in the debris. The only hitch was that these rats were incredibly dangerous; they had weapons and they shot back at you."[21]

Packed into two LVTs, Lieutenant Willard ("Bill") C. Hofer's B Company platoon was one of the few infantry units to ride their amtracs any distance inland. The two tractors ground their way four hundred yards into Japanese territory before stopping. Hofer, a stocky redhead who had played quarterback for Notre Dame, debarked to find his platoon all by their lonesome, far ahead of any of the other assault units and under increasing fire. Unrelentingly aggressive by nature, Hofer was undeterred. He led the platoon up toward the slopes of Mount Alifan and formed a defensive line.

They were not entirely alone. PFC Luther M. Flattum's B Company amtank was one of at least three that found their way forward as originally planned. Coming ashore, the crew spotted a machine-gun nest. As they took it under fire, a second amtank rolled by and hit a mine. Flattum's amtank plowed through a barricade and entered a blasted coconut grove, where the tankers paused, waiting for planes to drop a flare to show they had stopped strafing. When no flare materialized, they lumbered on. "I was expecting any second to get a big lift into the air but—thank God—we didn't hit a mine," he recalled.[22] After about fifteen hundred yards, they stopped to wait for the infantry. A lone troop-carrying tractor had followed them up, and the occupants piled out. Unable to raise anyone on his radio, Flattum ducked into the cargo compartment to help pass ammunition to the machine gunners exchanging fire with Japanese dug in on the slope. As one of the gunners bent over to pick up a box of ammo, a bullet punched through his gun shield, grazed his back, and ricocheted off the handle of the machine gun. Flattum looked back toward the beach. The rest of the infantry was still not in sight.

— • —

Steaming just off the Agat beaches, the gunboats and other support craft exchanged fire with Japanese shore positions located along Orote Point. LCI(G) 437 focused on a tiny islet called Pelagi Rock just offshore, about one thousand yards north of Yellow 1, using her 40mm guns so lavishly that a fire hose had to be turned on the red-hot barrels. The Japanese responded in kind with "exceedingly well directed fire," according to the gunboat's after-action report. "At least twelve near misses were reported on the port side close aboard and off the port bow. These shook the ship and threw considerable water and a small amount of shrapnel on deck." Shortly before 0900 the gunboat was struck by a 75mm shell, but the crew's luck held. The projectile passed through the steering room and out the other side of the ship just above the waterline without exploding.[23]

USS SC 1326, a 111-foot plywood subchaser serving as control vessel on the left side of the transfer line during the landing, was less fortunate. With a normal complement of twenty-eight men, the ship was armed with a 40mm mount, a 20mm gun, and a variety of antisubmarine weapons, including the "mousetrap," an array of small rocket-propelled depth charges designed to be fired in a pattern ahead of the vessel. The subchaser had already put her guns to use as she escorted the first wave of amtracs toward shore, opening fire at a range of three thousand yards and continuing until about sixteen hundred yards offshore.

As the LVTs lurched up onto the Yellow Beaches, a Japanese gun crew took notice of the subchaser. A shell sent up a cascade of water about seventy-five yards off the starboard bow. Skipper Lieutenant Howe J. Wheelock of Larchmont, New York, called for "left full rudder, all engines ahead, 8 knots." One minute later, while turning and increasing speed from a near-dead stop, two shells—possibly fired from a heavy mortar located on Orote Peninsula two thousand yards to the north of Yellow Beach 1—came in almost simultaneously. The nearest exploded about twenty yards off the port beam, spraying the pilothouse and signal bridge with shrapnel. Up on deck, news correspondent Howard M. Norton was covering the landings for the *Baltimore Sun*. He heard someone shout, "Duck! They've got us bracketed!" At the same instant a third shell exploded on the deck between the pilothouse and the 40mm gun, butchering members of the gun crew who were reloading the 40mm ready box. "The three men handling the ammunition were killed instantly," said Norton. "The steward's mate, beheaded and dismembered, lay beneath a gun. A pharmacist's mate, the only man aboard qualified to give expert first aid, was severely wounded in the chest and unable to move. Men crouching on the other side of me were badly hit and bleeding." A lieutenant junior grade clutched the bloody stump of his right arm, the lower part dangling by a thread of flesh.

Norton realized he was covered with blood, none of it his. A twenty-year-old coxswain near Norton dazedly examined a deep dent in the helmet that had just saved his life. "I wouldn't take a million dollars for this old tin hat," the coxswain observed to no one in particular. "The cabin was riddled with shrapnel, the magazine flooded, the radio knocked out, chunks of human flesh mingled with the kapok lining of shredded life preservers were spattered over the forward deck and there was a slippery film of blood underfoot," reported Norton. In addition to the three men who were killed instantly, twelve others were wounded, two of whom subsequently died.[24]

"This shell is believed to have struck one of the members of the gun crew in the chest, causing the shell to explode about four feet above the deck and killing five of the gun crew in that vicinity," noted the ship's after-action report. Several cases of 40mm ammunition, which had been brought on deck from the magazine to replace expended ready box ammo, were hit by shell fragments and caught fire. The flames spread to life jackets and one of the bodies. Fearing an explosion, sailors knocked down the flames with fire hoses and hastily dumped the damaged cases over the side. A shell fragment lodged in the cast TNT of one of the ship's mousetrap projectiles, which fortunately did not explode.

The ship remained on station two thousand yards from the beach and continued its control duties while taking care of the wounded, picking up body parts, and hosing down the bloody deck. Two of the more seriously injured were transferred by stretcher to a small boat for removal to the USS *Zeilin* for medical attention. One died en route to the *Zeilin* only minutes after leaving the ship. The other succumbed a few hours later. The body parts of the three men killed in the initial explosion were gathered up. "The bodies were later buried at sea as they were so mutilated and dismembered that preservation for later burial on land was impossible," observed the ship's report.

In retrospect, the report "respectfully" offered "several thoughts" for consideration in future operations involving submarine chasers in the role of control vessels during landings on hostile beaches. Foremost among these was the suggestion that "it might be wise" to use a ship with greater armor and armament, pointing out, "The plywood of a Submarine Chaser is not adequate shield for shrapnel."[25]

—✦—

Still aboard USS *George Clymer*, General Shepherd was anxious to get his tanks ashore as quickly as possible. Wave 5 Tare, composed of one LCT (Landing Craft, Tank) carrying four medium tanks, followed by a column of seven LCMs, each loaded with one tank, left the line of departure at 0815 and reached the reef off White Beach 1 at 0834, just as the first waves of infantry were arriving on shore. Problems arose almost immediately as the LCT came in two hundred to three hundred yards to the right of a channel cleared by underwater demolition teams two days before on the left flank of White Beach 1. It was later discovered the Japanese had apparently moved the buoys left to mark the channel. While attempting to guide boat traffic toward the channel, Ensign Thomas D. Nixon, a rangy twenty-nine-year-old naval reservist from Arkansas, became UDT-4's only fatality of the campaign when he was shot by a sniper concealed on Gaan Point. Shore party personnel managed to guide two of the tank lighters to the proper location, but the other tanks offloaded on the reef.

At 0858 Shepherd radioed the air liaison observer, "Are tanks landing?" Air liaison replied, "No dope yet. Tanks have not landed." A few minutes later, air liaison reported ominously, "Medium tanks landing off White beaches having trouble on reefs. Don't seem to be making any headway." The air observer subsequently added that the tanks were still about four hundred yards off the beach. "Water appears to be deep and tanks are sitting at cockeyed angle."[26]

Tank company commander Captain Phil Morell found the water deeper than reported where the armor tried to come ashore. Water depth on the front edge of the reef was relatively shallow but grew deeper toward the center, in a sort of geological saucer. Morell had one of his lieutenants, who stood six feet, six inches and had been a competitive swimmer in college, wade along in front of the tanks to verify the depth and locate any potholes as the vehicles edged slowly forward. At 0943 the air liaison observer reported the tanks were ashore, only to add a few minutes later that two of the Shermans remained stranded about four hundred yards offshore "with water about a foot from the top."[27]

Much of the brigade's radio equipment also fell victim to water. "Radio equipment was not effectively waterproofed because adequate waterproofing materials were never made available in spite of frequent requests," the brigade noted later. "Few air strikes were directed by air liaison parties because most vehicular radios had been damaged by salt water. These radios were the only ones capable of operating on the Support Air Direction Net."[28]

Due to the poor reef conditions off the Yellow Beaches, the tank company with the 22nd Marines was diverted to the White Beaches. Despite that precaution, Corporal William K. Anderson's tank managed to get stuck in a shell hole on the way in. His platoon commander, Lieutenant Sam W. Lane, a six-foot-tall, blonde, blue-eyed Texan, clambered out to hook them up to another tank for a tow. He didn't come back. A few minutes later, Anderson's captain came up on the radio, telling him to go out and hook up the tow. Anderson replied that the lieutenant was already taking care of it.

"The Japs shot his head off," said the captain. "You have to do it."

Anderson climbed out of the tank and was promptly shot in the arm. "It was only a minor flesh wound, but it hurt like hell and looked terrible," he recalled. He ducked back into the tank. The captain came up on the radio again, demanding to know why he hadn't hooked up the tow. "When I explained my wound, he told me in no uncertain terms what would happen if I didn't get my butt out and get the job done," remembered Anderson. "I was now the tank commander. My how I hated him at that moment, but I did it." Soon afterward, a Japanese armor-piercing round came through the tank. "It was deflected by my .45 hanging on the bulkhead and my radio," said Anderson. "If it had gone straight, it would have set off our 75mm rounds and turned us into a rolling torch."[29]

Once ashore, the Shermans turned left to join their own regiment. The change of plan paid a big dividend when the route took the tanks behind the Japanese burrowed into Gaan Point. The tankers paused to reduce the two guns—knocking out one of them at a range of only fifty yards—finally ending their contribution to the carnage off the Yellow Beaches. "[The] dead Nips were strewn around the large pillbox," observed Navy commander H. E. Smith. "They appeared as though thrown out of the concrete emplacement by a great force. Several little brown men in brown uniforms with wrap-around puttees, two-toed sandals and . . . mushroom helmets were huddled together in the fore section of the dugout, slumped over their wrecked cannon. One was leaning against a coconut tree on the top of the fort. A Marine approached cautiously and then kicked him over into a gulley."[30]

Even with its main guns silenced, the point remained a threat. "After the artillery pieces in this position were put out of action, the Japanese continued to harass personnel on the beach with rifle fire," reported the brigade intelligence officer, Major Robert W. Shaw. "Grenades and flamethrowers proved ineffective, and the fire was finally halted by sealing the openings by means of a bulldozer."[31]

An examination of the White Beach area to the south of Gaan Point indicated that Japanese plans for a similar ambush had fortunately failed. "On the extreme right flank of the beaches there were two small islands that were being fortified at the time of our landing," noted amtrac battalion operations officer Ralph Parker. "Upon landing we found whatever weapons were there had been abandoned but were *still loaded*. As I recall there was a small artillery piece set to deliver enfilade fire to the right beaches and a Nambu machine gun sighted also in the same area. Either the people did not have the chance to man the weapons because of heavy naval gunfire or they decided that now was the time to start a trek to the hills, we shall never know, anyway it was lucky for us they didn't stay."[32]

Supporting the 4th Marines, Phil Morell's tankers knocked out a machine gun on a rocky little point at the southern edge of the beach before heading inland, where Bill Hofer's platoon was about to get some much-appreciated support. Radio messages from Colonel Alan Shapley urged the tanks to silence a gun picking off landing craft from up on Mount Alifan less than two thousand yards inland from White 1. "It was in a cave," recalled Morell. "Mount Alifan was a kind of red clay mountain. They had some doors on that cave and the doors were plastered with that same red clay. The doors would open, and the gun would come out, fire about three rounds, and go back in."

Unable to spot the gun through the tank periscope, Morell climbed outside to get a better view. "I'm out there with just a shoulder-holstered pistol and here come about thirty Japs over this little grass ridge right in front of me." Morell had just enough time to think, "Oh, shit!" when the tank machine guns opened up and mowed the enemy soldiers down. About that time a Marine corporal came along and said he had spotted the elusive gun. The tankers fired a white phosphorus round, and the corporal guided them in on the enemy position. As the gun emerged from its lair, Morell's tanks cut loose. "There were boots with legs in them flying out, and pieces of the gun and helmets and everything else," observed Morell. "We slaughtered that thing."[33]

Shapley's 2nd Battalion, led by Major John S. Messer, broke into open country and pressed on through the sword grass toward Mount Alifan. Buck Daley's E Company platoon lost its first two men—Sergeant Joseph H. Dickson and twenty-one-year-old PFC Roscoe Fasnacht, both former Raiders—cut down by a hidden machine gun while working their way up a wooded ravine. They took more casualties when a mortar barrage descended on them as they reached Mount Alifan's lower slopes. The seriously wounded included Sergeant Joseph Latkovich, son of Yugoslavian immigrants who had settled in Pennsylvania coal country. "Sgt. Latkovich had been hit in the head behind the left ear with a mortar fragment that opened a wound in his skull, not deep and only about an inch and a quarter square [and] you could see his brain pulsating," remembered Daley. "I heard him moaning as he lay on a ledge just above us so I crawled up to where he lay and seeing he was alive I called for the corpsman." The corpsman said he had already checked the sergeant and the wound was fatal. Latkovich, a veteran of the 4th Raider Battalion, soon expired.[34]

PFC Neil L. Rogers, a flamethrower operator with F Company, sprayed an enemy pillbox with fuel, only to have his igniter fail. Undaunted, the stocky twenty-one-year-old from Warren, Ohio, crawled up to the pillbox and, though wounded, ignited the fuel-soaked emplacement with matches, immolating five Japanese. Heavy fighting followed as the Marines closed on the headquarters for the Japanese 1st Battalion, 38th Infantry, located on a small hill on the west side of Mount Alifan. According to Japanese accounts, about two companies of Marines broke through late in the morning in front of the headquarters. A fierce hand grenade battle developed. "At about 1000 [1100] hours the battalion commander, leading his troops, charged into the enemy and killed several with his sword, but he and almost all his men died a glorious death," observed the report.[35]

PFC Nick Zobenica came up short as two grenades suddenly plunked down next to him. "They were right there. I couldn't move," he recalled. The dual explosions blew his helmet and cartridge belt off. Dazed, he realized one side of his body was paralyzed, and he was having trouble with his vision. "My face was bleeding. I could kind of see the blood squirting out of my gut." Each time he took a breath, the blood pumped out. He seemed surrounded by chaos. Machine guns were yammering away. "There was a Polish kid by the name of Chuck Jendrasiak from Grand Rapids, Michigan," said Zobenica. "He was going to go over and contact George Company and the Japanese fire caught him and rolled him just like a tin can. Over and over."

The regimental chaplain, Father Paul Redmond, crawled up to Zobenica as the machine-gun fire continued. Zobenica had no idea how the priest had made it without getting shot. "You should have seen the way the guys were dropping. And he came right to me and he was saying that prayer to me and he says, 'You're a brave Marine. God will take care of you. Your wounds will be healed.' And then he took off." The next thing Zobenica knew, Platoon Sergeant Mike Dunbar had him by the ankles and was pulling him down the hill. "He was dragging me, really, because my whole side was paralyzed . . . and a sniper cut loose and hit him right [in the leg] and hit [an] artery. And my right hand wouldn't work, so he pulled his pants up and I grabbed that artery [with my left hand] and I stopped that bleeding. Just about then two corpsmen came by."[36]

Despite inflicting heavy casualties on the Marine Brigade during the landing, the Japanese shoreline defense was collapsing. Breaking through the beach defenses on Yellow Beach 1, Lieutenant Colonel Walfried H. Fromhold's 1st Battalion, 22nd Marines turned left and pushed toward Agat. Company B, advancing north along the shoreline, reached the outskirts of the village, where it ran into stiff resistance from Japanese infantry fighting from the rubble. Fromhold committed his reserve, Company C, and at 1020 reported, "We have Agat."[37] There wasn't much to the place. "A few chickens were about," remarked Sergeant Donald A. Hallman. "On one street was a dead donkey. That was all—that and a score or so of dead Japanese. A wilted and bedraggled flower bed could be seen by a house just off the main street."[38] A tin shed just outside town still housed a red and gray machine with a label identifying it as a "Case Rice Thresher."

Nineteen-year-old PFC Rudy Rosenquist arrived on White 2 with the reserve 3rd Battalion, 4th Marines two hours after the initial landing. "When we reached the beach, we were receiving light small arms fire," he recalled. As they rolled over the side of their tractor, one of the men in his company was wounded in the knee. They loaded him back into the amtrac, his battle over almost before it began. Rosenquist saw where shellfire had uncovered aerial bombs rigged as antivehicle mines. Here and there amtracs had been blown open like so many tin cans. "There were parts of bodies all over . . . a torso with no head, arms or legs was lying about fifteen feet to my right," he recalled. "Some bodies were still in the water. We were still getting small arms fire, but none of us were doing much firing. There was a smashed tractor at the water's edge and two Marines were firing over us at a small hill to our front, but we could locate no apparent signs of fire." As he started inland, Rosenquist paused to take a .38-caliber revolver from a dead Marine on the beach, using his knife to cut the ammunition belt with spare rounds off the body.

Not far inland, a tank was systematically reducing pillboxes, running up as close as possible, then depressing the turret gun to fire directly into the pillbox gun ports. "Several Japs were taken alive and wounded," Rosenquist recalled. "One enemy soldier had no apparent marks on him, but when we stood him up he was so dazed, he would simply fall on his face. All were stripped and marched back to the beach."[39]

As of 1034, the Marine Brigade had advanced approximately one thousand yards inland. General Shepherd and his forward command group disembarked from the *Clymer* at 1136. The brigade set up a command post in a coconut grove about two hundred yards southeast of Gaan Point, and at 1350 Shepherd assumed control of all troops in the brigade zone. Though advising III Amphibious Corps that ammunition and water were desperately needed ashore, Shepherd saw that the initial crust of opposition at Agat had been broken and ordered Shapley to continue the attack on Alifan with the 4th Marines. "I felt that if we had that piece of high ground, we would be all right," he observed.[40]

❧

Aboard ship off the 3rd Marine Division beaches, International News Service staff correspondent John R. Henry watched uneasily as wounded men started coming back less than an hour after the initial assault.

One man, unconscious, his head swathed in bandages, lay atop the engine compartment of an amphibian tractor bobbing in the water below. Shell fragments had torn through his skull. His dog tag identified him as a chief pharmacist's mate. Another casualty, shell-shattered leg dangling, was hauled onto the deck in a basket stretcher. Ashen-faced from blood loss, the wounded youngster noticed the sympathetic expressions of onlookers and managed a smile and a wave. "They shouldn't feel sorry for me," he protested. "I'm okay." When Henry checked a few hours later, he learned the youth had died.[41]

Back on shore, successive waves of LVTs continued to land men on the beaches: ten waves had come ashore by 0929, despite continuing fire from guns dug into Adelup Point. Destroyers did their best to knock out the enemy positions from the water, but reports persisted that "more help was needed."[42] PFC Calvin E. Rainey, came ashore on Red Beach 2 in the twelfth wave. The gunner watching from the machine gun on the tractor yelled, "Stay down!" recalled Rainey. "So we stayed down. We could hear bullets ricocheting off the [LVT] and he had a .50 caliber up there and he was shooting away. Finally he turned around and said 'Go!' So we all rolled over the side and got away from the [LVT] as fast as we can cause they ricochet bullets."

Rainey landed in the sand and never even got his feet wet. "And the kid I hit the beach with—good kid—got killed later. His name was Andy Anderson [PFC Charles V. Anderson] and he went haywire," recalled Rainey. "He saw a fella sittin' over there and a corpsman was wrapping his head up. A head wound can be serious or not. He just saw that blood. He couldn't stand the sight of blood. So I pushed him under a fallen tree for protection and I had to go on, so I went on."[43]

Combat correspondent Alvin Josephy waded in across the reef toward the Red Beaches, narrating his impressions into a microphone wired into a recording unit set up in a half-track lumbering by his side. A painted name on the side identified the vehicle as "Slapsie Maxie," a tribute to Maxie Rosenbloom, the popular light heavyweight boxing champion of the world in the early 1930s. Josephy could see the hills behind the beach. They seemed to go straight up. Machine-gun fire began to splash around the men slogging along through knee-deep water trying not to stumble on coral outcroppings. "[Oh], one boy's been hit—one boy's hurt now," he recorded.

They're putting him in the rubber boat—four men are putting him in the rubber boat—I don't know who he is—I can't see him. But he has been hurt and he's lying on his side—Hold it!—What!—Another boy's hit—another boy's just been hurt—I think he's been killed—our officer is yelling to get him. . . . There's a lot of fire around us now. We're almost ashore—I'd say a hundred feet or a little more from shore. . . .

And here, we're reaching the beach now—we're going to come up on it—and there's fire all around us, and the Marines are still on the beach! They haven't made any further

headway—at least, there's a whole—must be two or three waves here on the beach. . . .
Perhaps farther up there are some Marines in the hills, but I doubt whether they've gotten
there. There's very little cover here. There are Marines running forward around and men
seeking cover. . . . There are two—two amphibious tractors piled up next to us. . . . There's
one boy's been pretty badly hurt—lying on his back on the beach with his feet in the water.
One of our own boys has just been shot in the side. . . . It's a little round black hole. . . .

    Boy!—Something just hit very close—Here's rifle fire too! I don't see any Marines
firing. . . . [One] boy got up, started to run and fell down again. Don't know whether he
got hit—he's lying on his face. Here come more Marines in behind us—they're wading in.[44]

PFC Dale Fetzer had spent the morning watching planes strafing and bombing the landing area. "And I said, Oh my God, there's not going to be anything left. They've gotta kill them all. There's not going to be anything left." Now, wading toward shore, he could hear bullets zipping past him. A Marine wading nearby was hit. "He went down just like that," said Fetzer. "I said, 'Oh my God they're shootin' real bullets' and I got scared then."[45]

Heading toward the Red Beaches with the 3rd War Dog Platoon, First Lieutenant William W. Putney studied the landing area through his field glasses. The view was less than reassuring. A squad of men was visible climbing a nose projecting from the cliff, probably Marines from Geary Bundschu's A Company. They were almost to the top when explosions puffed among them, and they tumbled down the hill. Bailing out of the tractor just offshore, Putney waded in through hip-deep water. "Machine gun bullets kicked up water around us," he recalled. A major ran toward him as he emerged from the water. "Move your ass, lieutenant!" he yelled. A mortar shell exploded down the beach. Machine-gun bullets kicked up sand near the major's feet, but he appeared oblivious to his personal peril.

Putney led his men across the road and into a ditch as another shell exploded nearby. Behind him, the major stood in the open, continuing to yell at men to get off the beach and move inland. As he dove into a shell crater, Putney encountered his first dead Marines. There were three of them. One was lying halfway up the side of the shell crater without a visible mark on him, his rifle lying at his feet. Another had been struck down in midstride—one arm was stretched out before him; his other hand still clutched a box of .30-caliber machine-gun ammunition. "There was a hole in his forehead, and the blood that had run out of it and onto the ground was almost black, dry and crusted," recalled Putney. The third man was an officer, lying face down. His name was stenciled very clearly on his combat pack. Years later, it troubled Putney that vivid as his memories of that morning remained, he could not remember the name stenciled on that pack.[46]

Nineteen- year-old PFC Frank Hoban was among the follow-up waves streaming into the Red Beaches. The kid from Chicago was eager to see his first combat. "I was almost stale from all the training advice and I wanted to be in my first battle. I couldn't stand being a combat boot much longer," he confessed. Hoban's platoon climbed down the nets from troop transport USS *Rixey* at about 0800 and crammed themselves into the bobbing Higgins boats. "I remember I was more curious than scared so I looked over the side several times to see what all the noise was about," he recalled. As shells splashed around nearby boats, he decided to do what his sergeant had unceremoniously suggested—"keep our heads down, our mouths shut, and be ready to move out on one command by our sergeant." Arriving at the reef they transferred into an amtrac. "We moved swiftly over the remaining distance to shore without incident. If it hadn't been for the sound of mortars and small arms fire, it seemed only to be a routine exercise," he recalled.

The tractor bumped up onto the beach. The men went over the side on command, and Hoban got his first reality check. "Along the water's edge and to a short rise of a few feet, I saw dead and wounded lying in and out of the water as if they were mere pieces of driftwood," he recalled. He turned to his sergeant and asked if it was okay to put a round in the chamber of his rifle now. An amazed expression came over the noncom's face, but he managed to choke out, "Yes."[47]

Lieutenant Colonel Alfred Bowser, commanding one of the 12th Marine Regiment's four artillery battalions, had landed early by the Asan River outlet on Blue Beach to prepare for the DUKWs scheduled to bring his guns ashore. "There were still some Nips in and around the river bed and in the rubble of Asan Village, but the mortar and small arms fire was 'relatively' light,' so we proceeded, post haste, well dispersed," he said. The lull was relatively short-lived. "By [1020] the mortar and artillery fire and some small arms had increased considerably and the beaches were definitely unhealthy and uncomfortable," he observed. "Tanks, amphibians and DUKWs (the latter carrying the first radio jeeps) were all having difficulty getting over the bank about ten yards in from the water's edge."[48]

DUKWs carrying the guns were forced to pass through a cut in the bank—described by one artillery officer as a seawall—in order to move inland. "A Jap artillery piece was located in a mine shaft in Asan Point which was firing on the DUKWs as they slowed down to pass through this cut," reported Major Thomas R. Belzer, executive officer of the 4th Battalion. "At least one of the DUKWs was hit by this piece. Jap mortar fire was also directed at the artillery and a few hits were scored."[49]

Medium tanks, sporting the white elephant insignia of the 3rd Tank Battalion, had already begun coming ashore at the Asan beaches less than an hour after the initial landing. "Each tank was in its own lighter and backed into the Landing Ship Dock," recalled Corporal Walter R. Roose, who came ashore with B Company. "So we left on the lighter and got out there and there's ships all around . . . planes overhead . . . And here we're going toward shore *chuga chuga chuga chuga* . . . very slow." A tank radioman, Roose had skipped out of the malaria ward at the hospital on Guadalcanal to rejoin his outfit when he heard they were shipping out for combat. Now, heading toward shore, he saw one of the tankers perched on the tank lighter fender serenely thumbing through a Superman comic. "The shooting was going on all around him," marveled Roose. "Really. The guns from off shore and the guns toward us and the guns from the battleships behind us. And here he was totally engrossed in this comic book magazine. I couldn't believe it."[50]

Amtanks stationed on the reef helped secure the LCMs carrying the tanks. Cables from the LCMs were attached to the armored amphibs, which then acted as anchors to hold the lighters firmly against the reef. As the tanks rumbled off into the shallow water, the amtank crews led them around coral heads and potholes toward the beach. All the battalion's forty medium tanks were ashore by 1000, with one company already in action by 0930.

If there was a bright spot on the Asan beaches, it was in the center where Colonel Arthur H. ("Tex") Butler's 21st Marines had come ashore. Butler, a forty-one-year-old Naval Academy graduate who had earned kudos as executive officer of the regiment at Bougainville, had taken the warnings about Guam's terrain seriously. His regiment was expected to seize heights that included a sheer one-hundred-foot cliff about a mile inland. In planning conferences, Butler had advised his officers, "I've been told, gentlemen, that we can't get up on that cliff. Our best reports say that a trained cliff climber with line and spikes would have a hard time getting up there."[51]

Determined to overcome this daunting obstacle, Butler engineered a possible solution before his Marines ever stepped into a landing craft. An examination of aerial photos of Green Beach had revealed two steep defiles—one at either end of the regimental area—that appeared to offer access into the high ground. Butler decided to send the 3rd Battalion, commanded by Lieutenant Colonel Wendell H. ("Pete") Duplantis, to attack straight up the Asan River valley defile on the right. The 2nd Battalion, commanded by Lieutenant Colonel Eustace R. Smoak, would land behind Duplantis, turn, and attack up the defile to the left. No attempt would be made to maintain contact between the two battalions during the advance. Having penetrated inland and established a foothold on the plateau above the cliff face, the battalions would link up and establish a line across the top of the heights. The reserve 1st Battalion would secure the area below the "almost impossible" cliffs.[52]

The 3rd Battalion began taking casualties from mortar fire almost as soon as it started up the narrow passage on the regiment's right. Sherman tanks knocked out an enemy gun on the forward slopes, but a reinforced Japanese machine-gun platoon had dug into the defile. Fire was directed at the Marines from well-camouflaged caves, concrete shelters, and wooded areas along the corridor. Mortar and artillery fire was punctuated by headlong counterattacks by small groups of Japanese infantry. "The enemy showed a pointless disregard for their own lives as they charged the Marines, and even the tanks, with small arms and grenades," observed tank company commander Captain Bertram Yaffe. "Always grenades. . . . It was a bizarre scene: cows, goats and chickens wandered in a drunken daze among the Marines and Japanese. Our casualties were heavy."[53]

With supporting fire from the adjacent 1st Battalion, 9th Marines, as well as naval gunfire on a mortar position, Duplantis's battalion subdued the enemy position, capturing a reported fourteen machine guns and six mortars. The Marines also overpowered and seized two prisoners in the machine-gun position, believed to be the first prisoners taken on Guam. However, the heat and physical exertion of scaling the precipitous terrain began to take its toll after the long weeks of inactivity aboard ship. Men started to run out of water. Some began to fold up from exhaustion despite the urgings of officers and noncoms to keep moving. Finally, gasping and drenched with sweat, the exhausted men reached the top and began to dig in.

On the left, the 2nd Battalion, led by F Company, entered the defile channeling the east branch of the Asan River—now little more than a trickle—at noon and came up against a cliff blocking their way to the top. The rifle platoons started up the rocky cliff face, pulling themselves upward, clinging to scrub growth, pausing in the occasional crevice to catch their breath. "Through field glasses at the regimental OP the riflemen looked like so many flies crawling up the side of the living room wall," observed First Lieutenant Arthur A. Frances.[54] The Japanese apparently didn't believe anyone would be foolish enough to tackle the cliff, and there was little reaction to begin with, but forward scouts eventually began to draw enemy fire. The firing increased, raking the cliff and nearly decimating the platoon on the right. The Marines kept climbing. Finally reaching the top at about 1300, the F Company Marines came under machine-gun fire from a ridge only fifty yards away but were soon reinforced by Companies G and E. There was no sign of the 3rd Marines on the regiment's left, but after linking up with Duplantis, the battalion dug in, refusing its left flank to the edge of the cliff and covering the gap with mortars. For his part, due to the thick jungle vegetation, Duplantis was able to tie in with the 9th Marines on the right only with outposts, but that seemed like a minor issue for the moment. The slender, thirty-one-year-old Nevadan, probably the only member of the division to possess a college degree in philosophy, was more concerned—"shocked" as he put it later—to find his position dominated by two prominent hills "looking down my throat" from his left front. Neither of these hills appeared on the map he had been issued. That omission would cost the 21st Marines dearly over the next couple of days.

Over on Red Beach 1, desperate fighting continued for possession of Chonito Cliff. PFC Stephen F. Kuzma's L Company platoon was clawing its way up the height when a Japanese machine gunner directed a burst at PFC John S. Parker, a six-foot-two-inch BAR man from South Texas. Two or three slugs hit Parker in the right arm just above the elbow. Kuzma was trying to stop the blood with a tourniquet when "all of a sudden here comes a Jap at me out of a cave." Kuzma yelled in alarm, and a nearby automatic rifleman swung on the Japanese. "So he fires that rifle and cuts him down, just bang," recalled Kuzma. "And when he fell, he had a rifle with a bayonet on it, and when he fell, his head hit my knee." Kuzma picked up the dead man's rifle and found it had a perfectly good round in the chamber. "And he wouldn't shoot," he marveled. "He wanted to bayonet me. They were kind of crazy, I think you'd say. They'd rather bayonet you than shoot you." Kuzma stuck the bullet in his pocket as a souvenir of his good fortune; more than fifty years later, he still had it.[55]

PFC Frank R. Simone, a machine gunner with I Company, was also trying to scale the cave-riddled height. "Snipers were firing at us while we were trying to get up that hill," he recalled. "We'd run and fall, get up, go in a different direction until we got some vegetation where we could hide in there. We finally got where all the vegetation was on the higher ground." Unable to determine where the enemy fire was coming from, Simone and his gunner began hosing down the general area. "I was feeding a belt and he was doing the firing into these bushes even though we didn't see anything. . . . [T]o be sure, we fired into every bush or shrub that we could see." Finally the firing slackened. "We waited and there was no more shooting. So then we went around looking to see and that's where they were, in behind these bushes. . . . [They] were dead."

But Simone, only two days away from his twentieth birthday, was destined for a short battle. Small arms fire or, more likely, grenade or mortar fragments—he was never sure—tore into both his hands. "I was bleeding from both hands; [my] fingers were shot off. They called a corpsman and he ran over. Most of the fingers on my left hand were just hanging by a thread. He snipped them off." When the corpsman went to snip off another finger on the right hand that was "hanging down, twisted," Simone protested. "I said, 'No, don't cut any more fingers! Leave it alone. Just bandage that hand'; he bandaged both hands like two boxing gloves." After assuring the corpsman he could manage, Simone got up and walked back down to the beach.[56]

For Captain Geary Bundschu's A Company, fighting for what would subsequently become known as Bundschu Ridge just south of Chonito Cliff, things were going from bad to worse. Dug in on the high ground, the 320th Independent Infantry Battalion continued to sweep away every effort to move up the steep open slopes. To Bundschu's right, B Company, commanded by twenty-six-year-old Captain Joseph V. Millerick of Waterbury, Connecticut, had landed with instructions to locate "the first critical break in the terrain" and head inland.[57] Millerick quickly found there was no break. Preinvasion warnings that the height was impassable had been no exaggeration. Though enemy resistance was negligible, the company floundered in a nightmare landscape of rock precipices and deep fissures, all choked with thick brush.

Colonel W. Carvel Hall landed with the regimental command group on Red 1 at 1030. At the same time Major Henry Aplington reported that his battalion had managed to advance only about five hundred yards inland. Fifteen minutes later, Bundschu reported that his company had fought its way to within one hundred yards of the ridge top, where the near vertical slope and a hail of enemy grenades had forced the survivors to pull back. His executive officer, First Lieutenant Harry Gossard, asked for corpsmen, water, and stretcher bearers.

One of the few to make it almost to the top was PFC James S. Baldwin, whose platoon leader, Second Lieutenant William Shellhorn, had been killed on the beach. Baldwin's fire team leader, PFC Anthony Bufalini of Tunnelton, Pennsylvania, was killed as they struggled toward the crest, but Baldwin kept going, grabbing clumps of grass and pulling himself up the steep slope with both hands. He got a brief look at the activity on the beachhead behind him and had a moment to wonder what the hell he was doing there before a flurry of grenades drove him back down the slope past a litter of dead Marines. Bufalini's body would not be recovered until three weeks later.

About four hundred yards to the rear of A Company, the battalion's 81mm mortar platoon was also taking casualties. Colonel Hall's operations plan had called for the regiment's three mortar platoons to land with their parent battalions and then assemble as a group at the boundary of Red Beaches 1 and 2 in order to mass fires on Adelup Point. The 1st Battalion's platoon, commanded by twenty-two-year-old Second Lieutenant Walter F. J. Krawiec of Chicago, a student at Notre Dame with aspirations of a career in law before joining the Marines, had gone to ground in a scattering of shell holes just inland from the beach. Since arriving ashore with the sixth wave at about 0850, Krawiec had already lost five men wounded, including one of his sergeants.

Hoping to secure mortar support for another try at the hill, Bundschu sent a message arranging to meet Krawiec at the base of the ridge. Krawiec never got there. As he ventured into the open rice paddies, a rifle or machine-gun slug hit him in the shoulder and exited through his armpit, striking the equipment on his belt and fragmenting into his side. Stunned and in shock, he stumbled back to the beach and joined the parade of wounded awaiting medical treatment. Among them he found his wounded sergeant, who was now dying.

With hopes of timely mortar support dashed and his men being cut to pieces on the open slopes, Bundschu asked Aplington for permission to disengage. Feeling the company was already too heavily committed, Aplington ordered him to hold on. In an effort to divert some of the opposition facing Bundschu, he directed B Company, which had yet to become directly engaged, to shift left toward A Company. It was a good idea that came to naught when Millerick's company found all approaches to Bundschu from that side blocked by thick undergrowth and sheer rock faces.

With his battalion stalled, Aplington went forward to personally assess Bundschu's situation and reluctantly conceded that "attacking up the ridge frontally was an impossibility, men literally had to claw their way up." To continue was to invite a massacre. The only practical solution was to flank the enemy position on either the left or the right. It was now about 1120, and Colonel Hall was impatiently pushing for results. "How soon do you expect to capture O-A?" he messaged Aplington.

Aplington went to regimental headquarters and asked Hall to release his C Company, still in regimental reserve, so he could attempt a flanking movement on the ridge. Hall refused. He "was insistent on a frontal attack, and, with the battle spread in front of him, kept looking at the map and saying, 'But it's only two hundred yards,'" recalled Aplington. Hall didn't seem to realize that his map failed to accurately reflect the precipitous terrain facing Bundschu. What looked reasonable on paper was an entirely different story on the ground, but Hall was not prepared to listen, and his meeting with Aplington turned contentious.[58]

At the same time, there was some good news. By noon, Lieutenant Colonel Ralph L. Houser's 3rd Battalion had fought its way through the Chonito Cliff obstacle. Houser had managed to break the impasse with flamethrowers and the assistance of newly landed tanks from the 3rd Tank Battalion. Taking position on the coast road, the tanks fired directly into the caves in the slopes. Houser then sent in his reserve, Company L, down the beach road into the cut. L Company muscled its way through and out onto the flats beyond.

Having reduced the cliff, the thirty-year-old Houser—described by an acquaintance as "slender, hard bitten and incisive"—turned his attention to Japanese positions on Adelup Point, which extended out to sea on the battalion's left.[59] Organizing a tank-infantry fighting group, he went after those positions in fighting that would last well into the afternoon. Among the battalion standouts, Captain William G. H. Stephens led Company L over 250 yards of open terrain on the point. His Marines were credited with killing sixty-five Japanese and knocking out two 75mm field guns and one 37mm gun. The company suffered seventeen killed and twenty-five wounded during the day; K Company was hit even harder, losing seventeen killed and fifty-eight wounded. Nine of the corpsmen with the battalion were killed, and two were wounded.

Colonel Hall presumably welcomed Houser's success, but he was not pleased to learn that the battalion commander had personally participated in the assault. "God dammit," he snapped ungraciously, "if he wants to be a platoon leader, I'll make him a platoon leader!"[60] The Marine Corps was more appreciative. Houser was subsequently awarded the Navy Cross and Captain Stephens the Silver Star for their efforts at Chonito Cliff.

By 1130, three hours after H-Hour, twenty-four waves had landed over the Asan beaches, and the 3rd Division was ashore with all its essential equipment. Enemy fire had diminished somewhat, though one amtrac loaded with mortar ammunition ran over an artillery shell rigged as a mine on the beach. The blast killed four men and wounded several others, including the captain commanding Company C of the 3rd Amphibian Tractor Battalion. The captain was evacuated aboard a tractor heading out into the bay but was killed when the amtrac was struck by a mortar shell as it crossed the reef. By 1330, reports indicated that four amtanks, eighteen LVTs, and two DUKWs had been lost.

Only a few mines were found on the beach, most of them powerful Model 96 antivehicle, antiboat types. Intended for use either on land or in shallow water, the hemispherical mines were about twenty inches in diameter, weighed 107 pounds, and were fitted with a pair of lead alloy horns on top. Pressure on the horns crushed glass vials containing an electrolytic fluid that activated the fuse and detonated a forty-six-pound explosive charge. UDT-3 men removed about half a dozen of the mines from the beach. They loaded them into a landing craft, took them out to sea, and dumped them into deep water.

Frank Simone, both hands swathed in bandages, had arrived on the beach as amtracs struggled to get the large number of wounded to the ships offshore. A request for additional boats to evacuate casualties from Red Beach 1 had been made at noon; Beaches Green and Blue made similar requests at 1347, but the number of wounded on the beaches continued to pile up.

Adding to the problem were casualties among the medical personnel themselves, which included most members of the medical shore party from the USS *President Adams* on Blue Beach. The medical officer in charge, Lieutenant Walter G. Epply, was struck in the chest and killed by fragments from an exploding mortar shell, and several other members of the team were wounded. Twenty-year-old Pharmacist's Mate First Class Nicholas G. Dionisopoulos, who in civilian life had worked as a "pie conveyor" in a wholesale bakery in Saint Paul, Minnesota, took charge and began to send casualties to the ships as enemy fire continued to pound the beach. By day's end, the survivors under his supervision had processed about 250 casualties.

As Simone waited to be evacuated, a sniper shot him in the right side of his chest. "It didn't hit the bones or anything, just missed the ribs and the lungs," he recalled. He piled into a foxhole on the beach. "There were two guys there and they said, 'What are you doing in here? Get back out there.'"

"Fuck you!" said Simone.

"What?!"

"Fuck you!" he repeated, motioning to the blood leaking out of his chest.

The two foxhole occupants, apparently shore party personnel, relented. They took his evacuation tag and added "Chest Wound." "Now get back and wait for the amtrac to take you."

No way, said Simone. "I'm going to wait til that goddamned thing comes in and takes me right to the ship. I'm not going to lay out there."

And wait in the foxhole he did.

Finally loaded onto an amtrac, he headed out to the ships. Exploding shells sent water cascading into the tractor bay. "I thought, 'Oh, God, I'm never going to get out of here.' And finally when they pull up to the hospital ship I remember all the sailors looking down at us. There was two of us [wounded men]. And then they took us up."[61]

At noon a division air observer reported that troops appeared to have pushed as far as fifteen hundred yards inland from Asan Village. Somewhat more ominously, he also reported seeing numerous enemy troops moving along the road about a mile south of Adelup Point. Fighters from USS *Wasp* were dispatched to strafe the road area as efforts continued to solidify the beachhead toehold.

The last of the division artillery was ashore and going into position behind Blue Beach by 1300, though bypassed Japanese remained a threat. One battery of Colonel Bowser's 3rd Battalion was already in action by 1215. Eleven of his fifteen gun-carrying DUKWs had made it ashore without a hitch. Four others stalled or got caught at the reef edge, and three were mired down at the river mouth, but all were winched out and continued on in. The 4th Battalion was also ashore, though the crews had to wait for a tank to knock out two Japanese machine guns before they could set up in their designated position.

Two Marines, setting up a phone for an artillery CP in an abandoned thatched hut, received a shock when they went to move a heap of palm fronds inexplicably piled inside and a very live Japanese soldier scrambled out from underneath. The two wiremen bolted for the doorway, and when the Japanese emerged from the hut with his rifle in hand, some other Marines, attracted by the commotion, riddled him.

Corporal John Wardlow ran into another group of Japanese while stringing wire to an artillery position. Hearing some "jabbering," Wardlow peered over the edge of an embankment to see some Japanese moving along the streambed he and his buddy had climbed out of not ten minutes before. One of them, an officer with a sword, started to crawl up the embankment. Wardlow shouldered his carbine and squeezed the trigger only to find he had neglected to put a round in the chamber. He fumbled for a grenade, pulled the pin, and lobbed it toward the enemy officer before ducking back down. "Those things only have a five-second fuse, but it seemed like an hour before it went off," he recalled. When he looked out again, the Japanese officer was quite obviously dead, having been hit in the left jaw, side, and face. Hearing more jabbering, Wardlow ventured another look—this time making sure his carbine had a round in the chamber. A Japanese stuck his head up, and Wardlow cranked off three quick rounds. "Two of them hit—one in the face and one through the helmet." At that point, he and his buddy decided they'd had enough excitement and made a hasty withdrawal.[62]

Other Japanese, dug into the "devil's horn" of Asan Point, harassed the artillerymen with sniper fire until the cannon cockers finally retaliated with a few rounds from their 105mm guns, firing at point-blank range. "We weren't bothered after that," remarked one of the gunners.[63]

⌐◆⌐

In a bizarre twist, two of Captain Bundschu's A Company Marines somehow managed to walk through Japanese lines while their companions were being mowed down on the open slopes. Separated from Lieutenant Jim Gallo's platoon during the initial approach on the ridge, Sergeant Lloyd V. Erion of Hillsboro, Oregon, and eighteen-year-old PFC Mark Able of Berkeley, California, had wandered up a brush-choked ravine somewhere to the right of the company's line of attack. Clambering up toward higher ground, they saw only one live Japanese, a rifleman who emerged from a hole on the slope below them to take a shot at someone further down the hill. He had no idea the two Marines were just above him. Erion, a prewar Marine who had been aboard the battleship *Maryland* during the attack on Pearl Harbor on December 7, lobbed a grenade into the hole and killed the man.

The two Marines wandered around for hours—young Able fervently hoping the sergeant knew what he was doing—before coming across a cave position that appeared to be some kind of mortar emplacement. Assorted gear and equipment lay around the area, but there were no Japanese to be seen. Able nervously stood watch while Erion rummaged around inside, eventually emerging with a map that seemed important. By now they realized they had slipped through a hole in the enemy lines, and it was pure luck that they hadn't been noticed. Erion suggested they just sling their rifles and stroll back down the hill as if they belonged there. Hopefully any Japanese would think they were friendly troops or at least hesitate before reacting.

Slinging their rifles, they started back down the hill. Erion's ploy worked. They saw a couple of machine-gun emplacements in the near distance but didn't encounter any enemy soldiers, and no one shot at them. Finally reaching the bottom of the gulch, they rounded a boulder and narrowly avoided being shot by three Marines who had taken cover there. Rejoining A Company sometime after noon, Erion turned the map over to Captain Bundschu, who immediately sent a courier with the map and a note to Colonel Hall's headquarters. Just what the map depicted and what happened to it is unclear, though a IIIAC report dated July 23 mentions a captured map showing that the enemy planned to defend Asan with three battalions. Whatever the case, neither the map nor Sergeant Erion's uncontested tour of enemy positions seem to have figured in subsequent developments.[64]

Meanwhile, casualties in A Company continued to mount. Realizing he had strayed too far to the right and was unable to support Bundschu, who was on the other side of a wide gulch, Gallo brought his platoon back down the slope in an effort to slide over and coordinate with the rest of the company. Japanese, apparently bypassed during their climb, took them under fire as they descended. PFC Billy G. Copeland was shot as they started to dash one by one across the gulch toward Bundschu's position. Lying helpless, the dying seventeen-year-old from tiny Avant, Oklahoma, cried out, "I can't move either way." PFC John G. Zeller started toward Copeland but was shot through the head by a sniper. A sergeant was shot in the leg. A PFC had a close call when a bullet cut a deep furrow across his back. Gallo finally got his people through but lost two more men about an hour later after joining Bundschu.[65]

At regimental headquarters, an exasperated Colonel Hall decided to take matters into his own hands following his contentious exchange with Major Aplington. At 1300 Hall committed his reserve 2nd Battalion between the 1st and 3rd Battalions and apparently—at least in Aplington's estimation—assumed personal tactical control of the assault on the obstinate ridge. Supplanted in command of his battalion, at least for the moment, Aplington was relegated to watching developments unfold while seated on a log at regimental headquarters.

Hall ordered the renewed attack to jump off at 1500. By now, Bundschu's company had lost all its corpsmen, but as the assault was getting ready to start, Pharmacist's Mate Second Class Clyde T. Clark and Pharmacist's Mate Second Class Hugh P. Gresham Jr. arrived from the battalion aid station. They had volunteered to go forward to help with the many wounded but were under explicit orders not to go up on the ridge. A number of stretcher bearers had already been lost, and casualties among corpsmen had been severe. "Don't go up that hill with them," the battalion surgeon warned them as they left. "I can't afford to lose you guys."[66] Nevertheless, as they arrived at the base of the hill, a lieutenant—probably Second Lieutenant Henry S. Oliver of Company A's machine-gun platoon—told them to accompany the attack.

Clark explained that they were under orders not to go up on the ridge. Oliver, a former Phoenix, Arizona, high schoolteacher seeing his first combat, was generally considered by the men to be "a regular guy; easy to talk to," but he took a hard line with the two corpsmen, threatening to have them court-martialed if they refused.[67] Unimpressed, Clark dug in his heels, retorting that the lieutenant could do as he pleased. However, Gresham, an eighteen-year-old from Richmond, Virginia, who had joined the Navy just over a year before, agreed to accompany the attack. The Marines jumped off on time at 1500, and Gresham was shot in the chest. He survived evacuation to the USS *Warren* but died that same day. Lieutenant Oliver was also wounded. He was evacuated to the USS *DuPage*, where he died the following day. Both men were buried at sea. The attack made no more progress than its predecessors.

Aplington, who sat out the attack following his argument with Hall, soon found himself back on the hook, but not before he had a narrow escape of his own. Seated on the coconut log at the regimental CP alongside the regiment's "Grand Old Man," forty-seven-year-old World War I veteran Major John Winford, he heard a *wooosh* just before a Japanese mortar shell exploded in the sand between them. He picked himself up off the ground, spitting sand, to hear Winford calling, "Corpsman! Corpsman!" The veteran officer was "full of fragment holes," observed Aplington. "After five major engagements with the Marine Brigade in France and on his second World War II operation, the law of averages caught up with John Winford."[68]

Aplington returned to his own CP. At about 1600 Hall called him. "The progress of your A Company is unsatisfactory," he stated. "Do something about it." Aplington took this to mean he had tactical control of his battalion back. The colonel added that he intended to mount another assault at 1700. This time E Company from Lieutenant Colonel Hector DeZayas's 2nd Battalion would also participate, making a push on A Company's left. Fifty-five minutes later, Hall called again. Aplington was out getting his people ready for the attack, so his exec, Captain John Erickson, fielded the call. "What's the dope with Able Company?" demanded Hall. He then made it clear that he expected the ridge to be in Marine hands before dark. If Bundschu couldn't do it, he would find someone who could.

Colonel Hall later insisted he "did not specify a frontal assault" on the ridge, though that claim was contradicted by his executive officer, Colonel James Snedeker. The forty-year-old Snedeker, a 1925 graduate of the U.S. Naval Academy who had served in Nicaragua and Haiti, aboard the USS *Minneapolis*, and on the 3rd Division staff at Bougainville, stated he was present when Hall personally ordered Bundschu to resume the attack—adding that he himself had opposed a resumption of a frontal attack on the ridge. "I was present at the time this order was given and had recommended against it," he reiterated.[69]

Hall had a different recollection. "I clearly remember ordering another attack, but I did not specify a 'frontal assault.' I gave verbal orders to the executive officer of the 1st Battalion, 3rd Marines (in the hearing of the company commander of Company A) to again attack the ridge; but I left the scheme of maneuver to the battalion," he said.[70]

Snedeker vividly recalled the expression in Bundschu's eyes as the order was given. "He and I knew it was an order which demanded that he give up his life," observed Snedeker. But aside from that brief look, Bundschu gave no discernable sign of dissent or dismay. "He saluted crisply, and said to Colonel Hall, 'Aye, aye sir,'" remembered Snedeker.[71]

By now, A Company had only three officers left. Jim Gallo found Bundschu at the base of the ridge. "I came back to find out what was going on and there he was tending the wounded and he himself was wounded," he recalled. "I asked him what happened and he said he'd gotten word from the regimental commander that he had to take the hill by that night or he'd lose his command." Clearly agitated and upset, Bundschu exclaimed, "If I can't do it, nobody can."[72]

Bundschu and Gallo decided to mount a two-pronged attack up either side of the ridge. Bundschu and his company exec, First Lieutenant Harry E. Gossard, the muscular former light heavyweight boxing champion of Ohio Northern University, would take what was left of the 2nd and 3rd Platoons and attack up the left side, while Gallo's platoon pushed up the right. Gallo later estimated that A Company now numbered somewhere between 80 and 120 men out of the 240 that had come ashore that morning. Perhaps a third of the company had been killed, with the wounded bringing total casualties to about 50 percent. He had about thirty effectives in his platoon.

The attack was to begin in about twenty minutes, just before twilight. Gallo got his men into position 100 to 125 yards up the ridge, picking up a few strays as he went along. Some 40mm fire was exploding on the crest, along with shells from the battalion's 81mm mortars. As the platoon started to make its way up the ridge, fragments from an exploding mortar round peppered Gallo and the Marines to either side of him. Gallo kept moving. He came upon a badly wounded Marine. As bullets kicked up dirt around them, he dragged the wounded man down the slope out of the line of fire, but to no avail. The Marine died. Up on the crest, Japanese were taunting them, rolling grenades down the slope and shouting, "Maleen yellow! Maleen, you die!"[73]

In an effort to help as best he could, Colonel Snedeker had assumed fire direction of the 40mm guns from a battery of the 14th Defense Battalion, calling in fire while sitting on a sand dune with a portable radio. "Enemy machine gun fire kicked up the sand all about my exposed position," he recalled. "The 40mm fire was very effective, however, and a thin line of Company A men reached the crest. It was sickening though, to watch our men who were shot en route up the steep slope fall over backwards and tumble several hundred feet into one of the shallow ravines."[74]

Two of Gallo's men, PFC Bob Costen and twenty-two-year-old PFC Robert D. Conlon of Dedham, Massachusetts—a stocky youngster who stood only five feet tall—were among a handful of Marines who made it close to the crest. Conlon's brother Wilfred, a bombardier aboard the B-17 "Lightning Strikes," had been shot down over Germany in February and was now languishing in a prisoner of war camp. The two Marines worked their way along, firing their weapons until a grenade exploded at Conlon's feet, killing him. Though just a few feet from the enemy trench line, Coston was unable to go any further.

Over on the left, the 2nd and 3rd Platoons stalled, as did E Company, under the hail of machine-gun fire sweeping the slope. Bundschu had been wounded again, this time in the wrist by a shell or grenade fragment. He and Corporal Kenneth O. Roberts clung to the hillside, trying to knock out an enemy machine gun. Hampered by his damaged wrist, Bundschu passed grenades to Roberts, who lobbed them at the machine-gun emplacement, but the fire continued. Finally Bundschu exclaimed, "To hell with it—let's go!" Still swathed in bandages from the shoulder wound he had suffered that morning, he rose up out of the dirt and broke for the crest. Three Marines who attempted to follow were caught in a cross fire. One saved himself by jumping into an enemy foxhole. Bundschu disappeared up over the crest. He never came back.[75]

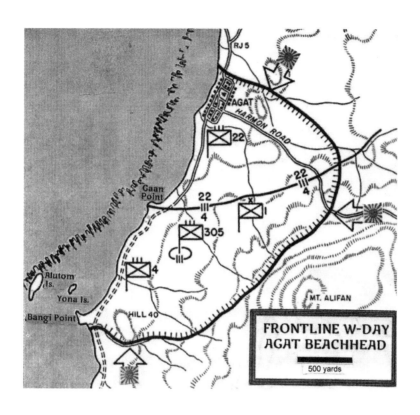

**FRONTLINE W-DAY
AGAT BEACHHEAD**

500 yards

RJ 5

AGAT

HARMON ROAD

22

22
|||
4

22
|||
4

305

|||

4

Gaan Point

Alutom Is.

Yona Is.

Bangi Point

HILL 40

MT. ALIFAN

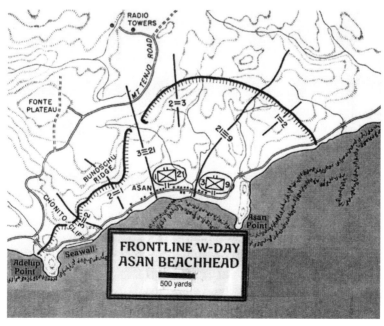

**FRONTLINE W-DAY
ASAN BEACHHEAD**

500 yards

RADIO TOWERS

MT. TENJO ROAD

FONTE PLATEAU

2≡3

2≡9

3≡21

2≡1

21

3≡9

BUNDSCHU RIDGE

ASAN

2≡1

2

3

CHONITO CLIFF

Asan Point

Adelup Point

Seawall

CHAPTER 14

COUNTERATTACK

Toward evening of that first day, Alvin Josephy became aware of a terrible odor. When he went down to the beach to help carry up water cans, he discovered the source. The beachhead was littered with unburied dead. Most of the dead were Marines, but here and there were enemy casualties, immediately recognizable by their wrap puttees. Lieutenant William Putney came across two Japanese who had been caught by a flamethrower. "Their bodies were naked and burned to a crisp, their external genitalia shrunk to the size of a newborn baby's," he observed. "The whole area smelled sickeningly of half-cooked flesh and kerosene." Overcome with nausea, an enlisted man with Putney sagged against a palm tree and started to vomit. Putney wet a handkerchief and tried to wipe the man's face, somehow managing to keep his own stomach under control.[1]

Josephy paused by a line of five bodies laid out in the sand. They were Marines killed when their amtrac was hit. The upended amtrac rested by the water's edge. A beach evacuation station had been set up nearby. It was crowded with wounded, a testament to the ferocity of the fighting for the inland heights. Most were bandaged and tagged and awaiting evacuation to the ships offshore. Corpsmen and less seriously wounded Marines knelt by stretcher cases holding plasma bottles aloft. By 1417, medical personnel on Red Beach 1 had run out of stretchers. Casualties during the day on this beach alone exceeded the division's entire losses during the Bougainville landing the previous November.[2]

A smaller collection of men who had broken mentally huddled by the aid station. "They shook and quivered like frightened puppies and their staring eyes were bloodshot," observed Josephy. "Every noise made them jump in terror." When a tractor pulled in to take aboard a load of wounded, the backfires from its exhaust sent the panicked men scrambling for cover in the sand. "A corpsman who looked about sixteen years old moved among them, patting them quietly and tenderly on the back and trying to reassure them," observed Josephy.[3]

PFC Harold B. Match was lucky to be alive as the day ended. A signalman with the 12th Marines, he had been helping to lay a line to an outpost during the morning when a mortar shell exploded behind him. He was aware of someone calling for a corpsman. One came running. He looked at Match, took his dog tag, and left. Prematurely consigned to the dead, Match heard one of his buddies exclaim, "Hey! He's alive! His eyes are open!" Another corpsman came along and gave Match a shot of morphine. He could hear the other Marines talking but was unable to move or respond. As he lay there, someone came along and remarked, "Dammit, Match, you finally got first in line for something, didn't you?" which Match took to be a caustic reference to his reputation for always being last in line. Loaded onto a stretcher, he was carried down to the beach aid station, where a doctor marked him for evacuation. He got the last space in an amtrac heading out to the ships with a load of wounded. Their first stop, USS *DuPage*, was already filled to capacity, so Match ended up on the USS *Elmore*, where he was sent directly to the operating room.

"All the doctors could see was a small piece of metal sticking out in back of my shoulder," he recalled. "They tried to remove the fragment without knocking me out, but each time they pulled on it I would let out a yell. Finally, they knocked me out." When he came to later, he learned it had taken over an hour to extract what turned out to be the entire tail assembly of a Japanese mortar shell. The nearly one-pound projectile had punched into his back and twisted down under his collar bone. "One of the fins on the tail assembly was missing," he remarked. "The others were all bent out of shape." Fortunately for Match, the thing had been so hot when it hit him that it cauterized the wound, and there was very little bleeding. Not only had he survived his brush with death, but the battered projectile would be his ticket to celebratory free drinks at Marine division reunions for years come.[4]

The attack transport USS *Wayne* took aboard casualties from the 3rd Marine Division beaches. The process started at the rail with classification of injuries. "Ambulatory patients were taken to the forward and after battle dressing stations and their adjacent troop berthing spaces," the ship reported. "The less seriously wounded stretcher casualties requiring surgery went to the after station in addition to a lesser number of ambulatory cases [that] were sent to the forward station. The more serious cases not requiring surgery, but requiring shock treatment and nursing care alone, were taken to the troop officer's quarters. Those requiring early major surgery went to the troop officer's mess opposite the operating rooms. The sick bay was reserved for serious post-operative cases requiring much and special care."[5]

The system for evacuating and treating casualties was severely taxed as the day wore on. Plans designated two LSTs as casualty receiving ships: one off the 3rd Division beaches and one off the Marine Brigade beaches. Onboard medical personnel treated wounded men evacuated from aid stations on the beaches. Once the LST had received one hundred casualties, the men were to be transferred en mass to better medical facilities aboard the transports offshore. The transports were supposed to fill this role until W+3, when the hospital ship USS *Solace* was due to arrive.

The evacuation plan was virtually the same as the one employed during the landings at Saipan where many wounded Marines died aboard the small landing craft before they could obtain proper medical attention. Similar problems arose at Guam, where coxswains of both DUKWs and LVTs reported long delays—as long as six hours in one instance—searching for a ship able to accept their load of casualties. Problems were exacerbated by the attrition of LVTs. At one point, the shore medical party from USS *Fayette* was reduced to sending casualties out to the reef on rubber rafts—an hour-long round-trip paddle for just those few hundred yards.

A medical officer reported, "The patients wait for hours in a ship [LST] where the medical facilities are such as to preclude the more through-going treatment possible in an APA [transport]. It also involves one added handling of the patient when they are put aboard the LST. Furthermore when a LST unloads 50 or 60 casualties onto an APA the sudden influx seriously overtaxes the Medical Department of the APA." The limited numbers of doctors and corpsmen were simply unable to keep up.[6]

Recognizing that the process was too cumbersome, Task Force 53 directed later in the afternoon that all casualties from the Asan beachhead be sent directly to transports.

One of the few amtank crewmen to get any distance inland, Luther Flattum returned to the Agat beachhead at about 1700. The shoreline was littered with knocked out amtanks and tractors, but command posts and aid stations had already sprung up; tanks and bulldozers were cutting exits leading inland. Medical teams on Yellow 1 were operating from a fifty-foot-long ditch scraped out by a shore party bulldozer. Except for the occasional sniper, the Japanese seemed to have fled into the hills. "I believe I saw a total of only three dead Japs that day," recalled Flattum. By contrast, unburied Marines lay in heaps along the beach and reef. One of the dead men had been run over by a tank or amtrac, "the mark of a grouser across his forehead and his guts lying all around him."[7] The sight of so many dead fellow Marines made Flattum feel sick.

As afternoon waned, elements of the Army's 305th Infantry began coming ashore. The regiment's 2nd Battalion had been floating around in landing craft since 0830 in case they were needed. Because so many LVTs had been lost during the day and the Marine Brigade's remaining amtracs were struggling to bring in ammunition and evacuate casualties, the GIs were forced to wade ashore. Some fell into potholes on the reef and were completely submerged. Platoons and companies became inter-mingled. Fortunately, there was little incoming fire as the Japanese were occupied with the Marine advance further inland. Units reorganized, and the battalion moved a short distance inland where the troops settled in to await developments. "They appeared old men, with an average age of around thirty," remarked a Marine amtank crewman watching them come ashore. The disparity in age was not lost on some of the GIs. One of them kidded eighteen-year-old Marine Creede Anderson, "Look closely, kid, you may find your father among us."[8]

Further inland, the 4th Marines had reached the slopes of Mount Alifan by 1730 and were directed to dig in for the night, just short of the objective line, which ran along the top of the height. It was easy to dig foxholes in the rich loamy soil of scattered yam patches, and the field of view was excellent—a far cry from the experi-ence in heavily jungled Bougainville, observed former Raider PFC Roger Spaulding. "Before nightfall, each man had his comfortable hole banked and surrounded with excavated dirt, dug in deep so that he could sleep on his back without his knees protruding above the surface where shrapnel could tear off a kneecap," he remarked.[9]

The main artery through the sector was the Harmon Road, which began at the little coastal village of Agat—or what was left of it—and ran toward Mount Alifan before making a climbing turn toward island water reservoirs located to the northeast of the mountain. The regiment's left was anchored at a roadblock on the Harmon Road, the line bending back along the lower slopes of Mount Alifan to Hill 40 and Bangi Point on the brigade right. The lines of the 22nd Marines on the left tied in with the 4th Marines and looped back to the shoreline just north of Agat.

Meanwhile, aboard the USS *Lamar*, Colonel Vincent J. Tanzola, commanding the 305th Infantry, received orders at 1530 to land the remainder of his combat team. The order had been delayed an hour in transit. By the time it reached Tanzola, it was already 1530. Tanzola replied that he only had sufficient boats to land his 1st Battalion; he would send in the 3rd Battalion as soon as those boats returned. Unfor-tunately, in a continuing sequence of foul-ups, the 1st Battalion's boats did not arrive until 1615. It took an hour to load, and then the Navy control officer insisted he had no orders to allow the battalion to proceed to the beach. It was 1730 before the battalion was finally permitted to disembark, wading in through chest-deep water. With darkness approaching, Tanzola had reservations about attempting to land his 3rd Battalion. At 1725 he contacted General Lemuel Shepherd: "Cannot complete unloading of teams before dark. . . . [S]uggest suspension of unloading."

Shepherd's reply came immediately and was unequivocal: "Land your combat teams at once."[10]

Anticipating the likelihood of a Japanese mass assault on his beachhead during the night or early morning, Shepherd wanted the GIs ashore and ready to fight if he needed them. To Colonel Tanzola's frustration, Murphy's law now intervened once again, and a submarine alert forced the transport carrying his 3rd Battalion to steam further offshore. By the time it returned to the transport area, it was 2120. The battalion did not begin landing over the reef until 0300, and some troops—wet and tired and some seasick—didn't get ashore until 0600.

By day's end, the southern beachhead was about forty-five hundred yards long and two thousand yards deep. At 1830 Shepherd fired off a brief situation report to General Roy Geiger: "Own casualties about 350. Enemy [losses] unknown. Critical shortage fuel and ammunition all types. Think we can handle it. Will continue as planned tomorrow."[11]

❧

The situation was more tenuous at the 3rd Division's beachhead at Asan. General Allen Turnage debarked from USS *DuPage* at 1600, arriving ashore aboard one of the ubiquitous DUKWs and assuming command at 1715. As his division struggled for a foothold on the high ground, the large number of casualties streaming back to the beaches taxed medical services and transport. Four LVT(A)s, eighteen LVTs, and two DUKWs were reported lost as of 1330. About half of all the LVTs assigned to Blue Beach alone had been put out of commission by enemy fire or had broken their tracks on the coral reef. Water, ammunition, and rations had to be dumped on the beach and moved inland by Marine working parties under constant enemy fire. An attempt to clear a road inland with a Sherman tank came to naught when the tank was disabled by a land mine.

Up in the hills, the day's best results had been obtained by Colonel Edward Craig's 9th Marines. Craig's assault battalions had secured a beachhead fifteen hundred yards deep at the cost of 231 casualties, including twenty officers killed or wounded. One of those officers was nearly Craig himself when he went forward to check on a holdup in the vicinity of Asan Point. "I was surprised to look to my left and see a couple of Japanese soldiers who had just come out of a cave," he said.

"One of them raised a square package in his hand and threw it at me. It landed some distance away and exploded with a terrific roar, knocking me off the road into a ditch filled with sharp stones." Some Marines came along and neutralized the position with the assistance of a jeep-mounted antitank gun. The colonel was uninjured, though pretty shook up. The concussion "really made my teeth chatter for a while," he admitted.[12]

Small arms fire from Japanese lurking in a maze of tunnels dug into Asan Point would continue to harass the beachhead for another few days before Marine combat teams finally cleaned them out. At one point, machine guns concealed on the western side of the point opened up on the Marines from the rear. Craig got a measure of revenge when he saw approaching LVTs being hit from the flank and spotted wisps of smoke from the enemy position. He ordered an antitank gun crew to fire on the spot. Eight dead Japanese soldiers were later found in the position.

In the division center, the 21st Marines clung to their ridgetop under machine-gun fire from yet another ridge less than fifty yards away. On the division left, the 3rd Marines had conquered Chonito Cliff and Adelup Point but remained stonewalled by the obstinate Japanese defense at Bundschu Ridge. At 1740 Turnage ordered the division to consolidate defenses for the night. Sunset was at 1852. By nightfall, the northern beachhead was about four thousand yards long and from one thousand to fifteen hundred yards deep.

The 3rd Division's fight for the beachhead had been costly—105 killed in action, 536 wounded in action, and 56 missing—but casualties might have been even worse had troop leaders been less aggressive in getting their men off the beach. Though the fire was intense, the Japanese gunners often seemed to be just a step behind. The 3rd Division war diary noted that hundreds of rounds of enemy mortar and artillery shells had been observed falling on areas just vacated by advancing Marines.

Though it may have come as a surprise to the average Marine dodging machine-gun fire on Guam's steep ridges, the Japanese were not escaping unscathed. The 320th Independent Infantry Battalion was taking heavy losses in its defense of the Asan Heights. The 3rd Battery of the 48th Independent Mixed Brigade's artillery battalion had inflicted considerable damage on the initial Marine landing. "Nevertheless, heavy naval and aerial poundings wiped out most of the battery's flank-defense artillery positions at Adelup Point and Asan Point while they were firing on enemy landing boats," observed a Japanese report. Firing on enemy troops that landed near Adelup Point, two batteries of the 10th Independent Mixed Regiment's artillery battalion lost one gun after another to counterfire by ships offshore. By nightfall, the battalion commander and most of his officers were dead, and the unit's 10cm howitzers installed at Fonte had been destroyed. At 1500, 48th Independent Mixed Brigade headquarters dispatched Major Shoji Fukushima, the senior adjutant, to the front to assess the situation in the Adelup Point–Asan Point area. The major never made it to his destination. He was killed somewhere between Bundschu Ridge and Mount Mangan.

In an effort to obtain more direct control over the defense, General Takeshi Takashina had moved his headquarters to a cave among the former manganese mines at Mount Mangan a few hundred yards west of Fonte. General Kiyoshi Shigematsu was not far away, having previously moved his command post to a mine shaft in the Mangan quarry. As the landings progressed, the Japanese commanders rushed to bring up reinforcements from the central massif. The 319th Independent Infantry Battalion, then stationed in the southern outskirts of Agana in brigade reserve, was dispatched to the area east of Adelup Point. The 321st and 322nd Independent Infantry Battalions were ordered from Agana and Tumon Bay, respectively, to positions near Mount Mangan behind the beleaguered 320th Battalion. Headquarters also took command of the main force of the 10th Independent Mixed Regiment, the 2nd Battalion of the 18th Infantry Regiment, and the 9th Company of the 38th Infantry Regiment as General Takashina attempted to contain the U.S. beachhead.[13]

Miles to the south, monitoring the situation from his command post on the slopes of Mount Alifan, Colonel Tsunetaro Suenaga had little cause to celebrate as the day drew to a close. His 38th Infantry Regiment, charged with defending the Agat sector, had been badly mauled resisting the American landing. The two companies of the 1st Battalion manning the Agat beach defenses had been overrun and were now mostly dead—the 1st Company could muster only thirty survivors that night. The two artillery batteries supporting the beach defense had been destroyed by naval gunfire and air attacks. Forward elements of the 2nd Battalion attempting to defend Agat Village had been eradicated by the 22nd Marines. Though the bulk of the battalion remained intact, it had lost communications with regimental headquarters as of noon. U.S. intelligence later learned that one force of over one hundred men stationed near Apra Harbor was not informed of the American landing until late afternoon, the news imparted by a straggler from Agat. To the south of the Marine Brigade beachhead, the 3rd Battalion's 8th Company had been destroyed when it was thrown into the fight for Hill 40 and Bangi Point during the landing. The remainder of the battalion, defending the area south toward Facpi Point, had otherwise escaped harm.

As American troops and equipment poured ashore under Japanese eyes on the slopes of Mount Alifan, Colonel Suenaga, "judging that every moment of delay would permit the enemy to strengthen his position," decided his only chance to regain the initiative was to launch a mass attack against the beachhead. With runners and what communications remained intact, he ordered his remaining units to assemble for a counterattack against the center and both flanks of the Marine Brigade. The plan called for all three of his battalions to participate, though regimental headquarters remained out of contact with the 2nd Battalion, which never got the word.

At about 1730 Colonel Suenaga telephoned 29th Division headquarters to advise General Takashina of his intentions. Takashina initially refused to grant permission for the counterattack "in view of the overall battle situation and the fact that the regiment was a holding force." However, he must also have recognized the 38th Infantry's isolated position at Agat. As Colonel Suenaga continued to argue his case, the general "finally gave way to the enthusiasm of the regimental commander who was determined to carry out an all-out attack [and] win posthumous fame for his regiment," observed the division's operations officer.

In what even General Takashina must have realized was a flight of unwarranted optimism, he directed Colonel Suenaga to reassemble his men and continue the defense of Mount Alifan following the attack. The colonel himself obviously considered that prospect—and the success of the counterattack itself—unlikely. Shortly after the phone call with General Takashina, he ordered that the 38th Infantry's regimental colors be burned.[14]

Commanding the 3rd Battalion, Captain Hiromi Naganawa distributed *sake* and issued orders to attack the enemy beachhead at midnight. The men began to sort through their personal belongings, burning letters and pictures from home before indulging in a last meal of canned salmon and rice washed down with *sake*. Many men turned their faces away and wept, recalled battalion surgeon Lieutenant Shigenori Yoshida. One of his fellow surgeons, a man named Ito, had always been very proud of his family album, often showing it off and bragging about family members. Yoshida noticed that Ito, apparently unable to bring himself to part with the album, had shoved it into a case with his medical supplies and tied it around his waist.

At a final briefing for 3rd Battalion officers, Captain Naganawa spoke calmly and with great composure. By contrast, Lieutenant Yoshida found he couldn't stop trembling. The captain and he had become good friends while stationed together in China. Now Naganawa turned to Yoshida and reminded him of his responsibility to tend to the battle's survivors. "As a medical man you do not have the right to act rashly and take your own life," he said sternly. Yoshida swallowed hard and bowed deeply without replying.[15]

—◦—

The 3rd Battalion, 4th Marines, which had landed that morning in reserve, came up before dark to anchor the right of the 1st Provisional Marine Brigade's beachhead line. The large proportion of former Raiders comprising the battalion were "rather hard-bitten characters," remarked battalion operations officer Major Anthony Walker, who was a rather hard-bitten character himself.[16] PFC Rudy Rosenquist's K Company platoon was directed into the line by Hill 40. The hill, three hundred yards inland from Bangi Point, had finally been captured by the 1st Battalion with the help of two tanks after a stiff fight earlier that morning. "It was dusk. . . . [T]he ground was wet as we dug in," recalled the nineteen-year-old from Fairhope, Alabama. Rosenquist set up his .30-caliber machine gun and drove an entrenching tool into the ground at one side so the gun wouldn't traverse too far and endanger friendly lines. His battalion commander, Major Hamilton Hoyler, formerly of the 3rd Raider Battalion, came along and asked the crew if they could hold until daylight. "We gave him some cocky assurances and settled in," observed Rosenquist. They had just opened their rations when they heard the clink and rattle of equipment coming from behind them. It was now almost dark. "We were scared, but it was a Marine ammo and water detail," remarked Rosenquist. The detail was loaded down with loose machine-gun belts they had salvaged from wrecked amtracs.

As darkness deepened, Navy ships sent up star shells, casting the unoccupied ground to their front in a garish light. K Company PFC Paolo DeMeis was crouched nervously in his hole when PFC Harry Reser, in a hole down the line, began calling out to him, "Kid, where are you?" Not wanting to reveal his position to any watching Japanese, DeMeis kept quiet, hoping Reser would give it up. But after a pause, Reser started calling again, this time calling him by name: "DeMeis, are you all right?" After seven or eight of these inquiries, DeMeis finally shouted back, "Shut up! Now they not only know where I am, they even know my name!"

"Well the whole line came alive laughing," he recalled. "Then the Japs started to talk to us in the dark saying, 'Eleanor sucks [cock]!' And all sorts of things. 'Franklin this' and 'Franklin that.' Marines would start to answer. 'Suck my [cock]. You eat shit!'"[17]

Corporal Dan Marsh's machine-gun crew set up in an abandoned enemy trench. A fifty-yard gap covered with tall grass separated them from L Company's machine-gun section to their left front. "[We] knew the enemy was beginning to infiltrate through the thick grass to the company's front," he recalled. Suddenly, L Company's gun opened up with a series of long bursts. "We were carefully searching the tall grass for signs of movement, when the air was split by a long, shrill, terrifying scream that I do not have words to describe," recalled Marsh. "We knew it came from the area of L Company's machine gun section, and we feared that the gun had been silenced."[18]

At 2330, units reported enemy activity out to their front as Captain Naganawa's 3rd Battalion began to move toward Hill 40. A single shot rang out just down the line from Rosenquist's machine-gun post. A Japanese had crept in close and picked off a BAR man by the light of a star shell. Twenty minutes later, they heard two sharp clicks from directly in front of their position. The Marines knew the sound all too well. Japanese grenades were armed by rapping them against a hard object such as the soldier's helmet. "In the dim light you could barely see the grenades glint as they came through the air toward us," recalled Rosenquist. They fell just short and exploded. Ducking his head, Rosenquist felt fragments glance off his helmet. He opened up with the machine gun, hosing down the area to their front.

A momentary lull was broken as six or eight more grenades were lofted toward them, trailing sparks. All fell short. "Again I hosed down the front and a few minutes later we could see a whole line of Japs all across our front trotting as they came into our positions," recalled Rosenquist. He opened up on them, and the line melted away, but there were more behind them. The Marine next to Rosenquist exclaimed, "Dammit, let me have some," and took over the gun just before the next wave of attackers came at them. Rosenquist was thinking his replacement should increase the gun's traverse when everything suddenly went to hell. "I heard a scream on my left, rolled over and found a Jap almost on top of me with his rifle and fixed bayonet. He pinned me to the ground as his bayonet went in the left side and out my lower chest. As he stepped over me, I grabbed his canteen strap and he jerked me all the way to my feet. . . . Someone else ran into me just as he tore loose. . . . He bayoneted me again in the gut." Rosenquist managed to pull out the .38-caliber pistol he had taken from the dead Marine on the beach earlier that morning and emptied it into his attacker. The Japanese fell back on the machine gunner. "Another Jap ran over me and the two of us went down together. . . . He was screaming something over and over. I had lost my revolver, but pulled my Ka-bar knife and stuck him good as we were rolling around. . . . I remember thinking . . . *How young he looks!* We were face to face in the star shell light. He showed no emotion when I cut him." As Rosenquist tried to struggle to his feet, something smashed into his head—"it was like a flare going off in my face"—and knocked him unconscious.[19]

BAR man PFC Emmitt Hays manned a position near a dry creek bed. "They hit our position hard," he recalled of the Japanese assault. Their mushroom-shaped helmets stood out but faces remained in shadow as they trotted forward in the light of the flares. Hays fired so many rounds, he nearly burned out the barrel of his BAR. "I couldn't touch it, since it was red hot. We had visible targets for an hour. They were in our faces." As they ran low on ammunition, someone passed machine-gun belts up the line. The men pulled rounds out of the belts and loaded them into clips and magazines. Hays made a conscious effort to conserve his ammunition, waiting until he saw three or four Japanese in a bunch and trying to get them all at once.[20]

Not far from Hays, twenty-year-old Sergeant Allen Shively, a former Indiana farm boy, was manning a machine-gun position. A grenade went off near the gun, and a lone Japanese officer, sword in hand, charged in on the heels of the blast. As Shively stood up, the officer lunged at him with the sword. Shively twisted away. The blade sliced through the right pocket of his dungaree trousers and out the back without touching him. As the Japanese came at him again, Shively got a grip on the officer's sword hand and managed to wrest the weapon away. In the light of a flare, he saw the officer reach toward his chest and pull out a pistol. The Japanese fired at him but the shot went wide as Shively grabbed his arm, forced it upward, and took the pistol away. "Then I literally beat the hell out of him with my hands," he recalled. "When I got him on the ground, I took his saber and rammed it through him about five times. I looked around for my buddy, and he was dead and I was alone."[21]

A brief lull followed the initial assault on K Company, but at 0100 the Japanese launched a concerted attack on the platoon holding Hill 40. Standing offshore, USS *Bennett* increased illumination using five-gun ripple salvos and began shelling suspected enemy assembly areas. The cruiser *Indianapolis* assisted with illumination, while the battleship *San Francisco* moved into firing position. Destroyers *Fullum* and *Halford* also stood in to assist.

The illumination exposed a mob of Japanese approaching Hill 40 across an open expanse. "I'll bet there were a thousand Japs and there were only two platoons of us up on this hill," recalled PFC Robert A. Powers.[22]

Not far from Powers, PFC Charles Meacham was also watching. "We could look down and see these guys wiggling through the grass," he observed. "They looked like brown maggots wiggling through the grass."[23] The Marine next to Powers was hit and went down. Explosions rocked the hill. Powers felt something warm on the back of his neck. He thought he had been hit, but when he reached back to check, he found a chunk of human skull still retaining some short black hair. Another explosion eviscerated two Marines further down the hill.

Forced off the hill, the Marines reorganized and counterattacked, retaking their positions, only to be shoved off once again. Help arrived in the form of an L Company platoon led by twenty-nine-year-old First Lieutenant Marvin C. Plock, a former running back on the University of Nebraska football team, who had volunteered to bring his men forward "without so much as asking for a vote," one of his Marines observed sourly. "That forced march guided by star shells went to prove the days of miracles are not over because we weren't fired on at all by our own troops," he added.[24]

The reinforcements made their way through a web of Japanese trenches, dropping men off in pairs as they went. "The trenches were full of dead bodies and we soon found ourselves with Japs on both sides and some of the dead were not dead but rose up to fight," recalled Corporal Luther Fleming. "One of them jumped up suddenly between Sgt. [Brian] Quirk and me and sent a burst of about twenty rounds at my head, but he was so close he missed. We only got powder burns and ringing ears"[25]

The Marines regained the hill, this time to stay. But the Japanese were far from finished. At about 0330, they mounted yet another assault against the 3rd Battalion. "We had a thin line of men," recalled PFC Nicholas J. Pappajohn. "The enemy rolled grenades into the trench killing two Marines on my right."[26] PFC Paolo DeMeis was trying to shove the bolt forward on his M-1 when he saw a Japanese with a bayonet-tipped rifle coming at him on the right. "It happened so fast all I could do was try to parry him with my rifle," he recalled. He wasn't sure what happened next. He remembered another enemy soldier jumping into his foxhole. They grappled until DeMeis managed to push his .45 automatic against the man and fire a couple of rounds. They collapsed together in the bottom of the hole.[27]

Under First Lieutenant Martin J. ("Stormy") Sexton, a former All-American lacrosse middle fielder at the University of Maryland, K Company stopped the main thrust, but numbers of Japanese leaked through the lines and into the pack howitzer positions to the rear. Working from the protection of a twelve- to fifteen-foot crater left by a one-thousand-pound bomb, Lieutenant Benjamin S. Read, executive officer of Battery A, challenged two figures edging along the crater at about 2330. The two turned out to be communicators checking a wire line, but thirty minutes later Read saw four more figures creeping along the same line. This time, when challenged, "they hit the ground and rolled away from the hole, muttering in Japanese," recalled Read.

A gunnery sergeant lobbed a grenade at them, killing one. The other three were subsequently picked off by the gun sections, but they were just the beginning of a concerted effort to get into the rear positions. Reports of infiltrating Japanese soon began coming in from gun sections and outposts all around the battery. At the same time, calls for fire missions began streaming in. "By about 0130, we were up to our necks in fire missions and infiltrating Japanese," recalled Read. "Every so often I had to call a section out for a short time so it could take care of the infiltrators with carbines and then I would send it back into action again. Somehow, one Japanese Nambu machine gunner managed to get between our guns and the front lines and all night harassed us with fire."[28]

A number of Japanese also bumped into the 1st Battalion, 305th Infantry positions inland from White Beach 1. The GIs had been forced to dig in hastily, and many of their slit trenches were less than a foot deep. "We had heard many tales about the famed *banzai* night attacks," recalled one soldier. "None of us could sleep. When we weren't pulling our turn at guard, we lay in our shallow holes trying vainly to relax but listening for the slightest noise that indicated the presence of the enemy."[29] Early in the morning, heavy firing broke out just outside the 1st Battalion's assembly area. "The men were surprised and confused," admitted the division historian. "It was impossible to discover the location of the enemy; sentinels who challenged when they heard movements received a burst of fire." Several Japanese broke through to the battalion command post but were cut down by an automatic rifle team before they could do any damage. The GIs counted twenty dead Japanese the next morning. The battalion lost seven men killed and ten wounded in exchange, at least a few of whom were victims of misdirected friendly fire.[30]

A few small groups of enemy infantry armed with demolition charges got as far as the beach, where they disabled two weapons carriers and three LVTs. A platoon from the 5th Field Depot's Ammunition Company intercepted another bunch headed for the brigade ammunition dump and killed fourteen of them, aided by a gunnery sergeant who had been brazenly using a flashlight while distributing ammunition. The 4th Marine Tank Company killed another twenty-three Japanese in and around the service park during the course of the morning. Tanker Phil Morell recalled that about a platoon of Japanese came toward them over a low hillock. "We thought maybe they were 4th Marines going back for ammunition. They didn't know the password, but we still said hold your fire." It was the wrong call. "They set a magnetic mine on my tank—it did no damage—and threw a Molotov cocktail on another tank that started a fire. These were diesel tanks and the crew put it out with their utility coats."[31]

Rudy Rosenquist came to his senses lying alongside a palm tree. He was still holding his Ka-bar. It felt sticky, as if it had been dipped in glue. "I couldn't see any of the bodies around me moving and I wondered which were Japs and which were Marines," he remembered. There was firing going on from somewhere off to his left. He realized his stomach area was soaked with blood, and he pulled his fatigue hat from his pocket and stuffed it under his belt over the bayonet wound in an effort to staunch the flow. He didn't feel much pain, "just a burning sensation." Struggling to his feet, he staggered back through a tree line by the light of the flares bursting behind him. Suddenly a challenge came out of the darkness. Unable to remember the password, he answered that he was wounded and needed help. He fell to his knees before his challengers could reply. "I was sure they would shoot me for moving so suddenly, but then I remembered the password and they let me crawl into their shell hole," he said. The hole was occupied by some Marines manning a pack radio. They sprinkled sulfa on his wounds, bandaged him up, and stuck him with a morphine syrette.

As Rosenquist lay there listening to the radio chatter, the men heard Japanese voices in the darkness beyond the hole. Some enemy soldiers were approaching along the same trail Rosenquist had used. "We could hear them talking and hear their gear working as they approached," he said. The Japanese paused as they emerged from the tree line just to the front. Crouched along the forward edge of the shell hole, the radiomen opened fire. When they stopped, there was a moment of silence, followed by the *pop-pop* of grenades being armed. Two or three grenades arched into the shell hole. "Everyone there bailed out and I could only stuff the radio between my legs as I watched the damn grenades go off. . . . [T]hen I belatedly rolled out of the shell hole," said Rosenquist.[32]

The radiomen slid back into the hole following the blasts. Someone reached out and dragged Rosenquist in. "The radio was completely wrecked and I had grenade fragments in both legs and one in the center of my chest and one through the palm of my right hand," he recalled. As the men wondered aloud whether the whole Marine line had caved in, Rosenquist decided he should try to get back to the beach. He crawled out of the hole on his hands and knees. He hadn't gone thirty feet when he came face to face with a wounded Japanese, also on his hands and knees. The enemy soldier jabbed at him with what appeared to be a short spear, sticking him between the fingers of his injured right hand, before turning and crawling away. Rosenquist crawled back to the shell hole and passed out again.

⌒⌒

While Hoyler's 3rd Battalion fought to hold Hill 40, a major assault was also developing in the 4th Marines center where the Japanese had been probing the 1st Battalion's lines since shortly before midnight. At about 0230, Marines blocking the

Harmon Road intersection heard the clank and squeal of armored vehicles from up around the bend toward Mount Alifan. "At the same instant, every man on the line was whispering that Japanese tanks were coming," recalled PFC George Aspley, who was dug in on the right side of the road. "My foxhole buddy and I immediately started to dig out our position a little deeper as we waited, using our field knives and helmets, placing the loose dirt in front of our position."[33]

As the metallic clanking grew louder, flares popped overhead, illuminating the roadway. The tanks—there were four of them—were Type 95 Ha-go light tanks from the 1st Company, 9th Tank Regiment. Weighing in at 7.4 tons, the Ha-go carried three crewmen and was armed with a 37mm main gun and two 7.7 machine guns. The Marines were aware of the presence of Japanese armored units on Guam and had taken the appropriate precautions earlier in the evening, positioning five Shermans from the regimental tank company in a hollow behind the lines. The Marine infantry was also armed with a small number of 2.36-inch rocket launchers. Popularly known as "bazookas," the rocket launchers had only recently been issued to the 4th Marines, but they had shown their worth against enemy armor at Saipan the month before. Operated by a gunner and a loader, the bazooka was essentially a tube about five feet long that fired a rocket with a shaped charge. The shoulder-fired weapon had a range of just over two hundred yards.

As the Japanese tanks clanked closer, Corporal Mel Heckt's machine-gun crew took them under fire, knowing full well the .30-caliber slugs wouldn't do much damage to the armor. "I remember my teeth chattered and my knees shook," he admitted. "I was more than slightly scared."[34] As the tanks continued along the road in column, accompanied by enemy infantry, twenty-three-year-old PFC Bruno Oribiletti and his loader, PFC Lee ("Russ") Polk, knelt in a ditch beside the road and readied their bazooka. Neither Oribiletti, a good-looking kid with an engaging grin from a big Italian family in Kenosha, Wisconsin, nor Polk, a solid twenty-two-year-old former bricklayer from Rochester, Michigan, had ever fired a bazooka in combat before.

Oribiletti had shot expert on the rifle range in boot camp, and he proved no less deadly with the bazooka. Waiting until the first tank was within fifteen yards of his position, he took careful aim and sent a rocket smashing into its side. Polk shoved another rocket into the launcher and attached the electrical contacts, and Oribiletti sent it at the second tank. As one of the enemy crew bailed out, Polk reloaded, and Oribiletti put another rocket into the first tank, which burst into flames. Polk reloaded again, and Oribiletti stood up to get a better line of sight on the damaged second tank. Corporal Leon Barr later wrote to Oribiletti's father, "The bazooka makes quite a large flash at night and after the third shot the Japs probably knew exactly where he was firing from. He was hit through the chest with a 37mm shell and went out instantly."[35]

Aspley was only twenty feet from the first tank when it was hit and burst into flame. Machine-gun and rifle fire was tearing into the supporting infantry. Aspley looked to his right at one of the machine guns and saw the barrel glowing red hot in the darkness. Two of the Sherman tanks that had been cached down the road now arrived on the scene. Unable to pick out his target at first, one of the tank gunners saw his tracers suddenly veer straight up as they glanced off the armor of an enemy tank. Using that as a guide, he let go with his 75mm gun and blew the turret off the tank, setting it on fire. In the confusion, the last Japanese tank in the column managed to escape back up the road. "We continued to fire at the tanks as they burned and at the remaining Japanese crewmen, now with their clothes on fire as they attempted to escape from their burning tanks," said Aspley. "Their blood-curdling screams and the stench of the burning flesh was [awful], but it was them or us." It wasn't completely one-sided. Hunkered down in his foxhole by the roadblock, Aspley could also hear the "wailing and moaning of our wounded." In the darkness, it wasn't safe to try to move from foxhole to foxhole, so many would have to wait until daylight for medical assistance. "It was heartbreaking having to sit and listen to the cries of the wounded and not being able to do anything to help them," he remembered.[36]

Dug in about twenty yards behind the forward foxholes, Sergeant Joseph Hiott saw a Marine staggering around out beyond the line. "He'd been wounded, shot through the chest," he recalled. "He was wounded and didn't know what he was doing." With all the shooting going on, Hiott couldn't believe the man hadn't been finished off already. He ran out and brought the wounded Marine—Corporal Robert A. Roth, a former Raider from Wisconsin—back in. A corpsman bandaged Roth's wound, and some men loaded him onto a poncho and carried him back to the command post. Hiott had a "pretty good feeling" the former Raider would make it but learned years later that Roth had died of his wound the next day aboard the USS *Fayette* and was buried at sea.[37]

While the armored thrust was destroyed on the road, a Japanese infantry assault down the slopes of Mount Alifan overran Company A dug in near a tree line to the right of the roadblock. Shrieking soldiers, led by an officer waving a flag on a blade-topped bamboo pole, surged through a draw toward the company. Defending his foxhole, twenty-six-year-old PFC Joseph V. Berault, a former bakery worker from Newark, New Jersey, was hit in the mouth by a live grenade. Berault managed to pick it up and throw it back before it exploded, but more grenades quickly followed. Berault got rid of four of them before he was finally wounded by a fifth. Crawling to a hospital corpsman for first aid, he was being tended to when still another grenade landed next to them. Berault kicked at it with his foot, at the same time shoving the corpsman out of the way. The explosion paralyzed his right leg and dislocated his knee. He would spend a year in hospital, but surgeons managed to save his leg.

Hunkered down with the 2nd Battalion on the other side of Harmon Road, PFC Roger Spaulding had been listening to the Japanese carry on out in the darkness in the wake of the failed tank attack. The Japanese were "whooping it up like cowboys at a rodeo," he recalled. "*Aaayeeee,* MALINE YOU DIE!" someone shrieked, accompanied by a lot of chatter, laughter, rattling rifle bolts, and the sound of glass *sake* bottles being smashed. An occasional grenade exploded near the road. "Every now and then we'd hear a bottle break," recalled Sergeant Hank Bauer. "Then you would hear this high shrill laugh the Nips had. You know—*yah-ta-ta, yah-ta-ta, yah-ta-ta*—that's what it sounded like." As the din began to rise to a crescendo—"it sounded like a hundred cats fighting in an alley," said Bauer—a Marine bellowed, "Don't shoot until they are so close they can piss on you. Keep your head, let them go by if your line of fire is not clear. Fix bayonets! Fix bayonets!"[38]

"Here come the bastards!" someone yelled.[39]

Bursts of machine-gun fire opened from Marine lines as a wave of Japanese charged across the road "yelling and screaming, staggering, falling and getting up again." Many of them ran right through, seemingly not even noticing the Marines in their foxholes. "They grunted as they ran, their straps and belts rattled and squeaked and they left the vinegar smell of *sake* behind to mingle with the cordite and the sulphur smell of explosions," recalled Spaulding. He saw a Japanese running behind him, aimed roughly with his M-1, and pulled the trigger, squeezing off shots until the man finally went down. Other Japanese were visible in the distance, still running.[40] Another G Company Marine, PFC Trenton Fowler, heard someone yelling, "Get some tanks up here! They've broken through!"[41]

———

Further to the left, at the north end of the brigade front, a company-sized enemy force made it to the vicinity of the 22nd Marines command post. There they ran into a reconnaissance platoon led by Lieutenant Dennis Chavez Jr., who personally killed five of the enemy at point-blank range with his Thompson submachine gun. Clerks, runners, and other headquarters personnel pitched in to help fight off the rest. Six

Marines were wounded, but morning revealed the bodies of three Japanese officers and sixty-six men scattered through the area. Intelligence later identified the enemy dead as members of a naval defense unit.

Holding down the shoreward end of the line, Captain Charles F. Widdecke's C Company had taken position in a web of Japanese trenches located at the base of a hill that had held them up most of the afternoon. As night approached, only 100 effectives remained of the 240 men who had stormed ashore that morning. Widdecke, a six-foot-one-inch Texan who had been awarded the Silver Star for heroism at Eniwetok, advised battalion he would need help if he was to get through the night, reporting, "Company C committed all platoons, no reserves, weak, could not hold counterattack."[42] Battalion sent up the reserve platoon from Company I at 1715. Bizarrely, as darkness fell, twelve enemy soldiers came strolling nonchalantly down a trail from the troublesome hill. Lugging one light machine gun and three heavy machine guns, they walked directly toward the center of the Marine-occupied trenches and were shot down to a man. "Those Nips were so heavy with slugs we couldn't lift them," quipped one of the Marines.[43]

Leading Widdecke's machine-gun platoon, First Lieutenant Cord Meyer spent a restless night in a shallow foxhole, changing watch every two hours with Platoon Sergeant George V. Tudor of Chicago. It had been a hard day for Meyer. Out of the forty-four men in his platoon who had come ashore that morning, just thirty remained to dig in beyond the ruins of Agat that night. The most painful loss for Meyer was the youngest Marine in his platoon, who was shot in the chest and abdomen. As the youngster arched his head back, gasping for breath, Meyer helped a corpsman try to stop the bleeding, though both knew it was hopeless. Meyer finally left to rejoin the platoon as the corpsman brushed flies away from the dying Marine's face. "I'll keep the flies away," he told Meyer. "They bother him." When Meyer returned later, the corpsman was gone, and the youngster was dead.

He had had his own close call during the day when a bullet tore through his breast pocket. The slug, which must have been nearly spent, knocked him down and nipped the end off a cigar he had been carrying in his pocket but left only a small welt on his chest. In a show of bravado, he lit the cigar with trembling fingers and pretended courage he did not feel. Now, clutching a Thompson submachine gun, Meyer watched and waited in fear as flares periodically popped softly overhead, reminding him of "the breaking of a Fourth of July rocket." The unearthly light as the flare swung overhead seemed only to accentuate the dangers beyond his hole as natural objects "assumed enormous and malevolent proportions in the shadows."

At about 0130, the Japanese finally came, charging out of the jungle growth with what seemed to Meyer like exultant cries. Firing broke out all along the line. Meyer had a brief glimpse of stooped figures running forward but could not manage to get a shot, though there seemed to be "strange foreign voices, high with excitement" all around. Someone screamed. And then the firing ebbed. "They're falling back," said Tudor. Meyer hadn't fired a shot.

A heavy object suddenly plunked in the hole and came to rest next to his leg. It was a grenade. Meyer groped for it, found it, and hurled it away. It exploded in the air, but another grenade bounced on the edge of the hole and rolled in. This one exploded as he reached for it, smashing into his face like a giant club. He clutched his head in agony. Blood ran down his neck, and he could feel fragments of teeth in his mouth. He reached out for Tudor, feeling a dungaree shirt and then a wound that left no doubt that the sergeant was dead. And then he realized that the darkness surrounding him was too impenetrable to be the night. He was blind.[44]

Clinging to their toehold on the high ground beyond the Asan beaches, 3rd Division Marines had their own troubles. "After dark, flares on parachutes lit up the beach," recalled amtank crewman Donald Scharf.

> As the flares swung from side to side, shadows moved making it look like Japs were moving among our tanks. I was never so afraid in all my life. All of us were jumpy and on edge. Suddenly all hell broke loose. There was a lot of yelling, grenades were going off on the hill, rifles and machine guns were firing, shells were landing on the beach and shrapnel was flying in all directions. We crunched ourselves deeper into the foxholes, and some crawled as far as they could under the tanks. I was shaking so hard my teeth were clicking.[45]

Up in the hills, Lieutenant Paul Smith and his runner lay out in a pouring rain trying to get some sleep. They had been unable to dig into the rocky ground, settling instead into a shallow crevice. Lying flat on his back, clutching a ten-inch stiletto in one hand, Smith suddenly heard "a muffled skid" and clatter. An instant later, something like a wet sack of flour fell on his left shoulder. In sheer panic, he swung his right arm around and plunged his knife into the "sack" up to the hilt. "The sack of flour gave a little lurch, then lay still, quivering, but not moving," he recalled. He was aware of a shocking stench as his victim's bowels let loose—he wasn't sure at first that they weren't his own. A second wave of panic washed over him as it occurred to him that he might have just killed one of his own men, but running his hand down the corpse's sodden leg, he found the split-toe canvas shoe worn by Japanese soldiers.

His foxhole companion asked what was going on, adding that the smell made him want to upchuck. He no sooner said it, than Smith himself vomited. He later found he had, by sheer luck, driven the knife under the enemy soldier's left shoulder blade, between his ribs and probably into his heart.[46]

Though Smith could not know it, General Shigematsu had been moving reserves up since late morning, including reinforcements to the defenders of Bundschu Ridge. The 2nd and 3rd Battalions of the 10th Independent Mixed Regiment were ordered from positions near Ordot to reinforce the 2nd Battalion, 18th Infantry fighting the 21st Marines. The 321st and 322nd Independent Infantry Battalions began moving south from Tumon Bay and Agana. Small groups of men were fed into the fighting as they became available. The bulk of the assaults in the center fell on Lieutenant Colonel Eustace R. Smoak's 2nd Battalion, 21st Marines, where Private Bill Baumheuter and his forward artillery observer team had spent the hours before nightfall settling in on the steep slope. Their tenuously held ridgeline was the boundary between life and death. "Some of the men crossed the crest to dig in," recalled team leader Lieutenant Bill Grissim. "The Japs, 100 yards away on the other side of the sky-line, picked them off as they crossed." Mortar fire kept knocking out the wires to the artillery, leaving Baumheuter's walkie-talkie as the only means of communication. "I was glad I had that radio," said Baumheuter, a twenty-year-old from Anna, Illinois, who was known to his buddies as "Tree Chopper," which was a loose translation of his German surname.

Just after dark, Baumheuter heard someone up on the lines warn, "They're coming." A rifle fired; then the whole line opened up. "Then we saw that we really had a mess of Japs out in front of us," said Baumheuter. Grissim yelled for Baumheuter to call for an emergency barrage. The wait seemed interminable, but the shells finally started thumping in. "We got some artillery fire down," said Grissim. "If the shells were to land among the Japs just over the hill, they had to skim the crest. They were parting our hair. I swear that if you reached up, you could have picked our shells out of the air as they sailed over us."

Everyone who could be spared from the forward observation team scrambled up to the line to add their rifles to the defense. With his radio the only link to the big guns, Baumheuter stayed huddled below the top of the ridge. Grissim was just above, banging away with his carbine. "We could hear the Japs and they could hear us," said Baumheuter. "They sort of washed against the top of the ridge once, and when they'd taken a pasting they washed away again. So the firing stopped for a while."

During the lull, Grissim and team member Corporal Martin Scanlon scrambled down to Baumheuter's radio. Scanlon, a big Irishman from Pittsburgh, had exchanged his carbine for an M-1. He'd been yelling at the Japanese and banging away up on the crest. "How many d'ja kill?" Baumheuter asked him. "I got a million of the bastards," said Scanlon.

They could hear attacks on the lines to both sides of them. Then it was their turn again. Baumheuter called for flares from the ships and then for artillery fire. This attack lasted a little longer than the first, maybe as long as twenty or twenty-five minutes and was pressed harder. "I couldn't see Scanlon," he remembered, "but I could hear his M-1 pumping away. The first time he'd been yelling at them. This time he wasn't doing any talking. No one was."

Grenades started to fall on their positions. A Marine just a short distance away from Baumheuter was hit in the head. As yet a third attack washed up against the crest, Baumheuter kept the artillery coming. The explosions lit up the men's faces with a reddish glow. One shell dropped short and blew off a Marine's legs. "The grenades started coming over thick then," said Baumheuter. He knew it was only a matter of time before he was hit.

> I took a sip of water from my canteen. I was thirsty and wanted more. I took another look at the guys falling and said to myself, 'I won't be here tomorrow to drink the rest of this.' So I drank it all down. I knew I was going to get it. It was simple as ABC. I knew I was going to get a grenade. I didn't know whether I was going to be killed or not but I knew I was going to get one. The Japs had plenty of grenades, but we didn't have many left. We threw everything at 'em but our shoes.

There were gaps in the line now. The Japanese were still coming. Baumheuter heard someone say something about using a flamethrower. Someone else said the wind was wrong, followed by, "Grenade! Watch that grenade!" Baumheuter ducked his head and lay flat as the grenade rolled down the hill. He heard it clank against his helmet. Then it went off. The side of his face went numb. He didn't know if he was alive or dead. His ears were ringing. Then sounds penetrated the fog, and he knew he was still alive. Somebody said, "You hit?"

"I think so," he replied.

It was Scanlon. "What the hell is this, don't you know?" he said unsympathetically.

Baumheuter felt someone jerk the radio away from him. There was another flurry of grenades. Scanlon was hit, and so was the E Company commander, Captain Sidney Altman. Baumheuter heard Altman talking on the radio. "This is Sid. I'm hit, I'm hit pretty bad. I've lost a lot of men. What do you want me to do?"

Word came to fall back. Scanlon picked up another Marine with a bad leg wound and stumbled down the sheer hillside. Baumheuter saw "a shadow fly by" and decided it was time for him to get out too. "I went back to the next ridge and sat there for a while. A corpsman came by and said: 'Come on, you walking wounded. We'll get aid.' That snapped me out of it. I went on back and later went aboard ship."[47]

Smoak had to withdraw his right company to the edge of the cliff, but the battalion held while U.S. artillery, mortars, and naval gunfire pounded the attackers. A wounded Marine reported that in the scramble to pull back, the shackle code effective from July 20 to 25, a working TBX radio, and Baumheuter's SCR 300 radio, tuned to channel 13, had been left behind and presumably captured. Word of that loss went all the way up to corps, which issued an alert that the codes could be compromised. Fortunately, no apparent security breach resulted. According to the Japanese, the 2nd Battalion, 18th Infantry lost two-thirds of its men killed or wounded; the 2nd Battalion, 10th Independent Mixed Regiment suffered comparable losses; and the regiment's 3rd Battalion lost "approximately 200 men" in the melee.[48]

The most organized push came against the beleaguered 3rd Marines clinging to Chonito Cliff, where a company commanded by First Lieutenant Shotaro Hashimoto of the 319th Battalion launched a flank attack on Colonel Ralph Houser's battalion. "In a fierce battle that followed, almost all members of the company perished," observed a Japanese report. Also on the move, the main force of the brigade's engineer unit, led by Captain Otomatsu Miyake, "launched a daring assault on enemy tanks that landed at Adelup Point," observed the report. "The commander plunged into an oncoming tank with eight kilograms of explosive charge in his arms. Most of his men died as heroically."[49]

Up by the cliff, Houser's battalion was handicapped as the W-Day fighting had left the three companies occupying three separate land masses. With no tie-in between companies and with definite routes of approach that could be exploited by the enemy between the units, the battalion was at a serious disadvantage. Worst hit was K Company. The company fought off three strong counterattacks during the night, but its line was finally breached when the fourth assault punched a fifty-yard salient into the perimeter. Machine-gun platoon leader First Lieutenant Vernon H. ("Whitey") Miller, a former University of Maryland football player who had dropped out of school in early 1942 to join the Marines, gathered up eighteen men and led an attack that eradicated the penetration. Miller, who obviously believed in leading from the front, personally destroyed two machine guns and killed eleven enemy soldiers despite being wounded by grenade fragments in the shoulder and hand.

PFC Luther Skaggs, a slightly built twenty-one-year-old from Henderson, Kentucky, also found himself in the thick of things. One of eight children, Skaggs had dropped out of school in the eighth grade and worked as a lineman for the Rural

Electrification Administration in Henderson and later as a carpenter before joining the Marines in October 1942. Months before, following the Bougainville campaign, he had written home to one of his brothers. "He said, 'If there is any way in the world you can stay out of this mess, do it,'" recalled his older brother Frank. Despite that admonition, Skaggs—who stood five feet, eight inches tall and weighed in at only 136 pounds—had a reputation as "a tough little guy." His 60mm mortar section had been ravaged by enemy fire upon landing on Red Beach 1 earlier in the morning, losing seven men, including their sergeant. When the section leader went down, Skaggs took charge and led the survivors into the high ground behind the beach, where they dug in and set up their mortars to support the assault on Chonito Cliff. Now, with the sea at their backs and the Japanese gathering, Skaggs told his men bluntly, "You're going to have to fight or die right here, and I'm not going to die."

As the first counterattack materialized out of the darkness, a Japanese hand grenade plunked into Skaggs's foxhole and exploded. Skaggs came to his senses to find he was still alive but grievously injured. The explosion had shattered his lower left leg. Still conscious but losing blood at an alarming rate, he used a belt as a tourniquet and rammed the shredded pulp of his lower leg into the dirt to help stem the bleeding. Having done what he could for himself and unwilling to call for a corpsman with Japanese all around in the darkness, Skaggs propped himself up behind his rifle. He had told his men he wasn't going to die, and he meant it.[50]

CHAPTER 15

HOLDING THE BEACHHEAD

TRYING TO FOLLOW THE PROGRESS OF THE ATTACK AGAINST THE MARINE BRIGADE, Lieutenant Shigenori Yoshida could see little from his hilltop position. Occasional flares silhouetted the distant figures of Japanese soldiers, but he was unable to determine the success of the assault. As the sky lightened to the east, men started straggling back. "Everybody is dead," mumbled one dazed soldier. "The battalion commander, the company commander. Everyone was killed." Another soldier was crying in a keening singsong wail.[1] Among the dead was Colonel Tsunetaro Suenaga, killed during the attack on the brigade center. Wounded in the leg by a mortar shell fragment, he had continued to hobble forward until he was killed by a bullet to the chest.

Among the survivors making their way back was Corporal Shoichi Yokoi. Despite their limited combat training, his transport company attached to the 38th Regiment had been ordered to participate in the attack. "Approach an enemy position stealthily; fight a close hand-to-hand combat; and do not expect to come back alive!" they were told. Instead, Yokoi spent most of the battle "flat, face down, trying to sink below the surface of the ground" as a hail of fire passed overhead. "*Ugh* . . . I heard someone groaning while I was still lying flat on the ground," he recalled.

"Yokoi, I have been shot!" exclaimed his close friend Higoyuki Fukaya. "When I turned my eyes on him, blood was pouring out of Fukaya's mouth," remembered Yokoi. "I wanted to go to him at once. However, *zip . . . zip . . .* enemy bullets were cutting through the palm trees. It was too dangerous even to raise one's head."

His group, led by a warrant officer named Kagawa, returned to their assembly point as the sun rose. Kagawa had been seriously wounded in the abdomen during the attack. Back at the assembly point, he borrowed the company commander's pistol, put the muzzle to his temple, and shot himself. "He was one year younger than I was," observed Yokoi. "He departed, I think, resolutely and honorably."[2]

The last of the counterattacks intended to erase the Marine Brigade beachhead ended around dawn. The approaches were littered with bodies, many Marines but far more Japanese—the 4th Marines alone reported counting over five hundred enemy dead in its area. Here and there, Japanese survivors remained on the field. Many appeared confused, some acting erratically, even suicidally. Weary Marines on Hill 40 watched in bewilderment as a Japanese heavy machine-gun crew approached as if on parade and proceeded to set up their weapon. The Marines cut them down. Shortly afterward, another crew came out and met the same fate. "One large group of Japs came right up to our lines facing the beach [and] sat down below a small rise where our men were dug in," recalled Lieutenant Glen M. Lewis of K Company. "They sat down, lit up cigarettes, and were chatting away among themselves as if there were no Marines within miles. We watched them for a while, then everyone opened up and we killed them where they were sitting."[3]

Near to where Rudy Rosenquist's machine gun had been overrun, a handful of diehards continued to harass the line from a nearby ditch. "They were throwing grenades and carrying on the fight," recalled PFC Herman E. Wooten. An exasperated Marine jumped into the ditch and emptied the twenty-round magazine of his BAR into the occupants, but the grenades kept coming. Finally a Sherman tank clattered onto the scene and fired its main gun into the ditch. "It was like a meat market with different cuts of meat flying around," remarked Wooten. "Later we counted over sixty dead bodies in that ditch."[4]

Lieutenant Benjamin S. Read's pack howitzer gunners found a dozen or more dead Japanese scattered around their gun positions. One artilleryman had been killed during the night and two wounded. "The dead Japs did not have weapons, but were loaded with demolitions and grenades," recalled Read. "They appeared to have been wounded prior to their attack on our position and gave the impression of being a suicide group bent on destroying our guns." One of the Japanese had a map with all of the Marine gun positions accurately plotted. "The only error on the map was the labeling of our position as that of a battalion and not a battery," observed Read. "The map had obviously been drawn from an OP on Mount Alifan."[5]

At the scene of the previous night's tank battle, Corporal Raymond R. Sullivan, manning the gun on one of the brigade's Shermans, spotted an enemy tank over a mile away, up by the mountain pass near the Maanot Reservoir. "I could barely make it out through the glasses," he said, "but I figured it was worth a few shots." Sullivan fired four armor-piercing rounds from his tank's 75mm gun. The fourth shot connected, and the enemy tank burst into flames. Skeptical of accounts of Sullivan's long-range shot—later determined to be 1,840 yards—their unit commander only credited the kill after coming up and seeing the knocked-out tank for himself.[6]

Corporal Luther Fleming's infantry platoon was one of the first to venture out in the field that morning to conduct what was generally referred to as "opossum patrol," making sure all corpses were actually dead. "We shot several wounded Japs for fear they had grenades," remarked Fleming. "There were hundreds of bodies. Arms, legs and body parts were everywhere. We had to shoot those in the head that weren't dead yet. We had to finish them off. If you thought they were breathing, you shot before they got you. There was banging up and down the line."[7]

During the day, five Japanese prisoners were evacuated from Beach White 1 to the USS *Ormsby*. All were from the 1st Battalion, 38th Infantry Regiment, which had been at the center of the Marine Brigade landings. They included three corporals and two first-class privates. Four had multiple shrapnel wounds—at least three of them apparently from grenades detonated by comrades committing suicide. Three also showed injuries to the throat that may have been self-inflicted. Their injuries were treated, and they were confined in a ship's compartment under armed guard prior to being transferred to the USS *President Polk* the next morning.

Prowling among the scores of fallen Japanese—some of whom had probably fallen victim to his BAR during the night—eighteen-year-old Emmitt Hays came across a badly wounded Japanese officer. "He was helpless, but alive," recalled Hays. A native of Camden, Arkansas, Hays had joined the Marines at sixteen years old, having lied about his age. He was still young in years, but his boyhood was long behind him. Taking out his combat knife, he coolly cut the enemy officer's throat before stripping him of his sword and pistol.[8]

Up by Harmon Road, scavengers from Roger Spaulding's outfit picked through the litter of dead Japanese looking for souvenirs. Swords were especially prized. Emblems were cut from uniforms, medals removed, bloody battle flags pulled from under shirts. A few hundred feet beyond the road where the Japanese had assembled for their attack, the ground was strewn with empty food tins, broken *sake* bottles, packs, and abandoned equipment. Discarded packs yielded up family photographs, Japanese money, silk scarves, and letters from home. One newly dead Japanese was found with a flag wrapped around his head and a self-inflicted wound to his midsection. He had apparently passed out, then awakened in time to kill himself before a Marine patrol found him. As big green flies descended on the carnage, the souvenir hunters retreated to build small fires to heat coffee and C rations.

Anchoring the 4th Marines' right flank, Company K had held Hill 40, but it had been a near thing. Regimental CO Lieutenant Colonel Alan Shapley later observed to K Company commander First Lieutenant Martin J. ("Stormy") Sexton, "If the Japanese had been able to capture Hill 40, they could have kicked our asses off the Agat beaches."[9] The 4th Marines reported 538 Japanese dead in their area; the 22nd Marines counted 70 dead. The Japanese 38th Regiment had been eliminated as an effective fighting force, its 1st and 3rd Battalions virtually wiped out in the counterattack. Only the 2nd Battalion, which had failed to receive the attack order, remained intact. Dazed survivors from the two shattered battalions gradually assembled in some woods northeast of Mount Alifan. The regiment's senior officer, the commander of the artillery unit, contacted 29th Division headquarters and was ordered to assemble what fragments he could and withdraw north to Ordot.

Some survivors would never get the word. Others were determined to keep fighting. A sergeant in Corporal Shoichi Yokoi's group refused to accompany the withdrawal north. "Even if I could survive longer, I have no hope for the future," said the noncom, who "had become a little mad," according to Yokoi. "I am going to attack enemy tanks." He left with a machine gun and five subordinates. Yokoi never saw any of them again.[10]

Marine Brigade casualties during the night totaled roughly fifty killed and twice that many wounded, including a high proportion of bayonet wounds. One platoon from Company A, 1st Battalion, 4th Marines was reduced to just four able-bodied men by repeated Japanese attacks down the wooded slopes of Mount Alifan. The company operated with only two platoons for the rest of the campaign since no replacements were available. Among the brigade's fatalities was one unlucky Marine whose head was crushed inside his helmet when he was struck by the heavy casing of a star shell plummeting out of the night sky.

As it grew light, Paolo DeMeis realized that he couldn't move. Lying in the bottom of his foxhole with a dead Japanese draped over him, he could hear sporadic rifle fire, mostly the occasional individual shot. As he tried to clear his head, his sergeant suddenly loomed overhead. "Hey, guys," the noncom called to unseen associates. "Come and see this. I got one wearing a Jap." The Marines pulled away the dead Japanese and lifted DeMeis out of the hole. "I was covered with blood and had a garlic aroma like the Jap that had died on me now," recalled DeMeis. A corpsman tended to a bayonet slash to DeMeis's stomach, gave him a shot of morphine, painted the letter

M on his forehead, and moved on to the next man. DeMeis later found out that Harry Reser—the Marine who had been so obsessed with checking on his welfare before the Japanese counterattack—had not been so lucky. He had been shot in the chest and killed during the night.[11]

Rudy Rosenquist woke up in the shell hole to find the sun high overhead. He was alone. He called for a corpsman, then stopped, afraid the Japanese would find him instead. He lay back and passed out again. When he came to, people were leaning over him. He thought at first they were Japanese, but his lucky angel was still watching over him: they were Navajo code talkers working as stretcher bearers. Rosenquist asked one of them to find his Ka-bar, but the Navajo just looked at him and silently shook his head. He probably thought Rosenquist would be lucky to just keep breathing. "They put me on a litter and carried me to a truck. . . . I could see dead Japs all around but only one dead Marine," said Rosenquist. He next woke up in a tent near the beach. Wounded Marines on litters were stacked all around. As he lay there, two rounds ripped through the tent canvas overhead. A doctor worked on him a while; next stop was the USS *Harry Lee* in what was to be a long series of hospitalizations.[12]

Over by Agat, Lieutenant Cord Meyer, in shock and unable to move, heard friendly voices speaking in hushed tones as he lay in his foxhole alongside his dead platoon sergeant. Someone leaned over him and exclaimed in surprise, "This one's alive!" He was loaded into an amphibious tractor and brought back to the beach. A corpsman or a doctor checked him and matter-of-factly observed, "This one's got about twenty minutes to live." Fortunately for Meyer, the diagnosis proved premature. He was transported out to an LST aid station, where a doctor got enough plasma into him to save his life. The left eye was a different story. It had been turned into a pulp by the grenade explosion and was unsalvageable. The doctor cleaned the swollen right eye and shined a flashlight on it. During the night, Meyer had forced the eye open and thought he could see stars. Now, to his incalculable relief, the doctors verified that hope. The eye still worked. He would not be blind.[13]

Attacks on the Asan beachhead continued into the daylight hours as elements of the Japanese 319th and 320th Independent Infantry Battalions launched an early morning counterattack on Colonel Ralph Houser's 3rd Battalion. Task Force 53 later reported enemy contacts "as close as eight yards."[14] As Houser clung to the ridge, Colonel W. Carvel Hall requested reinforcement from the division reserve. Shore party personnel were alerted to man defensive positions on order. Standing offshore, the commander of the destroyer *McKee* could see Japanese moving against the Marines on Chonito Cliff but was not able to obtain permission to fire from control parties on shore.

While some Japanese conducted frontal attacks on Houser's Marines, others made their way along the dry streambed between the cliffs and Adelup Point and began to climb the slopes behind the Marine foxholes. Spotting about twenty Japanese approaching from behind, twenty-six-year-old PFC Stephen Belas of Detroit, Michigan, launched a singlehanded attack. Alternately hurling hand grenades and firing his automatic rifle, he killed eight of the enemy and fatally wounded three others, disorganizing the assault before he was mortally wounded by Japanese fire.

Major Royal R. Bastian witnessed the action from the battalion command post located behind K Company. "Several attacks were made during the night and at daybreak an all-out attempt was made to reach the beach and set up machine guns on the tip [of the ridge spur] which had given K Company so much trouble the day before," he recalled. "Nips actually passed through the battalion CP and the dry stream bed to [the] rear and started up the ridge tip. Small arms fire from the battalion CP and amtracs on the beach stopped the Nips just short of their goal."[15]

The Japanese finally began to pull back at 0830. The Marines started to follow but were quickly brought up short by a barrage of artillery, mortar, and small arms fire. Among the morning's casualties was an L Company noncom from Delaware, Sergeant Paul L. Calk, whose brother had been killed in the torpedoing of the USS *Juneau* off Guadalcanal in November 1942—one of 687 crewmen, including the five Sullivan brothers, to perish in that catastrophe. Sergeant Calk died after a grenade blew his leg off.

K Company mortarman Luther Skaggs, grievously wounded during the night, was still alive at daybreak. Determined not to die, he had helped throw back three counterattacks over the past eight hours, encouraging the men around him, firing his rifle, and throwing grenades despite his shattered leg. His lieutenant later called his conduct that night "the greatest inspiration possible." When a withdrawal was finally ordered, Skaggs, aware of the many casualties, refused assistance and crawled out of the foxhole, dragging his ruined leg behind him. "I crawled behind the others for about 200 yards," he said. "After about fifty yards I dropped my rifle, then my ammunition. I heard my lieutenant's voice and crawled to the edge of his foxhole. Somebody pulled me in and put a dressing on my leg. Then I passed out." The next thing he knew, six men were carrying him in a poncho. "They had to drop me once when a shell hit close" he recalled. "Then they rushed me to the beach and I got two quarts of blood. I felt pretty good then."

Skaggs was evacuated from the beachhead, but his lower left leg was beyond salvation. Surgeons amputated what remained of the limb below the knee. His fortitude and determination to continue fighting despite his serious wounds was recognized eleven months later when, propping himself up on crutches, he was awarded the Medal of Honor in a ceremony on the White House lawn. Asked later about that night on Guam, he replied, "Somebody had to do it. It just happened to be me."[16]

At the other end of the Asan beachhead, PFC Edmund Topka, a Pennsylvania farm boy before joining the Marines, was dying. Part of the 3rd War Dog Platoon, Topka and his Doberman pinscher, Lucky, had gotten into a firefight with a dozen or more Japanese during the night. In the morning, Marines found the seriously wounded dog handler lying in a gully near a concrete bridge over the Asan River in the 21st Marine sector. Ten dead Japanese lay sprawled nearby. Lucky, unhurt, was watching over Topka.

The dog allowed a corpsman to tend to his wounded handler, but Topka had been hit too hard. When he died there in the gully, Lucky refused to let anyone come near the body. "He would not let you in," recalled PFC Dale Fetzer. "He would just stand there and bark at you and cry. He was going to guard his master dead or alive. That was his job." One of the handlers finally got a lead over Lucky's head and pulled him away. The dog was later reassigned to another handler but brooded so much over his missing friend that he was sent back to the United States and the family that had loaned him to the war effort.[17]

<hr>

Lieutenant Jim Gallo and a scattering of other survivors spent the night on the ridge that had eviscerated their company over the course of the day. "One Marine shot through both legs was asking for morphine," Cyril O'Brien reported of their ordeal. "Another's thigh was ripped by shell fragments. A PFC, his dry tongue swollen, tried to whisper the range of an enemy sniper."[18]

PFC Richard N. Moran and five other Marines had nearly made it to the top in the last effort the day before. They lobbed grenades over the crest but only provoked a rain of Japanese grenades in return. A BAR man was wounded in the head and leg. The others pulled back, but the BAR man couldn't move, so Moran stayed with him through the night. Every so often the Japanese would pitch a grenade in their direction, but they all passed over Moran's head and exploded down the hill.

Moran and others could hear the Japanese talking on the crest above, but except for the occasional grenade, the enemy made no concerted attempt to finish them off. "We couldn't understand what they were saying," said First Sergeant Charles V. Bomar, a thirty-three-year-old Texan and Pearl Harbor survivor who had served with the Marine detachment aboard the USS *West Virginia*. "We simply lay there as still as we could, waiting for daybreak."[19]

The 3rd Division had originally planned to attack with all three regiments abreast on July 22. The failure to seize Bundschu Ridge threw that plan into disarray as any advance by the 21st Marines would expose the regiment's left flank. Efforts to extend the flank of Colonel Eustace Smoak's battalion to the left to make contact with the 3rd Marines were confounded by the terrain. "No amount of maps, terrain models, or aerial photographs, nor advance intelligence from former island residents could do full justice to the nightmare of twisting ravines, jumbled rocks and steep cliffs that hid beneath the dense vegetation," observed a Marine officer. "With such terrain on its flanks and upper reaches, Bundschu Ridge was a natural fortress for the relative handful of Japanese troops that defended it."[20] There could be little progress on the division left or center until the troublesome ridge was secured.

Battalion executive officer Major John Ptak reported to Major Henry Aplington at dawn that Company A had lost nearly two-thirds of its men—including Captain Geary Bundschu—in the previous day's attacks on the ridge. Aplington asked regiment to let him to use C Company to try flanking the ridge from the right. Colonel Hall agreed but at 0830 announced an expanded effort that would include E Company from the 2nd Battalion in a double envelopment. Company A—or what was left of it—would again attempt a frontal attack on the ridge, while E Company flanked the objective from the left and C Company from the right. Regiment underestimated the time needed to organize for the assault—Hall "kept bugging me to attack," recalled Aplington—but the units were finally in position by 1150.[21]

Alvin Josephy watched from below as aircraft pounded the ridge with bombs, rockets, and machine-gun fire. Naval gunfire blasted the crest, joined by artillery from the beachhead and gunboats just offshore. Half-tracks and mortars chimed in. "Giant bursts of flame, followed by clouds of brown and yellow smoke, rose from the top of the hill," observed Josephy. Watching the continuous flash of explosions in an area only a few hundred yards square, it seemed impossible that anything could survive. The earsplitting din finally diminished as the assault got underway. The Japanese, emerging from the shelter of caves and positions on the reverse slope, were ready. "Wave after wave of green-dungareed Marines standing out in bold relief against the brown hillside, crawled and scrambled up, only to be hit and sent rolling back by machine guns, grenades and mortar shells," observed Josephy.[22]

Ignoring his shrapnel wounds, Jim Gallo led an assault on the left of the hill but was thrown back. Sergeant Bomar led eight Marines up the slope on the right. Five were killed as they left the cover of a small ravine. Bomar scrambled to the crest with the remaining three. Dozens of dead Japanese lay sprawled among a web of trenches. Bomar rushed two enemy soldiers manning a machine gun, killing the gunner with the butt of his rifle. The assistant gunner detonated a grenade, killing himself and eviscerating his already dead comrade. More grenades showered down on Bomar's tiny force. One exploded by a Marine's chest, blowing off his head. Another bounced off Bomar's helmet. It was a dud, but he was wounded by fragments from yet another.

Eighteen-year-old PFC Abel ("Billie") Aragon, a slender A Company mortar man from Price, Utah, had joined the assault as a rifleman the day before. Three Marines from the nine he started with had made it to the top, where they spent the night near Lieutenant Gallo below the crest. An excellent marksman in boot camp, Aragon silenced several Japanese positions with rifle fire before a Japanese grenade explosion tore into his left hip. Despite the injury, Aragon refused to give ground, continuing to fire on hostile positions for the next two hours. He survived his ordeal to receive the Navy Cross.

———

While A Company struggled, E Company's flank attack had run into heavy machine-gun fire. Hit in the leg, a squad leader shouted to his assistant to take over. A machine gun cut him down as he tried to hobble back to cover, and he tumbled to the bottom of the slope. The hail of fire from surrounding ridges stalled the advance before it had gone forty yards. Among the E Company Marines pinned down on the hillside was twenty-four-year-old PFC Leonard Mason, who had worked for a company that manufactured school bus bodies in Lima, Ohio, before joining the Marines. Trying to flank the high ground from the left, Mason's platoon worked slowly into a narrow gully. Any hopes that they had discovered an unguarded approach were dashed as two Japanese machine guns opened up at point-blank range. As they scrambled for cover, their platoon leader tried to regroup. "Don't go any further until I tell you to!" he shouted.

Twenty-one-year-old PFC Leon Slicner of Perth Amboy, New Jersey, hugged the slope next to Mason, whom he described as easygoing, though maybe a bit on the small side for the BAR he was assigned to carry. "The lieutenant's going around giving instructions here and there," recalled Slicner. The machine guns were hammering away, and he was content to stay right where he was for the foreseeable future.

"Bullshit with this!" Mason blurted suddenly, lurching to his feet. "I'll get them!"

Startled, Slicner reached out to pull him back down. "I grabbed him by his jacket and he just pulled away," he said.

Clutching his BAR, Mason clambered up the side of the gully and began making his way along the edge in an effort to get behind the Japanese gun positions.

"Cease fire! Cease fire! Mason's out there!" yelled Slicner.

"What's he doing out there?!" shouted the lieutenant. "Jesus Christ!"

Japanese riflemen on the higher ground immediately took Mason under fire. Struck in the arm and shoulder, he kept going, intent only on the pair of machine guns that had his platoon pinned down. As he reached the guns, he was hit again, this time by a burst of automatic weapons fire. Instead of going down, Mason raised his BAR and raked the Japanese machine-gun nest, killing five of the enemy and wounding a sixth. "There was so much fire going on you didn't even know who was who," said Slicner. Mason's BAR suddenly stopped. "And all of a sudden it's quiet," recalled Slicner. "Everything was real quiet. And here comes Mason back, real slow. He was all shot and his lower jaw was hanging. He knocked out the machine gun nests, but he was hurt real bad."[23]

Mason had eliminated the immediate threat, but other machine guns were already taking up the slack. Platoon commander Second Lieutenant Martin J. O'Brien, a six-foot, 180-pound former star basketball and baseball player at the College of the Holy Cross in Worcester, Massachusetts, reorganized his men and resumed the assault. The Marines struggled up the sixty-degree steep slope with no cover beyond some ankle-deep grass. "They knew there was not a prayer of a chance of getting up those slopes," said First Lieutenant French R. Fogle, the company's executive officer. "Yet they kept rushing and falling."[24]

The attackers grew fewer and fewer until finally only O'Brien remained, still advancing toward the crest. "It seemed for a while as if nothing could stop Lieutenant O'Brien," said Corporal Baker N. Sutton. "He charged the incline in a half crouch. Dust from enemy rounds was puffing up all around him."[25] Somehow, miraculously, O'Brien reached the top only to be finally cut down.

Things were going no better on the right where C Company's flanking attack bogged down in a tangle of thick undergrowth and sheer rock faces. Hanging on at the top of the ridge, Bomar's beleaguered force was running out of time. They were busy trying to bat away a seemingly endless succession of enemy grenades when a lieutenant scrambled into the trench. This was probably A Company executive officer First Lieutenant Harry E. Gossard, who had taken over after Bundschu was killed the day before. Witnesses from below had last seen the twenty-six-year-old former Marine Raider climb alone to the top of the ridge and disappear over the crest. If it was Gossard, he didn't last long. The officer had scarcely joined Bomar when he was shot in the head and killed. Bomar and his two fellow Marines—all of them wounded and with no help in sight—finally abandoned the trench and scrambled back down the hill. C Company, bogged down in the woods and rock faces to the right, never got into action. On the other flank, E Company sensed that Japanese resistance was weakening and managed to get up a little higher, though the crest remained in enemy hands by day's end.

The failed assault cost A Company an additional five dead and thirteen wounded. E Company suffered even more heavily, losing sixteen killed and thirty-four wounded during the day. Leonard Mason survived evacuation to the USS *Elmore*, an amphibious assault transport where he received medical attention, but his injuries proved too severe. He died aboard ship the following day and was buried at sea. His posthumous Medal of Honor was presented to his mother in Ohio a year later.

Shortly before 0800, lookouts aboard the USS *Wadsworth* patrolling off the southern end of Guam spotted a most unwarlike craft approaching. It was a large outrigger canoe paddled by six Chamorros. One of the occupants was waving a white flag fashioned from an undershirt. The destroyer hove to and lowered a Jacob's ladder as the canoe drew up alongside. One of the Chamorros grabbed onto the ladder to find the way blocked by an armed sailor looking down from above. "Uh, uh, not now," the sailor warned, pointing a carbine at the new arrivals. "What do you guys want?"

"We killed the Japanese guarding us and we are looking for help from the Americans," called one of the men. A few minutes later, the six emissaries from the uprising at Afate—Jesus C. Barcinas, Antonio L. G. Cruz, Jose M. Torres, Joaquin C. Manalisay, Juan M. Garrido, and Juan A. Cruz—were allowed on board, and the mood soon lightened. "Some of the crew members then started to hand out cigarettes, and, a short time later, they even brought us lunch," recalled Torres. "So excited were we that we hardly touched the food."[26] The Chamorros expressed profuse thanks to the ship's captain and crew for returning to liberate the islanders. "Liberate?" replied one of the Americans. "We are here to flatten this rock."[27]

Within an hour the six men were transferred to Rear Admiral Lawrence F. Reifsnider's flagship, the assault transport USS *George Clymer*, for a debriefing by intelligence officers. They reported that about seven hundred Japanese had moved up the east coast to Agana about two weeks before and that the bulk of the civilian population had been confined in camps located in the island interior.

A more immediately actionable bit of intelligence came from Torres, who said he had accompanied a work detail to an ammunition dump at Ordot in the center of the island about a week earlier. Munitions there were housed in bunkers, with some piled haphazardly on the ground. The Japanese had been very careful about daytime activities—particularly fires for cooking—for fear they would attract the attention of American aircraft, he said. U.S. officers showed him a photo mosaic of the island.

"I had hardly finished pointing out the precise location before an officer left the room," he recalled. He learned later that the site had been heavily bombed by carrier planes, resulting in huge secondary explosions.[28]

A "speed letter" alert from Admiral Reifsnider's Task Group 53-2 to various commands reported that the Japanese had apparently largely evacuated southern Guam nearly two weeks earlier, concentrating their forces, ammunition, and supplies in positions further north. "Japanese-speaking Chamorros have overheard [Japanese] army personnel discussing stores of poison gas believed located in northern part of island," the speed letter added ominously. Fortunately, that rumor proved unfounded. However, other troubling information was all too true. According to a synopsis of the intelligence information in the speed letter, "During past two weeks Japs have been threatening massacre of total native population. They report all natives are being concentrated in designated localities under guard to facilitate this. 'When Americans take Guam they were find nothing but flies' they were told. Hand grenades were thrown into [an] underground prison on 14 July where former native military personnel and 'blacklisted' natives had been imprisoned."[29] It was unsettling news, but until the Marines broke out of their beachheads, there was little to be done.

Having crushed the Japanese counterattack at Agat, the 1st Provisional Marine Brigade renewed the advance to Mount Alifan against light resistance early that morning. The 4th Marines were to seize the height, while the 22nd Marines continued the push up the coast toward Orote Peninsula. The newly arrived GIs would also join the fight, with the 305th Infantry (less the 2nd Battalion) passing through the 2nd Battalion, 4th Marines to attack toward Maanot Pass.

While official reports characterized resistance as light, it was far from nonexistent. PFC George MacRae accompanied the 4th Marines through the foothills to Mount Alifan. Noticing movement down in a small gully, he emptied his BAR's entire twenty-round magazine at the spot. "I reloaded and had started to fire a second burst when my BAR flew from my hands and a ringing was in my ears," he remembered. "My weapon was ripped from my hands and spun through the air and fell ten feet from me. My right arm was numb." His first thought was that he had stepped on a mine, then he realized that his feet seemed all right. "I looked at my right arm and knelt down to rest it on the ground as I could not see my hand doubled back underneath—only the white arm bones sticking out at the end of the arm." At about the same time a Japanese broke out of the brush with a bayoneted rifle in one hand and what looked to be a grenade in the other.

"It was like slow motion in a movie, as I could not believe what I was seeing," said MacRae. "All I could think of was that this was not going to be a fair fight. Since my arm was smashed, I tried with my left hand to reach my .45 under my left armpit but could not get it out of the holster. Just as I reached for my combat knife, someone—[PFC Francis G. Fitzpatrick], I think—hit the Japanese in the face with an incendiary round and he fell to the ground." MacRae, a former college track star once known in California newspapers as "The Glendale Greyhound," headed for the rear. He would spend the next two years in and out of military hospitals and, despite the best efforts of his surgeons, lose the use of his right arm.[30]

"The Japs occupied well defended caves connected by tunnels along the mountain side," noted a Marine Brigade report of the push up Mount Alifan. "In order to avoid unnecessary losses many of these caves were sealed by demolition parties."[31] The report's matter-of-fact tone failed to reflect the bitter nature of that effort. In one instance, an enemy rifleman in a cave on the seaward side of the mountain exchanged fire with approaching Marines. Someone threw a fragmentation grenade into the cave. The occupant promptly threw it back, inspiring a frantic scramble for cover by the Marines outside. A BAR man fired into the entrance, following up with a phosphorus grenade. That should have put an end to the nuisance, but when Marines started to investigate the smoke-filled interior, they were greeted by more shots. Finally, a demolition team shoved a pole charge inside. Poking through the wreckage, Marines found one lone Japanese soldier who had suffered multiple bullet wounds, as well as severe cuts and burns. One of his arms had been blown off. He had died with his rifle clutched in his one remaining hand.[32]

Continuing higher up Mount Alifan, the Marines entered a warren of sheer rock faces and thick thorny undergrowth. Thick roots from pandanus trees blocked trails, while vines snagged equipment and loose shale made for slippery footing. Fortunately, there was little resistance; the terrain was so bad even the Japanese couldn't construct a viable defense. A platoon finally reached the top and found it unoccupied.

———

Work to expedite the flow of supplies on the 3rd Division beaches resumed early on W+1. There were urgent calls for medical supplies and personnel. The hard-hit 3rd Marines requested twenty corpsmen as soon as possible. Stretchers were also requested as well as battle dressings, which were running critically low—all of this in addition to much-needed water and ammunition. The wide reef was a major headache, taking a toll even on the versatile amphibious DUKWs. At low tide, the reef was barely awash. At high tide there was as much as four feet of often rough water, with surf too deep to permit vehicles to come in under their own power. All cargo had to be manhandled, towed, pushed, paddled, pulled, or carried in amphibious vehicles over hundreds of yards of reef to the beach. Fuel drums were dropped off from landing craft and floated ashore by wading Marines, who soon developed coral cuts and painful saltwater sores. "Beach parties could more properly be called *reef* parties in this operation since the reef was where the beach parties were set up," observed one report. "They worked from life rafts, floats, in the water and generally all over the reef keeping things moving."[33]

Coming ashore at 0730 to personally check on the 3rd Division's situation at Asan, General Roy Geiger was greeted by heavy mortar and 75mm shell fire on the beachhead. At about 0830 a mortar shell made a direct hit on the division's message center. The explosion killed the operations officer, Lieutenant Colonel Chevy White. Twenty other men manning the division's radios were wounded. Geiger's aide noted in his diary that the same "mortar barrage was extremely close to us."[34]

Clinging to a hillside overlooking the Red Beaches, Sergeant Fred L. DiDomenico saw another shell make a direct hit on a machine-gun crew. "So we spent the morning holding the ponchos, picking up body parts," he recalled. "And one of the bodies, the mortar must have hit him directly or close by—there were no arms, no legs, no head. . . . [T]he chest cavity was there, but it was just like someone took his body and wiped out all the entrail parts of the body and wiped it clean."[35]

The shelling eased somewhat as the morning wore on. Bulldozers arrived ashore to construct road ramps from the beach to the coastal highway, allowing LVTs, DUKWs, and other vehicles easier access inland. Two cranes were positioned on the reef and by noon a steady flow of cargo was streaming in to supply dumps established on the other side of the coastal road.

To deal with the cliff in the 21st Marines area, engineers rigged up a hanging basket trolley. "Anchored at the top and bottom of the cliff on a 45-degree angle, a heavy line made the track," noted First Lieutenant Arthur A. Frances. "A pulley supported a navy wire stretcher. Guy lines at either end of the basket-stretcher guided its wounded cargo coming down, or ammunition and water going up. Once in operation, that basket made the trip up and down at practically all hours of the day and night."[36]

The continuing stalemate at Bundschu Ridge forced the 21st Marines to remain in place during the day on what was increasingly becoming a Japanese bull's-eye. Lieutenant Frances recalled one foxhole the morning of W+1 that contained a dead Japanese on the bottom, a dead Marine on top of him, and another dead Japanese on top of the Marine. Casualties mounted as the Marines endured enemy mortars and machine-gun fire from the two dominating hills that had not been marked on their invasion maps. Naval gunfire and artillery seemed to make little impression on the incoming fire. Corporal John Wlach, a twenty-three-year-old from New York City's Upper East Side, chronicled the carnage among one platoon from the 2nd Battalion. "Bodies were thrown out of foxholes," he said "Spinal columns were split open like melons. Some of the bodies were intact, but their skin had this strange purple color. Their mouths were agape and their eyes were bulging. That's when I realized they'd died from concussion."[37]

Hunkering low in their foxholes, the besieged Marines were startled by the sudden appearance of what to most would have considered a living relic—their forty-eight-year-old master gunnery sergeant, Israel Margolis. Short and wiry, the Russian-born Margolis had served with the army in France during World War I, then joined the Marines following demobilization. In the decades since, he had served all over the hemisphere, from the Caribbean to China. His present duty as an ordnance expert should have kept him off the front lines, but Margolis had apparently seen the stream of wounded coming down the hill and decided he was needed on the ridge.

He arrived as the Japanese singled out one of the 2nd Battalion's machine-gun positions. "In succession, five Marines tried to man that gun and each was hit," related Sergeant Alvin M. Josephy. "The fifth, though wounded, tried to drag the gun to a new position." Margolis went to the wounded Marine's aid and was himself badly wounded in the legs and hips in a mortar shell explosion. "We got Margolis out of there, but he was dying," recalled Corporal Emmanuel ("Bill") Ubertaccio.

Pharmacist's Mate Second Class Virgil Warren pulled the sergeant to the cliff edge. When Margolis opened his eyes, Warren asked if he wanted anything. The old veteran, probably realizing he was dying, managed a nod. "Please," he whispered. "Please sing God Bless America."

Warren swallowed and began a shaky rendition of "God Bless America." A few other men huddled nearby, joined in. "We did the best we could with it," recalled Ubertaccio. Margolis, a naturalized citizen from a Yiddish-speaking household in Philadelphia, took his last breath in the silence that followed.[38]

The best news for General Allen Turnage once again came from the right of the beachhead where the 9th Marines benefitted from less challenging terrain and weakening resistance. Jumping off at 0715 in a sweep to the south toward an eventual planned linkup with the Marine Brigade, the regiment overran numerous enemy positions—most abandoned—including a bivouac area large enough to accommodate a regiment. Only sporadic resistance was encountered from rearguard units of the Japanese 3rd Battalion, 18th Regiment, which had been ordered to withdraw into the hills to the east. Among the booty left behind were two new Japanese half-tracks abandoned by an enemy antiaircraft unit. Always on the lookout for more transport, both were quickly appropriated by the 9th Marines. Captain John L'Estrange from the III Amphibious Corps Motor Transport Battalion wandered through Piti Navy Yard, which was captured without a fight. "I walked into one of the buildings at the yard and the first thing I saw was a desk calendar," he recalled. "It was still open at December 10, 1941, the day the island had been captured. Not a thing had changed."[39] An American flag was still in its storage locker under the navy yard flagpole where it had rested undisturbed since the Japanese invasion.

As the 2nd Battalion secured Piti Navy Yard, Colonel Edward A. Craig ordered his 3rd Battalion to seize Cabras Island, a mile-long finger of an islet that formed the northern edge of Apra Harbor. A causeway connecting the islet to shore had been heavily mined, so the battalion made a shore-to-shore assault in amphibious tractors, supported by eighteen amtanks. Following a full-scale naval and air bombardment, the troop-carrying LVTs lurched ashore at 1425 under billowing black smoke from a burning fuel dump. Scaling ladders had been provided to help the Marines surmount the sheer face behind the landing beach, but fortunately there was no opposition.

"We went in there and I thought, well, we're going to lose the whole company here," recalled Sergeant Jim Milliff, a veteran of Bougainville. "And we jump out of the amtracs and there's a great big pillbox staring at us, a big, black hole, you know? So *bam, bam, bam, bam,* and we are all shooting at it. And I yell, 'Down men, let's sneak around.' We sneak up to it, and of course it's empty."[40] To their considerable relief, the landing was opposed only by heavy brambles and hundreds of mines, one of which claimed an LVT. After pausing for the night, the battalion finished occupying the island the next morning and turned it over to the 14th Defense Battalion.

Aboard the transport USS *Lamar*, preparations were underway that evening to commit the mortal remains of Corporal Daniel Francis Alfano to the sea. The severely wounded twenty-three-year-old New York native had been brought aboard the previous afternoon, having gone ashore with the 3rd Battalion, 4th Marines on the Agat beachhead earlier in the day.

In a letter to the chaplain of the 4th Marines, ship's chaplain B. C. Barrett noted that Alfano, who was unconscious when he arrived aboard ship, was not wearing his dog tags, which limited the information immediately available to medical personnel.

"Our men gave him the best," Barrett assured his fellow chaplain in the letter, which may have been intended for the young Marine's family. "We gave him transfusions and he was never alone for a single moment, but through the divine mercies of God, he was taken to his eternal rest before he awakened to much suffering." The former Marine Raider was committed to the sea at latitude 18° 16'N, longitude 144° 19'E at 1905 hours on W+1. "Nothing could be more beautiful than his burial at sea," wrote Barrett. "The sun was setting over the calm clear blue water of the Pacific. . . . He was a hero to us, for he gave his life for you at home and for us out here."[41]

Aboard the USS *Wayne*, also standing off Guam, chaplain Lieutenant Robert S. Toulman addressed the more practical aspects of burials at sea in a memo not intended for civilians back on the home front. He wrote,

At least twenty canvas pouches should be available for burial at sea. . . . The pouch should have an air hole at the head end for the escape of the air within the pouch when the body is committed to the sea or it will not immediately sink. The thirty-pound weight required to insure sinking should be secured between the legs at the ankle for proper balance. Our weights were one-gallon cans filled with cement and were made up ahead of time. Identification of the remains should be thorough and not dependent solely on the fingerprint. The most important item is a careful charting of the teeth by the dental officer.[42]

CHAPTER 16

TO THE TOP OF BUNDSCHU

GENERAL ALLEN TURNAGE REPORTED TO III AMPHIBIOUS CORPS ON JULY 22 THAT enemy resistance had increased "considerably" on the division left and center. One of his battalions in the 21st Marines was about 40 percent depleted. Colonel W. Carvel Hall had even more sobering news regarding his hard-hit 3rd Marines. Hall reported he had lost 615 men killed, wounded, or missing. Captain Geary Bundschu's Company A had been especially hard hit. The only remaining line officer in the company was Lieutenant Jim Gallo, and he was wounded and soon to be evacuated.

Hall planned to renew the attack on Bundschu Ridge in the morning, but his mood was grim. "I am going to try and advance up that mess in front of me," he advised division. "What I really need is a battalion whereas I have only 160 men to use on that 500-yard slope. They might move to the top but they couldn't advance on. Company A is down to about 30–40 men with an air liaison officer in charge. Company E is down to half strength. They have no strength to push on."[1]

<hr>

Sunday, July 23, arrived relatively clear with an occasional passing shower. Sunrise was at 0604. As Marines on the Asan front gathered themselves to renew the attack, all available weapons—offshore ships, artillery, half-tracks, and tanks—unleashed their guns on the ridges and gullies barring the way inland. In the center of the 3rd Marines lodgment, the 1st and 2nd Battalions jumped off at 0900 in another attempt to secure Bundschu Ridge. Colonel Hall had also given Major Henry Aplington a provisional infantry company formed from regimental weapons personnel. Captain William E. Moore's E Company, which had been badly shot up the day before, led the 2nd Battalion's assault on the left. At the same time, C Company, commanded by Captain David ("Dave") I. Zeitlin, moved once again to flank the ridge from the right. Company A, which was no longer combat effective with 65 percent casualties, was spared another try up the middle. Aplington pulled the survivors back to the CP area to regroup.

This time Zeitlin's company worked its way into a position looking down on an assortment of bunkers commanding the approaches to the ridge. Lieutenant Paul Smith could see Marines lying flat and motionless on the slopes below. "From my vantage point I couldn't tell which of the troops were dead and which alive, but some of the grotesque prone postures suggested that there were more dead than seemed justified by the filthy little bit of real estate involved," he observed. Smith's platoon brought up bazookas and knocked out thirteen bunkers from the flanking cliff, without casualties to themselves "How many Japanese were in them, I never knew," said Smith.[2]

At long last, Marines assaulting across the open slopes caught a break. Most of the Japanese—reinforcements from the 9th Company, 38th Infantry—had pulled back from the forward positions during the night. Scrambling to the top of the ridge, E Company found the forward edge furrowed with shallow trenches and spider holes. "They wound aimlessly about the summit like the tracks of a huge worm," observed a Marine.[3] Bodies and parts of bodies, many apparently butchered by mortar fire, littered the area. A dead Marine lieutenant knelt in front of a Japanese machine-gun pit, his carbine resting across his knees. The two Japanese inside had been shot through the head. An unexploded American grenade lay between them. The side of the Marine lieutenant's head had been stoved in. Two enemy officers, wearing new equipment, had evidently carried out some sort of suicide pact. One officer had a sword thrust through his neck; the other, his sword scabbard empty, sported a bullet hole in his forehead. Two other dead Japanese huddled together in what had been an unsuccessful effort to escape the mortar fire raining down on them. One live enemy soldier remained behind in the forward entrenchments. Both his legs had been blown off below the knees. The other survivors had withdrawn further back on the plateau. "Our 81 mortars pretty much cleared out their defenses, but there were still plenty of Japanese left in the spider trenches and foxholes," recalled PFC Charles G. Moore, a rifleman with E Company. "Our job was to flush them out."

Moore ran up an embankment and sprayed the trench just beyond with his BAR. "One hole was sheltered by a big boulder, and a soldier (tall for a Japanese) lunged at me with his bayonet," observed Moore. "I knocked away his piece with the barrel of my BAR and his weapon fell on the ground. He grabbed a knife from his belt and attacked me again." Having run the twenty-round magazine dry, Moore reversed his grip on the BAR, intending to club his assailant, but the barrel was so hot he dropped the gun. The Japanese lashed out with the knife and sliced open Moore's arm. "Then I pulled my Ka-bar and slashed him across the head," said Moore. "It was a deep gash and the skin fell off his brow and down to cover his eyes. It was an easy matter to dispose of him after that."[4]

Companies E and C linked up on top of the ridge about an hour before noon. The Marines finally had possession of the crucial height, but the Japanese had exacted a terrible price. Lieutenant Smith later ran into an A Company lieutenant—presumably Jim Gallo—who expressed bitterness over how long it had taken for the powers that be to agree to a flanking movement on the ridge. "His dead captain had suggested such a maneuver when the company was first held up, but a higher-ranking officer had told him to go and take the ridge frontally," said Smith.[5]

Ironically, Colonel Hall subsequently insinuated that he deserved credit for devising a plan to seize the ridge, observing with some self-aggrandizing latitude, "The 1st Battalion, 3rd Marines finally surmounted the cliff in their immediate front by a most unusual maneuver. Acting under orders, they abandoned their position in the front line, then moved in single file to the right and left, then moved forward over the easier terrain behind the units on their flanks, then (still moving in single file) they established a line on the high ground above the cliffs and filled the gap in the division line. The Japanese, probably thinking this area un-assailable, had only lightly covered this area."[6]

Cyril O'Brien trudged over the steep slope where half his old company—Company E—had been killed or wounded the day before. Had it not been for his transfer as a combat correspondent, he likely would have been among the huddled dead still scattered on the hillside or among the wounded now crowding the wardrooms of off-shore ships. "The Marine dead formed an uneven line across the slope. Most of them had their feet dug into the soil as if ready to charge again," recalled O'Brien. "There was Pappy, his name stenciled on his canteen cover. A bullet had ripped away the first 'P' in his name." O'Brien's former assistant squad leader—a man so physically strong he could throw full ammunition cases around as if they were empty—lay nearby. The first scout—O'Brien's tent mate for months—lay with his face turned toward the sky. "He was always promising himself a white Christmas in '45," observed O'Brien. There would be no more Christmases, white or otherwise, for him. A Marine dubbed "the Beast" because of his size had made it to within five yards of a machine-gun nest before a burst tore out his chest.[7]

Among the 2nd Battalion's casualties was a fifty-year-old corpsman who had been awarded the Croix de Guerre for bravery as a member of an ambulance company in World War I. In an outfit where a Marine over the age of twenty-five was routinely referred to as "Pops," Chief Pharmacist's Mate Paul B. Binder was a veritable dinosaur. Determined to get back into the service though well over the age limit, Binder, a former golf pro and insurance salesman from Pennsylvania, was repeatedly turned down by the Army and Navy until someone apparently got tired of listening to him and allowed him into the Navy. He had been cited for bravery at Bougainville, but his luck ran out on Guam when he was fatally wounded by a shell fragment that hit him in the face.

With "victory" finally in hand, Major Aplington's 1st Battalion also experienced what the major termed "the most unnecessary blow of the Guam campaign" that afternoon. At 1500, the last in a flight of Navy aircraft responding to a call for air support from the 2nd Battalion roared in low and dropped his bomb short—right in the middle of B Company's reserve position. Eight Marines were killed and three wounded. It was a tragic ending to a tragic chapter.

Possession of Bundschu Ridge finally helped stabilize the 3rd Division's grasp of the high ground immediately dominating the beachhead, but due to the heavy casualties, the line was thin, consisting in large part of widely separated strong points. The casualties on July 23 included Lieutenant Colonel Ralph Houser, whose battalion ran into fierce opposition when it threatened to interdict the Mount Tenjo Road leading into the heights overlooking Asan. Houser, who had been wounded on W-Day by a shell fragment in one arm, suffered a gunshot wound to his right hand and arm and had to be evacuated. He recalled that the Japanese who shot him "bobbed up just five feet away and fired point blank. He had played possum while I crawled up to look the situation over."[8] Turnage asked Roy Geiger for a combat team from the 77th Infantry Division to bolster his lines, but Geiger was unwilling to commit his reserve this early in the game. Still well short of the Force Beachhead Line (FBL) running along the dominating ground roughly a mile inland, Turnage would have to make do with what he had.

⚓

Deeper in the red clay ridges beyond the Asan beachhead, General Takeshi Takashina was also considering his options. As his defenses deteriorated on July 23, he called a late-afternoon staff meeting to review the situation. Though his men had inflicted heavy losses on the landing forces, they had suffered high casualties of their own. American naval gunfire and artillery were overwhelming. The enemy had been slowed but not stopped. The Americans had assembled large numbers of tanks and were constructing roadways to get them inland, where they would soon be positioned to overwhelm Japanese defenses.

"Most of our front-line commanders were killed by noon of the 23rd, about 70 percent of the men were lost, so the remaining fighting strength was small," observed Colonel Hideyuki Takeda. Small arms ammunition was running short, explosive charges for antitank defense were practically exhausted, and 90 percent of the artillery had been destroyed. Daytime movements were subject to strafing from planes descending to as low as thirty to forty meters; the shelling from warships seemed endless. Even water was in short supply. "There was a small stream running through the valley, but since the water was tinted with blood and the bodies of soldiers killed in the two-day-long battle lay in the stream giving off a putrid smell, the water was not fit to drink," noted Takeda. Drinking water had to be manhandled into the hills in drums.[9]

The situation in the Agat sector, where the 38th Infantry had lost 80 percent of its men and most of its artillery, was especially unfavorable. "Fortunately, however, the U.S. forces' pursuit is slow and they are only engaged in extending the final beach line toward Sumay Airfield at a slow pace," observed Takeda. "Therefore, the battle situation in the Adelup Point and Mt. Mangan sector will not be affected for the time being."[10]

As General Takashina saw it, he had two courses of action: he could withdraw into the jungled terrain of northern Guam for round two, or he could take the offensive in an attempt to drive the Marines into the sea. The second option was more compatible with "the Imperial General Headquarters' conventional policy on the island defense and was based on the concept characteristic of the Japanese Army to serve the country at the sacrifice of life," observed Colonel Takeda. Retreating to the north for a protracted battle "was very likely to become meaningless" as far as the final outcome of the campaign was concerned.[11]

Pondering input from his staff, General Takashina made his decision. He would attack. He would throw the bulk of his remaining strength at the Marine beachhead at Asan on the night of July 25–26 and "overwhelm and destroy" the enemy.[12]

❧

The beaches and hills at Asan had become reeking open-air graveyards by the second and third day of the landing. The 3rd Marine Division listed 239 men killed and 1,251 wounded as of July 23; the Marine Brigade reported 104 killed and 557 wounded. Nearly 1,300 Japanese—probably a conservative estimate—had been killed, according to IIIAC figures. Most of them lay rotting where they'd fallen. Major Louis Metzger found one of the latter the hard way. "While on the beach I put my hand on a 'sandbag' which turned out to be a very dead and decomposed

Japanese soldier," he related. "He had so deteriorated that my hand sank into his body." Metzger spent the next few hours repeatedly rinsing his hands in the ocean in an effort to rid them of the cloying stench.[13]

The 3rd Marine Division was the only unit with a regular graves registration section. The Marine Brigade had put together a provisional unit that also handled burials for the 77th Infantry Division. Both organizations got off to a slow start. "Some difficulty in getting ashore was experienced due to the desire of some units to keep the graves registration section on board for unloading ship until D+1 or D+2," observed a IIIAC report. "This resulted in large numbers of bodies of men killed in the initial phase remaining unburied along the beaches for one or two days and resulted in hasty burials which were unnecessary."[14]

A corps order directed that bodies be sprayed with sodium arsenite, a poisonous compound that retarded bacteria and decay, in an effort to prevent the spread of disease. "Bodies will be marked in a manner plainly indicating they have been sprayed," noted the order. "Personnel will be warned of danger of touching sprayed bodies."[15] Unfortunately, the 3rd Marine Division's supply of sodium arsenite failed to arrive on shore until the campaign was nearly over.

PFC Robert C. ("Cork") Blaemire, ashore at the Asan beaches with the 1st Armored Amphibian Battalion, found himself "volunteered" to a burial detail as hasty efforts were made to deal with the decomposing dead. "The sergeant says, 'You, you and you guys just volunteered. You're going to be on the burial detail,'" he recalled. "They're bringing the guys down from the hills that were killed, the infantry boys. You had to dig a hole. And they bring one body and put it alongside our hole. Some of the guys were real bloated and turned black. It was a mess. And all the unidentified were all in one pile, over here by themselves." The temporary burials were hastily done with the assumption that remains would later be moved to permanent cemeteries. "That night it rained and all the guys that we buried floated to the top of the grave," recalled Blaemire.[16]

Sergeant Buck Daley was shocked to see how dead Marines were handled as they were brought down from the hills. "I remember seeing one of the trucks down at the beach being unloaded," he said. "The bodies were stiff as boards, piled six feet deep in the truck box and being thrown off like cordwood."[17]

Among the 4th Marines dead, observed PFC Donald B. Heffron, was 1st Battalion runner PFC Robert W. Ball of Detroit, Michigan, who was listed as killed in action on July 23. The twenty-one-year-old Ball, former captain of his high school football team, had apparently been caught alive by the Japanese. "He was found staked to the ground with a 2x2 stake driven through his chest and about 24 inches into the ground," said Heffron. "His arms and legs were twisted grotesquely and his eyeballs were lying out on his cheeks. . . . I can never forget the sight of it."[18]

A day-by-day accounting of the carnage ashore was meticulously recorded by the medical officer about the USS *Fayette*, which had taken aboard 203 casualties since W-Day. Of that number, three were already dead when they arrived, and thirteen others died later. Broken down individually, casualties included bullet wound (91), shell fragment wound (77), bayonet wound (1), burn (1), blast (15), other injury (7), combat neurosis (5), malaria (3), hernia (1), diarrhea (1), gastric ulcer (1). A breakdown of wound sites noted: head (10 percent), neck (4 percent), chest (8 percent), abdomen (6 percent), genitalia (2 percent), upper extremity (28 percent), lower extremity (42 percent).

The ship's medical officer, Lieutenant Commander J. H. Wallace, wrote that he was "impressed" by the extreme violence of wounds inflicted by shell fragments, particularly from mortar fire. "These wounds were frequently ground so full of dirt that debridement was necessarily extensive and difficult." Medical personnel also found it difficult to differentiate between blast injuries and combat neurosis. "Several patients who had been subjected to violent blast presented the picture of neurosis or hysteria but it is difficult to know where organic brain damage ends and emotional trauma begins," he observed. In addition to the three patients who were already dead when brought aboard, four died the day they were admitted, seven lived one day, and two lived two days. Of the total of sixteen dead, ten had multiple wounds, and six had single wounds. In those having single wounds, four were of the skull with accompanying extravasation of brain tissue, one was a sucking wound of the chest, and one was of the abdomen.[19]

PFC Wayne Barham was hit in the legs by mortar shell fragments the first night ashore. He spent the next morning on Blue Beach amid a litter of discarded gas masks, fervently praying as shells exploded all around. A corpsman holding a bottle of plasma overhead was killed along with his patient, even as Barham futilely yelled at him to get down. A shell fragment punched a hole through the back of Barham's helmet and exited through the top, leaving a jagged tear but somehow only creasing his skull. Finally evacuated to a hospital ship, he was given a tongue depressor to bite down on and told to stand and hold onto a bunk while a doctor dug the metal out of his legs. The next day he was well enough to go topside and watch new casualties come aboard. One was a wild-eyed Marine who was hauled up and over the side. "He fell to the deck and crawled around on all fours looking for a place to hide," recalled Barham. "He whimpered and made strange sounds like a frightened dog." Two days later Barham was sent back into combat with instructions to have the bandages on his legs changed every day.[20]

Also evacuated from the Asan beachhead, PFC Frank Simone's combat days were over. Wounded the first day of the landing in the assault on Chonito Cliff, the Massachusetts youth lay in a bunk on a ship offshore. Around him, men were moaning in pain; some were dying. Medical personnel were hard-pressed to keep up. "They were so busy with everybody that they'd just come by and smell the bandages and this and that," he remembered. One day the smell was coming from his hand. "Apparently I was getting an infection in my left hand. They said it looks like gangrene is going to set in there." A doctor did some more surgery on his hand and returned him to his rack.

And there's this poor guy must have been shellshocked right over me [crying]: Mommy, I want to come home. Mommy, I want to come home. *And I'm looking at him; he had to be shellshocked. And I says, "Aw, be quiet, will ya?"*

Mommy I wanna go home. Mommy I wanna go home.

I says, "Jesus can you shut this guy up?" They say, "We can't do anything about it."

I says, "All right. I'm sorry."[21]

Sunset on July 23 found PFCs Russell Elushik and Joseph G. Basso dug in with B Company, 1st Battalion, 21st Marines along the high ground to the right of the 3rd Marines. The company had landed with 217 men; over the past three days it had been pared down to about 75. The depleted battalion had relieved Lieutenant Colonel Eustace Smoak's 2nd Battalion the day before and was now deployed over some two thousand yards of line, which spread the Marines very thin. In civilian life, the two PFCs would have been an unlikely pair. A big, easygoing twenty-four-year-old, Elushik was the son of a Ukrainian immigrant father and an Austrian mother who had settled in Racine, Wisconsin. A record-setting high school shot-putter, he had gone on to play center on his junior college football team before joining the Marines. Twenty-two-year-old Basso was from Brooklyn, New York, the son of an Italian immigrant. He had quit school after the eighth grade to go to work, eventually ending up in a machine shop before going into the Marines in August 1942.

Basso was trying to catch some sleep in the bottom of their forward foxhole when he was jolted awake by a long burst from Elushik's BAR. He grabbed for his rifle as Japanese swarmed out of the darkness. It was too late. The two Marines were quickly overwhelmed, pulled from the foxhole, and dragged, struggling and yelling for help, toward enemy lines. Elushik finally tore free and made a break back toward Marine lines. In the confusion, Basso's captors let go of him to chase after Elushik. Dashing back to the foxhole, Basso snatched up Elushik's BAR. The Japanese had overtaken Elushik and knocked him to the ground. Basso opened up with the BAR trying not to hit his buddy. Several Japanese went down; the others disappeared, leaving the shaken New Yorker alone in the hole.

Elushik was grievously wounded. His left hand had been chopped off, apparently by a sword; both his arms and legs were broken, and he had been bayoneted through the neck and back. He was still alive when help arrived to carry him out but soon succumbed to his injuries. Suffering from extreme shock, Basso was evacuated, though he later returned to his unit.[22] Over a dozen dead Japanese were found around the scene of the encounter. No one apparently gave much thought to why the Japanese had not simply killed the two Marines outright. Events would offer an explanation soon enough.

At IIIAC Headquarters, General Geiger was closely following the Marine Brigade's progress toward Orote and its all-important airfield. Having seized Agat on July 21, the 22nd Marines spent the next two days fighting through a succession of muddy coastal rice paddies against rear guard elements of the Japanese 2nd Battalion, 38th Infantry. "These paddies were about 200 square yards covered with two to three feet of water," recalled Platoon Sergeant Thomas R. O'Neill. "Around each paddy was a dike about three feet wide and used as foot paths."

O'Neill's platoon had been relatively lucky so far, having lost only two men on W-Day—one caught a machine-gun burst in the stomach as they moved off the beach; the other was hit soon afterward by another machine gun that took the top of his head off—but their first encounter with the paddies on W+1 was not encouraging. One man was wounded by artillery fire as they went forward. Then, as the first squad ventured out onto one of the dike paths, a Japanese machine gun promptly opened up. The initial burst knocked down two men, one killed and one shot through the knee.[23] O'Neill and two other men took to the water and hauled the wounded man back. In the 1st Battalion, bazooka man Jack Cadden of Orcas Island, Washington, won a Silver Star on July 23 for making three trips across one of the rice paddies to bring up his bazooka and more ammunition. During one trip, he was shot through the ear. Later, he admitted, "All I remember as I was running across that field with all them bullets flying was that I was scared stiff."[24]

The following day, in an effort to avoid the paddies, Shermans from the regimental tank company tried to advance down the road leading to Orote. Japanese antitank guns put one tank out of commission, and another hit a mine. Sergeant O'Neill's platoon made it to the top of a rise, where they formed a line in what had once been a village. "The place was swarming with Japs," he recalled. "Two Sherman tanks were having a field day, but one was in trouble. Japs were swarming all over it, pounding on the armor. Riflemen were picking them off by well-aimed shots. A third tank was on fire."[25]

Five Japanese tanks attempted to block the advance on the morning of July 24, only to be blown to pieces by Marine Shermans. The Shermans then slugged their way up the coastal road, blasting concrete and coconut log emplacements. At 1310, as the 22nd Marines broke through a Japanese roadblock along the coastal road, Geiger messaged General Lemuel Shepherd, "Take Orote as quickly as possible so that we can go on with the war X You will receive orders today for this attack for July 25 X Your Brigade has done splendid work congratulations to all hands X."[26]

Geiger may have hoped for a quick conquest, but everyone knew Orote was likely to be a tough nut. As the Marines closed on the peninsula neck, they came under fire from artillery concealed in the cliffs and on adjacent Neye Island. Six amtanks from the 1st Armored Amphibian Battalion took to the water parallel to the peninsula cliffs in an effort to beat down the enemy fire with their 37mm guns. "All went well for the first fifteen to twenty minutes," observed First Lieutenant Robert A. Fish, watching from the turret of his amtank. "Then I started seeing shell splashes and could hear projectiles going overhead." Through his field glasses, Fish spotted a muzzle flash from what looked like a cave position about one thousand yards away. Japanese soldiers with small arms were also visible firing on the amtanks from the shoreline.

Before Fish could react, his amtank was hit. "I think the shell exploded under the turret basket," he said. "The explosion stunned me, and I could see blood spurting from my legs. Knowing that others had been injured, I ordered the crew to abandon tank. The next thing I knew several of us were in the water, and the Japs on the beach were still sending small arms fire our way. We couldn't get on the reef because the small arms fire was heavy."[27] Another amtank took a direct hit on the turret, and the remaining tanks were so riddled with shrapnel and bullet holes that they were lucky to make it back into Agat without sinking. The foray cost the tankers two killed, one missing, and eight wounded.

Six LCI(G)s sailed up in another effort to knock out the enemy guns and also took a pounding. LCI(G) 366 and LCI(G) 439 were each hit several times by a gun located in a cave on Neye Island. LCI(G) 366 had three killed and fourteen wounded; LCI(G) 439 lost two dead and twelve wounded. The six gunboats directed 1,940 rounds of 40mm and 5,547 rounds of 20mm at the positions, and fire from the emplacements finally slackened.

Back with the 1st Armored Amphibian Battalion, PFC Luther Flattum and Platoon Sergeant Harvey B. ("Sacktime") Evans watched as the dead and wounded were removed from the amtanks. "When a dead CP [radioman] was lifted out feet first and they came to his head, which wasn't there, Sacktime cracked," Flattum recalled. "He was evacuated the next day."

Corporal Fred Addison and another crewman were detailed to clean up the interior of the damaged amtanks. They went in with rags and buckets. "I remember mopping blood out of the radioman's area," said Addison. "The interior of a tank is very hot in the tropics; the sweet sickly smell stuck with me for a long time."[28]

Despite the mauling of the LVT(A)s, by dusk the 22nd Marines had largely achieved their objectives. The 1st Battalion was dug in at the entrance to the peninsula, while the 3rd Battalion had eradicated Japanese hill positions and was settling in about four hundred yards short of Apra Harbor. The 2nd Battalion, which had swung around further inland while the main assault punched down the roadway, had advanced up the coast and occupied the high ground overlooking the harbor at the village of Atantano. Meanwhile, the 306th Infantry had come ashore to relieve the 4th Marines in the beachhead area, as Shepherd marshalled his brigade for the coming assault.

Trudging down from Mount Alifan on the way to help out at Orote, George Aspley's company of the 4th Marines passed through the detritus of the 38th Infantry's failed July 21 counterattack.[29] "The area had been completely devastated by naval gunfire and the stench from Japanese body parts that had been blown everywhere was terrible," he recalled. "If an intact corpse was encountered, they were so swollen and bloated that I was afraid it would explode if accidently touched. Many of the body parts were unrecognizable because of the huge mass of flies and maggots that were swarming all over them."[30]

Negotiating the rubble that had been Agat, the column passed some Marines sitting forlornly on the steps of a demolished house. Aspley recognized them as some of the men from the Marine Air Wing who had gone AWOL back at Eniwetok to join the invasion force. They informed the passing Marines they had been detained and ordered to await transportation back to their unit. A little further on, eight or ten Japanese POWs clad only in their *fundoshi* undergarments squatted in a barbed wire enclosure. "These were the first live captured Japanese that we had encountered and we immediately gave them the finger and other hostile signs," remarked Aspley. "The American guards moved between us and the captured Japanese, hoping that we wouldn't shoot them on the spot."[31]

Platoon Sergeant Thomas O'Neill got about an hour's sleep in a roadside culvert that night before he was awakened by Japanese mortar fire. "One round killed Foley," he noted. "The same burst left Williams without his right leg, although Gilispy was able to get to him with first aid, he cried with pain the rest of the night."[32]

The original schedule called for the attack on Orote to get off the next day (July 25), but Shepherd requested—and received from General Geiger—a twenty-four-hour delay to reorganize. The relief of the 4th Marines by the 306th Infantry had taken longer than expected. Furthermore, the successful expansion of the Agat beachhead over the past four days had come at a price. Casualties in the brigade totaled 924—137 killed, 700 wounded, and 87 missing—and the survivors were tired.

As it turned out, there was still considerable fighting during the Marine Brigade's "day of rest" as units maneuvered to shorten and straighten the line across the peninsula neck. Ray Gillespie's K Company was called up at 1400 from reserve to join the 3rd Battalion's attack on the right of the 22nd Marines. The company was quickly pinned down in a banana grove by two Japanese tanks about three hundred yards to their front. Machine gunners, supported by a line of enemy riflemen extending to either side of the tanks, were industriously shredding the large banana tree leaves overhead. Cries for corpsmen rose all along the line. Bazooka teams came up, but there seemed to be a problem with the rockets. "When they did fire, the shells only lobbed out about 60 yards in front of our line and hit the ground with no effect," said Gillespie.[33]

Gillespie was busy firing at two Japanese riflemen who kept popping up to take a shot in his direction before ducking down again. Lying by his side, his platoon leader, Lieutenant James W. Raynes, a former schoolteacher from Texas, nudged him and announced, "I just got the gunner." He directed Gillespie's attention to an enemy machine gun just to the right of the two riflemen Gillespie had been trying to pick off. "As we watched, the Japanese dragged their dead gunner back and the machine gun was manned again," recalled Gillespie. "We both opened up on the enemy around the gun and scored direct hits and the gun was silent again."[34]

The Japanese tanks finally backed down behind a knoll, and the firing tapered off. Dead and wounded Marines were gathered up as the company waited for its own tank support to make its way forward. To the company's misfortune, battalion commander Lieutenant Colonel Clair W. Shisler arrived first, resplendent "in his clean (band-box) dungarees, ordering us to move out," recalled Gillespie. The thirty-two-year-old Shisler had spent six years as an enlisted man before receiving a commission in 1937. He had been awarded a Silver Star for his "aggressive fighting spirit" leading the 3rd Battalion during the Marshall Islands campaign, but some worried that his insistence on results came with no regard for the cost.

K Company's commander, twenty-five-year-old Captain Harry D. Hedrick of Winter Haven, Florida, balked at Shisler's order to immediately resume the assault. "I need our tanks up here," he told the colonel.

Hedrick, who had graduated from the University of Florida in 1941 with a degree in forestry before joining the Marines, had narrowly escaped death during the Marshall Islands campaign when a Japanese bullet punched through the top of his helmet, grazing his skull. Considering the resistance his company had just encountered, prudence told him to wait for the armor—the Shermans were already on their way—but Shisler didn't want to hear it. "You're not waiting for any goddamn tanks, Captain," he snapped. "Move your line out now!"

Hedrick, now on his feet, yelled, "Move out!"

"All of us were up now and began walking forward," recalled Gillespie. "The captain and top kick [First Sergeant J. T.] Langley were about twenty feet in front of the line and my attention was drawn to them; they moved five feet and then five more feet when the whole Japanese line erupted. How many bullets hit the captain, I don't know. But his body turned and twitched a few times before he fell."[35] As the Marines went prone and opened fire in return, the Shermans belatedly arrived, knocking out an enemy tank with two rounds. Advancing alongside the Shermans, the Marines found a second enemy tank that had been abandoned. The Japanese had pulled out.

By late afternoon the brigade—with the 4th Marines taking position on the left and the 22nd Marines on the right—had cemented its grip on the narrow neck of the peninsula. Casualties in the 22nd Marines had been heavy—the 1st Battalion reported one officer left in each of its three companies—but the brigade was now poised to launch an assault down the peninsula the following day. Meanwhile, prospects of a linkup between the Asan and Agat beachheads were improving. On the previous day, a thirty-man patrol from the 9th Marines had scouted a mile and a half down the Piti-Sumay Road toward Orote Peninsula, encountering only sporadic small arms fire. It appeared the enemy had hastily withdrawn from the shore area. Roads and bridges remained intact, and "huge dumps of all classes of supply" were found, "enough to service a regiment, but no traces of the regiment," according to reports.[36] Now, on the afternoon of July 25, as his brigade secured the entrance to Orote Peninsula, General Shepherd notified IIIAC that the 22nd Regiment's 2nd Battalion had made contact with a patrol from the 9th Marines moving south from Piti. Point of contact was at the Big Gautali River bridge near the village of Atantano just north of Orote Peninsula.

Still piqued at General Turnage's refusal to allow him a few officers when he was struggling to put his brigade together, Shepherd took the opportunity to tweak his counterpart's nose. When his Marines reached the planned control point well before the 3rd Division, he messaged Turnage, "I am at point X, where in hell are you?"

"I don't think he liked it," Shepherd recalled. "But I was just that mad about his not letting me have a few of his officers that I could not help but needle him about the brigade having gotten to this objective before the 3rd Division."[37]

The prospect of finally consolidating the two beachheads had to come as good news to Expeditionary Force commander Lieutenant General Holland M. Smith, a man not celebrated for his patience or his tact, who was becoming increasingly concerned with the 3rd Marine Division's lack of progress. Even as patrols set out to make contact with the Marine Brigade, General Smith arrived to see the situation for himself. Accompanied by General Turnage, Smith inspected the division's front line, which he described as "a short distance inland from the beach." He was especially unimpressed with Colonel Hall's 3rd Marines. "The 3rd Regiment was dug in but I could see no evidence of Japanese in front of them," he wrote later. "Actually, the enemy was in very considerable force on the reverse side of the ridge, running beyond Agana. The situation did not please me."[38]

Assistant division commander Brigadier General Alfred H. Noble later acknowledged the difficulty of the division's position but made it clear that neither he nor General Turnage shared Holland Smith's concerns. "The enemy held the heights all around us there; we were in a pocket," he observed. "It was very difficult to get out of it. We had to take one little part after another. And I had a feeling that some of the higher echelons got a little impatient because we were in that pocket and they thought we weren't going to get out. We never had any such feeling. But we'd rather maneuver out than we would try to scale cliffs with ladders and have the Japs push the ladders back."[39]

General Turnage's plans for July 25 called for an assault on the next piece of high ground facing his division—the Fonte Plateau—which, though he did not know it, was also the location of General Takashina's 29th Division headquarters. In an effort to compensate for his heavy losses over the past four days, Turnage ordered all available men, including service and headquarters personnel, into the line. The most serious fighting during the day involved Lieutenant Colonel Robert ("Bob") E. Cushman's relatively fresh 2nd Battalion, 9th Marines. Cushman's battalion, which had been shifted over from the division right and attached to the 3rd Marines to replace Major Aplington's depleted 1st Battalion, had drawn the figurative short straw: he was assigned to assault Fonte Hill, a key point in the Japanese defense. Just getting into position for the assault was difficult, the twenty-nine-year-old Cushman later recalled, as his men were forced to follow "a tortuous single file path up the side of the cliff to [their] front" to an escarpment of "jumbled coral rock thickly overgrown with jungle trees, shrubs, and vegetation."[40]

To reach its objectives, the battalion would have to attack from its own ridgetop, down into a small valley or draw, and across the Mount Tenjo Road before advancing up a long, bare slope to the jungle-covered crest of Fonte Hill, which was actually more of a plateau. Just across the road was a low cliff roughly ten to twenty feet high dotted with a number of caves. "From the top of the cliff, and from elsewhere along the far side of the road, the ground [was] open and slope[d] up to the top of Fonte," Cushman observed. "Fonte Hill itself [was] covered with jungle growth. . . . Part of the power line [could be] seen where it [ran] up the hill and into the jungle on top."[41]

Apparently detecting the activity to their front, the Japanese dropped a mortar barrage on the Marines just as the two battalions were swapping positions. "The [Japanese] gun positions were so close to the battalion CP that the sound of the shells sliding down the tubes could be distinctly heard," recalled Cushman's executive officer, Major William T. Glass.[42] Despite the mortar fire, Cushman got his attack off at 0930 and secured the lower portion of the Mount Tenjo Road within an hour. The next few hours were spent reorganizing and mopping up pockets of resistance while Marine artillery and naval gunfire worked over the plateau. Tank support had been held up by mines and enemy fire, so at about 1430 Cushman resumed his assault without the hoped-for armor. E Company attacked on the right and F Company on the left, following on the heels of a barrage that included naval gunfire on the rear slopes, artillery fire on the summit, and close support from mortars and machine guns.

Commanding Company E was Captain Lyle Q. Petersen, a dark-haired, genial-looking twenty-five-year-old from Racine, Wisconsin, who had previously served as the company's executive officer. As he and executive officer Lieutenant Maynard W. Schmidt went to cross the road, a Japanese machine gun hidden in the brush on the other side opened up on them. "We were flat on the ground with little cover," said Schmidt. "We hit the dirt and tried to burrow in. Captain Petersen was beside me at the edge of the road. A Jap machine gun caught him in the chest and shoulders. He fell flat again and told me to take over. We pulled him behind some bushes. He died there a few minutes later."[43]

Leading F Company was twenty-four-year-old Captain Louis ("Lou") Hugh Wilson Jr., a drawling, bull-chested veteran of Bougainville, who had played football at Millsap College in Mississippi before joining the Marines. "A recruiter came around one day and had the red stripes down his trouser legs," he recalled of his introduction to the Marines. Wilson liked the look. After signing up, he took his then girlfriend (and future wife) out for a hamburger and informed her he had joined the Marine Corps.

"What is that?" she asked.

"Damned if I know," replied Wilson. "But I guess I will soon find out."

Now Wilson urged his company up Fonte Hill, shouting, "Keep moving! Keep moving!" as Japanese machine guns and mortars picked away at them. Running out to tie in two of his platoons, he felt himself suddenly spun around as if jerked by some invisible hand. His feet went out from under him, and he landed on his shoulder and face in a ditch. He heard his runner, PFC Ernest P. Hayes, who weighed about 135 pounds soaking wet, say to another Marine, "Let's pull the skipper out of there."

"Hell, boys," he reassured them. "I ain't hurt. I'm just scared to death."

Inspection revealed a machine-gun bullet had grazed him across his right knee-cap and another had torn through the tendon behind the knee. Climbing to his feet, Wilson found he could still walk, albeit with a limp. He took four of his sulfa pills— chewing them up dry since his canteen was empty—and hobbled on up the hill.

Fox Company scrambled into the brush at the crest of the hill and hastened to scrape out foxholes. On Wilson's right, half of Lyle Petersen's E Company had also reached the near edge of the jungle atop Fonte; the other half of the company had been held up by a knot of resistance hidden in a draw. Thanks to the lavish use of supporting fires, the afternoon assault up the hill had been accomplished in a matter of minutes, but the toehold was precarious. Wilson established a CP at the center of the line and called his platoon leaders together. By now it was about 1700 hours. He passed the word down the line of shallow foxholes, "No retreat. We've got the high ground and we're going to hold it through the night."[44]

At 1700, Cushman committed G Company on Wilson's left in an effort to reduce a gap between his battalion and the 3rd Marines. Elements of Weapons Company, reorganized as provisional infantry, were also brought up. G and E Companies were directed to dig in by the road near the bottom of the slope, leaving F Company in a salient on the rocky knoll a couple of hundred yards forward of the two flanking units.

No one realized that the battalion and the adjacent 1st Battalion, 21st Marines were now only a couple of hundred yards from General Takashina's command post. The Japanese had brought up reserves, concealing them in a natural depression and behind a low bluff in the vicinity of what had once been a penal farm. Commanding G Company, twenty-six-year-old Major Fraser West "went climbing up this hill up there and . . . looked over this precipice, just a cliff [and] there were thousands of Japanese down there." As West digested this unwelcome scene, Lou Wilson and his runner joined him. Talking in whispers, they decided to get out of there while they still could. "We almost got all the way across this little clearing and they opened up on us," recalled West. "Not one of us got hit. So we got back to our company."

After an intense day of fighting, ammunition had been practically exhausted, and the dribble of supplies making its way up the cliff trail could not be expected to relieve the shortage. Personnel from the CP and all men from the 81mm mortar platoon—leaving only two men per gun—were pressed into service carrying ammunition to the assault companies. As darkness fell, a tank platoon with ammunition and water made its way up the Mount Tenjo Road behind Cushman's battalion. Still shaken by the numerous Japanese he had stumbled upon earlier, Major West corralled the lieutenant in charge of the platoon and urged him keep his Shermans up front and within reach overnight. "Lieutenant, you're going to have to make a decision," West told him. "If you don't stay with us, I don't think we're going to be here in the morning."[45]

The lieutenant stayed, positioning the tanks behind the battalion line. It would prove to be a providential decision for the Marine riflemen.

Out in the sodden hills, the Japanese were on the move. General Takashina had been gathering his forces for two days after deciding on July 23 to launch a mass counterattack on the 3rd Marine Division's beachhead. The preliminary order was disseminated the evening of July 23, with the complete order following on the afternoon of July 24. Reserve forces were drawn from Tumon, Pago, and Agana. The assault on the beachhead the night of July 25–26 was to be coordinated with a breakout by the roughly twenty-five hundred Japanese troops now bottled up by the Marine Brigade on Orote Peninsula.

General Geiger and his staff were not oblivious to the danger. Expending all resources to defeat an enemy amphibious landing at the shoreline was standard Japanese military doctrine, coupled with an emphasis on taking offensive action under almost any circumstances. Marines from the most exalted general down to the lowliest private had come to expect a mass "banzai" attack on the heels of any amphibious landing. Such attacks typically came in the night or in the early morning hours after the initial landing. Surprisingly no such effort had yet been directed at the 3rd Marine Division.

Presumably motivated at least in part by Holland Smith's growing dissatisfaction with the progress of the 3rd Division, Geiger made a lengthy visit to the Asan beachhead on July 25. Coming ashore during the morning, he visited all three of the 3rd Division's infantry regiments over the course of the day. In the 21st Marine sector, he came upon a battalion making an advance along a ridge against stiff opposition from enemy riflemen and machine guns located on the reverse slope. Asked by the general about the view from the crest of the ridge, the battalion CO replied that it would not be safe for him to go any further. "Sorry, I can't see eye to eye with you on that," replied Geiger.[46] Accompanied by his aide, he proceeded cautiously up the slope to have a look.

What Geiger saw from the ridge was not recorded, but there were other signs that trouble was brewing. Chamorros filtering into Marine lines near Adelup Point reported seeing many Japanese in the Fonte–Mount Tenjo–Ylig Bay–Pago Bay area. Enemy troops were especially numerous on the Fonte Plateau. Other Japanese troops had been moving from the Tumon Bay region during the night, they reported, staying off the roads and using streambeds and ravines to get to the Fonte area. Units on the line had also begun to notice an uptick in enemy activity. At daybreak on July 24, a patrol from Lieutenant Colonel Wendell H. Duplantis's 3rd Battalion, 21st Marines "ambushed a group of about twelve quite senior officers who had come forward to orient themselves, a sure sign of a Jap night attack in force," noted the colonel. "Probing attacks had stepped up in frequency and intensity. Every sign pointed toward a major counterattack."[47]

Another apparent scouting party was spotted by Lieutenant Colonel Ronald ("Ron") R. Van Stockum, executive officer of the 1st Battalion, 21st Marines. During a "personal reconnaissance" along the newly established front lines, he noticed about a dozen men moving surreptitiously through a ravine. As the Japanese were so adept at concealment, he initially assumed it was a squad of Marines. "However, they were uniformly attired, and not quite as casual in their movements as our Marines were wont to be," he recalled. "Also, they had their helmets garlanded with small branches, instead of the camouflaged helmet covers worn by our Marines." The patrol had disappeared by the time Van Stockum belatedly realized they were Japanese. "Later we would appreciate more clearly why they were scouting our positions," he remarked.[48]

Whether or not General Takashina realized it, his best opportunity to eradicate the Marine beachhead had already passed. In retrospect, his more effective military option at this point would have been to use Guam's jumbled terrain, with its ridges and gullies, to fight a defensive battle to exact the greatest possible toll in blood. Only two months later, a Japanese colonel on Peleliu would do just that, ravaging the 1st Marine Division, but General Takashina remained wedded to the offense, though he must have known the mass attack was unlikely to throw the Americans back into the sea. A somewhat self-contradictory message from Imperial Headquarters in Tokyo also seemed to anticipate the worst, urging the garrison on July 24, "Defend Guam to the death. We believe good news will be forthcoming."[49] Just what that "good news" might be was a bit of a mystery. Takashina could expect no reinforcements—that hope had evaporated with the defeat of Admiral Jisaburo Ozawa's First Mobile Fleet just over a month earlier and the subsequent fall of Saipan. Many of his frontline officers were dead, and some heavily engaged units had suffered 70 percent casualties. All his forces were low on ammunition. The superiority of U.S. air and naval gunfire made movement in the daylight suicidal. He also feared the Marines might now move to outflank his existing defenses with another amphibious landing.

Whatever the outcome, this was to be no wild rampage. The attack was carefully planned, with specific instructions to various units designating objectives and routes of advance. The attack from the Fonte Plateau would be coordinated with a breakout from Orote Peninsula. Following the death of Colonel Tsunetaro Suenaga during the assault on the Marine Brigade beachhead the night of July 21, those forces were now under the command of navy commander Asaischi Tamai of the 263rd Air Group, who remained in communication with General Takashina as of the evening of July 25.

The 3rd Division's dispositions were already a largely open book to the Japanese thanks to their vantage point on the Mount Tenjo–Mount Alutom–Mount Chachao massif. The Marines would later find three big 20X telescopes emplaced on the height. Looking through the powerful telescopes, an observer could practically make out the individual features of Marines on the beachhead below. Studying the area at their leisure, the Japanese could pick out the gaps in the thinly manned U.S. line and make their plans accordingly.

According to Takashina's plan, the 18th Regiment and 48th Brigade would comprise the bulk of the attack force. The 18th Regiment (less the 1st Battalion) under the command of Colonel Hiko-Shiro Ohashi would attack the 21st Marines on a two-battalion front. The 2nd Battalion, commanded by Major Chusa Maruyama, would attack on the right into the 1st Battalion, 21st Marines, proceeding down the eastern draw of the Asan River to seize the high ground above Asan Point. The 3rd Battalion, commanded by Major Setsuo Yukioka, would attack on the left into the 3rd Battalion, 21st Marines, proceed down the Nidual River valley, and take the high ground southwest of Asan Point. Another unit, its identity unclear but probably a company of the 10th Independent Mixed Regiment, would protect the left flank of the assault in the sector of the 9th Marines.

To the right of the 18th Regiment's push, the 48th Independent Mixed Brigade would overrun the 3rd Marines and the foothold gained by Lieutenant Colonel Cushman's battalion on Fonte Plateau. The brigade would push toward Red Beach 2, then turn northeast to destroy ammunition and supply dumps at the foot of Chonito Cliff. Special demolitions teams were assigned to destroy artillery pieces, vehicles, and other installations. The entire operation would be supported by mortar and artillery fire.

As plans for the attack gelled, Imperial General Headquarters again radioed its encouragement from afar. "We are deeply moved by your hard fighting continued day and night," observed the message. "You have decided to launch the general attack. We wish you and your men every success in the attack."[50]

In what turned out to be a premature gambit, Commander Tamai launched a number of barges into Apra Harbor from Sumay shortly after dark on July 25 either in an attempt to join the main effort against the 3rd Division or possibly to take the Marines sealing off the peninsula from behind. Some individual Japanese were even observed attempting to swim across to the mainland. Spotted by the 9th Marines, the flotilla was quickly illuminated by star shells and then searchlight beams from the destroyer *Franks* and brought under fire by newly emplaced 90mm guns of the 14th Defense Battalion on Cabras Island. The barges were sunk or turned back. Whatever his original intent, Tamai's only option now was a frontal assault against the Marines blocking the neck of Orote Peninsula.

A more serious setback occurred late that same afternoon as Japanese units fought to hold on to jump-off positions for the counterattack against the 3rd Marine Division. Attacking on Cushman's right, the 1st Battalion, 21st Marines had spent a bloody and frustrating day attempting to seize a Japanese position dubbed Quarry Hill. Companies A and B had taken a pounding from Fonte Hill on their flank and met fierce resistance from Japanese in a warren of tunnels and caves in a large gravel pit on the east side of the hill. At the same time, C Company took heavy losses attempting to seize dome-shaped "Round Hill" (Mount Mangan) just to the right. The battalion was finally forced back to its original position on the ridge where B Company found itself down to two patched-up platoons numbering about seventy-five men; Able Company could count about 130 men from a normal strength of 215, and Charlie Company was in similar shape.

Late in the afternoon, tanks made their way up to the battalion along a newly cut roadway. Their arrival turned out to be bad news for twenty-four-year-old Second Lieutenant Arthur J. Kroncke of Jersey City, New Jersey. Kroncke was ordered to take his C Company platoon and support the tanks in a limited attack against the Round Hill strongpoint that had held them up earlier. The push, which finally got off at dusk, was a disaster for the platoon. As the tanks swung around behind the hill, the exposed infantrymen were cut down by a torrent of enemy fire. Kroncke was killed by rifle fire as he attempted to point out targets to the tanks. The Shermans took retribution with point-blank fire on the enemy positions before finally retiring. "The day had gone badly," observed Lieutenant Arthur A. Frances at battalion head-quarters. "We had taken a beating."[51] But though Frances did not know it, the attacks by Cushman's battalion and the 21st Marines had also taken a serious toll on the enemy. When the tanks finally withdrew, only about forty men remained of the 321st Independent Infantry Battalion. The loss of so many veteran infantrymen would be sorely felt when the Japanese counterattack got underway in only a few hours.

In the hills overlooking the 3rd Marine Division beachhead, officers from the 29th Division command post departed at sunset to check on units and offer encouragement. Documents were burned as officers and men "prepared to meet a heroic death," as Colonel Takeda, who would be the highest-ranking Japanese survivor of the battle, recalled. "Some took out photographs of their parents, wife, or children and bid farewell to them; some prayed to God or Buddha, some composed a death poem and some exchanged cups of water at final parting with intimate comrades. All pledged themselves to one another to meet again at the Yasukuni Shrine."

Takeda sensed that most of the men were afraid but resigned. Even those who were typically composed and considered fine soldiers "were struck with some fear to the last; few were able to be ready to rush out through the enemy line courageously," he admitted. "However, all of the officers and men were generally prepared for their fate, because of their honor, sense of responsibility and hate for the enemy."[52]

The 18th Regiment burned its colors at 1700 hours. General Takashina left his command post on the south side of Mount Macajna an hour later to establish an advance headquarters at Fonte. Behind him, approximately half of the officers and men of his headquarters were already dead, the victims of the seemingly nonstop enemy mortar and naval gunfire.

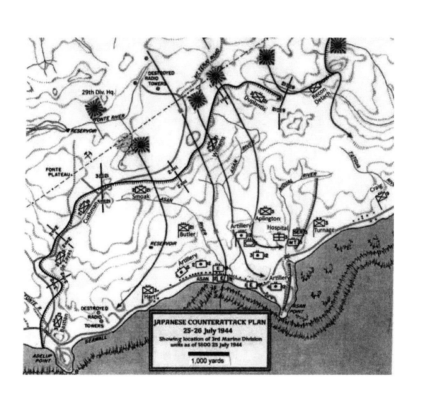

JAPANESE COUNTERATTACK PLAN
25-26 July 1944
Showing location of 3rd Marine Division
units as of 1800 25 July 1944

1,000 yards

CHAPTER 17

MARINE, YOU DIE!

As darkness closed in on Orote Peninsula, it was raining. Again.

A mixed bag of Japanese units—some twenty-five hundred men in all—were waiting in successive lines of defense across the narrow width of the 2.5-mile peninsula that formed the southern edge of Apra Harbor. They included elements of the 54th Keibitai; the 2nd Battalion, 38th Infantry commanded by Major Kiyoji Okujo, who had fought a successful delaying action against the 22nd Marines as the battalion fell back toward the peninsula; the 60th Antiaircraft Defense Unit; about seven hundred men from the 755th Air Group, which had been reorganized for ground combat; and some naval laborers. As one Marine officer observed, "Even if many of the Japanese were not trained in infantry tactics, they were apparently experts in the use of pick and shovel and well able to man the fixed defenses, which they had helped build."[1] Subsequent staff analysis concurred, observing that the Japanese on Orote Peninsula "offered the most consistent defensive action of the entire campaign."[2]

Ray Gillespie's company dug in that night along the neck of the peninsula about three hundred yards from a coastal mangrove swamp full of Japanese. Most of them, as intelligence would later determine, were from Major Okujo's battalion. Gillespie didn't like the position, which featured a small hill or knoll located between the Marines and the swamp. Adding to his discontent was his foxhole companion, whose nonstop predictions of doom and their impending demise were starting to wear on his nerves. "His negative predictions had already killed us at least a hundred times since we hit the beach," Gillespie observed sourly.[3]

Gillespie gave the pessimist the first watch but awoke about an hour later as mortar shells began to fall. The explosions were punctuated by taunts from the darkness beyond the foxhole line: *Maleeene going to die tonight!* He lay there in their wet hole watching trails of sparks from descending mortar shells. "If you could not see the descending sparks, then it was going to be your mortar," he remarked with the fatalism of a line rifleman. Inevitably, a shell finally landed in somebody's foxhole. One Marine died instantly; the other was less fortunate, moaning, "Help me. Please help me. Help me," until he died.[4] Out in the darkness, the Japanese were carrying on—screaming, yelling, laughing, and breaking *sake* bottles. It "sounded like New Year's Eve in the zoo," remarked one Marine wryly.[5] One worked-up Japanese soldier kept popping up and down on the small knoll out front as if daring them to fire.

Not far from Gillespie's position, PFC Charles Lepant of L Company was dug in with PFC S. J. Carpenter. It wasn't much of a hole; beneath the shallow layer of soil, they'd run into coral rock that defeated efforts to dig deeper. Lepant was shivering.

"Are you cold?" asked Carpenter.

"No." said Lepant. "But I'm scared."[6]

Captain Philip P. Santon, manning the fire direction center of the 22nd Marines Pack Howitzer Battalion, tried to contact the front to arrange artillery support, but the Japanese kept breaking in on his radio transmissions. Santon found that if he broadcast any sort of nonsense in another language—he started with German—the interference would stop for a moment, perhaps because the enemy thought they were on the wrong channel. The pause allowed Santon to establish a temporary connection in English, but the Japanese quickly returned.

Overlooking the mangrove swamp, Second Lieutenant Paul J. Dunfey, K Company's mortar section leader, had a clear phone line to Lieutenant Walter G. Barrett who had taken command of the company after Captain Harry Hedrick was killed the day before. Through a phone and radio patchwork ending with Santon at the fire direction center, Dunfey was able to designate targets on the edge of the swamp. By 2350, distances and directions were computed and the big guns prepared to register. It was none too soon. PFC George Popovich was deepening his foxhole when the BAR man next to him blurted, "My, God, here they come!"[7]

Punctuated by screams of *Marine, you die!* a wave of Japanese, seemingly well lubricated with *sake* and armed with everything from pitchforks and sticks to machine guns, swarmed out of the mangrove swamp. "They came in waves and like a solid wall, yelling and shrieking," said Platoon Sergeant Thomas O'Neill, dug in with L Company. "Every gun we had was blasting away, but that didn't stop them. The first wave broke through. They were all over the place."[8] Some paused to lob grenades, laughing drunkenly and yelling, "Fire in the hole!" Marine artillery and machine guns opened up, mowing them down. They "fell one on top of the other, some yet screaming and kicking," recalled Ray Gillespie.[9] Dunfey watched the results of his artillery calculations with grim satisfaction. "Arms and legs flew like snowflakes," he observed. "Japs ran amuck. They screamed in terror until they died."[10]

The survivors pressed on. "They broke through our lines. I just lay in my fox-hole. They jumped right over me," said Popovich.[11] Some attackers ran past Lepant and Carpenter so close that Lepant could have tripped them if he had wanted to reach out. It was bedlam. In a foxhole just behind them, a Marine whose leg had been blown off cried out over and over, "I don't want to die. I don't want to die."[12] Tracers from machine guns floated just overhead. Some of the Japanese seemed confused. "A few broke through and past our line and they just stopped as if they were lost or had forgotten something. In their moment of indecision we in the rear shot them down," remembered Gillespie.[13] Private Dale E. Watts, a BAR man with L Company, heard the machine gun in the adjoining hole go suddenly silent as the crew was overrun. Shadowy figures were visible setting up two heavy machine guns at the position. Watts stood up in his foxhole, ignoring the intense small arms and mortar fire, and took them under fire with his BAR, preventing them from putting the guns into action.

O'Neill's foxhole companion was hit. "I never found out what caliber weapon got him," said O'Neill. "He was instantaneously propelled against me by the force of whatever hit him. He made an attempt to grab me, then went lax. I was able to determine that he was dead. His face had been shot away."[14]

Over in the 2nd Battalion, Sergeant Alphons A. Pinter, leading a machine-gun section in G Company, experienced some frantic moments when both guns jammed. Pinter, a former star forward on the Texas Lutheran College basketball team, held off the Japanese with his submachine gun, intermittently throwing grenades while the crews scrambled to clear the guns. He killed eight of the enemy and kept the attack-ers at bay until the machine guns were finally restored to action, "thereby saving his entire sector," according to his subsequent citation for the Navy Cross.[15]

Three Japanese came after Corporal Webster J. Bachelot, a squad leader with Company E. Bachelot shot the first man even as the second thrust a bayonet at him. Twisting away as the blade sliced open his chest, Bachelot plunged his own bayonet into the enemy soldier. Jerking the blade free, he then impaled the third Japanese as the man passed by the side of the foxhole.

Later, in a letter home to Crowley, Louisiana, the twenty-two-year-old made light of his brush with death. "The Jap who came at me with a bayonet darn near had me, but I came out on top and stuck him instead," he wrote. "At least I got a Jap pistol and flag out of the deal. Later that same night I killed a Jap officer a few yards in front of my position and early the next morning a guy from another outfit went out and got his saber. Boy, did I beat my gums."[16]

During a lull between attacks, Charles Lepant heard a rustling from the sword grass out beyond his foxhole. He waited apprehensively, following the telltale sounds with the muzzle of his carbine. There was a sharp tap as the intruder activated a grenade against his helmet. Lepant braced, but the explosion, when it came, was out beyond his foxhole. The Japanese had killed himself.

The Japanese made three attempts on the Marine line—the last at 0300—before finally giving it up. Of the roughly five hundred men who had participated in the assault, the mangled remains of about four hundred were subsequently counted in the kill zone. Artillery had done most of the damage. Brigade, 77th Division, and corps artillery had rained over twenty-six thousand shells on the attackers. In its attempts to attack through this hellish maelstrom, the Japanese 2nd Battalion, 38th Infantry had virtually ceased to exist.

As relative quiet descended, Pharmacist's Mate Second Class Louis W. Jagoe, a former driver for a Birmingham, Alabama, funeral home, was giving in to exhaustion. The twenty-four-year-old sailor was dug in with two Marines from F Company. "It was about 3:20 a.m., darker than the inside of your hat, and there were three of us in a foxhole among the rocks at the base of the peninsula," he recalled. He had fallen half asleep when a Japanese suddenly loomed overhead and bayoneted him in the buttocks. Jagoe instinctively grabbed the bayonet with his right hand. "The Jap jerked away, cutting my hand pretty deep and stabbed the next guy and shot the third," he related.

A sergeant grabbed the enemy soldier by the throat, pulled him off his feet, and shot him. Jagoe shot him a second time for good measure. "Are there any more Japs?" he called.

"There's one here," the sergeant replied, gesturing.

Apparently realizing he had been spotted, the Japanese jumped out of a hole about five feet away. A machine gunner cut him down as he ran, adding him to the litter of corpses already scattered around the foxhole line. "When daylight came, we counted seventy-five dead Japs," recalled Jagoe.[17]

Just up the coast, General Takeshi Takashina's forces were also on the move as darkness fell. Unknown to the Marines dug in on the heights beyond the Asan beachhead, Japanese demolition teams had begun infiltrating the 3rd Division's lines twenty-four hours earlier. Equipped with magnetic mines and demolition packs, each containing about twenty pounds of TNT with ready detonators, the special teams were directed to head for rear areas and destroy American artillery and armor once the main attack got underway. In the interim, they laid low in caves, thickets, and other areas of concealment.

PFC Eugene Peterson and a buddy had dug in for the night on the bank of the Asan River—actually more of a stream at the moment—near the 12th Marines' command center. There had been intermittent showers during the day, but darkness brought a driving rain. "We had a big rainstorm and the creek just below our foxhole became a torrent," recalled Peterson. "It floated some dead Japanese bodies and dead animals to just below our foxhole. The stench was unbelievable. . . . [I]n an attempt to filter out the overpowering odor we bunched our blankets against our faces, but the stench was able to permeate through everything." Huddled under their dripping ponchos, the two Marines sensed movement out in the gully but didn't have any grenades. "We knew better than to fire our rifle at the noise so we sat in our foxhole expecting an assault at any minute," said Peterson.[18]

Also awake, PFC Jack Cross was puzzled by what sounded like dogs incessantly barking from somewhere out front. He couldn't remember having seen any dogs around. "Suddenly it dawned on me that it was Japs yelling at each other as they got into position after dark," he said.[19] Manning a foxhole on the edge of a gully where two platoons of his medium tank company had been positioned facing Fonte Ridge, Captain Bertram Yaffe could also hear the Japanese yelling, punctuated by the sound of breaking glass as empty *sake* bottles were shattered. Two things that never seemed to be in short supply on Guam, which had apparently served as a regional liquor supply center, were hand grenades and *sake*. "We responded with machine gun and mortar fire, but only sporadically, since there was a real concern about wasting ammunition," observed Yaffe.[20]

The first major clash occurred shortly after midnight in a ravine between the 9th and 21st Marines. An effort had been made before nightfall to plug the eight-hundred-yard gap with twenty-five men from the division Reconnaissance Company led by twenty-three-year-old First Lieutenant Oscar Salgo of the Bronx, New York. Salgo was no stranger to perilous situations. On Bougainville, he swam a mile through the surf to obtain help after his platoon was cut off and in danger of being annihilated—a feat that earned him the Silver Star—but now he was being asked to do the impossible.

Ordered to defend the gaping hole with only twenty-five men, the Recon Marines dug two-man foxholes, set up their machine guns, and settled in to await developments. Trouble was not long in arriving. At about 2330 an artillery forward observer reported an estimated fifty or more Japanese moving into the ravine. "A red flare went off, probably the Jap signal to attack," recalled Salgo. "I called for flares from our mortars and they lighted up the rugged country as the Japs rushed into our position. They were moaning and shrieking and shouting, *Banzai!*"

Four Japanese went after PFC Arthur L. Rodgers of Black Creek, South Carolina. "He got three of them with his carbine, the muzzle never more than six inches from the target," said Salgo. "His foxhole buddy got the fourth Jap." But Marines were also going down. Lieutenant Sidney Marlin was wounded by a grenade. Platoon Sergeant Claude F. Cole, who had joined the Marines in 1938 at the age of eighteen, was killed. PFC Eugene Beckman of Loretto, Tennessee, feigned death after being slashed across the forehead with a bayonet. A Japanese, apparently trying to catch his breath, sat on the twenty-three-year-old Marine's stomach. Beckman pulled out his combat knife and killed him. With four men killed and five wounded during the brief encounter, Salgo realized they would not survive another attack. He passed the word to pull out, and they made their way into the lines of the 1st Battalion, 9th Marines on the southern edge of the ravine.[21]

Another burst of activity occurred when about a dozen Japanese mounted a bayonet charge against the center of the 21st Marines. What they hoped to accomplish beyond a dignified exit into the hereafter is unclear. All were killed. Edgy Marines watched enemy signal flares—they were orange—arch into the rainy darkness. It was later learned the flares were intended to help guide Japanese assault units to their assembly points. Enemy mortar and artillery fire began to pick up. Marine artillerymen responded from gun pits that were knee deep with water from the pounding rain.

—◆—

Sergeant Werner H. Eubanks, a thirty-one-year-old career Marine from Jacksonville, North Carolina, had dug in alone. As acting machine-gun section leader, he was in charge of two light and two heavy machine guns assigned to Captain Donald M. Beck's B Company, 1st Battalion, 21st Marines, the same company that had lost Russell Elushik in a Japanese raid two nights before. Though Eubanks didn't know it, B Company was directly in the Japanese crosshairs. Toward midnight, the Japanese began throwing grenades. Some exploded in the air, showering the mud with metal splinters. The Marines responded with their own grenades. The Japanese were close—many no more than twenty yards away—gathered along a roadway that ran parallel to the Marine line where an embankment shielded them from direct fire. Peering into the rain, Eubanks thought he could hear activity even closer in a grassy area between his foxhole and the road. He called in mortar fire from time to time, and whatever activity was going on ceased for a while but then seemed to pick up again.

On watch further down the B Company line, PFC Arnaldo Martinez, the thin, twenty-year-old son of Mexican immigrants from Los Angeles, heard the clink of metal on metal in the darkness out front. It was now about 0300. He woke his companions, twenty-three-year-old PFC Grady C. Wimmer, a former brass foundry worker from Roanoke, Virginia, and Sergeant Gordon Garner, a prewar enlistee from Newport News, Virginia. As the three peered apprehensively into the night, an orange flare soared up from Japanese lines. From the darkness, Japanese soldiers began shouting in English, "American Marines, you die tonight!" The taunts were followed by grenades, trailing sparks as they descended on and around the Marine foxhole line. "It looked like lit cigarettes," recalled Martinez of the sputtering fuses arching down in the dark.

Screaming *Ban-zai-ai!* a wave of Japanese suddenly materialized from the rainy night in a rush toward the Marine foxholes. As flares cast the rushing figures in a garish light, Sergeant Eubanks's machine guns opened fire. Dozens of the screaming figures went down, but there were more behind them.

Martinez, Wimmer, and Garner fended off the first rush. During a momentary lull, Garner slipped out in search of more grenades. He had yet to return when the Japanese resumed the attack. Pressure built all along the line. About to be overrun, some Marines began scrambling down the slope to a secondary line of foxholes about thirty yards to the rear. Some were dragging their wounded. Another line of Japanese loomed up in front of Martinez and Wimmer. These soldiers advanced methodically, bayonets fixed, pausing to throw grenades, flopping to the ground, then following up in the wake of the explosions. A grenade blast shattered Wimmer's rifle, and the two Marines decided it was time to get out. As they emerged from their foxhole, screaming figures charged down the hill off to their right as the Japanese broke through the beleaguered company. Under the illumination shells from mortars and from ships offshore, the ridge "was floodlighted like a runway on an airfield," recalled a lieutenant.[22]

Companies A and C on either side of B Company held firm, refusing their flanks as Japanese poured into the hole. The commander of A Company was a six-foot-tall, 215-pound New Englander, Captain William G. Shoemaker. As a platoon commander on Bougainville, "Shoe" had won the Navy Cross for persisting in the attack despite multiple wounds. His men thought the world of him. Shoemaker's company beat back the first wave of Japanese, but follow-up mass attacks penetrated their lines. Japanese and Marines became intermingled, adding to the confusion and disorganization. As the situation deteriorated, there were shouts to withdraw. Wearing a captured Japanese raincoat that strained to contain his shoulders, Shoemaker stood up amid the withering fire to steady his men. "No, by God, we stay here and hold them!" he bellowed. "If we don't hold them here, the whole beachhead will go!"[23]

As Shoemaker stripped men from his front line to build up the flank and keep the penetration contained, B Company survivors fought on in isolated knots—small islands in a floodtide of Japanese. One of Eubanks's machine guns was knocked out by a grenade blast. The crew fixed it and resumed firing, but a second grenade hit the jacket and exploded, putting the gun out of action for good.

Clinging to their foxhole, PFC Edward G. ("Moose") Killian and Corporal John Dopp heard an unearthly screaming from the heavy machine-gun position manned by Corporal Carroll A. Herzberg and PFC Edward A. Krejci. By the light of the flares Killian saw Herzberg trying to pull a Japanese bayonet out of Krejci's body. At that same instant, another wave of Japanese swept over the machine gun. One of the Japanese thrust a bayonet into Herzberg's back.

Before Killian could fully process this waking nightmare, a mob of Japanese came at him and Dopp. He emptied his BAR at them, and they broke away. As he changed magazines, he looked up to see another a Japanese coming at him with a saber. He back-pedaled as the swordsman slashed at him. The blade struck the barrel of his BAR and glanced off his arm. Thrown off balance, the Japanese fell into the foxhole. Killian fired at him but either missed or just grazed him. Bleeding from the head, the Japanese rose up and again swung the sword, this time nicking Killian above the right eye. Killian pounded the stock of his BAR into the man's head. Dopp, who had been preoccupied with shooting at other attackers, saw what was going on at arm's length and drove his bayonet into the Japanese. Incredibly, the swordsman jumped up with a crazed shout and dashed down the ridge toward the beach.

Three Japanese took possession of Herzberg's machine gun. One pulled the trigger prematurely and sprayed a group of his own comrades running along the top of the ridge. They then tried to pick up the gun and turn it around on the Marines. Killian hosed them down with his BAR, knocking down two. The third held a grenade to his head and blew himself up. Still another knot of Japanese appeared at the gun. They had nearly managed to turn it around when an enemy soldier, apparently carrying a mine or demolitions, raced toward them, tripped over a body, and blew himself and the others to pieces.

Abandoning their foxhole, Martinez and Wimmer slid into a shell crater about ten yards below the crest of the ridge, where they found their platoon leader, Second

Lieutenant Edward W. Mulcahy, desperately trying to get through to someone on the field phone. It was a futile hope. The wires had been broken, and the line was dead. Bodies lay strewn all over the slope, and wounded men were screaming. Chaos raged all around, a horrific tableau of indistinct running figures, explosions, gunfire, and shrieks of pain or fear or rage. Mulcahy, who a year earlier had been studying history at Tufts College in his home state of Massachusetts, gave up on the phone and asked what was happening further up on the ridge. They told him most of their 1st Platoon was gone.

Martinez took up a position at the lip of the shell hole. All they had for weapons was Martinez's rifle, the lieutenant's carbine, and a .45 automatic Wimmer had been carrying in addition to his now shattered rifle. A group of Japanese suddenly appeared against the skyline. Martinez fired. The Japanese disappeared, but a moment later a flurry of hand grenades arched down toward the shell hole. Most rolled by to detonate harmlessly behind them, but one dropped into the hole and exploded, driving a chunk of metal into Martinez's chest. "It felt like somebody had thrown a rock at me," he recalled.

Martinez was the lucky one. Lieutenant Mulcahy absorbed the bulk of the blast. Only his helmet saved him as over fifty grenade fragments slammed into the left side of his body. His carbine was shattered. The left side of his helmet looked like a sieve. "There was so much going on," he said later. "It was like getting hit by a 2-by-4. That's about the way it felt." As he struggled to regain his senses, he became aware that Wimmer was trying to hand a pistol to him.

"You take it, Lieutenant," the Virginian said in a strained tone.

Mulcahy protested, replying that Wimmer would need the gun for his own protection.

"That's all right, Lieutenant," replied Wimmer, still composed. "I can't see any more."

"He was bleeding from his face and I put sulfa powder on him and wrapped his eyes," Mulcahy said.[24] Hearing firing up on the ridge, Mulcahy realized some men were still resisting. Covered with blood, he shouted into the night, "Hold them! Hold them!" in what was half sideline encouragement and half prayer.[25]

Manning the 1st Battalion command post at the foot of the cliff, officers were trying to get a handle on what was happening on the ridge above. "Mixed and confused reports, some frantic, reached our radios," recalled executive officer Lieutenant Colonel Ronald R. Van Stockum. As the din of machine-gun fire and explosions continued unabated, a forward observer stumbled down the cliff to report that the enemy had attacked, and "all hell" had broken loose on the front lines.[26]

Battalion called for fragmentation hand grenades to be sent up from the ammunition dump several hundred yards to the rear. After a painfully long delay, the grenades arrived, but instead of fragmentation grenades, they had been sent smoke grenades, useless in their present situation.

Overrunning B Company, a mob of Japanese swarmed into a draw where they ran into Captain Bertram Yaffe's two platoons of medium tanks from the 3rd Tank Battalion. Commanding one of seven tanks that had drawn up for the night not far from the edge of a steep drop-off behind the now broken infantry position, twenty-two-year-old Sergeant Louis Spiller and his crew had begun to see Japanese silhouetted against the skyline just before midnight. Knowing Marines would not be moving around after dark, they opened fire, but more and more Japanese appeared until they were like a swarm of ants descending on the Shermans. Enemy soldiers clambered up onto the tanks "oblivious of the vicious machine gun fire and frantically pounded, kicked and beat against the turrets in an attempt to get to the crew within," observed one account.[27] Some tried to shove grenades down the muzzles of the 75mm guns.

"They were trying to knock out a 33-ton tank," observed driver PFC Lawrence Ward. "They just got mowed down. Here was a 75mm cannon shooting at them and they would run up and grab the .30 caliber machine gun and try to wrestle it out of the tank. It was ridiculous."[28] Failing to get at the crews, survivors leaped to the ground and continued their rush down the draw, only to be replaced by more frenzied attackers.

Peering through the driver's periscope, Spiller was stunned to see Japanese charging the tanks with drawn sabers. Two enemy soldiers set up a machine gun under the back end of his Sherman. "We could hear them talking in Japanese and firing their machine gun in short bursts," he remembered. Two explosions—Spiller identified them as artillery rounds—slammed into the front slope of the tank, shattering his periscope and momentarily blinding him. No one was injured, but the shock jarred the bottom escape hatch open. Fearful the Japanese machine gunners behind the tank would take this opportunity to lob in a grenade or explosive charge, Spiller pulled the tank forward a few yards, then put it in reverse with one track locked. The heavy Sherman spun around, crushing the two Japanese and their machine gun.[29]

Further down the draw, tank company commander Bertram Yaffe had dug in on some higher ground with a radioman and a couple of other Marines. He could hear the tank machine guns going full blast down below. One of his Marines was firing his carbine at Japanese swarming along the gulch. As the situation grew evermore chaotic, the radioman turned and shouted, "Captain, let's get the hell out of here! Our artillery is going to pulverize this ridge!"

It was none too soon. As Yaffe, .45 pistol in hand, started to get up, two Japanese charged toward him from the left. "I aimed my pistol at the chest of the nearest as he came lunging toward me," he recalled. "When the bullet struck, it was as if he were a battered puppet being jerked back over the ridge, his grenade exploding simultaneously." Turning to the second Japanese, Yaffe squeezed off another shot. "Although I was aiming for his chest, the bullet obliterated what was his head while his ignited grenade rolled toward my foxhole. I bolted to my left, but most of the blast caught my chest; I tripped over a body and fell." Regaining his feet, Yaffe, tumbled down a steep trail leading down the cliff behind him. The fall broke some ribs but probably saved his life. As he landed at the bottom on a pile of bodies—some Japanese, some Marines—artillery shells began to explode on the ridge above. Gasping in pain, his undershirt soaked in blood from the grenade wounds, he found he had landed among the remnants of the battalion mortar platoon, which had been overrun and virtually wiped out by the surging Japanese.[30]

<hr>

While the 1st Battalion, 21st Marines fought for their lives, Major Setsuo Yukioka's 3rd Battalion, 18th Infantry slammed into Pete Duplantis's adjacent 3rd Battalion.

Though Duplantis had been anticipating this moment for nearly two days, the attack caught him at a disadvantage. With his L Company in regimental reserve, he had ended the day with his remaining two companies thinly stretched over several hundred yards of what one officer described as "nothing but ravines and ridges smothered in dense vegetation."[31] An eight-hundred-foot gap, soon to be assigned to Lieutenant Salgo's Recon Marines, yawned between his right flank and the adjacent 9th Marines. Just to his right rear and partially in the 9th Marines sector was a 460-foot hill—not shown on the maps but dubbed "Hill Item"—that promised to figure heavily in any enemy attack. The hill dominated the Asan and Nidual River valleys as well as the road network leading directly into the 3rd Marine Division command post and shore party dumps. The Japanese obviously recognized the importance of the height; they had fought stubbornly to hold it earlier and would presumably move quickly to take it back in any major counterattack.

Earlier, a worried Duplantis contacted regiment with his concerns. "I vigorously voiced these beliefs and more vigorously objected to being left in that position for the night with a wide-open flank and no reserve," he said in retrospect. Regimental commander Colonel Tex Butler concurred and released L Company to Duplantis's control just at dark. Duplantis positioned the men between I and K Companies to block a deep defile choked with jungle growth. He moved his command post into a pocket-like recess on the left side of Hill Item, pulling a reinforced squad back from K Company as his reserve in hopes of being able to hold onto the hill in the event of an assault. A blocking force with BARs and bazookas was sent out to guard a trail that skirted the battalion's right flank and led to the beach areas.

It was not enough. At about 0200 Duplantis heard the sounds of heavy fighting from the regiment's left flank. About an hour later, I Company reported a frontal attack in strength. A short time later, K Company came under assault and reported they were holding their position with extreme difficulty. "In a few minutes I heard the road block open up with everything they had and I knew the envelopment was coming," said Duplantis.[32]

The initial Japanese assault overran two of the battalion's machine-gun positions. The Marines counterattacked and retook the guns. Undeterred, the Japanese found the gap on the battalion's right flank. Guided by scouts carrying small metal lanterns, they headed down the ravine in column toward the 3rd Battalion command post. Marines at the trail block tried to stop them, but the outpost was overrun. "I don't know what time it was but here they come, screaming and hollering *banzai* and firing and throwing grenades," recalled PFC Hendon Edwards, a twenty-year-old former Western Union messenger boy from Mobile, Alabama. "The two men in front of our hole fired rifles just as fast as we could fire. The guy in the back of the hole he threw grenades just as hard as he could throw. We went through this two or three different times."[33]

PFC Rufus Belding heard the enemy screaming, "Die! Die, Marine!" as they swept forward. "And boy, I'm telling you, they came through," he recalled. A bullet slammed into his upper right shoulder by the collar bone and tore through the big muscle in his back. "I couldn't do nothing. This side was paralyzed. And I lost my rifle." Belding's foxhole buddy saw he had been hit hard. "Take my pistol," he told him. "Go on back to the CP and they'll take care of you." Belding made his way back to the CP, where he spent the rest of the night trying not to bleed to death. "When I got hit, I reached up and stuck my finger in the hole to stop the bleeding," he said. "First time I ever prayed in my life. . . . I asked the Lord don't let me down at this hour. I want to go home to mom and daddy."[34]

Duplantis called for an emergency artillery and mortar barrage and was informed that both the artillery and mortar positions were fighting with carbines to save their pieces. Though he did not know it, Lieutenant Salgo's reconnaissance team had also been shoved aside by this point. Duplantis attempted to reach regiment on the command radio net to warn division that Japanese troops were pouring around his right flank toward the division command post but could not get a response.

Bulling through, the Japanese enveloped Hill Item, surrounding the battalion CP. Setting up machine guns on the higher ground, they raked the rear of K Company. One Marine climbed a small tree and picked off several Japanese, but Duplantis was forced to commit the reserve force he had stripped from K Company. Led by Second Lieutenant Ralph H. Niehaus, a six-foot-four-inch, 215-pound former University of Dayton football tackle, the force launched a desperate assault up the hill. In a fierce hand-to-hand struggle employing hand grenades and bayonets, all but four of the men were killed or wounded. Niehaus himself was wounded twice but persisted in the attack until finally ordered to withdraw.[35]

Corporal Arthur Anderson of Independence, Iowa, took command of his team when the leader was hit early in the initial assault on the hill. Anderson pushed the attack until he was severely wounded in both legs. As orders came to retire from the uneven battle, Anderson, unable to move on his own, refused assistance. He continued to fire on the enemy as his men disengaged, until he was finally struck again and killed. PFC Howard Dodd of Fairmont, West Virginia, and twenty-year-old PFC Joshua Morris, a Native American who had grown up on the Gila River Indian Reservation, home to the Pima and Maricopa tribes, in Komatke, Arizona, were also killed when they remained behind to cover the withdrawal.

Lieutenant Niehaus was hit a third time during the withdrawal but returned under heavy fire to carry casualties to safety until prostrated by loss of blood. Platoon Sergeant Peter J. Renzo assumed command and directed evacuation of the wounded despite his own injuries. Renzo then settled in with those still able to fight—the reserve force had been reduced to just seven men—to defend the perimeter. "CP personnel were fighting desperately to keep from being wiped out, using the darkness of the pocket to conceal themselves and firing at the Japs silhouetted on the rim against the sky which was beginning to lighten," said Duplantis. "As it grew light, the Japs began to lob in knee mortars and deadly sniping began, which took a heavy toll of the corpsmen and communication personnel."[36] Both his forward artillery observers were among the casualties. One was killed by a gunshot to the upper back. The other was wounded in the upper left chest, then killed when he was shot in the head while being evacuated on a litter.

As the situation deteriorated, Duplantis notified division that he was burying his cipher device to keep it out of enemy hands should he be overrun.

To the north, the 2nd and 3rd Battalions of the 3rd Marines, holding the left of the division line overlooking Agana, came under attack by naval infantry—mainly former construction troops—operating under the auspices of the 54th Keibitai. The sailors, under the command of the senior naval officer, Captain Yutaka Sugimoto, were not well-trained infantry "but had excellent morale," observed a 29th Division staff officer.[37] Captain Sugimoto had greeted orders to attack with high spirits "expressing his determination to fight at the head of the unit." Sugimoto was also supposed to receive armored support from two tank companies that had been held near Ordot since W-Day. The tanks set out for the front after dark but somehow became lost on the trails leading toward Agana. The tanks returned to Ordot, leaving the sailors on their own. They attacked anyway.

Corporal Fred Hofmann Jr., a husky twenty-one-year-old from Hoboken, New Jersey, with the 2nd Battalion's Company E—the company that had helped to finally secure Bundschu Ridge—had charge of two machine-gun squads and ten riflemen guarding a draw that led into the battalion's lines about one thousand yards from Agana. Hofmann, a Navy corpsman, and two other Marines, one of whom was his runner, the other a machine gunner, roofed over a shallow foxhole with scavenged sheet metal to get out of the rain and settled in for the night, making periodic check-ins on their field phone.

Just before midnight Hofmann heard a noise outside and looked up from the field phone to see a Japanese soldier peering at him through the gap beneath their sheet metal roof. "He didn't do a thing. He just stared like he was doped or crazy," said Hofmann. "I stuck my .45 out to the edge of the hole and let go. I guess it blew his head off. He was on his hands and knees and just settled down flat. No sooner had I fired than another Nip, jabbering to himself, poked his head inside. I grabbed my carbine and fired at him point blank." He heard someone else in the hole start firing. "Then they started coming in from all around the front of the hole. And one came up from the rear. He started firing."

One of the men in the crowded hole handed Hofmann a grenade. Hofmann recounted,

We argued about who would throw it. I was afraid it would land right back in the hole. Finally, I decided to throw it. I tossed it out and after it went off we heard a lot of moaning around us. But then we heard a whole bunch of them coming in. It was a small shell hole we were in. Not big enough to stand up good in. We lay on our backs and kept looking around in all directions to see them when they popped over the edge. I saw one right over me and I emptied my .45 at him. I couldn't find any more clips and started yelling for someone to find some for me. By the time I got 'em the Nips started tossing grenades.

The man next to Hofmann yelled there was a grenade in the hole.

"Where?!" exclaimed Hofmann.

"Christ, I don't know," came the reply. "Right in here!"

Realizing the grenade was next to him, Hofmann clamped his helmet over it, pinning it down with his shoulder as it exploded. He could feel blood running out of him and thought he was dying. Another grenade exploded on top of the metal sheeting. "Then they started jumping up and down on it," recalled Hofmann. "There must have been about fifteen of them." He still had his .45 and was able to use his right hand. He began firing. The Japanese threw another grenade into the hole. This one wounded the corpsman in the chest and blew off part of their runner's foot.

As Japanese milled around the now roofless hole, the occupants played dead. "One Nip reached in and poked me in the leg with the butt of his rifle," said Hofmann. "I lay there with my eyes open, staring up, playing dead. So did the others." Assuming the Marines were dead, the Japanese left. "The corpsman had his hand on the calf of my leg," recalled Hofmann. "I tensed my muscles every once in a while to let him know I was alive. I had my hand around the leg of the runner. Whenever he started to move or groan, I grabbed him to keep him still. The machine gunner hadn't been hurt. He just lay still with the rest of us."[38]

Not far from Hofmann's shell hole, Corporal Charles E. Moore was also feigning death. "There were three attacks that night and by the third there was nobody left to fight, so they broke through," he recalled. "They came in droves throwing hand grenades and hacked up some of our platoon." Moore had only ten rounds left for his BAR—half a magazine. "I was holding those rounds if I needed them to make a break for it. I had no choice. Everybody was quiet, either dead or wounded. The Japanese came to take out their dead and wounded, and stepped on the edge of my foxhole. I didn't breathe."[39]

CHAPTER 18

THE FONTE HILL FIGHT

On Fonte Hill, holding down the right of the 3rd Marine Regiment, war dog handler PFC Ed Adamski and his Doberman, Big Boy, were out on the proverbial limb with Captain Lou Wilson's F Company. Adamski, a former amateur boxer from Chicago, was celebrating his twentieth birthday that day—and it was beginning to look as though it might be his last. Fox Company was holding a position on the top of the hill, well ahead of the companies on either flank. It was not a good spot, and it didn't seem to be getting any better when Big Boy began to periodically alert in the direction of Mount Tenjo. He was "the ugliest Doberman you've ever seen," said Adamski. "But I couldn't ask for a better animal."[1]

The dog alerted again, now straining frantically at his leash. Adamski dragged him back into the foxhole and passed word that the Japanese were coming. He wrestled with the dog on and off for the next thirty minutes until the cry *Banzai!* rose from the darkness and a wave of Japanese charged toward the foxhole line. "All of a sudden there was a lot of screaming going on," said Adamski. "They were throwing hand grenades. They were running. And it was chaotic. . . . They were all over hell. They'd get behind you already. Big Boy, he was pretty calm. I didn't have a real problem keeping him down except for when the Japs and the screaming got to within two or three yards of us."[2] At one point Big Boy sprang up on his hind legs, straining against the leash in an effort to get at a Japanese soldier coming directly at them. Adamski shot the man in the chest at point-blank range and again muscled the dog back down into the foxhole.

The Japanese attacks on F Company were mounted by elements of the 2nd Battalion of the 10th Independent Mixed Regiment. The regiment's 3rd Battalion had been badly mauled during the fighting earlier in the day, and the commander of the 2nd Battalion had been killed, but there seemed to be plenty of men left. "Waves of Japanese began coming over the hill right into us," recalled Wilson. The Marines shot them down, but there were more behind. Snipers moved onto a slight elevation to Fox Company's right and took the Marines under fire from that direction. "It was a nightmare, truly a nightmare," said platoon leader First Lieutenant Jack Eddy years afterward. "I can still remember the flares, the eerie green light [of illumination flares] over the battlefield. And it was like the lights in . . . in a disco, and all the people are jumping around, in slow motion, in a battle. It was completely eerie. . . . Our problem was that there weren't that many of us. They came in a big group and we were spread out. A group of fifty would hit a spot where there were only seven or eight people—you're convinced that they're going to run right over you."[3]

"We could hear the Japanese yelling at us throughout the night," remembered Wilson. "By the light of the flares we could see them drinking—presumably *sake*—laughing and preparing to charge. Then another charge would come. . . . We had called for some flares from the supporting destroyer, but the flares began to fall short so that we were being silhouetted to the enemy instead of the enemy being silhouetted to us. Naturally, communications failed and we couldn't halt the flares."[4]

At 2200 F Company had to pull back fifty yards to consolidate its lines. Cries for corpsmen multiplied as more and more Marines were hit. As Wilson did what he could to maintain his line, he heard a wounded Marine calling for help from their previous position. It was one of his gunnery sergeants, forty-year-old Lloyd A. Krummel, an old China Marine who had joined the Marine Corps in 1926 and whose varied career included chasing Sandinistas around Nicaragua. Wilson crawled out and found Krummel had been shot through both legs. He began dragging him back. "He was just a little guy, weighing no more than 100 pounds soaking wet," remembered Wilson. Under sporadic fire, he managed to drag the little gunny all the way back into the Marine perimeter. "I can't really say we were being fired on the whole way, but we were being fired on," he remembered. "We weren't hit, though, and we made it back."[5]

Ammunition began to run low, and men called out, trying to borrow clips from one another. G Company CO Major Fraser West, who had started the evening in a dual command post with Wilson before they decided it would be wiser to separate, organized volunteer details to bring up ammunition and grenades from the tanks parked down the road. The men hung bandoliers of ammo around their necks and shouldered boxes of grenades to pass out to the beleaguered line. At one point, some Marines were down to only two clips of rifle ammunition; mortar men reported as few as six rounds per tube. Getting on a tank radio, West called in naval gunfire within twelve hundred yards of his company. The margin of safety was typically nineteen hundred or two thousand yards, but West, aware that the ground dropped off out beyond the Marine line, took a chance that the topography would provide some protection from the barrage.

As casualties mounted, PFC Dale W. Whaley found himself alone on his F Company machine gun. Two men on the crew had been killed. Another, seriously wounded, was helped to the rear by a fourth Marine who never made it back. "One by one, the others were hit," recalled Whaley. "I was out front by myself and the company was not able to get to me. . . . The ground in front and on both sides was littered with bodies of Marines and enemy dead. I was the only one left in my squad. . . . When I found the bodies of my two buddies, I felt more alone than I had ever before or since that day."

Whaley was left to load and fire the gun by himself. Over the next several hours—what he later described as "the longest night of my life"—he lugged the forty-one-pound machine gun and tripod from one vantage point to another in the face of heavy fire, covering the flank of his rifle platoon. "Thank God my gun didn't jam," he said later. Though wounded in the left hand by shell or grenade fragments, the twenty-two-year-old from Montebello, California, killed an estimated fifty Japanese, the last six of whom came at his position as morning approached.[6]

Despite such tenacity, Wilson had serious doubts F Company could survive until morning as seven major attacks ate away at the defense. He did what he could to keep resistance organized but seemed to be surrounded mostly by mass confusion. At times it was not even clear who had control of the hill. "Most of the time throughout that night of battle, I didn't know what was going on. No one did," he admitted. There were no reinforcements available. "We were on our own."[7]

As Japanese swarmed in, the defenders just stayed put and shot anything that moved outside their holes. "I had expected to be in battle, but never anything like this," said Jack Eddy. "When you think about fighting, you think that you're 100 yards away, but this was pretty gruesome, fighting them from twenty feet away and they're running all around you and screaming. . . . They didn't give a shit if they got killed; they just wanted to make sure that you got killed."[8] At some time during the night, Wilson was wounded again. "It's confusion. You're lying in your foxhole hoping to live and you shoot your gun at whatever moves. . . . One time I looked up and saw someone bending over, looking into my foxhole," recalled Wilson. "I immediately shot him with my .45. It was a Japanese lieutenant and I took his sword."[9]

Attached to the 2nd Battalion, twenty-year-old Pharmacist's Mate Second Class Bernhard A. LeCaptain repeatedly ventured out to tend to the mounting number of casualties, at one point running seventy-five yards through heavy machine-gun fire to reach a wounded Marine. Retrieving another casualty from a fire lane, he continued to work on the man despite suffering multiple gunshot wounds. He finally collapsed from loss of blood when he attempted to rise from his kneeling position. His actions earned him the Navy Cross, but the award would be posthumous.

At about midnight, Wilson heard from Lieutenant Colonel Robert Cushman over the field phone. "How are you fixed up there?" asked Cushman. Wilson told him things were looking grim.

"Well, I don't want to lose all of you there," said Cushman. "If you have to retire off the peak, go ahead. We're going to be on this island a long time."[10]

Wilson said he'd hang on.

Despite fierce resistance on the ridges, large numbers of Japanese flowed through the widening gap in the center of the 21st Marines. Emerging from the draws, they rolled over the rearward mortar platoons from the 1st and 2nd Battalions.

Assigned to 2nd Battalion's Headquarters Company, nineteen-year-old PFC Frank Chuisano had been watching flares sporadically going off to his front. "We were beat—we were all trying to get some rest," he recalled. "Then a flare went up again, and like all of a sudden, I saw them [Japanese]. They were there, in front of us. Thousands . . . they were like ants. Oh man, they kicked the shit out of us. They just kept coming, coming." He and his buddy, fellow Brooklyn native PFC Tony Abbetamarco, opened fire. Between volleys, Abbetamarco kept repeating, "We're gonna get it. We're gonna die. We're gonna get it." Chuisano just urged him, "'Keep shooting. Keep shooting!" The Japanese kept coming. "They crawled, they climbed over their dead. They were all on top of each other, two or three high," said Chuisano. "We were yelling at each other, 'Keep spraying! Keep spraying! Kill them all!' because they would get up and start shooting again."[11]

Twenty-three-year-old Corporal Frederick W. Bechtold, a mortar man with the 2nd Battalion, managed to get out in time. "[We] had to leave our foxholes because they were overrunning us," he recalled. "They were all over the place." Bechtold's sergeant shouted for the men to get out, but he waited too long to go himself. A Japanese impaled him through the back with a saber. Amid the chaos one of the Japanese began calling Bechtold's platoon leader, Lieutenant Edward Coombs, by name, shouting, "Lieutenant Coombs, get back on your gun! Lieutenant Coombs, get back on your gun!"

Bechtold grabbed his carbine as they abandoned the mortars. "It only had eleven rounds in it. I didn't have my shoes on, didn't have my helmet. I started moving back up the hill with some of the other fellas." Flares lit up the scene like daylight. "We could see the Japs coming up the ravine. . . . [T]here were just swarms of them coming up this hill." At the top of the hill the mortarmen found a medium tank, but the crew was reluctant to fire, afraid they might hit Marines. "And our lieutenant said, 'Well, you get busy and start firing anyway because those are Japanese, they aren't Marines.'"[12]

As the breakthrough threatened to engulf the 1st Battalion CP, located on a slight rise up against a fifty-foot cliff, Second Lieutenant Joseph Y. Curtis of Glenwood, Alabama, pulled together an assortment of cooks, engineers, storekeepers, and clerks in the defense. Loaded down with grenades, the makeshift force worked their way up onto the slope above the CP. "It was good day[light] by then," said Curtis, "and there were the Japs below us. We let 'em have it. Whenever a Jap revealed his position, we'd toss grenades on him. There were five of them in one group and we were throwing one grenade after another on them. Finally, one of them sprang up with sword in hand and staged a lone banzai charge. I dropped him with my carbine. It was a cinch shot. Later when we were counting the dead, we found he was a Jap battalion commander."[13]

Major Thomas R. Belzer, executive officer with one of the 3rd Division's artillery battalions, saw shells exploding along the top of the ridge further inland. "Bodies could be seen flying in the air as the shells exploded," he recalled. Fearing the artillery was falling short, he ran to the operations tent where he quickly learned the truth.[14]

As Japanese leaked through his regiment's thin line, Colonel Tex Butler rushed the attached engineer company and three platoons of Weapons Company to the aid of the 1st Battalion CP, then established a reserve line overlooking the beach as a second line of defense. General Allen Turnage was also taking precautionary steps. Division headquarters put the 19th Marines on alert at 0420. The 2nd Separate Engineer Battalion was sent to backstop the 3rd Marines in the event of a breakthrough. Over the next hour all available men—some eight hundred in all—from division headquarters and the 3rd Service and 2nd Motor Transport Battalions were organized into makeshift combat units.

Major Henry Aplington's badly shot up 1st Battalion, 3rd Marines, now in reserve behind the 21st Marines, was alerted to stand by for possible action. Coming down from the hills after his battalion was relieved by Bob Cushman less than twenty-four hours earlier, Aplington had been hailed by a fellow officer, "Hey, Hank! I heard that you were killed." Aplington denied it, but the Japanese now seemed to be looking to get another chance at him.[15]

In reserve with Aplington's other companies, Lieutenant Paul Smith's C Company platoon had dug in in a sort of cul-de-sac between two ridges, two men to a foxhole, with little thought that they might have serious contact with the enemy so far to the rear. The men were exhausted. "It was then still daylight, but I noted that within minutes after the holes were dug everybody was asleep," said Smith. He himself settled in after dark, sharing a foxhole with his runner, PFC Herb White of Albany, Georgia. Mostly out of habit, he stretched out on his back with his .45 automatic on full cock and safety engaged, clutched to his chest.

It seemed only seconds later that he awoke in fear and confusion. Flares were bursting overhead; multiple explosions and screams of *Banzai! Banzai* pierced the night. He heard gunshots close by and dazedly realized he was firing his .45, though still not fully awake. A dead Japanese lay across the foot of his foxhole. Others, still very much alive, seemed to be all over the platoon's position. Hearing a moan from beside him, he put out a hand and found White drenched in blood. "Oh, Christ, Smitty," the young Georgian managed to say. "The son-of-a-bitch got me." He gurgled and choked and stopped talking.[16]

Back at battalion headquarters, Major Aplington was trying to figure out what was going on. "About 0430 my three companies on their hills erupted into fire and called for mortar support," he recalled. "Company commanders told me there were Japanese all around them." Getting on the horn with his C Company CO, Captain Dave Zeitlin, who seemed to be at the center of all the racket, Aplington, still not grasping the magnitude of the overall attack, said he'd better see some dead Japanese in the morning. Zeitlin, who would take a spray of grenade fragments in the chest before the night was over, assured him that was not going to be a problem.[17]

—◆—

Colonel John S. Letcher spent the night near the 12th Marines command post listening to the incessant din of gunfire from up in the hills. "The star shells fired by the warships kept the hilltops continuously lighted and the noise of the rifle and machine gun fire never ceased," he observed. His regiment's artillery batteries pounded away at the maximum rate. Despite all the noise, at some point Letcher dozed off. He was startled awake shortly before daybreak by an ashen-faced Marine shouting, "Colonel! Colonel! Wake up! We are being attacked!" Bullets cracking overhead lent credence to the news.

"Where are they?" asked Letcher.

"Right there, Colonel, right in the machine gun nest," exclaimed the Marine, pointing toward a gun emplacement only twenty yards away. Letcher was skeptical, but the Marine insisted. "Yes sir, yes sir, Colonel, they drove us out of it a minute ago." Belatedly recognizing the urgency of the situation, Letcher found a grenade and crawled toward the emplacement. Using a low earthen berm as cover, he made his way to within a few yards of the gun, pulled the pin on the grenade, and rose up to find the muzzle of the captured machine gun pointing directly at him. A Japanese soldier was fumbling with the breech. Letcher threw his grenade, dropping back down behind the berm as it exploded. He called for more grenades and threw another one, though as it left his hand, he saw it was unnecessary. "The Jap who had been pointing the gun was crumpled across the breech. Two others were lying behind him and one was crawling slowly along the ditch away from the nest." Only later did Letcher learn that the Marine who awakened him might well have saved his life: he had removed the bolt from the gun, rendering it inoperable, before abandoning the position.[18]

The Japanese incursion into the artillery CP area caught Jack Kerins with his pants down—literally. Just before dawn, he and two other Marines were sitting atop three steel fuel drums that had been sunk into the ground as a makeshift latrine when a bullet zipped overhead. It was quickly followed by another that smacked into the mud nearby. Kerins buttoned up, grabbed his carbine and pistol, and joined a defensive line forming around the artillery fire direction center. As shots continued to crack overhead, there was a tremendous explosion in a clump of bamboo on the hillside above, followed an instant later by a second blast. A Marine shouted that Japanese were throwing demolition charges down from the higher ground, but the charges were getting caught up in the bamboo. The Marines swept the slope with small arms fire, and a dead Japanese tumbled down to lodge in an irrigation ditch. "A Japanese officer rose waving his sword to direct his men," recalled PFC Eugene Peterson. A burst of machine-gun fire cut the officer down.

As the small arms fire intensified, nineteen-year-old PFC Caesare Adami ran up from the direction of the Asan River draw on the other edge of the perimeter. "He was coming for more grenades," recalled Corporal John Wardlow. "Johnny, those bastards are trying to kill me," exclaimed Adami. He showed Wardlow where a bullet had hit his helmet on one side, passed around the inside, and exited on the other, taking off his right earlobe. Grabbing a case of grenades, Adami headed back toward the river draw but hadn't gone far when he was shot again, this time in the abdomen.[19]

Directing fire on the slope from the recaptured .50-caliber machine gun, Letcher ordered Second Lieutenant Richard R. Rodgers, in happier times the HQ and Service Battery's athletic and morale officer, to take some men around behind the enemy penetration and "get those damn snipers." The lieutenant took five men around the base of the hill and up to the top. Tall sword grass and thick brush limited their vision as they edged cautiously down a narrow trail. Rodgers, a former University of California,

Los Angeles, basketball player who stood six feet, three inches tall, was in the lead, followed by Corporal John Wyly. He and Wyly edged around a bend in the trail but hastily retreated when they bumped into a group of Japanese. A firefight ensued. A couple of grenades fell among the men on the trail but failed to go off. As Marines at the foot of the hill began shooting toward his patrol, Rodgers jumped up and shouted, "Stop your goddamn firing! This is Lieutenant Rodgers!" Just to the rear of Rodgers and Wyly, PFC Robert Wolfe saw a khaki-sleeved arm emerge from the thick brush and drop a demolition charge at the lieutenant's feet. There was a terrific blast, and Rodgers simply disappeared.

Wyly was blown off his feet and severely wounded in the left leg, chest, and hand. Another Marine took a fragment in the leg. The trail was littered with pieces of flesh and clothing, some the remains of Lieutenant Rodgers, some parts of the Japanese soldier who had detonated the charge. "I remember seeing the Jap's hand and arm hanging in a nearby tree," recalled Wolfe. He and the other uninjured Marine, sure they were about to be overrun and killed, sat back to back, their carbines at the ready. "We could hear the Japs hollering all around us. There was a lot of shooting and we expected them to move in on us at any minute, but they never did," he said. After a while, things quieted down, and they dragged Wyly and the other wounded man out of there.[20]

A subsequent sweep finally cleared the hillside. The only identifiable part of Lieutenant Rodgers was one leg found caught in some tree branches. The lieutenant had visited sickbay the evening before to be treated for an infected toe, and the doc had packed cotton under the nail to relieve the pain. The cotton was still in place.

The same defiles leading down to the artillery command post also led to the division hospital set up in a narrow ravine along the Nidual River a few hundred yards inland from Blue Beach. At about 0630, corpsmen noticed enemy soldiers moving along the high ground just south of the hospital tents. As the Japanese approached, twenty-two-year-old Corporal Eulice L. Lowery of the 3rd Medical Battalion shot and killed an enemy officer and five soldiers, but another fifty to seventy Japanese had gotten through. A deluge of small arms and mortar fire descended on the hospital area. Inside the aid tent, Dr. Warren G. Parish finished working on a wounded man before ducking outside. Thirty-six years old, Parish came from a family of doctors—both his father and brother were MDs. He himself had left his practice in Ohio and a wife and two young children to join the Navy Medical Corps in 1942. Now, as he went to help a man wounded in the fighting outside the tent, he was hit in the abdomen and severely wounded.

Fearful they were about to be overrun, medical personnel helped those patients who were able to walk to evacuate the tents and head for the beach. Half-clothed, bandaged men—at least one wearing nothing but a hospital blanket—hobbled down the coast road, the less injured assisting the more seriously wounded. About forty less severely injured patients grabbed whatever weapons were at hand and joined doctors and corpsmen in a defensive cordon around the tents.

Alerted to the attack on the hospital, division headquarters ordered Lieutenant Colonel George O. Van Orden, normally the division infantry training officer, to take two companies of pioneers from the 19th Marines and clear the area. Van Orden responded immediately and, in three hours of fighting, finally corralled the intruders, killing thirty-three at the cost of three Marines killed and one wounded. Only one hospital patient had been wounded in the firefight, but medical personnel had paid a higher price. In addition to Lieutenant Parish, one dental officer, one Navy warrant officer, thirteen corpsmen, and sixteen Marines from the medical companies had been wounded defending the hospital area; one of the corpsmen subsequently died, and Parish was barely clinging to life.

Up on Fonte Hill, Lou Wilson's beleaguered company was again running low on ammunition. As morning neared, the Marines fixed bayonets. Wilson tried to rally his remaining men, urging them to conserve ammunition as best they could. "We stacked up Japanese bodies that were in front of us to serve as a barricade against the fire that was coming in," he recalled.

"This is it," said one wounded Marine, clutching his bayonetted rifle. "This is a hell of a place to die."[21]

Thankfully, their ordeal was nearly over. With daylight came the sound of tanks grinding forward, summoned by F Company executive officer Wilcie A. O'Bannon. The twenty-four-year-old Texan had made his way down the hill and was returning with two Shermans. Major Fraser West had also brought up armored support for G Company. The tanks turned what could have been a "last-stand" situation into a massacre. "The Japanese by this time were so psyched up that they would jump on the tanks and start slashing them with their sabers," recalled Wilson. "It was a field day for a while."[22] Watching a Japanese soldier beating futilely on one of the tanks with his sword, nearby Marines argued over who should get the privilege of terminating the maniac. Finally one of them shot the man off the tank.

Few could have been happier to see daylight than Sergeant Regilio Mercati. Late in the afternoon before the Japanese counterattack, the twenty-five-year-old

Chicago native had been posted as a temporary guard over three wounded G Company Marines. When stretcher bearers failed to arrive by twilight, Mercati stayed by their side as the Japanese attack began to build. At midnight, two Japanese infiltrated to within a few yards of his position. Mercati killed them both at point-blank range. Before dawn the next morning, three more Japanese attempted to close in on them. Mercati killed them but suffered a gunshot wound to his arm in the exchange. Nevertheless, he stayed with the incapacitated Marines until dawn when litter bearers finally arrived to evacuate them.

By 0900 it was over. Reinforcements were arriving and the Japanese were pulling out. "When we got up there, man, there was dead Japs laying everywhere," recalled PFC John W. Foley with G Company. "I don't guess we got over thirty, forty yards out in front of our front lines and somebody hollered at me and I looked around, and he was showing me there was a Jap crawling along over there. I didn't know whether he was wounded or what. . . . I just whirled around and shot him right through the side of the head and went right on."[23]

Over 350 enemy dead were found scattered about on Fonte Hill. Only about one hundred men from the 10th Independent Mixed Regiment survived the night. Cushman's F and E Companies had suffered about 75 percent casualties; G Company, "in reserve," reported 50 percent casualties. Among the latter was Major West, hit by a bullet that shattered his left femur as he was guiding a tank toward some pillboxes on the hill as the Marines exploited the enemy defeat. The phone on the back of the tank was out of order, so West stood out in front waving the driver forward, shouting, "C'mon! C'mon!" That bit of audacity earned the twenty-six-year-old Nevadan, a world-class skier in college, a Silver Star and put him in a body cast from the chest down for three months.[24]

In the charnel house manned by B Company, 1st Battalion, 21st Marines, Lieutenant Edward Mulcahy, Grady Wimmer, Arnaldo Martinez, Moose Killian, and a handful of others were still somehow alive. Despite multiple wounds from the Japanese grenade, Mulcahy had spent the early morning hours trying to organize some sort of a defense with the few survivors at hand. It was a sorry line indeed—it survived mostly because succeeding waves of Japanese were too intent on getting through to more profitable targets in the rear areas—but it was something.

With Mulcahy's acquiescence, Killian took the blinded Wimmer and a wounded corpsman in tow and struck out toward Captain William Shoemaker's A Company in hopes of getting medical help. The firing on the crest to their front had ceased—the last Marine positions there were apparently overrun—but judging from the shooting to their left, A Company was still hanging on. With Wimmer holding on to him for guidance, Killian took the corpsman by the arm and started across the battle-field. Along the way, he was hit in the arm by mortar fragments, but the three men staggered on. Finally, someone called out of the predawn darkness, "Jap or Marine?!" Killian answered quickly and found he had stumbled directly into Shoemaker's CP.[25]

Back at his own CP, 1st Battalion commander Lieutenant Colonel Marlowe Williams, struggling to get some idea of the situation up in the hills, turned to the battalion exec, Lieutenant Colonel Ron Van Stockum. "Van, get up there and see what's going on," he ordered. Van Stockum and his radio operator started up the bluff in the darkness. They had little idea where they were going but knew it had to be "up." Enemy mortar shells passed overhead, but their greater danger came from friendly artillery rounds that failed to clear the crest. At some point, the radio operator disappeared. Van Stockum didn't know where but suspected the man had developed a case of "leg bail," as he diplomatically put it.[26]

At about 0600, as the sun began to come up, a last Japanese wave charged over the hill at the 1st Battalion. A combat correspondent observed, "It was the wildest, most drunken group of all, bunched together howling, stumbling, and waving swords, bayonets and even sticks. Some were already wounded and swathed in gory bandages."[27] The Marines cut them down. Colonel Van Stockum plodded into C Company's lines "in time to see [an] enraged Gunnery Sergeant [Albert D.] Hemphill pick up a discarded Samurai sword and chop down the lone remaining enemy soldier."[28] On the flank, A Company's indomitable Captain Shoemaker ordered a barrage from his 60mm mortars on the Japanese approach route, then led a counterattack to restore his line. His stubborn stand during the night on the critical left flank of the enemy breakthrough would earn him the Navy Cross—his second—though he would not live to receive the decoration in person. Having survived the fierce counterattack of July 25–26, the captain was killed a week later by a stray enemy shell during the push north.

Buttoned up in one of the B Company tanks, Sergeant Tom Murphy's crew had lost radio contact when their antennas were shot off during the night. It seemed suddenly very quiet outside. "We waited a while and then came out of our tanks," he said. "It was a ghastly sight. Dead people all over the place. And then, from in between two tanks, came an unarmed Japanese soldier, running like hell." Sick of it all, Murphy impulsively yelled to his crew, "Don't shoot!" as the Japanese darted past them and disappeared into a gully. "He wanted to get the hell away from there," remarked Murphy. The tank sergeant couldn't blame him.[29]

An unearthly calm descended along the ridge, broken only by the occasional rifle shot. Surprised to be alive, Marines paused to light cigarettes with shaking hands, make coffee, or just sit in wonder. Stretcher bearers and corpsmen tended to the injured, dispatching a stream of walking wounded down the hill. "In some spots there were heaps of cadavers with a sprinkling of arms and legs that had been blown from bodies by our mortars," recalled Lieutenant Arthur A. Frances. "It was impossible to walk two paces without stepping on an already bloating body. . . . Light machine guns, rifles, mortars, knee mortars, and some heavy mortars lay where the Japs had dropped them."[30] Van Stockum used C Company's radio to advise battalion that the line—at that point at least—had held, though he doubted his message got through the jumble of traffic crowding the air waves.

PFC Moose Killian picked his way through the carnage around Corporal Carroll Herzberg's machine-gun position. The ground was littered with dead, the Marines in green dungarees, the Japanese sprawled like misshapen brown sacks of grain. A bayonet still protruded from nineteen-year-old Edward Krejci's body. Killian pulled a Japanese corpse off Herzberg and was astonished to find the twenty-five-year-old Chicagoan was still breathing. Sometime during the night, he had awakened and tied a belt around his leg as a tourniquet before passing out again. In addition to his being bayoneted as the Japanese overran his machine gun, grenade fragments riddled both his legs—sixty-three holes in one leg and thirty-five in the other. Despite the damage, he would survive.

Lieutenant Paul Smith had somehow gotten his wounded runner, Herb White, down to the battalion aid station in the dark even as the Japanese continued their attack. Later in the morning, he returned to their foxhole to retrieve his poncho, only to find it in shreds from a grenade or satchel charge. The dead Japanese lying at the foot of the hole was a major. He had gotten to White with his sword—which was still lying alongside his body—slicing the runner open from chest to groin. White was still alive when Smith carried him out, but he died of his terrible wound aboard the USS *Wharton*. He was buried at sea off Guam's northwest coast.[31]

Jack Kerins watched wounded survivors straggling down from the hills. They were "filthy and ragged and wore blood soaked bandages on different parts of their bodies." One distraught bunch was carrying a severely wounded Marine, who was unconscious if not already dead, a bloody bandage over his abdomen. As a makeshift stretcher, his buddies had inserted bamboo poles through the sleeves of his dungaree jacket and the legs of his trousers in order to lug him down the hill. The wounded man's arms extended over his head because of the poles through his sleeves; his head hung back, and his mouth gaped open. "Watch his head! Watch his head!" one of the Marines sobbed over and over as they stumbled and slid toward the hospital area.[32]

Of the 217 men that landed on Guam with B Company five days earlier, only 18 remained. The number was soon reduced to seventeen when one of the survivors sat down behind Herzberg's machine gun to see if it was still operable. A Japanese sniper shot him through the head. Another belated victim during the morning was Lieutenant Colonel Hector DeZayas, the swaggering, genial commander of the 2nd Battalion, 3rd Marines. Known to his Naval Academy classmates as "Hec" or "Diz," DeZayas was shot and killed by a sniper—or possibly just an enemy straggler who saw an opportunity—when he came forward during the morning to check on his battalion. He died in the arms of his regimental operations officer.

Fred Hofmann and his three companions had spent a traumatic night feigning death in the wreckage of their foxhole. Hofmann's wound stopped bleeding, and he remained conscious. During the night, large numbers of Japanese had passed by bound for the Marine rear. "About 4:30 in the morning I heard them coming back," he said. "I counted five crawl past the edge of the hole. I kept laying there with my eyes wide open, not moving." Some enemy soldiers glanced into the hole at the tangle of bodies but didn't investigate further. "I thought sure they would see the glint of my wristwatch and tear it off for a souvenir but they didn't," said Hofmann. Hours later, as the sun came up, help arrived, and Hofmann was evacuated back to the beach, then aboard ship, eventually ending up at Aiea Naval Hospital in Hawaii.[33] Corporal Charles Moore, who had played dead through the night not far from Hofmann and his companions, also escaped notice after being overrun by the Japanese. "They were milling around there until dawn, then they were gone," he recalled.[34]

Hofmann was subsequently awarded the Navy Cross for covering the grenade that landed in the shell hole. A newspaper reporter in Hawaii asked the wounded hero if he was willing "to go back."

"Back to where?" said Hofmann. "Sure, I'm ready to go back. Back to Hoboken."[35]

⌇

Colonel Pete Duplantis and his isolated command post remained in dire straits as day dawned. Enemy mortar and machine-gun fire virtually paralyzed any movement. He had approximately thirty wounded, some of whom were barely hanging on. Learning that the artillery was now back on call, he requested a barrage on top of Hill Item, about seventy-five yards to his right and now in the center of the Japanese position. While this posed some danger, Duplantis believed the artillery— which had fired numerous concentrations on the hill when it was first captured—

would be able to pull it off. "Under the circumstances, it seemed the only way to save the situation," he said. "The lightly armed CP personnel were almost out of ammunition and time was of the essence."[36]

Division headquarters refused his request, feeling the situation was too confused. Pressure was brought on Duplantis to pull troops back from K Company's forward position to defend the CP, but the colonel was unwilling to take the chance. "K Company was experiencing the utmost difficulty in holding and I preferred sacrificing the CP to what might prove a general collapse of the line," he said later.[37]

As an alternative, division ordered the adjacent 9th Marines—which had escaped the worst of the Japanese assault—to eradicate the penetration. The job fell to Colonel Edward Craig's regimental reserve, Company L, which was turned over to Major Harold C. ("Bing") Boehm, executive officer of Craig's 1st Battalion, as he was already familiar with the ground. While waiting for Boehm, the CP defenders set up a 60mm mortar and—with two wounded corpsmen serving as loaders—fired about ninety rounds into a mass of disorganized Japanese "who could be seen huddled like sheep in the valley far below," said Duplantis.[38] Boehm arrived later in the morning, working in behind Hill Item to within 250 yards of the Japanese before his Marines were detected. The assault carried the hill, killing twenty-three Japanese and driving most of the rest into a firing line manned by Duplantis's Marines.

"When dawn came, we had about thirty of them cornered in a little draw," said Lieutenant Tom Brock, who had come forward with L Company to reinforce the line the evening before. "They saw the situation and so everyone blew themselves up, and they used land mines to do it with. We found arms, legs, etc. all over in front of us." As one Marine officer observed sardonically, the Japanese were "saving their faces by blowing out their intestines."[39] Approximately three hundred dead Japanese were subsequently counted scattered around all sides of the CP and in the vicinity of K Company. Found among them were numbers of small lanterns with narrow slits on the rearward side, apparently used to keep order among files following guides in the darkness.

The scene was also grim up on Fonte Hill, where there were so many dead Japanese that Bob Cushman called division to ask for a bulldozer. "There are 800 Japanese here lying in the grass and I need a bulldozer to get rid of them," he reported. "They're beginning to stink."

Brigadier General Alfred Noble, Turnage's caustic assistant division commander, scoffed at the report. "There are no damned 800 Japanese up there, you must be dreaming," he told Cushman.

When Cushman persisted, Noble finally sent up a dozer and followed along to see for himself. He arrived to find Cushman was no dreamer. He then made his second mistake of the morning when he turned his ire on Lou Wilson. Exhausted and hobbling from his leg wound, Wilson, who had been hit a third time during the night—this time in the shoulder—had come down to Cushman's CP to report on his situation. Upon learning that the bedraggled officer was a company commander, Noble snapped, "That's typical, sitting back there in the damn CP instead of out there with his troops like he's supposed to be." Wilson's runner started to raise his rifle and for a horrified instant Cushman thought the youngster intended to put a bullet into Noble for disparaging his captain. Before the confrontation could escalate, another Marine grabbed the runner, told him to "put the damned gun down," and hustled him away.

Responding to Noble's criticism of Lou Wilson, Cushman replied coolly, "Well, sir, he's been wounded three times and I'm recommending him for a Medal of Honor."[40]

Most of the confusion in the 3rd Marine Division sector had abated by noon as Japanese stragglers were hunted down and killed. "By the next night there weren't any left," said Brigadier General Noble, who apparently had a better perspective on events following his visit to Fonte Hill. "We'd killed most of them. And the people were laughing and shooting. They'd go *There goes one!* and *bang*, knock him over just like you would a rabbit. It was sort of pitiful in a way. They were completely lost, disorganized. Some of them didn't even have any rifles."[41]

Forward observer PFC Joseph Kight cautiously emerged from his foxhole near the artillery positions, having spent the night "just laying there shaking like a dog passing peach seeds," as he put it. A dead Japanese lay nearby. "The only thing I could see was his heart, in one piece, on the outside of his chest," he recalled. The Marine who had killed him said he'd yelled the password at the straggler. "He went to jabbering and I shot him until I emptied that M-1," said the Marine.[42]

Two stubborn strays were cornered in a cave about one hundred yards from the 12th Marines' CP. Hoping to obtain a prisoner for interrogation, the process of extermination paused while an interpreter tried to coax them out. "Using a loudspeaker, he talked to them for half an hour, promising that they would be well-treated if they surrendered and not harmed in any way and telling them that if they would not surrender, they would be killed," observed Colonel Letcher. The Japanese answered with shouts of defiance and cries of *Banzai!*, so in the end a tank clanked up and "blasted them into eternity," reported Letcher.[43]

Accompanying a patrol flushing out strays in a ravine near the division artillery positions, a corporal saw a wounded Japanese trying to crawl to an open box of hand grenades. Picking up the wounded man's bayoneted rifle, the corporal stuck him through the throat. He told a news correspondent later that he intended to send the bayonet back to his home in Massachusetts as a souvenir.[44]

Ships standing offshore were advised by radio to prepare for large numbers of casualties from the night's fighting. Subchaser USS PC-555 was told at 0815 to expect up to 350 wounded. "Casualties soon started coming out," noted the ship's war diary. "All ships available blankets, toweling, sheets and mattress covers [were] turned over to Marines for first aid purposes."[45] Medical detachments were boated ashore to assist both the Marine Brigade and 3rd Division with the large numbers of wounded. "Upon arriving on the beach, casualties were strewn around that required immediate treatment," reported Lieutenant Francis J. Shiring, who arrived ashore at 1000 with medical personnel from USS *Zeilin*.[46]

Evacuation from the beaches continued through the day. "In a short while the main sick-bay dressing station was filled, whereupon, we opened the wardroom reception and dressing stations," noted the USS *Monrovia*. "Before very long this area was filled and casualties were awaiting their turn in the passageways. . . . At 2400 we were still receiving casualties. . . . A count showed that we received ninety patients, fifty two of whom were stretcher cases."[47] At noon the hospital ship USS *Solace* left with a load of casualties for the four-day voyage to the military hospitals at Kwajalein. The ship, which had been processing casualties since July 24, was filled to capacity with 585 wounded. Before departure, the remains of several men who had died aboard ship were sent back to the island for burial. Ten more would die of their wounds before the hospital ship arrived at Kwajalein.

Hundreds of other casualties were treated by medical teams aboard the transports. They included an artilleryman from the 3rd Division who was on the verge of a mental breakdown after a terrifying experience in the hours prior to the Japanese attack. After dark, he had taken shelter in a small dug cave trying to get some sleep out of the rain. He awoke during the night to find a group of Japanese—apparently one of the infiltrating demolition teams—crowded in with him. One of them was sitting on his carbine, others pushed against him in the confined space. Not daring to move, he could only lie there and hope they did not realize who he was.

"He stayed there all night without them discovering him," observed one of his officers. "They must have thought, jammed against him in the darkness, that he was one of them." Just before daybreak, the Japanese left the cave, and the shaken Marine scrambled out to safety, but the strain of those long hours had shattered him mentally, and he had to be evacuated.[48]

Among the evacuees from the 3rd Marine Division killing ground were Grady Wimmer, Lieutenant Mulcahy, and Arnaldo Martinez. Mulcahy had over sixty grenade fragments lodged in his body. Martinez had been hit in the chest near one of his lungs. Wimmer, blinded up in the hills, lost his left eye, but six or eight weeks later he recovered the sight in his right eye.

It was midnight before Rufus Belding, who had spent hours at Colonel Duplantis's CP with his finger plugging the hole in his shoulder, finally got off the island for medical treatment. "I went to a hospital ship that night and was worked on, operated on," he remembered. "I remember him cutting. They had a mirror up there and he was cutting all this stuff that was dead, you know."[49]

Another patient, Corporal Frank A. Bosse, had been wounded when a grenade landed in his foxhole. "[It] blew all the meat off my hip," he recalled. "I thought it blew my leg off. . . . I thought, well I'm dead." Bosse's lieutenant stuck him with a morphine syrette, and he was eventually brought back to an aid station. "I was there for maybe three or four hours and they put me aboard a hospital ship. They cleaned my hip as soon as I got aboard the ship, they took all the dirt out of my hip." Doctors saved his leg, but Bosse spent the next several months in the hospital. He later learned that the other Marine in his foxhole had been killed.[50]

Shot during the attack on the 3rd Division hospital, Lieutenant Warren Parish survived the trip out to the USS *Rixey*, where surgeons struggled to repair the extensive internal damage. "Lieut. (MC) USNR W.G.P. was struck by a bullet in the left axillary line seventh rib while defending his hospital from a Jap breakthrough," reported the ship's medical officer. "Profuse hemorrhage from a split spleen and retro-peritoneal hemorrhage from the left renal area was encountered. Splenectomy, closure of a perforated sucking hole in the diaphragm, packing of the retro-peritoneal bleeding area, and splenic flexure colostomy for a 2 cm perforation of the splenic flexure were performed while 1500 cc whole blood transfusion and 750 cc plasma were given." Despite all efforts, Parish succumbed two days later from hemorrhage and peritonitis.[51]

Also succumbing to his wounds aboard *Rixey* was PFC Caesare Adami, shot in the abdomen in the defense of the 12th Marines CP. With clinical detachment, the medical report chronicled the nineteen-year-old Marine's death: "PFC C.F.A.

with a bullet wound 3 cm in diameter in the right flank in the region of the liver was found to have a gushing hemorrhage from the region of the Foramen of Winslow which could not be controlled by pack or compression of the hepatic artery in the hepatic-duodenal ligament. The incision was hastily closed without determining the exact nature of the injury. (It is regretted that no personnel could be spared for autopsy on these patients.) He expired five minutes later."[52] The official telegram announcing the young Marine's death to his Italian-born father in Rockford, Illinois, would include none of these details.

General Hideyoshi Obata cabled Imperial General Headquarters at 0800 hours to express his apologies for the failure of the counterattack: "On the night of the 25th, the army with its entire force, launched the general attack from Fonte and Mount Mangan toward Adelup Point," he reported. "Command officers and all officers and men boldly charged the enemy. The fighting continued until dawn but our forces failed to achieve the desired objectives, losing more than 80 percent of the personnel, for which I sincerely apologize. I will defend Mount Mangan to the last by assembling the remaining strength. I feel deeply sympathetic for the officers and men who fell in action and their bereaved families."[53]

Even as General Obata's message made its way to Tokyo through the ether, survivors of the counterattack were trickling back to prearranged assembly areas. Some companies had been reduced to just a few men. Lieutenant Yasuhiro Yamashita of the 3rd Battalion, 18th Regiment returned with only nine survivors to find his assembly area "almost empty. . . . [T]here were only twenty soldiers, including those coming back alive from the battlefields."[54]

General Takeshi Takashina had thrown seven battalions or their equivalent against the Marines. The assault had successfully applied mass, force, and surprise on selected parts of the American line. Nevertheless, the gambit failed when the troops that did manage to break through were unable to maintain the contact or coordination required to seriously damage the Marine beachhead. Over three thousand men were dead with little to show for their sacrifice. "We had been thinking that the Japanese might win through a night counterattack, but when the star shells came over one after another, we would only use our men as human bullets and there were many useless casualties and no [chance] of success," observed an officer.[55]

Officers leading the assault had been among the first killed—95 percent died, including Colonel Hiko-Shiro Ohashi, commanding the 18th Infantry, who "died gallantly when he charged the enemy on the north side of Mount Libugon," according to Japanese accounts.[56] Majors Chusa Maruyama and Setsuo Yukioka, commanding the 2nd and 3rd Battalions of the same regiment, were also killed. Major Maruyama's body was discovered in the Asan River draw. Major Yukioka was found in the Nidual River area. A notated map recovered from Major Maruyama's body offered U.S. intelligence belated insight into the details of the failed attack and the units involved.[57]

The 2nd Battalion, 10th Mixed Regiment withdrew to Fonte with about one hundred survivors under the command of a first lieutenant. The battalion commander had been killed. The remnants of the 320th Independent Infantry Battalion had attacked with only about forty men. Half were killed, including the battalion commander; the remnants of the 321st Battalion were annihilated "after confused fighting," according to the Japanese. Major Aoki, commander of the 38th Infantry Regiment's artillery battalion, was wounded during the general counterattack and committed suicide. The commander of the 2nd Company of the 38th Regiment was killed by tank fire. Commanding the naval contingent's attack on the 3rd Marines, Captain Yutaka Sugimoto was shot dead during the initial charge. Executive officer Lieutenant Kiyokoza Kaburagi took over the command and continued to push forward until killed by an enemy shell. The few survivors of the naval force trickled back to their assembly area having accomplished nothing of consequence. According to Japanese sources, the long list of dead included a number of Japanese civilians from a "shock unit of seventy men [that] was organized at the earnest request of men having fencing experience." They suffered heavy casualties after joining the assault with General Kiyoshi Shigematsu's brigade.[58]

The shocking number of casualties sent morale plummeting among survivors. Over 90 percent of the available weapons had been destroyed, and remaining units were thoroughly disorganized. The situation on Orote Peninsula was unknown—communications had been lost with those forces by the evening of July 25—but it was assumed they had also taken part in the doomed counterattack and fared no better.

The Japanese had assured the Chamorros that if the Americans tried to return to Guam, they would find "nothing but flies" feasting on dead civilians.[59] Instead the flies were feeding on the thousands of slain Japanese. Describing the scene near the overrun 21st Marine mortar positions, Sergeant Francis H. Barr observed, "As far as you could see, dead Japs dotted the fields. On the crest of a hill, there was a long line of enemy dead, a line so straight that it appeared as if the Japs had been placed in that order."[60] PFC Tom Price was among the Marines trying to dispose of the scores of corpses in front of the 22nd Marines at Orote. "They were just dead all over the place," he recalled. "They dug a big hole with a bulldozer. We tied a wire around their leg or arm and drug them. It didn't take long to drag them over there, put them in a hole and cover them up."[61]

Many of the dead were simply covered with a few perfunctory shovelfuls of dirt and left to rot. Others didn't even receive that courtesy. PFC Joe Frank recalled, "One night, just as we were setting up and starting to dig in, I noticed a dead Jap. He had been there for a while and there was quite a stink so I got a rope around one of his arms and dragged him 20 to 30 feet out in front of us so we didn't have to smell him all night. I dragged him until his arm fell off and figured that would have to be far enough."[62]

Assigned to burial duty, PFC George Walden threw some dirt over two dead Japanese, only to find them uncovered the next morning. His lieutenant got after him about it, and Walden covered them again—and again, the next morning they were lying exposed. Walden decided to watch the bodies and find out what was happening. It turned out the culprits were Guam's large and ubiquitous toads, which had been imported to the island specifically to eat flies. As Walden watched, the toads pushed the dirt off the bodies so the flies would accumulate and provide their daily feast.[63]

In an effort to resolve two problems with one directive—the litter of dead bodies and the large number of unauthorized rear echelon scavengers looking for souvenirs—III Amphibious Corps authorized regiments to assign stragglers to burial details. Another, presumably short-lived order required anyone who shot a Japanese to bury the body, recalled PFC Frank Brandemihl. Suddenly men who had previously argued endlessly over who had fired the killing shot professed complete ignorance on the circumstances of any given fatality. "There was a lot of conjecture on how the Japanese troops had met their demise," observed Brandemihl. "Some of the theories were: heat exhaustion . . . heart attack . . . or finding and eating Marine rations."[64]

At about 1500 hours General Obata received a message from Imperial General Headquarters acknowledging his earlier missive apologizing for the failure of the counterattack: "The Army Commander and his men have fought bravely in a fierce battle from day to day, achieving brilliant battle results," observed the message. "However it is to be greatly regretted that many officers and men have been killed or wounded. The securing of Guam is a matter of urgency for the defense of Japan. We are confident that we will be able to meet your expectations. We hope that you will do your best to secure the island. Lastly, we pray for the success of the officers and men."[65]

The suggestion that General Obata might "secure the island" was a pipe dream, and the general and his staff officers knew it. The operations officer for the 29th Division later conceded that by noon on July 26, it was evident the Americans could not be dislodged from their beachhead. "After this it was decided that the sole purpose of combat would be to inflict losses on the American forces in the interior of the island," he observed.[66]

General Takashina called a staff meeting on the morning of July 27 to review plans to withdraw from the Fonte area. The shattered units would establish a new defensive line on northern Guam, where they would hold out as long as possible. An operational plan was already at hand, having been drawn up on July 23 during the debate over whether to drive for the beaches or pull back and fight a purely defensive battle. Despite reassuring messages from Tokyo, both Japanese generals knew there could be no outside rescue from their predicament, but they were determined to fight to the bitter end.

Under General Takashina's plan, all casualties and Japanese civilians were to be evacuated to the area north of Barrigada Hill starting the night of July 27. Combat units would begin to disengage after dark on July 28 and assemble at the village of Ordot—site of a Japanese supply point located on the dividing line between the mostly volcanic southern half of the island and the mostly limestone northern plateau—before moving into defensive positions at Barrigada Hill and the village of Finegayan. The field hospital would be relocated to the north side of Mount Santa Rosa, well to the north. A rear guard would remain at Ordot to delay the American advance while the new defensive line was established.

The withdrawal order came too late for General Kiyoshi Shigematsu, who was desperately attempting to reorganize the remnants of his shattered 48th Independent Mixed Brigade on the morning of July 26th. Only hours after crushing the assault at Fonte Hill, Lieutenant Colonel Bob Cushman's 2nd Battalion overran Shigematsu's command post in a quarry near Mount Mangan. Accepting his fate, General Shigematsu wrote a last report to General Takashina and gave it to his orderly to deliver before the position collapsed: "I took charge of the defense of the important front, but lost most of my men and now have no means to recover the situation," he observed. "I am really ashamed of myself. I will hold Mt. Mangan to the last with a small number of survivors, I pray for the battle success of the division commander and the survivors."[67]

Fierce fighting lasted all morning. With most of his men cut down, Shige-matsu "finally [died] a heroic death" around noon when a tank blasted his head-quarters. According to Japanese sources, only three men survived the fighting in the headquarters area.[68]

⌒⌒

For the 3rd Marine Division as a whole, July 26 was a day of adjustment and reorga-nization. It was badly needed. Shaken by the magnitude of the Japanese assault, U.S. commanders remained wary. A memorandum from General Turnage described his division's stubborn stand as "a grand victory for us" but at the same time expressed concerns that the Japanese might renew the attack the following night.[69] Preparing for that possibility, Turnage issued an order calling for the formation of an emer-gency division reserve composed of service and support troops. A battalion of the 307th Infantry in IIIAC reserve was directed to assemble in the vicinity of Piti Navy Yard. On the 3rd Division's right, the 9th Marines pulled back about fifteen hundred yards to better defensive positions. All hands were ordered to prepare strong defenses for the night, including the installation of barbed wire.

That same afternoon, General Roy Geiger came ashore and established his com-mand post near Agat in the Marine Brigade sector. "Snipers were near the beach at [the] time and we had to stop for a few minutes just as we reached the beach until the snipers could be cleared out," observed aide Roy Owsley.[70] Like Turnage, Geiger believed the Japanese might follow up with a second general counterattack, but he was also coming under pressure from Holland Smith to get things moving. Increas-ingly annoyed by what he viewed as the lack of progress by the 3rd Marine Division, Smith fired off a dispatch to Geiger "directing him to take more offensive action."[71]

Geiger's longtime chief of staff observed years later that Geiger "had a policy of never questioning an order. . . . If his immediate superior told him to do something, he did it."[72] This instance apparently proved to be the exception. Despite General Smith's exhortation, Geiger wisely opted to allow his battered troops a temporary respite to catch their breath and regroup. Thinly stretched over nine thousand yards of difficult terrain, the 3rd Division had prevailed but at a price. The division casualty report for July 25–27 listed 166 killed, 645 wounded, and 35 missing, the majority of which were incurred during the Japanese counterattack.

The 3rd Marine Division had absorbed a powerful blow. Not immediately recognized was that in delivering that blow, the Japanese had essentially destroyed themselves. Brigadier General Noble later observed that the mass attack "was the best thing that could have happened." Faced with a choice between bitter defense or full-scale offense, the Japanese chose to attack with all their reserves. "And they just threw those six battalions away and it broke their back," remarked Noble. Instead of the Americans' having to fight those battalions "piece by piece" over a period of days or weeks, they'd been obliterated in a single night. "The decisive battle had been fought finally right down on the beach," observed Noble with undisguised satisfaction. "Right in the beachhead."[73]

The feared Japanese counterattack on the night of July 26 failed to materialize. There was only an invasion by the dead. During the night, heavy rains filled foxholes and washed scores of corpses off the mountainside and sent them floating down the Asan River. Marines standing watch shot and threw grenades at the bobbing dead, mistaking them for live Japanese attempting to infiltrate by swimming down the river. Daylight revealed dozens of bloating bodies caught in the barbed wire belatedly strung across the watercourse following the counterattack of the preceding night.

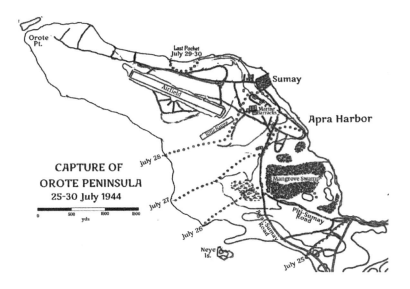

Captain George J. McMillin USN

顔横の虜俘 かる語を何

Japanese World War II propaganda sheet featuring some prominent POWs, including the USS *Penguin*'s Lieutenant James Haviland (bottom row, second from left) and Captain George J. McMillin (upper left corner).

Captain Geary Bundschu USMC

Private First Class
Luther Skaggs Jr. USMC

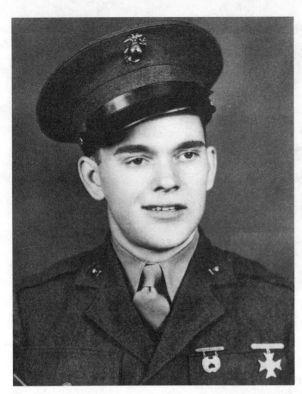

Private First Class
Leonard Mason USMC

Captain Louis H. Wilson Jr. USMC

Private First Class Frank Witek USMC

General Hideyoshi Obata
NATIONAL ARCHIVES

Lieutenant General Takeshi Takashina
NATIONAL ARCHIVES

Major General Roy S. Geiger
NATIONAL ARCHIVES

Major General Andrew D. Bruce NATIONAL ARCHIVES

Lieutenant General
Holland M. Smith USMC

Meeting on Guam as organized resistance comes to an end (l-r): Admiral Raymond A. Spruance, Admiral Chester W. Nimitz, Major General Allen H. Turnage, and Marine Corps Commandant Alexander A. Vandegrift. USN

Posing by the bronze plaque retrieved from the ruins of the former Marine Barracks on Orote Peninsula (l-r): Lieutenant Colonel Alan Shapley, Brigadier General Lemuel C. Shepherd, Colonel Merlin F. Schneider, and Lieutenant General Holland M Smith. USMC

CHAPTER 19

BATTLE FOR OROTE

WHILE THE EVENTUAL OUTCOME MIGHT HAVE BEEN ESTABLISHED THE NIGHT AND morning of July 25–26, the battle for Guam was far from over. As the 3rd Division took what passed for a breather, the Marine Brigade was preparing to attack down the Orote Peninsula toward the airfield in what would turn out to be some of the toughest fighting of the campaign.

The Japanese had organized a defense in depth with three successive lines. The first barrier, now broken, had defended the neck of the peninsula, covering the rice fields at the approaches. The second, three hundred yards behind the first, dominated a bottleneck along the Sumay Road created by a mangrove swamp on one side and marshy terrain on the other. The final and most formidable line had been organized along a low bluff that ran just below the airfield and old Marine rifle range all the way to Sumay. It included trenchworks and scores of pillboxes and fighting positions backed by weaponry that included four 120mm Type 10 guns that fired a forty-five-pound shell, fourteen 75mm Type 88 artillery pieces, and sixty 13mm machine guns and 25mm automatic cannons.

DAY 1: OROTE PENINSULA, JULY 26, 1944

Dug in with the 22nd Marines at the neck of the peninsula, PFC Ray Gillespie awoke in his sodden foxhole shortly before dawn. The chaos of the attempted enemy breakout from the peninsula during the early morning hours and the butchery on the low hill to his front seemed unreal in the relative quiet of morning. "There was a stillness all along the line, except for the weeping of a Japanese soldier on the top of the hill," he remembered.

As Marines began to stir in their muddy holes, Gillespie set out to check in with his lieutenant. "A few of the foxholes were empty and a few of the others had dead

Marines and Japs lying together," he observed. Down the line with L Company, a Marine in an advanced state of shock shared a foxhole with his dead buddy. "[He] was just sitting there," recalled his platoon sergeant, "a .45 in his hands, shaking all over. It took two men to get the .45 out of his hands."[1]

Gillespie was picking his way through the carnage when he heard an angry voice exclaim, "You goddamn bastards, why aren't you ready to move out?" Glancing up, he saw his ever-impatient battalion commander shaking his fist toward the weary riflemen. Years later, Gillespie's most striking memory of the scene was the stark contrast between his muddy, dirty platoon—some of them covered with dried blood, their own or that of their friends—and the angry colonel's "bandbox clean" dungarees.[2]

The morning attack did not get off well. As naval gunfire and artillery started to pound the Japanese positions prior to the 0700 jump off, shells began to fall on the waiting Marines, scattering men in all directions. Assuming he was the victim of misdirected friendly fire, regimental commander Colonel Merlin F. Schneider messaged brigade, "Naval gunfire and arty have completely disorganized my assault element." Brigade responded, "Front line infantry observers report that was Jap artillery."[3] Whatever the source of the shelling, the 22nd Marines were forced to delay their assault for an hour. PFC Fenton ("Gabby") Grahnert, who had scattered with the others, returned to his foxhole to find what was left of a Marine who had been killed by a shell. "Part of his guts was on my pack," he recalled. "And his head was lying there with his helmet on."[4]

Deployed with the 1st Battalion, 4th Marines on the brigade left, PFC George Aspley spent the night in a foxhole with his buddy, who kept complaining he had to move his bowels. Ordinarily he would have just dug their foxhole a little deeper, done his business, and covered it up, but they had hit coral while digging in. They could go no further down, and he couldn't leave the foxhole for fear of being shot. Finally, the Marine crapped in his helmet and dumped the contents out over the side of the hole.

They were still in their foxhole when word was passed just after daybreak to move out. Sherman tanks clanked up, and artillery shells whistled overhead, bursting in the brush and coconut trees beyond the foxhole line. Aspley fixed his bayonet as they went forward, scanning the ground for mines while remaining alert for any Japanese that might go after the tanks with a Molotov cocktail or demolition charge. He did not have long to wait. As he rounded a shell crater not fifty feet from his vacated foxhole, he encountered a Japanese soldier. "He sat with his rifle across his lap and for an instant we both froze and stared at each other before my trigger finger squeezed twice and the Japanese slumped forward." Aspley shot him twice more to make sure he was dead before moving on.[5]

The 22nd Marines finally jumped off at 0800 with the 2nd Battalion in the lead. Directly in their path to the right front was the coastal mangrove swamp used by the Japanese as an assembly area for the previous night's failed counterattack. Schneider opted to skirt the swamp except for patrols, which turned out to be a wise decision. Venturing in among the arching tree roots, through mud and water that was sometimes waist deep, the patrols encountered only a few snipers. Pushing up the Agat-Sumay Road, the main force enjoyed dry land but soon ran into the next Japanese defense line. Organized along a low ridge one hundred yards beyond Road Junction 15, the position took advantage of the natural bottleneck formed by the mangrove swamp on the battalion's right and a marshy area to the left. The Japanese had mined the narrow corridor with jury-rigged aerial bombs to keep the tanks at bay. The minefield was protected by a series of log emplacements—buttressed with earth-filled oil drums—spaced at ten-yard intervals overlooking the road junction. The positions were virtually invisible. "It was the most beautiful camouflage job I ever saw," remarked Major Robert S. Felkner. "It blended perfectly with the landscape. I had my field glasses focused directly on it a hundred yards away, and I thought I saw a tangle of vines."[6]

Watching from their vantage points, the Japanese allowed the assault platoon to proceed about halfway along the corridor before opening fire. The initial blast stopped the Marines cold and trapped the lead elements on the causeway. Stymied by the minefield, the accompanying Sherman tanks stood back and directed covering fire at the narrow gun slots in the bunkers, the shells and machine-gun fire passing only three or four feet over the prostrate Marines. They succeeded in suppressing the volume of enemy fire long enough for the trapped men to crawl back out of the kill zone, while the main assault stalled.

On the brigade left, the 4th Marines, made better progress initially, moving some four hundred yards against meager resistance. At 0930 the regiment reported finding twelve destroyed enemy tanks that had apparently fallen victim to artillery and naval gunfire. Opposition was described as "light."[7] That soon changed as the 1st Battalion on the far left encountered a warren of bunkers and pillboxes. In the desperate fighting that followed, three C Company Marines earned the Navy Cross. One went to eighteen-year-old PFC James M. Branch, who had joined the Marines immediately after graduating from high school in Duncan, Oklahoma. Branch's squad was advancing across a clearing when they came under intense automatic weapons fire from a well-concealed pillbox. In an effort to free his pinned-down squad, Branch stood up and went after the position with only his rifle, killing two Japanese before he was shot down. Next to give it a try was

Corporal Herbert Helpingstine, who crept forward with a bazooka. He managed to work his way in close to the emplacement but was shot as he rose to his knees to take aim. Though mortally wounded, Helpingstine shouldered his bazooka and knocked out the pillbox with a single rocket. The third recipient, Sergeant Albert J. Shaheen of Pawtucket, Rhode Island, was attacked from behind by a sword-wielding Japanese officer who slashed him twice on the shoulder. Shaheen shot him dead, then continued to lead his squad in the attack, personally killing seven more Japanese before allowing himself to be evacuated.

A fourth Navy Cross was earned during the day by Platoon Sergeant William J. Hunniford of Rockville, Connecticut, advancing with the 3rd Battalion's Company I. On W-Day the nineteen-year-old sergeant, a veteran of the 3rd Raider Battalion, had gone three times into an open rice paddy under heavy machine-gun fire to retrieve wounded men. Now, as his company ran into the enemy defense line, he went after one pillbox after another—three in all—using smoke grenades to blind the occupants before closing in and killing them. He knocked out yet another pillbox with rifle grenades, but his luck finally ran out when he attempted to tackle a fifth. Caught in a crossfire, he was killed by a gunshot to the head.

Unable to break through after hours of fighting, the brigade dug in for the night facing the web of Japanese defenses. Enemy casualties were unknown, but six enemy prisoners, including a warrant officer, had been captured during the day, bringing the total number of prisoners captured by III Amphibious Corps since W-Day to fourteen. Experience showed that prisoners usually possessed little useful information. "Prisoners taken were, or professed to be, extremely stupid, having no knowledge of any units or activity other than their own," noted a Marine Brigade intelligence report. "Nearly all tactical information obtained from prisoners of war proved to be thoroughly unreliable." This case turned out to be the exception. The newly captured POWs revealed that forces on the peninsula consisted largely of naval personnel, including Special Naval Landing Force troops, along with some army elements. Approximately two thousand enemy troops remained to defend the peninsula, including as many as one thousand armed "Jap Seabees." The defenders intended to make their major stand on the approaches to the airfield. "Information obtained later from prisoners disclosed that the Japs had been ordered to die on this final defense line," reported the brigade journal.[8]

DAY 2: OROTE PENINSULA, JULY 27, 1944

U.S. artillery, mortars, and offshore ships kept up harassing fire during the night, while Japanese guns remained comparatively quiet. The morning's jump-off, ordered for 0700, was briefly delayed due to fears the enemy had picked up the scheduled time on an SCR 300 radio channel. The attack got off fifteen minutes late without any interference that would indicate a security breach. On the brigade right, the 22nd Marines prepared to take another crack at the difficult bottleneck. On the left, the 4th Marines continued to face the multitude of pillboxes, trenches, and bunkers that had held them up the previous day. None seemed to have been seriously impacted by the heavy air support, naval gunfire, and artillery preparation.

Located roughly fifteen hundred yards southeast of Orote Airfield, the 3rd Battalion, 4th Marines would see some of the heaviest fighting of the day. The first obstacle was the low fortified ridge about three hundred yards to their front. Beyond the ridge, a coconut grove extended five hundred yards along gently rising ground to yet another ridge, site of the Japanese main position, which barred the way to the airfield.

The attack toward the first ridge had scarcely gotten underway when it ran into a minefield consisting of the ubiquitous converted aerial bombs. The mines had been set out with their noses projecting a few inches above the ground and were poorly camouflaged, allowing infantrymen to guide the supporting tanks around them. Watching from carefully camouflaged dugouts along the base of the ridge, the Japanese waited until the assault platoons were within two hundred yards before opening fire. As automatic weapons lashed the line, the Marine tanks rumbled forward to blast the dugouts at point-blank range. A return 75mm shell slammed into one of the Shermans but failed to penetrate. The only casualty inside was a crewman with a sprained wrist, but the fragmentation showered the unprotected infantry advancing alongside. As enemy fire gradually diminished, L Company moved onto the low ridge, mopping up with phosphorus grenades and BARs.

By 0900 the 3rd Battalion was moving down the back side of the ridge into the coconut grove beyond. Heavy smoke billowed from oil drums in a burning fuel dump. Enemy pillboxes scattered among the trees took the lead elements under fire. A mortar shell exploded in front of PFC Horace ("Cal") Frost as he moved up with his L Company machine-gun squad. Metal shards sliced open his hand. "It wounded three of us" he recalled. "The worst was the squad leader who had got it right through the neck." Though unable to use his right hand, Frost somehow managed to get a bandage in place on the squad leader's neck and applied pressure to control the bleeding.[9] An L Company corpsman, nineteen-year-old Pharmacist's Mate Third Class William E. Feshoh of Elmira, New York, was shot in the lung. PFC Nicholas Pappajohn tried to help the desperately wounded youth. "[There was] not much I could do, just plug the holes," he admitted. It was not enough. Feshoh died.[10]

Fighting for the coconut grove continued through the afternoon. By the time the grove was secured, Company L alone had had suffered seventy casualties. Following along with the 2nd Battalion, Sergeant Buck Daley came across Sergeant John J. Govaletz lying in an open area. The twenty-year-old from Perth Amboy, New Jersey, had been shot by a sniper; dying, he was no longer conscious, but "his chest was open wide, his heart still pumping slightly," noted Daley. Two officers stood nearby, talking unconcernedly. Daley assumed the sniper had been found and dispatched, or they wouldn't be so cavalier.[11]

The 3rd Battalion finally emerged from the coconut grove at about 1530, leaving clusters of Japanese dead, most of them scattered around knocked-out machine-gun emplacements. "Tank fire had killed many of the Japanese," noted Major Anthony Walker, the battalion operations officer. "Others, forced from their dugouts had been cut down by BARs and M-1s."[12] Up ahead, about four hundred yards away, lay the still higher ridge barring the way to the airfield.

The progress of the 4th Marines on the brigade left allowed the 22nd Marines to finally push across the narrow corridor that had held them up since the previous afternoon. Under the cover of smoke shells, a bomb disposal officer began disarming the aerial-bomb minefield, marking a path across the causeway for the tanks.

Leaving the mangrove swamp, Colonel Schneider took advantage of the expanded maneuver room and brought his 3rd Battalion up on the right of the 2nd Battalion, which had led the way across the causeway. Ray Gillespie was moving up with K Company when the Marine next to him was shot. The victim's body twisted, and he did a quick step backward before falling. "My reaction was to ease his fall with my left arm behind his back and rest him against the knoll," observed Gillespie. "When I looked at his face, I didn't know him. His heart was gushing thick streams of blood out with every beat. After I yelled for the corpsman, I felt his body go limp and he was dead."[13]

Despite the tank support, the 2nd Battalion took heavy losses in the push over and beyond the causeway. By midafternoon, the attack had ground to a halt in the face of intense mortar and automatic weapons fire from pillboxes and dugouts in the Japanese main position, barring the way toward the old Marine Barracks. Company G alone had over a dozen men killed by everything from blast concussion and multiple fragment wounds to gunshots to the head and chest. Among the dead was the company commander, big, blonde Captain Maurice Amundson of Cameron, Wisconsin, who was shot in the head when he went to help one of his wounded

Marines. Commanding Headquarters Company, twenty-eight-year-old Captain John F. Waddill was shot in the right thigh. Captain Donald B. Goverts of E Company was shot in the right arm. Also among the wounded was a Company E Marine who took a bayonet thrust through the leg.

In the 3rd Battalion, Lieutenant Colonel Clair Shisler suffered a minor leg wound from a mortar shell fragment, which was enough to earn him a Purple Heart, though he returned to duty almost immediately. Captain Robert L. Frank of Glendale, California, commanding L Company, was seriously wounded when he went forward with two runners to get things moving. "The Skipper was on a stretcher," recalled Platoon Sergeant Thomas O'Neill. "They had to hold him down, he kept trying to get off, saying he couldn't leave now. It was later in the day we got the news he had died at the battalion aid station."[14]

Also killed during the afternoon was the executive officer of the 4th Marines, thirty-eight-year-old Lieutenant Colonel Samuel ("Sam") D. Puller, younger brother of Marine Corps legend Colonel Lewis B. ("Chesty") Puller. Some officers thought Sam Puller might be trying to live up to his brother's reputation for fearlessness, but the exec wasn't doing anything rash when he was struck down. Checking on the status of the assault, he stopped to talk with some Marines waiting in reserve in what appeared to be a disused gravel pit when he was shot in the heart. Just where the shot came from—whether it was from a sniper or just a stray bullet—wasn't clear. Either way, the well-liked officer died on the spot.

Another casualty—this one administrative—was Lieutenant Colonel Donn C. Hart, commanding the 2nd Battalion, 22nd Marines. Hart, who had been awarded the Silver Star for his "skillful employment of his troops and weapons" in the seizure of Engebi Island in February, was relieved of command during the afternoon. His replacement was Major John F. Schoettel, a veteran of Tarawa now commanding the regimental Weapons Company, who was apparently brought in with the hope that he could get more out of the battalion.

As dusk approached, the brigade remained stalled under the guns of the final Japanese defense line. Flames from burning oil drums flickered up on the ridge, and Japanese infantry could be glimpsed moving behind the line of pillboxes facing the 4th Marines. In the gathering gloom, L Company Marines noticed a bizarre procession approaching. About three dozen Japanese infantrymen, led by an officer carrying a large rising sun battle flag, trudged toward them along the Sumay Road. A 75mm shell from one of the Marine tanks blew the Japanese officer and his flag into the air. Marine machine guns and BARs mowed down or scattered the rest.

On the brigade right, Merlin Schneider's Marines were about to catch a break after spending the day slugging against what the Marine Brigade described as "determined and fanatical" resistance.[15] In an effort to seize more defensible terrain before digging in for the night, Colonel Schneider stepped up the attack, requesting artillery support and strafing by carrier air elements on the enemy-held hills to his front. The strafing attack that followed at 1802 narrowly missed the Marines themselves—the 2nd Battalion reported the runs as "too close" for safety—though fortunately there were no casualties.[16] The air attack was followed by a devastating barrage from artillery and naval guns from offshore. As the impact area heaved in cascades of dirt and debris, the watching Marines were astonished to see enemy troops suddenly break and run, abandoning the defensive line. It was an almost unheard-of reaction from soldiers famous for holding positions to the death, though it is possible these particular defenders were poorly trained labor or support troops. Major Schoettel immediately ordered his battalion forward. Followed closely by the 3rd Battalion, the regiment surged past the 4th Marines on the left to seize the vacated higher ground.

It was not a complete rout. A few Japanese diehards remained. Entering a small stand of woods, Ray Gillespie's platoon came under close range fire from concealed positions. It took them a few confused moments to realize they were standing on a grouping of underground dugouts. As they got busy locating and grenading the entrances, a Japanese officer seemed to materialize out of the ground, swinging a sword over his head. He slashed at Corporal Ed Crouch, a twenty-two-year-old former farmer from Montpelier, Louisiana, slicing open Crouch's left arm and shoulder before another Marine jammed the muzzle of his M-1 against the enemy officer's chest and emptied the entire eight-round clip into him. "Crouch was as strong as a bull," noted Gillespie. "He took the sword away from the officer while the Jap was falling back, and with one powerful swing, nearly cut the poor bastard's head halfway off with his own sword."

Gillespie's platoon leader, Lieutenant James Raynes, was directing a flamethrower operator to burn out another emplacement when he abruptly crumpled to the ground. Gillespie knelt beside him. The lieutenant's face was a mask of blood seeping out of a bullet hole just over his left eye. The former Texas schoolteacher was probably dead before he hit the ground. The flamethrower operator saturated the cave with fuel, then lit it off. Three Japanese rushed out, burning like human torches. "Don't shoot them!" someone yelled. "Let the bastards suffer!"[17]

Despite the sour ending to an already tough day, the last-minute surge by the 22nd Marines marked a major turning point in the drive down the peninsula.

Seizure of the high ground above Sumay put the troops into position to flank the Japanese line extending along the rifle range and airfield. The 4th Marines dug in for the night about 250 yards from the ridge that had held them up all afternoon, while the 22nd Marines were now within three hundred yards of the former Marine Barracks on the right and the rifle range on the left.

Sometime during the fighting on Orote Peninsula, PFC Henry Block quipped himself into 4th Marines legend. Block had been assigned to assist the regiment's popular chaplain Father Paul Redmond, who was notorious for putting himself in harm's way on the front lines. "The day was especially hot as we were attacking the Japanese defending the approaches to Orote peninsula and our Marine Barracks," recalled Corporal Francis Hepburn. "Machine gun and rifle bullets buzzed across the dry grass where all of us were pinned down." Ignoring the fire, Father Redmond was moving around among the wounded giving comfort and, when necessary, last rites. "Henry of course, like the rest of us, was flat on the ground on his belly waiting for the firing to lift," observed Hepburn. Requiring Block's assistance, the priest called out, "Henry, I need you here, get over here!"

Block hollered back, "Not now, Father. I'll get killed. I'll get there when I can!"

Father Redmond was not to be put off. "Henry, get on over here," he called out over the din of small arms fire. "If you've lived a good life, you'll be okay." Nearby Marines laughed into the dirt as Block hollered back, "I haven't, sir, so I'm staying here till the shooting lets up!"[18]

Laughter was in short supply on Orote. PFC Nicholas Pappajohn recalled losing a steady stream of buddies: "PFC Max E. Bergfeld Jr. KIA July 27. Along with six men he stepped on a mine bomb. His buddy Claude M. Wilson lost a leg. PFC LeRoy Barr was KIA July 27 by a grenade in a trench next to me. PFC Joseph Sheridan was KIA July 26 by a sniper in front of me on a ridge on Orote Peninsula."[19] Between July 26 and July 29, Pappajohn's L Company, 3rd Battalion, 4th Marines lost 11 men killed and 63 wounded in the fighting on the peninsula.

Assigned to the 1st Battalion, 4th Marines, twenty-year-old Pharmacist's Mate Second Class Robert D. Law of Mansfield, Louisiana, found himself with eight wounded men to take care of during one push. One man's right leg had been shattered below the knee, requiring immediate amputation. Law had never before performed an amputation. "There was no time to think about it," he said later. "I just started on him first." Using a combat knife, Law took off the remainder of the leg. "He remained conscious all the time," he said of his patient. "I gave him morphine and when he asked for something to hold on to, I put a clod of earth in each of his hands for him to grip. He kept smiling even while I was bandaging the wound and giving him blood plasma." A surgeon who later examined the amputation pronounced it "an excellent job, considering the circumstances."[20]

As day followed day, PFC George Aspley couldn't remember if or where he even slept. "I couldn't wait until nightfall in order to lie down and then I couldn't wait until morning to see what kinds of insects had been eating on me all night," he recalled. During one advance through the underbrush, Aspley's squad emerged undetected alongside a Japanese bunker. A BAR man stuck his muzzle into the bunker and riddled the three occupants. "The Japanese must have been dozing," speculated Aspley, "or maybe they were so focused on covering the road with their well-positioned machine gun that maybe they never heard us coming. . . . Who knows?"[21]

Two of the casualties in his squad occurred when several Japanese were detected coming toward them along a path. The squad froze, ready to cut them down when they drew close enough. One Marine, apparently trying to obtain a better vantage point at the last minute, started across the path and was shot and killed by a squad mate who mistook him for a Japanese. The startled Japanese were gunned down as they started to run, but the Marine who had accidently shot his buddy was inconsolable, crying and talking to himself. "He completely cracked up and had to be led back and evacuated as a broken man," recalled Aspley.[22]

DAY 3: OROTE PENINSULA, JULY 28, 1944

An official campaign report described the night of July 27 as "uneventful" in the Marine Brigade zone.[23] The following morning's assault toward Orote Airfield would prove to be anything but uneventful.

General Lemuel Shepherd ordered a forty-five-minute air strike, thirty minutes of naval gunfire, and thirty minutes of artillery fire to precede the 0830 infantry assault. Six Army 105mm batteries and three 155mm howitzer batteries augmented the Marine Brigade's six pack howitzer batteries. They were joined by two corps artillery 155mm howitzer and two 14th Defense Battalion 90mm gun batteries. Boundaries for the brigade's two regiments placed the former Marine Barracks and Sumay Village in the zone of the 22nd Marines, while the old rifle range and the Japanese airfield remained in the 4th Marines area of attack.

With tanks in the lead, the 22nd Marines jumped off on time and rapidly outpaced the 4th Marines still facing the ridge fortifications on the left. As the gap between the two regiments widened, Colonel Schneider echeloned units to the left rear to maintain some sort of contact but continued the push. The 2nd Battalion seized the ruins of the former Marine Barracks shortly after noon. As a military objective, the barracks—reduced to just a frame with the odd piece of steel sticking up—had little worth, but the symbolic value of the capture was incalculable. The Marines were back. Sifting through the rubble, they found a cigar box containing Post Exchange papers and receipts and $104.33 in cash from the garrison's prewar recreational fund. They also turned up a star-spangled pillow some Japanese had apparently made from the blue field of an American flag, as well as the original bronze plaque identifying the barracks.

On the brigade right, Colonel Shisler's 3rd Battalion entered Sumay but found the place so infested with mines that the accompanying Sherman tanks were unable to continue. The village turned out to be one of the most heavily mined areas on the island—172 aerial bomb mines, 2 torpedo mines, and numerous conventional land mines were found in Sumay alone. Before the armor pulled up, one Sherman and its crew were blown up when they ran over a one thousand-pound bomb rigged as a mine. Two of the larger houses in the village were burning fitfully as the Marines entered the village. Inexplicably, a lone Japanese soldier emerged from somewhere and nonchalantly strolled over to a water point to fill his canteen. He was quickly riddled.

On the left, the 4th Marines were involved in heavy fighting. The Japanese had cut fire lanes through dense thorny brush fronting concrete and coconut log pillboxes organized in depth. Scattered bits of enemy equipment and clothing and the strong smell of what one sergeant described as "foo foo powder" indicated the Japanese were very close as the Marines pushed into the undergrowth.[24] "We kicked off late in the AM because a 'field' of aerial bombs blocked any tank approach to the airfield," recalled PFC Shirl Butler, advancing with the 2nd Battalion. "We were waiting for a bomb disposal unit to mark or defuse the bombs. I thought they were 500-pounders. I was impressed because the guy they sent came up without steel pot, pack, cartridge belt, etc., dressed in khaki versus dungarees. All he had was a pistol and a roll of white tape."[25] Buck Daley's platoon was also working through the aerial bombs. "We were told to find the bombs [and] lay a circle of gauze around them as a warning to all that came near," he said. "While doing so, avoid moving the vines woven into the propellors on the nose of the bomb because moving the vines detonated the bomb."[26]

Shirl Butler's platoon was moving cautiously forward when there was a terrific explosion from up ahead. Dirt and debris rained down. "I was knocked down from the concussion," said Butler "We were lucky not to be blown into one of the other bombs but picked ourselves up and moved ahead." He later learned that the explosion had obliterated two Fox Company Marines, one of whom apparently triggered a mine. The only remains of the two men "were small body parts in the surrounding trees," recalled a member of the company. They were subsequently listed as missing in action, though there was no doubt as to their fate. One of the victims had been very religious, recalled Butler. "He was at Catholic services at every opportunity, wore religious medals and did a lot of public praying." Now he had been blown to bits. "It certainly disabused any idea that being religious afforded any special protection," observed Butler.[27]

Sergeant Buck Daley's E Company squad reached the top of a grade. They were under fire but could not determine exactly where it was coming from. "There was fairly open terrain for about twenty-five yards in front of us that sloped down into a depression, then thick brush took over," recalled Daley. "And in there, somewhere, were the camouflaged bunkers." Word passed along the line to withdraw. The Marines hesitated—the order "just seemed too out of place," observed Daley. Moments later their platoon sergeant came loping down the line bellowing, "Belay that order! It's a Jap trick!"[28] Meanwhile, Shirl Butler's squad witnessed a bizarre scene out to their front. "Some Jap had donned a Marine poncho and helmet and was walking around within fifteen to twenty yards," he recalled. "I was both surprised and unsure whether it was a Marine or Jap. Someone else cut him down."[29]

As the squad ventured out into the clearing, the quick rip of Japanese Nambu machine guns was overwhelming. Daley took shelter behind a sprig of vegetation that wouldn't have stopped a slight breeze but offered a bit of concealment. A machine-gun crew poured bullets into the vegetation without noticeable effect. "We looked for dust from the enemy muzzle blasts, but the Nips had taken every precaution to clear away from in front of their guns any loose dirt or debris that would give away their position," observed Daley.

A Sherman tank clanked up, its turret slowly swinging in their direction instead of toward the Japanese. Fearing his men were about to be blown into the next world, Daley picked himself up out of the dirt and ran over to the tank holding his carbine up over his head with both hands. The driver's hatch swung open, and a head popped out. Before Daley could fill him in, the tanker's eyes shifted toward something over Daley's left shoulder, and he ducked back down into the tank, slamming the hatch shut behind him. Daley heard a shrieked *Banzai!* and spun around to see a Japanese officer charging toward him, sword held high. He tried to snap off a shot from the hip with his carbine, but the weapon failed to fire. Bizarrely, the officer continued past him and clambered up on the tank, slashing with his sword at the closed driver's hatch. Giving it up, he jumped back down. Again ignoring Daley, who was still fumbling with his carbine, he spotted Warrant

Officer Oliver Ostmeyer of F Company. A twenty-four-year veteran of the Corps, who was old enough to be the father of most of the Marines now struggling to seize the airfield, Ostmeyer had chosen that inauspicious moment to come looking for a tank to knock out enemy bunkers holding up the advance.

Screaming, "*Banzai! Banzai! Banzai!*" the enemy officer charged, bringing his sword down in a blow that would have split Ostmeyer from shoulder to crotch if the warrant officer hadn't partially blocked the stroke with the bolt action Springfield rifle he insisted on carrying. The deflected saber struck Ostmeyer's helmet and took out one of his eyes. Having finally cleared his carbine, Daley shot the Japanese officer in the torso and followed up with a bullet in the head before the swordsman could wreak any further damage. But now, more cries of *Banzai!* erupted as two more Japanese with rifles and fixed bayonets rushed out. He shot them both. They were followed by about a dozen others in what was apparently either a localized counterattack or a bypassed unit taking advantage of an opportunity. Fortunately for Daley, the tank crew now pitched in and mowed them down with the forward machine gun.[30]

As casualties mounted, anyone who was not directly engaged was assigned to litter duty to evacuate the seriously wounded, recalled Corporal Dan Marsh. "The ground was very rough, uneven and covered with holes that were hidden by the long grass," he said. "Because of the urgency we would run or half-run and frequently stumbled and fell. The screams, outcries or whimpering of the helpless victims was hard to endure, but increased our resolve to get them to the aid station. Sometimes, when we arrived we were rewarded by grateful smiles from the wounded. Frequently however, the corpsman would shake his head and we understood that we were too late."[31]

Returning from the stretcher detail, Shirl Butler noticed a knot of battalion officers gathered in a hollow engaged in sober conversation. "It was rumored they were discussing pulling back because of the high casualties," he remembered.[32] General Shepherd came forward early in the afternoon to assess the situation. Between W-Day and July 26, his brigade had suffered 1,266 casualties, and the number had only worsened over the past two days. Recognizing that the understrength assault platoons needed help breaking through the Japanese bunker line, he asked General Andrew Bruce for a platoon of the 77th Division's tank destroyers and a platoon of light tanks to augment the two platoons of Marine tanks already in action. He then issued verbal orders to Colonel Alan Shapley to organize a tank/infantry attack in a concerted effort to achieve a breakthrough.

Bruce came through with some tank support, and at 1530 Shapley launched an assault all along his regimental front. Marine tanks were augmented by a platoon of light tanks and two mediums from the 706th Tank Battalion. As the attack got off, the light tanks moved forward at fifty-yard intervals against coconut log bunkers and emplacements along a three-hundred-yard stretch of ridge. The structures reminded tank commander Phil Morell of hot dog stands at a football game. "They had a big window in front, open, maybe a foot and a half high and six or eight feet long," he recalled. Each contained several Japanese.[33]

A destroyer offshore recorded radio traffic in a tank unit attempting to punch through the web of defenses:

Red Three, this is Red One. Can you see that gun that's shooting at us?

Red One, I think that's our own gunfire.

Goddammit, it's not, I tell you. It's a high velocity gun and not a howitzer. Investigate over there on your left. But watch out for the infantry; they're right in there somewhere. . . . Red Three, what are you doing? Go southwest.

I am heading southwest, Red One.

For Christ's sake, get oriented. I can see you, Red Three. You are heading northeast . . .

Red One from Yellow One. I can see some Japs setting up a machine gun about a hundred yards to my right.

Those are our troops, Yellow One. Don't shoot in there.

The man at my telephone—I think he's an officer—says we have no troops in there.

Yellow Two, go over there and investigate. Don't shoot at them; that man at your telephone probably doesn't know where the troops are. If they're Japs, run over them.

Yellow Two, wilco . . .

Go ahead, Yellow Two. What in God's name are you waiting for?

I'm up as far as I can go and still depress my machine guns.

The hell with the machine guns. I told you to run over them. Run over them, goddammit, obey your orders . . .

Yellow One, what have you to report on that machine gun?

Red One, a Jap stood up and threw a hand grenade at us so I gave him a squirt.

Did you run over that gun like I told you?

No, Red One, we put an HE in it and wrecked it.

Chee-rist, won't you people ever learn to conserve your ammunition?[34]

The light tanks supporting I Company in the center fired on the bunkers from a range of only ten or fifteen yards, where even their less powerful 37mm guns were effective. When high-explosive shells failed to penetrate the log walls of the pillboxes, the gunners focused on the firing slots and crevices. As the line began to crack, the Marine infantry moved in. Commanding a platoon in I Company, Second Lieutenant John Von Wie Bergamini climbed up on one of the bunkers and called to Corporal Joseph Bartkiewicz, a former Raider from Chicago. The lieutenant was the son of missionary parents who were being held in a Japanese internment camp in the Philippines along with his younger brother and sister. He had joined the Marines shortly after graduating from Columbia University with the idea of avenging his parents.

Bartkiewicz would never find out what Bergamini wanted. As he started toward him, a sniper shot the lieutenant through the neck. "I caught him before he hit the ground, but that blood was coming out," recalled Bartkiewicz. "That blood was coming out purple. . . . [I]t was shooting up. We called the corpsman. We couldn't move him out of there [because of the enemy fire]. The army tanks came in to support us. So I banged on the tank and told him to move the tank in front so we could get the lieutenant out. Well, you figure he never would have made it anyway, but they moved the tank and we got him out of there." Bartkiewicz was right. Bergamini, who had turned twenty-four only four days earlier, died before he could be evacuated.[35]

The armored support broke the bunker line, and the 2nd Battalion finally punched through. The 3rd Battalion's I and K Companies followed on the right through a tangle of waist-high thorn bushes, advancing five hundred yards in just thirty minutes to positions just short of the former Marine rifle range and within sight of the airfield. The regiment later counted some 250 pillboxes and emplacements in the general area, most of which the enemy held to the death. In some places, as many as ten to fifteen enemy dead were found huddled in the confined spaces of concrete or log pillboxes. The light tank platoon supporting I Company had fired over ten thousand rounds of .30-caliber ammunition, one hundred rounds of high explosive, and twenty rounds of canister. The tankers had destroyed four pillboxes and numerous dugouts and killed an estimated 250 Japanese without suffering any casualties of their own.

It had been another tough day, and despite the successes, General Shepherd harbored growing concerns about the condition of his brigade. The Japanese still held the airfield and controlled Apra Harbor, and Shepherd's infantry was wearing thin. "I knew my depleted battalions had only one more day's good fight in them," he confessed later. He also knew they would prevail, but he dreaded the cost in lives. "After issuing my orders for the next day's attack, I went back to my tent, got down on my knees and prayed harder than ever before in my life that our objective would be taken with a minimum loss of life," he admitted years later.[36]

DAY 4: OROTE PENINSULA, JULY 29, 1944

The general's prayers were about to be answered. After a quiet night the brigade jumped off at 0800. The main effort was by the 4th Marines toward the airfield. The infantry assault was backed up by six artillery battalions, naval gunfire from eight cruisers and destroyers, and the heaviest air strikes since W-Day. Army and Marine tanks led the way, along with six M-10 tank destroyers on loan from the 77th Division.

Shirl Butler's outfit waited as artillery fire pounded an area just fifty yards beyond their positions near the open airfield runways. "A two-inch piece of hot, ragged shrapnel hit just one inch from my hand," he recalled. His platoon encountered no opposition when they finally ventured out onto the wide-open runway. "Crossing the airfield without receiving fire or casualties, we saw the results of our fire against the Jap positions," he said. "There were twenty-five to thirty bodies stacked around one heavy machine gun. This was just in the limited sector I was in. There must have been hundreds of dead enemy in the battalion front."[37]

Buck Daley's lieutenant led their platoon through a bowl-like depression that had held them at bay the day before. They could see now how cleverly the defense had been constructed. "The coconut log bunkers were mostly placed in the bottom of the bowl, their fire lanes sloping upward to highlight us against the green brush background when we had first come over the lip of the saucer," Daley noted. "Each bunker provided cross fire for the one next to it." Dead Japanese and parts of dead Japanese were strewn all around. "We said how in the hell was it possible for them to put up such a terrific firefight after the pasting given them by planes and artillery days before our advance on the defense line." In one position—possibly a battalion command center—they found seven Japanese officers in full dress uniform, sitting side by side in two rows, all dead. No blood or bullet wounds were in evidence. It also did not appear that they had been killed by concussion. The Marines could only conjecture that the officers had poisoned themselves.[38]

The extent of the Japanese collapse was further demonstrated by the fate of their wounded, numbers of which had been left in caves or sheltered areas with little or no treatment. Many died of wounds they might have survived given adequate medical care. Some of the badly wounded died by lethal injection administered by their own medical personnel. Others killed themselves or were killed by their comrades to avoid the shame of capture.

The 4th and 22nd Marines had advanced half the length of the airstrip by 1000, passing numerous wrecked aircraft scattered across the field and in revetments. "I remember looking over the airfield strewn with wrecked Zeros, and observing engines and equipment dispersed under the trees," recalled Major John T. Rooney of the 4th Marines, Regimental Weapons Company.[39] Two American dump trucks without wheels stood by the road along with a Japanese three-wheeled motorcycle. Straw men used for Japanese bayonet practice dangled from poles by the rifle range.

Shepherd reported to General Roy Geiger, "We have crossed our O-5 Line and are now advancing rapidly up the airstrip meeting meager resistance."[40] Colonel Shapley hitched a ride in a tank to the far end of the airfield, where he radioed the infantry battalion behind him to see what the holdup was. The battalion commander said he was still meeting resistance. "Goddammit," snapped Shapley, "I'm at the tip of the airfield, and you're at the other end of it. Just get your men up and run down here!" Eavesdropping on the exchange, tank commander Phil Morell quipped, "They raced down there like they were running a track meet."[41] The last significant resistance, offered by a strongpoint near the wrecked airfield control tower, was quickly overcome.

By 1400, the Marines had secured the entire airfield and established a defense line about 150 yards beyond. Marines coming up in support trudged past the corpse of a Japanese naval enlisted man lying in the middle of the road while demolitions men mopped up caves and holes. A Japanese ran out of one and was quickly shot down. Associated Press correspondent William Worden found a sand-bagged revetment cunningly dug under the roots of a massive tree. A heavy automatic weapon stood abandoned inside. It was still trained on Apra Harbor where the Americans had had failed to appear.

Colonel Shapley sent a tank patrol out to the shattered lighthouse at the tip of the peninsula. Their decks loaded with infantry, a pair of Shermans set out but encountered only two Japanese soldiers. When the patrol returned, General Shepherd declared the peninsula secure. "God had answered my prayer," he observed gratefully.[42] To eradicate the estimated twenty-five hundred Japanese troops— counted enemy dead numbered 1,633—on Orote Peninsula had cost the 1st Provisional Marine Brigade 115 killed, 721 wounded, and 38 missing in action. Casualties on the final day had been much lighter than Shepherd had feared.

Ironically, the daily toll included one Marine who didn't even have to be there: nineteen-year-old PFC Jose Francisco Duran of El Paso, Texas, who at the time of his death was officially carried on the rolls under "USMCR STRAGGLERS AND DESERTERS." Dissatisfied with the boring routine of his rear-area depot unit on

Guadalcanal, Duran had stowed away with the 4th Marines when they broke camp and left for Guam in late May. Taken in by G Company, he was killed during the company's advance on the airfield.

A formal ceremony took place late that afternoon as artillery boomed in the distance. High-ranking officers including Admiral Raymond Spruance, Lieutenant General Holland Smith, Major General Roy Geiger, soon-to-be Guam island commander Major General Henry L. Larsen, and Brigadier General Lemuel Shepherd assembled on the grounds of the former Marine Barracks to do the honors. Also in attendance were regimental commanders Shapley and Schneider and other lower-ranking officers and enlisted men not required on the line, including an honor guard from the 2nd Battalion, 22nd Marines, the unit that had captured the barracks area.

Upon command from General Geiger, a Marine sounded "To the Colors" on a captured Japanese bugle, and the Stars and Stripes was hoisted to the peak of a telephone pole in front of the wrecked barracks building. General Shepherd observed to the assemblage, "On this hallowed ground, you officers and men of the First Marine Brigade avenged the loss of our comrades who were overcome by a numerically superior enemy three days after Pearl Harbor. Under our flag this island again stands ready to fulfill its destiny as an American fortress in the Pacific."[43] Later that same day, the USS *Appalachian* steamed into Apra Harbor and dropped anchor, the first U.S. man-of-war to enter the harbor since USS *Penguin*'s demise in December 1941.

Over at the newly captured airfield, Buck Daley and a few of his buddies held their own celebration that afternoon on the steps of what was left of the concrete air control tower, toasting victory with "a sorry can of warm grapefruit juice." Orote Peninsula was now in U.S. hands, and they were still alive.[44]

Victory at Orote came just a day after a conference at III Amphibious Corps headquarters where General Holland Smith again urged Geiger to take more aggressive action to capture the remainder of the island. "Geiger replied that before he moved his troops forward across Guam in a general attack, he wanted to make sure Shepherd had cleaned up Orote, which would give us the use of an airfield we badly needed and also release the First Brigade for future employment," recalled Smith.

Smith did not agree. While reluctant to overrule Geiger, he thought the 3rd Marine Division and 77th Infantry Division should be directed to advance immediately. It was important to exert pressure on the enemy and "keep him on the run."[45]

Geiger could have replied that up to now, the Japanese hadn't done much running. But that was about to change.

CHAPTER 20

THEY ARE AMERICANS

MILES BEYOND THE BATTLE LINES, THE FUTURE WAS LOOKING INCREASINGLY BLEAK for the thousands of Chamorros herded into the half dozen or so detention camps scattered around the island's interior. The largest was located in the Manenggon Valley below Yona where as many as eighteen thousand Chamorros were crowded into a two-mile area along the Ylig River. There were no conventional buildings or latrines and no provision for medical care. "Everybody was told to just go to wherever they were standing and try to pitch camp," said Geraldine Torres Guiterez. "Cut coconut leaves, do whatever they needed to do to put up some kind of shelter for themselves." Most, like thirteen-year-old Isabel Bamba Montague's family, arrived with only the clothes they were wearing. "When we got to the camp there was nothing there," she recalled. "Nothing."[1]

"When we arrived at Manenggon there were already hundreds of Guamanians at the camp," recalled Irene Ploke. Her family built a rude shelter of coconut leaves and sticks. Fires were restricted for fear of U.S. aircraft. "It was very cold and wet as the rain kept on falling," said Ploke. "Sleeping was very difficult. We were very scared and only had a small space to rest. We slept sitting up and in constant fear of our lives. We prayed that the Americans would come and save us."[2]

With thousands of people packed into the area, sanitation soon became a major issue. "There was a river," said Irene Sgambelluri. "Everybody was taking a bath there. Everybody was taking drinking water there. Name it, they were doing it there."[3] People relieved themselves where they could. Diarrhea became rampant. "As human and animal wastes piled up each day, the odors grew more and more foul," recalled Ricardo Bordallo. "Soon, the whole camp reeked with a most horrible stench. The small stream that coursed through the valley was our only source of water. With several thousand people using it daily, it quickly turned into a cesspool."[4]

People inevitably became ill. The weak and elderly began to die.

The Japanese made no provision to feed the thousands of internees. Any food the refugees had brought along on the march was soon gone. "We barely brought enough food for the family," said internee Juan Baza. "We could only bring so much. We had no place to go. My father dug into the riverbank. That's where we stayed. No food. At night, my father would steal away to Yona and forage for food. That's what fed us. . . . Or I would swim across the river, climb coconut trees, bring coconuts. That's what we eat."[5]

Raymond Arceo Quintanilla's father had the foresight to butcher a pig before setting out on the march to Manenggon. They cut the meat into chunks and packed it in a kerosene can. When they took the pork out later, it was already going bad. "You could see the worms in the meat," said Raymond. "So then they put that over the fire. Over the cinders. They'd [worms] start falling off because they were dead. Then they'd barbecue that, and that's what the people ate."[6]

Some tried to subsist on green coconuts and boiled leaves from the elephant plant—but soon the valley and surrounding area had been stripped bare. "We kept looking for food," said Tomasa Cruz Salas. "There was nothing to eat. They picked *lemai* flowers, cut it up and cooked it for the kids." Breadfruit was harvested even though it was not yet mature—one Chamorro recalled it tasted like cotton. "The people were starving," related Raymond Arceo Quintanilla. "They were hungry. Some got together and would sneak out in the middle of the night to their ranches. But they didn't do that often because if [the Japanese] caught them, they'd kill them."[7]

Jesus Santos Okada remembered a boy at his camp near Yigo on the northern end of the island. "He was so hungry to the point that everything he saw that was moving he ate. He ate a gecko. He kept looking for things there, including snails. He broke it open and ate it because his stomach needed it. If what you wanted was water, even if polluted, you'd drink it because that's what you need."[8]

It was dangerous to build a fire. "If there is too much smoke, Japanese would come," said Juan Baza.[9] Virginia Lujan Unpingco came down with dysentery from drinking the dirty water in the river at Manenggon. When her grandmother built a small fire to sterilize their drinking water, Japanese guards accosted them. They were about to beat the old woman for building a fire, but Virginia's mother talked them into letting her take the beating in her place. Juan Baza's mother was beaten for a similar offense. "She was brutally whipped and all her body was swollen. There were bruises and clots," he recalled. "I put wet cloth around her body to lessen the swelling and the blood clots and told her to stop crying. She made me promise that I will not do anything drastic to avenge her beating."[10]

Terror weighed heavily on the captives as they struggled to subsist. Their Japanese guards kept them under close watch. Machine guns at Manenggon were positioned around the camp—facing inward. "Every day the Japanese would come and check us and somebody will be beaten up," said Guadalupe Perez Manglona. It was widely feared that the Japanese intended to eventually dispose of them all. "We are going to be killed. That's why they gathered us all in one place. Everybody was saying the Rosary," remembered Manglona. Their fears grew when an order came down for each family to dig a large hole by their campsite—"digging like a grave . . . every family was ordered to do that," said Rosa Gariddo Roberto.[11]

Ironically, the forced relocation to the island's interior may have saved more lives than it took by removing the civilians from battlefield areas. Except for one aged and sick civilian brought in by Marines on W+1, no civilians were seen by Civil Affairs personnel until July 24—three days after the landing—when eighteen Chamorro males came into 3rd Marine Division lines. The first civilians contacted by Marine Brigade Civil Affairs officers were sixteen who came into American lines on July 25.

However, the internees were right to be fearful of Japanese motives. The Chamorros were herded into camps not out of any pressing concern for their safety but because the Japanese viewed them as a security threat. They were Americans and not to be trusted. The Japanese had already shown they felt no compunction about disposing of them if they became inconvenient. Questions were already arising as young men from the camps were drafted to carry supplies and ammunition to positions to the north, never to be seen again. Their fate would soon be revealed in stark detail as the American breakout from the beachhead got underway.

While the Marines clawed their way up Guam's red clay hills, the 77th Infantry Division restlessly awaited its turn to join the battle. The 305th Infantry Regiment had landed on W-Day in something of a mess due to the lack of amphibian tractors. Ship-to-shore problems continued as division artillery and the 306th Infantry began coming ashore over the White Beaches on July 23, followed the next day by the 307th Infantry. "Vehicles had to be dragged by bulldozer from the reef to the beach, and most of them drowned out," observed the official Army history of the campaign. "Almost all of the radio sets, even those waterproofed, were ruined, and one tank disappeared altogether in a large shell hole."[12] A storm at sea raised heavy swells during the landing of the 307th Infantry on W+3. One company lost two men who fell from nets slung over the side of their heaving transport while descending toward their landing craft.

Initial orders were to take over the Force Beachhead Line (FBL) at Agat to free the Marine Brigade for the attack up the Orote Peninsula. Arriving ashore, the latecomers gawked at their first enemy dead like rubes on their first trip to the big city. "Out of sheer curiosity men left their holes to see what a dead Jap looked like," recalled Sergeant Henry D. Lopez, who arrived with the 307th Infantry. "In a large shell crater three corpses lay sprawled, face upwards, their bloated, blackened bodies blown up like gruesome balloons. Hundreds of small, slimy, white maggots squirmed on top one another and ate their way in and out of this stinking, rotten mess; through the opened, staring eyes; through the nose and gaping holes that once were their mouths. They slithered among torn guts and an exposed brain; and through bullet holes in arms, legs, and bodies. The disgusting sight, as well as the stench, made many men sick and caused them to throw up their recently eaten rations."[13]

Artilleryman Paul Russman came ashore the morning of W+1. Mortar and artillery fire was still falling. "There were dead men lying everywhere," he observed. "You have to step over them. It's a shock. Some of the bodies are blown apart and are in odd positions, some face up with their eyes open and flies are on them right away. The flies, they were awful."[14]

The GIs spent the next few days mopping up stragglers and probing beyond the FBL. Their education came at some cost. Sergeant Walter Jacobs remembered one three-man detail sent to burn down a shack to prevent its use by snipers. The GIs made the mistake of returning along the same route and fell into an ambush. One escaped. A rescue party found the bodies of the other two. They had been repeatedly bayoneted. "Just jabbed them all to pieces," observed Jacobs.[15]

General Andrew Bruce was not one to sit on his hands. On the afternoon of July 27, as the Marine Brigade attacked down the Orote Peninsula, he asked General Roy Geiger for permission to send a force out to investigate and possibly seize 1,022-foot Mount Tenjo. The height had been a key objective in the 3rd Marine Division sector, but the Marines had yet to reach the area, having been fully occupied with the struggle merely to hold and expand the Asan beachhead. Army patrols indicated Tenjo was lightly defended. Its seizure would deprive the Japanese of a valuable vantage point over the U.S. beachhead.

Geiger gave the Army general the green light, and a company from the 305th Infantry labored up the precipitous height that same morning, encountering only scattered sniper fire. Twenty-one-year-old PFC Benno Levi's job as platoon runner put him just behind the lead scout. "As we reached the summit, our objective, there was a big explosion, followed by another," he recalled. Six U.S. planes had mistaken them for an enemy unit and were now swinging around for another pass.

Levi, a German Jew whose family had fled to the United States before the war, grabbed a signal panel and began waving it at the diving pilots. They kept coming. He saw a small object detach itself from one of the planes. "I dropped the panel and ran like hell to the opposite side of Mount Tenjo," he said. A tremendous explosion showered him with dirt but caused no injury.

As the pilots circled for yet another run, Levi grabbed a second panel. Scrambling back to the summit, he arranged his panels in the form of an arrow pointing to Japanese positions. The planes veered off, tipped their wings by way of apology, and disappeared. Miraculously, no one had been killed. Adding insult to potential injury, the next day the conquerors of Mount Tenjo heard a broadcast from the United States that the height had been captured by the 3rd Marine Division.

Levi was later awarded the Silver Star medal for his actions. "I couldn't get over it," he admitted. "Here I was always so afraid I would be the first one to run in the face of fire, and now a big hero."[16]

Up on the Fonte Plateau, PFC Cull Forbus's 2nd Battalion, 3rd Marines was scheduled to launch a general attack against disorganized Japanese forces the morning of July 27, but the twenty-year-old Forbus would not be joining them. About two hours after midnight, a Japanese infiltrator armed with a bayonet crawled into his foxhole. "I thought I had been scared in my life, but not until then," he recalled. "I didn't know what to do. We had some knife training and bayonet training, but when you get right up to it, it's a different situation."

Forbus was severely cut up before he managed to kill his assailant. Doped up with morphine and wrapped in a wool blanket, he was taken out on a stretcher the next morning, loaded onto a Higgins boat with two other casualties, and brought out to the USS *Rixey*. The blanket was to help keep him from going into shock. "I was hot as could be and sweating, but this is what they stabilized your body with, a wool blanket," he observed.

A doctor came along as he lay on his stretcher on the deck and asked, "Son, can you walk?" Forbus said he could, but when he tried to stand up, he passed out from loss of blood. He was operated on later in the morning and woke up at about noon to find himself in a half cast. He would spend months recovering but eventually rejoined another battalion in time to be even more severely wounded on Iwo Jima.[17]

While Cull Forbus was being boated out to the USS *Rixey*, the general attack to finally secure the Fonte Plateau got underway at 0900. The main effort fell to Bob

Cushman's 2nd Battalion, 9th Marines, with the 2nd Battalion, 3rd Marines on their left and the 2nd Battalion, 21st Marines on their right.

The morning started on a sour note for Cushman's battalion. Jumping off amid scattered showers, the battalion was hammered at 0930 by a misplaced artillery barrage and air strikes, which held up the assault for an hour. Cushman did get one chuckle during the morning. He was walking next to a lieutenant when the other officer was hit in the foot. Instead of "hollering about it," Cushman recalled, the lieutenant gleefully exclaimed, "Boy, I'm on my way home!" It was his second wound. "Two wounds and you go home," observed Cushman "So they missed me, hit him and gave him a free ticket home."[18]

The rest of the day was considerably less humorous as the battalion engaged in fierce, small unit clashes as it pushed through heavy undergrowth, lagging behind the units on its flanks As the assault companies finally came up on line with the adjacent battalions at about 1300, a last counterattack by what Cushman described as "a screaming horde of Japs some 150 strong" came pouring over the crest of a small bluff.[19] The brunt of the charge fell on G Company, now commanded by Lieutenant Paul F. McLellan of Lantry, South Dakota, who had taken over after Major Fraser West was wounded the day before. Aided by tanks, the company managed to repulse the attack in a two-hour battle but soon had its third company commander in less than forty-eight hours when McLellan was hit in the face by a shell or grenade fragment and had to be evacuated. On Cushman's right, the 2nd Battalion, 21st Marines overcame machine-gun positions with the assistance of tanks and was just short of its objective by noon.

The fighting for Fonte Plateau during the day claimed the life of a Marine Corps legend. A grizzled forty-one-year-old, Lieutenant Milton C. ("Slug") Marvin had served his first hitch in the Marines as an enlisted man in the early 1920s. After a brief stint in the ring as a professional boxer, he returned to the Corps in 1926. In the years since, he had served all over the Caribbean, as well as hitches in China, where he accumulated a couple of wives and gained a reputation for going nose to nose with arrogant Japanese troops bullying Chinese civilians. On Bougainville, where he earned a Silver Star for rescuing five wounded men from the water after his landing craft was hit by a shell, he had reputedly killed a Japanese with a hatchet and scalped another with a machete. When word came that he was about to be ordered back to the United States following that campaign, Slug had accosted General Allen Turnage and demanded to remain with the division. He stayed. Oddly enough, considering his fearsome reputation, the former China Marine often spent his idle hours composing challenging crossword puzzles.

Promoted from warrant officer to lieutenant in June, Marvin landed on Guam with a flamethrower/demolition team from the 19th Marines. Over the next several days, his combat engineers blasted cave after cave, including one cavern that yielded up sixty-three enemy dead. On July 25, he led his men in an assault on a pair of pill-boxes, personally killing two of the enemy in close combat. The push to secure Fonte four days later found him in temporary command of a 21st Marines rifle platoon that had lost their lieutenant. He and two other Marines destroyed three enemy emplacements and started after a fourth. In the lead as usual, Marvin paused to shout facetiously to the youngsters following behind, "Come on up here, you men! I'm not a scout!"[20] The jibe was hardly out of his mouth when a bullet slammed into his car-tridge belt and tore into his midsection. The old veteran survived the journey back to the beach and transport out to the USS *Wharton* but succumbed to his wounds two days later and was buried at sea.

The day's action along the plateau gave little indication that the Japanese were getting ready to pull out. Enemy diehards continued to fight tenaciously from bunkers, caves, and trenches. Cushman's battalion alone had seven killed and forty wounded, according to battalion muster rolls for July 27. The guns on two of the tanks supporting the 21st Marines were knocked out when enemy soldiers shoved hand grenades into the muzzles. By the end of the day, the 3rd Marine Division had advanced to the last intermediate phase line before the crest of the ridge. If ever there was an indication of the perils of misplaced optimism during the planning stages of a campaign, this was it: planners had originally called for this objective to be secured by the 3rd Marines by evening on W-Day six days before.

General Hideyoshi Obata and key 31st Army staff members left 29th Division headquarters for the assembly area at Ordot at midnight of July 27. General Takeshi Takashina and his staff remained at the headquarters, located near an array of wrecked radio towers toward the head of the Fonte River, to oversee the withdrawal. Like his late colleague General Kiyoshi Shigematsu, he tarried too long. The general was still there the next morning when the 21st Marines arrived with tank support.

Officers and men from the headquarters unit fought desperately, committing virtual suicide as they climbed onto tanks with hand grenades or resorted to bayo-nets as they ran out of ammunition. Sergeant Granville G. Sweet of the 3rd Tank Battalion described the standard response to Japanese who rushed the tanks with magnetic mines or demolition charges. "We would call the platoon and tell them,

'Boy, scratch my back.' They would just spray the hell out of us [with machine-gun fire], but watching out that they didn't knock our periscopes out." He recalled one incident where a Japanese officer climbed onto his Sherman and rammed the blade of his sword down through the crack by the hatch. The sword broke off, leaving about eight inches of tempered steel blade projecting inside the tank; "the rest of it went with the Jap, because everybody in my platoon shot him off my tank with .30 calibers," remarked Sweet.[21]

General Takashina's headquarters personnel fared little better. Sherman tanks fired into cave positions, clearing the way for the Marine infantry. Dead bodies lay in heaps. The casualties included the commanding officer of the 10th Mixed Regiment, Lieutenant Colonel Ichiro Kataoka, who "met a heroic death," according to Japanese accounts. Takashina also joined the fight. "The division commander, lightly equipped with field sneakers, gaiters, etc., took command of the fighting with perfect composure," observed a staff officer.

As the position collapsed, General Takashina and his aide, Colonel Hideyuki Takeda, "stole out of the division headquarters, and ran straight between some enemy tanks, and jumped from a cliff," according to Takeda. Pursued by tracers from tank machine guns, the two officers escaped into a dead angle and began to make their way toward Ordot. Early in the afternoon, as they reached a stream at the northern foot of Mount Macajna, they were again spotted and fired on by tanks. Colonel Takeda escaped, but the general was struck by machine-gun fire "and died a heroic death, his heart having been penetrated by a bullet," observed Takeda.[22]

Combat efficiency for the 3rd Marine Division in the days immediately following the mass counterattack was listed as 80 percent, or "good." Despite that assessment, after a week of combat, the Marines were feeling the strain. The riflemen all began to look alike. Red dust caked their clothes and bodies when it was dry. Red mud did the same when the weather was wet. "And so pretty soon your uniform was red, your skin is red, everything is red. So if you had fallen down in the open, you pretty much disappeared," remarked PFC Billy W. Sherrill.[23] About halfway through the campaign, Sherrill's unit received new uniforms—theirs had literally rotted from the constant rain and sleeping in water-logged foxholes.

PFC Joe Frank vividly remembered digging in one night under a pouring rain. "We had dug holes maybe eighteen inches deep," he recalled. "The rain filled them up. It got to the point that if you had to urinate you just urinated in your pants; it didn't make a hell of a lot of difference because you were sopping wet from head to toe, and cold, oh my God, but it was cold on top of that mountain [Mount Chachao]."[24]

"We were haggard from lack of sleep and climbing hills," remembered PFC Wayne Barham, now back with Company K, 3rd Battalion, 9th Marines after being wounded the night of W-Day. "We never took our clothes off." The nineteen-year-old BAR man from Champaign, Illinois, found himself emotionally oblivious to the scores of enemy dead all around him. At the same time, he felt compelled to search the faces of any dead Marines, always hoping not to find a familiar face. "It only mattered if I knew the man," he admitted. He ate his rations surrounded by the dead, many of them grotesquely contorted in positions impossible to assume in life. "I used them as picnic tables on a Sunday afternoon," he said. "I sat with my back against a tree and placed my mess gear on the chest of one and my canteen cup on another."

He lived in a nightmare world. Stalking quietly over a hill he came upon a Japanese soldier drawing a bucket of water from a well. Barham found himself thinking of a similar well on his grandmother's farm as he squeezed the trigger on his BAR. The man toppled into the well. "I wonder if he is still there," he mused years later. A Marine walking in front of him stepped on a land mine. The explosion blew him into the air like a dummy in a movie, except that when he came down, he had no legs. "He pulled his body along the ground with his arms like a turtle when it walks," recalled Barham. "He never uttered a sound. He completed one small circle before he pitched forward on his face in the red mud and died." Barham was increasingly troubled by his own detachment. *How unfeeling can a man become*, he wondered.[25]

Lieutenant Paul Smith lost four more men from his platoon—wounded, not killed—and considered himself lucky not to be a casualty himself. "The trousers of my right leg were ripped by machine gun bullets," he recalled. "My .45 was shot off my belt. A wounded Japanese officer I thought was dead fired at me at point-blank range with a pistol he had concealed under his armpit, knocking my helmet askew, before he was finished off by PFC George E. Pugachoff, the BAR man walking behind me. I began to feel and to understand the dread sense of percentages that overtakes the combat soldier."[26]

In fact, the sacrifice was beginning to show tangible results. On July 30 a torpedo bomber from USS *Chenango* was first to touch down on the Orote airstrip after six hours of feverish work by engineers. The TBF's unannounced visit came much to the pique of the Marine brass, who had gone to some lengths to ensure that first landing honors would go to Marine Observation Squadron 1 (VMO-1). Lieutenant Colonel Frederick P. Henderson went out to the field with a radio to alert VMO-1 that the field was open for business but had scarcely sent his message when the Navy bomber came in, circled the field, made one pass, and then landed. The plane touched down just as a brisk fire fight broke out about three hundred yards from the airfield as a patrol flushed some Japanese from a cave. "All of us around the field hit the deck as some of the bullets started whizzing over the field," said Henderson. Apparently unprepared for a hostile reception, the "fame-happy Navy pilot," as Henderson described him, proceeded to taxi around and "took off in a hurry," to the mixed amusement and annoyance of the Marine onlookers.[27]

The TBF was followed about thirty minutes later by two VMO-1 observation planes from escort carriers *Sangamon* and *Suwanee* as the first elements of the air arm to operate from the field. Planes from Marine Air Group 21 would soon follow to provide close air support to ground units. Capture of Orote Peninsula by the Marine Brigade and expansion of the 3rd Marine Division beachhead had also opened Apra Harbor to development as a major forward fleet anchorage. Only a few days later, Admiral Raymond Spruance's flagship USS *Indianapolis* would steam triumphantly into the harbor.

Meanwhile, the 3rd Division continued to secure its hold on the ridges. The 9th Marines on July 28 overran a Japanese company-sized force defending a concrete emplacement on the summit of Mount Chachao. The following day, Colonel Cushman's 2nd Battalion went after thirty-five to fifty enemy soldiers dug into caves along the walls of a bowl-like depression on Fonte Plateau. The position presented a tactical issue in that anyone descending into the bowl from one point would be subject to enemy fire from at least three sides. Hoping to avoid sending his men into a meat grinder, Cushman asked regiment for an overnight delay so he could prepare demolitions and figure out a way to employ tank support against the bowl, but patience now seemed to be running short. "I had great trouble securing permission to delay the attack and it was understood that if I didn't succeed the next morning I could turn in my suit," he recalled.[28] The "honors" fell to G Company, which by noon on July 28 was down to one officer and its fourth commander since W-Day. Fortunately Cushman was able to position a tank to bring fire on the Japanese, and the Marines eradicated the bowl defenses without losing a man.

The advances of July 27 and 28 brought the 9th Marines into contact with the 77th Division troops on Mount Tenjo, finally linking the southern and northern beachheads solidly along the FBL. The belated success came too late for Colonel W.

Carvel Hall. The commander of the 3rd Marines, who days before had threatened to relieve the luckless Captain Geary Bundschu for failing to seize Bundschu Ridge, was himself removed from command of the regiment on July 28. He was reassigned to division supply after "showing signs of overstrain," according to one source.[29]

Officially, Hall's transfer came per an order that was subsequently described as "part of a division-wide shift in individual command and staff responsibilities," suggesting it was routine.[30] Circumstances indicated, and Major John A. Scott, 3rd Marines operations officer, later verified, that the reassignment was anything but routine. Scott testified that General Holland M. Smith, dissatisfied with the regiment's performance, "personally" relieved Hall of command, describing Smith's rage as "volcanic."[31] Scott's account was supported by Hall's executive officer, Colonel James Snedeker, who later revealed that Hall's relief "was personally demanded by Lt. Gen. Holland Smith on the ground that the regiment had been unable to advance earlier." Snedeker added that, in his opinion, the relief was "unnecessary and unconscionable," crediting Hall with coming up with the flanking plan that resulted in the belated seizure of Bundschu Ridge.[32]

The attempt to soft-pedal Hall's relief presumably fooled no one. Holland Smith was notoriously impatient with what he considered lack of performance—a month earlier on Saipan he had created an interservice firestorm when he fired 27th Infantry Division commander Major General Ralph Smith—and he was not likely to extend mercy to what he saw as an underperforming colonel. Hall's replacement was the division operations officer, forty-five-year-old Colonel James A. Stuart, an Annapolis graduate and member of the 1924 Olympics saber fencing team, who would receive the Legion of Merit for his leadership of the 3rd Marines during the second half of the campaign.

From a lofty observation post established alongside the empty swimming pool at the prewar U.S. officers' club—the clubhouse itself now a burned-out shell—the panorama of northern Guam stretched off into the distance. "Below was the destroyed city of Agana," observed an officer; "to its right the Pago Bay Road disappeared into the hills. Beyond the city and swamp the island appeared to be a jungle-covered plateau with only the outcroppings of Mounts Barrigada and Santa Rosa breaking the jungle. The slash of the airfield showed through the trees in the middle distance overlooking the flat of the coastal plain."[33]

Finally in command of the heights, General Geiger was ready to appease Holland Smith and move to pursue fleeing Japanese forces and secure the remainder of the island. "Almost every day he was up at the front lines," recalled chief of staff Colonel Merwin Silverthorn. "All the way out to battalion commanders' positions if not company positions."[34]

Geiger's plan called for a pivoting movement—the hinge being the Asan beachhead—to sweep out across the island and then north to the plateau area where it was believed the enemy would attempt to reorganize. Available intelligence indicated there were no strong defensive positions within two thousand yards of the FBL. Patrols found caves and dumps crammed with abandoned weapons, ammunition, and supplies of all kinds in the area fronting the IIIAC perimeter but no organized opposition.

An undated carrier pigeon message captured by the 3rd Marine Division indicated the Japanese were withdrawing at least to the Agana-Pago Road. "Because of unusual conditions," observed the message, "move to Sinajana or Ordot. Fire being received in depression to our front making movement difficult. . . . Hold on."[35] From a military standpoint, it made sense for the Japanese to continue the fight on the north end of the island. U.S. intelligence reports indicated that General Takashina had previously prepared for this contingency by establishing prepared positions, supply dumps, and an emergency headquarters with radio equipment capable of communicating with Tokyo.

To ensure that no organized Japanese units remained to threaten the rear of an attack to the north, the 77th Division Reconnaissance Troop mounted several long-range patrols, accompanied by Chamorro guides, into the unexplored southern end of the island. Sergeant Nunzio DePonto was a member of a five-man patrol that set out at dawn on July 28. They wore cloth caps instead of steel helmets and taped their dog tags together to prevent them from rattling. "We weren't supposed to engage the enemy," he recalled. "About a mile out, we saw a patrol. And they saw us. We ducked back into the jungle and they took off too. Those were the first Japanese I ever saw, except for dead ones on the beach."[36]

Another patrol, dubbed "Patrol Baker," returned on the afternoon of July 29 with five Chamorros who said there were only wounded Japanese at Talofofo and very few in the Ylig area, both along the eastern coast. About forty Japanese had previously left Ylig for the north, according to the Chamorros. The patrol itself had encountered no enemy. Chamorros coming into American lines reported that the Japanese had also evacuated Agana, moving at night and staying off the roads to avoid detection. The withdrawal to the plateau area was verified by Sergeant DePonto's team upon reaching the eastern side of the island. "There were trucks going along the road, moving north," he recalled. The team returned without casualty beyond providing a feast for the local mosquitoes. "We got bit something awful," DePonto recalled ruefully. "When we came in, my captain said he didn't recognize me because my face was so blown up with mosquito bites."[37]

Just over a week into the battle, IIIAC estimated roughly seventy-five hundred enemy had been killed. Intelligence believed at least another thirty-five hundred casualties could be added to the count, to include the wounded and fatalities that had been buried by the enemy. Of the survivors, two thousand to three thousand were thought to be poorly trained labor troops, many of them armed only with idiot sticks—knives or bayonets lashed to bamboo poles. A "native of American descent" told U.S. intelligence that Japanese construction personnel assembling in the vicinity of Yigo were "probably armed with nothing more than handmade spears."[38] Considering an original enemy strength of about 18,500, this would leave about 5,000 regular combat troops to oppose IIIAC's sweep to the north. Intelligence analyses indicated that though disorganized elements of all enemy units remained at large, the most formidable threat was posed by remnants of the 48th Independent Mixed Brigade, "of which the 319th [Battalion] may be intact."[39]

During the push inland in the days following the failed enemy counterattack, Sergeant Roy Buckner's outfit came across a macabre scene. Entering a deserted village, they found a parklike area with what appeared to be a swing set for local children. Two bodies were hanging by their feet from the overhead support. "Both of their throats were cut and they'd been hanging there all day, or a couple of days," observed Buckner.[40]

Miles away, at a detention camp in the hills outside Inarajan in southern Guam, a handful of Chamorro men were intent upon avoiding a similar fate. The men had stolen about a dozen Japanese rifles and ammunition from an enemy cache hidden in a cave and were plotting their next move on July 30 when they learned a U.S. Army patrol had been spotted only a half a mile away. Led by Second Lieutenant John R. Stringer, the four-man patrol, accompanied by a Chamorro guide, had been assigned to reconnoiter the Inarajan area. The excited Chamorros stopped them on the trail and advised Stringer of their plan to kill the eight Japanese camp guards and any other Japanese they could find. "American soldier, we strike tonight!" one Chamorro proclaimed dramatically.

Stringer was still absorbing this information when there was a rifle shot from the direction of the camp. Fearing the worst, the combined force of Chamorros and Americans set out for the camp. They had hardly gotten underway when two Japanese suddenly appeared, fleeing toward them. The Americans gunned them down. Upon entering the camp, they found the shot they had heard had been an accidental discharge by a Chamorro handling one of the stolen rifles, but it had been enough to send the few guards—already nervous about their changed fortunes—running off in a panic.

The people at the encampment were hastily packing up and striking out for nearby Merizo. "On our way down to the village, one Japanese soldier who was half naked came running after us," recalled Francisco Lujan. "He thought we were friendly." One of the Chamorros shot at him and missed. Realizing his mistake, the Japanese turned and fled, but another Chamorro quickly caught up to him. "He ran a saber through his back and killed him," observed Lujan.

Trudging into Merizo the next day, the refugee Chamorros found the village deserted. American ships were visible offshore out beyond Cocos Island, and planes droned constantly overhead. "Many of the people went up to the hills behind the schoolhouse to wave white sheets," said Lujan. As many as two hundred Chamorros had set up camp at the schoolhouse when rifle fire erupted from the jungle. Four men and a girl were hit. Following up on the fusillade, a half dozen Japanese broke out of the jungle and charged the schoolhouse. Armed Chamorros were ready for them. Twenty-two-year-old Tomas A. Fejerang shot one Japanese who was about to throw a grenade through a broken window. The grenade exploded in the soldier's hand, tearing open his chest and exposing his heart and lungs. Fejerang was so close that some of the fragments hit him in the stomach. "He thought at first he was going to die and was scared," recalled Lujan, but his wounds were not as serious as they seemed. The Chamorros killed four Japanese. Two others escaped, but the villagers were not bothered any further.

About a week later, Francisco Lujan returned to Merizo from Inarajan with some Marines. "There were four stumps of coconut trees with four clean skulls perched on them," he recalled. "One of the American Marines went over to the skulls on the stumps, took out his pliers and removed the gold teeth from the jaws, putting them carefully into a small bottle of alcohol. I noted there were already a number of small gold teeth resting in the bottom."[41]

<hr />

Having escaped the fate of General Takashina thanks to his early departure from Fonte, General Obata now assumed direct command of all Japanese forces on Guam. The transition was smoother than it might have been, as General Takashina had taken care to keep Obata thoroughly informed of his plans and intentions.

By now, U.S. intelligence was aware of the army commander's presence on Guam. An intelligence summary issued on July 27 noted that captured documents indicated he had arrived on Guam about June 24 and "will probably participate in the 29th Division headquarters."[42]

Obata established a temporary headquarters at Ordot on July 28 and spent the next twenty-four hours supervising the transfer of troops and matériel to the north. His immediate command consisted of about one thousand army infantry, eight hundred naval combat troops, and twenty-five hundred mixed personnel. These included the 29th Division tank unit and the 48th Independent Mixed Brigade artillery unit, which had been reduced to just six guns. Thousands of other Japanese remained scattered throughout the interior, most in disarray. Some would trickle in over the next few days; others would never contribute to any organized resistance. A very few opted not to fight to the death. Three army soldiers from the 3rd Battalion, 18th Infantry deserted their unit around July 28 and surrendered, deciding "the situation appeared hopeless." They said only about 250 men in the battalion remained alive. A POW from the 1st Battalion, 38th Infantry said he was the sole survivor of his 125-man company.[43]

At the Manenggon concentration camp, Rosa Garrido Carter saw clear evidence of the impending Japanese defeat as a line of enemy soldiers filed past on their way north. "I don't know how many [came through]," she observed. "Wounded ones as well as others, marched across the camp and left. I don't know where they were going."[44]

Among the surviving junior officers was Lieutenant Yasuhiro Yamashita, who had participated in the mass attack the night of July 25–26, despite being wounded in the ankle by mortar fire earlier in the day. Following the disastrous attack, his 18th Regiment was able to muster only about sixty survivors. Joined by about forty members of the 3rd Artillery Company, the fugitives considered launching a suicide attack on Marines at Mount Chachao, but unrelenting pressure from the American advance disrupted their plan for a glorious exit. They began instead to make their way north. "On the early morning of the 31st, we gathered in a valley east of [Mount Chachao]," reported the lieutenant. "Those suffering slight injuries were to move to the east, but it was difficult for me to walk with severe pains as injuries worsened. There was no food at all, and we clung to life by eating soft parts of grass stalks."[45]

Lieutenant Yamashita was far from alone in his misery. Joining the withdrawal following General Takashina's demise on July 28, Colonel Takeda described the overall "retrograde movement" as "pathetic." One Japanese soldier, whose leg had been shot off, arrived at Ordot having crawled about six kilometers, he recalled. Able-bodied men shouldered wounded comrades. Many died. "There was no drinking water available, and those who had died all expressed just before dying the desire for a drink of pure Japanese water," remembered Takeda.[46]

Japanese medical personnel retreating from Agana and Sinajana attempted to take their field hospital and patients with them, but the effort quickly broke down. The 29th Division hospital unit, which had originally consisted of fifteen doctors and two hundred enlisted men, had been shattered. Surviving doctors, medics, and more ambulatory wounded crept northward in a waking nightmare. Some patients succumbed to their wounds; others were killed by their own comrades when they could not keep up. Eventually, the hospital personnel could continue no longer. Realizing their situation was hopeless, orders were given to kill the patients. The three remaining doctors committed suicide. A IIIAC report later noted dispassionately, "That was the end of Japanese military medicine on Guam."[47]

Joining the sad procession north, sometimes moving at night by the light of American flares, were numbers of Japanese, Korean, and Okinawan civilians, including Minseibu and Kaikontai personnel and family members. Twenty-three-year-old Naoe Takano, a prewar immigrant who had operated a store in Agana, accompanied a mixed group of civilians and military personnel. The bodies of Japanese soldiers lay along the trail. Once, she recalled, "I felt a hand grab my leg. When I looked down, I saw and heard a dying soldier crying for water. But there was no water." Another soldier in the group had been badly injured and could no longer continue. "A hospital man put him to sleep with an injection," she said. The medic explained, "His injuries are serious and we couldn't take him with us."[48]

Arriving at Ordot, Takano's group, numbering about one hundred mostly elderly men, women, and children, found a large cave occupied by Japanese soldiers. When the refugees attempted to enter, the soldiers turned them away. They spent the night outside the cave and the next morning came under attack by U.S. aircraft. One man's head was shot off. Another man lost an arm. An Okinawan woman breast-feeding her baby was hit in the stomach and killed, while the infant survived.

General Obata was not oblivious to the carnage. Leaving Ordot on foot to go to Finegayan on the afternoon of July 29, the general found numerous wounded men had been abandoned along the roadside. Appalled, he ordered that they be evacuated by what few trucks remained and personally directed the rescue. "All of the wounded men shed tears of gratitude for his consideration to his men," observed a Japanese staff officer.[49] The general enjoyed at least one piece of good fortune. To his relief, the Americans did not seem to be on his heels as he tried to organize his scattered forces. Although the assembly point at Ordot was a scene of confusion, two traffic control stations helped keep units and stragglers moving. The respite also allowed truck units, operating after dark, to transport provisions stockpiled near Ordot further north to the anticipated new defense line.

Waiting on the newly won heights overlooking Agana, the 3rd Division Marines enjoyed a bird's-eye view of the once bustling capital, now a mile-long swath of shell-gutted buildings and heaped debris at the foot of the ridges. Intelligence indicated the enemy had pulled out, but at least one rear guard unit paused to figuratively thumb its nose at American spectators before departing.

To the astonishment of the Marine observers, a group of enemy soldiers suddenly appeared in a small open area on the outskirts of the city and proceeded to brazenly—and bizarrely—conduct what appeared to be a full-dress review of some sort. "Decked in full combat regalia, the Nips marched with militant precision while bewildered Marines looked down on them from the heights," noted the division history. "Cold steel of the bayonets and Samurai swords sparkled brilliantly in the morning sun."[50] The Marines called in an artillery concentration, but the Japanese had vanished by the time the barrage arrived, and the shells merely rearranged the vacant rubble.

Meanwhile, the 77th Infantry Division was moving into position to assist in the push north as General Geiger sought to bring a close to the campaign. Watching some elements of the division moving into position, one of Lieutenant Paul Smith's young enlisted men gave a low whistle. "Jeez," he exclaimed in bewilderment, "these guys are old men. Look at that guy driving that Jeep, Lieutenant Smitty. Why hell, he must be twenty-five or twenty-six if he's a day." Smith, just two months short of his thirty-sixth birthday, had no comment. He also couldn't help but notice that his astonished Marine might be only nineteen, but after more than a week of combat, he presently looked to be about thirty.[51]

Geiger planned to attack north with the two divisions abreast—the 77th Division on the right and the 3rd Marine Division on the left. The 307th Infantry, with a battalion from the 305th Infantry attached, began to get into position on the right side of the line on the morning of July 31, moving east from Mount Tenjo. The GIs pushed through the dense undergrowth under towering trees up to one hundred feet tall, snagged by vines, slipping down slopes, "straining, sweating and swearing" all the way, observed the division history.[52] They found signs of a hasty Japanese withdrawal. Medical instruments had been abandoned in a hut; elsewhere, a trunk crammed full of Japanese yen had been left behind. The GIs laughed as they lighted cigarettes with the bills, recalled their chaplain. A supply depot yielded up quantities of soft white military blankets. "Nothing could be done with them except use them as bedding in the night's slit trenches. They were fine to sleep on but they would be covered with mud and be useless the next morning," remarked the chaplain.[53]

Acting as point for a reinforced patrol, Sergeant Nunzio DePonto had one of the few contacts with the enemy—a chance encounter with the lead man of a Japanese patrol coming down the same narrow jungle trail. "When I saw him, he had his gun slung over his shoulder, not ready to fire," he recalled. "I had mine ready, and I shot from the hip. I think I put the whole clip into him, and everybody started firing—we were pretty trigger happy. I ran over and emptied the Jap's pockets—you can get a lot of information about the enemy that way. Then we got the hell out of there."[54]

The original schedule allowed two days for the 77th Division to extend across the island to the east coast before the push north. The lack of enemy resistance persuaded General Bruce to advance that timetable. Shortly before noon, an artillery liaison plane droned over the sweating, swearing GIs and dropped orders to advance to a line on the lower Pago River just north of Yona village by nightfall. It was 1730 and almost dark when the 307th Infantry's I Company finally reached the outskirts of the village. Situated on the south-north coastal road leading toward Barrigada, Yona had served as a rendezvous point for Japanese troops from southern Guam during the withdrawal. As scouts picked their way along a trail leading to the village, two Japanese soldiers darted across the opening up ahead. Moments later, the lead platoon reached a clearing on the edge of the village to find dozens of Japanese running among the grass huts.

Clearly taken by surprise, half-dressed enemy soldiers ran out of buildings and bolted for the jungle. A few riflemen fired on the GIs from dugouts and buildings, but the resistance was halfhearted. One luckless Japanese emerged from a dugout and tried to run but got tangled up in his gas mask straps. A private shot him dead. The GIs moved through the sprawl of huts and buildings, methodically grenading each. One building, now littered with dirt and trash, appeared to have been used as a barracks. By the time the GIs reached the far side of the village, the Japanese—estimated to number between fifty and one hundred—had fled into the jungle, leaving five dead and considerable quantities of grenades, small arms, and ammunition. A

Chamorro reported that Yona had originally been a supply center and garrison for several hundred soldiers, most of whom had left earlier for Barrigada about six miles further north. The Japanese encountered by the GIs were apparently laggards or had remained behind to tend to supplies.

⌇

While the 77th Division GIs bushwhacked their way into position on IIIAC's right, the 3rd Marine Division descended from the ridges the morning of July 31 and started toward the capital city, Agana. Liberation honors went to the 3rd Battalion, 3rd Marines, the conquerors of Chonito Cliff.

As Company I advanced along the heights overlooking the city—the term "city" being an exaggeration by most any but Guam standards—Company L, commanded by twenty-six-year-old Captain William G. H. Stephens, waited at Anigua on Agana's outskirts. Shellfire had reduced flimsy wooden houses to splinters. Broken trees, tin roofing, glass and sharp-edged shell fragments, and miscellaneous debris littered the narrow streets. Hibiscus, azalea, and flame trees still bloomed brightly in the front yard of a lone surviving house. Toward dawn, about a half dozen Japanese, probably trying to rejoin their units in the north, attempted to slip past Stephens's Marines. The Marines killed four of them, including two officers.

At 1000 hours L Company finally began their advance along the gravel seaside track running through the lowlands into Agana. Dead fish floated at the water's edge, killed by shell fire directed at now abandoned Japanese pillboxes in the beach area. Sheer seventy-foot cliffs loomed up on the right. "There were many caverns in the cliffs and they gave you the feeling of being looked at by someone unseen," observed Marine combat correspondent Sergeant Theo C. Link.[55] An archway at the entry of an old cemetery along the road bore a Latin inscription that translated to "Blessed are those who die"—not calculated to comfort any passing Marines who happened to be conversant in Latin. Glancing at the shell-toppled graves, a Marine remarked thoughtfully, "Even the dead can't rest in peace."[56]

Watching carefully for land mines, the Marines entered the city proper and fanned out along the three principal streets past sheared-off palm trees, roofless buildings, and broken walls webbed with hibiscus. Brass handrails stood incongruously in the debris of what had once been the Scenic Gaiety, one of Agana's two popular prewar movie theaters. A statue of the Madonna lay on the floor in one house amid a litter of broken china, smashed windowpanes, and water-logged papers. Abandoned medical supplies and surgical instruments and a pile of bloody clothing indicated the house had served as a temporary Japanese aid station. In another house, a Marine opened a closet to find a Japanese officer, sword in hand. The Marine slammed the door shut, riddled it with his automatic rifle, and walked away without bothering to verify the obvious results.

Private William "Bill" P. Morgan recalled one lone Japanese officer who chose to go down fighting. "Here is a combat platoon, hardened veterans looking for trouble," he remarked. "And when we got up to where our naval gun fire had flattened Agana, a Japanese officer comes running out from somewhere, with a samurai sword, waving it, yelling *Banzai! Banzai!* And he comes at the entire platoon. Well everybody was just thunderstruck. We just stood there and looked at him. And then finally somebody realized, hey this old boy's going to kill somebody. So we just cut him to ribbons. And around his neck he had a stalk of bananas."[57]

A sudden burst of automatic weapons fire marked the demise of another straggler found hiding in a pillbox built in the middle of the street. Otherwise, the capital seemed deserted as the Marines emerged onto the open expanse of the Plaza de Espana, scene of the Insular Force Guard's last stand two and a half years earlier. The Government Palace had been shattered by shell fire and air bombardment; holes gaped in what remained of the red tile roof. The nearby cathedral was a burned-out shell, windows gaping vacantly over a cluster of sandbagged antiaircraft positions, one of them occupied by a dead Japanese soldier. The prewar bandstand in the middle of the plaza remained intact—the Japanese had used it to store ammunition—but the nearby post office had been heavily damaged, the second floor nearly blown away. The streets had been seeded with antitank mines, but except for the dead man on the plaza and six others sprawled along nearby Esperanto Street—apparently the victims of artillery or naval gunfire—the enemy was gone. Taking advantage of the respite, a few weary Marines settled down in the shade by the bandstand. Four others stretched out on the chairs of an abandoned barber shop. Tanks rumbled up the street, followed by a motorized column. Engineers began to disarm the mines.

With Agana in hand, Turnage's Marines pushed north, moving past both Sinajana and Ordot by noon on July 31. During the advance to Ordot, a reinforced platoon from the 9th Marines came across what appeared to be a repair depot for a tank unit. In the main room of a house apparently used as a headquarters stood a small table with two neatly folded flags on top. One was an American garrison flag, the other a Japanese naval ensign. Lieutenant Colonel Edward Craig speculated they might have been removed from Agana during the retreat. Craig's Marines also discovered a large hospital with numerous dead Japanese and large quantities of medical supplies, but the main excitement of the day developed as the Marines headed away from the tank depot. Entering a small valley, they suddenly heard the sound of motors as two Japanese tanks rolled out of camouflaged positions at the side of the hill and started toward them. "Everyone opened fire at once, including the tanks," remarked Craig.[58] U.S. tanks were still well to the rear trying to get through Agana, but a bazooka man attached to one of the squads loaded his rocket launcher and calmly knocked out both enemy tanks as they sped toward the riflemen. Two more camouflaged tanks, dug into the hillside but unmanned, were discovered in the same area. Upon entering Ordot, the regiment also captured a number of abandoned Japanese trucks and some passenger cars, probably left by soldiers and civilians fleeing north.

An indication of the continuing confusion among enemy units occurred late in the afternoon when between fifteen and twenty Japanese led by an officer unwittingly approached a battalion command post being set up near a cluster of abandoned supply sheds or houses. The Marines took cover and sighted in on the approaching group but were ordered to hold their fire. As the Japanese drew within about 150 yards of the CP, an enlisted interpreter called out, demanding their surrender. "They were confused," said Major Edward A. Clark, the battalion exec; "apparently thinking we were friendly, they chattered amongst themselves, and after some more shouting from our interpreter, they started to break and run in confusion."[59] The Marines opened fire, killing or wounding about half of them, including the officer who appeared to be in charge. The officer was promptly stripped of his sword and other belongings. The others escaped into the jungle.

By dusk, the U.S. advance had seized twelve hundred to fifteen hundred yards of roads northeast of the capital, one of which led to Finegayan and the other to Barrigada. Information from Chamorros and patrols indicated the Japanese could be preparing to make a stand at Tiyan Airfield about two miles northeast of Agana or at Tumon Bay about four miles up the coast as the crow flies. Though the Japanese had not contested Agana, the extensive number of mines—both aerial bombs rigged with detonators and conventional horned mines—around the city and along the coast road remained a threat. White rags marked the location of many mines, but others remained undetected. Among their victims was Major John H. Ptak, executive officer of the 1st Battalion, 3rd Marines, who had taken such a prominent part in the fight for Bundschu Ridge immediately after the landing on July 21. The slender, mustachioed major was killed when the jeep he was riding in ran over a mine during the advance beyond Agana on August 1. "We barely had time to cover his body as we moved north," recalled a fellow officer.[60] Killed with Ptak in the same incident was the battalion intelligence officer, Lieutenant Arthur C. Vivian Jr., a former star baseball pitcher for Wake Forest who had been under contract with the New York Yankees when he joined the Marine Corps. The jeep driver and two other enlisted men were severely wounded.

Henry Aplington, Ptak's commanding officer and friend, got the news when an officer from regimental headquarters opened a phone message with "Hank, I'm sorry to hear about Ptak." Four days earlier, as Aplington and Ptak walked down from Fonte Hill, Aplington had mused aloud that if he were to be killed, he simply wanted to be wrapped in his poncho and buried where he fell. Ptak had replied, "I'll do it for you if you want, but I'm not going to be killed."[61] Temporarily interred on Guam, the major was brought home after the war and laid to rest at St. Leo Cemetery in tiny Tyndall, South Dakota.

❦

At the sprawling Manenggon detention camp, it was clear the battle was drawing near. "We could see the American planes flying overhead and hear the shooting and bombing," observed Irene Ploke. "Some Japanese guards had already left the camp and only a few were left behind."[62]

Despite Chamorro fears, the Japanese appeared more intent on saving themselves than on massacring their captives. On July 31, a patrol from the 307th Infantry found a camp containing about two thousand hungry and sick civilians near the village of Asinan on the south bank of the Pago River. The guards were gone, having joined the general retreat earlier that same morning. "The Chamorros were almost beside themselves with joy. Not sure whether to kiss their liberators, bow to them, or shake hands, they tried to do all three at once," noted the division history. Some produced small American flags they had secreted from the Japanese. "We wait long time for you to come," one exclaimed.[63]

The Manenggon camp was liberated the following day. Young Tony Palomo was among the first to see the Americans approaching. "I looked down and in the valley I saw a lot of soldiers going. They were big guys. They were white. I said, that's not Japanese, you know. They're big and they're white! A group of us run down, you know we figured they must be Americans. So we ran down the valley and met the Americans."

One of the GIs looked at Palomo and said, "Whaddya want, kid?"

Children being children, the thirteen-year-old blurted, "Do you have any chocolate candy?"[64]

Ben Blaz's sister Maria recalled that three Americans sauntered into the camp, weapons slung, helmets pushed back on their heads, "no urgency about them at all." One of them announced, "We've come to liberate you."

"Just the three of you?" responded one of the internees.

"Yup," replied a GI. "One, two, three. Just the three of us."[65]

Ricardo Bordallo was off by himself when he became aware of a lot of noise and commotion from the camp. People seemed to be laughing and shouting and whistling. Moments later, one of his friends raced up to him and exclaimed, "Hurry! The Americans are here!" The two boys ran down the hillside and into a mob of Chamorros surrounding nine dumbfounded American soldiers. "People were laughing and crying, hugging and kissing, shouting and jumping, dancing and singing," remembered Bordallo.[66]

Irene Ploke and her family joined the exuberant crowd. "We ran up to them, we hugged them and we kissed them with our dirty clothes on. . . . We all cried. People were crying because they were so happy," she recalled. "[The Americans] said, 'Follow me,' and we did."[67]

"One of the soldiers was shouting and holding his rifle above the surging mob," recalled Ricardo Bordallo. "*Follow* was all anyone heard." The word spread quickly: *Follow the Americans.*[68] Accompanying the 77th Division, news correspondent Robert Trumbull witnessed the ensuing exodus. "Coming suddenly over a ridge into the bivouac area, we were astonished to see an unending single-file line of civilians extending from the camp to the sea, winding snakelike over the hills on the crooked carabao trail, disappearing into the valleys and rising again on the green hilltops beyond," he wrote.[69]

"The American soldiers walked us through the hills towards Mount Tenjo," remembered Irene Ploke. "It continued to rain very hard but the soldiers helped us along the way and even covered me and my family with their ponchos. Along the way we passed many dead Japanese soldiers."[70]

Up to now, Chamorros had trickled into American lines by the twos and sixes. This column numbered in the thousands—men, women, and children of all ages, the strong assisting the weak, children in their parents' arms. "Some hobbled along on crutches," recalled PFC Benno Levi. "Others had to be carried and many had bandages. One old man with bleeding feet was carrying an old woman whose feet also were badly festered."[71]

"The people were clothed in ragbag remnants," observed Trumbull. "Some carried American flags which they had hidden from the Japs. Many were limping and sick. . . . The first soldier to meet the line was overwhelmed with kisses, and every Chamorro who passed through the camp insisted on shaking hands with every soldier. Some bowed, some saluted. Some would call out *God Bless you*."[72]

Stunned GIs hastened to share their K rations, cigarettes, and candy to profuse thanks from the starving Chamorros. "When the Americans came, they started giving us Hershey bars, chocolate candy, and until I started having diarrhea, I ate chocolate candy. I ate it until I got sick," remembered then thirteen-year-old Rosa Roberto.[73] "The phrase, 'Happy days are here again' was heard over and over again," recalled Levi. Others assured the soldiers, "We've waited a long time, but we knew you'd come back."[74] Levi confessed that he wasn't the only GI with tears in his eyes. Another onlooker remarked, "I didn't have anything to do with rescuing these people. . . . I'm just a goddamn spectator here, but I was so proud to be wearing an American uniform that I damned near busted."[75]

Among those rescued at Manenggon was young Beatrice Flores, who had somehow survived the horrific slash to the back of her neck and made a convoluted trek to Manenggon, where her wounds were cleaned for the first time by a former nurse. Maggots in the gash had eaten away the dead flesh, probably saving her life. She was taken to Asan and then sent out to one of the ships offshore for further treatment. Also rescued at Manenggon was Jose Cruz, who had survived the Fena Massacre, though he would go to the grave with bits of grenade shrapnel still in his leg. Fellow survivor Manuel Charfauros, who had managed to crawl to a shack near the massacre site, was evacuated to a hospital ship for treatment of his grenade wounds.

In one of the more humorous encounters, New Jersey–born PFC Joseph Friedman stopped an elderly Chamorro coming through the lines and questioned him in pidgin English, "Do you know-em where Japan man hiding positions are?"

The old gent looked at him and replied in clipped English, "No problem, Marine." Friedman's buddies went into hysterics and entertained themselves for some time, stopping him at every opportunity to inquire, "Say, you know-em where Japan man hiding?"[76]

Many more Chamorros would be liberated in the coming days, hungry, exhausted, and overjoyed. Getting a break from combat, PFC Wesley D. Bush's outfit moved through a gathering of Chamorros. "The youngsters ran alongside of us, holding on to our rifles," he recalled. "Old men held our hands and the women cried and cheered and patted our backs. All the hardship and misery and wounds we had suffered melted away at that moment and I said to myself, 'It has been worth it all.' I will never forget how grateful the people were."[77]

One group of men, women, and children perhaps spoke for all a few days after the liberation of Manenggon. Waving an American flag, they emerged from the bush to greet a column of Marines on the coastal road. Amid the ensuing hand shaking and back slapping, the children in the group stood stiffly at attention and bowed to the Marines as they had been taught by the Japanese occupiers.

Their parents quickly and happily corrected them. "You don't have to do that," they told the children. "They are Americans."[78]

CHAPTER 21

BARRIGADA

YEARS AFTER THE WAR, FATHER PAUL REDMOND, BELOVED CHAPLAIN OF THE 4TH Marines, recalled addressing a gang of dirty, battle-weary Marines one Sunday at the height of the fighting on Guam. There would be no full service that day, he advised his small congregation, only a short sermon based on Civil War general William Tecumseh Sherman's famous observation that "war is hell."

"Hell!" piped up some wise guy from the back of the group. "Sherman never even left the States!"[1]

The typical Marine enlisted man in World War II was in his late teens to early twenties. Junior officers were scarcely older. Colonel John Letcher felt that the officers and men he served with could be divided into three categories. The first, numbering somewhere between 15 and 20 percent, were men who apparently liked to fight. When ordered to advance, they responded instantly. "They were eager to come to grips with the enemy and seemed to be entirely lacking in fear."

The greater majority fell into the second category. These were men who did not look forward to fighting and who were afraid but whose sense of duty and pride kept them from giving in to their fear. They went forward when ordered and fought "with courage and resolution, if not with enthusiasm," observed Letcher.

The third category was made up of men who "had no stomach for fighting and who did everything possible to keep out of it. They could be gotten out of their foxholes and made to advance only by physical force or the threat of it." They would seize upon any excuse to lag behind or turn back. Their shoes would become untied, or they would say they didn't have enough ammunition and had to go back for more, or they remembered some urgent duty they were supposed to perform elsewhere. They would come up with any reason they could think of to get away from the fighting. Letcher remarked that officers and enlisted men seemed to fall into these categories in about the same proportions, and there was no way to determine which was which until they were actually exposed to combat.[2]

Corporal Richard Bush fought with the 4th Marines on Guam and later on Okinawa, where he earned the Medal of Honor for shielding wounded comrades from a Japanese grenade with his own body. "I was scared most of the time," he admitted years later. "Some of the guys I fought with seemed fearless and crazy, and I guess at the time they felt the same about me."[3] Second Lieutenant Noble Beck observed, "We prayed from time to time. We looked out for one another. It was camaraderie. We had been sort of brainwashed to believe that we were undefeatable. With that kind of confidence, that helps a great deal. Brood and think, 'Oh my God, will I live through another day?' You can't think like that. You've got to think positive."[4]

Nightmarish experiences could become weirdly surreal. PFC Russell Baker was helping a corpsman load a casualty onto a jeep on Chonito Ridge one day for evacuation down to the beach. "He had a guy in there with both legs blown off above the knee," recalled Baker. "He's sitting on a stretcher. He's talking and laughing and smoking a cigarette." Baker saw the corpsman later and asked how the wounded Marine made out.

"Hell, he was dead before I got back down there," replied the corpsman.[5]

"It was raining, raining, raining, and we were kind of in a small inlet, not an inlet but in a hole kind of between a couple of high hills," recalled Radioman Ralph M. Schultz of another tragic incident. "[We were] dug in and it was pouring rain and our radio generator guy was sitting on his stool with his poncho over his head and generator when Lt. [Caughey] Culpepper, for some unknown reason, rose up and started to walk. And the generator guy saw him and knowing that the rule was 'everybody stay in your hole even if you have to drown,' let go and killed him."[6]

Corporal Frederick Bechtold was struck by the randomness of death. "You can't understand why this fella right here gets shot and you don't. Beyond belief. You're just waiting to get hit and it doesn't happen. It's just the sort of thing that's unexplainable. Why me, why him?"[7]

Any small measure of compassion for a bitter enemy was short-lived. "One of my best friends, we hit the shore and he made a mistake and stuck his head out and he got it," remembered PFC George Bessette. "It makes you bitter. It hardens you when you see one of your own getting it. And you say to yourself, I can't get enough of these guys. And I think everybody felt like that. It takes the kid out of you."[8]

PFC Billy Sherrill was involved in a push gone bad when his platoon was shot up trying to cross open ground toward Japanese holdouts in a wooded gulch. "And all of our men, most of them were clearly down," he said. "You could see them before the firing stopped; the Japanese were really shooting them up—the ones already shot. You would see bodies jump."[9]

Japanese were viewed as subhuman. "I don't believe before the service I had ever really met an Oriental," remarked former PFC Sheldon Lansky. "I was trained so thoroughly by the Marine Corps that to go out and kill a Japanese was like going out hunting rabbits. I'm ashamed to say that, but that's the way we were trained. There was no remorse."[10]

PFC Fenton ("Gabby") Grahnert killed his first enemy soldier during the push toward Orote Peninsula. "I was pretty close behind this tank. Well, there was a hole in the ground, and I tiptoed up to peek in and there was a Jap, wearing one of those little bill caps. He shut his eyes. Well, he knew that I saw him, and so he come out of there with a grenade to throw at me. I wheeled around with my BAR." Grahnert fired three shots, hitting the enemy soldier in the chin, nose, and forehead. "He fell back down in the hole and the grenade went off, blew up between his legs. First live Jap I'd seen, and I shot him. Looked him right in the face. First man I ever killed. I was shook up as hell and then we moved out. I couldn't think straight because I killed a man."[11]

"The first time you kill a man is one feeling," said former PFC Charles Meacham years after fighting with the 1st Marine Provisional Brigade on Guam. "The first time you look him straight in the face and shoot first and kill him, that's another feeling, and after that it doesn't make much difference."[12]

During the mop-up of Japanese stragglers along the Sumay cliffs on Orote Peninsula, Ray Gillespie's 3rd Battalion picked up a prisoner. Many Marines—perhaps most—did not bother with prisoners, though the opportunity to capture one was not a common occurrence. Most Japanese preferred to fight to the death. "We were not looking to take prisoners because it was too difficult to take prisoners," admitted Lieutenant Noble Beck. "It's much easier to just shoot them and forget them." As of July 27, III Amphibious Corps G-3 Periodic Reports listed only fourteen POWs captured over the previous six days. By July 31, in the wake of the failed enemy counterattack, that number had risen to forty-one. "Taking them was pretty tricky because the Japanese were very suicidal," observed Beck. "They would die for the emperor. They were very brave and they would fight right to the bitter end. It was kill or be killed and it's not pretty."[13]

Even less "pretty" were instances involving outright murder. Sergeant Yoshio ("Victor") Nishijima, a nisei interpreter assigned to the 77th Division, recalled sending a Japanese prisoner back to headquarters. The man was escorted by two GIs. The three were intercepted by some Marines and "the Marines shot him [the prisoner] in front of these two guys that were bringing him in," said Nishijima. "They told our guys they don't take prisoners."[14]

The Japanese soldier picked up by Gillespie's outfit was wounded. He came in voluntarily, stripped and with his hands up. Seeing the Marines working to locate and defuse aerial bomb mines, he offered to help. "He was very excited about the bombs," recalled Gunnery Sergeant Ralph W. Paulk. "He showed us how to defuse the acid fuses and where all the bombs were located." The appreciative Marines gave him a cigarette and some K rations before escorting him to battalion headquarters. There the situation turned ugly as battalion commander Lieutenant Colonel Clair W. Shisler took notice of the prisoner. "Colonel Shisler, without listening to an explanation of how this man had helped locate the bombs—no one could get a word in—said 'Take the S.O.B. out and shoot him,'" recalled Paulk.

The order was directed at Second Lieutenant Buenos A. W. Young of Headquarters Company. Swallowing his apprehension regarding their difference in rank, the thirty-year-old Reservist from Connecticut flatly refused. "[It] just did not seem right to execute a prisoner who was, so obviously, no more than a boy; was so small and insignificant; was so badly wounded; and who by every decent, humane standard was entitled to better treatment," he said years later.

A number of other Marines in the headquarters had no such qualms. Grabbing the unfortunate captive, they hustled him outside. Corporal Russell Perry saw the prisoner, hands tied behind his back, being dragged along by three or four Marines. "More Marines, aware of what was to take place, began to follow the Marine-led prisoner to a landing strip nearby," he said. "Some word had been passed around that if anyone had a pistol and wanted target practice, this was an opportunity. Eventually, the Japanese was given a boot and made to run. He had taken three to five steps when he was gunned down by a number of weapons. I remember distinctly seeing one round enter the back left side of his head."

Paulk heard that Shisler was subsequently disciplined for the incident, but the colonel's personnel file does not indicate any formal action. As for the others, Paulk said only, "I hope the Marines who shot that poor Jap can sleep nights."[15]

On Guam's northern plateau, General Hideyoshi Obata was preparing as best he could to meet the American advance. He and Colonel Hideyuki Takeda visited Finegayan the night of July 29 to give instructions on defense. Site of an important road junction inland from Tumon Bay, the village was under concentrated naval bombardment, which inflicted heavy casualties, reported Colonel Takeda, "but officers and men calmly made preparations for the next battle."[16]

On July 31 the general inspected positions in the vicinity of Mount Barrigada, a little over a mile to the southeast of Finegayan, to evaluate the ground for a potential main line of resistance. "This inspection showed that the positions were unsuitable for the fighting because of the jungle which would make firing impossible and provide no room for counterattack," observed a staff officer. "As a result, he decided to engage the enemy . . . on the Mt Santa Rosa Mt. Mataguac line," still further north.[17]

In an effort to slow the American advance, General Obata established delaying positions at Finegayan and Barrigada, about six miles forward of his planned main defense line. The right sector unit at Finegayan would face the 3rd Marine Division. The left unit, positioned at Barrigada, would face the 77th Infantry Division. A second defense line was to be established just below Ipapao, with the final stand to take place at Mount Santa Rosa.

The Finegayan–Mount Barrigada defense was placed under the direction of forty-seven-year-old Major General Yoshitomo Tamura, former chief operations officer of the Northern China Area Army. Tamura was serving as General Obata's chief of staff when they were stranded on Guam in mid-June by the American landings at Saipan. His orders now were to check the enemy advance as long as possible. As enemy pressure became unmanageable, he was to gradually extract as many units as possible and shift them into positions at Mount Santa Rosa.

General Obata located his headquarters in an extensive underground command bunker previously built at Mount Mataguac northwest of Yigo. Here he formed a scratch unit—the so-called Mount Santa Rosa Garrison Force. Composed of oddball naval units, including air squadron, hospital, and construction personnel and even a weather observation unit, the force was organized into four and a half companies. Three companies were placed under the command of a Captain Otori to defend Mount Mataguac and General Obata's command post. The other company was sent, along with two machine-gun squads, to Mount Santa Rosa to build dummy positions "to fool U.S. troops."[18]

Joining this mixed bag of ill-trained combatants was Atsuo Takeda, a member of the navy's 4th Weather Unit. Takeda had arrived on Guam in late May, but the unit's duties measuring wind direction and speeds soon became secondary to building defenses against the expected invasion. Toward the end of July, as organized resistance began to collapse, the weather unit received a message from Imperial Headquarters on their one remaining radio exhorting, "Persevere doggedly until the last soldier and wait for the arrival of friendly forces."[19]

During the withdrawal north, Takeda was assigned to a 250-man "naval brigade with no guns." Their main duty was to transport food and ammunition. Despite not being committed to direct ground combat, by early August the unit had lost fifty men killed and ten missing as the incessant American aerial and naval bombardments took their toll. A subsequent Japanese study observed, "The enemy air force seeking our units during the daylight hours in the forest bombed and strafed even a single soldier." Darkness brought little respite as naval units took up the harassment, "shelling our position from all points of the perimeter of the island."[20]

Facing probable annihilation, survivors of the 29th Division defiantly celebrated the fourth anniversary of the unit's organization. "In an environment [so] different from last year, I was deeply moved," an officer confided to his diary. "There was only a little *sake* to drink to each other's health. The American mortar shelling is awful and a wounded man, Corporal Nakaji, committed suicide."[21]

Following the seizure of Agana on July 31, General Roy Geiger expected August 1 to be another day in pursuit of a fleeing disorganized enemy. The Pago River, reached by 77th Division troops the day before, was the first natural barrier the Japanese might have used in an effort to stop the American advance, but GI patrols probing beyond the watercourse found no sign of defense works. The army division now realigned its advance to head north parallel to the coast and secure a line delineated by the cross-island Agana-Pago Road.

The hard-surfaced, two-lane road was more than a convenient objective line on military maps—it was badly needed to supply the continuing advance. Geiger's two divisions were moving so rapidly they had left their supply dumps well behind. Roads—particularly in the 77th Division zone of operations—were either nonexistent or insufficient. Lack of water had already become a serious problem for the GIs struggling through the thick jungle. "I can remember it was damned hot and we never had enough water at first. We were taking water out of seeps in the hillsides and putting halazone tablets in it," observed Colonel James E. Landrum, commanding the 1st Battalion, 305th Infantry. "We were short of water—our logistics failed us. Cutting across the island we didn't get water for two and a half days."[22]

The difficulty of supplying the 77th Division's advance had been recognized beforehand. Plans called for construction of a new road about ten miles long, connecting the Harmon Road leading out of Agat to the coastal surfaced highway near Yona to support the army division's advance up the island. Theoretically, the solution made good sense. From a practical standpoint, it proved to be a nightmare. The first two- to three-mile stretch took engineers five days to build, working on a twenty-four-hour schedule. Bulldozers leveling a two-lane strip found no firm foundation, only seemingly bottomless clay. Constant rain turned the clay into a quagmire. Drainage proved impossible. Bulldozers trying to scrape the mud away only lowered the level of the "roadway," allowing more water to flow into what was already a muddy ditch.

Facing reality, General Andrew Bruce asked permission from IIIAC to share the coastal road in the 3rd Marine Division area to bring in supplies, especially water and ammunition. Permission was granted, and the original road project was abandoned. The solution was far from ideal—the heavy use of the single artery for an entire corps created traffic issues and compounded maintenance problems—but it had to suffice. "The books would say it can't be done," Bruce observed later, "but on Guam it was done—it had to be."[23]

Bruce now had a way to get supplies north, but he still needed to seize the Agana-Pago cross-island roadway in the 77th Division's zone of operations to bring those supplies east to his advancing division. Meanwhile, he continued to receive complaints about shortages of food and water. "Capture that road," Bruce told 307th Infantry commander Colonel Stephen S. Hamilton, "and we'll bring up your breakfast."[24]

Jumping off at 0700 on August 1, the 307th saw no Japanese but did find an arms dump containing knee mortars, light machine guns, rifles, and bayonets. The discovery of canned salmon, *sake*, and strawberry gumdrops was greeted with considerably more enthusiasm. Substituting *sake* for halazone-treated creek water, some enterprising GIs mixed the lemonade powder from K rations along with sugar to create a sort of jungle Tom Collins. By noon, General Bruce had his road, and breakfast was on the way. By nightfall, the 77th Division was in position about fifteen hundred yards south of Barrigada. "So far, the advance to the north had been easy," observed the official Army history of the campaign.[25]

━━●～●━━

Up on Mount Chachao with the 9th Marines, PFC Wayne Barham would not have described the day as "easy." On August 1 he lost the best friend he ever had. His name was Jack Rich. A nineteen-year-old redhead from South Dakota, Rich was mortally injured when a Japanese hand grenade exploded between his legs. Running to his aid, Barham felt his friend's shattered legs, and "they felt like a rabbit that had been shot a close range by a 12-gauge shotgun." Rich had been injected with morphine but was still conscious. "It was pouring rain and his foxhole was full of water and blood," remembered Barham.

Rich looked up at Barham, who was weeping. He smiled. "Don't cry, buddy," he said. "Remember to go see my mom and dad. Okay? It doesn't even hurt. Honest. Please don't cry."

Rich was still alive when they carried him down the hill. Surgeons amputated his legs in an effort to save him, but he died later that same day. Back up on Mount Chachao, Barham sat there in the bloody water and cried for a long time. "No one came near me," he said. "I don't even know where we were that day. We were on top of a mountain."[26]

That evening General Geiger informed his command that it appeared the enemy had fallen back to Yigo about ten miles above the waist of the island. Field intelligence indicated that Tiyan Airfield and the Barrigada area had been organized as delaying positions. Determined to close on the Japanese before they could dig in, he ordered both divisions to move with all possible speed to regain contact. The 3rd Marine Division jumped off the following morning with two regiments abreast to secure the airfield.

Accompanying the push, radioman Ralph M. Schultz had been sent over to the 3rd Battalion, 9th Marines after his forward observer team's gunfire officer "cracked up." He considered himself fortunate to be assigned to Captain William K. Crawford. "We're not here to get the Congressional Medal of Honor," Crawford advised Schultz when he reported in; "we're here to keep our asses whole" while calling in gunfire when needed by the infantry. "Keep your head down. We'll do our job and let them do their job."

But now, moving cautiously along in the shelter of a ditch by the airfield, Crawford peered over the embankment toward the runways and spotted a prize he couldn't resist. "There's an airplane up there," he said. "There's two guys working on it. We're gonna take it, but don't hit the airplane." The Marines eased their way up onto the embankment and opened fire. "And I think the Japs thought the whole Marine Corps was there," remarked Schultz. The squad moved up on to the field, he recalled, "and the airplane wasn't touched, but the tools were still laying on the wings when we walked by."[27]

The coral strip had been hacked out of a large coconut grove with taxiways and revetments scattered among the trees, which were now a mass of shattered trunks and shredded fronds interspersed with wrecked aircraft. Despite cautionary intelligence reports, resistance was limited to one lone enemy soldier manning a light machine gun. The 9th Marines had the objective in hand by 0910. "The field looked like a country airport back home, though not so good," observed Alvin Josephy. "A few scattered buildings had been smashed to ruins. About twenty-five Jap planes lay in the bushes and among trees along the strip."[28]

On the right, the 77th Infantry Division was advancing on Barrigada, which wasn't much of a metropolis even by Guam standards. Located at Junction 306 on the roadway east from Agana, the settlement consisted of less than two dozen buildings clustered in the corner of a large clearing. With the exception of a two-story temple and a large tin-roofed shack, notable mostly because it had been painted green and stood by the roadway leading north, the place was pretty nondescript. But Barrigada's main attraction wasn't its architecture—it was a well and pump station. Located one hundred yards northwest of the road junction, the pump station was capable of providing thirty thousand gallons of pure water a day to thirsty troops. The northern part of the island had few streams, and the subsurface coral quickly absorbed even heavy rains. With water points near the beaches too far away for rapid delivery, and with weapons and ammunition having first priority on the already constricted roadway, Barrigada's water was a valuable prize.

Having received a report during the night that as many as two thousand Japanese could be in transit on the road between Barrigada and Finegayan, General Bruce opted for caution. He ordered a preliminary reconnaissance at 0630 by twelve light tanks from the 706th Tank Battalion. The tankers clattered off down the road but were back within an hour. They reported they had come under fire from the outskirts of the village but had seen only eight Japanese and a machine gun during the foray. Skeptical, Bruce ordered them back out for another look.

At 0800, the tanks once again rattled off toward the village. Pushing aside a flimsy roadblock on the road to Finegayan, they came upon three Japanese trucks and took them under fire, destroying the vehicles and killing an estimated thirty-five Japanese. So far everything had gone their way, but as they headed back to investigate Barrigada, dense jungle closed in on both sides, confining them to the track. When one tank got hung up on a stump a few hundred yards from the road junction, the jungle on both sides of the roadway suddenly erupted with gunfire. A Japanese dashed out and attempted to climb on one of the tanks, but the tank to the rear shot him off before he could do any damage. The stuck vehicle managed to rock its way off the stump, but the company commander, twenty-eight-year-old Captain Leonard H. Seger, whose prewar command performance had been as a member of the glee club at Miami University (Ohio), had seen enough. He radioed division, "Can I come home?"

"Why?" replied a staff officer.

"Damn it to hell," yelled Seger. "There are a hundred and fifty Japs trying to climb on my tanks. They've got grenades, machine guns and a 20mm gun. Can I come home?"

"Come home," agreed the officer.[29]

<hr>

Staff Sergeant Chester B. Opdyke's first glimpse of Barrigada came at 0930 as his squad emerged into the open by a draw leading toward the southern edge of the village. What he later learned was a two-story temple was visible about three hundred yards to his left, rising above the roofs of more modest structures.

Opdyke's squad was the tip of the spear for the 1st Platoon, I Company, 3rd Battalion, 305th Infantry. The company was supposed to sweep around to the right of Barrigada while elements of the 307th Infantry assaulted the village itself. The GIs could detect no movement in the village, but it quickly became apparent they were not alone. PFC John Andzelik, acting as scout, spotted three Japanese soldiers crossing a trail two hundred yards ahead. Opdyke called a halt and sent Andzelik and Private Salvatore Capobianco to check out a shack off to their right. The two had gone only a few yards when they came under rifle fire. Andzelik was killed instantly, and Capobianco was hit in the arm and leg. As the squad scrambled for cover, Opdyke started for the shack and was shot in the arm. Firing broke out from their front and left front as the rest of the platoon came forward, followed by the 2nd Platoon and I Company commander Captain Lee P. Cothran.

Opdyke's platoon commander, twenty-six-year-old Second Lieutenant Edward C. Harper of Greenville, South Carolina, began to send the men in intervals across the small open draw toward the woods on the other side in an effort to get around the enemy's flank. A few men had already gotten across when a machine gun opened up from the left, catching others still in the open. Private Arthur Haberman had almost reached the far side of the draw when he was killed. Staff Sergeant William Hunt was fatally wounded. Nineteen-year-old Private George W. McElroy Jr. tried to get back out of the draw; he had almost made it when he was killed by a shot to the chest.

"For Christ's sake, go back and tell Cothran a machine gun has opened up," Harper shouted.[30]

As the advance stalled, machine gunners and mortar men attempted to suppress the fire but had difficulty finding targets in the thick jungle. Enemy snipers began to pick away at them. Taking the place of a wounded machine gunner, PFC Edwin L. O'Brien picked up the air-cooled gun and sprayed a tree. A Japanese rifleman tumbled through the branches and thudded to the ground, but such visual rewards were rare. By 1030, the advance remained at a standstill, with the GIs estimating they faced a company-sized unit dug in with automatic weapons.

To I Company's left, the 307th Infantry, which had been assigned to seize the village itself, was also running into trouble. The plan was for the regiment to maintain contact with the 3rd Marine Division on its left, push through the town, and continue for a little over a mile to occupy 694-foot Mount Barrigada. The 3rd Battalion would seize the town while the 1st Battalion advanced on the left. However, as the GIs began their advance at 1030, enemy fire, thick undergrowth, and poor maps caused Company A to veer toward the village and into the 3rd Battalion's zone. Compounding the problem, the 1st Battalion's radio batteries had worn down to the point that they were ineffective beyond a range of about two hundred yards. The result was a wide gap on A Company's left and crowding on the right.

Lead elements entering Barrigada found the first few houses unoccupied. Two light tanks reported having seen no Japanese, but as soon as the armor clattered off, the GIs came under small arms fire from deeper in town. The volume of fire gradually increased "until it sounded like the steady cracking roar of a rifle range."[31]

Desmond Doss, a medic with B Company, scraped out a shallow hole in the dirt and tried to make himself as small as possible as the firing picked up. A devout Seventh-day Adventist, the bespectacled twenty-six-year-old from Lynchburg, Virginia, refused to so much as touch a weapon. He had driven his officers to distraction with his Saturday Sabbaths and uncompromising religious observances, but he was also conscientious to a fault. Watching from his hole, he saw a green-clad GI get up and begin to advance at a crouch. The soldier abruptly collapsed in a heap. Doss scrambled to his feet and ran toward him, trying to stay low as bullets snapped overhead. The soldier lay on his face where he had fallen. Doss crossed one of the GI's legs over the other as he had been taught and turned the man over on his back. His chest was soaked in blood. Doss ripped open the bloody fatigue jacket and saw that a shell fragment had torn a big hole in his chest. Knowing it was probably hopeless, he opened his medical bag and took out a large battle dressing. As he was securing it in place, the wounded man exhaled a last dying breath. It was Doss's first fatality but far from his last.[32]

As the firing intensified, Second Lieutenant Willis J. L. Munger, whose B Company platoon was approaching the village on the Agana Road, was ordered to proceed diagonally across a wide grassy field on Company A's left. Across the field, on the east side of Finegayan Road about two hundred yards north of the village proper, stood a green-painted two-story building with a metal roof. Referred to by the GIs simply as the "green house," it appeared to be a good spot to put down flanking fire on the enemy positions. "That looks like good protection," observed Munger. "Let's take it."[33]

Munger took his platoon across the field in short two- and three-man rushes, but as they started across the road toward the green house itself, a machine gun opened up from the woods beyond the building, driving the men into a shallow ditch by the roadway. Their situation became even more precarious as 3rd Battalion machine gunners and mortars focused on a grass shack along the roadway, setting it on fire. As flames licked up, a Japanese medium tank burst out of the shack and started toward the men in the ditch. Three Japanese infantrymen riding on the deck were quickly knocked off by small arms fire, and the tank turned away and headed for the village where A Company had taken position near the two-story temple.

PFC John E. Raley, a twenty-eight-year-old former textile mill worker from Frostburg, Maryland, had set up his heavy machine gun at a corner of the temple building. As the tank drew near, he took it under fire. The tank kept coming, but Raley stuck to his gun. Ramming into the side of the building, the tank paused, shifted gears, and ground forward, crashing out through the other side, the tracks narrowly missing Raley. As it was, the roof of the building collapsed and pinned him in the wreckage.

With a piece of thatched roofing partially obscuring the vision slit, the tank continued its rampage, running over another machine-gun position. A Company had three bazookas: two failed to work, and the team on the third was so excited they neglected to pull the safety pin on the rocket before firing. Hanging up on a coconut log, the tank continued to fire wildly while rocking back and forth in an effort to break loose. Concentrated small arms fire knocked ammunition boxes off the deck but had little other effect. The tank finally freed itself and proceeded down the road through a battalion aid station, a battalion command post, and the 307th Infantry headquarters, leaving wounded men, scattered equipment, and confusion in its wake before disappearing off into the 3rd Marine Division sector.

While A Company battled the tank, most of Munger's platoon had abandoned the shallow roadside ditches and made a dash for the green house. It proved to be a dubious refuge. Automatic weapons fire from a pillbox only twenty yards behind the house and from other emplacements in the woods tore through the flimsy walls. A BAR man was shot as he returned fire from a window. An attempt to bring in two wounded men from the road attracted a hail of fire. One of the casualties was dragged into the house; the other man remained lying near the road pleading for help until he finally died.

Belatedly realizing that the house offered scant protection against mortar or artillery fire, Munger, a stocky former steel company police officer, gave his men the option to get out while they could. "Anyone who wants to leave—I wouldn't blame you," he said. "But I'm sticking."[34] Sergeant Charles J. Kunze volunteered to go back to company headquarters to get some direction. Darting out of the house, the twenty-two-year-old Texan flopped into the roadside ditch, crawled through a culvert, and sprinted across the open field to find company commander Captain Frank J. Vernon. After hearing Kunze's report, Vernon said, "Tell Munger to come back. That shack isn't worth it."[35] Kunze ran back to the house. As he was giving Munger the order to withdraw, artillery fire from the division's own guns rocked the building, erasing any doubts that it was time to get out.

The GIs bolted from the green house, running and dropping to cover, then rising to dash a few more feet as Japanese machine-gun fire raked the field. Originally in position to provide covering fire for the withdrawal, almost all of Company A fell back from the temple area to avoid the artillery fire. One exception was PFC Raley. Having recovered from his face-to-face with the Japanese tank, Raley, though injured, stuck with his machine gun in an effort to protect litter bearers evacuating casualties over the open ground.

Back at battalion, an officer belatedly realized the men were under fire from their own artillery. Getting on the phone, he located the artillery liaison officer and had the barrage stopped. In the meantime, several men, including Kunze, making his fourth trip across the field, were hit by enemy fire. Kunze survived, but Lieutenant Munger was killed as he exited the green house.[36] As the last wounded were carried toward the rear, PFC Raley finally left his gun and also started back, only to be shot and killed.

The situation had not markedly improved at the other end of the line where Captain Lee Cothran's I Company remained stalled at the draw southeast of the village. At 1330 Company K, reinforced with five light tanks from the 706th Tank Battalion, moved up and deployed in some thick woods to Cothran's right, parallel to the lower end of the troublesome draw. Mortar and machine-gun fire had been directed on the supposed Japanese positions over the past three hours with little noticeable effect. The tanks now took their turn.

Four of the tanks, accompanied by infantry, clattered across the draw without incident, but the fifth came under machine-gun and cannon fire from hidden positions to the left. Ricochets off the tank killed an infantry sergeant, wounded two other men, and drove the rest to cover. Unwilling to advance without infantry support, the tanks pulled back. Believing he had one of the Japanese emplacements spotted, platoon leader Lieutenant Edward Harper stepped up and offered to guide one of the tanks into a firing position. Climbing aboard "Dirty Detail," commanded by Second Lieutenant Charles J. Fuchs, he guided the light tank to within a few yards of the suspected enemy position, but they quickly found they had a tiger by the tail. As Fuchs opened fire, a Japanese gun responded, scoring hits on the trailing idler and drive shaft. Another shell punched through the side armor, missing Harper by inches. Fuchs tried to back up but lost a track. Newly arrived Shermans from the 706th Tank Battalion laid down covering fire while Harper and the crew of Dirty Detail bailed out and ran back to friendly lines. The Shermans then destroyed the damaged tank with their 75mm guns to keep it out of Japanese hands.

In one last effort, four medium tanks, with the indomitable Lieutenant Harper again acting as guide, had better luck. Moving out abreast toward the suspected enemy position, they raked the area with machine-gun and 75mm fire, stripping away the camouflage to reveal an enemy tank.

"Is that a *tank*?" an excited crewman exclaimed over the radio.

"Hell, yes!" the commander shouted back.

"Ours?"

"No!"

The Shermans quickly knocked out the enemy tank, but by now it was almost dark, and there was no opportunity to follow up.[37]

After hours of fighting, the Japanese opposing the 307th Infantry at Barrigada remained in command of the Finegayan Road and the water station. Shortly after 1400, an impatient General Geiger weighed in, radioing General Bruce, "You are holding up advance of 3rd Marine Division. Make every effort to advance your left flank to maintain contact."

Bruce replied with a rundown of the difficulties the 307th Infantry was encountering at Barrigada. "I do not expect to capture Mount Barrigada today," he advised.[38] However, in one last effort to at least seize the village area before dark, he committed the 2nd Battalion to the 307th Infantry's assault.

Battalion commander Colonel Charles F. Learner decided to send G Company in a two-pronged attack toward the green house. The 2nd Platoon, under First Lieutenant Robert C. Smith, would follow four light tanks up Agana Road, approaching the house from the south. The 1st Platoon, under twenty-six-year-old First Lieutenant James T. Whitney, would attack toward the Finegayan Road north of the house. This movement would allow the platoons to skirt the open field that B Company had been forced to cross under heavy fire in the failed attack earlier in the day.

Once again, Murphy's Law prevailed. When Lieutenant Smith reported for orders, G Company commander Captain John F. Gannon was not available. Smith talked on the phone with Colonel Learner, who directed him to move his platoon up on the left of the 1st Battalion. Believing those were the complete orders—and not aware that the plan called for his platoon to support the tanks—Smith brought his men up on the left of B Company and advanced onto the open field in a series of squad rushes. Reaching the top of a rise, they came under sniper fire and took cover in shell holes. At this point, a runner arrived from Captain Gannon informing Smith he was "to follow the tanks" through town.[39]

With the tanks already on the move two hundred yards away, it was too late for Smith to comply. He decided instead to continue across the field in an effort to arrive at the green house simultaneously with the tanks. The gambit worked. In a series of rushes, the platoon overtook the tanks on the Finegayan Road near the green house. Tank fire into the building and the woods behind momentarily quieted resistance from that direction. Meanwhile, to the northwest, Lieutenant Whitney's 1st Platoon, forming the other pincer of the movement on the green house, received orders to extend further to the left, nearer the woods bordering the north side of the field. Whitney didn't like this scenario at all. Though the woods were presently quiet, any Japanese positions there would have a clear—and point-blank—field of fire on his men as they advanced across their front. As a precaution, he moved his platoon out with the squad on the far left trailing behind where it would be able to react to any developing threat from the woods.

Whitney's well-placed caution was not appreciated by Colonel Learner. Seeing the squad hanging back, he messaged the platoon, "Get that left flank up!"[40]

As the squad ran to catch up, the tanks at the green house were disappearing back down the road. As if on signal, Japanese machine gunners and riflemen dug into positions in the woods to Whitney's left directed a concentrated fire on the platoon. The 2nd Platoon at the green house also came under heavy fire, both from the north and from the woods east of the house. Caught in the open, a few of Whitney's men broke for the Finegayan Road, but most hit the ground where they were. A lucky few found cover in shell holes; the others lay in the foot-tall grass, easily visible to the Japanese dug into an embankment just inside the woods.

Manning a skirmish line east of the green house, Smith's platoon was also being shot to pieces. Two men were hit and dragged into the house. Four GIs ran around the right side of the house in an effort to knock out an enemy machine gun in the woods. All were shot. Following behind the platoon, Captain Gannon was hit in the leg. The skirmish line dissolved as the platoon withdrew to the protected side of the green house. Staff Sergeant Edward E. Whitemore volunteered to run back over the open field to seek help. He made it to company headquarters and found the company exec, First Lieutenant Garrett V. Rickards. "The 2nd Platoon are almost all casualties," he told Rickards "They are over there in that green house. We need stretchers and help to get them out."[41] Rickards ordered First Lieutenant Walter E. Seibert to take his 3rd Platoon to Smith's aid while he contacted 1st Battalion to obtain tanks to cover the evacuation of the trapped platoon.

With Whitemore as a guide, Seibert brought his platoon up the road toward the green house. Encountering heavy fire, the GIs set up a machine gun and sprayed the treetops. Return fire wounded the first and second gunners. Two heavy machine-gun crews from Company H arrived, along with an 81mm mortar section, and began hammering the woods. Two tanks clanked up and joined in. Under their protection, the eighteen men of 3rd Platoon began evacuating casualties from 2nd Platoon. Some were loaded onto the tank decks; others were lugged out on stretchers. All were retrieved with the exception of one man, who could not be located. (He lay out by the green house all night and was picked up the next morning.) As it started to grow dark, the platoons pulled back across the field.

Seibert arrived back at the company headquarters to be greeted with more bad news. Lieutenant Rickards informed him that the 1st Platoon was trapped in the field to the northeast near the woods and had been almost completely wiped out. Another rescue needed to be mounted.

Under the leadership of 1st Battalion commander Lieutenant Colonel Joseph B. Coolidge and Lieutenant Rickards, the 3rd Platoon and three tanks immediately set out for Whitney's trapped platoon. The tanks turned their guns on the woods as the 3rd Platoon began collecting casualties scattered across the length of the field. Having come under fire from positions less than one hundred yards away, the only men who had escaped were those who had managed to find some kind of hole in the open field. The others, scratching at the ground, were an easy mark, their location betrayed by their backpacks protruding above the grass. Running out of stretchers, the rescue party improvised litters using rifles and coats. A later count revealed that 1st Platoon had lost twenty-six men, most of them killed. One squad alone lost eight killed and one wounded. Among the dead was Lieutenant Whitney. Colonel Coolidge was wounded during the evacuation. By contrast, Seibert's 3rd Platoon was lucky: the day's action had cost them only three wounded.

The GIs withdrew and dug in for the night. The division had lost twenty-nine killed and ninety-eight wounded during the day. The two regiments claimed 105 Japanese killed, which was almost certainly wildly optimistic. Few GIs had so much as seen an enemy soldier. The Japanese positions at Barrigada had, as the U.S. Army official history subsequently conceded, been "barely dented."[42] The division history was more blunt, observing, "Throughout the day great courage but little tactical skill had been demonstrated."[43]

CHAPTER 22

THE ROAD TO FINEGAYAN

An undersized but infinitely precious Stars and Stripes fluttered from the flagstaff in front of the shell-torn Government Palace on the Plaza de Espana on August 2. Instead of forty-eight stars, this flag had only twelve. Instead of thirteen stripes, it had but nine.

The flag had been presented to General Hal Turnage by twenty-five-year-old Maria Guevara Arceo, who had fashioned it while hiding in the hills. She brought it with her when she finally made her way into Marine lines, accompanied by a cow and a flock of children. While Arceo and the children stood by the general's side, a Marine corporal sounded Colors. A color guard of military police snapped to attention as the gallant little banner rose to the peak of the flagstaff.

Maria Arceo's homemade flag aptly reflected the civilian situation, which was both pathetic and defiant at the same time. The destruction of major population centers had left thousands of civilians homeless. Ruined Agana was left to the elements, inhabited by a few military police, medical personnel at the former naval hospital, and a shell-shocked cat that lived under a house commandeered by some news correspondents hanging around looking for stories. "The cat mews all day and wanders around all night, yowling dismally," remarked Associated Press reporter William L. Worden.[1]

Now and again some civilians wandered through, vainly hoping to salvage their few possessions. "There is some battered furniture, some abused stoves, but all textiles, dishes, personal possessions, papers, mementoes and pictures either were lost or ruined," observed Worden. "The bombing blew this stuff to pieces, the ship bombardment shoved it out the windows and the rain completed the ruination." It was pretty much the same or worse at Asan, Piti, Sumay, and Agat. Still, he added, the Chamorros seemed to harbor no resentment about the destruction of their property—they only shrugged. "Everybody is poor and nobody seems to care," he remarked.[2]

Trudging over the ridges in the rain, Irene Ploke's column of refuges from Manenggon was met by military trucks that took them to Pigo Cemetery at Agana. "They gave us army tents, so each family [had] a tent," she recalled. The refugees pitched their tents between the graves, using the mounds as pillows. "Nobody was afraid. We didn't care," she said. When tents became too crowded, some of the boys took up residence in graves blown open by shell fire. "My brother and my cousin, each one got into the hole, pushed out all these bones that [were] there, and they slept," remarked Ploke.[3]

Prior to sailing for Guam, twelve Civil Affairs officers had joined IIIAC on temporary duty. While on Guadalcanal they formulated plans to handle normal civil affairs functions. A platoon of fifty men was assigned to the Civil Affairs Section and given special training. Instructions to troops and military police were prepared, and efforts were made to procure supplies and transportation. A request for two thousand shelter tents, tarpaulins, screening, canned milk, rice, and tools was approved. However, these items were stowed on a ship with low unloading priority—the tarpaulins never made it aboard at all—and would not reach the beach until some fifteen thousand civilians had already swarmed into friendly lines. Some days, as many as a thousand or more arrived in search of succor as the battle line moved north.

Protective compounds rapidly evolved into sprawling ramshackle refugee camps with families living in scrounged-up tentage or shelters cobbled together from whatever was at hand. At their peak, about eighteen thousand civilians were housed in three camps. The first camp was established on July 25 in the ruins of Agat, but due to lack of room, its seventy-one occupants were moved to a better location about a mile and a half to the south on July 30. Within hours the seventy-one civilians had become seven hundred, reaching a peak population of 6,689 by August 5. Another camp was established on August 1 at Anigua on the outskirts of Agana.

Ironically, a third camp took form at Manenggon at the former Japanese detainment area in a last-minute effort to accommodate over four thousand refugees streaming in from the Talofofo area. As it was accessible only by a trail that was too narrow to accommodate trucks, all supplies had to be brought in by hand or by bull cart. Refugees were fed with captured Japanese food stores, including 87.5 tons of rice, 185 gallons of soya sauce, 150 cases of canned noodles, and 500 cases of canned fish. Using machetes and local materials—including fiber fastenings instead of nails—workers erected buildings, including two small chapels and a hospital for thirty patients. Improvements to drainage eliminated much of the standing water, though the site remained muddy. A Marine guard and members of the Insular Force provided security against roving Japanese. Seven Japanese were killed in the area during the first two days of occupancy.

Many civilians arrived at the camps in dire need of medical attention. PFC Ray Gillespie was part of a patrol sent out to assist a group of Chamorros hiding in a cave. "The civilian women had been raped by the Japanese and some were murdered," he observed. Before the Japanese left, they had thrown grenades in the cave and many of the survivors were wounded. "The one with the worst wound was a very pretty sixteen-year-old girl," he recalled. "The heel on her right foot had been blown away and gangrene had set in. The girl smelled to high heaven. For the wounded we made stretchers, using our ponchos and cut poles. Some of the children we had to carry on our backs."[4]

Civil Affairs had tried to arrange for medical supplies during the planning stages, but priority had to be given to military units. "Civilians will be treated if and when facilities are available over and above the necessity of service personnel," observed a Marine Brigade order two months before the Guam landings.[5] No medical supplies, tents, cots, or equipment were specifically designated for civilians during the assault phase, forcing Civil Affairs to beg for critically needed items. The Army loaned tentage for a one-hundred-bed medical facility that Civil Affairs managed to wheedle out of the hospital ship USS *Bountiful*. The corps medical battalion provided wards and hospital care for about three hundred of the most seriously ill and wounded refugees. Despite best efforts, medical care in the three camps was "completely inadequate," admitted a subsequent Civil Affairs report. As many as eighteen hundred civilians were reporting for sick call each day. "Malnutrition and exposure over a long period of time have been the chief causes of illness and respiratory diseases are prevalent," noted Civil Affairs. "Wounds inflicted in the course of the occupation have been frequent."[6]

With military physicians and hospitals struggling to cope with large numbers of wounded Marines, war dog veterinarian Lieutenant William Putney found himself pressed into service providing medical care for civilians. Accompanied by four corpsmen, he proceeded to Mount Tenjo, where about four hundred Chamorros had gathered after passing through American lines. "Many of them had escaped from a concentration camp, many in rags, and some half-naked," recalled Putney. "They were all undernourished, dehydrated and sick from vitamin-deficient diets." Climbing down from their jeep, Putney and his corpsmen were greeted by "a loud chorus of crying children and babies." Seabees were distributing water in whatever containers were available. One of Putney's corpsmen started the night by delivering a baby boy under a shelter half in the pouring rain. By morning, he had delivered two more. The division provost marshal arrived soon afterward with two trucks—one loaded with C rations, the other with tarpaulins—and the hillside began to take on the ambiance of a small tent city. A large tent served as a sickbay where civilians lined up for treatment of cuts, sore throats, dysentery, and other ailments. By evening, field kitchens were in operation, serving hot C rations in mess kits brought up from the division supply dump. It wasn't by the book, but it worked.[7]

Twenty-two-year-old PFC Frank Witek woke up the morning of August 3—the fourteenth day of the battle for Guam—turned to his buddies and remarked, "This is my day."[8] Later they would wonder about that comment. But for the moment, busy getting ready to head up the road toward Finegayan, most probably didn't give it much thought.

Witek himself could be a bit of an odd duck. Enlisting in the Marines less than two months after Pearl Harbor, he had been working as a laborer at the Standard Transformer Company in his hometown of Chicago when the war broke out. Assigned to the 9th Marines, he ended up in Sergeant Robert ("Rabbit") Pavlovich's B Company squad, mostly because nobody else wanted to deal with him, according to Pavlovich. "I got Frank because I had the reputation of getting all the eight balls," he recalled. "Every time somebody couldn't handle somebody in their platoon or in their squad, they said, 'Take him to Rabbit. Give him to Rabbit.' So anyway, that is how I ended up getting Frank."

In Witek's case, the issue was his nonchalance about certain basics. "When you told Frank, 'Hey, Frank, you haven't taken a shower in a week,' he'd look at you and say, 'So what?'" said Pavlovich. "What I did, I just left Frank on his own. I mean if Frank wanted to walk around in brown skivvies, well, they're his skivvies. If he didn't want to wear shoes—he wanted to go barefooted—fine. But when it came time for us to stand inspection, then I expected Frank to do what he was supposed to do. And if you talked to Frank, he did it. But in the meantime, Frank was his own man." Whatever his deficiencies in camp, Bougainville proved Witek was thoroughly dependable in combat. "Once the battle started, once the shooting started, you would get, in my mind, a different Frank," remarked Pavlovich.[9]

Witek's company spearheaded the 1st Battalion's push up the unpaved Mount Santa Rosa Road toward Finegayan the morning of August 3. "My company was ordered to move very quickly [that morning]," recalled company commander Captain Burtis Anderson. "I don't know what the distance was, whether it was a mile or two or just what, to an important crossroads, [Road Junction (RJ) 177]. The Japs were reported to have it heavily defended. As I recall, they even had an artillery piece pointing point-blank."[10]

Shortly after 0900, still about five hundred yards short of RJ 177, Company B ran into an ambush by what turned out to be a company-sized force. "The Japs had had two road blocks in parallel lines across the road, about a hundred yards apart," recalled combat correspondent Sergeant Alvin Josephy. "There were mines in the roads, then antitank and heavier guns on both sides of the road. . . . The first row of Japs let most of our men through, then opened fire on their backs. At the same moment, the second row of Japs opened fire on our men's faces."[11] Spotting some Japanese in a depression almost at his feet, Witek brashly remained standing and emptied a full magazine from his BAR at point-blank range, killing eight of them. As his platoon tried to regroup, he stayed to watch over a casualty who had been hit too badly to get out on his own, then laid down covering fire when help arrived to retrieve the man.

Twenty minutes after the initial contact, B Company took another stab at the enemy roadblock. Again the push went bad. Witek's platoon was pinned down by a heavy machine gun. As the advance stalled, Witek picked himself up out of the red dirt, charged to within ten yards of the machine gun, and shot down the crew. PFC Jimmy Ganopulos was working through some abandoned huts along the road when Witek made his assault. "What he did, he ran in front of our squad," he recalled. "He was a BAR man. He just started spraying the bushes and everything else and the first thing you know, we saw him go down. That was it! He was killed outright. He went down like a block of cement. He was hit right in the head."[12]

Moving toward the fighting soon afterward, Josephy came across two Marines lying on their backs, talking in a low voice. "They were a single color, clay-red, from helmet to shoes," he recalled. The two saw a corporal they knew. "Witek just got it," they reported. "But he took thirteen Nips with him. Just stood up and sprayed them. Funny thing. He woke up this morning and said it was his day."[13]

B Company overran the ambush site with the help of tanks, finding 105 enemy dead sprawled in the grass and bushes. "A Jap 77, with big wooden wheels stood silently against the trunk of a breadfruit tree; around it sprawled dead Japs," observed Josephy. "In from the road was a line of spider pits—round holes about two feet across and three feet deep. In each one there were two dead Japs, mashed and gory. Some had been hit with grenades, others looked as if tanks had run over them."

Unused ammunition, hand grenades, and Molotov cocktails—green *sake* bottles filled with gasoline to use against tanks—were strewn around by the edges of the foxholes. One Marine came upon a human leg lying in the grass. "It looked like a bloody hambone," observed Josephy.[14]

Frank Witek was awarded a posthumous Medal of Honor for his actions that morning. When his body was recovered, he had only eight cartridges left for his BAR. "He wasn't crazy or anything," remarked Jimmy Ganopulos sixty years after the battle for Guam. "He wasn't reckless. But he was reckless that day."[15]

◦━◦

Wayne Barham's luck also ran out on the way to Finegayan. The Marines were moving along the road heading north, stepping over, on, and around the many dead Japanese scattered about. Colorful birds flitted among the trees. Barham was daydreaming when a machine gun suddenly shattered his reverie, followed by shouts and the crackle of rifle fire. He dove for cover behind a Japanese corpse, firing his BAR over the dead man's chest. A live Japanese suddenly burst out onto the road and ran directly at him. The man was armed with a bayonet lashed to the end of a bamboo pole. Barham knocked him down with a burst from his BAR, then raised up slightly to find himself looking at a Japanese hand grenade on the ground directly in front of him. He had just enough time to think, *Where the hell did that come from?* when it went off in his face. Stunned and blinded, he felt blood gushing from his head. Someone nearby was yelling, "Corpsman!"

It seemed like only seconds before the corpsman flopped down alongside him. Heavy fire continued along the road. "Grab my ankles with your hands and crawl out behind me," the corpsman told him. They crawled for perhaps fifty yards in Barham's estimation before the corpsman stopped. He sprinkled sulfa over Barham's wounds and wrapped his head with gauze to keep the flies off. Through his mental fog, Barham heard somebody say, "He's just about had it. Give him a shot of morphine, load him up and get him out of here."

He was vaguely conscious of being lifted into a jeep, followed by a bumpy ride to a landing craft at the beach. The last thing he remembered was being taken aboard a hospital ship. He was still clutching his helmet to his chest—the helmet with the hole through it from the mortar round that exploded next to him on the beach the morning of W+1. "Please don't lose my lucky helmet," he said. "See, it has a hole right through the top. It's the only thing I want to take back with me."

A voice said, "Don't worry about a thing, mate. We'll take care of it for you." Barham never saw it again.[16]

—◦—

After an uneasy night, the 77th Division GIs resumed their assault on Barrigada that same morning, following on the heels of an artillery barrage. The attack proved anticlimactic. The Japanese had pulled out during the night, taking their dead and wounded with them. A subsequent Japanese report did not enumerate losses, observing only, "Shiina Platoon (two field guns) holding the position in Barrigada destroyed two enemy tanks, but the field guns were destroyed."[17] The delaying action had been well executed, but the Japanese had overlooked at least one crucial item: the village's water point had been left intact. Division engineers jacked up a jeep as a power plant, improvised a belt from a Japanese fire hose, and soon had the precious water flowing.

With Barrigada finally in hand, the division's 307th Infantry pushed toward the height of the same name about a mile northeast of the village. A Japanese sniper wounded five GIs before he was located and killed, but there was no organized resistance. Friendly artillery proved a greater hazard: a misdirected artillery barrage that landed on E Company during the morning killed or wounded several men, the latter including 2nd Battalion commander Colonel Charles F. Learner. Both the 77th Division artillery and the 12th Marines denied shooting into the area, but the culprit was soon identified. "The next day the 77th Division presented us with a nose fuse ring from a 75mm pack howitzer which had been taken from the stomach of one of the Army casualties," recalled Marine lieutenant colonel Frederick Henderson. "As the 77th Division did not have any pack howitzers, the round had obviously come from the 12th Marines."[18]

Shortly after midday, the 3rd Battalion pushed through scattered resistance on the lower slopes and started up the eight-hundred-foot height, reaching the summit at 1500. East of Mount Barrigada, the 1st Battalion, 305th Infantry advanced up a road that gradually deteriorated into a narrow trail. A series of close-quarter fights ensued in vegetation so thick that tanks had to make trails for the infantry to follow. In one adrenalin-fueled encounter, a sergeant fell into a hole occupied by two Japanese soldiers. "Bring me a bayonet!" he shouted, somewhat irrationally as he was already armed with a BAR. A Japanese tried to grab him by the leg. The sergeant kicked him in the face, scrambled out of the hole, turned, and squeezed the trigger on his BAR. One of the Japanese had already armed a grenade. Whether he intended to commit suicide or was shot before he could throw it was unclear; whatever the case, the grenade exploded in the hole between the two occupants, killing them both.[19]

Enemy resistance along the remainder of the division front was limited. A tank/infantry patrol from the 706th Tank Battalion attempting to establish contact with the Marines on the division's left knocked out a hastily erected roadblock on Finegayan Road. Fifty yards up the road, one of the three tanks struck a mine, which blew off the left track. Enemy guns immediately opened fire from the brush, but the crew of the stricken Sherman managed to bail out and make it back to the two accompanying tanks. Unable to advance due to other mines and without sufficient infantry to hold the position, the tankers destroyed the damaged Sherman to keep it out of Japanese hands and withdrew.

Over in the 3rd Marine Division area of operations, General Turnage was thinking breakout. Even before the fight on the road to Finegayan that claimed the life of Frank Witek, the division had laid plans to exploit Japanese disorganization with a motorized thrust to the northern end of the island. The idea was not as reckless as it might seem at first glance: the 3rd Marines were meeting little resistance in their advance up the coast on the division left, and the 9th Marines had seized Tiyan Airfield with unexpected ease. Held to only five thousand yards during the first eight days of battle, Marines and GIs had advanced five thousand to twelve thousand yards in just the last three days.

Still, if not exactly reckless, the plan was certainly audacious. At 0750, only fifty minutes after Frank Witek set off up the road toward Finegayan and his posthumous Medal of Honor, the 21st Marines were alerted to provide one company for a motorized reconnaissance patrol to Ritidian Point roughly eight miles beyond the village. As fighting developed outside Finegayan, the patrol waited in a state of uncertainty a little over a mile below the village. As it waited, additional units continued to straggle in to add muscle to the column. The additions included one section of the Reconnaissance Company with two half-tracks and four radio jeeps; Company A and staff tanks of the 3rd Tank Battalion; an engineers squad from the 19th Marines equipped with mine detectors; and six trucks to transport Company I, 3rd Battalion, 21st Marines.

Forty-year-old Lieutenant Colonel Hartnoll J. Withers, commanding officer of the 3rd Tank Battalion, had charge of the column. The reinforced infantry unit was commanded by Major Edward A. Clark, executive officer of the 3rd Battalion, 21st Marines, who was later critical of the foray, citing a "lack of understanding and appreciation on the part of the higher commander of what it takes in time and preparation for such an operation."[20] Despite having all morning to organize, the last-minute addition of various components contributed to an increasingly haphazard situation. This included the six trucks, which had been transporting rations to a forward dump when they were simply redirected to join the patrol column. "After the hasty decision to motorize this patrol, the first six trucks to unload at the forward dump were assigned or ordered to this patrol by parties unknown," reported Lieutenant Colonel Thomas R. Stokes, commanding the 3rd Motor Transport Battalion. "Neither the platoon, company or battalion motor transport commander were aware of this until some time afterward."[21] As a result of the last-minute orders, the trucks arrived without enough gas to get to Ritidian Point; the drivers were not well oriented as to their new mission, and there was confusion about the route to be followed. That confusion would contribute to serious trouble later on.

The column finally received word to move out at 1245. Two hours later, Colonel Withers, held up by fighting along the planned route of advance, began to question the wisdom of continuing so late in the day. He messaged division headquarters, "Patrol is held up at front lines where firefight is going on. Recommend patrol remain together behind front lines tonight and clear at 0730 tomorrow. Insufficient time remains today to accomplish mission."[22]

Headquarters responded a half an hour later. Withers was ordered to continue with the assigned mission at once but to return by 1800. He was to cover as much ground as he could during that time frame. As Withers mounted up, Lieutenant Colonel Carey A. Randall, whose 1st Battalion had been in combat along the road all day, advised him to stay put. "You'd better not go any further. They've got some heavy stuff up there," warned Randall.

"I've got to go," replied Withers. He'd already asked to wait until morning, only to be told, "No. Go do it now."[23]

Against Withers's better judgement, the column continued up the road, where the colonel's bad luck continued when the lead vehicle missed the left fork at RJ 177. Instead of heading up the road toward Ritidian, the patrol proceeded east in the direction of Yigo. It did not get far. At 1610, only about two hundred yards beyond RJ 177, the column fell into a well-organized ambush. Fire raked the vehicles from 75mm guns, automatic weapons, small arms, and tanks. The Japanese, later determined to be members of the Navy Special Landing Force, were well dug in and in battalion strength.

Over the next two hours the two sides slugged it out in the first and only mechanized engagement ever fought by the 3rd Marine Division. Enemy field pieces fired directly down the road. One Marine half-track was knocked out, a tank was hit in the suspension system and slightly damaged, and one of the six-by-six trucks was damaged, taking a large round through the door just as the driver threw it open to bail out. The driver was not hurt, but the truck had to be abandoned. The Marines knocked out two 75mm guns, a tank, and several machine guns but finally disengaged, having lost one officer and twelve men killed or wounded. Enemy casualties were unknown. Examining the enemy defenses later, Colonel Edward A. Craig concluded, "If the patrol had not pulled back when it did, it would have been annihilated."[24]

Japanese sources indicate that the resistance at Finegayan was built around an artillery unit equipped with two 75mm howitzers and four field guns. The unit claimed to have disabled more than ten tanks and destroyed several others. "Unit under the command of its senior noncommissioned officer continued to direct fire against the enemy who had attacked with more than ten tank guns. When the artillery pieces were destroyed the men engaged in a hand-to-hand fight. The infantry units fought back with machine guns, but suffered heavy losses before darkness," according to Japanese reports.[25]

Around August 3, Lieutenant Colonel Frank M. Reineke, executive officer of the 9th Defense Battalion, happened to be visiting the IIIAC operations tent when General Roy Geiger came in. The general, who was wearing neatly creased khakis, summoned the operations officer over to the map board, where he proceeded to point out areas with his swagger stick. "I'll have the brigade go up this way, have the 3rd Marine Division attack thusly, and send the 77th Division up the east coast in this manner and we'll wind this affair up in about a week," he stated matter-of-factly. Reineke, who referred to Geiger as "one of my favorite Marines," was greatly impressed by the general's confident, no-nonsense performance as he deftly mapped out the finale to the campaign.[26]

Things were a lot less neat and orderly for the Marines and GIs out in the boondocks, well removed from General Geiger's map board. The next four days would be a severe trial—particularly for the 77th Division—as the GIs struggled north through nearly impenetrable jungle. Tropical downpours were a daily occurrence, creating a sticky red mud that clung to wet uniforms and equipment. "At night, when the men most needed warmth, they sat in flooded foxholes, their teeth chattering; during the day their mud-encrusted uniforms remained wet with sweat," noted the 77th Division history.[27] Daylight hours brought steaming humidity and nagging thirst.

Spotter planes droned low overhead as observers tried to see below the thick jungle canopy, relaying radio messages from the ground forces when reception was problematic and calling in targets for the artillery batteries. The aircraft were not immune. Lieutenant Colonel Frederick Henderson recalled one instance when a spotter reported he was being fired on by a 20mm gun and requested that the artillery take care of it. While the artillery crews were adjusting, the spotter reported he "got the SOB's picture," said Henderson. "After the gun was knocked out and he landed, we developed the pictures he had taken with his hand camera and clearly saw that two Japs were manning the gun and firing directly at him."[28]

Laboriously hacking their way forward through the thick jungle, columns on the ground often had only a vague idea of their actual location. "In places the jungle was almost trackless; the few existing trails led nowhere and only served to confuse the troops," observed the U.S. Army history of the campaign. The location of individual units was "a nightmare," noted the official account. "Unit commanders rarely knew exactly where they were, and the reports they sent back to higher echelon could not be relied on."[29]

"We just got lost, we couldn't see where we were going," remembered battalion commander Lieutenant Colonel Joseph B. Coolidge. "We had our compasses and that's the only thing that led us along, but to maintain contact on either side was impossible and I know the Marines were having the same trouble on my left. We really had no contact for almost twenty-four hours; we had contact between individuals but it was very hard to maintain this even between squads. We also had problems with our radios; we had very little use from them when we needed them badly."[30] In some instances, the GIs were forced to rely on artillery observers to fix their position. The unit would set off a smoke round or a flare; artillery observers would mark the round and compute it in the fire direction center. The position would then be relayed to the infantry units, which were often hundreds of yards from where they thought they were.

The confusion resulted in at least one serious friendly-fire incident involving Marines and GIs. A section of Army tanks and infantry knocked out two Japanese roadblocks on the Finegayan-Barrigada Road. Encountering a third roadblock, the tankers opened up with a barrage of machine-gun and 75mm fire, stopping only when a Marine officer jumped up, waving his helmet at the advancing tanks. The roadblock was manned by Marines, some of whom were wounded in the encounter. Through some foul-up, they had not been told that they were to use red smoke grenades to identify themselves as friendly. The smoke grenades thrown by the soldiers after the action got underway meant nothing to them.

In another mishap that same day, also attributable to liaison difficulties, two B-25s flying support for the 77th Division strafed a Marine battalion command post. Incidents of American artillery fire falling on friendly troops became so common that GIs blamed their own artillery even when the culprit was Japanese. On August 4, General Andrew Bruce felt compelled to warn his infantry regiments to "stop accusing our own artillery of firing on [our] own troops until the facts are known."[31]

The morning of August 4, General Geiger notified both division commanders that he was temporarily holding up the advance of the 3rd Marine Division "until 77th Division lines are a little better organized and gap between divisions is closed."[32] By now, it had become apparent to General Bruce that any effort to conduct a shoulder-to-shoulder sweep north through the forbidding terrain would be futile. "I pointed out that it was far better to get through the jungle regardless of flanks until they [the attacking troops] arrived at a trail or road where liaison and contact could be established with adjacent units," he recalled. The lack of vision in the jungle negated the effectiveness of tactics devised for open ground. "In brief, my idea was to push boldly forward and then take up a strong all-around defense at night," said Bruce.[33]

Over in the 3rd Marine Division, General Turnage came to a similar conclusion. Between July 31 and August 2, resistance had been relatively light, but the ratio of Marine dead to wounded—forty-four killed in action to fifty-two wounded in action, or nearly 50 percent killed—was well above normal as Marines moving through dense jungle bumped into enemy rear guard units without warning. "At close quarters, the point-blank fire could not miss and resulted in the disproportionate death toll," observed a Marine officer.[34]

The division's experience over the past couple days indicated that Japanese delaying forces were confining themselves to positions along the roads and trails. Rather than thrash through uninhabited jungle simply to maintain physical contact with adjacent units, Turnage decided to attack in columns along the roads and trails. When faced with heavy cover, columns would sweep each side of the roadway for a couple of hundred yards. In more open terrain, the edges of the nearest cover would be checked. Contact with adjacent units would be established at open areas and along lateral roadways as terrain allowed, much as Bruce had suggested.

Geiger, who continued to press for speed, seems to have recognized the practicality of a change in tactics as early as August 3, when IIIAC approved General Bruce's plan to advance past Mount Barrigada "without regard to contact."[35] Had the enemy been better organized, the change in tactics might not have been possible, but the Japanese were experiencing similar difficulties. Colonel Hideyuki Takeda later observed, "They were forced to fight in the jungle where it was very hard to cooperate and communicate with each other." In a nod to the effectiveness of the amended U.S. tactics, he added, "And as American armored troops drove along the highways and trails in [the] jungle to cut off the front line into several pockets, our troops were forced to be isolated."[36]

⎯ ⎯

Prior to W-Day, U.S. intelligence estimated the Japanese had sixty-four tanks available on Guam. This was a gross overestimate—subsequent information puts Japanese armored strength at no more than thirty-eight Chi-ha and Ha-go medium and light tanks and possibly even fewer—but this had not been recognized as IIIAC continued its push north. U.S. forces reported the destruction of twenty-eight tanks between W-Day and noon on July 29, with another six "probably destroyed."[37] In one much-talked-about incident on August 2, a Japanese light tank raced down a road through the 9th Marines sector past astonished Marines waiting in reserve. "At this time a Japanese stuck his head out of the turret and started to fire in all directions with his pistol," said Colonel Edward Craig, who witnessed the scene. "The tank did not fire."[38] The excitement ended abruptly when the tank—probably the same one that had raised havoc with the GIs at Barrigada before disappearing into the Marine sector—finally ran off the road. The crew bailed out and fled into the jungle.

As of August 5, it was calculated that thirty-five enemy tanks had been destroyed. Three others had been captured and another six probably destroyed. By those estimates, the enemy now possessed no more than nineteen or twenty tanks, according to intelligence. While the number of tanks reported destroyed was clearly inflated, the number of estimated survivors may have been somewhat closer to the mark. A subsequent Japanese study indicated that ten medium tanks and three light tanks remained in action as of about August 4.[39]

One of the surviving tanks was the centerpiece of a bizarre encounter similar to the August 2 incident, but this one occurred in the 21st Marines' sector. Lieutenant George Cavender's tank platoon was waiting by the roadside when they heard the sound of a vehicle approaching at high speed. Moments later, to their disbelief, a Japanese tank sped by. The tank commander, bleeding visibly from a head wound, stared at them from the top turret hatch as the tank passed. "I suppose he was just as surprised as we were," speculated Cavender.

As the tank disappeared down the coral highway, Cavender's crew piled into their Sherman, revved the six-cylinder diesel engines to an ear-splitting roar, and took off in hot pursuit. "We were gaining on the Jap and had our 75mm gun loaded and zeroed on his rear, but we held our fire," observed Cavender. "We were heading toward our own rear area and there was danger of hitting Marines bivouacked there." Soon they were passing dozens of Marine infantrymen who had been attracted by the sound of wound-out engines and were lined up on either side of the road, point-ing after the escaping tank and cheering the pursuing Sherman. "It seemed more like we were playing a game," admitted Cavender.

After about a mile, the Japanese tank veered off onto a secondary road and dis-appeared behind a long strip of heavy brush in an open field. Cavender took a guess and maneuvered the Sherman cautiously around the further corner of the hedgerow. There, at the other end, its gun trained on the wrong approach route, waited the enemy tank. Cavender's gunner put two rounds of HE into the tank, which had never fired a shot during the entire escapade. "The last I saw of the enemy tank, it was rocking with inner explosions" remarked Cavender.[40]

The enemy tank crew's comrades were not long in exacting retribution as the 1st Battalion, 305th Infantry dug in under a heavy rain the night of August 5. The downpour let up around midnight, leaving overcast skies. About two hours later, GIs of Company A, manning the northern end of the battalion perimeter, heard the rattling squeal of approaching armored vehicles. The GIs had been warned that friendly tanks were operating in the area—and these seemed to be approaching from the area held by the regiment's 2nd Battalion—but the timing was suspicious. The entire division had also been on edge, anticipating a last-ditch banzai attack, and the men crouching in their wet foxholes were not taking anything for granted.

Their caution was well taken. As the moon emerged from behind a cloud, two Japanese tanks loomed up, accompanied by infantry who appeared to be setting up a machine gun. The GIs immediately cut down the exposed foot soldiers. A Japa-nese atop the first tank shouted, "American tank—okay! American tank—okay!" as the armored vehicles charged into the perimeter.[41] Having stopped for the night in an area with just a few inches of soil overlying hard coral, the GIs had been unable to dig in deeply. Their shallow foxholes offered little protection as the tanks split up and tore through their positions. Rifle and machine-gun fire merely ricocheted off the steel sides. A number of men broke and ran. A wounded man staggered to his feet only to fall under the grinding tracks. One of the Japanese tanks collided with an American Sherman tank that was unable to fire for fear of hitting friendly troops in the confusion. The Japanese crew backed away, crushing a jeep and spray-ing other vehicles with machine-gun fire before joining up again with their fellow tank and heading back the way they came. Pressed flat in their shallow holes, a number of GIs escaped harm as the tanks rolled over them, though two men had their rifles crushed in narrow escapes.

As the tanks finally disappeared back into the night, someone picked off a Japanese who had been clinging to the top of one of the vehicles since the beginning of the attack, but fifteen Americans had been killed and forty-six wounded, many of them casualties of wild friendly fire. An artillery forward-observation team had been almost wiped out, losing six men. Smashed and bullet-riddled equipment littered the area. A wounded Japanese, one of the infantry component shot down in the initial assault, lay out beyond the lines moaning. The GIs took periodic shots at him throughout the night, and come daylight he was dead.

The Japanese tankers were not yet through. Unbeknownst to the GIs, one of the tanks had broken down after fleeing the perimeter, and both had stopped along a nearby trail as crews tried to make repairs. The two tanks were in hull defilade, with guns covering the trail for a distance of two hundred yards. They might have gone undetected except that the 2nd Battalion, which had spent the night somewhat forward and to the west of its sister 1st Battalion, was forced to backtrack during the morning in search of a better route north. As the lead elements started back down the trail, the four-man point bumped into an enemy soldier. The Japanese gave them a dumfounded look, then shouted a warning to his companions somewhere in the undergrowth, and with that, the jungle exploded.

The Japanese tanks and riflemen were well positioned and raised havoc with the American column. A call went back for aid men and stretcher bearers as shells burst among the trees, the fragments slashing into soldiers on the crowded trail. Medium tanks made their way forward, but as the first Sherman rounded a slight bend, it was hit by a shell. As the tank stopped, GIs spread out to either side, unable to locate the source of the fire tearing into them.

Technical Sergeant James F. Walters set up his heavy machine gun slightly behind the Shermans. The crew got off only a few bursts before they were blanketed by return fire. Walters heard someone yell, "I'm hit," and turned to see one of his ammunition carriers propped against a tree, blood streaming from a deep gash in his shoulder. "Goddammit, I'm hit!" another of his gun crew screamed as a bullet smashed into his leg. A third man was on his knees, blood pouring from his neck "like a broken wine bottle," recalled Walters, who was himself then hit in the leg.[42] A shell burst fatally wounded two other men. Medic Howard N. Conwell, a twenty-year-old former office clerk from Pennsylvania steel country, crawled from man to man, bandaging wounds until he was hit in the chest by shell fragments.

Men began breaking and crabbing backward under the heavy fire. Afraid of losing his infantry protection, the commander of the lead Sherman tank began backing out, which only added to the chaos on the crowded trail. The battalion's executive officer, thirty-one-year-old Captain Charles T. Hillman, was hit by machine-gun fire as he came up the trail in an effort to regain control of the situation. Despite his wound, which would prove fatal, he and a wounded sergeant managed to get a grip on some of the retreating men. Mortar crews set up their tubes further back in the column but found few openings in the jungle canopy. One man's arm was blown off as the Japanese continued to rake the trail. Finally, one crew began to put shells down on the Japanese position. The enemy fire slackened and then abruptly stopped.

Creeping cautiously forward, riflemen found the two enemy tanks had been abandoned. A dead Japanese, clad in what appeared to be a new uniform, lay near one tank. Two others, killed by mortar fire, were sprawled just off the trail. The rest had disappeared into the jungle, but not before exacting a heavy price. The 2nd Battalion lost fifteen men killed and thirty-one wounded seriously enough to require evacuation. It took hours to get the casualties out over the rudimentary trail, and the battalion made little progress that day.

—

Corporal Masashi Ito was among the Japanese opposing the 77th Division's tank/infantry push around Barrigada. "Some [Japanese] soldiers disappeared in the jungle, either casualties or lost," he recalled. "We established a position about two kilometers from Mount Barrigada. There we saw some tanks drive through a nearby village. They stopped not far from us." Ito and another soldier crept up to investigate and found one of the tanks had pulled up by the side of the road. Seven infantrymen were eating lunch in the rain.

"Eat this instead," Ito thought to himself, lobbing a grenade into their midst. The explosion killed four and wounded three of the seven, he wrote later. The Americans loaded the wounded onto the tank—painted with the nickname "Lori" or "Loralei"—and rumbled away, leaving the four dead GIs. The Japanese rifled their pockets, finding cigarettes and dried biscuits. "I smoked a cigarette and found it to be good," observed Ito. "I also took a carbine from one of the dead soldiers."[43]

Another chance ambush on August 6 took the life of the 77th Division's conscientious and energetic chief of staff, thirty-seven-year-old Colonel Douglas McNair. A 1928 West Point graduate who began his career as an artillery officer, McNair had joined the division in June 1943 and earned praise from General Bruce for his selfless attitude and commitment.

Accompanied by some men from the Division Reconnaissance Troop and two light tanks, McNair was reconnoitering a location for a new division command post in what passed for a "secure" area one thousand yards from the front lines when he noticed movement in a shack set in the thick underbrush off the road. He summoned one of the Reconnaissance Troop men and ordered, "Spray it, Sergeant." The sergeant cut loose with his BAR.

A single shot came in return. It hit McNair in the chest, killing him almost instantly.[44]

One of the tanks belatedly blasted the shack. The remains of three Japanese soldiers were later found in the wreckage, but they were just the tip of the iceberg. A subsequent sweep located as many as 150 Japanese only a third of a mile from the planned division command post. Many of them had dug individual foxholes at the base of ironwood trees. "These trees with their impenetrable trunks and buttress-like root formations usually gave these foxholes 270-degree protection against small arms fire," observed General Bruce.[45] A six-hour fire fight that included support from a platoon of Sherman tanks ended at dark with seven GIs killed and seventeen wounded. Among the dead was Lieutenant Edward Harper, who had famously guided the tanks during the fighting around Barrigada. The Japanese fled after nightfall, leaving thirty-seven dead.

Colonel McNair was interred in Cemetery No. 3 at Agana. He left his wife, a young daughter, and his mother. Compounding the family tragedy, his death came less than two weeks after his father, Lieutenant General Lesley J. McNair, was killed when U.S. planes mistakenly bombed their own lines in Normandy.

Corps intelligence officer Lieutenant Colonel William F. Coleman recalled another incident involving bypassed Japanese that could have had even greater consequences. After IIIAC headquarters was established on the bluff above recently captured Agana, two of Coleman's enlisted photo interpreters asked his permission to go souvenir hunting in the vicinity. "Seeing no particular harm in it, since we were well removed from combat operations, I assented, warning them to stay away from the front lines," remarked Coleman. The two had been gone only about fifteen minutes when the command post personnel heard a flurry of gunshots erupt very close by. "Shortly after the sounds of the firing died out, the two men came back, scared to death, one of them pretty well covered with blood and clutching a bloody Japanese rifle," said Coleman. "It developed that they walked just a couple of hundred yards from the CP, saw a cave opening looking out toward the CP and wandered into it. They found a small Japanese field piece set up in the opening, a fair amount of ammunition for it stacked nearby, and two Japs sitting on the ammunition." Both sides were startled, but the Marines recovered first and started shooting. "In the scramble both Japs were killed and one of them, as he fell, landed on one of the Marines, which accounted for the latter's bloody condition," observed Coleman.

Aside from putting a damper on souvenir hunting, the incident prompted a thorough search of the surrounding area to be sure no other enemy stragglers lurked in the vicinity. "We didn't want any more Jap field pieces trained in the direction of the general's mess," remarked Coleman. "Why the Japs hadn't opened up on the CP is a question we will never have answered."[46]

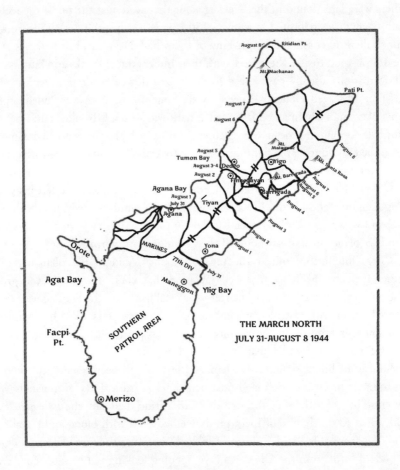

THE MARCH NORTH
JULY 31-AUGUST 8 1944

CHAPTER 23

SHOOTOUT AT YIGO

THE EVENING OF AUGUST 6 FOUND THE 77TH DIVISION "IN A POSITION TO CON-tinue the attack to the sea," according to the division operations officer.[1] That same day, the 3rd Marine Division, attacking with three regiments abreast, finally eradi-cated the last Japanese resistance around Finegayan and advanced forty-five hundred to five thousand yards all along the front. The ground included an unfinished airfield southwest of Road Junction 366 where the trees had been cut and leveling begun, but little else.

The past four days of close combat had cost the Marines 18 killed and 141 wounded. Large numbers of Japanese had died defending the important road junc-tion, finally losing their last 75mm gun to a Marine half-track on the afternoon of August 5. Less than a third of the island now remained in enemy hands. Behind them lay the five-hundred-foot cliffs of Guam's northern coast and an endless expanse of ocean. Still, no one expected them to quit. "I don't know anybody that's going to fight better than the Japanese did," said 3rd Division assistant commander Brigadier General Alfred H. Noble. "They fought until they died. And they had nothing much to fight with. The end was very plainly in sight for all of them."[2]

The Japanese had no illusions. "On 6 August in the Barrigada area, the enemy tanks advanced toward Ipapao and fierce hand-to-hand fight[ing] took place," noted a Japanese summary of events. "On the central force front, the enemy tanks advanced along the main roads toward the south side of Ipapao and intense fight-ing followed in the jungle. The situation of fighting, however did not improve. The enemy tanks also attacked on the right flank force front and fighting ensued in the jungle. Although the Japanese force fought gallantly, Lt. Col. Fujii and many of his men died in this fighting."[3] According to U.S. intelligence assessments, roughly two thousand Japanese troops remained in condition to resist the push north. A captured map, reports from Chamorros, and air observation indicated that the bulk of these forces were located in the vicinity of Yigo village and Mount Santa Rosa in the 77th Division's zone of operations.

The village of Yigo was an unimpressive collection of dust-covered houses and thatched huts along with a church, Our Lady of the Lourdes Chapel, which happened to stand at a major road junction (RJ 415) on the Finegayan Road. The hub of a network of roads and trails branching off to the north, east and west, Yigo also barred the way to the last key terrain feature in the 77th Division area: eight-hundred-foot Mount Santa Rosa, which rose less than two miles east of the village and a mere mile inland from the coast. Recognizing that the area offered the last terrain suitable for a serious defensive stand, General Roy Geiger had anticipated a fight here for days.

Preparing for what was expected to be the last major attack of the campaign, Geiger positioned the 1st Provisional Marine Brigade on the far left (west) covering a zone extending 1.75 miles inland from the coast. The 3rd Marine Division was responsible for a three-mile front in the center. The 77th Infantry Division, which would make the main effort toward Yigo and Mount Santa Rosa, occupied the remaining frontage extending to the east coast. As an indication of the magnitude of the effort, only one battalion from the 77th Division and one from the 3rd Marine Division would remain in reserve. All others were committed to the assault.

General Andrew Bruce planned to use all three of his infantry regiments in a pivoting maneuver to isolate and then clear Mount Santa Rosa. Supported by a company of Sherman tanks, the 306th Infantry would sweep around the western side of Yigo village before turning east to seize the ground north of Mount Santa Rosa. As the regiment would have the farthest to go, it was ordered to advance without regard to other units. The 307th Infantry, in the center, would drive straight up the Finegayan Road through Yigo, supported by Companies C and D of the 706th Tank Battalion. C Company had ten medium tanks, and D Company had ten light Stuarts. After taking Yigo, the battalion would turn east and seal off the western side of Mount Santa Rosa. Rolling open ground along the roadway and east of Yigo offered fairly good tank country as compared the what the armored battalion had experienced up to that point. On the division right, the 305th Infantry (less the 3rd Battalion) would drive north past the eastern edge of the village to seal off any escape southward from Mount Santa Rosa. Success by all three regiments would leave any defenders of the height and its environs hemmed in on three sides and pinned against the sea on the fourth.

Promptly at 1138, the first of hundreds of shells began to rain down on Yigo as the division's three 105mm howitzer battalions commenced firing. At 1148 the shelling ceased. Two minutes later, at 1150, all four battalions of division artillery and the three 155mm battalions of corps artillery roared to life with a final overwhelming ten-minute preparation. An artillery air observer circling overhead reported Japanese soldiers fleeing in all directions as the barrage tore into them, destroying the church, leveling houses, and pounding the road junction. Some of the panicked soldiers ran directly into the guns of the waiting GIs; others were shredded as they fled along a trail to the north. "My God, this is slaughter!" the observer exclaimed over the radio.[4]

The artillery barrage lifted at 1200, but due to a lack of coordination between the 307th Infantry and the 706th Tank Battalion, the ten Stuart light tanks that were to spearhead the assault through the village remained mired in the press of men and vehicles on the narrow road leading up to the line of departure. Having been ordered to follow immediately on the heels of the barrage, the 307th Infantry's 3rd Battalion waited anxiously for the armored support. When it failed to materialize, the battalion jumped off without it. By 1220, when the tanks finally caught up, the infantry had advanced about 250 yards from the line of departure, fortunately without meeting significant opposition.

That soon changed. As the attack neared the village, small arms fire began to pick up. Up ahead, where the woods gave way to open ground on the right, the Japanese had sited machine guns in dugouts and pillboxes. Gunning their engines, the Stuarts fanned out across the field as the medium tanks continued along the roadway. The enemy fixed positions were quickly overrun, either knocked out or bypassed, the few survivors left to be mopped up by the infantry. As usual, they fought to the death. The occupants of one damaged pillbox resisted a hail of rifle and machine-gun fire. GIs lobbed six grenades at the emplacement before one finally landed inside, still with no apparent effect. Finally a flamethrower operator sent a long blast of flame into the pillbox. A solitary Japanese staggered outside to be riddled by the waiting GIs.

The light tanks proceeded in a wedge formation across the rolling ground toward the southern edge of Yigo. Manning the tank at the right rear of the wedge, company commander Captain Leonard Seger suddenly saw an explosion on the side of the tank directly ahead of him. "There's a burst in front of me—could be a mine or AT [antitank] gun," he radioed his battalion commander. "Call for the mediums."[5] More explosions erupted among Seger's tanks. The fire seemed to be coming from guns emplaced in dense woods on the other side of the roadway to their left, but the tankers were unable to pinpoint the location due to the lack of flash and smoke.

A shell slammed into the turret of the tank commanded by thirty-seven-year-old Sergeant Joe Divin, shredding his legs. The blast also knocked the turret off center, blocking the driver and bow-gunner hatches. The only remaining exit was through the turret hatch, now blocked by the badly wounded sergeant. Divin tried to center the turret to clear the forward hatches, but the mechanism wouldn't budge. As his strength ebbed, Divin tied a tourniquet around his leg and by sheer force of will dragged himself out of the turret and tumbled down onto the rear deck. It was none too soon. The tank began to burn as the rest of the crew clambered out under fire from machine-gun positions only fifty yards away. As Divin, still lying on the open deck, urged his crew to cover, he was killed by a burst of machine-gun fire. Minutes later, another Stuart commanded by Second Lieutenant Ernest Pardun, a former elementary schoolteacher from Swiss, Wisconsin, was hit three times and burst into flames. Pardun got out, but his three crewmen were killed.

Rushing forward, the medium tanks also came under well-aimed fire. A shell hit the gas tank of one of the Shermans. The crew bailed out as flames erupted from the bottom and enveloped the sides of the vehicle. Moments later the tank's ammunition began to cook off. A second tank was also hit and started to burn. Exiting one of the stricken tanks, Corporal Gerald Rowe saw that their cannoneer, PFC Emil Conrad, had suffered multiple fragmentation wounds and was unable to follow. As Rowe went back to assist Conrad, he too was hit and seriously wounded but managed to secure help to pull Conrad from the tank before it went up in flames.

The Shermans briefly slugged it out with the unseen guns before pushing on toward Yigo, leaving the Japanese to the infantry moving up along the road. Heavy fighting ensued, but the ambushers were about to fall victim to an attack from an unexpected quarter. Commanding the 3rd Battalion, 306th Infantry, assigned to skirt around the left of the village, Lieutenant Colonel Gordon Kimbrell heard the heavy gunfire to his right and decided to investigate. Commandeering a platoon from K Company, he came upon the enemy position from the rear. The Japanese were so intent upon the tanks and infantry in the field to their front that they failed to notice the approach of the GIs from behind. The platoon shot them down while the rest of K Company rolled up positions along the roadway further north.

The enemy trap at Yigo had been built around two tanks, a 47mm antitank gun, two 20mm guns, six light machine guns, two heavy machine guns, and an undetermined number of infantrymen. Documents captured by the 77th Division revealed that the Japanese had anticipated that the attack on Yigo would be spearheaded by tanks. Their carefully laid trap had worked well for as long as it lasted. Four U.S. tanks—two lights and two mediums—were left burning in the field as the infantry passed through toward the village. The tank battalion lost ten wounded and five killed, including PFC Conrad, who subsequently died of his wounds.

The fight outside Yigo proved to be the main event of the day. By 1408, the 3rd Battalion, 307th Infantry had reached the southern edge of the village, or what was left of it—little remained of the church or dwellings after the intense artillery barrage. Aside from fifteen abandoned trucks and a handful of food and ammunition drops, there was no sign of the Japanese, who had apparently been completely routed. General Geiger, for one, expressed surprise at the relative ease of the advance. "I thought we'd have a real hard fight at Yigo," he remarked to news correspondents gathering for the final bell.[6] It had been hard enough for the few men at the tip of the spear, but Geiger was right. In the grand scheme of things, the Japanese had not put up much of a fight.

The lack of major resistance at Yigo did nothing to ease fears that the Japanese would launch a final mass banzai attack. Those concerns and the belief that the enemy had major forces somewhere in the Santa Rosa area had already prompted General Bruce to ask Geiger to bolster his forces at Yigo. Logic indicated that any attack from down the Salisbury Road or from Mount Santa Rosa would be directed at the important road junction. Geiger denied Bruce's request, though he too continued to anticipate a counterattack. He advised subordinate units that reserves would be available should the situation warrant.

As dusk fell over Yigo, an enemy patrol probed the line of Lieutenant Colonel Gordon Kimbrell's 3rd Battalion, 306th Infantry, which straddled a trail running north from the village. A second incursion occurred around midnight. Two sleepless hours later, hunkered down in their slit trenches, the GIs heard the clatter of tanks approaching from the north. The squeak and squeal grew louder as a Japanese medium tank—one of three—loomed up over a slight knoll and opened fire on the perimeter with its cannon and machine guns. A second tank appeared a short distance behind the first and joined in. The machine-gun fire went high, but high explosive shells from the main guns detonated in the trees overhead, showering the GIs with shell fragments and wood splinters. A platoon of Japanese infantry following behind the tanks added to the volume of fire.

A GI with a bazooka was hit as he tried to get a shot at one of the tanks. A flamethrower operator gave it a try and was also shot. A few men scrambled out of their foxholes and headed for the rear under the onslaught, but others hung tight. Manning a light machine gun, Privates Everett W. Hatch and Joseph P. Koeberle waited for the first tank to draw within point-blank range. They opened up at the last moment, concentrating on the vision slits at the front of the vehicle. The two GIs fired without pause until the barrel on their machine gun finally burned out. The tank ground to a halt within five yards of them, its guns now silent and with no sign of life inside.

Taking command when his platoon leader was wounded, thirty-seven-year-old Technical Sergeant Charles E. Schafer of Baltimore, Maryland, was struck in the neck by a shell fragment. Though paralyzed, he was still able to speak. He ordered one of his men to keep him propped up in his foxhole where he could see the action and continued to direct the platoon for the next hour.

The second tank finally fell victim to bazooka rockets and rifle grenades. The third withdrew along with the remaining infantry. Eighteen dead Japanese—including three officers—were subsequently found in the vicinity. The 3rd Battalion lost six men killed and sixteen wounded. Sergeant Schafer survived evacuation but died of his wound aboard a hospital ship ten days later. He was posthumously awarded the Distinguished Service Cross.

Colonel Kimbrell's battalion exacted a measure of revenge the next morning in the drive north to cut off escape from Mount Santa Rosa. It soon became apparent that the Japanese were finished as the advance turned into what the 77th Division unit history called a "massacre." Dozens of demoralized Japanese had taken shelter in huts along the trail leading north. Each hut had three or four Japanese inside; one had eighteen. "They had weapons and ammunition, but many showed little stomach for fighting," noted the division. "They simply waited in the huts to be killed, sometimes firing a few shots and then destroying themselves."[7]

U.S. tanks blew the wood-and-thatch huts to splinters with high explosives or riddled them with machine-gun fire. Flamethrower operators turned others into infernos. A Japanese crawled out of one with his hair and clothes on fire in a vain effort to escape death. Venturing into a two-story building, GIs noticed a large pool of blood on the cement floor. Cautiously ascending to the second floor, they found eight newly dead Japanese—apparent suicides—leaking blood through the floor into the room below. Over one hundred Japanese were killed during the 306th Infantry advance, which took the GIs well past Mount Santa Rosa and within one thousand yards of the ocean. The only casualty among the leading battalion elements was a man who was fatally knifed by a cornered enemy soldier.

While the 306th Infantry swept around Mount Santa Rosa, the 307th Infantry tackled the height itself in what turned out to be more of a whimper than a bang, considering the days of careful planning and constant air and sea bombardment that preceded the assault. A prisoner—the first captured by the division in over a week—stated that three thousand Japanese waited in caves on the height. The man was either a consummate liar, or the three thousand defenders were long gone. "As I recall, prisoner or documents taken later stated our fires were so effective that they prevented the so-called defense force from even getting established, and completely demoralized them so that they withdrew off toward Ritidian Point," said a III Amphibious Corps artillery officer.[8] The GIs killed thirty-five Japanese during the approach to the mountain but found the slopes undefended. The height was entirely under control by 1400 hours.

⸺•⸺

West of the 77th Division, a patrol from the 21st Marines stumbled across a horrific scene while scouting along a bull cart trail near the village of Chaguian north of Yigo. Investigating a terrible stench from the undergrowth, the patrol found the butchered remains of dozens of Chamorros. The bodies lay scattered through the weeds about ten yards off the trail. Most had been decapitated. "They had their legs drawn up against their chests and had their arms tied behind their backs," recalled PFC Joe Young. "They lay in awkward positions—on their sides and their stomachs, and on their knees—like swollen purple lumps. And none of them had heads, they had all been decapitated. The heads lay like bowling balls all over the place." An abandoned 1937 Ford truck contained more bodies and severed heads. "It looked as if the Japs had been loading all the bodies and heads into the truck, but had been frightened away and left everything behind," said Young. He estimated there were forty bodies, all males, ranging from youths to older men.[9]

United Press correspondent Charles Arnot visited the site soon afterward. "There in an open bomb crater with the heavy smell of death so thick we could taste it for hours afterward, were forty-three headless bodies," he observed. "The heads were within a few feet of the severed trunks, which lay for the most part twisted on the ground." Some of the decapitated bodies were still kneeling or sitting on their haunches as they had died. Their hands were tied. Some had their feet bound as well. There was no sign of a struggle. "The heads lay where they had rolled after being lopped off by a single clean blow. . . . The upturned faces were fixed in expressionless death masks. One man's head that rested on the ground near his right shoulder bore a faint smile on its dead lips. On another bodiless head, a straw hat remained perched jauntily."[10]

A patrol led by Lieutenant Tom Brock attempted to obtain an accurate count of the bodies. Brock personally counted fifty-one. Arnot counted forty-three dead in three groups, the largest of which numbered twenty-four victims. Fellow correspondent William L. Worden counted forty-two. The official count eventually settled on forty-five, which included three corpses later found a short distance away. All were males. The youngest was only fifteen; the oldest, seventy-six. It appeared they had been killed two to three days earlier. Decomposition was well underway, although the features were not beyond recognition. "Half a dozen bodies bore large welts and tears on the backs, indicating beatings before death; but there was no other evidence of torture," noted Worden. "Most of the men had been slain while kneeling, death having come through one or more slashes with a sword at the back of the neck."[11]

The discovery settled any mystery about what had befallen the young Chamorro men from the internment camps who had been drafted to carry ammunition and supplies to the Mount Mataguac area defense line. Having outlived their usefulness, they had simply been eliminated.

＊

Hiding in George Tweed's cave in the cliffs high above the ocean on the northwestern coast, the Artero family was in dire straits even as the Americans drew ever closer. Mrs. Artero, who was pregnant, lost the baby during their ordeal. She began to hemorrhage, and Antonio had difficulty staunching the bleeding. Eight-year-old Carmen was coughing and developed a fever. There was little left to eat or drink. "My mom and dad started saying the Rosary," recalled Carmen.

In a fit of hopelessness, Carmen hurled her own rosary against the wall of the cave. "I don't want to pray anymore!" she cried. "God doesn't want to hear us! He doesn't care to hear us." She stalked out of the cave and sat up on the cliff overlooking the wide expanse of ocean. In the distance she could see a scattering of ships with the men looking like "little ants." Planes flew overhead. She began waving in frustration and despair, shouting, "Over here! We're over here! Come on! Let's be done. I can't take it anymore." A voice calling from below the cave broke in on her despairing rant. It was her cousin. "No, no, no. The Americans are here!" he called.

Led by her cousin, a couple of Marines made the steep climb toward the cave. Ever cautious, Antonio called for one of them to remove his helmet so he could be certain they were in fact Americans. Reassured, the family rushed to greet them. "I was watching my mom and dad," remembered Carmen. "They were hugging these two men and they were crying. Mom and dad were crying. The Americans were crying. They were all hugging and kissing and crying."

It was August 8, 1944, Carmen Artero's ninth birthday.[12]

By nightfall, the 3rd Marine Division was within a mile and a half of the sea. To the division's left, the 22nd Marines had pressed up along the coast and reached Ritidian Point, the northernmost point of Guam, by midafternoon. In the Marine Brigade's sector, the advance was so swift that riflemen climbed on the tanks to keep pace.

That same evening, a Radio Tokyo news broadcast braced the Japanese public, already reeling from the loss of Saipan, for yet another defeat, admitting that the Americans now controlled 90 percent of Guam. Still, Geiger remained wary. A similar situation on Saipan in July had seen a mob of three thousand to four thousand enemy troops from a variety of fragmented units launch a last frenzied assault—a *gyosukai*—that overran and decimated two U.S. Army battalions. Determined not to repeat that disaster, Geiger issued warnings and repositioned reserves as his forces neared the northern end of the island.

On August 9 it appeared intelligence had hit the jackpot when a Chamorro reported the presence of two thousand to three thousand enemy in an area known as Savana Grande just southwest of Pati Point. It was believed this force was gathering "for a final stand and a last banzai charge," recalled IIIAC artillery officer Lieutenant Colonel Frederick Henderson. "We put an air spotter over the area, who saw a few individuals through the very dense forest growth, which apparently confirmed the previous report." Over a period of two and a half hours, the 7th 155mm Gun Battalion sent an unprecedented one thousand rounds into the area. Division artillery chipped in with another 2,280 75mm and 105mm shells. "When the mission was over, the gun crews flopped to the ground exhausted, and the tubes were really smoking," observed Henderson.

As it turned out, the effort was all for naught. When the 9th Marines moved into the kill zone in the wake of the barrage, they met no resistance and found only a few bodies. "The intelligence information on which all the firing had been based was wrong, and we had made this great effort for nothing," said Henderson. It did, however, "provide a bang-up end to the campaign," he conceded.[13]

By 1800, the 9th Marines had reached Pati Point on the east coast and the cliff overlooking the beach further to the north. Resistance was light, but one Marine was shot through the head, and two others were wounded in the thick jungle. They were the last casualties of the regiment's active campaign. In the brigade sector, patrols from the 22nd Marines descended from the cliffs at Ritidian, and the 4th Marines gained the coastal plain just south of Mergagan Point. At 1800 General Lemuel Shepherd reported that all resistance had ended in the brigade zone. The following morning a platoon of Shermans with the 2nd Battalion, 3rd Marines caught up with two surviving Japanese Type 97 Chi-ha medium tanks and destroyed them both. Seven other mediums, still in working order, were found abandoned. Captain Hideo Sato, commanding the 24th Tank Company, later told interrogators the tanks had been "scuttled" due to lack of fuel.[14] They were the last of the thirty-eight Japanese tanks on Guam.

"Exhausted of tanks and guns, we engaged the enemy in a close quarter combat and lost heavily," noted a Japanese account of the situation as of August 9. "The remaining strength in the evening was estimated at about 300 men in the Mt. Mataguac area, 200 men in the Mt. Santa Rosa area and about 300 men fighting in the jungle area in front of these mountains."[15]

That night, bypassed and still undetected in his headquarters cave at Mount Mataguac northwest of Yigo, General Hideyoshi Obata made a decision. All remaining strength—including wounded men still able to fight—would be assembled in the Mount Mataguac area the evening of August 10 to launch a last attack the following morning. In a final message to Imperial Headquarters in Tokyo, the general conceded that the situation was hopeless and abjectly apologized for his failures.

> *I accepted the important position of the army commander, and although I exerted all-out effort, the fortune of war has not been with me. The fighting has not been in our favor since the loss of Saipan. We are continuing a desperate battle on Guam, Officers and men have been lost, weapons have been destroyed and ammunition has been expended. We have only our bare hands to fight with. The holding of Guam has become hopeless. I will engage the enemy in the last battle with the remaining strength at Mt. Mataguac tomorrow the 11th. My only fear is that the report of death with honor (annihilation) at Guam might shock the people at home. Our souls will defend this island to the very end; we pray for the security of the Empire.*[16]

Oblivious to General Obata's last-ditch plans, at 1131 on August 10 General Geiger announced that all organized resistance on Guam had ended. In fact, as a staff campaign analysis later observed, "The enemy had actually offered no effective resistance during the course of the preceding ten days."[17] That same day the USS *Indianapolis* steamed into Apra Harbor with Admiral Raymond Spruance and General Holland M. Smith aboard. Later in the afternoon Admiral Chester Nimitz, Commander in Chief, Pacific Ocean Areas, and Marine Corps Commandant Alexander A. Vandegrift arrived by air at Orote Airfield for high-level conferences on Guam's future role in the continuing advance on the Japanese home islands. "It is believed that the remaining enemy on Guam is totally disorganized with no further alternative than individual resistance or surrender," noted an intelligence summary. "Remnants and stragglers are hiding out, functioning only in small isolated groups or as snipers."[18]

Attempting to organize a final attack from his now isolated headquarters at Mount Mataguac, General Obata might have viewed General Geiger's victory lap as slightly premature. Geiger himself recognized that thousands of Japanese remained on the loose, most of them in the heavily jungled northern end of the island. Shortly after announcing the end of organized resistance, he directed that the 77th Division and 3rd Marine Division establish a cordon across the island from Fadian Point to just northwest of Tumon Bay to seal off the northern area. Emphasis now would be on mopping up stragglers and preventing the enemy from moving south, where the civilian population was being resettled.

U.S. forces were also closing in on General Obata. Intelligence information indicated the Japanese had built an underground command center and radio station at Mount Mataguac. Chamorros who had been forced to work on the installation said it consisted of two large, concrete-reinforced U-shaped tunnels that opened into a hidden gulch. This area had been bypassed during the 77th Division's push to Mount Santa Rosa but had not gone completely unnoticed. A couple of days earlier, the 9th Marines had unknowingly set up their command post for the night among some small knolls within three hundred yards of the enemy installation. A number of Japanese officers were killed in the area, and there were signs of activity near a low jungle-covered hill in the adjacent Army sector. A well-worn trail led to the site, and steps had been cut into the hillside. Two small patrols immediately drew fire when they attempted to investigate. The patrols were withdrawn, and regiment notified the Army units responsible for the sector, assuming they had merely run into a small delaying position or bypassed group. A patrol from the 77th Reconnaissance Troop went for a look on August 8 but was unable to penetrate what now appeared to be a fortified gully—actually a natural limestone sinkhole—protected by numerous cave positions. The depression was about one hundred yards long and forty feet deep and was well hidden in the heavy vegetation.

On August 10, as General Obata laid plans for a final assault—an effort almost certainly doomed from the start, considering the condition of his forces—the 1st Battalion, 306th Infantry entered the area in force "to investigate caves reported to contain one thousand Japs."[19] After tangling with enemy diehards all day, the GIs succeeded in sealing caves in the surrounding rim but were unable to force access to the tunnels. The battalion withdrew at dusk having lost eight men killed and seventeen wounded. Nevertheless, the day's fighting had severely eroded the enemy defense and certainly put an end to any thoughts of a last mass banzai. "From about

1400 hours on August 10, enemy infantry launched an attack on the summit of Mount Mataguac and enemy machine guns began to fire on our headquarters from the top and the slope of Mount Mataguac," noted a Japanese report. "This heavy fighting continued to the evening. Since the enemy withdrew about 800 meters in front of Mount Mataguac, our units made preparations for next day's fighting. Our unit commanders died in this day's engagement, leaving only three officers."[20]

The GIs returned the next day, supported by mortars and a tank platoon from the 706th Tank Battalion. The tanks were unable to access the steep-sided depression, but the volume of fire was too much for the exhausted Japanese survivors. Two infantry companies advanced into the gully and mopped up the outer defenses of the underground facility. "Few were still alive," reported a division historian of the outlying defenders; "most of them had crept into shallow holes and covered themselves with brush and dirt, to no avail."[21]

The command facility was now revealed on one side of the sinkhole where the foliage had been blasted away. Four cuts in the slope led to heavy concrete entrances to the tunnels. A rifle shot from a darkened entrance hit one of the soldiers as they approached. His companions retaliated with pole charges and white phosphorus grenades. Two Japanese carrying rifles ran out and were immediately shot.

As the GIs set demolition charges at the tunnel entrances, they could hear the Japanese deep inside "singing a sort of chant."[22] Two attempts to blow the entrances failed to close the tunnels or stop the chanting. As evening approached, demolition teams assembled four four-hundred-pound charges of TNT—one for each entrance—and set them off. The massive blasts finally sealed the tunnels. Four days later, one of the entrances was opened up, releasing an odor so vile that the men donned gas masks before entering the large, elaborately constructed facility. More than sixty dead Japanese were found inside, along with a large new radio transmitter and other communications equipment. Among the dead was General Obata, whose body reportedly bore a bullet wound suggesting he had committed suicide.[23]

That same day, Graves Registration belatedly laid Captain Geary Bundschu to rest. Recovered from the ridge that now bore his name, he was interred in Grave #4, Row #8, Plot A at Cemetery No. 3 at Agana. Marine Corps records listed his date of death as July 22, though it is clear from witness testimony that he was killed during the last attack on the ridge late in the day on July 21. Cause of death was attributed to small arms fire, though considering the date of burial, that determination may have been mostly guesswork. The captain was subsequently awarded a posthumous Navy Cross for his dogged efforts to seize the high ground overlooking Red Beach 2. Lieutenant Jim Gallo, the company's sole surviving rifle platoon leader, thought it should have been a Medal of Honor.

CHAPTER 24

THE WAR GOES ON

Victory officially in hand, General Roy Geiger left Guam on August 12 to join the upcoming operation to seize Peleliu in the Carolines. Writing to a friend eight days later, he observed, "Yes, I was particularly pleased to get the Guam assignment, and I hope we lived up to the expectations of those of you back in the States. We had some pretty hard fighting at times, but from the time of our landing there was never any question in our minds as to the outcome."[1]

Marine major general Henry L. Larsen assumed full operational control of Guam on August 15. Engineers and Seabees were already hard at work transforming the island into a major air and naval base. Admiral Chester Nimitz had announced plans on August 9 to make Guam the forward base for Central Pacific Command as planners contemplated an assault on Formosa. Work would soon begin on his headquarters on the Fonte Plateau, eventually to become known as "Nimitz Hill."

Life was also looking up for the tired Marines and GIs. PFC Billy W. Sherrill's outfit finally got a chance to wash up under showers rigged from empty gasoline drums. "It was interesting, as I was going to the showers, I see these guys look at me with a funny look," he remembered. "And as I finished my shower and started back, the guys, as they were headed for it, they smelled terrible. I can understand why they were looking at me like that. So it made a difference whether you had a shower or not."[2]

In retrospect, U.S. planners were satisfied with the execution of the Guam operation, despite the inevitable snags and fierce fighting for control of the beachhead. Ray A. Robinson, 3rd Marine Division chief of staff, viewed the operation as "nearly perfect. It was the school solution of how a battle should go."[3]

Of course, even success has its price.

The Guam campaign was the second costliest of the war to date, though there would be worse—much worse—to come at Iwo Jima and Okinawa. For the moment,

Saipan led the list with 11,727 casualties, while there had been a "mere" 4,420 casualties at Guadalcanal. Losses at Guam, as of General Geiger's announcement on August 10 that organized resistance had ended, totaled 1,741 killed in action or died of wounds, 6,053 wounded in action, and 22 missing in action and presumed dead. The number of known enemy dead was put at 10,984 to date. Civilian deaths during the war are estimated at 1,170, which includes perhaps as many as 600 who were killed or died between W-Day and early August.

Among military units, the 3rd Marine Division suffered most heavily, reporting 993 killed in action or died of wounds and 3,244 wounded in action, for a total of 4,237. The 1st Provisional Marine Brigade reported 464 killed in action or died of wounds and 1,600 wounded, for a total of 2,064. The 77th Infantry Division, which saw less action, lost 177 killed in action and 662 wounded, for a total of 839. Casualties in various other units, including III Amphibious Corps troops and Navy shore elements, totaled 124 killed in action, 22 died of wounds, and 504 wounded in action, for a total of 650. That number included heavy losses among Navy medical personnel serving in Marine units, which reported 46 killed in action or died of wounds and 103 wounded, for total of 227.

The roster of dead on both sides would continue to lengthen over the next several months. Only three days after General Geiger decreed organized resistance at an end, a Marine sergeant, Peter B. Saltonstall, was one of two men killed in a skirmish with Japanese holdouts. Sergeant Saltonstall's death would have gained little attention except that he was the son of Massachusetts governor Leverett Saltonstall. The twenty-three-year-old, who could trace his roots to the *Mayflower*, had left Harvard in his junior year to enlist in the Marines, perfectly content to serve in the ranks. When his patrol ran into a Japanese ambush along a jungle trail, Saltonstall rose up to close with the enemy and was shot in the head. The governor, a veteran of World War I who had served in France, received official notice of his son's death five days later as he left the statehouse for the day.

U.S. intelligence analysis indicated "that a minimum of 2,000 Japs remained on the island after organized resistance ceased."[4] That number was a woeful understatement. Enemy dead as of August 12 was put at 11,340. Even if too low, that number was far removed from the 18,500 Japanese believed to have been present on Guam as of W-Day. American patrols killed 1,802 Japanese alone between August 13 and August 31.

"They asked us how many were left when the high command said it was now safe for democracy," recalled 3rd Marine Division chief of staff Ray A. Robinson, "and we said five thousand. Well, in a month we killed five thousand and they asked us again and we still said five thousand. And that was about right. They were the damnedest holding-up people you've ever seen."[5] In July 1945, as the war neared its end, Island Command reported that since August 10, 1944, when organized resistance was declared at an end, U.S. forces had killed 7,381 Japanese and taken 1,026 prisoners.[6]

At least two senior officers remained at large following the American declaration of victory—31st Army chief of staff Major General Yoshitomo Tamura and the ever-resilient 29th Division operations officer Lieutenant Colonel Hideyuki Takeda—who apparently were not present at General Hideyoshi Obata's headquarters when it was finally overrun. Survivors also included a lower-ranking staff officer, Major Seihachi Sato, and a number of junior officers.

General Tamura, who inherited command following General Obata's death, reportedly committed suicide on August 22. A Japanese civilian subsequently told U.S. interrogators that a general officer—whom she believed to be General Takeshi Takashina—had committed suicide in a cave next to one where she had been hiding in the Pati Point area. She said she was told that his body had been consigned to the sea.[7] As General Takashina had been killed in action on July 28, it is likely that the officer was actually General Tamura. Tamura's death left Colonel Takeda as the ranking survivor of the Guam garrison. He and Major Sato would figure prominently in organizing bands of fugitives in the months ahead, but the majority of Japanese remained leaderless, alone or in small groups, at least for the time being.

Typical was Hoshi Kazuo, a member of a Japanese navy meteorology unit. Kazuo had fled north in early August with a mixed group of fellow meteorology workers and servicemen, many of whom had been injured. Finally arriving at the cliffs above Tarague Beach near Yigo, they could go no further. One of their leaders declared they would detonate their explosives in one suicidal blast as the Americans approached, but another officer intervened. "You guys are young," he said. "Go in the jungle and try to survive." Kazuo clambered down the steep cliff in a pouring rain and took to the bush as American gunfire broke out behind him.[8]

Most of the fugitives quickly found themselves in a nightmare struggle for survival. A Japanese navy corpsman wrote in a diary later found on his corpse,

12 August—Fled into a palm grove feeling very hungry and thirsty. Drank milk from five coconuts and ate the meat of three.

15 August—Tried eating palm tree tips but suffered from severe vomiting in the evening.

23 August—Along my way I found some taro plants and ate them. All around me are enemies only. It takes a brave man indeed to go in search of food.

10 September—This morning I went out hunting. Found a dog and killed it. Compared with pork or beef it is not very good.[9]

"It was raining every day and we were wet to the skin," recalled Corporal Masashi Ito. "Americans were patrolling constantly. We moved to another area we thought might be a little safer." On August 19, Ito wrote in his diary, "First-class Private T., also from Kofu, committed suicide with a grenade. He had been sick. Corporal S. also killed himself by grenade. He had been a model non-commissioned officer. . . . For many days we had nothing to eat but papayas."[10]

Some survivors attempted to escape from the island by raft, none successfully so far as is known. In September a group consisting of three officers, a warrant officer, and an enlisted man embarked on a crude raft hoping to either reach Japanese-held Yap or be picked up by a friendly plane. "Indicative of the desperate measures these Japs would take rather than surrender is the fact that food supplies discovered on the raft consisted of 2 canteens of water and a box of bananas, coconuts, avocadoes and citrus fruit—hardly sufficient for the trip planned," observed a U.S. report on the incident. Spotted by a U.S. Navy PBY, they were intercepted thirty miles offshore by the destroyer USS *Straus*. At the last moment before capture, the warrant officer and enlisted man shot themselves with a pistol. The three officers surrendered. In another case, a raft was seen to break up in the surf just offshore, and in a third a U.S. plane strafed a raft, which "blew up," with no sign of survivors.[11]

Perhaps the most bizarre "straggler incident" occurred on August 16 when a grenade-laden Japanese sneaked into a VMF-216 Corsair at Orote Field sometime in the early morning hours. Squeezing behind the pilot's seat, he hid there for hours, apparently waiting for a pilot to take the plane into the air before he blew them both to oblivion. Fortunately for this bold soul's potential victim, fate conspired against him in two ways he could not have predicted. First, the Corsair he chose was on standby alert—it was manned by a pilot but would remain on the ground unless called. In a second lucky fluke, a pilot had fitted an extra piece of armor to the bottom of the seat on this particular aircraft in hopes of protecting his nether regions from ground fire.

A little after noon, twenty-one-year-old Lieutenant Lowell Wilkerson of Notus, Idaho, relieved the pilot who had spent the morning on call completely unaware of the would-be assassin hiding behind his seat. Wilkerson settled in and was writing a letter to his sister-in-law about how "dull" things were when he heard a tapping sound. "Suddenly a blast under my feet blew the letter out of my hands," he said. "I thought it was just an oxygen bottle exploding, so I jumped out and was examining the wrecked flooring when [a] second explosion occurred, blasting a hole farther back."

Apparently losing patience, the stowaway had detonated a grenade under Wilkerson's seat, but the makeshift armor plate had absorbed the blast. The Japanese then detonated another grenade, killing himself. Still oblivious to what had actually happened, Wilkerson examined the cockpit and was stunned to find a shattered corpse behind the seat. The body was lying face down on a control rod with four more unexploded grenades, pins pulled, around his waist. Ground crewmen spent two anxious hours gingerly extracting the grenade-laden remains from the cockpit.[12]

An Insular Patrol Force, consisting of Chamorros, was created in mid-August to help track down fugitive Japanese in what one Marine described as "a rabbit hunt."[13] Other patrols were accompanied by war dogs. Sergeant Jim Milliff was surprised to learn from a handler that the dogs had rank, just like a regular Marine. "I said to the guy, 'What rank's your dog?' He says, 'sergeant.' And I said, 'What're you?' He says, 'I'm a corporal.' His dog outranked him."[14]

"When we first started doing these patrols on Guam we were laughed at," recalled war dog handler Richard Reinauer.[15] Other Marines would bark and howl at the handlers and ask them why they'd brought their pet from home. But the comedians soon changed their tune as they came to realize the dogs and their highly developed sense of hearing and smell increased their chances of staying alive. "We trusted the dogs completely," remarked Chamorro scout George C. Flores. "They saved our lives more than once. The Japanese would set up an ambush in a cave or in the jungle and the dogs would sense it. When the dogs started to hunch down and crawl in a certain direction, glancing over their shoulders at us, we would know that something was wrong. Most of the time the enemy was ahead and we were ready for him."[16] Realizing their peril, the Japanese began shooting the dogs, and canine casualties in the war dog platoons rose drastically. By the end of the campaign, twenty war dogs had been killed and twenty wounded.

PFC Hendon Edwards accompanied patrols trying to induce surrenders from Japanese along the northern cliffs. "We had a Japanese with us and we had an interpreter and a speaker system and they would try to talk these Japanese into coming out of the caves or pillboxes, whatever they had down there."[17] There was no room for misunderstandings. Eighteen-year-old PFC William Morgan, whose 3rd Marine Regiment had been decimated in the fighting for the beachhead, was guarding a communications man stringing telephone wire to an outpost when a Japanese suddenly got up from a clump of kunai grass by the side of the trail where he had been chopping at a coconut. The man was unarmed except for a hatchet in his hand. Morgan motioned for him to drop the hatchet, which he did. "And we were going to take him back. I said 'su su . . . march.' And he kind of grinned with his hands up and he reached inside his jacket and I shot him right in the face. And killed him. And we looked and all he had was some pictures and a little money."

It was an unfortunate outcome, but Morgan had no second thoughts, no apologies. "You never let your guard down," he recalled. "Never. That'll get you dead."[18]

The cruelty tended to be more nonchalant than malicious. PFC Ralph M. Contreras was with a patrol that caught some Japanese hiding in a hut. "A few of them got away, a few of them were shooting at us," he recalled. As Contreras tried to clear a jam in his BAR, one of the "dead" Japanese at his feet picked up his head and looked at him. Contreras's squad leader promptly shot the man through the head. Clearing his BAR, Contreras test fired it at the dead Japanese and "just shot his head completely off." It was almost gratuitous, he admitted years later. "I didn't think anything of it. It was just like stepping on an ant."[19]

PFC George Aspley was with a patrol that killed several Japanese stragglers up by Ritidian Point. "Someone got the bright idea to behead one of them and place the severed head on a rock wall as if it were keeping watch on the road." The following day, another patrol spotted the head and opened fire, thinking they were about to be ambushed. They were not amused to find they were the victims of a "joke" after the head was blasted off the wall in pieces. The unit's chaplain was also displeased and "gave us the standard lecture about how it was all right to kill as many Japanese as we could find, but it was not all right to desecrate the dead," observed Aspley, who, like his buddies, remained unimpressed.[20]

Though there was no shortage of cruelty, mercy was not entirely extinct. Out on patrol one day, PFC Joe Friedman found a Japanese soldier trying to hang himself when he went to check out a native shack. Friedman quickly cut the man down. "As the rest of my platoon came up, the Jap started screaming in Japanese with his arms raised; it seemed to me as though he was pleading not to be killed," Friedman recalled. The prisoner had a wide cotton bandage over what was apparently a serious chest wound. As the man continued to carry on at the top of his lungs, the platoon leader told Friedman to kill him. Friedman refused.

"Damn it, Friedman, kill him!" snapped the lieutenant. "He's calling out to his buddies!"

Again Friedman refused, suggesting they take the man back for interrogation. Again the lieutenant ordered Friedman to kill him. Turning to the terrified man, Friedman yelled a Japanese phrase he had learned that supposedly meant "shut up." The soldier promptly stopped screaming.

The lieutenant finally relented. Cutting the patrol short, they returned with their prisoner to a very unhappy major who berated the lieutenant for returning prematurely. Months later, when Friedman failed to make corporal, he learned from his sergeant that the lieutenant blamed him for the reprimand he had received and had pledged that he would never get another promotion. Friedman remained a PFC, but he was a PFC with a clear conscience.[21]

Admiral Nimitz took up residence at his newly constructed forward headquarters on Guam on January 27. Located on Fonte Ridge—soon to become known as "CinCPac Hill" and still later as "Nimitz Hill"—the complex featured a two-story wooden building with manicured walkways and cottages for flag and general officers and visiting dignitaries. The view, as the previous but now permanently departed occupants of the high ground could have attested, was spectacular.

Both Orote and Tiyan airfields were now operational. Plans called for two B-29 fields to be built on the northern end of the island as well as construction of Depot Field, a B-29 aircraft depot and maintenance base, outside Agana. However, the transformation of Guam into a major B-29 base proved to be a slow process, lagging well behind airfield construction on Saipan and Tinian as the Navy gave priority to transforming the island into a major naval base—soon to be widely touted in the press as "a second Pearl Harbor."[22] With construction assets in Navy hands, priority was given to naval installations, harbor facilities, and staging requirements for ground troops. The construction of B-29 fields remained on the back burner for the time being.

As military construction began to rapidly transform Guam, efforts were also underway to resettle displaced civilians. As early as August 3 General Larsen established a policy allowing civilians to return to areas that were relatively clear of Japanese—primarily the southern end of the island. The refugees were turned loose from the encampments with a supply of foodstuffs to tide them over and could return for more if needed. As of September 30, 1944, only 5,410 civilians remained in refugee camps, many with little more than the clothes on their backs.

Some help was provided by the American Red Cross. In September alone, the Red Cross sent two shipments of clothing, including 1,445 women's slacks, 2,594 women's panties, 1,204 children's playsuits, 1,656 pairs men's underwear, 2,657 boys' overalls, 748 boys' suits, 2,121 boys' shirts, 490 boys' pants, 1,957 children's dresses, 1,883 children's panties, 1,264 girls' dresses, 1,510 women's dresses, 5,225 women's blouses, 2,029 men's trousers, and 1,667 men's undershirts.

The last of the camps—the facility at Anigua—would finally close in April 1945, but housing remained a problem. With Agana, Agat, and even small villages in complete ruin, many of the displaced Chamorros had no home to return to. Of the 3,286 dwellings prior to the war, about 80 percent had been destroyed. Other civilians found themselves the victims of military priorities as the government appropriated their property for base and airfield construction. In April 1945 alone, 272 families were relocated to make way for military facilities or construction. Within a year, there would be more than two hundred thousand military personnel on Guam, and they needed room. The military forbade resettlement of Sumay. Agana was also off limits due to plans to build an entirely new capital on the site.

From August 1944 through September 1945, the military government constructed over fourteen hundred dwellings in new communities at Agat, Asan, Sinajana, Barrigada, Yona, Talofofo, and elsewhere. Civilians themselves built about fifteen hundred dwellings in new communities as well as in existing villages in the south, though these were not always greeted with enthusiasm by the authorities. "Unsightly and unsanitary shanty towns have sprung up in different localities, with hovels constructed of salvaged boxes, canvas and tin sheet," noted Island Command. "It is planned to dismantle these shanties and replace them with semi-permanent dwellings as soon as possible, or relocate the civilians concerned in other new villages as soon as dwellings there become available." The report then conceded, "The low priority which must necessarily be given on areas needed for civilian communities poses a problem of some difficulty because of the constantly expanding requirements of military activities."[23] There was little the Chamorros could do to protest, but the disregard for private property rights would spawn a tangle of landowner claims that would linger for years come.

Meanwhile, the units that had conquered the island were reorganizing and receiving replacements to fill the holes left by casualties. The 1st Provisional Marine Brigade left at the end of August for Guadalcanal, where it would form the nucleus of the 6th Marine Division under the command of Lem Shepherd. The 77th Infantry Division spent the next three months at Camp McNair—named after the division chief of staff killed on August 6—located in the hills east of Agat, where heavy rains and lack of tentage made for a miserable existence. The division finally departed Guam in November when it shipped out to assist in the seizure of Leyte in the Philippines.

The departure of the 77th Division left the 3rd Marine Division home-based on Guam. General Allen Turnage had returned to the States to serve as director of personnel. His place was taken by Major General Graves Erskine, a World War I veteran of the famous Marine Brigade, who had served as Holland M. Smith's chief of staff during the Saipan operation. Erskine, who had a reputation for high intelligence and little personal warmth, was not impressed with his new division. The men were living in "wet and mud," and the division "seemed at low ebb," observed his new chief of staff, Colonel Robert E. Hogaboom.[24] Erskine also felt the three combat teams were too independent and immediately took steps to centralize control from a divisional level.

Adding to the headaches, at least some men in Erskine's division—some of them apparently recent replacements—were also involved in one of the more volatile racial clashes of the war, though the military managed to conceal the incident from the American public for some months. The trouble began in late August when whites balked at sharing the attentions of local women with blacks from the newly arrived service units. Verbal abuse and efforts at intimidation led to rock throwing and even gunfire. The provost marshal urged island commander Major General Henry L. Larsen, to take action in an effort to rein in the troublemakers.

Larsen issued a statement stressing the common ideals and standards that should unite all service personnel regardless of race, religion, or political beliefs and urging all personnel to conduct themselves "as becomes Americans," but the trouble continued to escalate. A subsequent complaint noted, "For weeks a few Marines had been throwing bricks, empty beer bottles, and upon three occasions, hand grenades and smoke bombs into camps occupied by Negro Navy men. When no attempt was made by the authorities to stop the attacks or punish the attackers, the colored men in despair determined to defend themselves when next attacked." As tensions increased, a black Marine was shot and killed by a white sailor in a quarrel over women at what was evidently a house of ill repute. At about the same time, a black sentry from one of the depot companies shot and fatally wounded a white Marine, who had reportedly been harassing him.

Things came to a head on Christmas Eve when a rumor that a black serviceman had been killed by a white Marine spread through the Naval Supply Depot. A number of black personnel started toward Agana for revenge but encountered Marine military police, who managed to defuse the situation. However, on Christmas night, after some whites in a jeep drove up to their encampment and made threats, over forty black servicemen from the depot armed themselves and gathered on a bridge, blocking the road to Agana. This time, they refused to disband when confronted by military police, and some shots were fired. While there were no fatalities, the "rioters" were subsequently arrested and charged with unlawful assembly, rioting, theft of government property, and attempted murder.

A subsequent court of inquiry indicated there was no organized pattern of racial discrimination but acknowledged numerous individual incidents of racial violence and harassment by both white and black sailors and Marines. This was not considered an excuse for the so-called riot, and the court sentenced forty-three participants to prison terms ranging from four months to four years. When news of the incident finally made it into stateside newspapers in July, the National Association for the Advancement of Colored People (NAACP) went public, putting pressure on both the Navy and the White House. "While the NAACP makes no defense for any illegal acts which the defendants may have committed, we do charge that these men were goaded by attacks and failure of island authorities to check repeated physical and verbal attacks on Negro sailors or to punish these attackers," the organization noted in a formal statement. Bowing to pressure—and perhaps to logic—the Department of the Navy subsequently overturned the verdicts, and the men were released from prison in 1946.[25]

At Hirohata prison camp southwest of Kobe and only 130 miles from Hiroshima, PFC Garth G. Dunn and his fellow prisoners were focused mostly on not starving to death as they rang in the new year. Since their arrival aboard the *Argentina* Maru on a frigid night three years earlier, the men captured at Guam had experienced hunger and privation, though their privations paled in comparison to what American and Allied servicemen captured in the Philippines and elsewhere had to endure. Early on, a Japanese colonel disabused Sergeant Earl Ercanbrack's group of any illusions the captives might entertain about their new place in the world. The colonel told them, in effect, "we were cowards, else we would have killed ourselves as brave Japanese soldiers would have done, that we could not forget our comrades in arms were killing Japanese brothers and husbands, that we chose the disgrace of a cowardly surrender and that we must suffer," said Ercanbrack.[26]

The first POW camp was located in a former Japanese army facility at Zentsuji on Shikoku Island south of Honshu. In retrospect, Zentsuji proved to be among the better of the camps. Crowded into a barracks building that had housed Russian prisoners during the Russo-Japanese War some forty years earlier, the men slept on a wooden platform elevated about two feet off the floor. Early on, the prisoners killed a rat in the barracks and threw the corpse outside in disgust. Two years later, when he was starving, one of the prisoners would remember that bit of fastidiousness ruefully, "thinking how much [he] regretted the waste of some perfectly good meat."[27]

Dissension among POW ranks appeared early. Senior officers offered little or no direction. Most were eventually transferred away to more distant camps or simply ceded their authority to others. Chief Donald Lane, who had accompanied Commander Donald T. Giles across Plaza de Espana to surrender the Guam garrison, was designated by the Japanese to be camp administrator—apparently on the basis of that previous interaction. Fairly or unfairly, the chief became a despised figure among the lower ranks. POW Tony Iannarelli alleged that Lane and his fellow chiefs reserved more and better food for themselves and recalled one instance when Lane berated prisoners on a Japanese forced labor detail for "not doing an honest day's work for their daily 'stipends.'"[28] Author and veteran Roger Mansell, who accumulated a huge archive of interviews and data regarding the Guam POWs, noted that Lane's "basic honesty would never be questioned." However, he added, "the concept of officers and higher ranks caring for the welfare of subordinates was noted more for its absence. Lane, along with a few other Navy chiefs, exhibited a distinct lack of concern for the general welfare of his subordinates."[29]

In the months following their arrival, some of the Guam contingent remained at Zentsuji, while others were sent to other camps to be exploited as forced labor under their new masters. Marine PFC Garth Dunn was among eighty more recalcitrant prisoners—soon to become known as the "Eighty Eightballs"—who were sent in October 1942 to a camp at Hirohata west of Osaka, where they worked on the docks as stevedores unloading ships. It was hard, dirty, backbreaking labor, involving everything from shoveling coal to manhandling heavy iron and lead ingots, subject to the whims of guards who ranged from tolerant to openly sadistic.

Now removed from Chief Lane's authority, the Hirohata POWs were administered by Chief Don Barnum and Sergeant Earl B. Ercanbrack. It was a change for the better. Tony Iannarelli recalled that Barnum and Ercanbrack "would often stand toe to toe with the guards on our behalf. To do this required a great deal of courage because the guards were always quick to take their anger out on anyone who questioned their authority. However, courage was one thing neither of these men was short of."[30]

"All of them carried clubs and used them freely," noted Ercanbrack of their guards and the civilian bosses—called *hanchos*—who supervised the POW work parties. "They would cause men to hold a shovel or bar of pig iron over their heads until they dropped from exhaustion, they beat one man during the winter until he was insensible and then threw him into the ice-covered lake."[31] Beatings could be for the most trivial reasons or for no reason at all. Marine Sergeant George J. Shane recalled, "For some reason, the Japs took a particular hatred towards anyone who was tall, especially if they were blond or red haired. They would stand up on chairs just so they could punch you in the face and bash your head."[32]

The one benefit of laboring on the docks was that it provided a chance to steal food. There never seemed to be enough to eat, and as the war turned against Japan, the shortages grew even worse. For Garth Dunn's eighty-man group doing hard labor, the Japanese provided less than thirty pounds of rice and six heads of cabbage a day. Hirohata prisoners lost an average of forty-five pounds while in captivity. When captured on Guam, Dunn had weighed about 175 pounds. When he arrived at Hirohata in October 1942, he had lost about thirty-five pounds. By July 1945 he weighed 118 pounds—and this was while supplementing his diet with food pilfered on the docks.

"In 1944, and especially in 1945, we stole anything edible in order to stay alive, including garbage and stuff that we found on the ships, trains or docks, anything that even looked edible," said Dunn. When some prisoners began trading a bowl of rice for cigarettes, Dunn quit smoking in order to trade for more food. As the war dragged on, the men in all the camps were eating virtually anything that grew, walked, or crawled. "The diet included rice (almost always full of weevils), seaweed, grasshoppers, frogs, silkworms, ants, roaches, dogs, cats, rotten vegetables, tangerine peelings—literally anything," remembered Dunn. Once, as the prisoners were walking to work at the nearby steel mill, a puppy ran playfully out into the line of men. A skinny Marine scooped him up and tucked him inside his coat front. As the puppy happily licked his neck, the Marine reached down and strangled it. That afternoon, the prisoners skinned it, boiled it, and ate it.[33]

Soon after being captured on Guam, Hugh Myers and some of his fellow prisoners had taken bets on when the war would end. Now, as the summer of 1944 headed into fall, all but two of those predicted dates had passed. The next date, December 1944, was obviously going to lose as well. That left only one. Navy chief machinist's mate Henry E. ("Whitey") Strauch had been ridiculed when he predicted the war would last until July 1945. Now, as the clear winner regardless of how long hostilities continued, he slightly modified his prediction, citing the impact of a coal strike in the United States he had read about in a smuggled newspaper. Thanks to the strike, he said, the war would now drag out until August 1945. Unfortunately, Whitey Strauch would not live to see his prediction come true.

Still, from stray newspapers and information gleaned from civilians and ship's crewmen on the docks where they labored, the Guam POWs realized that the war had turned against Japan. "All in all, it looked like we were doing all right," observed

Marine corporal Martin Boyle.[34] Fewer and fewer ships arrived in port, and some of those that did showed war damage. Contrails from high-flying B-29s began to appear overhead starting around late January 1945. Pharmacist's Mate Third Class Al Mosher witnessed a B-29 attack on Kobe in March. "Lots of flames, bomb explosions, and an endless stream of bombers," he said. "It felt pretty good to see Kobe going up in flames."[35]

Tragically, another raid on Kawasaki and its steel mill on July 25 killed nearly two dozen POW forced laborers, including five from the Guam contingent: Ensign Frank Carney, Chief Machinist's Mate (CMM) Vernon M. Small, CMM Bernard J. Snater, CMM Henry E. Strauch, and Machinist's Mate First Class Arthur E. Foote. Ensign Carney, a thirty-year-old civil engineer from Newport, Rhode Island, suffocated when an air raid shelter collapsed. He was found with a rosary still clutched in his hand. Whitey Strauch, who had predicted the war would end in August, missed seeing that happy day by a mere three weeks.

Treatment by the guards became harsher as bombing raids laid waste to Japanese cities. "When things really started going badly for them, it got worse for us too," recalled Captain Charles S. Todd, formerly of the Guam Insular Patrol. "A few times they lined us up facing their soldiers with fixed bayonets. We thought that was it, but for some reason they changed their minds."[36] In late April, the Japanese at Zentsuji forced the POWs to dig a large trench—measuring about eight feet wide, five feet deep, and one hundred feet long—in the prison compound. For the prisoners, who had been repeatedly assured they would be killed should Japan be invaded, the purpose of this excavation was all too obvious.

Lest there be any confusion about their fate, PFC Garth Dunn and the prisoners at Hirohata were marched up a hill one Sunday morning to a bamboo stockade fitted with machine-gun platforms. A Japanese lieutenant ordered the captives to stand at attention. Any effort by the Americans to invade Japan would fail, he informed them. The entire population would resist. But first, he screamed in conclusion, all the prisoners would be brought to this location and shot. He then marched them back to the compound to ruminate on their future. The prisoners did not doubt the lieutenant. "I think the most frightening thing to me that I saw, toward the end of the war, elderly women and little kids sharpening . . . practicing bayonet thrusts with sharpened bamboo sticks there in the factory where we were working," remarked former *Penguin* crewman Ed Howard.[37]

Determined not to be slaughtered like sheep after surviving more than three years of captivity, groups of POWs in the various camps prepared to fight back, should it become necessary. They hid clubs and knives and put together contingency plans. At Hirohata, Sergeant Ercanbrack organized squads with specific missions to attack guard posts, seize weapons, and set up a defense before escaping into the hills. No one could have any illusions about their chances, but they were prepared to resist as best they could. "When it came to that moment, we'd take our chances with the guards, and at least take some of them with us," Garth Dunn observed darkly.[38]

As weeks turned into months, Guam's jungles were taking their toll on die-hard Japanese stragglers. "We found hundreds of them that were dying of dysentery or they had died of dysentery," recalled PFC Sheldon Lansky. Many were trying to subsist on unripe coconuts that made them sick. They were just lying in their own excretions. "It was awful. The Marine Corps officers were putting a round through their head. There was no medical assistance you could render them," said Lansky.[39]

U.S. forces reported killing 1,803 Japanese and capturing 72 between August 13 and 31, 1944. As of September 15, a total of 239 POWs were in custody. In October, General Erskine ordered his 3rd Marine Division to conduct a sweep of northern Guam in an effort to eradicate the numerous stragglers still hiding out in the jungle. The division's chief of staff estimated there were perhaps a thousand Japanese still at large, though he subsequently admitted that the number was just "drawn out of a hat."[40] In fact, no one really had any firm idea. Erskine's sweep lasted nearly a week and killed 205 Japanese by the time it reached the northern cliffs. Another sixteen were taken prisoner. Hundreds of others found it a fairly simple matter to elude the sweep in the nearly impenetrable jungle.

"The Japs were concerned mainly with remaining hidden," observed a report; "they fought when routed out by aggressive Blue patrols, and even then many attempted to escape rather than risk engagement, some even dropping their rifles before fleeing." Most were poorly armed. "Probably typical of the prevailing state of Jap armament is a study of the weapons found in the possession of 48 Japs killed by the 3rMarDiv on 28 August," observed the report; "17 had rifles, 5 only had bayonets, 24 had only grenades, and 2 were unarmed."[41]

Among the fugitives was battalion surgeon Shigenori Yoshida. Following the 38th Infantry Regiment's futile counterattack on the Marine Brigade the night of W-Day, Yoshida had attempted to evacuate the wounded to Ordot. Now, hiding in the jungle, he had managed to dodge U.S. patrols. During one sweep, he climbed into a tree to wait for the Americans to pass. He saw a Japanese soldier come out with his hands up, attempting to surrender. The Americans shot him. Weeks later, during another encounter with U.S. patrols, an Okinawan comfort girl with Yoshida's group was shot in the leg. Unable to walk, she asked the Japanese soldiers to kill her. Yoshida urged her to surrender. Since she was a woman and a civilian, he said, the Americans wouldn't kill her. The other men also tried to persuade her to surrender. But the woman insisted, "I can never be a captive because I am Japanese. Please kill me." One of Yoshida's fellow officers, a medical captain, strangled her. That night the same captain loaned his pistol to a man to shoot another soldier who was badly wounded.[42]

Despite the debilitated condition of many stragglers, the jungle remained dangerous to U.S. servicemen who ignored prohibitions against unauthored junkets into the bush. In one incident, seven sailors from the submarine *Sea Fox* were ambushed when they went off into the bush with a Chamorro guide in search of souvenirs. Ignoring a pile of fresh coconuts, indicating stragglers in the area, they continued down a trail and were hit by a volley of small arms fire. Two men at the tail end of the group managed to escape. A rescue party returned to find five sailors and the Chamorro guide dead. The men had been stripped of their shoes and clothes. Powder burns on some of the bodies indicated that wounded men had been finished off at close range. The Chamorro guide's throat had been slit.

At least two organized groups of Japanese—each numbering about one hundred men—were at large and retained some semblance of military discipline. One, under command of Colonel Takeda, was located in the north; the other was led by Major Seihachi Sato, who according to U.S. records had been a "staff officer in charge of Rear Echelon" with the 29th Division in the south.[43] Lieutenant Yasuhiro Yamashita led another group that hid out near Fena along the upper reaches of the Talofofo River a couple of months after Erskine's sweep. "By that time there had been suicides and people had gone insane," he recalled. "The more people joined with us the more difficult it became to hide from the U.S. military and find food. . . . I tried to limit the number as much as possible."[44]

Efforts to induce stragglers to surrender included leaflets and loudspeaker broadcasts aimed at suspect areas. The best results came from sending POW volunteers back into the jungle to encourage fugitives to give up. Given the Japanese military mantra that death was preferable to the dishonor of surrender, a surprising number of officers and men emerged from the jungle to turn themselves in.

Private Robert W. Amstutz accompanied a patrol that went out to Talofofo to pick up nine Japanese who had decided to give up. Eight had stripped to the waist as directed in surrender leaflets; the ninth was in full uniform and still wearing his sidearm. He informed the Marines he wanted to surrender to an officer. The highest-ranking Marine in the patrol was a private first class named "Mugan," recalled Amstutz. Unimpressed with the prisoner's rank—and still less with his attitude—Mugan unceremoniously relieved the Japanese of his sidearm, followed up with a kick in the ass, and ordered him to "Get your butt in there," motioning toward their vehicle. He then added by way of explanation, "I don't even like American officers." The Japanese meekly complied. "They weren't going to do anything," said Amstutz. "They were glad to get out of that place."[45]

One night Lieutenant Yoshida and two of his men climbed up to some high ground overlooking the shore area. They were amazed to see electric lights extending in almost every direction. "It was like another world," he recalled. In April, after a lengthy discussion, his group agreed it was time to give up. He and his twelve men stripped to the waist and walked out of the jungle in single file holding pieces of white cloth. An islander led them to Merizo, where Yoshida walked up to an American standing by a tent and announced, "We want to surrender." Telling them to wait, the American ran into the tent exclaiming, "Many Japs!" About fifteen men emerged, holding rifles. Yoshida asked the American squad leader if they were going to be killed. The squad leader replied they would simply be taken to the prison stockade at Agana for processing. Yoshida reassured his nervous men they would not be harmed. "Their faces beamed with joy," he recalled.[46]

Navy meteorologist Atsuo Takeda found one of the thousands of surrender leaflets scattered in the jungle. "We laughed through our nose," he said. "Damn it! No one becomes a captive."[47] But as time went on and food became scarcer, Atsuo's will weakened. Many stragglers were killed foraging for food in American garbage dumps. While food was more plentiful in the south, the stragglers on the northern end of the island struggled to get enough to eat. In one instance, two Japanese, one of them a warrant officer, surrendered "in a dying condition from eating some poisoned wheat set out by rat control agencies," according to a U.S. report.[48] They died a few hours later.

In January, one of the thirty men in Atsuo Takeda's group was captured. Several days later he returned to the cave and advised the others to surrender. They refused, declaring they would endure until friendly forces returned to Guam. But Atsuo had finally had enough. "I could no longer endure staying there . . . and resolved to get out even if I was killed," he recalled. "My last desire was to die after eating something delicious. That was all I thought." Weak from malnutrition, he struggled through the jungle to an American radio post consisting of three Quonset huts surrounded by barbed wire. "When I climbed up the fence, about thirty Yankees came out and arrested me," he recalled. After about fifteen minutes of questions, including "What have you been eating to live?" he was taken by jeep to Agana.[49]

At least two stragglers turned to more horrific measures to survive. As the new year arrived, Seaman First Class Koju Shoji was starving in Guam's northern jungles. The twenty-four-year-old former member of the 54th Naval Guard Unit had set up a camp with three other military escapees: Superior Private Kiyoshi Takahashi, who had served with the 29th Division tank company, Superior Private Masami Ohura, and Superior Private Isei Ito. About eight hundred meters from Shoji's hideaway, four Okinawan civilians—Saburo Oshiro and Haruichi Yamauchi, along with Seiichi Kikuchi and his twelve-year-old son, Shigeru Kikuchi—were also struggling to survive.

In early January, Seiichi Kikuchi mysteriously disappeared. Accompanied by Seiichi's son, Oshiro visited the other encampment to ask if any of the soldiers had seen the missing man. They suggested Kikuchi might have "gone to the mountain" to search for food. About a week later, still with no sign of Kikuchi, Seaman Shoji showed up and invited twelve-year-old Shigeru to return with him to his camp to feast on some lizard meat. Three days later, when the boy failed to return, Oshiro and Yamauchi went to inquire about him. "The last time we saw him he started back to your place," said the soldiers. They invited Oshiro and Yamauchi to share their meal with them. "It tasted ill," recalled Oshiro. Their hosts told them it was lizard meat.

Oshiro and Yamauchi stayed the night at the camp. Oshiro awoke the next morning to the sound of a quarrel between Shoji and Ohura. "I sat up, and Shoji called me outside," he recalled. When he asked Shoji what seemed to be the matter, Shoji replied, "Didn't you ever come to think what meat you ate last night? Well, that meat is human being's (child) meat." Shoji subsequently confessed to Oshiro and Yamauchi that he had killed the father and son. The two had been butchered, cooked, and eaten.[50]

—⁓—

On March 21, 1945, hundreds of Chamorros gathered for a solemn ceremony at St. Joseph Church in Inarajan. A small, polished wood casket adorned with a simple bouquet of white flowers rested on a draped, candle-lit platform. Inside lay the remains of Father Jesus Baza Duenas, the beloved priest who had been tortured and beheaded only days before the American landings.

The location of Father Duenas's execution and burial had remained unknown until March, when his colleague, Father Oscar Calvo, visited the POW stockade at Agana Heights. Among the inmates was a Saipanese interpreter who had witnessed Father Duenas's last moments.

Guided by the interpreter, an exhumation party went to the execution site at Tai and found four graves. The first to be opened contained the remains of Father Duenas, who was identified by his belt and religious medals. Another grave yielded the remains of his cousin, Eduardo Duenas, who was identified by his dentures. The priest's remains were carefully removed and transported to Inarajan for burial beneath the altar at St. Joseph Church, where he had presided through most of the occupation. "Almost the entire population of Inarajan was standing or kneeling inside the church," wrote Kyle Palmer, a *Los Angeles Times* news correspondent who came upon the ceremony by happenstance and did not realize its significance at first. "We thought we were witnessing the funeral rites for an infant, so small was the coffin, and so light when it was lifted from its resting place."

Although it was a weekday, all the men, women, and children were dressed in their Sunday best. "Brilliant native costumes, showing the influence of their centuries-old Spanish origin, ranged beside cotton-print house dresses just received from the United States. Most of the men wore blue dungarees or khaki shirts and trousers. A majority were barefoot," observed Palmer. Some were weeping. The feeling of reverence was palpable.

Many of the mourners had known Jesus Duenas since he was a boy and had seen him grow to young manhood when he left for Manila in 1926 to study for the priesthood. During nearly three years of Japanese occupation, their fondness for the young priest had been transformed into something deeper as he sought to protect them "in complete humility and serenity, but with a firm and fearless spirit," observed Palmer. And now they had gathered to enshrine him at the church he had served so faithfully.

As Palmer left the church, a very old woman who had been weeping smiled at him and murmured something in Chamorro. He later learned she had said simply, "He was so young." The priest would have been thirty-three that month.[51]

CHAPTER 25

HOME ALIVE IN '45

As July arrived, the 3rd Marine Division was training for the upcoming invasion of Japan. It was not the same division that had landed on Guam in 1944. Thrown into battle at Iwo Jima in February, the division had suffered 5,326 casualties, including 1,193 dead, before returning to its home base on Guam in March. Only the 3rd Marines—which had suffered so heavily during the fighting for Guam—escaped the carnage, remaining aboard ship in reserve throughout the battle while the 9th and 21st Marines were called ashore. Rested and reequipped, its depleted ranks filled with replacements, the division was now preparing for what promised to be the bloodiest campaign of the war.

The transformation of Guam into a major base had brought a huge influx of nearly 202,000 service men and women to the once idyllic island. No less than forty-seven construction battalions—Seabees, aviation engineers, stevedores, and 3rd Marine Division engineers—worked on airfields, warehouses, barracks, fuel depots, roads, and harbor improvements, even leveling Chonito Cliff in a frenzy of activity. Starting on February 25, B-29s began lumbering into the air from Northwest Field on the northern plateau to join in the continuing devastation of Japanese cities.

Planning at the highest levels called for the invasion of southern Kyushu ("Operation Olympic") in November, followed by landings at the Kanto Plain near Tokyo in March 1946 ("Operation Coronet"). As of July, it was estimated that U.S. casualties could range as high as 1.7 million to 4 million, with between 400,000 and 800,000 killed; Japanese dead—military and civilian—could be anywhere from 5 million to 10 million. Guam veterans were listed on the upcoming order of battle. The 3rd Marine Division and 77th Infantry Division were slated for Olympic. The 6th Marine Division, formed from the expanded 1st Marine Provisional Brigade and recouping from heavy casualties suffered in the seizure of Okinawa, which had just concluded in June, was scheduled for the Coronet landings. Known collectively as "Operation Downfall," the assault would be the largest amphibious operation in history.

That grim scenario was about to be dramatically transformed. On July 25, a plane arrived on Guam carrying Captain William S. Parsons, a naval ordnance officer who was involved with the top-secret Manhattan Project. Parsons brought films of the first atomic bomb test that had taken place at Alamogordo, New Mexico, nine days earlier. A stunned audience that included Admiral Chester Nimitz, Admiral Ray Spruance, XXI Bomber Command chief General Curtis LeMay, and selected staff watched as an unimaginable fireball rose over the New Mexican desert. Days later, Brigadier General Thomas Farrell, deputy to Major General Leslie R. Groves, commanding the Atomic Bomb Project, flew to Guam to confer with General LeMay and General Carl Spaatz, commanding U.S. Strategic Air Forces. The 509th Composite Group would deliver the "first special bomb" as soon as weather permitted after about August 3, revealed Farrell.

Farrell met with Admiral Nimitz to ask that the Navy station submarines along the route and that flying boats be ready to rescue the atomic bomb crew should they need to bail out or ditch. Nimitz agreed, then called Farrell over to a window and pointed toward the island of Rota off to the north. The Japanese garrison there, numbering about three thousand men, was a nuisance, he remarked. They constantly radioed information regarding air operations on Guam, but he didn't really want to invest the time and effort to invade the island. "Haven't you got a small bomb you can drop on Rota?" he asked.

"Unfortunately, Admiral," replied Farrell tactfully, "all our bombs are big ones."[1]

On the morning of August 6, Tony Iannarelli was working by the docks at Hirohata with a crew of fellow POWs when the ground began to vibrate. "The trembling lasted for about thirty seconds before subsiding," he observed.[2] The POWs assumed it was "just another earthquake," a not uncommon occurrence in that part of Japan. None could have imagined the truth—that a B-29 flying from an airfield on Tinian, less than 120 miles north of their old haunts at Guam, had obliterated a city and an estimated 140,000 people in a radioactive holocaust—but it soon became clear from the "awe-struck, frantic behavior of the civilians" that something major had taken place, recalled Ed Hale.[3]

Reporting for work at a steel mill the next morning, Iannarelli was told by the Japanese manager that the Americans had destroyed Hiroshima, killing thousands of people with a single bomb. "One man, hastening to talk to us, told us that a little bomb no bigger than a football had come down in a parachute, and when it exploded it had wiped out a town and killed 500,000 people," recalled Ed Hale. Another Japanese made reference to something called an "adum bum," he observed.[4] "The Japanese told us that the Americans had dropped a bomb that had killed 100,000 people," said POW Garth Dunn. "There was a big cloud over the Inland Sea, and they told us if the cloud blew our way we were all going to die."[5]

A few days later the prisoners learned a second "adum bum" had devastated Nagasaki. Guards warned, "If you see a lone plane, hide quickly—kills everything in sight."[6] Japanese civilians they encountered during work details began to say the war was a bad thing, but the Americans would not let them surrender.

More ominously, a camp guard told prisoners he expected an invasion to take place very soon, but they would never live to see it. "We have our orders," he said. "We are going to have to kill all of you and fight the enemy to the death."[7]

NORTHWEST FIELD, GUAM, AUGUST 14, 1945

B-29 crews in the 315th Bomb Wing on Guam found themselves in a state of limbo—half at war and half at peace—following the atomic bomb attacks on Hiroshima and Nagasaki on August 6 and August 9. "Rumors had spread like wildfire, but most of us could not comprehend the concept of an atomic bomb nor of the extent of damage it might do," recalled Robert F. Griffin, a bombardier with the 331st Bomb Group.[8] A small celebration broke out at the airfield late in the night on August 10—a year to the day after General Roy Geiger declared victory on Guam—when a surrender offer was broadcast by Japanese radio, but the elation ebbed as peace talks seemed to bog down.

"We had planned for a mission on the 13th, but it was postponed in hopes the Japs might accept our peace terms," recalled Walter King, a navigator with the 502nd Bomb Group.[9] But as the talks dragged on, the mission—a raid on Japanese oil reserves at the Nippon Oil Refinery at Tsuchizake near Akita located on the northern part of Honshu—was rescheduled for August 14. Comprised of 143 B-29s, it would be the longest continuous combat mission ever flown from the Marianas—a seventeen-hour flight over 3,760 miles.

Whether or not the mission would actually get off remained in doubt right up to takeoff from Northwest Field that afternoon. As Colonel Boyd Hubbard's B-29, "Fleet Admiral Nimitz," taxied out to the runway, a jeep intercepted the plane and an officer signaled Hubbard to cut engines. Climbing into the cockpit, the officer announced, "Admiral Nimitz says the war is over." The mission was scrubbed. The bearer of this happy news had scarcely departed when another Jeep raced up with another message: "Get going. LeMay hasn't received word that the war is over." Such was the confusion that Brigadier General Frank A. Armstrong, waiting in his B-29 at the head of the takeoff line, sent an officer to Wing Operations to verify that no surrender had occurred. Assured that it had not, he gave the go-ahead to proceed with the mission.[10]

The big bombers began lumbering into the air at about 1640 hours. "Planes left every minute," navigator Marvin Martin wrote in his diary. "Trying to get off the ground with a full bomb load and maximum fuel for a 3,000- to 4,000-mile flight was a challenge. Our runway ended abruptly with a several hundred-foot cliff that dropped down to the ocean. There was a 'point of no return' on the runway where the pilot must either cut the engines and abort the mission or totally commit to the flight."[11]

Even now, as the aerial armada turned to westward, the mission could be cancelled should word of a peace settlement arrive during the long flight to target. "We were given instructions to salvo our bombs into the ocean and return to Guam if we were radioed to do so while we were en route to our target," recalled King. "We never received such instructions, even though we listened hopefully all the way." Bombardier Griffin's crew was also on edge. "As we headed to Iwo Jima, we listened for a call on the radio to abort the mission," he recalled. "Several hundred miles past Iwo we decided that we had gone too far to abort and would no longer listen for an abort message."[12]

The 315th Bomb Wing was not the only unit in the air that night. In an effort to prod the Japanese into a settlement, many hundreds of aircraft were in action over targets. "We met over 300 B-29s and passed through them as they departed Tokyo leaving it an inferno," recalled Colonel Hubbard. "All [aircraft] had landing lights on and [were] flying at assigned altitudes, but even so it was a bit unnerving."[13] It was nearing midnight when the bombers from Guam finally reached the refinery complex. "By the time we flew over the target in the middle of the formation at midnight, it was ablaze," recalled First Lieutenant Bob Wachter. "It was one big terrible fire below us with dozens of explosions everywhere."[14]

Also approaching the target area, Robert Griffin bent over his bombsight, guiding the aircraft during the final run. "About a minute from the target we could see what appeared to be a huge cloud, a thunderhead, ahead of us," he observed. "There had been some questionable reports of potential thunderstorms around the target. We were at 11,000 feet and this cloud towered over us reaching up to 15,000 or 16,000 feet." Reaching the release point, Griffin sang out, "Bombs away!" As the captain took the plane off the bombsight, Griffin stood up and leaned far forward in order to see the bomb impacts. The large black cloud was just ahead.

"We touched the cloud and *Whoosh!*, the plane jerked violently upward," he recalled. "I was thrown up into the air and then dropped unceremoniously with my feet pointed upward, my backside where my feet should be and my head leaning back upon my seat. As I lay there looking upward at the Plexiglas and the edges of the aluminum ribs of the plane's nose, it seemed that they were alive with fire. Sparks jumped all over. I thought, 'This is it, the end of the line.'" Then, as suddenly as it started, the phenomenon ceased as they emerged from the cloud.

"The thunderhead wasn't a rain cloud. It was a violent thermal cloud of smoke and debris that was drawn thousands of feet into the air by the heat of the huge fires and explosions from the bombing on the refinery," said Griffin. "The sparking that I had seen on the Plexiglas was akin to St. Elmo's fire that sailors see in the rigging of ships in a storm, it was electrical discharges from all the charged particles thrown up into the cloud from the explosions on the ground."[15]

The return trip to Guam from the B-29 raid on Tsuchizake was uneventful, though crews carefully monitored their gasoline consumption. They were still in the air when a radio message arrived that the Japanese had accepted peace terms. The war was over.

Back on Guam, a sleepy Marine listening to Guam's radio station WXLI burst out into the street in his skivvies, shouting, "It's over! It's over!"[16] Hundreds of excited men in the 3rd Marine Division encampment poured out of their tents into the streets. Private First Class Bill Morgan was walking down the company street, coming from the mess hall, when it suddenly dawned on him that the crazed mob was shouting that the war was over. "This buddy of mine . . . came running out of his tent with his steel helmet on and shorts, leggins' and his toothbrush, yelling, 'I'm going home!' Well everything just stopped. Discipline went out the window. The officers lost control. There's nothing they could do. The men were just absolutely wild. . . . My gosh, we made it after all."[17]

The division band formed up to lead an impromptu parade. Precious cans of beer were opened as celebratory gunfire punctuated the night. The war was over, and they were still alive.

Work parties at Zentsuji went out as usual to the local railyard the morning of August 15. But shortly before noon the POWs were ordered to stand down. Mystified, they watched as the Japanese guards and supervisors gathered around a radio. Similarly, at the Futatabi POW camp near Kobe, prisoners saw their guards assemble around the office radio, face north toward the Imperial Palace, and bow. Hugh Myers, who was friendly with one of the guards, walked over and asked in Japanese, "Baseball on the radio today?"

"No," replied the guard soberly. "The emperor speaks about the war."[18]

It was much the same at POW camps throughout Japan as the emperor addressed the nation. It would be days before many of the POWs learned that the emperor was announcing Japan's acceptance of the Potsdam Declaration, demanding the unconditional surrender of the Japanese military. For most, what was happening became obvious when they were not called out to work the next day. "The optimists are saying, 'the war's over,'" remembered Ed Howard. "The pessimists are saying, 'they're getting ready to move us.' You know, that sort of thing. I decided in my own mind—and I think most of the people agreed—that the next day would tell the story. That if we didn't go out to work the next day, then the war was over."[19]

Held at the Shinjuku camp outside Tokyo, former *Penguin* crewman Machinist's Mate First Class Norman S. Tattrie, was in high spirits the next morning as work details were cancelled. "Watch me," he said. "I will go down and walk through the yard without bowing to anyone and we will see what happens." As the other POWs watched, the twenty-seven-year-old Illinois native did just that, strolling past "Baby Face," one of the camp's meanest guards, without the slightest acknowledgment. "Baby Face" and the other guards simply ignored Tattrie. There were no slaps, no beatings, no outraged shouts.[20]

Over the following days many of the Japanese guards disappeared. Camp officials began burning records. On August 22 one of the remaining guards at Hirohata admitted to a prisoner that Japan had surrendered. The next morning Sergeant Earl Ercanbrack marched into the camp commandant's office and demanded that he turn over control of the camp. The officer, a Lieutenant Takenada, bowed and agreed. Ercanbrack assembled the squads he had prepared to resist a possible massacre; the Japanese guards were disarmed, and their weapons distributed to the POWs, who took position at the gates. The storerooms were opened, and for once the POWs had all the rice and beans they could eat. Garth Dunn remembered that joyous moment. "In a second we'd ripped the locks off of the storeroom door, taken sacks of rice into the galley and said, 'Cook it up.' We started eating as much as we could eat: rice, rice, rice. Naturally everybody got the shits, but still we ate."[21]

The camp commander at Rokuroshi, located in the mountains northeast of Ono, gathered all the prisoners together for an announcement, recalled Captain

Charles S. Todd, formerly of the Guam Insular Patrol. "He told us that Japan had quit fighting in the interest of world peace," remarked Todd.[22] At Futatabi camp, the news was greeted with stunned silence. "Then, in a moment, with a sudden surge of emotion, everyone went stark raving made with joy," recalled Jim Thomas. "We jumped, screamed and yahooed with ecstasy. Working off four years of frustration, the inmates smashed furniture and threw it out the windows. Grown men began to cry. Everyone hugged everyone else."[23]

At camps throughout Japan, prisoners painted the letters "PW" on the roofs of barracks, and soon U.S. planes arrived overhead to drop food, medicine, and other supplies by parachute. "We put PW up on top of the roof and then American planes came over and parachuted food and clothing and stuff to us," said Howard. "Some of the parachutes didn't open. . . . [W]e're out there running around, waving, and here are these beautiful parachutes. They're coming down with all the stuff, and the first thing we did was get sick. . . . We ate peaches and ham and then we'd go vomit. . . . Then go back and eat again."[24]

Swiss delegates of the Red Cross arrived at Hirohata on August 30 to verify that that the surrender would formally become effective on September 2. "Meanwhile one of our sergeants began to make an American flag," recalled the new camp commander, Sergeant Earl Ercanbrack. "He used the white of a parachute and the blue of two Japanese sport shirts. For the red we took the lining of a blackout curtain in the Jap officers quarters." As far as Ercanbrack was concerned, "It was the most beautiful flag in all the world." On September 2, Ercanbrack ordered their former captors to assemble and stand at attention in the courtyard. He then marched his own men—some three hundred of them, many now armed with Japanese rifles—in for a flag-raising ceremony. "Most of us were crying like babies," he admitted, "but we didn't care." As his men stood at attention, Ercanbrack gave a brief speech referring to Japan's unconditional surrender. The former camp commander then lowered the Japanese flag and handed Ercanbrack his sword. As the Stars and Stripes was hoisted aloft, the Americans presented arms while the Japanese were forced to salute.

"Somebody started singing 'God Bless American' in a husky voice and soon we all joined in to that song," said Ercanbrack. "We didn't sing loud because most of us were crying with joy and emotion."[25]

Once celebratory hangovers dissipated on Guam, efforts were stepped up to inform the remaining enemy stragglers to come out. The war was over. Japanese surrenders had already been on the increase since May. On June 11, Major Seihachi Sato had finally surrendered with his aide and thirty-three enlisted men. A total of 121 prisoners were taken during June alone. In July, forty-seven Japanese—including four officers—surrendered. One group of twenty-four surrendered in a body near Agat. "It can be stated, however, that several hundred Jap fugitives are still at large, scattered over almost every unoccupied section of the island," observed the monthly report by Island Command.[26]

Intelligence officers with Island Command—with the assistance of Major Sato—sent out POW officers and men to contact stragglers and inform them of the Imperial Rescript ordering the surrender of all Japanese forces. Leaflets in the form of an order from Major Sato were widely distributed by airdrop and by hand. On August 31, three Japanese emissaries, including two officers, appeared on behalf of Lieutenant Colonel Hideyuki Takeda to discuss the surrender of his group. Two officers from the Language Section, accompanied by Major Sato, met with the colonel personally later in the day. Takeda claimed he controlled about 150 men in the north-central area, adding that he had seen Major Sato's leaflet and had issued a "cease firing" order five days earlier.[27] He agreed to come in as soon as his men could be rounded up from their various hideouts. Word was also received from Second Lieutenant Yasuhiro Yamashita that he intended to come in with some fifty men from the south-central area. Meanwhile, the largest group of fugitives actually received during August consisted of sixty-three men who gave themselves up near Mount Barrigada on August 27. All told, 137 prisoners were taken during August. Another twelve Japanese were killed.

Colonel Takeda surrendered on September 4 with sixty-seven men in accordance with his agreement of August 31. Another group of forty-six surrendered in the Tarague area a few days later in compliance with the colonel's orders. On September 12, Lieutenant Yamashita surrendered his group, consisting mostly of survivors from the 18th Infantry Regiment. They had spent the past year in various encampments along the upper reaches of the Talofofo River, surviving on cattle and pigs, freshwater shrimp, bananas, and pineapples. One camp was close to the garbage disposal area of a U.S. rifle range, which supplied tobacco and canned goods as well as discarded American magazines, the latter giving the fugitives a general idea of what was happening in the outside world. "On August 20 a U.S. observation plane dropped fliers, and we knew about Japan's unconditional surrender," recalled Yamashita. The flyers included Major Sato's order for immediate surrender. "Upon seeing them, opinions among my subordinates were divided whether to surrender or continue the war," admitted Yamashita. He decided to "negotiate with the U.S. military as equals" for what he called "disarmament, not surrender." He dispatched two subordinates with a white flag to make arrangements. "To persuade subordinates who were opposed to the meeting, I ordered them to wait in the rear, ready to attack if I shot a gun as a sign of a failed meeting."

But the meeting did not fail. At 0900 on September 12, Yamashita's holdouts "disarmed themselves" and prepared to go into captivity. They were the last organized group of fugitives to emerge from the jungle. "When we formed a line to get on the trucks of the US military, I asked them to permit Chako, our dog, to come with us, but this was not approved," recalled Yamashita, a former teacher who had been drafted into the army. He had survived, but like so many others, his life had been forever changed. "If there had been no war, I would have advanced to a graduate school and become a researcher," he observed years later.[28]

Not all Japanese POWs would be returning home. Even before the war ended, a process had begun to bring accused war criminals to trial. Men accused or convicted of war crimes were housed in the war criminal stockade in the village of Tumon. Watched over by forty-eight Marine guards, the stockade was enclosed with a double fence of barbed wire and flood lit after dark. Some of the prisoners would later allege they were routinely abused by the guards—offenses ranging from beatings to sexual assaults. One former prisoner claimed a guard made him get down on his hands and knees, forcing him to crawl around and chant, "I am a horse," while the guard sat on his back and shouted, "I am Hirohito!" Another prisoner claimed two guards had knocked him down and urinated on him. "They then forced me to lick the urine on the floor." There were allegations that prisoners were forced to perform oral sex. Investigators subsequently concluded that the accusations had been fabricated.[29]

A Navy court operating in a specifically designated building on Nimitz Hill would eventually hear allegations of war crimes against nearly 150 individuals from throughout Micronesia, including Guam, over the next two and a half years. Of that total, 123 of the accused were military personnel. Some of the most horrific charges were leveled against Japanese officers from Truk and Chichi Jima, some of whom were accused of murdering captured airmen and eating their livers. The doctor in command of the hospital on Truk was hanged for performing medical experiments on prisoners.

The trials would last until mid-1949. Of the military personnel placed on trial, eight were acquitted, two committed suicide, thirty were sentenced to death, and thirty-six received life sentences. In the end, only ten death sentences were carried out on Guam—including those imposed on three admirals and one lieutenant general—all by hanging. Civilians tried by the Guam War Crimes Commission included over a dozen Saipanese Chamorro "interpreters" and other police personnel charged with murder, torture, and assault during the occupation. Five of the thirteen Saipanese arrested for committing war crimes on Guam were initially sentenced to death or to life in prison. One Chamorro from Guam who served as a Japanese district official was sentenced to one to ten years in prison. A Japanese naval police investigator was hanged for beheading a Guamanian U.S. Navy veteran shortly before the American landings, but the majority of sentences involving police criminality were subsequently commuted to lesser punishments. It appears that few if any of those sentenced to prison actually served significant time.

The most prominent civilian to face trial for his actions on Guam was Takekuna ("Samuel") Shinohara, who had walked into U.S. lines on August 3. Thought to have been a spy for the Japanese before the outbreak of hostilities, he was promptly taken into custody. Prosecutors ultimately charged him with treason for his efforts on behalf of the Japanese invaders throughout the occupation. Though there was no doubt that Shinohara had done his utmost to assist the Japanese, the treason charge was problematical as he was not a U.S. citizen. Though he had resided on Guam since 1905 and was married to a Chamorro woman, he had never relinquished his Japanese citizenship. Nevertheless, following a lengthy trial that concluded on July 28, 1945, the former restauranteur was sentenced to death by hanging. That sentence was subsequently commuted to fifteen years in prison. He eventually served eight years in Sugamo Prison in Japan before returning to Guam, where he quietly lived out the remainder of his years.[30]

Among the Japanese captives at the prison stockade on Guam, two prisoners— Seaman First Class Koju Shoji and Superior Private Kiyoshi Takahashi—found themselves under particular scrutiny by U.S. investigators. Takahashi had surrendered to 314th Bomb Wing perimeter guards on February 19. Shoji had given up eight days later. Takahashi, who was recovering from shrapnel wounds suffered earlier to his chest and right arm, was listed as being in "fair" condition. Shoji was not wounded but was considered to be in "poor" condition, suffering from malnutrition and leg ulcers. The two were soon identified by three civilians—including, presumably, Saburo Oshiro and Haruichi Yamauchi—as having been among the group that had allegedly killed and eaten father and son Seiichi and Shigeru Kikuchi sometime in January. Confronted with the allegations, the two men confessed.

Both said the descent into cannibalism had originated with the acknowledged leader of their group, Superior Private Masami Ohura. Members of their group were afraid of Ohura, who seemed to be almost mentally unhinged at times. While their accounts varied somewhat, according to Shoji they lured Seiichi Kikuchi out by himself with the promise of food, then murdered him. "I hit the rear of Kikuchi's head with a wooden club, but because he didn't die, Ohura held him down and Takahashi hit him again with the wooden club, killing him," confessed Shoji. The skull made a crackling sound, recalled Takahashi. Blood poured from the wound, and the skin rapidly began to appear transparent. Undressing his victim, Takahashi "thought about how strange a man's navel is." The four of them then cooked and ate their victim's flesh. "I was afraid of danger from Ohura if I didn't eat it and since I had no alternative, I ate it," Shoji claimed to investigators.

"On or about 17 January," said Shoji, "we four discussed whether we should kill the son also, because we had killed the father." Shoji was reluctant, he said, but Ohura pressured him into luring the child to their camp with a promise of food. Takahashi later claimed that they fed the boy meat from his father's body. When the child said it was "delicious," Shoji "started to laugh almost hysterically," claimed Takahashi. When the child asked about this father, the others said he had probably gotten lost in the jungle. "But when he returns he'll have a nice meal waiting for him," Takahashi assured the boy.

Sometime afterward, Ohura killed the child, according to both Takahashi and Shoji. In one statement, Takahashi claimed, "I was making a fire at the time and heard a cry and a thud and when I looked up, surprised, I saw Ohura with a razor in his hand and killing the child." In another statement, he admitted that he had clubbed the child in the neck. According to Shoji, "The child started to cry, then Ohura cut the child's throat with a razor and killed him. Then I went to sleep. Ohura cut up the kid and came along with the meat. I didn't want to eat it, but out of fear for Ohura I finally did." Shoji buried the skulls of both victims in a crevice in the cliff. Isei Ito threw the remaining bones into the ocean.

Both Shoji and Takahashi professed to have been deeply disturbed by these events. "After having partaken of Kikuchi's meat, to eat part of the child's too must have been due to insanity," said Takahashi. When Ohura suggested that Oshiro should be their next victim, Shoji finally balked. Instead of cooperating, he warned Oshiro. He, Oshiro, and Yamauchi fled into the jungle and eventually surrendered.

The others did not last long. Ito became sick. Leaving to scavenge for food, Takahashi and Ohura returned to the campsite to find he had disappeared. Soon afterward, the two men made a fatal mistake. "One day, the two of us divided up a frog not knowing the eggs were poisonous and Ohura died despite what I could do for him," said Takahashi. "I was laid up for a day and a half, paralyzed." Alone now, he walked out of the jungle and surrendered.

Both men were subsequently charged with murder in the first degree for killing Seiichi and Shigeru Kikuchi. Their trial before a military commission began on August 30 and concluded on September 8, 1945. Evidence included the skulls of the two cannibalized victims retrieved by an investigator from the crevice near the campsite. Testimony from men who had served with the two men that both were of good character was of little consequence in light of their own confessions. Even those who knew them could offer no persuasive rationale for what they had done. "My own idea is that perhaps the jungle life has effected Takahashi," observed a petty officer who became acquainted with the accused murderer in the prison stockade. Both men were found guilty and sentenced to death by hanging. "Now there is nothing," Takahashi wrote from his cell. "I have no emotion in me. I am merely in a boxed hole. Time passes and I know death is coming. For me there is no tomorrow."[31]

As Lieutenant Yamashita's men emerged from the jungle, Americans who had been captured on Guam three and a half years earlier were heading home from prisoner of war camps scattered throughout Japan. Many of them passed through Guam. The transformation of the island into a major base had brought a huge influx of military personnel. The end of the war brought an almost overnight transformation of another sort. Admiral Nimitz and his staff left Guam for Hawaii in late August. The rank and file were soon to follow as "Magic Carpet," the rapid demobilization of military forces, got underway. Within ten months, the number of military personnel on Guam had been reduced from over 200,000 to only 36,923. But behind them they left an island that would never be the same.

"Guam is dead," former POW Ed Hale wrote to his sister in September.

Dead as the dodo, or perhaps I should say just erased; or gone. Gone are the coconut groves, the quiet beaches, the flame trees; you still see a few natives, beautiful Chamorran girls here and there, an occasional thatched-roof hut that the bulldozers missed. But quiet, peaceful Agana is gone—only a few piles of rubbish, a solitary smokestack, the old bandstand where 150 of us swapped shots with 7,000 invaders, the four walls of the jail, two walls of the Post Office. . . . Today I saw more servicemen than natives, more paved highway than coral reef, more B-29's than grass shacks. Instead of a whispering breeze, the incessant roar of engines; instead of a lapping surf, the rattle of riveters; instead of the smell of coconut forest and salt air, the fumes of oil and gasoline.[32]

Reunited with his family, Chief Pharmacist's Mate John Ploke didn't waste much energy fretting about the changes to his adopted island. He swore he would never leave Guam again. His family scarcely recognized the wraithlike former POW. "We ran away," said daughter Irene. "We were looking at a skeleton. He was skin and bones."[33] Over three years before, Irene's mother had made her put aside her best pair of shoes against the day that her father would return. Now that he was back, she discovered they no longer fit her.

Other endings were more tragic. Released from a Japanese prison camp, Ed Howard was put on a plane and sent back to Guam to reunite with his islander wife Mariquita, whom he had met after arriving to serve aboard the USS *Penguin* in 1939. The couple had two children, the youngest of whom had been born just before the Japanese invasion. Howard was sent to the hospital when he arrived back on the island. "And the first Guamanian that I saw, I told him who I was and said, 'Hey, I want to see my wife and my kids.' He said, 'Well, your wife's been killed.'"[34]

Howard learned that twenty-three-year-old Mariquita had been forced to become a domestic to a Japanese agricultural officer in the village of Tai. The implications of that servitude were obvious. Whether because she was married to a U.S. sailor or because she was uncooperative, on July 18, only three days before the American landings, Mariquita was taken into the jungle and never seen again. Her remains were never found.

The end of the war found former machine gunner Frank Simone back in his home state of Massachusetts. Wounded on W-Day, he had become one small part of what might be described as the "detritus of victory." Hurriedly treated aboard ship following his evacuation from the 3rd Marine Division beaches, Simone arrived at the naval hospital in Hawaii where doctors tended to the gangrene affecting his mangled hands. From there, he was eventually forwarded to the naval hospital in Chelsea, Massachusetts, not far from his home in Revere. Unable to use his hands, he was virtually helpless. Hospital personnel had to feed him, bathe him, and even help him when he needed to use the bathroom.

"It was very embarrassing to me; it really was, but I knew it had to be done," he said. At one point someone came through the ward and tossed a Purple Heart medal on his bed. "I was laying on the bed when he came in . . . and he was throwing one on every sack that somebody was in there. . . . [H]e went right down the line."

His mother called and wanted to know when he was coming home. Simone said he didn't want to come home. She asked him why.

"My hands are a mess," he said. "I don't want you to see me like this."

His father called from work, and Simone told him the same thing.

"What are you talking about," his father told him. "Come home. It means nothing. We want you. We love you."

Still Simone resisted. "And the corpsman and the doctor talked to me and said 'Don't be ridiculous. Go home. That will be healed and you go home.' So I stayed extra time in the hospital 'til it healed before I would go home. I didn't want to shock them."

Finally, he summoned up his courage and returned home. "It went a lot easier than I thought," he remembered. "They didn't make a lot of it. They didn't comment on it. They served food just like they would any other time. 'Thank God you're home. Thank God you're alive. That's what counts.'"[35]

Wounded by a Japanese hand grenade that exploded in his face on August 3, PFC Wayne Barham woke up in a hospital in the Russell Islands. He was twenty years old and blind. Doctors told him his right eye was a total loss. There was a slight chance he might regain some vision in his left eye. He was sent to the naval hospital on Mare Island and from there to Philadelphia Naval Hospital. In October a surgeon operated on his left eye. Afterward Barham had to lie flat on his back for three days with his head immobilized between sandbags.

Then came the moment of truth. As patients and nurses crowded around, the bandages were removed. He could see light, color, and some blurred movement. The surgeon said he had removed the lens from the eye. He handed Barham a magnifying glass with a long handle. "Tell me what you see through this," he said.

Barham couldn't believe it. Looking through the glass, his vision was clear. "I can see you!" he exclaimed to cheers. Later that day he walked over to the window and peered through the magnifier at the park below. The October leaves were yellow, orange, and red.

Barham's formal discharge from the Marine Corps came through before his twenty-first birthday. He couldn't vote or legally buy a glass of beer. Standing on a downtown Philadelphia street corner, he overheard two middle-aged men talking. One of them said, "The next thing you know, these young kids will think they have the right to vote. Now what the hell does a twenty-year-old kid know about life anyway?"[36]

After nearly a year in a prison cell, Superior Private Kiyoshi Takahashi's day of reckoning finally arrived on June 18, 1947. Summoned before a military panel that afternoon, he was informed that his execution had been scheduled for the following day. About fifteen minutes after Takahashi's appearance, Koju Shoji received the same in-person announcement. The sentences were read in English and translated into Japanese.

Takahashi listened closely to the Japanese translation but appeared unmoved by the news that he had approximately twenty-four hours to live. He spent what seemed to be a restful night in his cell and passed the next morning writing and smoking. "He appeared very cheerful," observed a report. After a brief afternoon visit by a Buddhist priest who had been brought in from Honolulu, he lay on his stomach on his bed, singing softly, whistling, drawing pictures, and smoking a great number of cigarettes. "He was continually cheerful and at no time exhibited any traces of sadness," noted the report.

Shoji, by contrast, appeared shocked, looking "quite upset and nervous, swallowing rapidly and continually moistening his lips." He seemed somewhat more composed after a visit from the Buddhist priest but passed a restless night, "kicking his blanket off on numerous occasions and throwing his arms wildly about." Arising early the next morning, he appeared deep in thought and by evening seemed to have accepted his fate. "He declined to eat his evening meal and asked if he might have a piece of bacon," observed the official report.[37]

The two enlisted men were among six Japanese—including two admirals—sentenced to hang for war crimes that day, the first such executions to be held on Guam. The condemned men were transported by army ambulances to the gallows. Erected in an isolated Quonset hut warehouse, the wooden gallows stood so high that the upper braces touched the curved roof of the building. A stretcher stood on end at the foot of the trap for the removal of each body. Six coffins waited in two stacks behind a blue canvas screen. Just behind the scaffold twenty chairs had been set up for the various witnesses and recorders. The noose had been carefully tested earlier by dropping a two-hundred-pound gun barrel through the trap.

The hangman was forty-three-year-old First Lieutenant Charles C. Rexroad, U.S. Army, who was made available from the Provost Marshall's Office, U.S. 8th Army, Yokohama, Japan. A former San Quentin prison guard and son of a Methodist minister, Rexroad would soon gain notoriety as "MacArthur's Hangman" for carrying out scores of executions. "He is an extremely efficient man at the job," wrote a witness. "He is a big, shaggy, slow voiced man whose gray eyes glow coldly behind thick spectacles."[38]

The condemned were processed in order of rank. The first to die at 2030 was Vice Admiral Koso Abe, former ranking navy commander in the Marshalls convicted of ordering the execution of nine Marines captured during the famous Makin Island raid in 1942. Abe was followed by Rear Admiral Shigematsu Sakaibara, former commander on Wake, found guilty of the machine-gun massacre of ninety-eight Americans on that island late in the war when an American invasion was feared. He was also convicted of personally beheading one American who had escaped the machine guns.

Next, at 2103, came Lieutenant Colonel Kikugi Ito, who had ordered two American fliers, downed on Chichi Jima, bayoneted to death and then personally beheaded the corpses. He was followed by Captain Noboru Nakajima, convicted of beating an American flier to death on Chichi Jima.

Clad in a simple shirt and trousers—the trouser legs tied securely around his ankles and arms handcuffed behind his back—Kiyoshi Takahashi arrived at the place of execution at 2132. Takahashi's hands were rehandcuffed in front of his body; a binding strap was placed around his arms and body, and the straps for his leg shackles were placed around his ankles. He remained composed, a smile still on his face as he mounted the ten rough, unpainted steps to the gallows platform. The leg shackles and hood were put in place, and the hangman adjusted the noose over his head. It was all done in a matter of a few seconds. Takahashi was dropped through the trap at 2133 and declared dead by two official medical observers at 2146.

Koju Shoji, the last of the six, arrived as Takahashi was being certified as dead. Accompanied by the Buddhist priest the navy man had "a bewildered and worried expression on his face" but did not struggle or resist. Mounting the gallows at 2147, he was fitted with hood, leg shackles, and noose and dropped through the trap at 2148, plunging eighty-four inches before the rope brought him up short. He was declared dead at 2201.

The bodies of the executed men were buried in six varnished plywood coffins. The burial place was not made public, ostensibly "to prevent possible desecration of the graves by angry Guamanians who suffered under the Japanese occupation."[39]

EPILOGUE

RUMINATIONS ON "THE GOOD WAR"

MILITARY HISTORIANS DO NOT SEEM TO HAVE DEVOTED MUCH TIME TO A CRITICAL analysis of the Guam operation. General Roy Geiger's chief of staff, Colonel Merwin H. Silverthorn, opined after the war, "All together, the Guam operation was considered from the corps standpoint as sort of a school solution, a classic that went off as contemplated and with a minimum of difficulties."[1] That accolade might have raised eyebrows among veterans of frontline combat on Guam, but Silverthorn, of course, was looking at the picture from the more rarefied perspective of higher command. Geiger himself wrote in his report on the operation, "It is my considered opinion that the Guam operation is the best executed of any in which I ever participated, or of which I have personal knowledge."[2]

There is little question, as Stephen R. Taaffe observes in his study *Commanding in the Pacific: Marine Corps Generals in World War II*, that "seizure of the island involved good planning, thorough preparation, fine interservice cooperation and ruthless implementation."[3] The lack of interservice conflict, such as that which plagued the Saipan operation, reflects well on the personalities involved and must certainly have come as a relief to Admiral Chester Nimitz, who found himself in the unenviable position of playing peacemaker between the services throughout the war. Major General Andrew D. Bruce remarked in retrospect, "To me the big picture of Guam is unification. Starting with Admiral Nimitz's command with the most unified and integrated staff of World War II, we find in Guam the Army, Navy and Marine Corps truly working under a unified command. Of course, there were differences of opinion, but these are found even in a squad of one service."[4]

This is not to say the Guam campaign did not have its share of issues and errors. One early and very serious miscalculation involved the original invasion timetable. The decision to schedule the Guam landings a mere three days after D-Day at

Saipan seems ludicrous in retrospect. It grew out of a severe miscalculation regarding the resistance U.S. troops could be expected to encounter on Saipan and on Guam and underestimated the likelihood that the incursion into the Marianas would lead the Japanese to seek a major naval confrontation. The subsequent postponement of the Guam landings to July 21 and the benefit of additional intelligence allowed more realistic preparations. However, the initial overly optimistic W-Day date left thousands of Marines floating aimlessly around in the ocean for unnecessary weeks. "Contrary to popular opinion, this prolonged voyage had no ill effect upon the troops and they were landed on W-Day in excellent physical condition," maintained the III Amphibious Corps after-action report.[5] Common sense and recollections by the troops themselves argue otherwise. Years later, Louis Wilson, then a general officer and Commandant of the Marine Corps, said the confinement aboard ship was "a terrible thing for troop conditioning," adding he was "sure there were many casualties" because of it.[6]

From a tactical standpoint, the decision to land on two widely separated beachheads has been viewed in the retrospect of success as an acceptable risk, though Geiger later expressed little enthusiasm for trying it again. Colonel Silverthorn subsequently observed, "The 3rd Division around there by Piti and the 1st Brigade being over by Agat and it was some days before they joined up. And before they join up, the supply problems become enormous. For logistic reasons. And I remember General Geiger saying, 'If I can ever help it, I'll never land on separated beaches [again].'"[7] In this case, the tactic worked, which isn't the same thing as enthusiastically adopting it as normal doctrine.

Particular praise was lavished on Admiral Richard Conolly's lengthy preinvasion bombardment. While not as effective as Conolly and others initially believed, it certainly saved Marine lives by knocking out numbers of guns and positions that would otherwise have taken their toll. It was also an aberration brought about by the unanticipated delay caused by the situation on Saipan. An admiral subsequently discouraged hopes that such bombardments would become standard practice, observing, "I think it is a grave error to set up the Guam operation as the standard for the future. It is erroneous to lead the Marines or other troops to expect any such support prior to landing. It never happened anywhere else and probably never will again."[8] The admiral was correct. Marines would not receive similar support in future operations. A Marine historian who was in a position to know noted that "nearly all top naval commanders" familiar with the operation agreed that Conolly had "spent entirely too much ammunition."[9] As for criticism that the effects of the Guam bombardment and subsequent gunfire support were overblown, Conolly himself observed, "Effectiveness cannot be measured in either case by a total absence of opposition but by what might have been had this been lacking."[10]

While there were snags at Guam, it would be a mistake to regard every rough spot in the operation as a failure. Few things go exactly as planned or as hoped in any battle. Many of the problems that arose at Guam had been anticipated, and steps had been taken to overcome them as far as possible. Perhaps most notable was the problem posed by Guam's wide reef. Planners knew the reef was going to be trouble—and it was—but the obstacle was overcome nonetheless. There was no repeat of the catastrophe of Tarawa. There were sufficient tracked vehicles to get the men ashore. The high rate of attrition among LVTs, notably at the Marine Brigade beaches, created logistical difficulties, but these were not insurmountable. The transfer of men and supplies at the reef line was often cumbersome, but it worked. Tanks and artillery made it ashore very early and contributed greatly to securing the beachhead.

Intelligence on enemy forces was excellent, thanks in large part to documents captured on Saipan. However, one major—and almost inexplicable—shortcoming was the lack of information on the island itself after its more than forty years as an American territory. One officer declared that he and others who had served on Guam in previous years knew the island "like the inside of my hand," but the deficiencies in maps and lack of appreciation for the true nature of the terrain argue otherwise.[11] Officers that came ashore on the 3rd Marine Division beaches thought they were prepared for the inland ridges, but the terrain—particularly behind the Red Beaches—far exceeded their worst expectations.

Since it ultimately succeeded—and because options were sorely limited—no one seems to have expressed any postbattle criticism of the decision to land the 3rd Marine Division in a natural amphitheater with Japanese occupying the high ground all around. Plans called for seizing that high ground during the shock of the initial assault, but the Japanese rebounded more quickly than had been anticipated. Marines hoping to seize their objectives before the enemy recovered his equilibrium instead found themselves being gunned down on the open slopes, and General Allen Turnage's division ended up in a bloody days-long struggle for the high ground overlooking the beachhead. Despite that failure, the Japanese could not hold out indefinitely, and a U.S. breakout was already imminent by July 25 when General Takeshi Takashina decided to launch his mass counterattack, thereby hastening his own destruction. Nevertheless, returning to Fonte Hill years after the war, Medal of Honor recipient Louis Wilson was presumably only half joking when he remarked about the landing, "Had I ever been up here before [the battle] I would never have been down there."[12]

As for execution, one major criticism of the Guam operation focused on the quality of close air support. There were numerous "friendly fire" incidents involving bombing and strafing runs. The Marine Brigade made sparing use of close air support, later citing "rather severe casualties to our troops from bombing by our supporting aircraft."[13] The 3rd Marine Division, which made more frequent use of close air support to within five hundred yards of friendly lines, reported at least four incidents of misdirected strikes on Marine units. The division also noted that very few strikes arrived in a timely fashion—delays of forty-five minutes to an hour or more were not unusual. In one case, an air strike called in by the 3rd Marines came in an hour late and hit the wrong target square, killing eight Marines. Improvements in training and ground-to-air communications were clearly necessary.

Any examination of the Guam operation must also address the inadequacy of preparations to take care of displaced civilians. Most of these shortcomings were simply a matter of priorities. Planners working to secure a military victory over a tenacious enemy naturally—and rightly—gave priority to matériel and valuable cargo space that would contribute directly to that victory. In the cold calculations of war, provision of food, shelter, medicine, and such for some twenty-one thousand civilians was not at the top of the list. The destruction of Agana and other towns prior to the landings may be more debatable, and the outcome was unfortunate. Nevertheless, this decision too was made in an effort to contribute to the main goal, which was military success.

Marine Corps Commandant A. A. Vandegrift subsequently expressed satisfaction with the operation and the conduct of Generals Geiger, Turnage, and Lemuel Shepherd, but he may not have fully shared Geiger's glowing and somewhat self-aggrandizing appraisal. In his memoir published in 1964, Vandegrift mentioned a visit he made to Guam shortly before the end of organized resistance. "For three days Geiger and Turnage briefed me on the appalling battle, one still being fought in the north," he observed.[14] The word "appalling" would not seem to reflect an unqualified satisfaction with events.

The battle could have been more appalling by far had the Japanese exercised better coordination. In their landmark 1951 study *The U.S. Marines and Amphibious War*, Jeter A. Isely and Philip A. Crowl noted that despite many advantages of defense, the Japanese seemed to "operate in a daze" with little coordination. "From the very beginning the Japanese appeared to be completely disorganized and incapable of anything but the most sporadic and ill-planned counter-measures," they observed.[15]

In 1962, the Japanese army's Guam Military History Investigation Team headed by Major General Haruo Umezawa conducted an on-the-spot postmortem on the 29th Division's defense of the island. While the study concluded that "the Japanese defense garrison on Guam had been highly effective against the US landings," it also pointed out a number of serious errors. One of these, which was no fault of General Takashina or his division, was the failure to move strong forces to Guam much earlier than March 1944, which would have provided time to organize a better defense. Tactical errors included adherence to the Imperial General Headquarters "defeat-the-enemy-on-the-beach" policy and Takashina's decision to accept battle "on two widely separated, and not mutually supporting fronts" instead of focusing on defending the crucial Apra Harbor. "If Gen Takashina had defended the vital area of Guam, Apra Harbor, he would have seriously delayed subsequent US operations," observed the study. "By so doing he could have delayed the devastating B-29 raids on his homeland. Instead, he located his forces behind the landing areas and thus violated the cardinal rule of island defense—defend the vital area."

The defense was further weakened by ill-advised counterattacks, two of the more notable being Colonel Tsunetaro Suenaga's assault on the Marine Brigade the night of W-Day and General Takashina's own mass attack on July 25–26. "These attacks, launched piecemeal, could only be indecisive," according to the study. The latter attack had merely hastened the Japanese defeat. Unfortunately for the U.S. Marine Corps, the Japanese finally accepted this lesson—as well as the futility of staking everything on a beach defense—following the Marianas campaign and made changes that cost their enemy dearly at Peleliu, Iwo Jima, and Okinawa in the closing months of the war.[16]

For some participants, war never really ends. Pulitzer Prize–winning author Dale Maharidge's father Steve, a veteran of intense combat on Guam and Okinawa, rarely talked about the war, but there were signs that it always lurked beneath the surface. One evening in the 1960s, as he and Dale, then an adolescent, worked side by side grinding tool parts in his basement machine shop, Maharidge spontaneously began to talk about the July 25 Japanese counterattack that nearly overran his unit on the neck of Orote Peninsula. He was then a nineteen-year-old private first class with L Company, 3rd Battalion, 22nd Marines. There were dead men all around him, he said. He took the body of an unusually large Japanese he had shot and stacked him on top of a dead Marine as a bulwark in front of his shallow foxhole. Someone was crying for his mother. As Dale listened mutely, his father slammed metal parts into the grinding machine. Becoming more and more agitated, he began shouting, "Fuck you! You don't have NO fucking mother! She's not here! Shut the fuck up! SHUT THE FUCK UP! Your mother isn't going to help you NOWWWW!"

Dale kept working at his own machine. Familiar with the inexplicable, often unfocused rage that seemed always to lurk just beneath his father's personality, he knew better than to ask questions.[17]

They say that time heals all wounds. It doesn't, but age and time can make men more pensive. Louis E. Smith joined the 3rd Marine Division after the bulk of the fighting on Guam was over. The nineteen-year-old Kentuckian was looking forward to combat. "I couldn't wait to get in it," he admitted.

During a sweep on the island's northern beach area one morning, Smith saw a Japanese armed with a rifle approaching his patrol. The Japanese spotted one of the Marines. "He didn't see me. And he raised his rifle up." Smith shot him through the neck. "That was the first Jap I ever killed. It sounds great. I was real proud of it," he said. As the dead man lay there with his mouth agape, Smith noticed his victim's gold teeth. He knocked them out and pocketed them as a macabre souvenir. "It was spur of the moment stuff and you do it," he said.

Smith, who was later wounded on Iwo Jima, kept the gold teeth for years. "After that Jap I was a hero," he mused in retrospect. "I got a Jap and this and that and everything else.... But as you get older it grows on you. You always think, did I really have to kill him? I mean you realize you've killed another human being. . . . That's something you live with for the rest of your life." Smith eventually came to an accommodation of sorts with what he had done. Returning to Guam for the 55th anniversary of the battle, he brought the teeth with him and buried them on the island.[18]

Combat veterans heading back into civilian life found they had unwittingly joined an exclusive club—a sort of secret society that was secret only because outsiders were incapable of understanding the brutality involved in the price of admission. Many were like Sheldon Lasky, who came home from the war and finished high school but found he didn't fit in with the other students; they seemed like children to him. He and an Army veteran skipped graduation and went out and got drunk. "He'd liberated concentration camps so he knew what it was about too," Lasky said of his companion.[19] On a more humorous note—but perhaps no less illustrative of the disconnect between two worlds—Marine Anthony N. De Martino sent a prized Japanese sword home for safekeeping. When he returned home after his discharge, he found his father had been using the sword to cut weeds in the garden. "It looked like an old saw blade," he said ruefully.[20]

After cutting the Japanese officer's throat in the aftermath of the enemy counterattack on the Marine Brigade beachhead the night of W-Day, PFC Emmitt D.

Hays was wounded by a mortar round in the fighting for Orote Peninsula. The injury left him comatose for ten days. He was still a month short of his eighteenth birthday when he landed in the hospital. Looking back on the war in an interview with author Patrick K. O'Donnell, Hays admitted, "The war has been difficult for me to forget. . . . When I go to a reunion, it's to see the guys, and we sit around and talk. Very seldom do we talk about battle. It's like just going to visit brothers. There's a few battles that are re-fought, but most of it is the comical stuff. If we talk about the combat, it reawakens things that have been buried for all these years. I get to a point where I can't even talk if we talk about it in depth."[21]

Captain George J. McMillin, who opted for reason and surrendered Guam to the Japanese hours after the enemy landing, retired from Navy in 1949 as a rear admiral, then served for eight years as postmaster of Long Beach, California. He was active in a variety of community and civic organizations. He died in 1983 in California at the age of ninety-three. Judging by his postwar life, Admiral McMillin was luckier, or perhaps emotionally stronger, than some of the others who went into captivity, though his decision almost certainly saved numerous lives.

Ed Howard, who returned to Guam from prison camp to find that his wife had been murdered, leaving him with two small children, stayed in the Navy. He remarried, but something inside him seemed to be broken or missing. "I had to have the radio on all the time. Movement. I had to move. I had to keep active. Nothing satisfied me," he said. "A lot of people committed suicide after they got out. A lot of people became incurable alcoholics. Others changed their personality entirely; just something snapped. But that was the kind of thing that happened. . . . [Y]ou couldn't be happy; you couldn't be content. [It was as if] that big, ol' beautiful cloud up there in the sky, it had a hole in it and you kept falling through."[22]

The family moved to Bloomington, Indiana, after Howard retired from the Navy. He tried farming, working at a car dealership, and a few other ventures, but none seemed to work out. His children found him remote. Finally he enrolled in college, eventually obtaining a master's degree in library science. He got a job as director of the county library system, where he was highly regarded. But during the 1970s, he began to struggle with posttraumatic stress syndrome. He couldn't bear to be around Asian men. He began missing work.

"Beginning about 1975 I wound up in the hospital once every year for headaches and exhaustion, a kind of nervous breakdown," he wrote to the U.S. Board of Veterans Appeals in a filing for full disability benefits. The annual hospitalizations typically occurred in early December, the anniversary of his capture on Guam years before. "It was as if I had never left the POW camp. It hung over me like a huge dark cloud, always menacing and ever frightening."

He went to the Mayo Clinic in Minnesota, where a psychiatrist told him he had managed to function through the years by suppressing his POW experience, but those barriers were breaking down as he grew older. The doctor prescribed medication, but it didn't help much. He checked into the psychiatric ward at the Veterans Administration (VA) hospital in Indianapolis but made little progress. A VA psychiatrist finally admitted, "We don't know what to do for you. The psychotherapy may help you to survive, but it will be rough. We could put you on medication and send you back out, but you'd be back in within six months." Howard considered suicide. "I do believe that the [dead] POWs whom I watched being burned in the furnace in Japan were the lucky ones," he wrote in a self-described "testimonial."

Ed Howard's torments finally ended in 1990 when he passed away a month after his seventieth birthday. The official cause of death was listed as respiratory failure, but there were those who felt the Japanese had finally managed to kill him forty-five years after his liberation as a prisoner of war. He was laid to rest in the Marion National Cemetery, where his marker notes that he was a Navy veteran of World War II and Korea and was an ex-POW.[23]

There were happier endings. Carlisle E. ("Ki") Evans joined the Marines after going to the movies in his hometown of Chicago and seeing *The Shores of Tripoli* starring John Payne. A BAR man with the 22nd Marines, the teenager was already a veteran of the Marshall Islands campaign when Guam rolled around. On July 29, two days after his nineteenth birthday, his company was fighting its way up Orote Peninsula when a mortar shell exploded a few feet off to his left side and riddled him. He survived the trip back to the naval hospital at Pearl Harbor, but the prognosis was not good. "I happened to be on one knee [when I got hit] and so it penetrated my left hip and into my stomach and I had blast concussion, peritonitis in my kidneys, paralyzed left arm. . . . They told me they didn't know if they were going to keep me alive. Then they said I'd probably never walk, never work and never participate in any sports," he recalled. Their pessimism only made Evans more determined to live. "When you're nineteen you don't like to have somebody tell you you're not going to walk anymore and so you fight that much more," he remarked. Three months later, he was walking. He was transferred to Oak Knoll Hospital and then to San Leandro Hospital in California. While he was hospitalized, his girlfriend from home came to see him, and they got married. "I snuck out with one of my nurses and a Marine friend, who was my best man."

After his discharge Evans received a degree in architecture from the University of Illinois and later a master's in professional management from Florida Tech. He spent thirty-five years as chief architect for U.S. Army Material Command, located at the Rock Island Arsenal. He and his wife raised four children. A baseball fanatic, he coached Little League baseball and played softball in the senior league until he reached his mid-seventies.[24]

A significant number of officers who fought on Guam went on to notable careers. Following his oversight of the campaign, General Roy Geiger went on to command the IIIAC in the battles for Peleliu and then Okinawa, where he assumed command of the Tenth Army after Lieutenant General Simon Bolivar Buckner Jr. was killed in action by artillery fire. He led Tenth Army until relieved by General Joseph Stillwell and to this day remains the only Marine to have ever held command of a field army. His career was cut short when he died on January 23, 1947, two days before his sixty-second birthday, from complications from lung cancer.

After leaving the 3rd Division, General Allen Turnage was assigned to Headquarters Marine Corps as director of personnel and later served as assistant commandant. He retired from active duty in 1948 and was advanced to four-star rank by reason of having been commended for heroism in combat. He died in 1971 and is interred at Arlington National Cemetery. His Army counterpart at Guam, General Andrew D. Bruce, was awarded the Navy Distinguished Service Medal for his performance at Guam and went on to lead the 77th Division at Leyte and Okinawa. He retired from the Army in 1954 and was named president of the University of Houston in Houston, Texas. He died in 1969. Marine Brigade commander General Lemuel C. Shepherd went on to command the 6th Marine Division at Okinawa and participated in the landing at Inchon and the Chosin Reservoir campaign during the Korean War. He was named Marine Corps commandant in 1954 and was the first commandant to become a member of the Joint Chiefs of Staff. He died from bone cancer in 1989 at the age of ninety-four.

Two other Marines who fought on Guam also became commandant in later years. Captain Louis Wilson received the Medal of Honor for his actions at Fonte Hill. He subsequently served in a variety of command and administrative posts and as a staff officer with the 1st Marine Division in Vietnam. He was promoted to four-star rank and named commandant in 1975. He died at his home in Birmingham, Alabama, on June 21, 2005. Wilson's battalion commander at Guam, Robert Cushman, received the Navy Cross for Guam and commanded the battalion in bitter fighting at Iwo Jima. He commanded all Marine forces in Vietnam for several months in 1967 and served as deputy director of the Central Intelligence Agency from 1969 to 1971 before being named Marine Corps commandant in 1972. He died at his home in Maryland on January 2, 1985.

Among those who figured directly in the nightmare at Bundschu Ridge, Colonel W. Carvel Hall received a measure of redemption in 1950, the year he retired from the service, when was promoted to the rank of brigadier general and awarded the Navy Cross for his efforts to seize the high ground behind Red Beach 2. All regimental commanders at Guam eventually received the Navy Cross: Arthur H. ("Tex") Butler also received his decoration in 1950, while Edward A. Craig, Alan Shapley, and Merlin Schneider all received the award in 1947. Brigadier General Hall died on August 20, 1977, in California and is buried at Arlington National Cemetery. He was eighty years old.

Commanding Hall's 1st Battalion at Guam, Henry Aplington remained in the Marines after the war. Following his retirement as a full colonel in 1967, he was recruited by the National Security Agency. He later lived in New Hampshire, where he was active in civic affairs, but eventually retired to Maine where he died on September 8, 2002. In the 1980s he penned an unpublished memoir of his World War II service, which included an unvarnished account of his experiences at Bundschu Ridge. Lieutenant Jim Gallo, the sole surviving rifle platoon leader of Geary Bundschu's A Company, received a Silver Star for his actions on Guam and also stayed in the Marines. He served in Vietnam and retired from the service as a colonel. He died in Arizona on April 23, 2012, and is buried in Arlington National Cemetery.

Excluding Carvel Hall's 1950 Navy Cross award, one Medal of Honor and three Navy Crosses were awarded for actions involving Bundschu Ridge. PFC Leonard Mason received a posthumous Medal of Honor for his actions during E Company's assault on July 22. Mason's company commander, Captain William E. Moore Jr., was awarded the Navy Cross for his repeated and ultimately successful assaults on the left side of Bundschu. Commanding A Company, Captain Geary Bundschu received a posthumous Navy Cross. The other A Company recipient was eighteen-year-old PFC Abel ("Billie") Aragon, who survived the wounds he suffered at the crest of the ridge on July 22. Aragon returned to Utah, where he found work in the coal mines, married, and had five children. In 1957, in another act of heroism, he saved the life of a fellow miner, braving toxic gas to carry the man to safety during an accident that claimed the lives of three other miners.

Unfortunately, Aragon subsequently fell on hard times. In 1961, despondent and desperate at being unemployed and unable to find work, Aragon—up to that time a model citizen who had never been in any sort of trouble—shot and killed a woman, seriously wounded her companion, and kidnapped the woman's fifteen-year-old daughter in a roadside robbery gone horribly wrong. On July 7, when his car was pulled over by two FBI agents investigating the case, he shot himself in the head with a .22-caliber pistol. He died at the hospital the next day, two days after his thirty-fifth birthday, without gaining consciousness. Despite an intensive search, the missing girl was never found.

The general consensus in the community was that Aragon—a dedicated family man, hard worker, and "nice guy"—had snapped under the stress of being broke and out of work. Desperate to find some way to provide for his wife and five children ranging in age from three to fourteen, he had resorted to the roadside robbery. The confrontation had gone wrong, and in fear or panic, he had shot his victims and taken the girl. A sheriff's deputy who knew Aragon said he did not believe Aragon had originally intended to kill anyone, but he was desperate. "If you had five children to feed, what would you do?" the deputy asked a reporter.[25]

As of January 1946, Guam Island Command reported having taken nearly 1,550 POWs since the Japanese surrender. Other fugitives remained obdurate. It was estimated that about 130 hardcore Japanese continued to refuse—out of fear, disbelief, or stubbornness—to come out of Guam's jungles. From a military standpoint, most were more concerned with personal survival than mayhem, though there were rare exceptions. On December 8, 1945—nearly three months after the war formally ended—a lieutenant and two enlisted Marines were killed and one wounded in an ambush while scouting a restricted area near Asan Point. Another Marine, a member of a combat patrol from the 3rd Marines operating in the Piti area, was killed six days later.

The Guam Police Combat Patrol, formed in November 1944 and consisting of armed Chamorros, operated until the end of 1948, following up on tips from farmers whose crops or livestock had been pilfered or who saw signs of habitation in remote areas. There was little patience with the holdouts. Over the course of its existence, the patrol took only five prisoners and killed 117 stragglers.[26] Among the latter was a wounded Japanese who begged patrol members to shoot him and put him out of his misery. They obliged him.

In May 1948, a pair of military policemen patrolling in a truck came upon two Japanese standing in the middle of the road. One of the ragged men was clutching a discarded American magazine. He showed it to the bemused Americans, bowing and calling their attention to a photograph of Emperor Hirohito pictured in the company of U.S. military police. It turned out that the photo had persuaded the two army privates that the war was actually over, and all was well in Japan. They climbed aboard the truck and were soon on their way home.

The Police Combat Patrol stood down after its last kill on Christmas Day 1948, though no one thought the stragglers had been completely eradicated. Just a few months later, forty-one-year-old Private Shigero Arimoto, a former ammunition carrier with the 43rd Shikohu Regiment who had arrived on Guam in November 1943, negotiated his surrender through a Guamanian rancher at Yigo. He said he decided to give up after his seven companions committed suicide.

Early in the morning of September 25, 1951, two fishermen heading out along a remote beach a couple of miles from Andersen Air Force Base at the northern end of the island came across four stragglers asleep in the sand. Three bolted, leaving behind a U.S. carbine, but the fishermen caught the fourth. He turned out to be thirty-eight-year-old Taira Koshin,[27] who had arrived on Guam with an air unit in early 1944. He said he knew Japan had lost the war but thought Germany still had a chance to prevail and might come to his rescue. Persuaded otherwise, he led Guam police to four comrades who had taken refuge in a cave high in the northern cliffs. They too gave up after assurances from Koshin that they would not be harmed.

Ranging in age from thirty to forty-one, the group of former enlisted men included a former radio operator and two airplane mechanics. They said they had avoided detection by remaining concealed by day, only emerging at night to forage for food. They traveled in single file, the lead man cautiously scrutinizing every step, while the last in line swept away their footprints. They tried never to break twigs in an unnatural fashion, dislodge stones, or trample patches of grass. They spoke in whispers and, when picking fruit from trees, were careful not to strip the tree lest it arouse someone's attention.

Three days later, another straggler, thirty-one-year-old Seichi Kimachi, a wartime weather observer who had heard Koshin's loudspeaker pleas to his comrades, flagged down a bus carrying civilians to work. Removing his sandals before climbing aboard, he was taken directly to the provost marshal's office. Kimachi led U.S. patrols into the jungle in search of his two companions—Private Kosaku Kaitamura and navy weather observer Kazuo Hoshi—leaving them a note in their now vacant hideout. Those two subsequently showed up at the air force base sporting white U.S. Navy mess jackets they had presumably liberated off someone's unattended clothesline.

The emergence of the eight stragglers from the jungle generated much interest in tracking down any others who remained on the loose. Representatives of the Japanese government provided letters to be left in the jungle, and patrols scoured the boondocks, but without success. In late 1953, reported sightings led to "Operation Straggler," a concerted effort to contact any fugitives, but again without success. Nevertheless, reports of sightings continued in subsequent months and years.

In 1957 a woman golfing at the Windward Hills Golf and Country Club reported seeing a ragged, scrawny figure with a beard, but it was not until May 21, 1960, that another straggler was captured. Spotted and overpowered by two Guamanians who were out checking coconut crab traps in the jungle not far from the golf course, this elusive fugitive turned out to be Corporal Bunzo Minagawa, a former member of a Japanese artillery unit, who had ventured out of hiding in hopes of stealing a chicken. Minagawa initially refused to cooperate or to concede that Japan had lost the war, but he eventually led police to his camp. As they explored the site, a second straggler, Corporal Masashi Ito, emerged from the bushes with a white cloth in hand. He said he could not bear the thought of remaining in the jungle alone now that Minagawa had been captured. Both men remained stubbornly suspicious of authorities, even after receiving reassuring phone calls from family members. Only after returning home—to a Japan far changed from the country they remembered— did they finally accept that no one was trying to trick them: the war was actually over.

It was widely believed that Ito and Minagawa were the last remaining holdouts on Guam—a 1962 book about the pair referred to them as the "straggliest" of the stragglers, but that dubious honor proved premature. In a rather bizarre incident in April 1962, thirty-nine-year-old Joaquin Q. Cruz, his son, and two nephews were trespassing on restricted government property about three miles from the U.S. naval magazine in search of betel nuts when what was believed to be a Japanese straggler lurking in the bushes threw a hatchet at them. As the assailant turned and ran, Cruz, who was carrying an unlicensed shotgun, fired at him, hitting him in the shoulder. Chasing the man, he fired again, knocking him down. Approaching his prostrate victim, he fired a final blast at the man's chin when the man tried to kick him.

Fearful of being prosecuted for being on Navy property and carrying an unlicensed firearm, Cruz did not report the encounter. By the time word got out nearly three weeks later and the authorities got to the scene, the victim's body had been devoured by wild boars, and the bones were strewn over a one-hundred-foot area. Searchers found a Japanese-style sandal among the remains. A thatched roof shack was also discovered nearby.

Somewhat surprisingly in light of previous incidents involving stragglers, Cruz was arrested. He pleaded guilty to manslaughter and was given a three-year suspended sentence. The judge in the case, U.S. judge Paul D. Striver, cited extenuating circumstances, observing that Cruz had lived through thirty-one months of Japanese occupation during the war, during which the civilian population was subjected to numerous atrocities. Furthermore, he added, the straggler had had many opportunities to return to civilization during the last seventeen years, "but the hatred imbued in his mind made him more willing to die than surrender."[28]

It appeared that Guamanians had finally seen the last of the stragglers, but once again that assumption proved premature. Nearly ten years later, on January 24, 1972, Jesus M. Duenas and his brother-in-law, Manuel T. DeGracia, were slogging along a tributary of the Talofofo River intending to set shrimp traps when they noticed someone approaching through the tall reeds. Moments later they found themselves face to face with a wizened scarecrow of a man who was also carrying shrimp traps. Duenas, who was armed with a sixteen-gauge shotgun, blurted in surprise, "He's Japanese!"

The stranger recoiled in surprise and apparent terror as Duenas pointed the shotgun at him. He dropped his traps and raised his hands in supplication, but then grabbed at Duenas—ironically, a distant relative of the martyred Father Jesus Duenas—who pulled away and knocked the man down. The two Guamanians then fell on him and tied his hands. They realized now that he was not as ancient as they had thought—probably only in his fifties. Their captive seemed resigned as they walked him out of the swamp, so they untied him and gave him a pancake they had brought to snack on. The scarecrow broke it in half and carefully stored one half in his pocket before consuming the rest in small pieces. They escorted their now compliant prisoner to Duenas's house near the mouth of the Talofofo River, fed him, and contacted the authorities.

Their captive identified himself as Corporal Shoichi Yokoi. Now fifty-eight years old, his shattered unit had fled into the jungle following the 38th Regiment's doomed counterattack at Agat on the night of July 21–22. Unable to reestablish contact with higher authority, the men had roamed aimlessly in the bush, dissolving into smaller and smaller bands as discipline broke down. Yokoi had originally joined a group of about ten men, but their number gradually dwindled to three. Eight years earlier, his two remaining companions had died, leaving him alone. He had lived in a tunnel-like cave he dug in a dense thicket and subsisted on a diet of coconuts, papaya, shrimp, frogs, and rats. A former tailor, he made his own clothes from pago tree bark. He had a frying pan crafted from a Japanese canteen he cut in half; the other half was flattened for use as a plate. He made his own shrimp and rat traps, fashioned rope from coconut husk fiber, and contrived a small light fueled by coconut oil.

Yokoi said he had known for at least twenty years or more that the war was over. Eking out a primitive existence, he had seen the massive B-29s—and later the

B-52 bombers—flying overhead. He had also heard the broadcast pleas to give up but had been unable to accept the shame of surrender. When his captors attempted to reassure him by playing tape-recorded messages from relatives and old friends, Yokoi, having no idea what a tape recorder was, attempted to converse with them as if it were a telephone.

Fearful about his return to Japan, Yokoi was gratified to be greeted as a celebrity. Cheering crowds met his plane at the airport in Tokyo. "Though I am ashamed, I am alive and have come home again," he said.[29] He had no siblings. His father had died when he was a boy. His mother had died in 1958, still hoping for his return, said old neighbors.

Inside an old temple gate in Yokoi's home city of Nagoya, his mother had erected a stone cenotaph inscribed with the words, "The Late Sergeant Shoichi Yokoi, decorated with the Eighth Order of Merit. He died at the age of 30." Another stone, adjacent to the first, was inscribed, "Died in 1944 on Omiya-jima when his entire unit fought like heroes to the death."

Ever the survivor, Yokoi adapted well, though he remained perplexed by what he considered the material greed and spiritual desolation of modern Japan. He married a few months after returning home and traveled around Japan giving lectures on survival techniques. Over 350,000 Japanese visited an exhibit of the clothes he had made while in hiding. In 1974 he even ran unsuccessfully for the House of Councilors—Parliament's upper house. He also admitted in an interview that he had shot and killed two Guamanians several years before his capture. He later retracted that statement—his handlers attributed it to mental confusion—but the people of Guam continued to wonder, and Yokoi lost some of his luster there.

Yokoi died of heart failure on September 22, 1997, at JR Tokai General Hospital in Nagoya. Despite the official cause of death, he had been suffering from Parkinson's disease, and it was widely rumored he had starved himself to death so that he would not be a burden to his wife, who had recently suffered an accident. He was eighty-two years old. "I never intended to stay in the jungles for twenty-eight years," he admitted a couple of years after his return. "I was just scared and ashamed to surrender."[30]

On January 16, 1989—seventeen years after Shoichi Yokoi emerged from the Guam jungle—emergency personnel responded to a motor vehicle accident north of Crescent City, California, twenty miles from the Oregon state line. A car had veered off the rain-slick roadway and crashed into a telephone pole, killing the driver, identified as eighty-six-year-old George R. Tweed.

Newspapers throughout the country ran a brief wire service report noting that the victim had gained notoriety for evading Japanese forces on Guam for nearly three years during World War II. The low-key coverage was in sharp contrast to the lionization of Tweed in the public eye following his rescue just prior to the U.S. landings on Guam nearly forty-five years earlier. Dubbed the "Ghost of Guam" by the American press, he was immediately promoted from radioman first class to chief petty officer. The Navy awarded him the Legion of Merit with Combat "V" in recognition of his copious information regarding Japanese troop movements and defenses prior to the invasion—including "an undamaged hostile battery of six-inch guns concealed on Point Adelup"—thereby "making a vital contribution to the recapture of this strategic American possession."[31]

Despite the laudatory outpouring—which eventually included a movie about his exploits—Tweed remained a controversial figure on Guam, where many blamed him for contributing to the death and suffering among the civilian population. They noted that Tweed refused to give himself up even as the Japanese tortured and even executed Chamorros suspected of helping him—many had indeed helped him, but many others had known nothing of his whereabouts. Some who had had contact with Tweed during the war viewed him as unlikeable, reckless, demanding, and seemingly ungrateful. It was said he made unseemly efforts to procure female companionship and was even "picky about food" that was provided to him by people who risked their lives to protect him.[32]

The undercurrent of ill feeling exploded in 1946 after a book about Tweed's experiences, *Robinson Crusoe, USN*, published under Tweed's name but ghostwritten by Blake Clark, asserted that the much-idolized Father Duenas had betrayed the confessional under torture and given the Japanese information that led them to Tweed's protector, Antonio Artero. Enraged by those allegations, a crowd of protestors organized by Father Oscar Calvo turned out when Tweed returned to Guam in late 1946. The visit had been arranged so Tweed could present his former benefactor and friend, Antonio Artero, with a brand new four-door Chevrolet sedan as a token of his gratitude for hiding him for nearly two years. The car was provided free by Chevrolet after Tweed inquired about it with the company. The grateful gesture toward the Artero family only aggravated many other Chamorros who felt their own sacrifices on behalf of Tweed remained unappreciated.

The protestors jeered Tweed and brandished signs reading, "338,000,000 Catholics Resent Your Accusations," "Our Necks for a Chevrolet," "Remember Father Duenas," and "We Resent Tweed's Appearance on This Island." Infuriated by one sign that asked, "What About Tweed's Desertion in the Face of the Enemy?" Tweed stalked over to the protestors, tore the sign from their hands, ripped it to pieces, and stomped it underfoot. Tweed later retracted his allegation about Father Duenas, saying he had been misinformed, but he never returned to Guam.[33]

His marriage, already in a shambles before he became a fugitive in December 1941, was beyond salvation. Tweed was granted a formal separation decree only days after returning to the United States following his rescue. He remarried on July 2, 1945, to a twenty-nine-year-old War Department employee named Delores Kramer, a union that would last until his death. The couple had a son and a daughter and eventually settled in Grant's Pass, Oregon, where he operated a TV and radio repair shop.

A war film about his experiences as a fugitive on Guam, titled *No Man Is an Island* and starring Jeffrey Hunter as Tweed, appeared in 1962. Billed as his "true" story, it was a ludicrous, highly fictionalized yarn in which the Chamorros hide Tweed in a leper colony run by a priest. The film was shot entirely in the Philippines, and all the supporting actors spoke Tagalog rather than Chamorro, to the mixed amusement and annoyance of Chamorros who saw the film. As for Tweed's standing among survivors of his radio unit on Guam, former radioman Harold M. Winters may have spoken for all when he remarked years after the war, "I heard Tweed had a TV shop in Oregon somewhere, but I never cared to find out."[34]

Though many Guamanians remained ambivalent about Tweed, he also had his supporters, including Wayne "Wenceslao" Santos, who had helped him while he was on the run in the early months. "He was a very good man," Santos told a news reporter in 1984. "When we talked, he would always tell me that if he knew that the people he touched were going to be tortured on account of him, he would surrender. He told me that if I was ever taken in for interrogation, he told me to tell the truth because they would kill my family. For me, he was a hero. Those people who say that Tweed is no good never even knew the man."[35]

Tweed also remained close to the Artero family, who had sheltered him for twenty-one months. They corresponded through the years, and family members visited Tweed in Oregon several times. Following Tweed's death, the Arteros organized a memorial Mass for him at the Agana Cathedral-Basilica. Only thirty-five people attended. Among them was Joe T. Duenas, the grandnephew of Father Jesus Duenas.

In the end, said Carmen Artero Kasperbauer, who as a child so many years before had given up her much-anticipated lemon pie so the radioman could have a happier Christmas, none of it was really about Tweed the man. It was about what Tweed, imperfect though he may have been, represented. "Our parents did what they did because of their love and belief in God and their love for America," Kasperbauer said. "The Japanese tortured and killed our people because of our love and belief in America and [for] protecting an innocent person against an enemy."[36]

⁓

For the people of Guam, the war remains a watershed event, one that changed their island forever and is remembered with mixed feelings.

As of June 1946, nearly two years after liberation, the makeshift refugee camps had finally emptied out, but thousands of Chamorros were unable to return to their previous homes. The government had summarily taken over huge tracts of land for military use—including Sumay and the entire Orote Peninsula. The resulting legal tangle over land ownership and compensation would continue for years; it also left as many as ten thousand people in temporary government-provided housing. By 1947 a total of 1,350 families had lost their land and homes due to military policy.[37] The old way of life was also gone. The Navy encouraged Chamorros to return to farming and copra production, but with little success. With most of the island's prime agricultural land taken for Navy and Air Force military bases and airfields, farming on any larger scale was not possible. As Guam took its place as a major U.S. Pacific bastion in what would eventually become known as the Cold War, the lure of regular salaried jobs with military and civilian contractors was simply too great. By the end of 1946, some six thousand Chamorros were regular wage earners, about half of them working for the Navy.

Still, even as life has moved on, the war and its remembrance continue to pervade what may be described as "the Guamanian psyche." The strong feelings developed during the wartime experience are reflected in a letter six prominent Chamorros sent to Admiral Nimitz soon after Guam's recapture. "What kept us throughout the thirty-two months of Japanese oppression was our determined reliance upon our mother country's power, sense of justice, and national brotherhood," they wrote.[38]

Liberation Day is a major celebration that takes place each year on July 21, the anniversary of the landings. First held with modest observances in 1945, the celebration now features a mile-long parade with floats, bands, and marching units. Families often camp out along the parade route to reserve the best views. Young women from villages throughout the island compete to become the annual Liberation Day queen. There are fireworks, sports competitions, speeches, a carnival, and more, with past events featuring wrestling matches, agricultural fairs, bicycle races, a battle of the bands, and even pig wrestling. American veterans of the battle have been welcome guests over the years. For the fiftieth-anniversary Liberation Day in 1994, over a thousand veterans of the battle were flown to Guam on special tours and honored at the various ceremonies. The event also highlights the stories of Chamorros who endured the Japanese occupation, along with solemn observances at memorials and visits to the massacre sites.

Over the years a handful of critics have emerged to disparage Liberation Day, one arguing that the event should be titled "Reoccupation Day" as a celebration of the island's "reoccupation" by returning colonial forces.[39] They cite the seizure of land for military bases, lack of self-determination, and the second-class citizenship bestowed upon the islanders. It has also been pointed out that the liberation was less about the islanders and more about the island itself and its value as a military base. There is some truth to these observations, though the dissidents have generally met with scorn from those who actually lived through the war. In fact, while the commemoration is indeed an expression of gratitude toward the liberators, it is also a celebration of Chamorro loyalty, patriotism, courage, and fortitude during a time of great suffering.

As for that experience, lingering hurts remain. Animosity toward the Saipanese Chamorro "interpreters" and police has been long lasting, with islanders viewing their brutality as a betrayal of fellow Chamorros. Anger ran so deep that the islanders for a time preferred to be called Guamanians rather than "Chamorros," lest they be confused with Chamorros from Saipan.

Progress toward full U.S. citizenship has also been slow. Following the war, the civilian population continued to live under the authority of a naval governor with limited constitutional rights. While Guamanians were nationals of the United States, they did not become citizens until the passage of the Guam Organic Act of 1950. The act finally gave the islanders a congressional form of citizenship and replaced Navy rule with a civilian government, though Guam remains an unincorporated territory and residents still do not have full rights. Under a bill passed by Congress in 1968, Guam now has an elected governor. Another bill passed in 1972 allowed Guam a delegate to the U.S. House of Representatives. This delegate can vote in committee but not on the floor of the House. Guam's citizens still cannot vote in presidential elections.

One issue that remained unresolved for decades was the question of reparations for victims of the Japanese occupation. A 1945 law allowed residents to apply for recompense for war damages, but the bulk of the $8 million in payments was for property loss, not death and injury. Guam also was omitted from later legislation that provided compensation to U.S. citizens and others who were captured by Japan during the war. Another blow came with a 1951 peace treaty that relieved Japan of the responsibility to pay Guam reparations.

A powerful advocate for recognition of Chamorro suffering emerged in Beatrice Perez, who, as a fourteen-year-old, had survived her attempted decapitation outside Agana just before the U.S. landings. The terrible wound to her neck eventually healed, but Beatrice suffered from a nervous disorder for rest of her life. She attended school for a while but was unable to continue as she had been too traumatized. Interviewers through the years remarked on her strange detachment whenever called upon to recount her story. "Beatrice tells her story . . . in a flat voice without emotion," wrote a reporter for the *Guam Daily News* in 1952. "Tonelessly, she continues." Writing in the July 1964 issue of *Pacific Profile*, interviewer Howard Handleman echoed that observation. "The girl showed no emotion as she talked," he wrote. "Her almond eyes show neither a reflection of the terror that was part past nor a hint of happiness. She relayed her memories in factual manner while her face remained a stoic mask."[40]

Beatrice eventually married and raised a family and in 1993 recounted her horrific story in front of the U.S. Congress during the push to compensate Guamanian war victims. That testimony before Congress also reflected the conflicted feelings of so many survivors, who were "grateful for American liberation, loyal to the American nation, but [wanted] to be acknowledged for their suffering and sacrificing," as one reporter put it. "All I am trying to ask," Beatrice told the committee, is "recognize us, please. We are American."[41]

After years of haggling, President Barack Obama signed the Guam War Claims Measure in 2016. The measure provided payments of $10,000 to those who underwent forced marches or internment or hid to escape internment; $12,000 to those who experienced forced labor or personal injury; $15,000 to people who were severely injured or raped; and $25,000 to children, spouses, and some parents of those killed during the occupation. To date, about 2,000 of the estimated 3,762 war claims received in 2017 and 2018 have been adjudicated, paid, or recommended for payment.

Ironically, by the time the war claims measure was signed, the Japanese were back on Guam in force. The termination in 1962 of travel restrictions imposed by the Naval Security Clearance Policy opened the door wide for tourism on the island. As Guam is so distant from the U.S. mainland, Japan was the logical market. What would become a flood of tourists began modestly enough in May 1967, with 109 Japanese debarking from a Pan American World Airways flight. Those numbers exploded in succeeding years. In 2019, nearly 685,000 Japanese visited Guam, comprising over 41 percent of the total number of tourists.

Japanese tourists flock to an island far removed from the Guam of 1941. Attracted by its beaches, duty-free shopping, seven public golf courses, and entertainment venues—even the largest Kmart in the world—they pump an estimated

$700 million or more a year into the economy. In response, Guam has adapted to Japanese culture with an alacrity that is disquieting to some aging survivors of the wartime occupation. In high-traffic tourist areas, shop signs often include Japanese translations, employees speak Japanese, and some businesses accept yen as payment. The island has even adopted some Japanese celebrations as tourists and money have gradually softened postwar hostility toward the former occupiers.

The island's transformation from Pacific backwater into prime tourist destination would astonish any serviceman or woman who served there during the war. Much of the development has been funded and carried out by Japanese companies. Luxury hotels ring Tumon Bay where Japanese forces landed in 1941. Harmon (originally Depot) Field is now part of the Guam International Airport. Northwest Field, launch site for the last B-29 raid on Japan, is gone. What used to be North Field is now Andersen Air Force Base, which figured prominently in the B-52 raids on North Vietnam during the late 1960s and early 1970s. The capital of Hagåtña—formerly known as Agana—looks more like a midsize city in the Hawaiian Islands than the quaintly picturesque town destroyed during the 1944 battle.

Physical reminders of the war remain scattered about the island. Three Japanese 140mm coastal defense guns emplaced on the ridge near Piti are a popular attraction. Concrete blockhouses remain along the shoreline; the Gaan Point emplacement, which wreaked such havoc on the 22nd Marines on W-Day, also remains. Tweed's cave on the northwestern coast attracts its share of curious visitors. A variety of commemorative plaques and monuments include a plaque at the Plaza de Espana honoring the Guam Insular Guardsmen and their gallant fight against the invading Japanese on December 10, 1941. A statue at Father Duenas Memorial School at Tai honors the courageous priest executed for defying the Japanese occupiers. Commemorative plaques are also located at the sites of the Manenggon camp and the massacre sites at Tinta, Faha, and Chaguian. Another poignant site is the War Dog Cemetery with the graves of the twenty-five dogs from the 2nd and 3rd War Dog Platoons killed during the liberation of the island. A statue dedicated in 1994 depicts a life-size bronze Doberman pinscher on a base inscribed with each dog's name.

The U.S. government took formal action to commemorate the liberation of Guam with the establishment in 1978 of the War in the Pacific National Historic Park, which preserves various historic sites on the island. The overlook at the Asan beaches where the 3rd Marine Division landed includes a Memorial Wall of Names listing the 1,888 U.S. servicemen who died in the 1941 and 1944 battles, as well as the 1,170 Guamanians who died and the 14,721 who were victimized during the Japanese occupation.

Tentative steps toward a reconciliation with the former enemy began in the 1960s as Japanese "bone collectors" visited the island to retrieve the remains of their war dead. In 1965 former wartime priest Monsignor Oscar Calvo started the South Pacific Memorial Association, which included both local and Japanese participation, with the goal of building a peace memorial. Despite objections from some U.S. veterans groups infuriated at the prospect of a monument on American soil commemorating Japanese war dead, the project went forward. The result was the Peace Memorial Tower, a fifty-foot rendition of hands clasped in prayer, dedicated in 1970 at Mount Mataguac near the site of General Hideyoshi Obata's final stand.

As the years have gone on, fewer and fewer veterans of the battle for Guam have been able to attend the annual Liberation Day festivities. The seventy-fifth anniversary Liberation Day in 2019 was attended by only two veterans of the battle and one veteran who assisted with the island's reconstruction. Former pharmacist's mate Peter Marshall, the last surviving prisoner of war captured at Guam in 1941, passed away in early 2021 at the age of one hundred. Remembrances of Guam's war will no doubt continue, but as the last survivors—veterans and civilians—pass on, time and death may finally put an end to lingering hurts.

In 1994, as preparations were underway to celebrate the fiftieth anniversary of Guam's liberation from Japanese occupation, a letter arrived at the island's office for veterans' affairs. The letter was written by William C. Jerdonek of Parma, Ohio. Jerdonek observed that he understood Guam's governor was inviting former servicemen who took part in the liberation in 1944 to come and participate in the anniversary activities. He was writing, he noted, on behalf of his brother, former PFC Paul J. Jerdonek. His brother had served with B Company, 1st Battalion, 3rd Marines, which had been heavily involved in the struggle to seize the high ground behind Red Beach 2 immediately after coming ashore. "He was the B.A.R. man in his squad and was mortally wounded on the first day (July 21, 1944) of the invasion of Guam," wrote William. "He was unable to be evacuated until the following day and suffered greatly until he was transferred to the U.S.S. *Solace* hospital ship, upon which he passed away from the wounds on July 27, 1944. He was buried on Kwajalein Atoll in the Marshall Islands until after the war ended."

William related that twenty-one-year-old Paul was from Cleveland, Ohio, one of a family of fifteen children born to immigrant parents and raised through tough years of the Depression. He had served in a Civilian Conservation Corps camp in Idaho in the late 1930s. When the war started, he worked in a defense plant in

Cleveland until enlisting in the Marine Corps in February 1943. While stationed with a guard detachment in Virginia, he volunteered for overseas duty. Shortly afterward, he shipped out with a replacement battalion and joined the 3rd Marine Regiment in the Solomon Islands. "The rest is history," wrote William. A letter to Paul's mother from the chaplain aboard the USS *Solace* assured her that her twenty-year-old son had "passed away peacefully" at 7:30 a.m. "As he breathed his last he held the miraculous medal in his hand as it hung from the chain around his neck," he wrote.

William attached a small photo depicting his brother, smiling slightly, rifle slung over his right shoulder, left hand on his hip, looking calm and confident. He explained that he wrote only to recognize one of the liberators of Guam—one of the over one thousand men who gave up their lives in that battle and who "deserve the unending gratitude of all the citizens of Guam and our country. . . . All of the family had been saddened by the loss of our brother and son Paul and as the years have passed he surely has not been forgotten," he wrote. "His remains lie here at Calvary cemetery in Cleveland. Please remember the great sacrifices made by these valiant men."[42]

NOTES

INTRODUCTION

1. Guam, Wake Island, and two islands in Alaska's Aleutian chain, Kiska and Attu, were the only U.S. territory to be occupied by enemy forces in World War II. Wake was captured soon after Guam and held throughout the war; Kiska and Attu were seized by the Japanese in mid-1942 and recaptured by American forces a year later.

2. Steve Liewer, "Vets Recall Guam's Day of Infamy," *San Diego Union-Tribune*, December 7, 2009.

PROLOGUE

1. Hugh Myers, *Prisoner of War World War II* (Portland, OR: Metropolitan Press, 1965), 6.

2. Donald T. Giles Jr., ed., *Captive of the Rising Sun: The POW Memoirs of Rear Admiral Donald T. Giles* (Annapolis, MD: Naval Institute Press, 1994), 110.

3. Ibid.

4. Ibid., 28.

5. Ibid., 26.

6. Alice Rogers Hager, "Men Cut in Half by Jap Bombs; Dust, Destruction, Wake's Story," *The Tennessean* (Nashville), January 13, 1942.

7. Estimates of the number of detainees vary somewhat.

8. Tony Palomo, *An Island in Agony* (Agana, Guam: privately published, 1984), 2.

CHAPTER 1. DOLLARS CANNOT BUY YESTERDAY

1. Martin Boyle, *Yanks Don't Cry* (New York: Bernard Geis and Associates, 1963), 6.

2. "Study of the Theater of Operations Island of Guam," Marine Corps Schools, Marine Barracks, Quantico, Virginia, 1939.

3. Maj. O. R. Lodge, *The Recapture of Guam* (Washington, DC: Historical Branch, G-3 Division, Headquarters, U.S. Marine Corps, 1954), 4.

4. Palomo, *An Island in Agony*, 71.

5. Roger Mansell, *Captured: The Forgotten Men of Guam* (Annapolis, MD: Naval Institute Press, 2012), 69.

6. Ibid., 68.

7. Russell A. Apple, *Guam: Two Invasions and Three Military Occupations: A Historical Summary of War in the Pacific National Historical Park, Guam* (Mangilao, Guam: Richard F. Taitano Micronesian Area Research Center, University of Guam, 1980), 4.

8. Earl S. Pomeroy, *Pacific Outpost: American Strategy in Guam and Micronesia* (Stanford, CA: Stanford University Press, 1951), 90.

9. Ibid., 102; Wakako Higuchi, *The Japanese Administration of Guam, 1941–1944: A Study of Occupation and Integration Policies, with Japanese Oral Histories* (Jefferson, NC: McFarland & Co., 2013), 14.

10. Samuel Eliot Morison, *History of United States Naval Operations in World War II*, vol. 1: *The Rising Sun in the Pacific, 1931–April 1942* (Boston: Little, Brown and Company, 1988), 32–33; Colt D. Denfeld, *Hold the Marianas: The Japanese Defense of the Mariana Islands* (Shippensburg, PA: White Mane Publishing Company, 1997), 141.

11. Harry Gailey, *The Liberation of Guam, 21 July–10 August 1944* (Novato, CA: Presidio, 1988), 21.

12. "Borah Opposes Defenses," *Madera Tribune* (California), February 28, 1939.

13. Pomeroy, 157.

14. Robert F. Rogers, *Destiny's Landfall: A History of Guam* (Honolulu: University of Hawaii Press, 1995), 161.

15. Adm. Harry Hill, interview by John Mason, Columbia Center for Oral History, Columbia University.

16. Henry I. Shaw Jr., Bernard C. Nalty, and Edwin T. Turnbladh, *Central Pacific Drive: History of U.S. Marine Corps Operations in World War II* (Washington, DC: Historical Branch, G-3 Division, Headquarters, U.S. Marine Corps, 1966), 3:439.

17. Lt. George B. Todd, "Early Navy Radio Communications in Guam, Marianas Islands" (prepared for the Old Timer Communicators, n.p., n.d.).

18. Edward E. Hale, *First Captured, Last Freed: Memories of a P.O.W. in World War II Guam and Japan* (Sebastopol, CA: Grizzly Bear Press, 1995; Westport, CT: Praeger, 1996), 12.

19. Mansell, *Captured*, 7–8.

20. Todd.

21. Rogers, 134.

22. Boyle, 7.

23. Palomo, *An Island in Agony*, 32.

24. Frederick D. Parker, *Pearl Harbor Revisited: United States Navy Communications Intelligence, 1924–1941* (Fort George C. Meade, MD: Center for Cryptologic History, National Security Agency, 1994), 73.

25. Tony Palomo, "1941: Fateful and Tragic Year," in *The Defense of Guam* (Mangilao, Guam: Richard F. Taitano Micronesian Area Research Center, University of Guam, April–September 1972).

26. Mansell, *Captured*, 14; Rogers, 161.

27. Thomas Wilds, "The Japanese Seizure of Guam," *Marine Corps Gazette*, July 1955.

28. Rogers, 162; Parker, 76.

29. Rogers, 162.

30. Palomo, *An Island in Agony*, 9.

31. Harold E. Joslin, interview, National World War II Museum Oral History Collection, New Orleans, Louisiana.

32. Boyle, 11.

33. Mansell, *Captured*, 5.

34. "Vision of Old Glory in Disgrace Fortified McAllen Guam Captive," *The Monitor* (McAllen, TX), October 15, 1945.

35. Roger Mansell, "Testimony of USMC Pfc Captured on Guam: Pfc Carroll D. 'Barney' Barnett," Roger Mansell Collection, http://www.mansell.com/pow_resources (hereafter cited as Barnett interview).

36. Edward J. Drea, *In the Service of the Emperor* (Lincoln: University of Nebraska Press, 1998), 27.

37. Toyoko P. Kang, "Japanese Offensive Operations Immediately after the Outbreak of War: The Cooperative Operation of the Army and Navy to Occupy Guam," *Micronesian Journal of the Humanities and Social Sciences* 2, no. 1–2 (December 2003), 41–42.

38. "Operations in the Central Pacific, Japanese Studies in World War II" (Japanese Monograph No. 48, U.S. Army Historical Division) (cited hereafter as Japanese Monograph No. 48).

39. *Reports of General MacArthur: Japanese Operations in the Southwest Pacific Area* (Washington, DC: U.S. Government Printing Office, 1966), vol. 2, pt. 1, 16–17.

40. Higuchi, *The Japanese Administration of Guam*, 169.

41. Ibid., 177.

42. Japanese Monograph No. 48; "How the Guam Operation Was Conducted" (Tokyo: Japanese Self Defense Force Staff School, 1962).

43. Japanese Monograph No. 48.

CHAPTER 2. WAR COMES TO PARADISE

1. Esther Figueroa and Jim Bannan, dirs., *An Island Invaded—Guam in WWII*. Pacific Storytellers Cooperative video (Honolulu: PREL, 2004.

2. Myers, 7.

3. Frank Nichols, Mansell Collection interview, http://www.mansell.com/pow-index.html.

4. Palomo, *An Island in Agony*, 194.

5. Palomo, "1941."

6. Mansell, *Captured*, 18.

7. Ibid.

8. Edward N. Howard, interview with Darlene Norman, 1980, Vigo County Public Library/Wabash Valley Press Club, Terre Haute, Indiana.

9. Edward Wayne Settles, interview, Edward Wayne Settles Collection (AFC/2001/001/02917), Veterans History Project, American Folklife Center, Library of Congress.

10. Joslin interview.

11. Myers, 9.

12. Hale, 13–14.

13. Filipe S. Cruz, "Chamorro Sailor Tells His Story," *Guam Daily News*, July 21, 1969.

14. Jillette Tore Guerrero, *Coming of Age in War-Torn Guam: The WWII Memoirs of Justo Torre Leon Guerrero* (Hagatna Heights, Guam: Guamology Publishing, 2021), 11.

15. Ben Blaz, *Bisita Guam: Let Us Remember Nihi Ta Hasso* (Guam: University of Guam, 2008), 15–16).

16. Hale, 14.

17. Franklin D. Roosevelt, Papers as President: Map Room Papers, 1941–1945 Series 2: Military Files Box 36, Franklin D. Roosevelt Presidential Library and Museum.

18. Some accounts say five were caught, but McMillin's official report says three. Translation of a Japanese report refers to them as "spies," but "agents" may be more accurate.

19. Miguel Angel Olano y Urteaga, "Diary of a Bishop," *Guam Recorder*, April–September 1972, Richard F. Taitano Micronesian Area Research Center, University of Guam.

20. Capt. George J. McMillin, "Surrender of Guam to the Japanese," *Guam Recorder*, April–September 1972.

21. Todd.

22. Alfred Mosher, interview, National World War II Museum Oral History Collection, New Orleans, Louisiana.

23. Andre Sobocinski, "Peter Marshall's Journey: The Story of the Last Living American POW on Guam," U.S. Navy Bureau of Medicine and Surgery, Defense Visual Information Distribution Service, March 26, 2021.

24. Giles, 39–40.

25. Palomo, "1941."

26. Giles, 40.

27. Hale, 17–18. Hale remembered five sailors, but there were actually six.

28. Kang, 45–46.

29. Japanese Monograph No. 48.

30. Kang, 46.

31. Japanese Monograph No. 48.

32. Ibid.

33. Kang, 46.

34. Manuel T. Charfauros, "Merizo Massacre," *Pacific Profile*, July 21, 1965.

35. Apple, 26–27.

36. Hale, 18.

37. Ray Church, interview, National World War II Museum Oral History Collection, New Orleans, Louisiana.

38. Maj. Ralph S. Bates Sr., An American Shame: The Abandonment of an Entire American Population (CreateSpace, 2016), 67.

39. Palomo, *An Island in Agony*, 20.

40. Hale, 18.

41. Bates, 67.

42. Todd.

43. Hale, 18.

44. Mansell, *Captured*, 28.

45. Palomo, *An Island in Agony*, 26.

46. Hale, 18.

47. Hale, 20.

48. Giles, 46. McMillan, who hoped to be eligible for prisoner exchange due to his status as island governor, had also donned civilian garb. While Giles did not say so in his memoir, he may have had similar hopes as vice governor.

49. Church interview.

50. Giles, 46.

51. Church interview.

52. Harris J. Chuck, interview, National World War II Museum Oral History Collection, New Orleans, Louisiana.

53. Barnett interview.

54. Mansell, *Captured*, 32. Another account notes that Kauffman had a perpetual facial tic and suggests that the Japanese may have thought he was making faces at him.

55. McMillin, "Surrender of Guam."

56. This according to Giles; McMillin does not mention it in his official report.

57. Hale, 20–21.

CHAPTER 3. THE SURRENDER

1. "Vision of Old Glory in Disgrace."

2. Nichols interview.

3. Barnett interview.

4. Myers, 17–18.

5. Donald F. Schram, "It Happened in Michigan," *Detroit Free Press*, May 8, 1942.

6. Maj. Gen. Haruo Umezawa and Col. Louis Metzger, "The Defense of Guam," *Marine Corps Gazette*, August 1964.

7. McMillin, Captain George J. Report. to Secretary of the Navy, September 11, 1945, "Surrender of Guam to the Japanese."

8. Kang, 47.

9. Ibid.

10. Ibid., 48.

11. Higuchi, The Japanese Administration of Guam, 174–75.

12. Ibid., 170.

13. Giles, 54.

14. Marion Olds, "Navy Nurse: The Story of the Capture of Guam," *Sensation*, February 1943.

15. Todd.

16. Sobocinski; Peter B. Marshall, *1368 Days: An American POW in WWII Japan* (Eugene, OR: Luminare Press, 2017), 53.

17. Barnett interview; Mansell, *Captured*, 34–35.

18. Settles interview; Mansell, *Captured*, 40–41.

19. Juan U. Baza, testimony during Guam War Claims Review Commission public hearings held in Hagåtña, Guam, December 9, 2003 (hereafter cited as Baza testimony).

20. Guerrero, 16.

21. Rogers, 170.

22. Higuchi, *The Japanese Administration of Guam*, 170.

23. Olano y Urteaga; Palomo, *An Island in Agony*, 42.

24. Higuchi, *The Japanese Administration of Guam*, 24.

25. Palomo, *An Island in Agony*, 29.

26. "Americans Have Probably Lost the Island of Guam," *Pensacola News Journal*, December 14, 1941.

27. "380 Americans Captured in Guam Foray," *St. Louis Star-Times*, December 17, 1941.

28. Drew Pearson and Robert S. Allen, "The Washington Merry-Go-Round," *Spokane Chronicle*, December 24, 1941.

29. "Derides Excuse for FBI Failure to Guard Hawaii," *Chicago Tribune*, February 4, 1942.

30. Giles, 55.

31. Joslin interview.
32. Myers, 43.
33. Todd.
34. Hale, 32.
35. Giles, 60.
36. Hale, 36.
37. Giles, 60.
38. Anthony Iannarelli and John Iannarelli, *The Eighty Thieves: American POWs in World War II Japan* (Phoenix: Bridgewood Press, 2006), 36; Settles interview.
39. Giles, 61.
40. Mansell, *Captured*, 57–58.

CHAPTER 4. THE GREATEST GIFT OF ALL

1. Ricardo J. Bordallo and C. Sablan Gault, "The Journey to Manengon," in *Liberation—Guam Remembers: A Golden Salute for the 50th Anniversary of the Liberation of Guam* (Maite, Guam: Graphic Center, 1994) (edited volume henceforth cited as *Liberation—Guam Remembers*).
2. According to Wakako Higuchi, a more accurate meaning of Omiyajima would be "the island of the Imperial Court" or "Shinto shrine"; Tony Palomo, "Rising Sun Dawns on Guam," in *Liberation—Guam Remembers*.
3. Paul Boria, "Sablan Never Afraid to Preach," in *Liberation—Guam Remembers*.
4. Palomo, "Rising Sun Dawns on Guam."
5. Rogers, 171.
6. Blaz, 51.
7. Ibid.
8. Ibid., 52.
9. Diary of Fumitoshi Yasuoka, National Archives, RG 153, Box 1.
10. Blake Clark, *Robinson Crusoe, USN: The Adventures of George R. Tweed, RM1C, on Jap-Held Guam* (New York: McGraw-Hill Book Co., 1945), 21.
11. Todd.
12. Clark, 41.
13. Higuchi, *The Japanese Administration of Guam*, 181.
14. Ibid., 86.
15. Clark, 60.
16. Ibid., 62.
17. "Report Interview with Governor of Guam Now Held Prisoner in Japan," *Journal-Standard* (Freeport, IL), January 19, 1942.
18. "Union Nurse, Stationed at Guam, Believed Prisoner of Japanese," *Journal Herald* (Dayton, OH) January 18, 1942.
19. "Guam Commander Says He Is Well," *News-Herald* (Franklin, PA), February 3, 1942.
20. "L.A. Captives Send Messages," *Los Angeles Times*, February 16, 1942.
21. "Wife, Parents Hear Message from Former Valley Man in Jap Prison," *The Monitor* (McAllen, TX), April 20, 1942.
22. "Son in Marines at Guam Dead, Parents Learn," *Chicago Tribune*, May 7, 1942.

23. Jose M. Torres, *The Massacre at Atate* (Guam: University of Guam Press, 2014), 26.

24. Baza testimony.

25. Guerrero, 25.

26. Higuchi, *The Japanese Administration of Guam*, 184.

27. Ibid., 74.

28. Higuchi, *The Japanese Administration of Guam*, 171.

29. Ibid., 273.

30. Ibid., 133.

31. Torres, 27.

32. "War Survivor: Jose Santos Torres: The Musician and Soldier from Fena," Guampedia, https://www.guampedia.com/war-survivor-jose-santos-torres; Haidee Eugenio Gilbert, "Surviving the Odds: Guam WWII Survivor Reflects on Getting an Education at a Time of War," *Pacific Daily News*, February 3, 2019.

33. Torres, 26.

34. Higuchi, *The Japanese Administration of Guam*, 70.

35. Mac R. Johnson, "Slave Work, Little Food, Lot of Chamorros under Jap Rule," *Honolulu Advertiser*, August 9, 1944.

36. Palomo, *An Island in Agony*, 117.

37. "Story of Father Duenas—Martyred by the Enemy," *Guam Daily News*, July 21, 1952.

38. Palomo, *An Island in Agony*, 180.

39. Higuchi, *The Japanese Administration of Guam*, 201.

40. III Amphibious Corps, Report of Operations for the Capture and Occupation of Guam Island, Marianas, July 21–August 1944 (hereafter cited as IIIAC Report of Operations).

41. Higuchi, *The Japanese Administration of Guam*, 203.

42. Ibid., 225–26.

43. Case of Samuel T. Shinohara, July 28, 1945, Record of Proceedings of a Military Commission Convened at Agana, Guam, by Order of the Island Commander.

44. Higuchi, *The Japanese Administration of Guam*, 202.

45. Case of Kanzo Kawachi, September 17, 1945, Record of Proceedings of a Military Commission Convened at Agana, Guam, by Order of the Island Commander.

46. Case of Jose P. Villagomez, October 22, 1945, Record of Proceedings of a Military Commission Convened at Agana, Guam, by Order of the Island Commander.

47. Blaz, 47–49.

48. Case of Pedro Sablan Leon Guerroro, April 1945, Record of Proceedings of a Military Commission Convened at Agana, Guam, by Order of the Island Commander.

49. Palomo, *An Island in Agony*, 104.

50. Ibid., 105–6.

51. George Ray Tweed, interview with Commander Wright, August 25, 1944, Office of the Chief of Naval Operations, Intelligence Division, National Archives, RG 38, Records of the Office of the Chief of Naval Operations.

52. Clark, 157.

53. Ibid., 195, 197.

54. Ibid., 2011.

55. Carmen Artero Kasperbauer, interview, in Figueroa and Bannan.

CHAPTER 5. UNDER THE HEEL

1. Keith L. Camacho, "Cultures of Commemoration: The Politics of War, Memory and History in the Mariana Islands" (PhD diss., University of Hawaii, August 2005), 106.
2. Higuchi, *The Japanese Administration of Guam*, 253
3. "They Staked Their Lives So They Can Hear the News," *Pacific Profile*, July 21, 1965.
4. "How the Guam Operation Was Conducted."
5. Japanese Monograph No. 48.
6. Higuchi, *The Japanese Administration of Guam*, 210.
7. Ibid., 211.
8. Palomo, *An Island in Agony*, 138; Case of Kanzo Kawachi.
9. Case of Kanzo Kawachi.
10. Manuel Mafnas Merfalen, testimony during the Guam War Claims Review Commission, public hearing held in Hagåtña, Guam, on December 8, 2003.
11. Palomo, *An Island in Agony*, 139.
12. Ibid., 112–113.
13. Camacho, "Cultures of Commemoration," 287.
14. Ibid., 288.
15. Lonnie Gene Vining, "Guam Native Woman, Once Pupil of Shreveporter, Saved Tweed," *Shreveport Journal*, May 14, 1945.
16. E. B. Potter, *Nimitz* (Annapolis, MD: Naval Institute Press, 1976), 280.
17. Higuchi, *The Japanese Administration of Guam*, 276.
18. Ibid.
19. Blaz, 95.
20. "How the Guam Operation Was Conducted."
21. IIIAC Report of Operations.
22. Higuchi, *The Japanese Administration of Guam*, 227.
23. "How the Guam Operation Was Conducted."
24. Ibid.; Umezawa and Metzger.
25. "How the Guam Operation Was Conducted"; Umezawa and Metzger.
26. "How the Guam Operation Was Conducted."
27. Omi Hatashin, *Private Yokoi's War and Life on Guam 1944–1972: The Story of the Japanese Imperial Army's Longest WWII Survivor in the Field and Later Life* (Folkestone, UK: Global Oriental Ltd., 2009), 70.
28. Ibid., 10–11.
29. Gene Linn, "Blood and Sands of Guam (The Sakito Maru)," *Pacific Daily News*, December 13, 1981.
30. Lodge, 10; Sources disagree on the number of casualties, but it appears between 1,400 and 2,200 men were lost.
31. Shaw, 443.
32. Japanese Monograph No. 48.
33. Hatashin, 14–15.
34. Masashi Ito, *The Emperor's Last Soldiers* (New York: Coward-McCann, 1967), 14–15.
35. Hatashin, 17.
36. Pedro Peredo, "Wartime Memories," *Pacific Profile*, July 1965.
37. Higuchi, *The Japanese Administration of Guam*, 186.

38. Ibid., 62.
39. Blaz, 86–87.
40. Shannon J. Murphy, "Guam Is Attacked," Guampedia, https://www.guampedia.com /wwii-oral-war-histories-of-the-chamorro-people.
41. Apple, 39.
42. Higuchi, *The Japanese Administration of Guam*, 122.
43. IIIAC Report of Operations.

CHAPTER 6. THE MARIANAS

1. Commander Task Force 51 (Joint Expeditionary Force, Marianas), Report of Amphibious Operations for the Capture of the Marianas Islands (Forager Operation), August 25, 1944.
2. Samuel Eliot Morison, History of United States Naval Operations in World War II, vol. 2: New Guinea and the Marianas, March 1944–August 1944 (Boston: Little Brown and Company, 1959), 374.
3. Gen. Robert E. Hogaboom, interview with Benis M. Frank, April 1970, United States Marine Corps, History and Museums Division, Washington, DC.
4. Shaw, 433.
5. Gen. F. P. Henderson, "The First Air-Ground General," *Marine Corps Gazette*, April 1995.
6. Ibid.
7. Coleman letter, USMC Publication Background Files (Guam), National Archives, RG 127, Entry A1 1038 (hereafter cited as Publication files).
8. Dick Camp, Leatherneck Legends: Conversations with the Marine Corps' Old Breed (Saint Paul: Zenith Press, 2006), 118–19.
9. Roy H. Owsley, Diary, October 14, 1943–September 3, 1945, General Roy Geiger Papers, History and Museums Division (Gray Research Center), Quantico, Virginia (archive hereafter cited as Geiger Papers).
10. Fletcher Pratt, *The Marines' War* (New York: William Sloane Associates, 1948), 269.
11. Shaw, 451.
12. Holland M. Smith and Percy Finch, *Coral and Brass* (New York: Charles Scribner's Sons, 1949), 213.
13. Louis A. Metzger, "Guam 1944," *Marine Corps Gazette*, July 1994.
14. Henry Aplington II, "To Be a Marine," unpublished memoir, Special Collections, Firestone Library, Princeton University, Princeton, New Jersey, 1986 (hereafter cited as Aplington memoir).
15. IIIAC Report of Operations.
16. Lodge, 24.
17. Gen. Ray A. Robinson, interview with Benis M. Frank, United States Marine Corps, History and Museums Division, Washington, DC, 1968.
18. Craig letter, Publication files.
19. IIIAC Report of Operations.
20. John Seymour Letcher, *One Marine's Story* (Verona, VA: McClure Press, 1970), 291–92.
21. Dave Bouslog, *Maru Killer: War Patrols of the USS* Seahorse (Placentia, CA: R. A. Cline Publishing, 1996), 151–52.

22. VD-3 (Fleet Air Photographic Squadron Three), War Diary, entry for April 1944.

23. VD-3, Aircraft Action Report, Photographic Reconnaissance, Guam, May 7, 1944; VD-3, War Diary, entries for May; Task Force 56, Headquarters, Expeditionary Troops, Report on Guam Operation (G-1. G-2. G-3. Periodic Reports. etc.), October 2, 1944.

24. Charles F. Maier, interview, Charles F. Maier Collection (AFC/2001/001/52741), Veterans History Project, American Folklife Center, Library of Congress.

25. Jack Kerins, *The Last Banzai* (privately printed, 1992), 62.

26. Ibid., 67.

27. Letcher, 290; Kerins, 67.

28. Kerins, 68.

29. Shaw, 215.

30. Gen. Alfred H. Noble, interview with Lloyd E. Tatem, 1968, United States Marine Corps, History and Museums Division, Washington, DC.

31. Gen. Lemuel C. Shepherd Jr., interview with Benis M. Frank, 1967, United States Marine Corps, History and Museums Division, Washington, DC.

32. Camp, 110–11.

33. Henry Berry, *Semper Fi, Mac: Living Memories of the U.S. Marines in World War II* (New York: Arbor House, 1982), 345.

34. Shepherd interview.

35. Hogaboom interview.

36. IIIAC Report of Operations.

37. Alvin M. Josephy Jr., *The Long and the Short and the Tall: The Story of a Marine Combat Unit in the Pacific* (New York: Alfred A. Knopf, 1946), 7.

CHAPTER 7. A FORCED CHANGE OF PLANS

1. Josephy, 10.

2. Aaron S. Fox, interview, Aaron S. Fox Collection (AFC/2001/001/05232), Veterans History Project, American Folklife Center, Library of Congress.

3. Josephy, 5.

4. Paul C. Smith, *Personal File* (New York: Appleton-Century, 1964), 367.

5. Josephy, 19.

6. IIIAC Report of Operations.

7. VF-24, Aircraft Action Report, June 11, 1944; USS *Belleau Wood*, Report of Action against Guam, Rota, Haha Jima, Chichi Jim, Iwo Jima, and Pagan Islands and the Japanese Fleet, June 11–24, 1944.

8. USS *Hornet* (CV-12), Action Report, June 11–24, 1944.

9. VF-24, Aircraft Action Report.

10. Carl LaVO, *Slade Cutter: Submarine Warrior* (Annapolis, MD: Naval Institute Press, 2003), 155.

11. USS *Stingray*, Patrol Report of War Patrol Number 11, May 1944–July 1944; Dave Lotz, *Patrol Area 14: US Navy World War II Submarine Patrols to the Mariana Islands* (Bloomington, IN: Xlibris, 2018), 206. This appears to be the only successful "periscope rescue" of the war.

12. Harold R. Graham, interview, Harold R. Graham Collection (AFC/2001/001/3885), Veterans History Project, American Folklife Center, Library of Congress.

13. Aplington memoir.

14. Hogaboom interview.

15. Morison, New Guinea and the Marianas, 377.

16. USS *Honolulu* (CL48), Action Report, Bombardment and Fire Support of Guam, July 17, 1944–August 9, 1944, including preliminary bombardment on June 16, 1944.

17. Philip Crowl, *United States Army in World War II: The War in the Pacific, Campaign in the Marianas* (Washington, DC: Office of the Chief of Military History, Department of the Army, 1960), 321; Denfeld, 169.

18. USS *Aloe*, AA Action Report, June 17, 1944, East of Guam Island, Marianas; Japanese Monograph No. 48.

19. LCI(G) 468, AA Action Report, June 17, 1944, Southeast of Saipan Island.

20. LCI(L) 471, AA Action Report, June 17, 1944, East of Guam.

21. Aplington memoir.

22. Smith, *Personal File*, 368.

23. LCI(L) 471 report.

24. James A. Gallo, interview, James Aloysius Gallo Collection (AFC/2001/001/44217), Veterans History Project, American Folklife Center, Library of Congress.

25. *Daily Mountain Eagle* (Jasper, AL), July 13, 1944; *Clovis News-Journal* (New Mexico), July 9, 1945.

26. Japanese Monograph No. 48.

27. Blaz, 96.

28. Higuchi, *The Japanese Administration of Guam*, 239–40.

29. Crowl, 323–24.

30. Magdalena San Nicolas Bayani, testimony during the Guam War Claims Review Commission public hearing held in Hagåtña, Guam, on December 9, 2003; Baza testimony.

31. Palomo, *An Island in Agony*, 144.

32. Ibid., 144–45.

CHAPTER 8. TURKEY SHOOT

1. *Belleau Wood*, Report of Action.

2. Ibid.

3. A variation of the Zero or Zeke.

4. USS *Bunker Hill*, Aircraft Action Reports, Air Group Eight, Marianas Operations, June 11–24, 1944.

5. Gerald Astor, *Wings of Gold: The U.S. Naval Air Campaign in World War II* (New York: Presidio Press, 2004), 287.

6. USS *Hornet*, Action Report.

7. Diem was shot down and killed a month later.

8. Astor, 288.

9. Eric Hammel, *Aces Against Japan* (New York: Pocket Books, 1992), 224–28.

10. USS *Cabot*, Action Report—First Phase of Marianas Operation and Action against Japanese Surface Force, June 6–24, 1944.

11. Astor, 288.

12. Barrett Tillman, *Clash of the Carriers: The True Story of the Marianas Turkey Shoot of World War II* (New York: NAL Caliber, 2005), 183.

13. Hammel, 230–33.

14. Lodge, 108–09.

15. James H. Hallas, *Saipan: The Battle That Doomed Japan in World War II* (Guilford, CT: Stackpole Books, 2019), 268.

CHAPTER 9. HURRY UP AND WAIT

1. Aplington memoir.

2. Joseph L. Frank, *My First and Only Paid Vacation, 1942–1945* (Victoria, BC, Canada: Trafford Publishing, 2007), 79.

3. Ibid., 162.

4. Aplington memoir.

5. Ibid.

6. Neil Stiles, interview with Dwight Daniel, August 17, 2003, National Museum of the Pacific War, Fredericksburg, Texas.

7. Dan Marsh's Raider History, http://www.usmcraiders.org/history.

8. James L. Swain, interview, James Lowell Swain Collection (AFC/2001/001/4487), Veterans History Project, American Folklife Center, Library of Congress.

9. Ibid., 163.

10. Ibid.

11. Cord Meyer, *Facing Reality: From World Federalism to the CIA* (New York: Harper & Row, 1980), 13–14.

12. Frank, 85.

13. Ibid., 164.

14. Vice Adm. George C. Dyer, *The Amphibians Came to Conquer: The Story of Admiral Richmond Kelly Turner* (Washington, DC: Department of the Navy, 1972), 2:932.

15. Ibid.

16. Shaw, 444; Dyer, 933.

17. Fifth Fleet, Final Report on the Operations to Capture the Marianas Islands.

18. Morison, New Guinea and the Marianas, 176–77.

19. Shepherd interview.

20. Scott W. Carmichael, *Bundschu Ridge: At the Tip of the Spear during the Liberation of Guam* (Kindle edition, 2014).

21. Dale L. Barker, *Hitting the Beaches: The First Armored Amphibian Battalion in World War II, 1943–1945* (Atlanta: First Armored Amphibian Battalion, 1996), 4.

22. Actually "Chorito Cliff" but misspelled "Chonito" on American maps and in subsequent accounts, a spelling that will be continued here in order to avoid confusion.

23. Aplington memoir.

24. Raymond P. Gillespie, *The K-Company Marines: 3rd Battalion-22nd Regiment* (n.p.: privately printed, 1992), 12.

25. Anthony A. Frances, "The Battle for Banzai Ridge," *Marine Corps Gazette*, June 1945.

26. Letcher, 294.

27. Morison, New Guinea and the Marianas, 12.

28. Umezawa and Metzger; "How the Guam Operation Was Conducted."

29. Ito, 17.

30. Shaw, 447.

31. Reports: Expeditionary Troops, Task Force 56, Forager, June–August 1944; Shaw, 447.

32. CinPac Operations in the Pacific Ocean Areas during the Month of July 1944, Commander in Chief U.S. Pacific Fleet and Pacific Ocean Areas.

33. "How the Guam Operation Was Conducted."

34. Ibid.; Shaw, 450.

35. "How the Guam Operation Was Conducted."

36. Ibid.

37. *Ours to Hold It High: The History of the 77th Infantry Division in World War II* (Washington, DC: Infantry Journal Press, 1947), 59.

38. IIIAC Report of Operations.

39. "Draft Board Calls Man Who Was Killed on Guam," *Burlington Free Press* (Vermont), July 13, 1944.

40. Barker, 168.

41. Stiles interview.

42. Edward C. Schubel, interview, Edward C. Schubel Collection (AFC/2001/001/33269), Veterans History Project, American Folklife Center, Library of Congress.

43. Smith, *Personal File*, 369.

44. Gillespie, 61.

45. Lodge, 30.

46. Cmdr. H. E. Smith, "I Saw the Morning Break," *USNI Proceedings*, March 1946.

47. Berry, 193.

CHAPTER 10. RESCUE

1. "Guam 'Visitor' Sees No Japs," *Wisconsin State Journal*, July 23, 1944.

2. Robert Trumbull, "Navy Pilot, Shot Down, Spends 13 Nights on Guam Undetected," *Honolulu Advertiser*, July 24, 1944; Jeremy Lyons, "7 Days at Sea: One Soldier's Story of Survival," FOX 26 KNPN, May 25, 2015.

3. Lt. R. W. Kiser, interview, OpNav-16-V-# E553, February 16, 1945, United States Naval Air Station, Pensacola, Florida.

4. Trumbull, "Navy Pilot."

5. Tweed interview.

6. Tony Palomo, "A Time of Sorrow and Pain," War in the Pacific National Historical Park, U.S. Department of the Interior, National Park Service, 2004.

7. Guerrero, 35.

8. Bruce Petty, *Saipan: Oral Histories of the Pacific War* (Jefferson, NC: McFarland & Company, 2002), 81.

9. Tweed interview. There is some confusion over the pilot's identity. Chamorros and Tweed identified him as a "Lt. (jg) Hamilton," or "J. J. Hamilton," but no aviator by that name was lost in the Marianas. It is possible he was actually Ensign Thomas E. Hallowell from San Jacinto's VF-51, who was shot down over Guam on June 19.

10. Petty, 81.

11. Task Force 56, Report on Guam Operation.

12. "Operations Report on Marianas," Headquarters 77th Infantry Division, August 19, 1944.

13. Alternate Plan Employment 77th Division in Corps Reserve, July 14, 1944, Geiger Papers.

14. Crowl, 317.

15. "How the Guam Operation Was Conducted."

16. Col. W. A. Wachtler, Memorandum for the Commanding General (Geiger), 77th Division Alternate Plan, July 18, 1944, Geiger Papers.

17. Crowl, 318. Bruce would finally get his chance to execute an amphibious end run at Leyte, where his division made a highly successful landing at Ormoc in December 1944.

18. Exchange of letters/notes between Generals Geiger and Smith, all dated July 23, 1944, Geiger papers, Personal Papers Collections, Archives Branch, U.S. Marine Corps History Division, Quantico, Virginia.

19. "Local Sailor Decorated for Rescue of Tweed, Is Home," *Lancaster New Era* (Pennsylvania), February 13, 1946.

20. Clark, 239–245; Tweed interview.

21. USS *Wasp*, War Diary, Action Reports of *Wasp* and Carrier Air Group Fourteen in the Final Phase of the Operation against Guam and in the Operation against Palau, July 6–30, 1944.

22. Bordallo and Gault.

23. Masako Watanabe, "Woman Recalls Life during, after World War II," *Pacific Sunday News*, August 11, 2013; Amanda Francel Blas, "War Leaves Lasting Impression on Survivor," *Pacific Daily News*, July 20, 2014.

24. Hatashin, 21–22.

25. Higuchi, *The Japanese Administration of Guam*, 64.

26. Rlene Steffy and Robert Steffy, prods., *Historic Context: Manenggon March and Concentration Camp Survivor Accounts* (DVD) (Guam: Micronesian Publishing, 2015).

27. Higuchi, *The Japanese Administration of Guam*, 281.

28. Luis Untalan, "The Long Trek to Manenggon," Pacific Profile, July 1965.

29. Edward Aguon, testimony during the Guam War Claims Review Commission public hearing held in Hagåtña, Guam, on December 8, 2003.

30. Steffy and Steffy.

31. Ibid.

32. Ibid.

33. Accounts of Hannah Torres's death vary in their details but agree that it resulted from a beating by a Japanese soldier.

34. Higuchi, *The Japanese Administration of Guam*, 280; Wakako Higuchi, "The Japanisation Policy for the Chamorros of Guam, 1941–1944," *Journal of Pacific History* 36, no. 1 (June 2001): 19–35.

35. Judge Joaquin V. E. Manibusan, "In Tai, a Day of Terror and Tragedy," in *Liberation— Guam Remembers*.

36. "Political Martyr: Last Hours of Father Duenas," *Pacific Profile*, July 1965.

37. Apple, 44–45.

38. Palomo, *An Island in Agony*, 181.

39. Joaquin Limtiaco, "The Last Days of Fr. Duenas," *Guam Daily News*, July 21, 1960.

40. Figueroa and Bannan.

41. "He Went to Round Up Cattle and Found a Wanted Sailor," *Guam Daily News*, July 21, 1960.

42. Figueroa and Bannan.

43. "He Went to Round Up Cattle."

44. Figueroa and Bannan. This is how Carmen remembered the encounter. The two Chamorros told a different story, claiming they warned Antonio that the Japanese had learned he was hiding Tweed and advised him to flee.

45. "Three Guamanians, Beheaded by the Japanese, Still Alive," *Guam Daily News*, July 21, 1952; testimony of Beatrice Perez Emsley at the Hearing before the Subcommittee on Insular and International Affairs of the Committee on Interior and Insular Affairs House of Representatives, Washington, DC, July 27, 1989; Beatrice Emsley testimony before the US Congress on May 27, 1993; "The Survivors: Woman Lives to Tell about Grisly Execution," *Pacific Daily News*, July 21, 1984.

CHAPTER 11. FROGMEN AND TETRYTOL

1. Barker, 168.
2. Aplington memoir.
3. Coleman letter.
4. IIIAC Report of Operations.
5. Meyer, 11.
6. Dale Maharidge, *Bringing Mulligan Home: The Other Side of the Good War* (New York: Public Affairs, 2013), 83.
7. USS *Dickerson*, Action Report at Guam, July 28, 1944.
8. Chet Cunningham, *The Frogmen of World War II: An Oral History of the U.S. Navy's Underwater Demolition Units* (New York: Pocket Books, 2005), 221.
9. Metzger.
10. UDT #3, Action Report, Guam Operation; *Dickerson*, Action Report.
11. Martin Jacobson, interview, National World War II Museum Oral History Collection, New Orleans, Louisiana.
12. UDT #3, Action Report.
13. Morison, *New Guinea and the Marianas*, 380; Cmdr. Francis D. Fane and Don Moore, *The Naked Warriors* (New York: Appleton-Century-Crofts, 1956), 119.
14. Fane and Moore, 116.
15. IIIAC Report of Operations.
16. Coleman letter.
17. Lodge, 33; IIIAC Report of Operations.
18. Denfeld, 182.
19. Ibid.; Lodge, 116.
20. "How the Guam Operation Was Conducted."
21. Hatashin, 24.
22. Crowl, 336.
23. Apple, 44.
24. Crowl, 336; "How the Guam Operation Was Conducted."
25. Ito, 17–19.
26. Cyril J. O'Brien, *Liberation: Marines in the Recapture of Guam* (Washington, DC: Marine Corps Historical Center, 1994), 8.
27. Hatashin, 25–26.
28. Commander Task Force 53, Report of Amphibious Operations for the Capture of Guam, August 10, 1944.

29. Ibid.; IIIAC Report of Operations; Crowl, 325.

30. "Farewell Message Penned before Priest Met Death," *Republican and Herald* (Pottsville, PA), August 30, 1944.

31. Cruz.

32. Ibid.

33. Palomo, *An Island in Agony*, 186–87; Charfauros.

34. Charfauros.

35. "The Fena Massacre," hearing.

36. Torres, 51–55.

CHAPTER 12. ACROSS THE REEF

1. Aplington memoir.

2. USS *Rixey*, Action Report on Occupation of Guam, Marianas Islands, July 21–29.

3. Barker, 168.

4. Ibid.

5. Josephy, 26.

6. Kerins, 76.

7. George R. Aspley, *Amphibious Assault, First Wave on Guam and Okinawa: A Marine Raider's Account of War in the Pacific* (n.p.: privately printed, n.d.), 40.

8. "Lieut. Tom Brock Reveals Guam Battle Experiences," *Columbus Telegram* (Nebraska), December 9, 1944.

9. Josephy, 27.

10. Kerins, 76.

11. Joseph Friedman, *God Shared My Foxholes* (New York: iUniverse, 2010), 90.

12. William W. Putney, *Always Faithful: A Memoir of the Marine Dogs of World War II* (New York: Free Press, 2001), 140.

13. Barker, 177–78.

14. Leo A. Remaklus, interview, Leo A. Remaklus Collection (AFC/2001/001/69026), Veterans History Project, American Folklife Center, Library of Congress.

15. Barker, 176.

16. Harris Done, dir., *War Dogs of the Pacific* (Harris Done Productions, 2009).

17. Smith, *Personal File*, 370.

18. Robert Leckie, *Strong Men Armed: The United States Marines Against Japan* (New York: Random House, 1962), 360.

19. Bertram A. Yaffe, *Fragments of War: A Marine's Personal Journey* (Annapolis, MD: Naval Institute Press, 1999), 37.

20. Kerins, 78.

21. Eugene H. Peterson, *Still a PFC: Guadalcanal, Bougainville, Guam, Iwo Jima* (n.p.: privately printed, 2000), 58.

22. Ito, 19–20.

23. John R. Silvestrini, interview, John R. Silvestrini Collection (AFC/2001/001/14286), Veterans History Project, American Folklife Center, Library of Congress.

24. Kerins, 78.

25. Aplington memoir.

26. LaVarre Daley, *United States Marine Corps Raiders: A Personal Account by LaVarre Daley* (Erie, CO: MJ Clark Publisher, 2002), 133–35.

27. Aspley, 41.

28. Hendon H. Edwards, interview, Hendon H. Edwards Collection (AFC/2001/001/4510), Veterans History Project, American Folklife Center, Library of Congress.

29. O'Brien, *Liberation*, 8.

30. Frank, 98–99.

31. Done.

32. Barker, 175.

33. Tony Palomo, and Paul J. Borja (eds.), "Liberation—Guam Remembers.": A Golden Salute for the 50th Anniversary of the Liberation of Guam. Maite, Guam: Graphic Center, 1994.

34. USS *Ringgold*, Action Report, Guam.

35. Maharidge, 85.

36. 1st Provisional Marine Brigade Operations and Special Action Report, August 19, 1944 (henceforth cited as Marine Brigade Report).

37. Barker, 180.

38. Parker letter, Publication files. A number of accounts indicate there were two 75mm guns at the point, but it appears there was just one, the other being a 37mm gun.

39. Shaw, 462.

40. Barker, 180.

41. Ibid., 187.

42. *Ringgold*, Action Report.

43. Linn.

44. George McMillan et al., *Uncommon Valor: Marine Divisions in Action* (Washington, DC: Infantry Journal Press, 1946), 100.

45. Robert A. Aurthur et al., *The Third Marine Division* (Washington, DC: Infantry Journal Press, 1948), 146.

46. Kunz letter, Publication files.

47. Rogers, 184.

48. PC-555, Action Report, July 21–29, 1944.

49. Frank, 99.

50. Palomo and Borja, *Liberation—Guam Remembers*.

51. Ibid.

52. "Lieut. Tom Brock Reveals Guam Battle Experiences."

53. John Foley, interview with Richard Misenhimer, March 26, 2002, National Museum of the Pacific War, Fredericksburg, Texas.

54. George L. Bessette, interview, George L. Bessette Collection (AFC/2001/001/18556), Veterans History Project, American Folklife Center, Library of Congress.

55. Kerins, 79.

56. John McClure, interview, John McClure Collection (AFC/2001/001/9534), Veterans History Project, American Folklife Center, Library of Congress, Washington, DC.

57. Edwards interview. Creamer was actually a corporal at the time.

58. "Lieut. Tom Brock Reveals Guam Battle Experiences."

59. Robert M. Dent, interview, Robert Miller Dent Jr. Collection (AFC/2001/001/70650), Veterans History Project, American Folklife Center, Library of Congress.

60. Kerins, 83.

61. Barker, 200–01.

62. Billy Wayne Sherrill, interview with Mark Cunningham, April 22, 2015, National Museum of the Pacific War, Fredericksburg, Texas. Sherrill believed the officer was a captain, but my research indicates it was Lieutenant Shelly.

63. Wayne Barham, "Guam: D-Day Plus 30 Years," *Argosy Magazine*, July, 1974.

64. Frank, 102.

65. John B. Davis, interview with John K. Driscoll, 2004, Wisconsin Veterans Museum Research Center.

66. Joseph R. Anderson, interview, Joseph Robert Anderson Collection (AFC/2001/001/59011), Veterans History Project, American Folklife Center, Library of Congress.

67. Kerins, 114–15.

68. Josephy, 32.

69. Lawrence F. Radel, interview, Lawrence Frank Radel Collection (AFC/2001/001/86891), Veterans History Project, American Folklife Center, Library of Congress.

70. Shaw, 463.

71. Ibid.

72. Aplington memoir.

73. Bastian letter, Publication files.

74. Shaw, 466.

75. Carmichael.

76. Ibid.

77. Ibid.; Gallo interview.

78. Carmichael.

79. Ibid.

80. Smith, *Personal File*, 372.

81. Aplington memoir.

82. Smith, *Personal File*, 373.

83. Palomo and Borja, *Liberation—Guam Remembers*.

84. Henry Karbin, interview, Henry Karbin Collection (AFC/2001/001/42144), Veterans History Project, American Folklife Center, Library of Congress.

85. Carmichael.

86. Barker, 198.

87. Remaklus interview.

88. Friedman, 92–93. Friedman did not name the lieutenant in his memoir, but a check of the casualty records indicates it was almost certainly twenty-nine-year-old Ferris Wharton of Newark, Delaware.

89. Gen. Edward Arthur Craig, interview with Lloyd E. Tatem, May 16, 1968, United States Marine Corps, History and Museums Division, Washington, DC.

90. Camp, 127.

91. *Third Division's Two Score and Ten History* (Paducah, KY: Turner Publishing Company, 1992), 89.

92. Frank, 102.

93. Joseph Kight, interview with Richard Misenhimer, December 27, 2007, National Museum of the Pacific War, Fredericksburg, Texas.

94. Rex Alan Smith and Gerald A. Meehl, *Pacific War Stories in the Words of Those Who Survived* (New York: Abbeville Press, 2004), 423.

95. Lodge, 39.

96. Camp, 127–28. Records indicate Henderson suffered a gunshot wound to the arm, not the throat. Craig may have been confused by the blood from Henderson's earlier neck wound. The captain survived.

CHAPTER 13. THE FIGHT FOR THE BEACHHEADS

1. Shaw, 462.

2. Marine Brigade Report.

3. Thomas E. Backman, interview, Thomas E. Backman Collection (AFC/2001/001/2912), Veterans History Project, American Folklife Center, Library of Congress.

4. Marine Brigade Report.

5. Richard M. Pfuhl, *Chasing the Sun* (Saint Louis, MO: Ten Square Books, 1979), 138.

6. George H. Hall, "He Has a Lot of Notches in His Gun," *St. Louis Post-Dispatch* (Missouri), November 29, 1944.

7. O'Brien, *Liberation*, 13.

8. Weber was subsequently awarded the Navy Cross for his actions at Gaan Point; Bevan Cass, *History of the Sixth Marine Division* (Washington, DC: Infantry Journal Press, 1948), 14–15; "Schaghticoke Soldier Gets Navy Cross," *Troy Record* (New York), April 9, 1945.

9. St. John O'Neill, personal diary, John O'Neill Papers, USMC History and Museums Division (Gray Research Center), Quantico, Virginia.

10. Backman interview.

11. James Bradshaw, interview, James Bradshaw Collection (AFC/2001/001/90054), Veterans History Project, American Folklife Center, Library of Congress.

12. Hall, "He Has a Lot of Notches."

13. Ralph Contreras, interview with Mark DePue, May 20, 2011, #VR2-A-L-2011-015, Abraham Lincoln Presidential Library; Ralph M. Contreras, interview, Ralph Martin Contreras Collection (AFC/2001/001/9127), Veterans History Project, American Folklife Center, Library of Congress.

14. Shepherd interview.

15. Parker letter, Publication files.

16. Barker, 189.

17. Ibid., 190.

18. Ibid., 187–88.

19. Patrick K. O'Donnell, *Into the Rising Sun* (New York: Free Press, 2002), 143.

20. R. G. Rosenquist, Martin J. Sexton, and Robert A. Buerlein, *Our Kind of War: Illustrated Saga of the U.S. Marine Raiders of World War II* (Richmond: American Historical Foundation, 1990), 133.

21. Aspley, 43–44.

22. Barker, 185.

23. LCI(G) 437, Action Report, Guam, July 20, 1944, to August 12, 1944.

24. Howard Norton, "We Retake Guam, Eyewitness Report," *Baltimore Sun*, September 3, 1944; "War Writer Escapes Death in Guam Drive," *Miami Herald*, August 13, 1944.

25. USS SC 1326, Action Report, July 21, 1944.

26. Marine Brigade Report.

27. Oscar E. Gilbert, *Marine Tank Battles in the Pacific* (Conshohocken, PA: Combined Publishing, 2001), 184.

28. Marine Brigade Report.

29. William K. Anderson Jr., "The Bravest Man I Have Ever Known," *Marine Corps Gazette*, November 2006.

30. Smith, "I Saw the Morning Break."

31. Shaw letter, Publication files.

32. Parker letter, Publication files.

33. Gilbert, *Marine Tank Battles*, 185–87.

34. Daley, 137; *Raider Patch*, May 1986.

35. "How the Guam Operation Was Conducted."

36. Nicholas Zobenica, interview with Thomas Saylor, September 26, 2002, Minnesota Historical Society, Saint Paul, Minnesota.

37. Shaw, 473.

38. Sgt. Donald A. Hallman, "Marine on Guam Recalls Former Beauty of Isle," *Chevron*, August 26, 1944.

39. Rudolf G. Rosenquist, "Rosenquist: Guam Banzai Attack," *Raider Patch*, September 1980.

40. Camp, 130.

41. John R. Henry, "Reporter's Guam Notebook Yields Colorful Items," *Honolulu Star-Bulletin*, August 3, 1944.

42. Commander Task Force 53, Report of Amphibious Operations for the Capture of Guam Island, Marianas, June 4–August 10, 1944.

43. Calvin E. Rainey, interview, Calvin Earl Rainey Collection (AFC/2001/001/65850), Veterans History Project, American Folklife Center, Library of Congress.

44. Josephy, 218–19.

45. Done.

46. Putney, 146–48.

47. Francis J. Hoban, *Marines Don't Cry: The True Story of a Few Good Men* (Long Beach, CA: Seaside Printing Company, 1985), 69–70.

48. Bowser letter, Publication files.

49. Belzer letter, Publication files.

50. Walter R. Roose, interview, Walter R. Roose Jr. Collection (AFC/2001/001/57455), Veterans History Project, American Folklife Center, Library of Congress.

51. Frances.

52. Some historians would later attribute Butler's well-planned use of the defiles to a stroke of luck; it was far from luck. Lodge, 40.

53. Yaffe, 45.

54. Frances.

55. Stephen F. Kuzma, interview, Stephen Fred Kuzma Collection (AFC/2001/001/45015), Veterans History Project, American Folklife Center, Library of Congress)

56. Frank R. Simone, interview, Frank Robert Simone Collection (AFC/2001/001/79036), Veterans History Project, American Folklife Center, Library of Congress.

57. Aplington memoir.
58. Ibid.
59. Robert Martin, "Notes from Guam," *Marine Corps Gazette*, October, 1944.
60. Aplington memoir.
61. Simone interview.
62. Kerins, 110–11.
63. Ibid., 115.
64. Carmichael.
65. Ibid.
66. Ibid.
67. Ibid.
68. Winford survived. Aplington memoir.
69. Snedeker letter, Publication files.
70. Hall letter, Publication files. In the margin of Hall's letter, Marine Corps historian Maj. O. R. Lodge, who compiled the official monograph on Guam, notes of Hall's claim, "Too many people don't agree, including R-Exec who tries to cover Hall on most things."
71. Snedeker letter.
72. Gallo interview; Carmichael.
73. Carmichael.
74. Snedeker letter.
75. Carmichael; Snedeker letter; O'Brien, *Liberation*, 16.

CHAPTER 14. COUNTERATTACK

1. Putney, 151.
2. Aurthur, 1467.
3. Josephy, 45.
4. Kerins, 112.
5. USS *Wayne*, Action Report of Landing Operation on Guam, August 25, 1944.
6. USS *Fayette*, Report—Action and Operations–Guam, July 21–25, 1944.
7. Barker, 194.
8. Ibid.; Creede John Anderson, interview, Creede John Anderson Collection (AFC/2001/001/10040), Veterans History Project, American Folklife Center, Library of Congress.
9. Rosenquist, Sexton, and Buerlein, 129.
10. *Ours to Hold It High*, 64.
11. Lodge, 53.
12. Camp, 133–34.
13. "How the Guam Operation Was Conducted."
14. Ibid.; Shaw, 479–80.
15. Linn.
16. Walker letter, Publication files.
17. Paolo S. DeMeis, *The Bazooka Kid* (N.p.: privately published, n.d.), 69.
18. Dan Marsh's Raider History.
19. Rosenquist.
20. O'Donnell, 137.

21. Ibid., 138.

22. Robert A. Powers, interview, National World War II Museum Oral History Collection, New Orleans, Louisiana.

23. O'Donnell, 139.

24. Luther Fleming account in the *Raider Patch*, January 1987.

25. *Raider Patch*, May 1987.

26. Ibid., May 1978.

27. DeMeis, 70–71.

28. Read letter, Publication files.

29. Charles O. West et al., *Second to None! The Story of the 305th Infantry in World War II* (Washington, DC: Infantry Journal Press, 1949), 112.

30. Kenneth Condit and Edwin T. Turnbladh, *Hold High the Torch: A History of the 4th Marines* (Nashville: Battery Press, 1989), 66.

31. Gilbert, *Marine Tank Battles*, 189.

32. Rosenquist.

33. Aspley, 46.

34. O'Donnell, 142.

35. "Kenosha Marine, Killed in Action, Wins Navy Cross," *Kenosha News* (Wisconsin), March 17, 1945. Understandably, considering the darkness and general chaos, there was some confusion over the number of tanks involved and how many were knocked out by PFC Oribiletti. Some accounts indicate there were five enemy tanks, but witnesses counted four. Both Barr and the 6th Marine Division history credit Oribiletti with three kills, but his Navy Cross citation and other witnesses put the number at two.

36. Aspley, 47–49.

37. Joseph Hiott, interview, Witness to War Foundation, https://www.witnesstowar.org/combat_stories/WWII/717.

38. Berry, 124; Rosenquist, Sexton, and Buerlein, 130–31.

39. Berry, 124.

40. Rosenquist, Sexton, and Buerlein, 130–31.

41. Trenton Fowler, interview with Floyd Cox, January 17, 2001, National Museum of the Pacific War, Fredericksburg, Texas.

42. Lodge, 50.

43. Millard Kaufman, "Attack on Guam," *Marine Corps Gazette*, April 1945; Shaw, 474.

44. Meyer, 15–28.

45. Barker, 206.

46. Smith, *Personal File*, 374–75.

47. Sgt. James E. Hague, "One Night at Asan," *Leatherneck*, February 1947; Sgt. James E. Hague, "Big Irishman Piles Up Dead Japs," *Chevron*, September 9, 1944.

48. Shaw, 485.

49. "How the Guam Operation Was Conducted."

50. Patrick W. Wathen, "Marine Shunned Wounds, Hurled Back Enemy," *Evansville Courier & Press* (Indiana), May 29, 1995; "'The Tough Little Guy' Isn't Tough at All," *Courier-Journal* (Louisville, KY), July 8, 1945.

CHAPTER 15. HOLDING THE BEACHHEAD

1. Linn.
2. Hatashin, 31.
3. *Raider Patch*, September 1980.
4. Ibid., November, 1981.
5. Read letter, Publication files.
6. "Herman Tanks Win Guam Scrap," *Intelligencer Journal* (Lancaster, PA), August 12, 1944); Shaw, 483.
7. O'Donnell, 141; *Raider Patch*, May 1987.
8. O'Donnell, 137–38.
9. O'Brien, *Liberation*, 17.
10. Hatashin, 31.
11. DeMeis, 71.
12. Rosenquist.
13. Meyer, 32.
14. Task Force 53, Report of Amphibious Operations for the Capture of Guam, August 10, 1944.
15. Bastian letter, Publication files.
16. "Officer Calls Skagg's Conduct Greatest Inspiration Possible," *Ames Daily Tribune*, February 22, 1945; "The Tough Little Guy"; Wathen.
17. Putney, 5; Done.
18. O'Brien, *Liberation*, 16.
19. "One Guam Hill Proves Costly," *Daily Oklahoman*, August 6, 1944.
20. Shaw, 488.
21. Aplington memoir.
22. Josephy, 50–51.
23. Leon Slicner, interview with author.
24. Cyril O'Brien, "A Saga of Bravery: Chonito Ridge," *Chevron*, August 12, 1944.
25. Jim McCulley, "Athletes and Dividends," *New York Daily News*, October 14, 1944.
26. Torres, 63–64.
27. Vincent Diaz, "Simply Chamorro: Telling Tales of Demise and Survival in Guam," *Contemporary Pacific* 6, no. 1 (spring 1994): 29–58.
28. Torres, 64.
29. Marine Brigade Report.
30. John McCarthy, *Gung Ho Marines: The Men of Carlson's Raiders* (n.p.: ReView Publications, n.d.), 284.
31. Marine Brigade Report.
32. Rosenquist, Sexton, and Buerlein, 126.
33. Dyer, 943.
34. Owsley.
35. Fred L. DiDomenico, interview with Richard Misenhimer, October 27, 2005, National Museum of the Pacific War, Fredericksburg, Texas.
36. Frances.

37. James Kinall, "On Guam Paradise Turned Ugly," *Newsday* (New York), August 10, 1994.

38. *Third Division's Two Score and Ten History*, 100; Kevin Hall, "World War II Battle Changed Ubertacci's Life," *Moultrie Observer* (Georgia), November 10, 2012. The story of Margolis's final request sounds like something out of romantic fiction, but it appears to be true.

39. Berry, 179.

40. Smith and Meehl, 424.

41. *Raider Patch*, September 1979.

42. USS *Wayne*, Action Report.

CHAPTER 16. TO THE TOP OF BUNDSCHU

1. Lodge, 62.

2. Smith, *Personal File*, 377.

3. O'Brien, "A Saga of Bravery."

4. *Third Division's Two Score and Ten History*, 102.

5. Smith, *Personal File*, 377–78.

6. Hall letter, Publication files.

7. Capt. Patrick O'Sheel and S/Sergeant Gene Cook, eds., *Semper Fidelis: The U.S. Marines in the Pacific—1942–1945* (New York: William Sloane Associates, 1947), 188–89.

8. "Lieut. Col. Ralph L. Houser Is Awarded Navy Cross for Heroism on Guam Beachhead," *Iowa City Press Citizen*, March 28, 1945.

9. "How the Guam Operation Was Conducted."

10. Ibid.

11. Ibid.

12. Ibid.

13. Metzger.

14. IIIAC Report of Operations.

15. Marine Brigade Report.

16. Robert C. Blaemire, interview, Robert Chester Blaemire Collection (AFC/2001/001/66968), Veterans History Project, American Folklife Center, Library of Congress.

17. Daley, 149.

18. *Raider Patch*, November 1980.

19. USS *Fayette*, Report.

20. Barham.

21. Simone interview.

22. Josephy, 57–58.

23. O'Neill.

24. McMillan et al., 208.

25. O'Neill.

26. Marine Brigade Report.

27. Barker, 214.

28. Barker, 215.

29. Aspley, 52.

30. Ibid.

31. Aspley, 53.

32. O'Neill. O'Neill's diary/memoir, written shortly after the campaign, often employs pseudonyms or names that do not appear on L Company muster rolls, as is the case here.

33. Gillespie, 64.

34. Ibid.

35. Ibid., 65–66.

36. Shaw, 493.

37. Shepherd interview.

38. Smith and Finch, 217.

39. Noble interview.

40. Robert E. Cushman, "The Fight at Fonte," *Marine Corps Gazette*, April 1947.

41. Ibid.

42. Glass letter, Publication files.

43. "'Led His Company Fearlessly,' Story of Racine Captain's Death," *Journal Times* (Racine, WI), October 7, 1944.

44. General Louis H. Wilson, interview with Brigadier General Edwin H. Simmons, 1988, United States Marine Corps, History and Museums Division, Headquarters, Washington, DC; Fletcher Knebel, "The Courageous Americans: Captain Holds the High Ground," *San Fernando Times* (California), September 24, 1960; Mark A. Kiehle, "The Battle of Fonte Hill, Guam, 25–26 July 1944," *Marine Corps Gazette*, July 2003.

45. Fraser E. West, interview, Fraser Edwards West Collection (AFC/2001/001/71918), Veterans History Project, American Folklife Center, Library of Congress.

46. Owsley.

47. Duplantis letter, Publication files.

48. Ron Van Stockum, "30 Years in the Marines: The Rest of the Story (1942–1967) Part 7: The Battle for Guam (1944)," *Sentinel News* (Shelbyville, KY), July 26, 2017.

49. Gailey, 129.

50. "How the Guam Operation Was Conducted."

51. Frances.

52. "How the Guam Operation Was Conducted"; Umezawa and Metzger.

CHAPTER 17. MARINE, YOU DIE!

1. Shaw, 517.

2. Headquarters Expeditionary Troops, Task Force 56 Report on Marianas.

3. Gillespie, 67.

4. Ibid., 68.

5. Lodge, 78.

6. Maharidge, 86.

7. George Popovich, interview, George Popovich Jr. Collection (AFC/2001/001/31157), Veterans History Project, American Folklife Center, Library of Congress.

8. O'Neill.

9. Gillespie, 68.

10. Kaufman.

11. Popovich interview.

12. Maharidge, 87.

13. Gillespie, 68.

14. O'Neill.

15. Pinter was killed the next day by a mortar shell fragment that hit him in the stomach.

16. "Crowley Marine Who Killed Japanese Officer on Guam Loses Battle Prize to Fellow Warrior," *Crowley Post-Signal* (Louisiana), August 30, 1944.

17. Robert Trumbull, "Japs Search Guam Foxholes with Bayonets Tied on Poles," *Honolulu Advertiser*, August 9, 1944.

18. Peterson, 68.

19. Kerins, 124.

20. Yaffe, 51.

21. Salgo survived Guam but was killed on Iwo Jima. Sergeant James E. Hague, "Blades Flash in Weird Night Battle," *Chevron*, September 16, 1944; Shaw, 509.

22. Josephy, 59–61; Frances.

23. Frances.

24. Josephy, 61; "Marines Injured by Grenade in World War II Reunited," *News Leader* (Staunton, VA), November 2, 1992.

25. O'Sheel and Cook, 66–67.

26. Van Stockum.

27. Lodge, 81.

28. Kinall.

29. Gilbert, *Marine Tanks*, 193–94.

30. Yaffe, 52–53.

31. Shaw, 508.

32. Duplantis letter, Publication files.

33. Edwards interview.

34. Rufus Belding, interview, Rufus Belding Collection (AFC/2001/001/73075), Veterans History Project, American Folklife Center, Library of Congress.

35. Duplantis recalled that the reserve consisted of a reinforced squad. Niehaus's Navy Cross citation indicates it was a platoon or its approximate equivalent.

36. Duplantis letter, Publication files.

37. "How the Guam Operation Was Conducted."

38. Earl Albert Selle, "Night of Horror on Guam Told by U.S. Fighting Men," *Honolulu Advertiser*, August 11, 1944; Gene Sherman, "Japs Outwitted by Ruse of Yanks," *Los Angeles Times*, August 13, 1944; Hofmann Navy Cross citation.

39. O'Brien, *Liberation*, 26.

CHAPTER 18. THE FONTE HILL FIGHT

1. Decades later Adamski remarked, "There is not a day that goes by that I don't think of that dog." Tom Berg, "The Four-Legged Platoon That Helped Win a War," *Orange County Register*, July 17, 2009.

2. Done.

3. Palomo and Borja, *Liberation—Guam Remembers*.

4. Kent Delong, *War Heroes: True Stories of Congressional Medal of Honor Recipients* (Westport, CT: Praeger, 1993), 156–57.

5. Ibid., 157.

6. *Third Division's Two Score and Ten History*, 123; "Sixty Japs Die as Montebellan Battles Alone," *Los Angeles Times*, August 25, 1944.

7. Delong, 158.

8. Palomo and Borja, *Liberation—Guam Remembers*.

9. Delong, 158.

10. Kiehle.

11. Palomo and Borja, *Liberation—Guam Remembers*.

12. Frederick W. Bechtold, interview, Frederick William Bechtold Collection (AFC/ 2001/001/90415), Veterans History Project, American Folklife Center, Library of Congress.

13. Sergeant Harold Breard, "Glenwood Officer Leads 20 Volunteers on Guam to Wipe Out 43 Japanese," *Troy Messenger* (Alabama), December 4, 1944; "Lieut. Joe Curtis Is Hero at Guam," *Huntsville Times* (Alabama), December 24, 1944. Curtis, whose younger brother had been killed in a military plane crash in 1942, did not survive the war. He was killed on Iwo Jima at the very end of the campaign.

14. Belzer letter, Publication files.

15. Aplington memoir.

16. Smith, *Personal File*, 379–80.

17. Aplington memoir.

18. Letcher, 307–08.

19. Kerins, 126.

20. Ibid.

21. Kiehle; Wilson interview.

22. Wilson interview.

23. Foley interview.

24. West interview.

25. O'Sheel and Cook, 71–72.

26. Van Stockum.

27. O'Sheel and Cook, 72–73.

28. Van Stockum.

29. Tom Bartlett, "3d Tank Battalion: Warriors of World II," *Leatherneck Magazine*, January 1989.

30. Frances.

31. The official record erroneously lists White as suffering a bayonet wound.

32. Kerins, 129.

33. Sherman.

34. O'Brien, *Liberation*, 25.

35. Philip G. Reed, "Wounded Marine Corporal Plays Dead to Stay Alive on Guam," *Fort Worth Star-Telegram*, August 12, 1944.

36. Duplantis letter, Publication files.

37. Ibid.

38. Ibid.

39. "Lieut. Tom Brock Reveals Guam Battle Experiences"; Maj. Frank O. Hough, *The Island War: The United States Marine Corps in the Pacific* (Philadelphia: J. P. Lippincott and Company, 1947), 274.

40. General Robert E. Cushman, interview with Benis M. Frank, 1982, United States Marine Corps, History and Museums Division, Washington, DC.

41. Noble interview.

42. Kight interview.

43. Letcher, 310.

44. Sergeant Jim Healey, "Greater Boston Marines Heroes on Guam's D-Day," *Boston Globe*, November 13, 1944.

45. PC-555, Action Report.

46. USS *Zeilin* (APA3), Action Report, July 21–26, 1944.

47. USS *Monrovia* (APA31), Report of Operations during Amphibious Assault on Guam.

48. Letcher, 312–13; Lodge, 85.

49. Belding interview.

50. Frank A. Bosse, interview, Frank A. Bosse Collection (AFC/2001/001/31887), Veterans History Project, American Folklife Center, Library of Congress.

51. *Rixey*, Action Report.

52. Ibid.

53. "How the Guam Operation Was Conducted."

54. Higuchi, *The Japanese Administration of Guam*, 236.

55. Task Force 56, Report on Marianas.

56. "How the Guam Operation Was Conducted."

57. Lodge, 80.

58. "How the Guam Operation Was Conducted."

59. Task Force 56, Report on Marianas.

60. Sergeant Francis H. Barr, "Jap Night Raid Fails. Thin Line of Marines Beats Off Banzai Charge," *Chevron*, August 19, 1944.

61. Maharidge, 152.

62. Frank, 113.

63. *Third Division's Two Score and Ten History*, 99.

64. Ibid., 104.

65. "How the Guam Operation Was Conducted."

66. Lodge, 87.

67. "How the Guam Operation Was Conducted."

68. Ibid.

69. Lodge, 87.

70. Owsley.

71. Smith and Finch, 217.

72. General Merwin H. Silverthorn, interview with Benis Frank, March 1969, United States Marine Corps, History and Museums Division, Washington, DC.

73. Noble interview.

CHAPTER 19. BATTLE FOR OROTE

1. O'Neill.

2. Gillespie, 68–69.

3. Marine Brigade Report.

4. Maharidge, 102.

5. Aspley, 55.

6. Sixth Marine Division Association, *Sixth Marine Division: The Striking Sixth* (Paducah, KY: Turner Publishing Co., 1987), 65.

7. The numbers of tanks reported destroyed during the campaign were invariably inflated, probably at least in part because of multiple reports about the same tanks. Marine Brigade Report.

8. Marine Brigade Report; IIIAC Report of Operations.

9. Horace "Cal" Frost, interview, Horace Calvert Frost Collection (AFC/2001/001/23790), Veterans History Project, American Folklife Center, Library of Congress.

10. *Raider Patch*, September 1979.

11. Daley, 149.

12. Maj. Anthony Walker, "Advance on Orote Peninsula," *Raider Patch*, November 1983.

13. Gillespie, 69.

14. O'Neill.

15. Marine Brigade Report.

16. Shaw, 522.

17. Gillespie, 70.

18. *Raider Patch*, July 1983.

19. Ibid., September 1979.

20. Sergeant Murrey Marder, "Battlefield Surgery on Guam Doctors, Corpsmen Invasion Heroes, Pharmacist's Mate Amputates Leg of Marine In Foxhole," *Chevron*, August 26, 1944.

21. Aspley, 56–57.

22. Ibid, 57.

23. Lodge, 21.

24. Daley, 157.

25. *Raider Patch*, May 1999.

26. Daley, 160.

27. *Raider Patch*, May 1999.

28. Daley, 160.

29. *Raider Patch*, May 1999.

30. Another account claims the officer was killed by Ostmeyer's runner. Ibid.; Daley, 163–69.

31. Dan Marsh's Raider History.

32. *Raider Patch*, May 1999.

33. Gilbert, *Marine Tanks*, 197.

34. "Tanks on Guam," *Marine Corps Gazette*, October 1944.

35. Joseph F. Bartkiewicz, interview, Joseph Francis Bartkiewicz Collection (AFC/2001/001/85860), Veterans History Project, American Folklife Center, Library of Congress.

36. *Raider Patch*, January 1982.

37. *Raider Patch*, May 1999.

38. Daley, 171.

39. Palomo, *An Island in Agony*, 200.

40. Marine Brigade Report.

41. Gilbert, *Marine Tanks*, 197.

42. *Raider Patch*, January 1982.

43. Lodge, 95.

44. Daley, 172.
45. Smith and Finch, 218. In 1952, when asked to comment on a draft of O. R. Lodge's official study of the campaign, three years after the publication of his own controversial *Coral and Brass*, Smith responded, "No comment is made on the enclosures other than the suggestion that all mention of my efforts to speed up the attack on Guam be omitted." Note dated October 13, 1952, in Publication files. In a separate comment to Lodge, General Silverthorn objected to the implication that Smith "built a fire" under Geiger, saying, "Nobody ever had to prod General Geiger into action." Note dated October 16, 1952, in Publication files.

CHAPTER 20. THEY ARE AMERICANS

1. Steffy and Steffy.
2. Erin Thompson, "Retracing Old Steps: War Survivor Returns to Manenggon 66 Years After Imprisonment," Pacific *Daily News*, July 25, 2010.
3. Steffy and Steffy.
4. Bordallo and Gault.
5. Ibid.
6. Steffy and Steffy.
7. Ibid.
8. Ibid.
9. Juan Baza testimony, Guam War Claims Review Comission, Hagatna, Guam, December 9, 2003.
10. Ibid.
11. Steffy and Steffy.
12. Crowl, 355.
13. Henry D. Lopez, *From Jackson to Japan: The History of Company C, 307th Infantry, 77th Division in World War II* (privately published, 1977), 73.
14. Grace Rishell, "A Soldier Returns to the Battlefield," *Pittsburgh Post-Gazette*, July 14, 1994.
15. Walter Jacobs, interview, 2020, National World War II Museum Oral History Collection, New Orleans, Louisiana.
16. Stephen G. Ostrander and Martha A. Bloomfield, *The Sweetness of Freedom: Stories of Immigrants* (East Lansing: Michigan State University Press, 2010), 188–89.
17. Cull W. Forbus, interview with Chuck Nichols, February 17, 2005, National Museum of the Pacific War, Fredericksburg, Texas.
18. Cushman interview.
19. Ibid.
20. Josephy, 66.
21. Gilbert, *Marine Tanks*, 195.
22. "How the Guam Operation Was Conducted."
23. Sherrill interview.
24. Frank, 107.
25. Barham.
26. Smith, *Personal File*, 378.
27. Henderson letter, Publication files.
28. Cushman letter, Publication files.

29. Pratt, 280.

30. Shaw, 531.

31. Brigadier General John A. Scott, "Scott: Guam Was Destroyed to Be Saved," *Pacific Daily News*, July 21, 1984.

32. Snedeker letter, Publication files.

33. Aplington memoir.

34. Silverthorn interview.

35. *Guam: Operations of the 77th Division (21 July to 10 August 1944)* (Washington, DC: Historical Division, War Department, 1946), 70.

36. Kevin Lollar, "Nerve-wracking Mission," *Fort Myers News-Press* (Florida), July 28, 1994.

37. Ibid.

38. Task Force 56, Report on Guam Operation.

39. IIIAC Report of Operations.

40. Roy Buckner, interview with Rishi Sharma, http://www.youtube.com/watch?v=ewZn-PzmGGHk

41. Francisco G. Lujan and Joaquin Aflague Limtiaco, "Inarajan Uprising," *Pacific Profile*, July 1965.

42. Task Force 56, Report on Guam Operation.

43. Ibid.

44. Steffy and Steffy.

45. Higuchi, *The Japanese Administration of Guam*, 236.

46. "How the Guam Operation Was Conducted."

47. IIIAC Report of Operations.

48. Higuchi, *The Japanese Administration of Guam*, 221; Palomo, *An Island in Agony*, 190.

49. "How the Guam Operation Was Conducted."

50. Aurthur, 157.

51. Smith, *Personal File*, 381.

52. *Ours to Hold It High*, 84.

53. Thomas J. Donnelly, *"Hey Padre": The Saga of a Regimental Chaplain in World War II* (New York: 77th Division Association, n.d.), 76–77.

54. Lollar.

55. Sergeant Theo C. Link, "Japs Deserted Agana during Marine Attack," *Courier-News* (Bridgewater, NJ), October 7, 1944.

56. Martin, "Notes from Guam."

57. William P. Morgan, interview, William Paul Morgan Collection (AFC/2001/001/30140), Veterans History Project, American Folklife Center, Library of Congress.

58. Ibid.

59. Clark letter, Publication files.

60. Scott.

61. Aplington memoir.

62. Thompson.

63. *Ours to Hold It High*, 85.

64. Figueroa and Bannan.

65. Blaz, 139–40.

66. Bordallo and Gault.

67. Watanabe, "Woman Recalls Life."

68. Bordallo and Gault.

69. Robert Trumbull, "Liberated Chamorros Tell Dramatic Story of Two and a Half Years of Jap Misrule," *Honolulu Advertiser*, August 8, 1944.

70. Thompson.

71. Ostrander and Bloomfield, 191.

72. Trumbull, "Liberated Chamorros."

73. Palomo, *An Island in Agony*, 224.

74. Ostrander and Bloomfield, 191.

75. Larry McManus, "When the Japs Held Guam," *Yank Magazine*, September 22, 1944.

76. Friedman, 100–101.

77. Paul Borja, "Liberators Meet the Liberated," in *Liberation—Guam Remembers*.

78. *Third Division's Two Score and Ten History*, 94.

CHAPTER 21. BARRIGADA

1. *Raider Patch*, September 1979.

2. Letcher, 314.

3. *Raider Patch*, September 1982.

4. Noble L. Beck, interview, Noble L. Beck Collection (AFC/2001/001/9125), Veterans History Project, American Folklife Center, Library of Congress.

5. Russell Baker, interview, Abraham Lincoln Presidential Library and Museum Oral History Collection, Springfield, Illinois.

6. Ralph M. Schultz, interview with Richard Misenhimer, July 29, 2019, National Museum of the Pacific War, Fredericksburg, Texas.

7. Bechtold interview.

8. Bessette interview.

9. Sherrill interview.

10. Sheldon L. Lansky, interview, Sheldon L. Lasky Collection (AFC/2001/001/42311), Veterans History Project, American Folklife Center, Library of Congress.

11. Maharidge, 99.

12. O'Donnell, 140.

13. Beck interview.

14. Yoshio "Victor" Nishijima, interview, August 28, 1998, Go for Broke National Education Center Oral History Project.

15. Gillespie, 76–77; Maharidge, 88–89, 102.

16. "How the Guam Operation Was Conducted."

17. Ibid.

18. Crowl, 378.

19. "How the Guam Operation Was Conducted."

20. Ibid.; Crowl, 378.

21. Lodge, 122; Pratt, 286.

22. Gailey, 161.

23. Maj. General A. D. Bruce, "Administration, Supply, and Evacuation of the 77th Infantry Division on Guam," *Military Review*, December 1944.

24. Crowl, 382.

25. Ibid.
26. Barham.
27. Schultz interview.
28. Josephy, 67.
29. *Ours to Hold It High*, 93.
30. *Guam: Operations of the 77th Division*, 82–83.
31. Ibid.
32. Less than a year later, Desmond Doss would earn the Medal of Honor for his actions on Okinawa. Booten Herndon, *The Unlikeliest Hero: The Story of Desmond Doss* (Mountainview, CA: Pacific Press Publishing Association, 1967), 66.
33. Ibid., 59.
34. *Guam: Operations of the 77th Division*, 89.
35. Herndon, 60.
36. Kunze was killed in action in May 1945 on Okinawa.
37. *Guam: Operations of the 77th Division*, 92.
38. Crowl, 393.
39. *Guam: Operations of the 77th Division*, 94.
40. Ibid., 96.
41. Ibid., 97.
42. Ibid., 101; Crowl, 396.
43. *Ours to Hold It High*, 100.

CHAPTER 22. THE ROAD TO FINEGAYAN

1. William Worden, "The Battle of Guam's Agana Over but Its Peace Has Not Yet Begun," *Honolulu Star-Bulletin*, August 23, 1944.
2. Ibid.; "Guam Farmers in Good Shape: Townspeople Have Nothing Left," *Reno Gazette-Journal* (Nevada), August 22, 1944.
3. Watanabe, "Woman Recalls Life."
4. Gillespie, 78.
5. Operations Plan No. 1, 1st Provisional Marine Brigade (TG 53.11), May 15, 1944.
6. Guam Island Command War Diary, March 30–August 15, 1944.
7. Putney, 173–74.
8. O'Sheel and Cook, 61.
9. Robert Pavlovich, interview with author.
10. Burtis Anderson, interview with author.
11. Josephy, 69.
12. James Ganopulos, interview with author.
13. O'Sheel and Cook, 61.
14. Ibid.; Josephy, 69–70.
15. Ganopulos interview.
16. Barham.
17. "How the Guam Operation Was Conducted."
18. Henderson letter, Publication files.
19. *Guam: Operations of the 77th Division*, 104.
20. Clark letter, Publication files.

21. Stokes letter, Publication files.
22. Lodge, 138.
23. Kight interview.
24. Shaw, 547.
25. "How the Guam Operation Was Conducted."
26. Reineke letter, Publication files.
27. *Ours to Hold It High*, 101.
28. Henderson letter, Publication files.
29. Crowl, 406.
30. Gailey, 166.
31. Crowl, 406.
32. Lodge, 137.
33. Crowl, 397.
34. Lodge, 129.
35. Ibid., 398.
36. Gailey, 167.
37. Task Force 56, Report on Marianas.
38. Craig letter, Publication files.
39. Crowl, 334; *Guam: Operations of the 77th Division*, 111; Japanese Monograph No. 48.
40. Sergeant John W. Chapman, "Guam Incident Better Than Movies," *Chevron*, August 4, 1945. Eyewitness descriptions indicate that this was in fact a separate incident.
41. *Ours to Hold It High*, 110.
42. Ibid., 111.
43. Craig Smith, *Counting the Days: POWs, Internees, and Stragglers of World War II in the Pacific* (Washington, DC: Smithsonian Books, 2011), 64–65.
44. Crowl, 416.
45. Bruce letter, Publication files.
46. Coleman letter, Publication files

CHAPTER 23. SHOOTOUT AT YIGO

1. *Ours to Hold It High*, 113.
2. Noble interview.
3. "How the Guam Operation Was Conducted."
4. *Ours to Hold It High*, 116.
5. Ibid., 117.
6. "Enemy in Wild Flight on Guam," *Holdredge Daily Citizen* (Nebraska), August 8, 1944.
7. *Ours to Hold It High*, 119–20.
8. Henderson letter, Publication files.
9. Josephy, 91.
10. Charles P. Arnot, "Heroic Yanks Seize Vital Jap Position," *Long Beach Sun* (California), July 31, 1944.
11. William Worden, "Japs Leave Grisly Scene: 42 Guam Natives Slain," *Salt Lake Tribune*, September 3, 1944.
12. Figueroa and Bannan.
13. Henderson letter, Publication files.

14. Denfeld, 204.
15. "How the Guam Operation Was Conducted."
16. Ibid.
17. Task Force 56, Report on Marianas.
18. Ibid.
19. 706th Tank Battalion, After Action Report, July 21–August 9, 1944.
20. "How the Guam Operation Was Conducted."
21. *Guam: Operations of the 77th Division*, 131.
22. *Ours to Hold It High*, 123.
23. Months later, a group of Japanese POWs were permitted to pick through the debris to retrieve the skeletal remains of their former leaders from the headquarters bunker. The bones were cremated.

CHAPTER 24. THE WAR GOES ON

1. Letter to Cmdr. David G. Click, August 20, 1944, Geiger Papers.
2. Sherrill interview.
3. Robinson interview.
4. Guam Island Command War Diary, August 1944.
5. Robinson interview.
6. Guam Island Command War Diary, July 1945.
7. Ibid., September 1944.
8. Masako Watanabe, "Japanese Straggler Recalls Nearly 8-Year Survival in Jungle," *Pacific Daily News* July 12, 2017.
9. Gailey, 194.
10. Smith, *Counting the Days*, 165.
11. Guam Island Command War Diary, September 1944.
12. S/Sergeant Harold Powell, "Fanatic's Little Trick Backfires," *Honolulu Star-Bulletin*, August 25, 1944; "'Human Bomb' Explodes in Corsair, Jap Stays Hidden in Ship 9 Hours Awaiting Flight," *Chevron*, September 16, 1944.
13. *Raider Patch*, September 1986.
14. Smith and Meehl.
15. Done.
16. *Raider Patch*, September 1986.
17. Edwards interview.
18. Morgan interview.
19. Contreras interview.
20. Aspley, 60.
21. Friedman, 110–12.
22. Al Dopking and Elmont Waite, "Guam Fast Becoming Second Pearl Harbor," *Rhinelander Daily News* (Wisconsin), February 27, 1945.
23. Guam Island Command War Diary, April 1945.
24. Hogaboom interview.
25. Tina Ligon, "The Christmas Shootings on Guam: Charges of Unlawful Assembly and Rioting Followed," *Prologue: Quarterly of the National Archives and Records Administration* 46,

no. 4 (winter 2014): 46–51; Bernard Nalty, *The Right to Fight: African-American Marines in World War II* (Washington, DC: Marine Corps Historical Center, 1995).

26. Earl B. Ercanback, "Letter to International Red Cross Representative, Report of Treatment While Held as Prisoner of War," August 30, 1945, http://www.mansell.com /pow_resources.

27. Smith, *Counting the Days*, 78.

28. Iannarelli and Iannarelli, 59–60.

29. Mansell, *Captured*, 73.

30. Iannarelli and Iannarelli, 64–65.

31. Ercanback.

32. Mansell, *Captured*, 137.

33. Smith, *Counting the Days*, 137–45.

34. Boyle, 137.

35. Mansell, *Captured*, 178.

36. Raj Sood, "Marine Endures War in POW Camp," in *Liberation—Guam Remembers*).

37. Howard interview.

38. Smith, *Counting the Days*, 186.

39. Lansky interview.

40. Hogaboom interview.

41. Guam Island Command War Diary, August 1944.

42. Linn.

43. IIIAC Report of Operations.

44. Higuchi, *The Japanese Administration of Guam*, 237.

45. Robert Amstutz, interview with Richard Misenhimer, July 28, 2008, National Museum of the Pacific War, Fredericksburg, Texas.

46. Linn.

47. Ibid., 242.

48. Guam Island Command War Diary, May 1945.

49. Higuchi, *The Japanese Administration of Guam*, 243.

50. Case of Koju Shoji and Kiyoshi Takahashi, August 30, 1945, Record of Proceedings of a Military Commission Convened at Agana, Guam, by Order of the Island Commander.

51. Kyle Palmer, "Priest Who Defied Japanese Revered," *Los Angeles Times*, April 1, 1945; "Story of Father Duenas."

CHAPTER 25. HOME ALIVE IN '45

1. Potter, 384–85.

2. Iannarelli and Iannarelli, 161–63.

3. Hale, 135.

4. Ibid., 136.

5. Smith, *Counting the Days*, 186.

6. Mansell, *Captured*, 182.

7. Iannerelli and Iannerelli, 163.

8. *315th Bomb Wing (VH) Anthologies* (Cocoa Beach, FL: 315th Bomb Wing Association, 1987).

9. Ibid.

10. Ibid.

11. Beccy Tanner, "Kansan Was Aboard B-29 for Last Mission of World War II," *Wichita Eagle*, August 8, 2016.

12. "315th Bomb Wing Anthologies."

13. Ibid.

14. Don Moore, "War Tales: 1st Lt. Bob Wachter Flew Last B-29 Mission over Japan in WWII," *War Tales*, December 26. 2011, https://donmooreswartales.com/2011/12/26/bob-wachter.

15. "315th Bomb Wing Anthologies."

16. Aurthur, 330.

17. Morgan interview.

18. Myers, 175.

19. Howard interview.

20. Myers, 178.

21. Smith, *Counting the Days*, 187.

22. Sood.

23. Mansell, *Captured*, 187.

24. Howard interview.

25. "Vision of Old Glory in Disgrace."

26. Guam Island Command War Diary, July 1945.

27. Ibid., August 1945.

28. Higuchi, *The Japanese Administration of Guam*, 238.

29. Keith L. Camacho, *Sacred Men: Law, Torture and Retribution in Guam* (Durham, NC: Duke University Press, 2019), 57.

30. In 1982, Shinohara's son, then a U.S. Air Force master sergeant, mounted a legal effort to erase his father's treason conviction, an effort that met with a chilly reception. Case of Samuel T. Shinohara, July 28, 1945, Record of Proceedings of a Military Commission Convened at Agana, Guam, by Order of the Island Commander.

31. Linn; Case of Koju Shoji and Kiyoshi Takahashi.

32. Hale, 3–4.

33. Blas.

34. Howard interview.

35. Simone interview.

36. Barham.

37. Case of Koju Shoji and Kiyoshi Takahashi (addenda).

38. Harold Martin, "Hangings Went Off with Dispatch if Rexrod Presided, Martin Says," *Atlanta Constitution*, December 23, 1948.

39. Case of Koju Shoji and Kiyoshi Takahashi (addenda).

EPILOGUE. RUMINATIONS ON "THE GOOD WAR"

1. Silverthorn interview.

2. Stephen R. Taaffe, *Commanding the Pacific: Marine Corps Generals in World War II* (Annapolis, MD: Naval Institute Press, 2021), 130.

3. Ibid., 129.

4. Bruce letter, Publication files.

5. IIIAC Report of Operations.

6. Wilson interview.

7. Silverthorn interview.

8. George W. Garand and Truman R. Strobridge, *Western Pacific Operations: History of U.S. Marine Corps Operations in World War II* (Washington, DC: Historical Division, Headquarters, U.S. Marine Corps, 1971), 4:280.

9. Hoffman letter, Publication files.

10. Conolly letter, Publication files.

11. Silverthorn interview.

12. *Third Division's Two Score and Ten History*, 113.

13. Marine Brigade Report.

14. Robert Asprey, *Once a Marine: The Memoirs of General A. A. Vandegrift, U.S.M.C* (New York: W. W. Norton and Company, 1964), 267.

15. Jeter A. Isely and Philip A. Crowl, *The U.S. Marines and Amphibious War* (Princeton, NJ: Princeton University Press, 1951), 379.

16. "How the Guam Operation Was Conducted"; Umezawa and Metzger.

17. Maharidge, 20.

18. Louis E. Smith, interview, Louis Edward Smith Collection (AFC/2001/001/76351), Veterans History Project, American Folklife Center, Library of Congress.

19. Lansky interview.

20. Anthony N. De Martino, interview, Anthony N. De Martino Collection (AFC/2001/001/68521), Veterans History Project, American Folklife Center, Library of Congress.

21. Hays passed away on September 3, 2020; he was ninety-five years old. O'Donnell, 136.

22. Howard interview.

23. Ibid.; Sam Jacobs, "Survival and Salvation: Ed Howard, Once a POW, Shaped Terre Haute's Library System," *Terre Haute Tribune-Star*, August 14, 2020.

24. Carlisle E. Evans, interview, Carlisle E. Evans Collection (AFC/2001/001/13282), Veterans History Project, American Folklife Center, Library of Congress.)

25. "Unemployed Miner Had Problems," *Daily Herald* (Provo, UT), July 9, 1961.

26. Another source claims twelve POWs and 174 killed.

27. Spelling varies in accounts.

28. "Suspended Term Given Killer of Jap War Straggler," *Palladium-Item* (Richmond, IN), July 20, 1962.

29. Tetsuro Morimoto et al., *Twenty-Eight Years in the Guam Jungle* (Tokyo and San Francisco: Japan Publications, 1972), 110.

30. Matthew J. Seiden, "Japanese Soldier Who Hid on Guam 27 Years Prefers Jungle," *Baltimore Sun*, April 23, 1974.

31. Legion of Merit citation.

32. Jasmine Stole Weiss, "George Tweed, Controversial War Hero, Refused to Surrender When Japanese Forces Invaded," *Pacific Daily News*, July 15, 2019.

33. "Ghost of Guam Hissed and Booed on His Return," *Spokane Chronicle* (Washington), September 16, 1946.

34. Todd.

35. Lourdes Pangelinan, "Tweed, to Some a Hero, to Some Only Ungrateful," *Pacific Daily News*, July 15, 1984.

36. Weiss.

37. Anne Perez Hattori, "Guardians of Our Soil: Indigenous Responses to Post–World War II Military Land Appropriation on Guam," in *Farms, Firms and Runways: Perspectives on U.S. Military Bases in the Western Pacific*, ed. L. Eve Armentrout Ma (Chicago: Imprint Publications, 2001), 190.

38. Letter, Photographic Reference File, National Archives, RG 127, Box 14, Folder 89.

39. Camacho, *Sacred Men*, 177; Angel Santos, "U.S. Return Was Reoccupation, Not Liberation," *Pacific Daily News*, July 21, 1991.

40. Samantha Marley Barnett, "The Influential Voice of Beatrice Perez Emsley," *Stars and Stripes*, July 12, 2019; Howard Handleman, "Condemned, 'Executed' by Japanese Headsmen, Guamanian Boy, Girl Escape Guam Grave: Youths Were Charged with Aiding Yankees," *Pacific Profile*, July 1964.

41. Barnett.

42. Paul Borja, "The Lasting Legacy of a Liberator," in *Liberation—Guam Remembers*.

BIBLIOGRAPHY

ORAL HISTORIES AND INTERVIEWS

Amstutz, Robert. Interview with Richard Misenhimer, July 28, 2008. National Museum of the Pacific War, Fredericksburg, Texas.

Anderson, Burtis. Interview with author.

Anderson, Creede John. Interview. Creede John Anderson Collection (AFC/2001/001/10040), Veterans History Project, American Folklife Center, Library of Congress, Washington, DC.

Anderson, Joseph R. Interview. Joseph Robert Anderson Collection (AFC/2001/001/59011), Veterans History Project, American Folklife Center, Library of Congress, Washington, DC.

Backman, Thomas E. Interview. Thomas E. Backman Collection (AFC/2001/001/2912), Veterans History Project, American Folklife Center, Library of Congress, Washington, DC.

Baker, Russell. Interview. Abraham Lincoln Presidential Library and Museum Oral History Collection, Springfield, Illinois.

Barnett, Carroll D. Interview, February 10 and October 27, 2000. Roger Mansell Collection. http://www.mansell.com/pow-index.html.

Bartkiewicz, Joseph F. Interview. Joseph Francis Bartkiewicz Collection (AFC/2001/001/85860), Veterans History Project, American Folklife Center, Library of Congress, Washington, DC.

Baza, Juan U. Testimony during Guam War Claims Review Commission Public Hearings Held in Hagåtña, Guam, December 9, 2003. https://www.guamwarsurvivorstory.com.

Bechtold, Frederick W. Interview. Frederick William Bechtold Collection (AFC/2001/001/90415), Veterans History Project, American Folklife Center, Library of Congress, Washington, DC.

Beck, Noble L. Interview. Noble L. Beck Collection (AFC/2001/001/9125), Veterans History Project, American Folklife Center, Library of Congress, Washington, DC.

Belding, Rufus. Interview. Rufus Belding Collection (AFC/2001/001/73075), Veterans History Project, American Folklife Center, Library of Congress, Washington, DC.

Bessette, George L. Interview. George L. Bessette Collection (AFC/2001/001/18556), Veterans History Project, American Folklife Center, Library of Congress, Washington, DC.

Binn, Donald A. Interview with Luke Thompson, May 9, 2009. Kansas Historical Society, Topeka, Kansas.

Blaemire. Robert C. Interview. Robert Chester Blaemire Collection (AFC/2001/001/ 66968), Veterans History Project, American Folklife Center, Library of Congress, Washington, DC.

Blaz, Ben. Interview with Ronald E. Marcello, October 8, 1994. University of North Texas Oral History Collection (No. 1042). https://texashistory.unt.edu/ark:/67531 /metapth1606451.

Blaz, Vicente (Ben). Interview with Jerry Mannering, November 17, 2006. National Museum of the Pacific War, Fredericksburg, Texas.

Bosse, Frank A. Interview. Frank A. Bosse Collection (AFC/2001/001/31887), Veterans History Project, American Folklife Center, Library of Congress, Washington, DC.

Botts, Robert H. Interview with Mark Van Ells, 1997. Wisconsin Veterans Museum Research Center.

Bowser, Alpha. Interview with Bill Alexander, March 12, 1998. National Museum of the Pacific War, Fredericksburg, Texas.

Bowser, Gen. Alpha L. Interview with Benis M. Frank, 1970. United States Marine Corps, History and Museums Division, Washington, DC.

Bradshaw, James. Interview. James Bradshaw Collection (AFC/2001/001/90054), Veterans History Project, American Folklife Center, Library of Congress, Washington, DC.

Brandt, Donald C. Interview. Donald C. Brandt Collection (AFC/2001/001/15861), Veterans History Project, American Folklife Center, Library of Congress, Washington, DC.

Buckner, Roy. Interview with Rishi Sharma. https://www.youtube.com/watch?v=ewZn- PzmGGHk.

Buege, Frederick H. Interview. Frederick Herman Buege Collection (AFC/2001/001/ 89324), Veterans History Project, American Folklife Center, Library of Congress, Washington, DC.

Chuck, Harris J. Interview. National World War II Museum Oral History Collection, New Orleans, Louisiana.

Church, Ray. Interview. National World War II Museum Oral History Collection, New Orleans, Louisiana.

Contreras, Ralph M. Interview. Ralph Martin Contreras Collection (AFC/2001/001/ 9127), Veterans History Project, American Folklife Center, Library of Congress, Washington, DC.

Contreras, Ralph. Interview with Mark DePue, May 20, 2011. Abraham Lincoln Presidential Library and Museum Oral History Collection, Springfield, Illinois.

Craig, Gen. Edward Arthur. Interview with Lloyd E. Tatem, May 16, 1968. United States Marine Corps, History and Museums Division, Washington, DC.

Cushman, Gen. Robert E. Interview with Benis M. Frank, 1982. United States Marine Corps, History and Museums Division, Washington, DC.

Davis, John B. Interview with John K. Driscoll, 2004. Wisconsin Veterans Museum Research Center, Madison, Wisconsin.

De Martino, Anthony N. Interview. Anthony N. De Martino Collection (AFC/2001/001/ 68521), Veterans History Project, American Folklife Center, Library of Congress, Washington, DC.

Del Valle, Gen. Pedro A. Interview with Benis M. Frank, November–December 1966. United States Marine Corps, History and Museums Division, Washington, DC.

Dent, Robert M. Interview. Robert Miller Dent Jr. Collection (AFC/2001/001/70650), Veterans History Project, American Folklife Center, Library of Congress, Washington, DC.

DiDomenico, Fred L. Interview with Richard Misenhimer, October 27, 2005. National Museum of the Pacific War, Fredericksburg, Texas.

Dunbar, Calvin Warner. Interview. Calvin Warner Dunbar Collection (AFC/2001/001/51656), Veterans History Project, American Folklife Center, Library of Congress, Washington, DC.

Edwards, Hendon H. Interview. Hendon H. Edwards Collection (AFC/2001/001/04510), Veterans History Project, American Folklife Center, Library of Congress, Washington, DC.

Erskine, Gen. Graves B. Interview with Benis M. Frank, 1970. United States Marine Corps, History and Museums Division, Washington, DC.

Evans, Carlisle E. Interview. Carlisle E. Evans Collection (AFC/2001/001/13282), Veterans History Project, American Folklife Center, Library of Congress, Washington, DC.

Foley, John. Interview with Richard Misenhimer, March 26, 2002. National Museum of the Pacific War, Fredericksburg, Texas.

Forbus, Cull W. Interview with Chuck Nichols, February 17, 2005. National Museum of the Pacific War, Fredericksburg, Texas.

Fowler, Trenton. Interview with Floyd Cox, January 17, 2001. National Museum of the Pacific War, Fredericksburg, Texas.

Fox, Aaron S. Interview. Aaron S. Fox Collection (AFC/2001/001/05232), Veterans History Project, American Folklife Center, Library of Congress, Washington, DC.

Frost, Horace. Interview. Horace Calvert Frost Collection (AFC/2001/001/23790), Veterans History Project, American Folklife Center, Library of Congress, Washington, DC.

Gallo, James A. Interview. James Aloysius Gallo Collection (AFC/2001/001/44217), Veterans History Project, American Folklife Center, Library of Congress, Washington, DC.

Ganopulos, James. Interview with author.

Graham, Harold R. Interview. Harold R. Graham Collection (AFC/2001/001/3885), Veterans History Project, American Folklife Center, Library of Congress, Washington, DC.

Hill, Adm. Harry W. Interviews with John T. Mason, Jr., 1967 and 1968. Columbia Center for Oral History, Columbia University, New York, New York.

Hiott, Joseph. Interview. Witness to War Foundation. https://www.witnesstowar.org/combat_stories/WWII/6195.

Hogaboom, Gen. Robert E. Interview with Benis M. Frank, April 1970. United States Marine Corps, History and Museums Division, Washington, DC.

Howard, Edward N. Interview with Darlene Norman, 1980. Vigo County Public Library/Wabash Valley Press Club, Terre Haute, Indiana.

Howard, Edward N. Interview with William Pickett, 1981. Vigo County Publish Library/Wabash Valley Press Club, Terre Haute, Indiana.

Jacobs, Walter. Interview, 2020. National World War II Museum Oral History Collection, New Orleans, Louisiana.

Jacobson, Martin. Interview. National World War II Museum Oral History Collection, New Orleans, Louisiana.

Joslin, Harold E. Interview. National World War II Museum Oral History Collection, New Orleans, Louisiana.

Judd, Robert. Interview, December 20, 2021. National World War II Museum Oral History Collection, New Orleans, Louisiana.

Karbin, Henry. Interview. Henry Karbin Collection (AFC/2001/001/42144), Veterans History Project, American Folklife Center, Library of Congress, Washington, DC.

Kasperbauer, Carmen Artero. Interview in *An Island Invaded*, directed by Esther Figueroa and Jim Bannan. Honolulu: PREL, 2004.

Kerins, John J. Interview. John J. Kerins Collection (AFC/2001/001/2607), Veterans History Project, American Folklife Center, Library of Congress, Washington, DC.

Kight, Joseph. Interview with Richard Misenhimer, December 27, 2007. National Museum of the Pacific War, Fredericksburg, Texas.

Kiser, Lt. R.W. Interview. OpNav-16-V-# E553, February 16, 1945. United States Naval Air Station, Pensacola, Florida.

Kuzma, Stephen F. Interview. Stephen Fred Kuzma Collection (AFC/2001/001/45015), Veterans History Project, American Folklife Center, Library of Congress, Washington, DC.

Lansky, Sheldon L. Interview. Sheldon L. Lasky Collection (AFC/2001/001/42311), Veterans History Project, American Folklife Center, Library of Congress, Washington, DC.

Maier, Charles F. Interview. Charles F. Maier Collection (AFC/2001/001/52741), Veterans History Project, American Folklife Center, Library of Congress, Washington, DC.

McClure, John. Interview. John McClure Collection (AFC/2001/001/9534), Veterans History Project, American Folklife Center, Library of Congress, Washington, DC.

Morgan, William P. Interview. William Paul Morgan Collection (AFC/2001/001/30140), Veterans History Project, American Folklife Center, Library of Congress, Washington, DC.

Morimoto, Shinji. Interview, June 12, 2008. Japanese American Military History Collective. https://ndajams.omeka.net.

Mosher, Alfred. Interview. National World War II Museum Oral History Collection, New Orleans, Louisiana.

Nichols, Frank. Interview. Roger Mansell Collection. http://www.mansell.com/pow-index.html.

Nishijima, Yoshio "Victor." Interview, August 28, 1998. Go for Broke National Education Center Oral History Project. https://goforbroke.org.

Noble, Gen. Alfred H. Interview with Lloyd E. Tatem,1968. United States Marine Corps, History and Museums Division, Washington, DC.

Pavlovich, Robert. Interview with author.

Popovich, George. Interview. George Popovich, Jr. Collection (AFC/2001/001/31157), Veterans History Project, American Folklife Center, Library of Congress, Washington, DC.

Powers, Robert A. Interview. National World War II Museum Oral History Collection, New Orleans, Louisiana.

Radel, Lawrence F. Interview. Lawrence Frank Radel Collection (AFC/2001/001/86891), Veterans History Project, American Folklife Center, Library of Congress, Washington, DC.

Rainey, Calvin E. Interview. Calvin Earl Rainey Collection (AFC/2001/001/65850), Veterans History Project, American Folklife Center, Library of Congress, Washington, DC.

Randall, Carey. Interview with Floyd Cox, February 18, 2005. National Museum of the Pacific War, Fredericksburg, Texas.

Remaklus, Leo A. Interview. Leo A. Remaklus Collection (AFC/2001/001/69026), Veterans History Project, American Folklife Center, Library of Congress, Washington, DC.

Richardson, Gus. Interview. Witness to War Foundation. https://www.witnesstowar.org/combat_stories/WWII/717.

Robinson, Gen. Ray A. Interview with Benis M. Frank, 1968. United States Marine Corps, History and Museums Division, Washington, DC.

Roose, Walter R. Interview. Walter R. Roose Jr. Collection (AFC/2001/001/57455), Veterans History Project, American Folklife Center, Library of Congress, Washington, DC.

Roslansky, Marvin. Interview with Thomas Saylor, June 25, 2004. Concordia University Library, Department of History Oral History Project, Saint Paul, Minnesota.

Schubel, Edward C. Interview. Edward C. Schubel Collection (AFC/2001/001/33269), Veterans History Project, American Folklife Center, Library of Congress, Washington, DC.

Schultz, Ralph M. Interview with Richard Misenhimer, July 29, 2019. National Museum of the Pacific War, Fredericksburg, Texas.

Settles, Edward W. Interview. Edward Wayne Settles Collection (AFC/2001/001/02917), Veterans History Project, American Folklife Center, Library of Congress, Washington, DC.

Shapley, Gen. Alan F. Interview with Thomas E. Donnelly, January 19, 1971. United States Marine Corps, History and Museums Division, Washington, DC.

Shepherd, Gen. Lemuel C., Jr. Interview with Benis M. Frank, 1967. United States Marine Corps, History and Museums Division, Washington, DC.

Sherrill, Billy Wayne. Interview with Mark Cunningham, April 22, 2015. National Museum of the Pacific War, Fredericksburg, Texas.

Silverthorn, Gen. Merwin H. Interview with Benis Frank, March 1969. United States Marine Corps, History and Museums Division, Washington, DC.

Silvestrini, John R. Interview. John R. Silvestrini Collection (AFC/2001/001/14286), Veterans History Project, American Folklife Center, Library of Congress, Washington, DC.

Simone, Frank R. Interview. Frank Robert Simone Collection (AFC/2001/001/79036), Veterans History Project, American Folklife Center, Library of Congress, Washington, DC.

Slicer, Leon. Interview with author.

Smith, Louis E. Interview. Louis Edward Smith Collection (AFC/2001/001/76351), Veterans History Project, American Folklife Center, Library of Congress, Washington, DC.

Spangler, Charles. Interview with Dwight Daniel, June 17, 2003. National Museum of the Pacific War, Fredericksburg, Texas.

Stiles, Neil. Interview with Dwight Daniel, August 17, 2003, National Museum of the Pacific War, Fredericksburg, Texas.

Swain, James L. Interview. James Lowell Swain Collection (AFC/2001/001/4487), Veterans History Project, American Folklife Center, Library of Congress, Washington, DC.

Tweed, George Ray. Interview with Commander Wright, August 25, 1944. Office of the Chief of Naval Operations, Intelligence Division. National Archives, RG 38, Records of the Office of the Chief of Naval Operations.

West, Fraser E. Interview. Fraser Edwards West Collection (AFC/2001/001/71918), Veterans History Project, American Folklife Center, Library of Congress, Washington, DC.

Wilson, Gen. Louis H. Interview with Brig. Gen. Edwin H. Simmons, 1988. United States Marine Corps, History and Museums Division, Washington, DC.

Zobenica, Nicholas. Interview with Thomas Saylor September 26, 2002. Minnesota Historical Society, Saint Paul, Minnesota.

BOOKS AND ARTICLES

Aguon, Tina D. "Combat Patrol Hunts for Stragglers." In *Liberation—Guam Remembers: A Golden Salute for the 50th Anniversary of the Liberation of Guam*. Maite, Guam: Graphic Center, 1994.

"Americans Have Probably Lost the Island of Guam." *Pensacola News Journal*. December 14, 1941.

Anderson, William K., Jr. "The Bravest Man I Have Ever Known." *Marine Corps Gazette*. November 2006.

Apple, Russell A. *Guam: Two Invasions and Three Military Occupations. A Historical Summary of War in the Pacific National Historical Park, Guam*. Mangilao, Guam: Richard F. Taitano Micronesian Area Research Center, University of Guam, 1980.

Arnot, Charles P. "Heroic Yanks Seize Vital Jap Position." *Long Beach Sun* (California), July 31, 1944.

Arnot, Charles, and Mac R. Johnson. "Find Bodies of Natives Beheaded by Japanese." *Sheboygan Press* (Wisconsin). September 2, 1944.

Asprey, Robert. *Once a Marine: The Memoirs of General A. A. Vandegrift, U.S.M.C.* New York: W. W. Norton and Company, 1964.

Astor, Gerald. *Wings of Gold: The U.S. Naval Air Campaign in World War II*. New York: Presidio Press, 2004.

Aurthur, Robert A., et al. *The Third Marine Division*. Washington, DC: Infantry Journal Press, 1948.

Barham, Wayne. "Guam: D-Day Plus 30 Years." *Argosy Magazine*. July 1974.

Barker, Dale L. *Hitting the Beaches: The First Armored Amphibian Battalion in World War II, 1943–1945*. Atlanta: First Armored Amphibian Battalion, 1996.

Barnett, Samantha Marley. "The Influential Voice of Beatrice Perez Emsley." *Stars and Stripes*. July 12, 2019.

Barr, Sgt. Francis H. "Jap Night Raid Fails. Thin Line of Marines Beats Off Banzai Charge." *Chevron*. August 19, 1944.

Bartlett, Tom. "3d Tank Battalion: Warriors of World II." *Leatherneck Magazine*. January 1989.

Bartley, Lt. Col. Whitman S. *Iwo Jima: Amphibious Epic*. Washington, DC: Historical Branch, G-3 Division, Headquarters, U.S. Marine Corps, 1954.

Bates, Maj. Ralph S., Sr. *An American Shame: The Abandonment of an Entire American Population*. CreateSpace, 2016.

Berg, Tom. "The Four-Legged Platoon That Helped Win a War." *Orange County Register*. July 17, 2009.

Berry, Henry. *Semper Fi, Mac: Living Memories of the U.S. Marines in World War II*. New York: Arbor House, 1982.

Blas, Amanda Francel. "War Leaves Lasting Impression on Survivor." *Pacific Daily News*. July 20, 2014.

Blaz, Ben. *Bisita Guam: Let Us Remember Nihi Ta Hasso*. Guam: University of Guam, 2008.

"Body of Japanese Straggler Found Near Guam Shack." *Honolulu Star Bulletin*. May 9, 1962.

Bordallo, Ricardo J., and C. Sablan Gault. "The Journey to Manengon." In *Liberation—Guam Remembers: A Golden Salute for the 50th Anniversary of the Liberation of Guam*. Maite, Guam: Graphic Center, 1994.

Borja, Paul. "In Asan, Banzai and Bravery." In *Liberation—Guam Remembers: A Golden Salute for the 50th Anniversary of the Liberation of Guam*. Maite, Guam: Graphic Center, 1994.

———. "The Lasting Legacy of a Liberator." In *Liberation—Guam Remembers: A Golden Salute for the 50th Anniversary of the Liberation of Guam*. Maite, Guam: Graphic Center, 1994.

———. "Liberators Meet the Liberated." In *Liberation—Guam Remembers: A Golden Salute for the 50th Anniversary of the Liberation of Guam*. Maite, Guam: Graphic Center, 1994.

———. "Sablan Never Afraid to Preach." In *Liberation—Guam Remembers: A Golden Salute for the 50th Anniversary of the Liberation of Guam*. Maite, Guam: Graphic Center, 1994.

Bouslog, Dave. *Maru Killer: War Patrols of the USS* Seahorse. Placentia, CA: R. A. Cline Publishing, 1996.

Boyle, Martin. *Yanks Don't Cry*. New York: Bernard Geis and Associates, 1963.

Breard, Sgt. Harold. "Glenwood Officer Leads 20 Volunteers on Guam to Wipe Out 43 Japanese." *Troy Messenger* (Alabama). December 4, 1944.

Bridgewater, Lt. Col. F. Clay. "Reconnaissance on Guam." *Cavalry Journal*. May–June 1945.

Bruce, Maj. Gen. A. D. "Administration, Supply, and Evacuation of the 77th Infantry Division on Guam." *Military Review*. December 1944.

Burrus, L. D. *The Ninth Marines: A History of the Ninth Marine Regiment in World War II*. Washington, DC: Zenger Publishing, 1985.

Bush, Elizabeth K. *America's First Frogman: The Draper Kauffman Story*. Annapolis, MD: Naval Institute Press, 2004.

Bywater, Hector C. *The Great Pacific War*. New York: St. Martin's Press, 1991.

Camacho, Keith. *Cultures of Commemoration: The Politics of War, Memory, and History in the Mariana Islands*. Honolulu: University of Hawai'i Press, 2011.

———. *Sacred Men: Law, Torture and Retribution in Guam*. Durham, NC: Duke University Press, 2019.

Camp, Col. Richard D. *Lieutenant General Edward A. Craig: Warrior Six: Combat Leader in World War II and Korea*. Philadelphia: Casemate, 2023.

Camp, Dick. *Leatherneck Legends: Conversations with the Marine Corps' Old Breed*. Saint Paul: Zenith Press, 2006.

Carmichael, Scott W. *Bundschu Ridge: At the Tip of the Spear during the Liberation of Guam*. Kindle edition, 2014.

Carter, Lee, William L. Wuerch, and Rosa Roberto Carter, eds. *Guam History: Perspectives*. Vol. 1. MARC Educational Series, no. 20. Mangilao, Guam: Richard F. Taitano Micronesian Area Research Center, University of Guam, 1997.

Cass, Bevan. *History of the Sixth Marine Division*. Washington, DC: Infantry Journal Press, 1948.

Caven, Wesley Frank, and James Lea Cate. *The Army Air Forces in World War II*. Vol. 5: *The Pacific: Matterhorn to Nagasaki, June 1944 to August 1945*. Washington, DC: Office of Air Force History, 1983.

Chapman, Sgt. John W. "Guam Incident Better Than Movies." *Chevron*. August 4, 1945.

Charfauros, Manuel T. "Merizo Massacre." *Pacific Profile*. July 21, 1965.

Clark, Blake. *Robinson Crusoe, USN: The Adventures of George R. Tweed, RM1C, on Jap-Held Guam.* New York: McGraw-Hill Book Co., 1945.

Condit, Kenneth, and Edwin T. Turnbladh. *Hold High the Torch: A History of the 4th Marines.* Nashville: Battery Press, 1989.

Crosley, Robert L. "Picture Makes Last Guam Jap Surrender to U.S." *Daily American* (Somerset, PA). June 23, 1948.

Crowl, Philip. *United States Army in World War II: The War in the Pacific, Campaign in the Marianas.* Washington, DC: Office of the Chief of Military History, Department of the Army, 1960.

"Crowley Marine Who Killed Japanese Officer on Guam Loses Battle Prize to Fellow Warrior." *Crowley Post Signal* (Louisiana). August 30, 1944.

Cruz, Filipe S. "Chamorro Sailor Tells His Story." *Guam Daily News*. July 21, 1969.

Cunningham, Chet. *The Frogmen of World War II: An Oral History of the U.S. Navy's Underwater Demolition Units.* New York: Pocket Books, 2005.

Cushman, Robert E. "The Fight at Fonte." *Marine Corps Gazette*. April 1947.

Daley, LaVarre. *United States Marine Corps Raiders: A Personal Account by LaVarre Daley.* Erie, CO: MJ Clark Publisher, 2002.

Del Valle, P. A. "Massed Fires on Island of Guam." *Marine Corps Gazette*. December 1944.

"Derides Excuse for FBI Failure to Guard Hawaii." *Chicago Tribune*. February 4, 1942.

Delong, Kent. *War Heroes: True Stories of Congressional Medal of Honor Recipients.* Westport, CT: Praeger, 1993.

DeMeis, Paolo S. *The Bazooka Kid.* N.p.: privately published, n.d.

Denfeld, D. Colt. *Hold the Marianas: The Japanese Defense of the Mariana Islands.* Shippensburg, PA: White Mane Publishing Company, 1997.

Diaz, Vincent. "Simply Chamorro: Telling Tales of Demise and Survival in Guam." *Contemporary Pacific* 6, no. 1 (spring 1994): 29–58.

Donnelly, Thomas J. *"Hey Padre": The Saga of a Regimental Chaplain in World War II.* New York: 77th Division Association, n.d.

Dopking, Al, and Elmont Waite. "Guam Fast Becoming Second Pearl Harbor." *Rhinelander Daily News* (Wisconsin). February 27, 1945.

"Draft Board Calls Man Who Was Killed on Guam." *Burlington Free Press* (Vermont). July 13, 1944.

Drea, Edward J. *In the Service of the Emperor.* Lincoln: University of Nebraska Press, 1998.

Dyer, Vice Adm. George C. *The Amphibians Came to Conquer: The Story of Admiral Richmond Kelly Turner.* 2 vols. Washington, DC: Department of the Navy, 1972.

"Enemy in Wild Flight on Guam." *Holdredge Daily Citizen* (Nebraska). August 8, 1944.

Fane, Cmdr. Francis D., and Don Moore. *The Naked Warriors.* New York: Appleton-Century-Crofts, 1956.

"Farewell Message Penned before Priest Met Death." *Republican and Herald* (Pottsville, PA). August 30, 1944.

Farrell, Don A. *The Pictorial History of Guam: Liberation 1944.* Tamuning, Guam: Micronesian Productions, 1984.

"The Fena Massacre." Hearing before the Subcommittee on Insular and International Affairs of the Committee on Interior and Insular Affairs, House of Representatives, One Hundred First Congress, Washington, DC, July 27, 1989.

"Find Reported Straggler's Remains." *Guam Daily News*. May 10, 1962.

Fink, Stanley. "Co-prosperity." *Marine Corps Gazette*. October 1944.

Forrestel, Vice Adm. E. P. *Admiral Raymond A. Spruance, USN: A Study in Command*. Washington, DC: U.S. Government Printing Office, 1966.

Frances, Anthony A. "The Battle for Banzai Ridge." *Marine Corps Gazette*. June 1945.

Frank, Benis M., and Henry I Shaw Jr. *Victory and Occupation: History of U.S. Marine Corps Operations in World War II*. Vol. 5. Washington, DC: Historical Branch, G-3 Division, Headquarters, U.S. Marine Corps, 1968.

Frank, Joseph L. *My First and Only Paid Vacation, 1942–1945*. Victoria, BC, Canada: Trafford Publishing, 2007.

Friedman, Joseph. *God Shared My Foxholes*. New York: iUniverse, 2010.

Gailey, Harry. *The Liberation of Guam, 21 July–10 August 1944*. Novato, CA: Presidio, 1988.

Garand, George W., and Truman R. Strobridge. *Western Pacific Operations: History of U.S. Marine Corps Operations in World War II*. Vol. 4. Washington, DC: Historical Division, Headquarters, U.S. Marine Corps, 1971.

"George Tweed: The Final Chapter." *Pacific Daily News*. March 26, 1989.

"Ghost of Guam Hissed and Booed on His Return." *Spokane Chronicle* (Washington). September 16, 1946.

Giangreco, D. M. *Hell to Pay: Operation Downfall and the Invasion of Japan, 1945–47*. Annapolis, MD: Naval Institute Press, 2009.

Gilbert, Haidee Eugenio. "Surviving the Odds: Guam WWII Survivor Reflects on Getting an Education at a Time of War." *Pacific Daily News*. February 3, 2019.

Gilbert, Oscar E. *Marine Tanks Battles in the Pacific*. Conshohocken, PA: Combined Publishing, 2001.

Giles, Donald T., Jr., ed. *Captive of the Rising Sun: The POW Memoirs of Rear Admiral Donald T. Giles*. Annapolis, MD: Naval Institute Press, 1994.

Gillespie, Raymond P. *The K-Company Marines: 3rd Battalion-22nd Regiment*. N.p.: Privately printed, 1992.

Guam: Operations of the 77th Division (21 July to 10 August 1944). Washington, DC: Historical Division, War Department, 1946.

"Guam 'Visitor' Sees No Japs." *Wisconsin State Journal*. July 23, 1944.

Guerrero, Jillette Tore. *Coming of Age in War-Torn Guam: The WWII Memoirs of Justo Torre Leon Guerrero*. Hagatna Heights, Guam: Guamology Publishing, 2021.

Hager, Alice Rogers. "Men Cut in Half by Jap Bombs; Dust, Destruction, Wake's Story." *The Tennessean* (Nashville). January 13, 1942.

Hague, Sgt. James E. "Big Irishman Piles Up Dead Japs." *Chevron*. September 9, 1944.

———. "Blades Flash in Weird Night Battle." *Chevron*. September 16, 1944.

———. "One Night at Asan." *Leatherneck*. February 1947.

Hale, Edward E. *First Captured, Last Freed: Memories of a P.O.W. in World War II Guam and Japan*. Sebastopol, CA: Grizzly Bear Press, 1995; Westport, CT: Praeger, 1996.

Hall, George H. "He Has a Lot of Notches in His Gun." *St. Louis Post-Dispatch* (Missouri). November 29, 1944.

Hall, Kevin. "World War II Battle Changed Ubertacci's Life." *Moultrie Observer* (Georgia). November 10, 2012.

Hallas, James H. *Killing Ground on Okinawa: The Battle for Sugar Loaf Hill*. Westport, CT: Praeger, 1996.

———. *Saipan: The Battle That Doomed Japan in World War II*. Guilford, CT: Stackpole Books, 2019.

Hallman, Sgt. Donald A. "Marine on Guam Recalls Former Beauty of Isle." *Chevron*. August 26, 1944.

Hammel, Eric. *Aces against Japan*. New York: Pocket Books, 1992.

Handleman, Howard. "Condemned, 'Executed' by Japanese Headsmen, Guamanian Boy, Girl Escape Guam Grave: Youths Were Charged with Aiding Yankees." *Pacific Profile*. July 1964.

Hatashin, Omi. *Private Yokoi's War and Life on Guam, 1944–1972: The Story of the Japanese Imperial Army's Longest WWII Survivor in the Field and Later Life*. Folkestone, UK: Global Oriental Ltd., 2009.

Hattori, Anne Perez. "Guardians of Our Soil: Indigenous Responses to Post–World War II Military Land Appropriation on Guam." In *Farms, Firms, and Runways: Perspectives on U.S. Military Bases in the Western Pacific*, ed. L. Eve Armentrout Ma. Chicago: Imprint Publications, 2001.

"He Went to Round Up Cattle and Found a Wanted Sailor." *Guam Daily News*. July 21, 1960.

Hebert, James A. "Japanese Abandoned, Hunted, Shot." *Pacific Daily News*. July 21, 1974.

Henderson, Gen. F. P. "The First Air-Ground General." *Marine Corps Gazette*. April 1995.

Hennessy, Duane. "2 Jap Admirals Hanged in Mass Guam Execution." *Fort Myers News-Press* (Florida), June 20, 1947.

Henry, John R. "Reporter's Guam Notebook Yields Colorful Items." *Honolulu Star-Bulletin*. August 3, 1944.

"Herman Tanks Win Guam Scrap." *Intelligencer Journal* (Lancaster, PA). August 12, 1944.

Herndon, Booton. *The Unlikeliest Hero: The Story of Desmond Doss*. Mountainview, CA: Pacific Press Publishing Association, 1967.

Higuchi, Wakako. *The Japanese Administration of Guam, 1941–1944: A Study of Occupation and Integration Policies, with Japanese Oral Histories*. Jefferson, NC: McFarland & Co., 2013.

———. "The Japanisation Policy for the Chamorros of Guam, 1941–1944." *Journal of Pacific History* 36, no. 1 (June 2001): 19–35.

History of the Medical Department of the United States Navy in World War II: A Compilation of the Killed, Wounded and Decorated Personnel. Vol. 2. Washington, DC: Government Printing Office, 1953.

Hoban, Francis J. *Marines Don't Cry: The True Story of a Few Good Men*. Long Beach, CA: Seaside Printing Company, 1985.

Hough, Lt. Col. Frank O., Maj. Verle E. Ludwig, and Henry I. Shaw Jr. *Pearl Harbor to Guadalcanal: History of U.S. Marine Corps Operations in World War II*. Vol. 1. Washington, DC: Historical Branch, G-3 Division, Headquarters, U.S. Marine Corps, 1958.

"How the Guam Operation Was Conducted." Tokyo: Japan Self-Defense Force Staff School, 1962.

"'Human Bomb' Explodes in Corsair, Jap Stays Hidden in Ship 9 Hours Awaiting Flight." *Chevron*. September 16, 1944.

Hough, Maj. Frank O. *The Island War: The United States Marine Corps in the Pacific*. Philadelphia: J. P. Lippincott and Company, 1947.

Iannarelli, Anthony, and John Iannarelli. *The Eighty Thieves: American POWs in World War II Japan*. Phoenix: Bridgewood Press, 2006.

Isely, Jeter A., and Philip A. Crowl. *The U.S. Marines and Amphibious War*. Princeton, NJ: Princeton University Press, 1951.

Ito Masashi. *The Emperor's Last Soldiers*. New York: Coward-McCann, 1967.

Jackson, Leona. "I Was on Guam." *American Journal of Nursing* 42, no. 11 (November 1942): 1244–46.

Jacobs, Sam. "Survival and Salvation: Ed Howard, Once a POW, Shaped Terre Haute's Library System." *Terre Haute Tribune-Star*. August 14, 2020.

"Jap Surrendering on Guam Didn't Know War Was Over." *Great Falls Tribune* (Montana). October 5, 1947.

Josephy, Alvin M., Jr. *The Long and the Short and the Tall: The Story of a Marine Combat Unit in the Pacific*. New York: Alfred A. Knopf, 1946.

Kahn, E. J., Jr. *The Stragglers*. New York: Random House, 1962.

Kang, P. Toyoko. "Japanese Offensive Operations Immediately after the Outbreak of War: The Cooperative Operation of the Army and Navy to Occupy Guam." *Micronesian Journal of the Humanities and Social Sciences* 2, no. 1–2 (December 2003): 41–49.

Kaufman, Millard. "Attack on Guam." *Marine Corps Gazette*. April 1945.

"Kenosha Marine, Killed in Action, Wins Navy Cross." *Kenosha News* (Wisconsin). March 17, 1945.

Kerins, Jack. *The Last Banzai*. Privately printed, 1992.

Key, Jennie. "Brant's WWII Ordeal a Timeless Story of Heroism." *Cincinnati Enquirer*. May 24, 2000.

Kiehle, Mark A. "The Battle of Fonte Hill, Guam, 25–26 July 1944." *Marine Corps Gazette*. July 2003.

Kinall, James. "On Guam Paradise Turned Ugly." *Newsday* (New York). August 10, 1994.

Klein, Edwin H. "The Handling of Supplies at Guam." *Marine Corps Gazette*. February 1945.

Knebel, Fletcher. "The Courageous Americans: Captain Holds the High Ground." *San Fernando Times* (California). September. 24, 1960.

LaVO, Carl. *Slade Cutter: Submarine Warrior*. Annapolis, MD: Naval Institute Press, 2003.

Leckie, Robert. *Strong Men Armed: The United States Marines against Japan*. New York: Random House, 1962.

LeMay, Curtis, and MacKinlay Kantor. *Mission with LeMay*. Garden City, NY: Doubleday & Co., 1965.

"'Led His Company Fearlessly,' Story of Racine Captain's Death." *Journal Times* (Racine, WI). October 7, 1944.

Letcher, John Seymour. *One Marine's Story*. Verona, VA: McClure Press, 1970.

"Lieut. Col. Ralph L. Houser Is Awarded Navy Cross for Heroism on Guam Beachhead." *Iowa City Press Citizen*. March 28, 1945.

"Lieut. Joe Curtis Is Hero at Guam." *Huntsville Times* (Alabama). December 24, 1944.

"Lieut. Tom Brock Reveals Guam Battle Experiences." *Telegram* (Columbus, NB). December 9, 1944.

Liewer, Steve. "Vets Recall Guam's Day of Infamy." *San Diego Union-Tribune*. December 7, 2009.

Ligon, Tina. "The Christmas Shootings on Guam: Charges of Unlawful Assembly and Rioting Followed." *Prologue: Quarterly of the National Archives and Records Administration* 46, no. 4 (winter 2014): 46–51.

Limtiaco, Joaquin. "The Last Days of Fr. Duenas." *Guam Daily News*. July 21, 1960.

Link, Sgt. Theo C. "Japs Deserted Agana during Marine Attack." *Courier-News* (Bridgewater, NJ). October 7, 1944.

———. "Tupelo Man Killed off Coast of Guam." *Clarion-Ledger*. September 13, 1944.

Linn, Gene. "Blood and Sands of Guam." *Pacific Daily News*. December 13, 1981, January 24, 1982.

Lodge, Maj. O. R. *The Recapture of Guam*. Washington, DC: Historical Branch, G-3 Division, Headquarters, U.S. Marine Corps, 1954.

Lollar, Kevin. "Nerve-wracking Mission." *Fort Myers News-Press* (Florida). July 28, 1994.

Lopez, Henry D. *From Jackson to Japan: The History of Company C, 307th Infantry, 77th Division in World War II*. Privately published, 1977,

Lotz, Dave. *Patrol Area 14: US Navy World War II Submarine Patrols to the Mariana Islands*. Bloomington, IN: Xlibris, 2018.

———. *World War II Remnants: Guam, Northern Mariana Islands: A Guide and History*. Guam: Making Tracks, 1994.

Lujan, Francisco G., and Joaquin Aflague Limtiaco. "Inarajan Uprising." *Pacific Profile*. July 1965.

Maga, Timothy. "Away from Tokyo: The Pacific Islands War Crime Trials, 1945–1949." *Journal of Pacific History* 36, no. 1 (June 2001): 37–50.

Maharidge, Dale. *Bringing Mulligan Home: The Other Side of the Good War*. New York: Public Affairs, 2013.

Manibusan, Judge Joaquin V. E. "In Tai, a Day of Terror and Tragedy." In *Liberation—Guam Remembers: A Golden Salute for the 50th Anniversary of the Liberation of Guam*. Maite, Guam: Graphic Center, 1994.

Mansell, Roger. *Captured: The Forgotten Men of Guam*. Annapolis, MD: Naval Institute Press, 2012.

Marder, Sgt. Murrey. "Battlefield Surgery on Guam Doctors, Corpsmen Invasion Heroes, Pharmacist's Mate Amputates Leg of Marine in Foxhole." *Chevron*. August 26, 1944.

"Marine Corporal Who Wins Navy Cross Too Excited to Remember." *Greenville News* (South Carolina). April 29, 1945.

"Marines Injured by Grenade in World War II Reunited." *News Leader* (Staunton, VA). November 2, 1992.

Marshall, Peter B. *1368 Days: An American POW in WWII Japan*. Eugene, OR: Luminare Press, 2017.

Martin, Harold. "Hangings Went Off with Dispatch if Rexroad Presided, Martin Says." *Atlanta Constitution*. December 23, 1948.

Martin, Robert. "Notes from Guam." *Marine Corps Gazette*. October 1944.

McCarthy, John. *Gung Ho Marines: The Men of Carlson's Raiders*. N.p.: ReView Publications, n.d.

McCulley, Jim. "Athletes and Dividends." *New York Daily News*. October 14, 1944.

McManus, Larry. "When the Japs Held Guam." *Yank Magazine*. September 22, 1944.

McMillan, George, et al. *Uncommon Valor: Marine Divisions in Action*. Washington, DC: Infantry Journal Press, 1946.

McMillian, Cmdr. I. E. "Naval Gunfire at Guam." *Marine Corps Gazette*. September 1948.

McMillin, Capt. George J. "Surrender of Guam to the Japanese." *Guam Recorder*. April–September 1972.

Metzger, Louis A. "Guam 1944." *Marine Corps Gazette*. July 1994.

Meyer, Cord. *Facing Reality: From World Federalism to the CIA*. New York: Harper & Row, 1980.

Moore, Don. "War Tales: 1st Lt. Bob Wachter Flew Last B-29 Mission over Japan in WWII." *War Tales*. December 26, 2011. https://donmooreswartales.com/2011/12/26/bob-wachter.

Morimoto, Tetsuro, et al. *Twenty-Eight Years in the Guam Jungle*. Tokyo and San Francisco: Japan Publications, 1972.

Morison, Samuel Eliot. *History of United States Naval Operations in World War II*. Vol. 2: *New Guinea and the Marianas, March 1944–August 1944*. Boston: Little Brown and Company, 1959.

———. *History of United States Naval Operations in World War II*. Vol. 1: *The Rising Sun in the Pacific, 1931–April 1942*. Boston: Little, Brown and Company, 1988.

Murphy, Shannon J. "Guam Is Attacked." Guampedia. https://www.guampedia.com/wwii-oral-war-histories-of-the-chamorro-people.

Myers, Hugh. *Prisoner of War World War II*. Portland, OR: Metropolitan Press, 1965.

Nalty, Bernard. *The Right to Fight: African-American Marines in World War II*. Washington, DC: Marine Corps Historical Center, 1995.

North, Oliver. *War Stories II: Heroism in the Pacific*. Washington, DC: Regnery Publishing, 2004.

Norton, Howard. "We Retake Guam, Eyewitness Report." *Baltimore Sun*. September 3, 1944.

O'Brien, Cyril J. *Liberation: Marines in the Recapture of Guam*. Washington, DC: Marine Corps Historical Center, 1994.

———. "A Saga of Bravery: Chonito Ridge." *Chevron*. August 12, 1944.

O'Donnell, Patrick K. *Into the Rising Sun*. New York: Free Press, 2002.

"Officer Calls Skagg's Conduct Greatest Inspiration Possible." *Ames Daily Tribune*. February 22, 1945.

O'Sheel, Capt. Patrick, and S/Sgt. Gene Cook, eds. *Semper Fidelis: The U.S. Marines in the Pacific—1942–1945*. New York: William Sloane Associates, 1947.

Olano y Urteaga, Miguel Angel. "Diary of a Bishop." *Guam Recorder*. April–September 1972. Richard F. Taitano Micronesian Area Research Center, University of Guam.

Olds, Marion. "Navy Nurse: The Story of the Capture of Guam." *Sensation*. February 1943.

"One Guam Hill Proves Costly." *Daily Oklahoman*. August 6, 1944.

Ostrander, Stephen G., and Martha A. Bloomfield. *The Sweetness of Freedom: Stories of Immigrants*. East Lansing, MI: Michigan State University Press, 2010.

Ours to Hold It High: The History of the 77th Infantry Division in World War II. Washington, DC: Infantry Journal Press, 1947.

Palmer, Kyle. "Priest Who Defied Japanese Revered." *Los Angeles Times*. April 1, 1945.

Palomo, Tony. *An Island in Agony*. Agana, Guam: Privately published, 1984.

———. "A Man of Courage and Conviction" (Father Duenas). In *Liberation—Guam Remembers: A Golden Salute for the 50th Anniversary of the Liberation of Guam*. Maite, Guam: Graphic Center, 1994.

———. "1941: Fateful and Tragic Year." In *The Defense of Guam*. Mangilao, Guam: Richard F. Taitano Micronesian Area Research Center, University of Guam. April–September 1972.

———. "Rising Sun Dawns on Guam." In *Liberation—Guam Remembers: A Golden Salute for the 50th Anniversary of the Liberation of Guam*. Maite, Guam: Graphic Center, 1994.

———. "A Time of Sorrow and Pain." War in the Pacific National Historical Park, U.S. Department of the Interior, National Park Service, 2004.

Palomo, Tony, and Paul J. Borja, eds. *Liberation—Guam Remembers: A Golden Salute for the 50th Anniversary of the Liberation of Guam*. Maite, Guam: Graphic Center, 1994.

Pangelinan, Lourdes. "Tweed, to Some a Hero, to Some Only Ungrateful." *Pacific Daily News* (Agana Heights, Guam). July 15, 1984.

Parker, Frederick D. *Pearl Harbor Revisited: United States Navy Communications Intelligence, 1924–1941*. Fort George C. Meade, MD: Center for Cryptologic History, National Security Agency, 1994.

Pearson, Drew, and Robert S. Allen. "The Washington Merry-Go-Round." *Spokane Chronicle*. December. 24, 1941.

Peredo, Pedro. "Wartime Memories." *Pacific Profile*. July 1965.

Peterson, Eugene H. *Still a PFC: Guadalcanal, Bougainville, Guam, Iwo Jima*. N.p.: Privately printed, 2000.

Petty, Bruce. *Saipan: Oral Histories of the Pacific War*. Jefferson, NC: McFarland & Company, 2002.

Pfuhl, Richard M. *Chasing the Sun*. Saint Louis, MO: Ten Square Books, 1979.

"Political Martyr: Last Hours of Father Duenas." *Pacific Profile*. July 1965.

Pomeroy, Earl S. *Pacific Outpost: American Strategy in Guam and Micronesia*. Stanford, CA: Stanford University Press, 1951.

Porter, Cameron. "This 103-Year-Old Vet Served 22 Years in the Navy—after Being a POW." *The Mighty* (newsletter). U.S. Department of Veterans Affairs. May 31, 2018.

Potter, E. B. *Nimitz*. Annapolis, MD: Naval Institute Press, 1976.

Powell, S/Sgt. Harold. "Fanatic's Little Trick Backfires." *Honolulu Star-Bulletin*. August 25, 1944.

Pratt, Fletcher. *The Marines' War*. New York: William Sloane Associates, 1948.

Putney, William W. *Always Faithful: A Memoir of the Marine Dogs of World War II*. New York: Free Press, 2001.

Raider Patch newsletters, Marine Raider Association, 1980–1999.

Redman, Judith L. *Duty Bound: One Marine's Story of World War II and the Cold War*. Ashland, OR: Hellgate Press, 2018.

Reed, Philip G. "Wounded Marine Corporal Plays Dead to Stay Alive on Guam." *Fort Worth Star-Telegram*. August. 12, 1944.

Rishell, Grace. "A Soldier Returns to the Battlefield." *Pittsburgh Post Gazette*. July 14, 1994.

Rogers, Robert F. *Destiny's Landfall: A History of Guam*. Honolulu: University of Hawaii Press, 1995.

Rosenquist, Rudolf G. "Rosenquist: Guam Banzai Attack." *Raider Patch*. September 1980.

Rosenquist, R. G., Martin J. Sexton, and Robert A. Buerlein. *Our Kind of War: Illustrated Saga of the U.S. Marine Raiders of World War II*. Richmond: American Historical Foundation, 1990.

Santos, Angel. "U.S. Return Was Reoccupation, Not Liberation." *Pacific Daily News*. July 21, 1991.

"Schaghticoke Soldier Gets Navy Cross." *Troy Record* (New York). April 9, 1945.

Schram, Donald F. "It Happened in Michigan." *Detroit Free Press*. May 8, 1942.

Scott, Brig. Gen. John A. "Scott: Guam Was Destroyed to Be Saved." *Pacific Daily News*. July 21, 1984.

Seiden, Matthew J. "Japanese Soldier Who Hid on Guam 27 Years Prefers Jungle." *Baltimore Sun*. April 23, 1974.

Selle, Earl Albert. "Night of Horror on Guam Told by U.S. Fighting Men." *Honolulu Advertiser*. August 11, 1944.

Shaw, Henry I., Jr., Bernard C. Nalty, and Edwin T. Turnbladh. *Central Pacific Drive: History of U.S. Marine Corps Operations in World War II*. Vol. 3. Washington, DC: Historical Branch, G-3 Division, Headquarters, U.S. Marine Corps, 1966.

Sherman, Gene. "Japs Outwitted by Ruse of Yanks." *Los Angeles Times*. August 13, 1944.

Simmons, Brig. Gen. Edwin H. "Memorandum from the Director: Guam Redux." *Fortitudine: Bulletin of the Marine Corps Historical Program* 24, no. 2 (fall 1994): 3–12.

Sixth Marine Division Association. *Sixth Marine Division: The Striking Sixth*. Paducah, KY: Turner Publishing Co., 1987.

"Sixty Japs Die as Montebellan Battles Alone." *Los Angeles Times*. August 25, 1944.

Smith, Cmdr. H. E. "I Saw the Morning Break." *USNI Proceedings*. March 1946.

Smith, Craig. *Counting the Days: POWs, Internees, and Stragglers of World War II in the Pacific*. Washington, DC: Smithsonian Books, 2011.

Smith, Holland M., and Percy Finch. *Coral and Brass*. New York: Charles Scribner's Sons, 1949.

Smith, Paul C. *Personal File*. New York: Appleton-Century, 1964.

Smith, Rex Alan, and Gerald A. Meehl, eds. *Pacific War Stories in the Words of Those Who Survived*. New York: Abbeville Press, 2004.

Sobocinski, Andre. "Peter Marshall's Journey: The Story of the Last Living American POW on Guam." U.S. Navy Bureau of Medicine and Surgery, Defense Visual Information Distribution Service. March 26, 2021.

Sood, Raj. "Marine Endures War in POW Camp." In *Liberation—Guam Remembers: A Golden Salute for the 50th Anniversary of the Liberation of Guam*. Maite, Guam: Graphic Center, 1994.

Souder, Paul B. "The Problems of Feeding, Clothing and Housing 18,000 War Refuges." *Pacific Profile*. July 1965.

"Story of Father Duenas—Martyred by the Enemy." *Guam Daily News*. July 21, 1952.

"Suspended Term Given Killer of Jap War Straggler." *Palladium-Item* (Richmond, IN). July 20, 1962.

Swann, Maj. Ralph L. *A Unit History of the 315th Bomb Wing: 1944–1946*. Maxwell Air Force Base, AL: Air Command and Staff College, Air University, c. 1985.

Taaffe, Stephen R. *Commanding the Pacific: Marine Corps Generals in World War II*. Annapolis, MD: Naval Institute Press, 2021.

"Tanks on Guam." *Marine Corps Gazette*. October 1944.

Tanner, Beccy. "Kansan Was aboard B-29 for Last Mission of World War II." *Wichita Eagle*. August 8, 2016.

"They Staked Their Lives So They Can Hear the News." *Pacific Profile*. July 21, 1965.

Third Division's Two Score and Ten History. Paducah, KY: Turner Publishing Company, 1992.

"Three Guamanians, Beheaded by the Japanese, Still Alive." *Guam Daily News*. July 21, 1952.

Tillman, Barrett. *Clash of the Carriers: The True Story of the Marianas Turkey Shoot of World War II*. New York: NAL Caliber, 2005.

Todd, Lt. George B. "Early Navy Radio Communications in Guam, Marianas Islands." N.p.: Prepared for the Old Timer Communicators, n.d.

Toland, John. *The Rising Sun: The Rise and Fall of the Japanese Empire*. New York: Bantam Books, 1970.

Torres, Jose M. *The Massacre at Atate*. Guam: University of Guam Press, 2014.

"'The Tough Little Guy' Isn't Tough at All." *Courier-Journal* (Louisville, KY). July 8, 1945.

Trumbull, Robert. "Japs Search Guam Foxholes with Bayonets Tied on Poles." *Honolulu Advertiser*. August 9, 1944.

———. "Liberated Chamorros Tell Dramatic Story of Two and a Half Years of Jap Misrule." *Honolulu Advertiser*. August 8, 1944.

———. "Navy Pilot, Shot Down, Spends 13 Nights on Guam Undetected." *Honolulu Advertiser*. July 24, 1944.

Umezawa, Maj. Gen. Haruo, and Col. Louis Metzger. "The Defense of Guam." *Marine Corps Gazette*. August 1964.

Untalan, Luis. "The Long Trek to Manenggon." *Pacific Profile*. July 1965.

Van Stockum, Ron. "30 Years in the Marines: The Rest of the Story (1942–1967) Part 7: The Battle for Guam (1944)." *Sentinel News* (Shelbyville, KY). July 26, 2017.

"Veteran 'Mop-Up' Officers Detailed to Find Straggler." *Guam Daily News*. March 11, 1955.

Vining, Lonnie Gene. "Guam Native Woman, Once Pupil of Shreveporter, Saved Tweed." *Shreveport Journal*. May 14, 1945.

"Vision of Old Glory in Disgrace Fortified McAllen Guam Captive." *The Monitor* (McAllen, TX). October 15, 1945.

Walker, Maj. Anthony. "Advance on Orote Peninsula." *Raider Patch*. November 1983.

War in the Pacific National Historical Park: Hearing before the Subcommittee on National Parks, Forests, and Public Lands, Committee on Natural Resources, House of Representatives, One Hundred Third Congress, First Session, on H.R. 1944, to Provide for Additional Development at War in the Pacific National Historical Park . . . Hearing Held in Washington, DC, May 27, 1993. Vol. 4.

"War Writer Escapes Death in Guam Drive." *Miami Herald*. August 13, 1944.

Watanabe, Masako. "Japanese Straggler Recalls Nearly 8-Year Survival in Jungle." *Pacific Daily News*. July 12, 2017.

———. "Woman Recalls Life during, after World War II." *Pacific Sunday News*. August 11, 2013.

Wathen, Patrick W. "Marine Shunned Wounds, Hurled Back Enemy." *Evansville Courier & Press* (Indiana). May 29, 1995.

Weiss, Jasmine Stole. "George Tweed, Controversial War Hero, Refused to Surrender When Japanese Forces Invaded." *Pacific Daily News*. July 15, 2019.

West, Benny. "A Marine's Marine." *Leatherneck* (July 1947).

West, Charles O., et al. *Second to None! The Story of the 305th Infantry in World War II*. Washington, DC: Infantry Journal Press, 1949.

"Wife, Parents Hear Message from Former Valley Man in Jap Prison." *The Monitor* (McAllen, TX). April 20, 1942.

Wilds, Thomas. "The Japanese Seizure of Guam." *Marine Corps Gazette*. July 1955.

Willock, Roger. *Unaccustomed to Fear: A Biography of the Late General Roy S. Geiger*. Princeton, NJ: Privately published, 1968.

"Woman Lives to Tell about Grisly Execution." *Pacific Daily News*. July 21, 1984.

Worden, William. "The Battle of Guam's Agana Over but Its Peace Has Not Yet Begun." *Honolulu Star-Bulletin*. August 23, 1944.

———. "Guam Farmers in Good Shape: Townspeople Have Nothing Left." *Reno Gazette-Journal*. August 22, 1944.

———. "Japs Leave Grisly Scene: 42 Guam Natives Slain." *Salt Lake Tribune*. September 3, 1944.

———. "Yanks Find Guam's Airport a Litter of Wrecked Jap Ships." *Battle Creek Enquirer* (Michigan). August 3, 1944.

Yaffe, Bertram A. *Fragments of War: A Marine's Personal Journey*. Annapolis, MD: Naval Institute Press, 1999.

UNPUBLISHED

Alternate Plan Employment 77th Division in Corps Reserve, July 14, 1944. General Roy Geiger Papers, History and Museums Division (Gray Research Center), Quantico, Virgina.

Analysis of Pacific Air Operations (Marianas Operations, June 11–30, 1944). Commander Air Force, Pacific Fleet.

Aplington, Henry, II. "To Be a Marine." Unpublished memoir. Special Collections, Firestone Library, Princeton University, Princeton, New Jersey, 1986.

Battle Experience: Supporting Operations for the Capture of the Marianas Islands (Saipan, Guam, and Tinian), June–August 1944. United States Fleet, Headquarters of the Commander in Chief, December 21, 1944.

Camacho, Keith L. "Cultures of Commemoration: The Politics of War, Memory and History in the Mariana Islands." PhD diss., University of Hawaii, 2005.

Case of Jose P. Villagomez, October 22, 1945. Record of Proceedings of a Military Commission Convened at Agana, Guam, by Order of the Island Commander.

Case of Kanzo Kawachi, September 17, 1945. Record of Proceedings of a Military Commission Convened at Agana, Guam, by Order of the Island Commander.

Case of Koju Shoji and Kiyoshi Takahashi, August 30, 1945. Record of Proceedings of a Military Commission Convened at Agana, Guam, by Order of the Island Commander.

Case of Pedro Sablan Leon Guerroro, April 1945. Record of Proceedings of a Military Commission Convened at Agana, Guam, by Order of the Island Commander.

Case of Samuel T. Shinohara, July 28, 1945. Record of Proceedings of a Military Commission Convened at Agana, Guam, by Order of the Island Commander.

Chapman, Maj. Raymond T., et al. "Armor in Operation Forager: A Research Report." Prepared by Committee 8, Officers Advanced Course, the Armored School, Fort Moore, Georgia, 1948–1949.

CinPac Operations in the Pacific Ocean Areas during the Month of July 1944. Commander in Chief U.S. Pacific Fleet and Pacific Ocean Areas.

BIBLIOGRAPHY

Commander Task Force 51 (Joint Expeditionary Force, Marianas). Report of Amphibious Operations for the Capture of the Marianas Islands (Forager Operation), August 25, 1944.

Commander Task Force 53. Report of Amphibious Operations for the Capture of Guam Island, Marianas, June 4–August 10, 1944.

Ercanbrack, Earl B. "Letter to International Red Cross Representative, Report of Treatment While Held as Prisoner of War," August 30, 1945. http://www.mansell.com/pow_resources.

Fifth Fleet. Final Report on the Operations to Capture the Marianas Islands.

First Provisional Marine Brigade. Operations and Special Action Report, August 19, 1944.

Fumitoshi, Yasuoka. Diary. National Archives, RG 153, Box 1.

Geiger Papers. Personal Papers Collections, Archives Branch, U.S. Marine Corps History Division, Quantico, Virginia.

Guam Island Command War Diary, March 30–August 15, 1944.

Guam War Claims Review Commission. Public hearings in Hagåtña, Guam, December 8–9, 2003, testimony of various witnesses.

Japanese Studies in World War II. "The 'A-Go' Operations Log, Supplement May–June 1944" (Monograph No. 91). U.S. Army Historical Division, c. 1946.

Japanese Studies in World War II. "Operations in the Central Pacific" (Monograph No. 48). U.S. Army Historical Division, 1946.

Japanese Studies in World War II. "The A-Go Operation, May–June 1944" (Monograph No. 90). U.S. Army Historical Division, c. 1946.

LCI(G) 365. Action Report, Guam, July 23, 1944.

LCI(G) 437. Action Report, July 20, 1944, to August 12, 1944.

LCI(G) 468. AA Action Report, June 17, 1944, Southeast of Saipan Island.

LCI(G). Division Fifteen Action Reports, August 17, 1944.

LCI(L) 471. AA Action Report, June 17, 1944, East of Guam.

LST 207. Action Report, June 17, 1944.

O'Neill, Sgt. John, Personal Diary. John O'Neill Papers, USMC History and Museums Division (Gray Research Center), Quantico, Virginia.

Operations Plan No. 1, 1st Provisional Marine Brigade (TG 53.11), May 15, 1944.

"Operations Report on Marianas." Headquarters 77th Infantry Division, August 19, 1944.

Owsley, Roy H. Diary, October 14, 1943–September 3, 1945. General Roy Geiger Papers, History and Museums Division (Gray Research Center), Quantico, Virginia.

PC-555. Action Report, July 21–29, 1944.

Roosevelt, Franklin D. Papers as President: Map Room Papers, 1941–1945, Series 2: Military Files Box 36, Franklin D. Roosevelt Presidential Library and Museum.

706th Tank Battalion. After Action Report, July 21–August 9, 1944.

"Study of the Theater of Operations Island of Guam." Marine Corps Schools, Marine Barracks, Quantico, Virginia, 1939.

Takeda, Lt. Col. H. "The Outline of Japanese Defense Plan and Battle of Guam Island." October 4, 1946. Lester A. Dessez Collection, 1920–1946. USMC History and Museums Division (Gray Research Center), Quantico, Virginia.

Task Force 53. Report of Amphibious Operations for the Capture of Guam, August 10, 1944.

Task Force 56, Headquarters, Expeditionary Troops. Report on Guam Operation (G-1, G-2, G-3, Periodic Reports, etc.), October 2, 1944.

III Amphibious Corps. Report of Operations for the Capture and Occupation of Guam Island, Marianas, July 21–August 10, 1944.

Transport Division Four. Action and Operation Report, Guam.

UDT #3. Action Report, Guam Operation, July 14 to July 28, 1944.

UDT #4. Report of Its Activities during the Guam Operation, August 15, 1944.

USMC Publication Background Files (Guam), 1947–1989. National Archives, Record Group 127, Box 12, Entry A1 1038.

USS *Aloe*. AA Action Report, June 17, 1944, East of Guam Island, Marianas.

USS *Belleau Wood*. Report of Action against Guam, Rota, Haha Jima, Chichi Jim, Iwo Jima, and Pagan Islands and the Japanese Fleet, June 11–24, 1944.

USS *Bunker Hill*. Aircraft Action Reports, Air Group Eight, Marianas Operations, June 11–24, 1944.

USS *Cabot*. Action Report—First Phase of Marianas Operation and Action against Japanese Surface Force, June 6–24, 1944.

USS *Corregidor*. Aircraft Action reports, June 10–28, 1944.

USS *Crescent City* (APA-21). History, October 10, 1941–December 1, 1945.

USS *Dickerson*. Action Report at Guam, July 28, 1944.

USS *Enterprise*. Report of Operations, June 6–29, 1944.

USS *Essex*. Report of Air Operations Conducted by Carrier Air Group Fifteen, June 19–July 3, 1944, inclusive.

USS *Fayette*. Report—Action and Operations–Guam, July 21–25, 1944.

USS *Flying Fish* (SS229). Report of 4th War Patrol; Area 14. January 6, 1943–February 28, 1943.

USS *George Clymer*. Action Report, Assault Landing on Guam, July 21–August 2, 1944.

USS *Honolulu* (CL48). Action Report, Bombardment and Fire Support of Guam, July 17, 1944–August 9, 1944, including preliminary bombardment on June 16, 1944.

USS *Hornet* (CV-12). Action Report, June 11–24, 1944.

USS *Lexington*. Action Report, Attacks on Guam and Pagan, June 25, 1944–July 5, 1944.

USS *Monrovia* (APA31). Report of Operations during Amphibious Assault on Guam, July 22–28, 1944.

USS *Permit*. Report on Seventh War Patrol, February 1943–May 1943.

USS *Ringgold*. Action Report, Guam, July 21–30, 1944.

USS *Rixey*. Action Report on Occupation of Guam, Marianas Islands, July 21–29, 1944.

USS *San Jacinto*. Action Report: Operations against Saipan, Tinian, and Guam, June 6–30 and July 14–August 5, 1944.

USS SC 1326. Action Report, July 21, 1944.

USS *Snapper*. Sixth War Patrol—Comments on, January 27–March 14, 1943.

USS *Stingray*. Patrol Report of War Patrol Number 11, May 1944–July 1944.

USS *Wasp*. War Diary, Action Reports of *Wasp* and Carrier Air Group Fourteen in the Final Phase of the Operation against Guam and in the Operation against Palau, July 6–30, 1944.

USS *Wayne*. Action Report of Landing Operation on Guam, August 25, 1944.

USS *Whale* (SS239). Report of Fourth War Patrol, May 5–June 21, 1943.

USS *Yorktown*. Report of Operations in Support of the Occupation of the Marianas Islands, June 30–July 21, 1944.

USS *Zeilin* (APA3). Action Report, July 21–26, 1944.

VD-3 (Fleet Air Photographic Squadron Three). Aircraft Action Reports, April 25 and May 7, 1944.

Wachtler, Col. W. A. Memorandum for the Commanding General (Geiger), 77th Division Alternate Plan, July 18, 1944. General Roy Geiger Papers, History and Museums Division (Gray Research Center), Quantico, Virginia.

Wellons, Maj. James B. "General Roy S. Geiger, USMC: Marine Aviator, Joint Force Commander." School of Advanced Air and Space Studies, Air University, Maxwell Air Force Base, Alabama, June 2007.

VIDEOS AND OTHER RESOURCES

Dan Marsh's Raider History, http://www.usmcraiders.org/history.

Done, Harris, dir. *War Dogs of the Pacific*. DVD. Harris Done Productions, 2009.

Pacific Storytellers Cooperative. *An Island Invaded—Guam in WWII*, dir. Esther Figueroa and Jim Bannan. Honolulu: PREL, 2004.

Ramage, James, and Don Gordon. "Philippine Sea, June 19–20, 1944." USS Enterprise CV-6, http://www.cv6.org/1944/marianas/default.htm.

Steffy, Rlene, and Robert Steffy, prods. *Historic Context: Manenggon March and Concentration Camp Survivor Accounts*. DVD. Guam: Micronesian Publishing, 2015.

315th Bomb Wing (VH) Anthologies. Cocoa Beach, FL: 315th Bomb Wing Association, 1987.

INDEX

Note: Photo insert images indicated by *pA, pB,* etc.